SCOTLAND

Aberdeen, Banff & Moray	271	Highlands (North)	298
Argyll & Bute	273	Highlands (Mid)	299
Ayrshire & Arran	277	Highlands (South)	301
Borders	280	Lanarkshire	307
Dumfries & Galloway	284	Perth & Kinross	309
Dundee & Angus	288	Renfrewshire	312
Edinburgh & Lothians	289	Stirling & The Trossachs	313
Fife	294	Scottish Islands	314
Glasgow & District	296		

WALES

Anglesey & Gwynedd	317	Pembrokeshire	326
North Wales	320	Powys	327
Carmarthenshire	324	South Wales	331
Ceredigion	325		

REPUBLIC OF IRELAND 333

Special Welcome Supplements

Non-Smoking	335
Special Diets	337
Disabled	338

Bed & Breakfast Stops 2006

© FHG Guides Ltd, 2006
ISBN 1 85055 378 5

Maps: ©MAPS IN MINUTES™ 2005. ©Crown Copyright,
Ordnance Survey Northen Ireland 2005 Permit No. NI 1675.

Typeset by FHG Guides Ltd, Paisley.
Printed and bound in Great Britain.

Distribution. Book Trade: ORCA Book Services, Stanley House,
3 Fleets Lane, Poole, Dorset BH15 3AJ
(Tel: 01202 665432; Fax: 01202 666219)
e-mail: mail@orcabookservices.co.uk
Published by FHG Guides Ltd., Abbey Mill Business Centre,
Seedhill, Paisley PA1 ITJ (Tel: 0141-887 0428 Fax: 0141-889 7204).
e-mail: admin@fhguides.co.uk

Bed & Breakfast Stops
is published by FHG Guides Ltd,
part of Kuperard Group.

Cover design: FHG Guides
Cover picture supplied by Still Digital

Bed & Breakfast Stops

FHG
·K·U·P·E·R·A·R·D·

tos: Acton Scott Farm, Church Stretton, Shropshire   Lyne Farmhouse, Peebles, Scottish Borders   Caebertran Farm, Felinfach, Brecon, Powys

VALUE FOR MONEY ACCOMMODATION
England, Scotland, Wales & Ireland
With special sections for Non-Smokers, Disabled & Special Diets

For Contents see page 2, 3

Plus Website Directory

For Index of towns/counties see back of book

2006

Contents

Colour Section	1-48
Guide to Tourist Board Ratings	5, 270
Readers' Offer Vouchers	53-90
Directory of Website Addresses	339-370
Family-Friendly Pubs	371-378
Pet-Friendly Pubs	379-392
Index of Towns/Counties	393-398

ENGLAND

London (Central & Greater)	91
Bedfordshire	98
Berkshire	99
Cambridgeshire	101
Cheshire	103
Cornwall	106
Cumbria	120
Derbyshire	138
Devon	141
Dorset	159
Durham	167
Essex	168
Gloucestershire	170
Hampshire	176
Herefordshire	183
Hertfordshire	186
Isle of Wight	186
Kent	188
Lancashire	193
Leicestershire & Rutland	195
Lincolnshire	196
Merseyside	199
Norfolk	200
Northamptonshire	205
Northumberland	206
Nottinghamshire	210
Oxfordshire	211
Shropshire	215
Somerset	219
Staffordshire	233
Suffolk	234
Surrey	237
East Sussex	239
West Sussex	242
Tyne & Wear	243
Warwickshire	244
Wiltshire	247
Worcestershire	250
East Yorkshire	254
North Yorkshire	255
West Yorkshire	267

Bed & Breakfast Stops

Please mention Bed & Breakfast Stops when enquiring

Ratings You Can Trust

ENGLAND

The *English Tourism Council* (now *VisitBritain*) has joined with the *AA* and *RAC* to create an easily understood quality rating for serviced accommodation, giving a clear guide of what to expect.

HOTELS are given a rating from One to Five *Stars* – the more Stars, the higher the quality and the greater the range of facilities and level of services provided.

GUEST ACCOMMODATION, which includes guest houses, bed and breakfasts, inns and farmhouses, is rated from One to Five *Diamonds*. Progressively higher levels of quality and customer care must be provided for each one of the One to Five Diamond ratings.

HOLIDAY PARKS, TOURING PARKS and CAMPING PARKS are now also assessed using *Stars*. Standards of quality range from a One Star (acceptable) to a Five Star (exceptional) park.

Look out also for the new *SELF-CATERING* Star ratings. The more *Stars* (from One to Five) awarded to an establishment, the higher the levels of quality you can expect. Establishments at higher rating levels also have to meet some additional requirements for facilities.

VisitBritain has launched a new *Quality Accredited Agency Standard*. Agencies who are awarded the Quality Accredited Agency marque by VisitBritain are recognised as offering good customer service and peace of mind, following an assement of their office polices, practices and procedures.

SCOTLAND

Star Quality Grades will reflect the most important aspects of a visit, such as the warmth of welcome, efficiency and friendliness of service, the quality of the food and the cleanliness and condition of the furnishings, fittings and decor.

THE MORE STARS,

THE HIGHER THE STANDARDS.

The description, such as Hotel, Guest House, Bed and Breakfast, Lodge, Holiday Park, Self-catering etc tells you the type of property and style of operation.

WALES

Places which score highly will have an especially welcoming atmosphere and pleasing ambience, high levels of comfort and guest care, and attractive surroundings enhanced by thoughtful design and attention to detail

STAR QUALITY GUIDE FOR

HOTELS, GUEST HOUSES AND FARMHOUSES
SELF-CATERING ACCOMMODATION
(Cottages, Apartments, Houses)
CARAVAN HOLIDAY HOME PARKS
(Holiday Parks, Touring Parks, Camping Parks)

★★★★★	Exceptional quality
★★★★	Excellent quality
★★★	Very good quality
★★	Good quality
★	Fair to good quality

In England, Scotland and Wales, all graded properties are inspected annually by Tourist Authority trained Assessors.

Bed & Breakfast Stops 2006

London(Central & Greater)

BED AND BREAKFAST IN LONDON
IDEAL LONDON LOCATION

Comfortable, centrally located quiet Edwardian home. Great base for sightseeing, close to the river, traditional pubs, lots of local restaurants and antique shops. Excellent transport facilities – easy access to West End, Theatreland, shopping, Harrods, museums, Albert Hall, Earls Court and Olympia Exhibition centres. Direct lines to Eurostar (Waterloo), Airports: Heathrow, Gatwick (Victoria), Stansted (Liverpool Street). Bed and Continental Breakfast Prices: Double/Twin/Triple £24 pppn; Single £34.00; Children's reductions. Smoking only in garden.

Sohel and Anne Armanios
67 Rannoch Road, Hammersmith, London W6 9SS
Tel: 020 7385 4904 • Fax: 020 7610 3235
www.thewaytostay.co.uk

Barry House Hotel
12 Sussex Place, Hyde Park, London W2 2TP
- Comfortable, family-friendly B&B
- Most rooms with en suite facilities
- Rates include English Breakfast
- Near Hyde Park and Oxford Street
- Paddington Station 4 minutes' walk

www.barryhouse.co.uk
hotel@barryhouse.co.uk
fax: 020 7723 9775

Call us now on: 0207 723 7340
We believe in family-like care

CHARLIE'S HOUSE HOTEL
BED & BREAKFAST

Singles • Doubles • Triples • Family Rooms
- All rooms en suite
- Central heating
- TV in rooms
- Tube Station: Tufnell Park

63 Anson Road, London N7 0AR
Tel: 0207 607 8375 • Fax: 0207 697 8019
www.charlieshotel.com

Hotel Columbus

141 Sussex Gardens, Hyde Park, London W2 2RX
Tel: 020-7262 0974 • Fax: 020-7262 6785

e-mail: hotelcolumbus@compuserve.com
website: www.delmerehotels.com

This charming Bed and Breakfast hotel is the ideal choice for individuals and families who seek both value for money and a quality B & B in the "Heart of London".

Situated in an elegant tree-lined avenue close to Hyde Park and Oxford Street, it is a former residence of the aristocracy and has now been converted to provide modern, comfortable accommodation. All rooms have en suite shower, telephone, TV, etc.

Look no further for London's Best B&B !

Bed & Breakfast Stops 2006

London (Central & Greater)

Elizabeth Hotel

Quiet, convenient townhouse overlooking the magnificent gardens of Eccleston Square. Only a short walk from Buckingham Palace and other tourist attractions. Easy access to Knightsbridge, Oxford Street and Regent Street.

Extremely reasonable rates in a fantastic location.

Visa, Mastercard, Switch, Delta and JCB are all accepted.

37 Eccleston Square, Victoria, London SW1V 1PB
info@elizabethhotel.com
www.elizabethhotel.com
Tel: 020 7828 6812
Fax: 020 7828 6814

- Central London
- ★★ B&B Hotel
- Family friendly • Est. 30 years
- Tranquil position
- Set in a garden square
- 2 mins Paddington Station
- Airlines check-ins 15 mins Heathrow on Express Link

- e-mail: info@aafalcon.co.uk
- website: www.aafalcon.co.uk
- Tel: +44 (0) 20 7723 8603
- Fax: +44 (0) 20 7402 7009
- 11 Norfolk Sq., Hyde Park North, London W2 1RU

FALCON HOTEL

Our guests first and always
Affordable prices from: Singles £35, Doubles £55
For latest seasonal prices please call

- En-suite facilities
- Very clean and comfortable
- Close to tourist attractions and shops
- Triple and Family rooms
- Full freshly cooked English breakfasts

UNBEATABLE VALUE IN THE HEART OF LONDON, FACING HYDE PARK

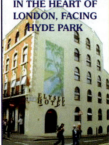

THE ELYSEE HOTEL
25/26 CRAVEN TERRACE, LONDON W2 3EL
TEL: 020 7402 7633 • FAX: 020 7402 4193
e-mail: information@hotelelysee.co.uk
website: www.hotelelysee.co.uk

Near London's famous tourist and shopping areas. Rooms with attached bath/shower and toilets. Lifts to all floors. Tea/coffee making facilities, Sky and cable TV, security safe, hairdryer. Rates include Continental breakfast. Three minutes from Lancaster Gate Underground and six minutes from Paddington Station for Heathrow Express.

**Single £49, Twin/Double £59.50 (for room),
Family (3 persons) £75, Family (5 persons) £95**

London(Central & Greater)/Berkshire/Cheshire

WHITE LODGE HOTEL

White Lodge Hotel is situated in a pleasant North London suburb, with easy access via tube and bus to all parts of London. Alexandra Palace is the closest landmark and buses pass the front door. Prices are kept as low as possible for people on low budget holidays, whilst maintaining a high standard of service and cleanliness. Many guests return year after year which is a good recommendation. Six single, ten double bedrooms, four family bedrooms (eight rooms en suite), all with washbasins; three showers, six toilets; sittingroom; diningroom

Cot, high chair, babysitting and reduced rates for children.
No pets, please.
Open all year for Bed and Breakfast from £32 single, £42 double.

White Lodge Hotel, No. 1 Church Lane, Hornsey, London N8 7BU
e-mail: info@whitelodgehornsey.co.uk • website: www.whitelodgehornsey.co.uk
Tel: 020 8348 9765 / 4259 • Fax: 020 8340 7851

Netherton Hotel

96 St Leonards Road, Windsor SL4 3DA
Tel: 01753 855508 • Fax: 01753 621267

This recently refurbished hotel offers a comfortable and friendly atmosphere. All rooms are en suite, with colour TV, direct-dial telephone, and tea/coffee making facilities. Also available are hairdryers and ironing facilities. There is a TV lounge for guests use. Full English breakfast. We have a private car park and are easy to find. Children welcome.

- Walking distance to Windsor Castle, town centre, train stations and Legoland is only one mile away.
- Central London can be reached in 35 minutes by train.
- M4 only two miles, Heathrow seven miles.

e-mail: netherton@btconnect.com

The Compton Swan Hotel

High Street, Compton, Near Newbury, Berkshire RG20 6NJ

Situated in the heart of the Berkshire Downlands. The Hotel has 6 en suite bedrooms with TV, radio alarms, hairdryers, beverage facilities, telephones and sauna. An extensive menu with traditional, exotic, vegetarian, and special diets catered for. Our home-cooked meals are a speciality. Downlands Healthy Eating Award winner. Large walled garden where we have al fresco eating; BBQs. Near the famous ancient Ridgeway National Trail and is an ideal base for walking, horse-riding, and golf. Stabling and horsebox available. Real Ales and Bar Meals available. Entry in CAMRA Good Beer Guide and Good Pub Guide. A friendly reception by staff and our Jack Russells "Mushy & Bonnie".

Tel: 01635 578269 • Fax: 01635 578765

e-mail: info@comptonswan.co.uk • www.SmoothHound.co.uk

Friendly, medium sized, family-run hotel near Chester Railway Station and City Centre. Ground floor, family, non-smoking and four poster bedrooms available. All of the en suite bedrooms have direct dial telephone, satellite TV, tea making facilities and hairdryer. There is a comfortable residents' lounge bar where you are able to enjoy drinks and snacks, or alternatively you can dine in our pleasant restaurant which serves freshly prepared English fayre.

The ancient city of Chester is world famous for its walls, parts of which date back to Roman times. Chester is the ideal location from which to tour the North West and North Wales resorts.

STAFFORD HOTEL
City Road, Chester CH1 3AE
Tel: 01244 326052/320695
Fax: 01244 311403
e-mail: enquiries@staffordhotel.com
website: www.staffordhotel.com

Bed & Breakfast Stops 2006

Cheshire/Cornwall

Green Cottage
The Green, Higher Kinnerton,
Chester CH4 9BZ
Tel & Fax: 01244 660143
★★★ Guest House

A homely, friendly, peaceful and comfortable country retreat just over the Welsh border, ideally situated for exploring the historic City of Chester under seven miles away. Easy access to all routes (five minutes from the A55) makes this an ideal base for touring North Wales, West Cheshire and North Shropshire.

Beryl and John, previous winners of a Prince of Wales' Award, will offer you warm hospitality and invite you into their home, which has recently been renovated and furnished to a high standard. A double room and a twin room are available, overlooking open countryside. Tea/coffee making facilities, TV, shared private bathroom with bath and shower, central heating, off-road parking, pleasant gardens. There are two pubs within the village offering excellent cuisine. Non-smoking.

Bed and Full English Breakfast from £25 per person, with reductions for weekly stays. Please send or telephone for our brochure.

LONG CROSS HOTEL & VICTORIAN GARDENS
TRELIGHTS, PORT ISAAC PL29 3TF • www.portisaac.com

Stay in one of Cornwall's most unusual hotels. Set in our own magnificent gardens in an Area of Outstanding Natural Beauty, and visited by thousands of garden lovers every year. Restaurant, Bar and Terraces with panoramic views. Spacious, newly refurbished, en suite rooms. Children's adventure play area.

Tel: 01208 880243
e-mail: longcross@portisaac.com

ROCKLANDS

"Rocklands" is situated overlooking part of Cornwall's superb coastline and enjoys uninterrupted sea views. The Lizard is well known for its lovely picturesque scenery, coastal walks and enchanting coves and beaches, as well as the famous Serpentine Stone which is quarried and sold locally. Open Easter to October. Generations of the Hill family have been catering for visitors on the Lizard since the 1850s. Three bedrooms with sea views, two en suite, tea/coffee making facilities and electric heaters; sittingroom with TV and video; sun lounge; diningroom with separate tables. Children and well trained pets welcome.

Bed and Breakfast £23pppn, en suite £25pppn; reductions for children under 10 years.

Mrs D. J. Hill, "Rocklands", The Lizard, Near Helston TR12 7NX • Tel: 01326 290339

THE TOWNHOUSE ROOMS
20 Falmouth Road, Truro TR1 2HX
Tel: 01872 277374 • Fax: 01872 241666

The Townhouse is different - relaxed, friendly, flexible - and our guests seem to love it! We are not a hotel or a traditional bed and breakfast. We aim to give you lovely rooms, real value for money, and the flexibility you need to enjoy your stay. You have your own key - come and go as you please. There is an all day breakfast/dining room - use it whenever you want. And if you fancy a night in - grab a takeaway and a bottle of wine and chill out. We are just five minutes from restaurants, bars, shops and the theatre. And within a short drive, you can be sunning yourself on the beach, walking the Coastal Path, or checking out the Eden Project. *Please ring for brochure.*

e-mail: info@trurotownhouse.com • website: www.trurotownhouse.com

Cornwall/Cumbria

Boscean Country Hotel
St Just, Penzance, Cornwall TR19 7QP

The Boscean Country Hotel, located amidst some of the most dramatic scenery in West Cornwall, is somewhere very special just waiting to be discovered. This country house offers a wonderful combination of oak panelled walls, a magnificent oak staircase and open log fires. The natural gardens, extending to nearly three acres, are a haven for wildlife including foxes and badgers.

Situated on the Heritage Coast in an Area of Outstanding Natural Beauty close to Cape Cornwall and the Coastal Footpath, this is an ideal base from which to explore the Land's End Peninsula. The moors of Penwith are rich in Iron and Bronze Age relics dating back to 4000BC. Penzance, St Michael's Mount, St Ives, Land's End and the Minack Theatre are all a short distance away.

12 en suite rooms, centrally heated throughout, licensed bar. Excellent home cooking using fresh local produce. *Unlimited Desserts!!*

Open all year. English Tourism Council ♦♦♦♦

Bed & Breakfast £23.00 Dinner, Bed & Breakfast £36.00

Tel/Fax 01736 788748 • E-mail: Boscean@aol.com
Website: www.bosceancountryhotel.co.uk

Tel: 01900 822644
e-mail: AmandaVickers1@aol.com

Mosser Heights
Mosser, Cockermouth, Cumbria CA13 0SS

Expect a warm welcome at our family-run farm, just off the beaten track, yet near to the fells and lakes of Loweswater (two miles) and Cockermouth (four miles). Comfortable spacious en suite bedroom, cosy lounge and dining room with log fires. A hearty breakfast to set you up for the day. An ideal base for walking, cycling, touring and bird watching. Arrive as guests and leave as friends.
We are a hidden jewel awaiting your discovery!

This beautifully appointed famous shooting lodge stands in its own private 700 acre estate. It is traditionally furnished with antiques, oil paintings, sporting trophies and log fires. Amenities include a wonderful traditional English bar, a gun room and snooker room. All bedrooms are individually styled, each double and single room has a four poster bed.
The Lodge is well known for its professionally run activities, weddings, corporate entertainments and Country House weekends. Guests may enjoy a wide range of sports including clay pigeon shooting, fishing and falconry on the estate. Locally there is riding and sailing in the Lake District. Boarding Kennels on site. Single, double and twin rooms. B&B £35 per person per night.

Bracken Bank Lodge

Tel: 01768 898241 • Fax: 01768 898221
e-mail: info@brackenbank.co.uk
www.brackenbank.co.uk

Lazonby, Penrith CA10 1AX

Bed & Breakfast Stops 2006

Cumbria

The Shepherds
HOTEL & RESTAURANT

B&B £24.50 to £49.

26 en suite rooms, single, double, twin and family, all furnished to a high standard. The restaurant is open throughout the day, serving a selection of bar meals and snacks, and the extensive evening menu is freshly and skilfully prepared by our chef. Enjoy a full English breakfast before exploring this breathtaking part of the Lake District.

Restaurant • Bar Meals • Ensuite facilities • Colour TV
Trouser Press & hair dryer • Direct dial telephone • One wheel chair accessible room • Office services • Retail gifts & wool shop • Visitor centre • Live sheep show (Seasonal)

Egremont Road, Cockermouth, Cumbria CA13 0QX
Telephone & Fax: 01900 822673
e-mail: reception@shepherdsotel.co.uk
website: www.shepherdshotel.co.uk

Mrs S. Park, Langdale
14 Leonard Street, Keswick CA12 4EL
Tel: 017687 73977
website: www.langdaleguesthouse.co.uk

Victorian town house, quietly situated, yet close to town, park, lake and fells. All rooms furnished to a very high standard, having quality en suite facilities, central heating, colour TV, tea/coffee making facilities throughout. Family, double or twin available. Enjoy a good home cooked English or vegetarian breakfast or our popular Continental breakfast. We have a non-smoking policy throughout the house.
We will ensure your stay is a pleasant one.
Bed and Breakfast from £25; Theatre Breaks.

The Dower House

**Wray Castle, Ambleside
Cumbria LA22 0JA
Tel: 015394 33211**

Lovely old house, quiet and peaceful, stands on an elevation overlooking Lake Windermere, with one of the most beautiful views in all Lakeland. Its setting within the 100-acre Wray Castle estate (National Trust), with direct access to the Lake, makes it an ideal base for walking and touring. Hawkshead and Ambleside are about ten minutes' drive and have numerous old inns and restaurants. Ample car parking; prefer dogs to sleep in the car. Children over five years welcome.

Bed and Breakfast from £30.00
Optional Evening Meal from £15.00
Open all year round

~ Mrs Dorothy Nicholson, Gill Farm, Blackford, Carlisle, Cumbria CA6 4EL ~

In a delightful setting on a beef and sheep farm, this Georgian-style farmhouse, dated 1740, offers a friendly welcome to all guests.

Near Hadrian's Wall • Gretna Green • Lake District Golf • Fishing • Swimming • Large agricultural auction markets • Cycle path passes our entrance.

Accommodation is in one double room en suite, one family and one twin/single bedrooms. All rooms have washbasins, shaver points and tea/coffee making facilities. Two bathrooms, shower; lounge with colour TV; separate diningroom. Open all year. Reductions for children; cot provided. Central heating. Car essential, good parking.

B&B from £21 to £25. Telephone for further details or directions. Tel: 01228 675326 • mobile: 07808 571586

Gill Farm

Cumbria

Ambleside Lodge

Heart of the English Lake District. This elegant Lakeland home, dating from the 19th century, has been sympathetically converted and now offers a high standard of accommodation. All bedrooms are en suite, with colour TV, tea/coffee making facilities and delightful views. The Premier suites and king-size four-poster rooms with jacuzzi spa baths offer relaxation and indulgence. Leisure facilities available at a private club just 5 minutes' drive away include swimming pool, sauna, steam room, squash, gym and beauty salon. Free parking.

www.ambleside-lodge.com

AMBLESIDE LODGE, ROTHAY ROAD, AMBLESIDE, CUMBRIA LA22 0EJ
015394 31681 • Fax: 015394 34547 • e-mail: enquiries@ambleside-lodge.com

Ferndale Lodge

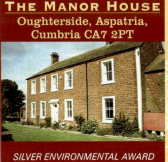

Lake Road, Ambleside, Cumbria LA22 0DB
Tel: 015394 32207
e-mail: stay@ferndalelodge.co.uk
website: www.ferndalelodge.co.uk

Ferndale Lodge is a small, family-run guesthouse where you will find a warm, friendly welcome and personal attention at all times. Offering excellent accommodation with good home cooked English or Vegetarian breakfast. Our 10 attractive bedrooms have all been individually decorated and furnished, each with full en suite facilities, colour television and tea/coffee making tray. Full central heating throughout, several rooms having views of the fells, and including ground floor bedrooms. The Ferndale is open all year round with a car park, offers packed lunches, hair dryer, clothes/boot drying and ironing facilities. A wide choice of places to dine, within minutes' walking distance, ranging from excellent pub food to superb restaurants of many varied cuisines will complete your day.

Bed and Breakfast £28.00 - £30.00 pppn. Weekly £182 - £196 pp. **Please phone for brochure.**

THE MANOR HOUSE
Oughterside, Aspatria,
Cumbria CA7 2PT

Tel & Fax: 016973 22420
e-mail: richardandjudy@themanorhouse.net
website: www.themanorhouse.net

Our lovely manor farmhouse dates from the 18th century and retains many original features as well as several acres of land. Rooms are spacious with large en suite bathrooms, tea and coffee making facilities, full size TVs, views and lots of little extras. Our double rooms have kingsize beds and our twin room has double beds. The grounds are home to many species of birds, including barn owls. Set in peaceful surroundings we enjoy easy access to the magnificent scenery of the Western Lakes and Solway Coast. Pets and children welcome. Bed & Breakfast from £25. Evening meals by arrangement.

SILVER ENVIRONMENTAL AWARD

publisher's note

While every effort is made to ensure accuracy, we regret that FHG Guides cannot accept responsibility for errors, misrepresentations or omissions in our entries or any consequences thereof. Prices in particular should be checked. We will follow up complaints but cannot act as arbiters or agents for either party.

FHG

Cumbria/Derbyshire

Book with this advert and claim a FREE Bottle of house wine at dinner.

Elterwater, Langdale, Cumbria LA22 9HP
Tel: 015394 37210

A 500 year-old quintessential Lakeland Inn nestled in the centre of the picturesque village of Elterwater amidst the imposing fells of the Langdale Valley. Comfortable, newly refurbished en suite double and twin-bedded rooms. Dogs welcome. Enquire about our Winter Mid-Week Special Offer of three nights B&B for the price of two. Relax in the oak-beamed Bars or Dining Room whilst sampling local real ales and dishes from our extensive menu of fresh, home-cooked food using lots of Cumbrian produce.

www.britinn.co.uk • e-mail: info@britinn.co.uk

St John's Lodge
Lake Road, Windermere, Cumbria LA23 2EQ
Tel: 015394 43078 • Fax: 015394 88054
e-mail: mail@st-johns-lodge.co.uk • www.st-johns-lodge.co.uk

This pretty Lakeland B&B is ideally situated between Windermere village and the lake (10 minutes' walk) and close to all amenities. The guesthouse caters exclusively for non-smokers and has been awarded 3 AA Red Diamonds for excellence. The choice of breakfast menu is probably the largest in the area. From a touring visitor's point of view, or if you prefer healthier alternatives, this is a refreshing change. There is a wide choice of cereals and fresh fruit and a good selection of traditional English breakfasts, but there are also over 20 other tasty dishes, including vegetarian/vegan, fresh fish, and a number of house specialities. All guests are offered free access to a nearby local luxury leisure club (about 2 minutes by car). Free internet access is provided via a dedicated computer. For laptop owners, radio connectivity is available, or you can simply plug in and use ASDL technology.

GREEN GABLES
37 Broad Street, Windermere LA23 2AB

A family-owned and run licensed guesthouse in Windermere centrally situated one-minute's walk from village centre with shops, banks and pubs and only five minutes from the station or bus stop. Accommodation comprises two doubles, one family triple/twin and one single room, all en suite; one family (four) and two family triple/twin rooms with private facilities; all with central heating, colour TV, hairdryers, kettles, tea & coffee. Comfortable lounge bar on the ground floor. No smoking in bedrooms. We can book tours and trips for guests and can advise on activities and special interests. B&B from £20 to £30 pppn. Special Winter offers available. Open just about all year round. Contact **Carole Vernon and Alex Tchumak**.

Tel: 015394 43886 • e-mail: greengables@FSBdial.co.uk • e-mail: info@greengablesguesthouse.co.uk

Stone Cottage

A charming cottage in the quiet village of Clifton, one mile from the Georgian market town of Ashbourne.
Each bedroom is furnished to a high standard with all rooms en suite, with four-poster bed, TV and coffee making facilities.
A warm welcome is assured and a hearty breakfast in this delightful cottage.
There is a large garden to relax in.
Ideal for visiting Chatsworth House, Haddon Hall, Dovedale, Carsington Water and the theme park of Alton Towers.
B&B from £22.50 pp. Good country pubs nearby serving evening meals.

Enquiries to: *Mrs A. M. Whittle, Stone Cottage, Green Lane, Clifton, Ashbourne, Derbyshire DE6 2BL* • **Telephone: 01335 343377**
Fax: 01335 347117 • e-mail: info@stone-cottage.fsnet.co.uk

14 Please mention Bed & Breakfast Stops when enquiring

Derbyshire/Devon

Ye Olde Cheshire Cheese Inn
How Lane, Castleton, Hope Valley S33 8WJ
Telephone: 01433 620330 • Fax: 01433 621847
website: www.cheshirecheeseinn.co.uk • e-mail: kslack@btconnect.com

This delightful 17th century free house is situated in the heart of the Peak District and is an ideal base for walkers and climbers; other local attractions include cycling, swimming, gliding, horse riding and fishing. All bedrooms are en suite with colour TV and tea/coffee making facilities. A "Village Fayre" menu is available all day, all dishes home cooked in the traditional manner; there is also a selection of daily specials. Large car park. Full Fire Certificate. B&B from £25.00. All credit cards accepted.

SPECIAL GOLF PACKAGES ARRANGED.
PERSONAL TRAINING INSTRUCTOR AVAILABLE.

Devon • The English Riviera
WOODLANDS GUEST HOUSE
Parkham Road, Brixham, South Devon TQ5 9BU

Overlooking the beautiful Brixham Harbour

Victorian House with large car park at rear and unrestricted on-road parking to the front. All bedrooms en suite, with colour TV, tea/coffee making facilities, mini fridges etc. Four-Poster bedroom with panoramic views over Brixham Harbour and Torbay. Just a short walk away from the picturesque harbour, ancient fishing port with its quaint streets full of varied shops, pubs and restaurants. Ideal holiday base from which to explore the glorious South-West, romantic Dartmoor, boat trips, Paignton and Dartmouth Steam Railway.

Walkers can explore the marvellous Devon countryside. Fishing trips available from the harbour. Bed and Breakfast from £20pppn.
We hope to see you soon and make your stay a memorable one.

Phone 01803 852040, Paul and Rita Pope for free colour brochure and details, or fax 01803 850011
www.woodlandsdevon.co.uk • e-mail: woodlandsbrixham@btinternet.com

---

Glenorleigh
HOTEL

26 Cleveland Road
Torquay
Devon TQ2 5BE
Tel: 01803 292135
Fax: 01803 213717

As featured on BBC Holiday programme

David & Pam Skelly
AA ◆◆◆◆

Situated in a quiet residential area, Glenorleigh is 10 minutes' walk from both the sea front and the town centre.
• Delightful en suite rooms, with your comfort in mind.
• Good home cooking, both English and Continental, plenty of choice, with vegetarian options available daily. • Bar leading onto terrace overlooking Mediterranean-style garden with feature palms and heated swimming pool. • Discounts for children and Senior Citizens. • Brochures and menus available on request. • B&B £30–£40; Dinner £14.

e-mail: glenorleighhotel@btinternet.com • website: www.glenorleigh.co.uk

Bed & Breakfast Stops 2006　　　　　　　　　　　　　　　　　　　　　15

Devon

A family-run, licensed, non-smoking hotel, in a quiet level location near Cary Park and Babbacombe Downs. Close to beaches and South West Coastal Path. Within easy reach of harbour and town. Ideal base for many attractions in the area. All rooms en suite. Full central heating. Car park. Gardens. Children welcome. Rates from £25 to £30 B&B per person per night, evening meal optional. All major debit/credit cards accepted. Sign Language.

COMMITMENT TO QUALITY AWARD — **AA**

Telephone: **01803 326622**
e-mail: **avelandhotel@aol.com**
website: **www.avelandhotel.co.uk**

Aveland Hotel
Aveland Road, Babbacombe, Torquay, Devon TQ1 3PT

Fairmount House Hotel

Enjoy a taste of somewhere special in the tranquillity, warmth and informal atmosphere of our small hotel of character. Set above the picturesque Cockington Valley, Fairmount House, with its mature gardens and sun-filled terraces, is a haven for the discerning visitor seeking a peaceful setting for their holiday or short break. All our bedrooms are tastefully furnished, clean and comfortable, with en suite bathroom or shower, remote-control TV, tea and coffee making facilities. Relax with a drink in our conservatory bar, or choose from an extensive menu in our fully licensed restaurant. Bed and Breakfast from £24.

website: www.fairmounthousehotel.co.uk
e-mail: stay@fairmounthousehotel.co.uk

Herbert Road, Chelston, Torquay TQ2 6RW
Tel: 01803 605446

BROOKSIDE GUEST HOUSE

160 NEW ROAD, BRIXHAM TQ5 8DA • 01803 858858

Tess and Joan Harris, the resident proprietors, will be pleased to welcome you to Brookside.

Brookside is a small, friendly guest house situated on a level position on the main approach road into Brixham. All accommodation offers the best in comfort, with tea and coffee making facilities, remote-control colour TV and refrigerators in all rooms. There is ample off-road parking, both at the front and rear of the property. To add further to your comfort Brookside is a no smoking establishment. After a hard day's sightseeing, relax on our large outside terrace.

B&B (standard) from £22pppn • B&B (en suite) from £25pppn • B&B (superior suite) £30pppn.

HEATHCLIFF HOUSE HOTEL
16 Newton Road, Torquay, Devon TQ2 5BZ
Telephone: 01803 211580
e-mail: heathcliffhouse@btconnect.com • www.heathcliffhousehotel.co.uk
Owners: Adrian & Terri Bailey

This former vicarage is now a superbly appointed family-run hotel equipped for today yet retaining its Victorian charm. All the bedrooms have full en suite facilities, colour TV and drink making facilities. The elegant licensed bar boasts an extensive menu and unlike many hotels, the car park has sufficient space to accommodate all vehicles to eliminate roadside parking. Torquay's main beach, high street shops, entertainment and restaurants are all nearby and with full English breakfast included, it is easy to see why guests return time after time.

Tariff for B&B ranges between £21 and £32pppn. Four-poster & Family rooms available.
So, be it main holiday, touring or business, make the Heathcliff your 1st choice.

Devon

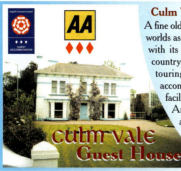

Culm Vale Guest House, Stoke Canon, Exeter EX5 4EG

A fine old country house of great charm and character, giving the best of both worlds as we are only three miles to the north of the Cathedral city of Exeter, with its antique shops, yet situated in the heart of Devon's beautiful countryside on the edge of the pretty village of Stoke Canon. An ideal touring centre. Our spacious comfortable Bed and Breakfast accommodation includes full English breakfast, colour TV, tea/coffee facilities, washbasin and razor point in both rooms. Full central heating. Ample free parking. Bed and Breakfast £20 to £27.50 pppn according to room and season. Credit cards accepted.

Telephone & Fax: 01392 841615
e-mail: culmvale@hotmail.com
www.SmoothHound.co.uk/hotels/culm-vale.html

ALVERDISCOTT Tel & Fax: 01271 858230

Our family-run working farm of 240 acres, with a pedigree herd of suckler cows and sheep, is situated in a small rural village between Barnstaple and Torrington. Many local attractions and beauty spots. Comfortable accommodation with family room, twin beds, single and double rooms; private bathroom with shower; double room en suite. Guest lounge with TV and tea/coffee making facilities. Good farmhouse cooking. Ample parking. No pets. Non-smoking.

B&B from £20. Reduced rates for children under 12; weekly terms on request.

Mrs J. Ley, West Barton, Alverdiscott, Near Barnstaple, Devon EX31 3PT

A most attractively situated working farm. The house is a very old traditional Devon farmhouse located just three miles east of Honiton and enjoying a superb outlook across the Otter Valley. Enjoy a stroll down by the River Otter which runs through the farmland. Try a spot of trout fishing. Children will love to make friends with our two horses. Lovely seaside resorts 12 miles, swimming pool, adventure parks and garden nearby. Traditional English breakfast, colour TV, washbasin, heating, tea/coffee facilities in all rooms.

Bed and Breakfast £17.50-£20 • Reductions for children.

Mrs June Tucker, Yard Farm, Upottery, Honiton EX14 9QP •• 01404 861680

WENTWORTH HOUSE

Wentworth House, a friendly family-run private hotel built as a gentleman's residence in 1857, standing in lovely gardens only a stone's throw from the town and minutes from the sea, harbour and Torrs Walks. En suite rooms with colour TV and tea/coffee making facilities. Family rooms sleeping up to four persons. Home-cooked food with packed lunches on request. Spacious bar/lounge. Secure storage for bicycles etc. Private parking in grounds. Open all year.

Bed & Breakfast from £19.50. Bed, Breakfast & Evening Meal from £28.00.
PRICES HELD FOR 2006. Discounted rates for weekly bookings.

Stay a few days or a week, Geoff & Sharon will make your visit a pleasant one.
2 Belmont Road, Ilfracombe EX34 8DR • Tel & Fax: 01271 863876
E-mail: wentworthhouse@tiscali.co.uk

Devon

Eggworthy Farm
Sampford Spiney, Yelverton, Devon PL20 6LJ

Holiday on Dartmoor! In the beautiful Walkham Valley. Moorland and Valley walking within yards of the accommodation or just relax in the garden and adjoining woodland. Many local attractions. Comfortable rooms, one double en suite, one family suite with private bathroom. Both rooms have colour TV, tea/coffee facilities, and fridge. Full English breakfast. Non-smoking. Pets welcome. Open all year except Christmas. Brochure available. Terms from £22-£28. We look forward to seeing you.

**Tel/Fax Linda Landick on 01822 852142 • e-mail: eggworthyfarm@aol.com .
www.eggworthyfarm.co.uk**

Cat lovers' paradise in charming 16th century farmhouse set in beautiful Otter Valley with two acre gardens including stream and pond. Only four miles from beach at Sidmouth. Central heating. All rooms en suite. Dogs welcome free of charge. Lovely touring and walking country.
Bed and Breakfast from £25 per person per day.

Ottery St Mary, Devon EX11 1RJ

Fluxton Farm

Tel: 01404 812818
www.fluxtonfarm.co.uk

VALLEY HOUSE
Lynbridge Road, Lynton EX35 6BD
Tel: 01598 752285

A secluded Victorian country house, five minutes' walk from Lynton. Set into the rock face high above the West Lyn River, with magnificent views of the National Trust Woodland and sea.

All rooms are stylishly decorated, en suite with tea/coffee making facilities, hairdryer, colour TV and beautiful views. Interesting breakfast menu; scrumptious evening meals most days; packed lunches available. Relax in the bar/lounge, the new conservatory room or the front terrace. A walkers' paradise, with some of the best horse riding in the country; also golf and surfing. Rates from £27.50 pppn.

e-mail: info@valley-house.co.uk   website: www.valley-house.co.uk

Devoncourt Hotel
Douglas Avenue, Exmouth EX8 2EX
Tel: 01395 272677 • Fax: 01395 269315

Standing in four acres of mature subtropical gardens, overlooking two miles of sandy beach, yet within easy reach of Dartmoor and Exeter, Devoncourt provides an ideal base for a family holiday.

Single, double and family suites, all en suite, well furnished and well equipped; attractive lounge bar and restaurant.

**indoor & outdoor heated pools * sauna * steam room
spa & solarium * snooker room * putting * tennis &
croquet * golf * sea fishing * horse riding nearby**

B&B from £75 single, £115 double; self-catering/room only from £60 single, £90 double. Weekly rates available.

Devon/Dorset

LOWER PINN FARM Peak Hill, Sidmouth EX10 0NN
Tel: 01395 513733
e-mail: liz@lowerpinnfarm.co.uk • www.lowerpinnfarm.co.uk

19th century built farmhouse on the World Heritage Jurassic Coast, two miles west of the unspoilt coastal resort of Sidmouth and one mile to the east of the pretty village of Otterton. Ideally situated for visiting many places, and for walking, with access to coastal path.

Comfortable, centrally heated en suite rooms with colour television and hot drink making facilities. Guests have their own keys and may return at all times throughout the day. Good hearty breakfast served in the dining room. Ample off-road parking. Children and pets welcome. Lower Pinn is a no smoking establishment. Open all year.

Bed and Breakfast from £24 to £28

Just off the A3072, five miles from Dartmoor, this 16th century farmhouse with barn conversions offers a total of twelve rooms, all en suite, family suites available. There is a non-smoking lounge with TV, games and books, to meet friends or to relax in, as well as a separate bar with a residential licence. You are assured of plenty of hearty Devonshire food and a warm welcome. Babies and well-behaved dogs are welcome by arrangement. We have farm walks, ponies, goats, rabbits, plus a working sheep flock and suckler cow herd. Walkers and cyclists on the Tarka Trail are catered for, with cycle sheds and packed lunches etc. B&B from £27.50, Dinner from £12.50.

AA ♦♦♦♦

Higher Cadham Farm, Jacobstowe, Okehampton, Devon EX20 3RB • www.highercadham.co.uk

Tel: 01837 851647

Cromwell House Hotel
Lulworth Cove, Dorset

Catriona and Alistair Miller welcome guests to their comfortable family-run hotel, set in secluded gardens with spectacular sea views. Situated 200 yards from Lulworth Cove, with direct access to the Jurassic Coast. A heated swimming pool is available for guests' use from May to October. Accommodation is in 17 en suite bedrooms, with TV, direct-dial telephone, and tea/coffee making facilities; most have spectacular sea views. Restaurant, bar wine list. Two nights dinner, Bed and breakfast (fully en suite) from £90 per person. Off peak mid week breaks available. Open all year except Christmas.

Cromwell House Hotel, Lulworth Cove, Dorset BH20 5RJ
Tel: 01929 400253/400332 • Fax: 01929 400566

ETC/AA/RAC ★★

Kingfishers

Come to Kingfishers and relax on your large sunny balcony overlooking the river and gardens. Set in beautiful surroundings on the banks of the River Char, Kingfishers offers a secluded setting yet is only a short stroll to the beach and village amenities.
- 2 Miles Lyme Regis • Adjoining National Trust Land
- South Coast Path • Free Access • Ample Parking
- Home Cooked Food including clotted cream teas available throughout the day.

**Mr & Mrs Derham,
Kingfishers, Newlands Bridge,
Charmouth, Dorset DT6 6QZ
Tel: 01297 560232**

Bed & Breakfast Stops 2006

Durham/Essex/Gloucestershire

Bushblades Farm
Harperley, Stanley, County Durham

Comfortable Georgian farmhouse set in large garden. Twin ground floor en suite, and double first floor en suite bedrooms. All rooms have tea/coffee making facilities, colour TV and easy chairs. Ample parking. Children over 12 years welcome. Sorry, no pets.
Bed and Breakfast £25 to £30 single, £48 double.
Self-catering accommodation also available.

Near Durham, Metro Centre, Beamish Museum; Hadrian's Wall, Northumberland Coast under an hour.

Telephone: 01207 232722

RETREAT GUEST HOUSE
12 Canewdon Road, Westcliff-on-Sea, Essex SS0 7NE
Mr & Mrs Bartholomew
Tel: 01702 348217/337413 • Fax: 01702 391179

Quality accommodation ideally situated in the quieter more picturesque side of Southend. Close to the Cliffs Pavilion and beautiful gardens. Conveniently by Westcliff station and near to the seafront leading to Southend's main attractions.

● *All remote-control colour TV* ● *Some rooms with video* ● *Tea/Coffee making facilities* ● *Choice of English Breakfast* ● *Private secure parking.*

Most bedrooms en suite, some on ground floor. **En suite rooms also available with own kitchen.**
B&B from £25 per person • Major debit/credit cards accepted

e-mail: retreatguesthouse.co.uk@tinyworld.co.uk

Roylands Farm Cottage Bed & Breakfast

Fernhill, Almondsbury, Bristol, Gloucestershire BS32 4LU Tel: 07791 221102; 07768 286924

Roylands Farm Cottage is a comfortable home from home situated within a working farm, with classic styling to blend in with its rural surroundings. Rooms are spacious, bright and welcoming with all usual en suite and private facilities, lounge and kitchen. One single, one twin and a double bedroom, all with full English breakfast, towels, TV and tea and coffee making facilities. Uniquely guests can take advantage of their own lounge, or relax and take in the beautiful views of the Severn estuary and the surrounding countryside from the adjoining conservatory or large country garden. Ample secure and secluded off road parking.

e-mail: jane@roylandfarmcottage.co.uk
website: www.roylandfarmcottage.co.uk

'Brymbo'   ETC ♦♦♦♦
Honeybourne Lane, Mickleton, Chipping Campden, Gloucestershire GL55 6PU
Tel: 01386 438890 • Fax: 01386 438113
e-mail: enquiries@brymbo.com • www.brymbo.com

A warm and welcoming farm building conversion with large garden in beautiful Cotswold countryside, ideal for walking and touring.

All rooms are on the ground floor, with full central heating. The comfortable bedrooms all have colour TV and tea/coffee making facilities. Sitting room with open log fire. Breakfast room. Children and dogs welcome. Parking. Two double, two twin, one family. Bathrooms: three en suite, two private or shared.
Bed and Breakfast: single £25 to £40; double £40 to £55. Brochure available. Credit Cards accepted.
Close to Stratford-upon-Avon, Broadway, Chipping Campden and with easy access to Oxford and Cheltenham.

Gloucestershire/Hampshire

Hunters Lodge
Dr Brown's Road, Minchinhampton Common,
Near Stroud GL6 9BT • Tel: 01453 883588 •
hunterslodge@hotmail.com
www.cotswoldsbandb.co.uk

Premier Collection

HUNTERS LODGE is a beautiful stone-built Cotswold country house set in a large secluded garden adjoining 600 acres of National Trust common land at Minchinhampton. The accommodation comprises - one double room en suite; two twin/double-bedded rooms both with private bathrooms. All have tea/coffee making facilities, central heating, dressing gowns and colour TV and are furnished and decorated to a high standard. Private lounge with TV and a delightful new conservatory. Car essential, ample parking space. Ideal centre for touring the Cotswolds, Bath, Cheltenham, Cirencester, with many delightful pubs and hotels in the area for meals. You are sure of a warm welcome, comfort, and help in planning excursions to local places of interest.
Bed and Breakfast from £25-£30pp; single from £40. Non-smoking. Children over 10 years only. Sorry, no dogs. SAE please, or telephone.

Tel & Fax: 01452 840224

Quality all ground floor accommodation. "Kilmorie" is Grade II Listed (c1848) within conservation area in a lovely part of Gloucestershire. Double, twin, family or single bedrooms, all having tea tray, colour TV, radio, mostly en suite. Very comfortable guests' lounge, traditional home cooking is served in the separate diningroom overlooking large garden. Perhaps walk waymarked farmland footpaths which start here. Children may "help" with our pony, and "free range" hens. Rural yet perfectly situated to visit Cotswolds, Royal Forest of Dean, Wye Valley and Malvern Hills. Children over five years welcome. No smoking, please. Ample parking.

*Bed, full English Breakfast and Evening Dinner from £31
Bed and Breakfast from £21.*

S.J. Barnfield, "Kilmorie Smallholding", Gloucester Road, Corse, Staunton, Gloucester GL19 3RQ
e-mail: sheila-barnfield@supanet.com

Aston House, Broadwell, Moreton-In-Marsh GL56 0TJ

ASTON HOUSE is in the peaceful village of Broadwell, one-and-a-half miles from Stow-on-the-Wold, four miles from Moreton-in-Marsh. It is centrally situated for all the Cotswold villages, while Blenheim Palace, Warwick Castle, Oxford, Stratford-upon-Avon, Cheltenham and Gloucester are within easy reach. Accommodation comprises a twin-bedded and a double room, both en suite on the first floor, and a double room with private bathroom on the ground floor. All rooms have tea/coffee making facilities, radio, colour TV, hairdryer, electric blankets for the colder nights and fans for hot weather. Bedtime drinks and biscuits are provided. Open from March to October. No smoking. Car essential, parking. Pub within walking distance. PC and internet access available. Bed and good English breakfast from £27 to £29 per person daily; weekly from £195 per person.

Tel: 01451 830475 • e-mail: fja@netcomuk.co.uk • www.astonhouse.net
RAC ♦♦♦♦ Warm Welcome Award, Sparkling Diamond Award • ETC ♦♦♦♦ Silver Award

---

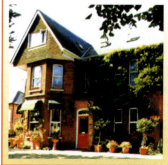

OAKLEA GUEST HOUSE
London Road, Hook RG27 9LA
Tel: 01256 762673 • Fax: 01256 762150

Friendly, family-run Guest House. All bedrooms en suite and non-smoking. Guest lounge with SKY TV, licensed bar. Evening meals available on request. Easy access from J5 M3, London 55 mins by train.

GOLF: Many excellent courses within 10-mile radius.
HORSE RACING at Sandown, Ascot and Goodwood.
SHOPPING at The Oracle, Reading and Festival Place, Basingstoke.
DAYS OUT: Thorpe Park, Chessington, Legoland, Windsor Castle, Hampton Court, RHS Wisley, Milestones.

AA ♦♦♦

Hampshire/Herefordshire

MAYS FARM

Twelve minutes' drive from Winchester, (the 11th century capital city of England), Mays Farm is set in rolling countryside on a lane which leads from nowhere to nowhere. The house is timber framed, originally built in the 16th century and has been thoroughly renovated and extended by its present owners, James and Rosalie Ashby.

There are three guest bedrooms, (one double, one twin and one either), each with a private bathroom or shower room. A sitting room with log fire is usually available for guests' use. Ducks, geese, chickens and goats make up the two acre "farm". Booking is essential. Please telephone or fax for details.

**Longwood Dean,
Near Winchester SO21 1JS**

Tel: 01962 777486
Fax: 01962 777747

Tel: 02380 812552

Simon and Elaine Wright, Bushfriers, Winsor Road, Winsor, New Forest, Southampton, Hampshire SO40 2HF

Bushfriers is an individual forest cottage having wonderful countryside views, character and charm with delightful accommodation, comfy double bed and spacious en suite, TV, hair dryer and hospitality tray. A restful sitting room with log fire and timbered ceiling reflect the warm and friendly atmosphere, or relax in the secluded pretty garden.
An excellent breakfast is cooked to suit the individual tastes of guests. Local fresh farm produce, home-made organic bread, preserves from our organically grown fruit. The traditional village pub serves good food. A perfect base to explore the New Forest. Hire a bike, ride a horse or visit the coast.

B&B from £26.50 per person
DISCOUNT THREE NIGHTS

e-mail: bushfriers@waitrose.com
website: www.newforest-uk.com/bushfriers.htm

Hedley Lodge lies two miles to the south of the City of Hereford and is superbly located for visiting this wonderful Marches City or for touring the beautiful towns and villages of Herefordshire and the Wye Valley.
Set within the grounds of historic Belmont Abbey, this modern, comfortable venue offers a warm, friendly welcome to all visitors and is ideal for short stays, holidays, conferences, retreats and wedding receptions.

• 17 en suite bedrooms with tea and coffee making facilities, colour TV and direct-dial telephone • Fully licensed restaurant is surrounded by beautiful gardens • B&B from £40 per room.

HEDLEY LODGE
Belmont Abbey, Hereford HR2 9RZ
Tel: 01432 374747 • Fax: 01432 374754 • e-mail: hedleylodge@aol.com • www.hedleylodge.com

---

Sink Green Farm

Rotherwas, Hereford HR2 6LE • Tel: 01432 870223
e-mail: enquiries@sinkgreenfarm.co.uk
website: www.sinkgreenfarm.co.uk

A friendly welcome awaits you at this our 16th century farmhouse overlooking the picturesque Wye Valley, yet only three miles from Hereford.
Our individually decorated en suite rooms, one four-poster, all have tea/coffee making facilities, colour TV and central heating. Relax in our extensive garden, complete with summer house and hot tub, or enjoy a stroll by the river. Fishing by arrangement.
Prices from £25 per person. Children welcome. Pets by arrangement.

AA ♦♦♦♦

Isle of Wight/Kent

SANDHILL HOTEL

6 Hill Street, Sandown, Isle of Wight PO36 9DB
Tel: 01983 403635 • Fax: 01983 403695

Trevor Sawtell and family welcome you to a friendly family hotel five minutes' walk from the beach and train station. All rooms are en suite, with colour TV, tea/coffee and telephone with internet ports. We have a reputation for quality food served in our comfortable dining room, and after dinner, why not take a stroll in nearby Los Altos Park. Bed and Breakfast from £22. Bed, Breakfast and Evening Meal (five courses) from £32 per night. Special rates for children. Disabled friendly. Please call for brochure.

e-mail: sandhillhotel@btconnect.com • www.sandhill-hotel.com

FERNSIDE HOTEL

30 Station Avenue, Sandown, Isle of Wight PO36 9BW
Tel: 01983 402356 •• Fax: 01983 403647
e-mail: enquiries@fernsidehotel.co.uk •• www.fernsidehotel.co.uk

This family-run hotel is ideally situated within walking distance of sandy beaches, town centre and visitor attractions - the perfect location for a relaxing and enjoyable holiday or short break.

- Bed & Breakfast accommodation
- 11 comfortable en suite rooms (all non-smoking). Ground floor and family rooms (cots available).
- Remote-control colour TV and tea/coffee in all rooms, comfortable lounge with books, magazines and games
- Traditional full English breakfasts served in our dining room.

Frenchman's Cove
ALUM BAY OLD ROAD, TOTLAND, ISLE OF WIGHT PO39 0HZ

Our delightful family-run guesthouse is set amongst National Trust downland, not far from the Needles and safe sandy beaches. Ideal for ramblers, birdwatchers, cyclists and those who enjoy the countryside. We have almost an acre of grounds. Cots and high chairs are available. All rooms are en suite, with colour TV and tea/coffee making facilities. Guests can relax in the the attractive lounges. Also available is the Coach House, a delightfully appointed apartment (ETC 3 Stars) for two adults and two children.

Please contact Sue or Chris Boatfield for details.
Tel: 01983 752227 • www.frenchmanscove.co.uk

THE WHITE LION

Taking its place proudly amongst Tenterden's attractive Tudor buildings, this fine 15th century hostelry retains its convivial character, the bar invariably buzzing with animated conversation between locals and visitors to this neat little town of tree-lined streets and interesting shops. All around is a peaceful and verdant countryside and the coast may be reached in little over half-an-hour. A spacious bar restaurant offers excellent home-cooked fare with both traditional and modern influences. Delightfully appointed en suite bedrooms with the option of a luxury four-poster bed. Children and pets welcome.

The White Lion, High Street, Tenterden, Kent TN30 6BD
www.whitelion-tenterden.co.uk
e-mail: whitelion@celticinnspubs.co.uk

ETC/AA

TEL: 01580 765077 FAX: 01580 764157

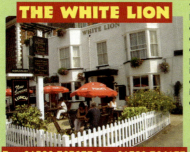

Bed & Breakfast Stops 2006

Kent/Lancashire

Bolden's Wood
Fiddling Lane, Stowting, Near Ashford, Kent TN25 6AP

Between Ashford/Folkestone. Friendly atmosphere – modern accommodation (one double, two singles) on our Smallholding, set in unspoilt countryside. No smoking throughout. Log-burning stove in TV lounge. Full English breakfast. Country pubs (meals) nearby. Children love the old-fashioned farmyard, free range chickens, friendly sheep and... Llamas, Alpacas and Rheas. Treat yourself to a Llama-led Picnic Trek to our private secluded woodland and downland and enjoy watching the bird life, rabbits, foxes, badgers and occasionally deer. Easy access to Channel Tunnel and Ferry Ports.

Bed and Breakfast £25.00 per person.
Contact: Jim and Alison Taylor

Tel & Fax: 01303 812011
e-mail: StayoverNight@aol.com
www.countrypicnics.com

Great Field Farm
Stelling Minnis, Canterbury, Kent CT4 6DE
Tel: 01227 709223

Situated in beautiful countryside, our spacious farmhouse provides friendly, comfortable accommodation.
• Full central heating and double glazing.
• Traditional breakfasts cooked on the Aga.
• Courtesy tray and colour TV in each suite/bedroom.
• Cottage suite with its own entrance.
• Annexe suite ideal for B&B and self-catering.
• New detached ground floor "Sunset Lodge".
• Ample off-road parking.
• Good pub food nearby. • Non-smoking establishment.
Bed and Breakfast from £25 per person; reductions for children.

Bed & Breakfast • Self Catering • www.great-field-farm.co.uk

Sunnyside & Holmsdale Hotel
25-27 High Street, North Shore, Blackpool FY1 2BN

Two minutes from North Station, five minutes from Promenade, all shows and amenities. Colour TV lounge. Full central heating. No smoking. Children welcome; cots available. Reductions for children sharing. Senior Citizens' reductions May and June, always welcome.

Special diets catered for, good food and warm friendly atmosphere awaits you. Bed and Breakfast from £18. Morning tea available. Overnight guests welcome when available. Small parties catered for.

Elsie and Ron Platt
Tel: 01253 623781
e-mail: elsieandron@amserve.net

Rakefoot Farm
Chaigley, Near Clitheroe BB7 3LY
ETC ♦♦♦♦
ETC ★★★/★★★★
Tel: (Chipping) 01995 61332 or 07889 279067 • Fax: 01995 61296
e-mail: info@rakefootfarm.co.uk • website: www.rakefootfarm.co.uk
Family farm in the beautiful countryside of the Ribble Valley in the peaceful Forest of Bowland, with panoramic views. Ideally placed for touring Coast, Dales and Lakes. 9 miles M6 Junction 31a. Superb walks, golf and horse riding nearby, or visit pretty villages and factory shops. Warm welcome whether on holiday or business, refreshments on arrival.

BED AND BREAKFAST or SELF-CATERING in 17th century farmhouse and traditional stone barn conversion. Wood-burning stoves, central heating, exposed beams and stonework. Most bedrooms en suite, some ground floor. Excellent home cooked meals, pubs/restaurants nearby. Indoor games room, garden and patios. Dogs by arrangement. Laundry. Past winner of NWTB Silver Award for Self-catering Holiday of the Year.

B&B £20 - £30pppn sharing, £20 - £35pp single
S/C four properties (3 can be internally interlinked)
£90 - £570 per property per week. Short breaks available.

24   Please mention Bed & Breakfast Stops when enquiring

Lincolnshire

Bed & Breakfast at No. 19 West Street
Kings Cliffe, Near Stamford, Peterborough PE8 6XB
Tel: 01780 470365 • Fax 01780 470623

A beautifully restored 500-year-old Listed stone house, reputedly one of King John's Hunting Lodges, situated in the heart of the stone village of Kings Cliffe on the edge of Rockingham Forest. Both the double and twin rooms have their own private bathrooms, and there is colour TV and a welcome tray in each. In the summer breakfast can be served on the terrace overlooking a beautiful walled garden. Off-street parking is behind secure gates. Within 10 miles there are seven stately homes, including Burghley House famous for the Horse Trials, Rutland Water, and the beautiful old towns of Stamford and Oundle. Imaginative evening meals are available on request and prices range from £12 to £18. Open all year.

A non-smoking house • Bed and Breakfast from £22.50 per person • Proprietor: Jenny Dixon
e-mail: kjhl_dixon@hotmail.com • www.kingjohnhuntinglodge.co.uk

---

Baumber Park

Spacious elegant farmhouse in quiet parkland setting, on a mixed farm. Large plantsman's garden, wildlife pond and grass tennis court. Fine bedrooms with lovely views, period furniture, log fires and books. Central in the county and close to the Lincolnshire Wolds, this rolling countryside is little known, quite unspoilt, and ideal for walking, cycling or riding. Championship golf courses at Woodhall Spa. Well located for historic Lincoln, interesting market towns and many antique shops. Enjoy a relaxing break, excellent breakfasts, and a comfortable, homely atmosphere.

Double, twin, single/family suite. All en suite or private bathroom.
Bed and Breakfast from £26.

Mrs C.E. Harrison, Baumber Park, Baumber, Near Horncastle LN9 5NE
01507 578235 • Fax: 01507 578417 • mobile: 07977 722776
http://uk.geocities.com/baumberpark/thehouse

Mrs S. Evans, Willow Farm,
Thorpe Fendykes, Wainfleet,
Skegness PE24 4QH
Tel: 01754 830316
Email: willowfarmhols@aol.com
Website: www.willowfarmholidays.co.uk

In the heart of the Lincolnshire Fens, Willow Farm is a working smallholding with free range hens, goats, horses and ponies. Situated in a peaceful hamlet with abundant wildlife, ideal for a quiet retreat – yet only 15 minutes from the Skegness coast, shops, amusements and beaches.

Bed and Breakfast is provided in comfortable en suite rooms from £20 per person per night, reductions for children (suppers and sandwiches can be provided in the evening on request). Rooms have tea and coffee making facilities and a colour TV and are accessible to disabled guests. Friendly hosts! Ring for brochure.

We offer a warm and friendly stay at our delightfully converted 18th century coaching inn, so get away from the 'hurly burly' of modern life, and escape to the peace and quiet, although Lincoln is only 12 miles away and many other attractions are nearby.

The Black Swan Guest House

21 High Street, Marton,
Gainsborough, Lincs DN21 5AH
Tel & Fax: 01427 718878
info@blackswan-marton.co.uk
www.blackswan-marton.co.uk

All rooms en suite, with full facilities; Comfortable guest lounge. Breakfasts are made with the best quality local produce and should set you up for the day. We are a non-smoking establishment.

Single from £35, double/twin from £58.

Merseyside/Norfolk

Holme Leigh Guest House
93 Woodcroft Road, Wavertree, Liverpool L15 2HG

Recently fully refurbished • All rooms comfortably furnished complete with TV, tea and coffee and en suite facilities • Full central heating • Award-winning breakfast room • Close to Sefton Park, just two miles from the M62 and 20 minutes from the airport, 2½ miles from city centre.

Tel: 0151-734 2216
e-mail: info@holmeleigh.com
website: www.holmeleigh.com

Single rooms available from £22 per night, doubles and twins from £44. Family rooms also available. All rates include VAT and Continental breakfast.

The ideal base to explore East Anglia & The Norfolk Broads

Simon and Heather welcome you to this former village school, fully refurbished in 2005, with views over the quiet Tas Valley, south of Norwich. Oakbrook House is an excellent touring base for East Anglia, centrally situated in the region. Nine warm comfortable rooms of various sizes and prices to match individual budget and comfort, each with en suite wc and basin, colour TV, clock radio and hospitality tray, en suite or private shower. All diets catered for, central heating, smoke-free, pets by arrangement. Evening meals and daytime use of the facilities available.

Contact us for brochure. Long stay discounts. B&B from £19 pppn.

OAKBROOK HOUSE

Oakbrook Guest House, Frith Way, Great Moulton, Norwich NR15 2HE
Tel: 01379 677539 • mobile: 07885 351212
e-mail: simonandheather@btopenworld.com • www.oakbrookhouse.co.uk

---

DOLPHIN LODGE

Friendly welcome from the proprietors of this bungalow accommodation. Bed and Breakfast in a village setting just two-and-a-half miles from beaches. Many rural walks locally; within easy reach of all Norfolk's attractions including the Norfolk Broads. All rooms en suite, with tea/coffee making facilities, TV, hairdryer.

Mrs G. Faulkner, Dolphin Lodge,
3 Knapton Road, Trunch,
North Walsham NR28 0QE
Tel: 01263 720961

Shrublands Farm

Shrublands farm is a working arable farm in the village of Northrepps, two and a half miles south-east of Cromer and 20 miles north of Norwich. This is the ideal situation for exploring the wonderful coast of North Norfolk, National Trust properties and The Norfolk Broads. The Victorian/Edwardian house has three bedrooms, all with private facilities, colour TV, and tea and coffee making facilities. There is full central heating and plenty of parking space. This is a non-smoking house. Children over 12 years. Sorry, no pets. Prices: £27-£29 per person per night. Single supplement £10.

Mrs Ann Youngman, Shrublands Farm, Northrepps, Cromer, Norfolk NR27 0AA
Tel and Fax: (01263) 579497   e-mail: youngman@farming.co.uk
Website: www.broadland.com/shrublands

Norfolk/Northumberland

MARINE BAR with accommodation

Pets are very welcome at a small charge of £1 per night. We do not have en suite rooms but every room has its own basin. Bar meals available all day. Colour TV in all bedrooms. Most rooms have a view. £22.50 pppn, including breakfast. Town centre location. Open all year.

10 St Edmunds Terrace, Hunstanton, Norfolk PE36 5EH • Tel: 01485 533310

Stamfordham Bay Horse Inn
South Side, Stamfordham NE18 0PB

Family-run 16th century village inn serving lunches and evening meals; real ales, pool and darts. Four double, one twin/family and one single en suite rooms with TV and hot drinks facilities; central heating. Newcastle Airport six miles. Children and pets welcome. Parking available. Open January to December.

B&B from £33 single, £58 double & £68 to £78 (for four) family room.

Tel: 01661 886244

e-mail: stay@stamfordham-bay.co.uk • www.stamfordham-bay.co.uk

---

South Hazelrigg is situated between the market town of Wooler and the coastal village of Belford, approx. 10 minutes off the A1 road, ideally placed for trips to the beach, Farne Islands, Holy Island, the Cheviot Hills and the many castles. Rooms are spacious and comfortable with hospitality trays and colour TV. Breakfast is served in the elegant dining room and the local village inns provide an extensive menu. Local activities include birdwatching, fishing, horse riding and golf, Bamburgh being the most scenic English course.

Sheila Dodds, South Hazelrigg, Chatton, Alnwick NE66 5RZ
01668 215216 • mobile: 07710 346076

e-mail: sed@hazelrigg.fsnet.co.uk
www.farmhousebandb.co.uk

❖ Struthers Farm ❖
Catton, Allendale, Hexham NE47 9LP

Struthers Farm offers a warm welcome in the heart of England, with many splendid local walks from the farm itself. Panoramic views. Situated in an area of outstanding beauty. Double/twin rooms, en suite bathrooms, central heating. Good farmhouse cooking. Ample safe parking. Come and share our home and enjoy beautiful countryside. Near Hadrians Wall (½ hour's drive). Children welcome, pets by prior arrangement. Open all year. Bed and Breakfast from £25; Optional Evening Meal from £12.50.

Contact Mrs Ruby Keenleyside ❖ **01434 683580**

Bed & Breakfast Stops 2006

Oxfordshire/Shropshire/Somerset

The Close Guest House
Witney Road, Long Hanborough, Oxfordshire OX29 8HF

We offer comfortable accommodation in house set in own grounds of one-and-a-half acres. Three family rooms, four double rooms; all en suite; one double and one single. All have colour TV and tea/coffee making facilities. Full central heating. Use of garden and car parking for eight cars. Please mention FHG when booking.

Close to Woodstock, Oxford and the Cotswolds. Babysitting. Open all year except Christmas. Bed and Breakfast from £20.
Mrs I.J. Warwick (01993 882485).

The Four Alls Inn & Motel
Newport Rd, Woodeaves, Market Drayton TF9 2AG

A warm welcome is assured at the Four Alls, situated in a quiet location of Woodeaves yet only a mile from the town of Market Drayton, and within easy reach of Shropshire's premier attractions.

Relax in our spacious bar, sample our home-cooked food and excellent traditional beers, then enjoy a good night's sleep in one of our nine en suite chalet-style rooms with central heating, TV and tea/coffee making facilities. The function room is available for weddings, celebrations or as a conference venue and can accommodate 50-100. Large car park.

Tel: 01630 652995 • Fax: 01630 653930
e-mail: inn@thefouralls.com • www.thefouralls.com

Lovely 17th century farmhouse in peaceful village amidst the beautiful South Shropshire Hills, an Area of Outstanding Natural Beauty. The farmhouse is full of character and all rooms have heating and are comfortable and spacious. The bedrooms are either en suite or private bathroom with hairdryers, tea/coffee making facilities, patchwork quilts and colour TV. There is a lounge with colour TV and inglenook fireplace. Children welcome. We are a working farm, centrally situated for visiting Ironbridge, Shrewsbury and Ludlow, each being easily reached within half an hour. Touring and walking information is available for visitors. Bed and full English Breakfast from £23pppn. Non-smoking. Open all year excluding November, December and January.

Mrs Mary Jones, Acton Scott Farm, Acton Scott, Church Stretton SY6 6QN • Tel: 01694 781260
Fax: 0870-129 4591 • e-mail: fhg@actonscottfarm.co.uk • www.actonscottfarm.co.uk

---

Clanville Manor
18th century elegance: 21st Century comfort!

Stay for a few days and really explore the Somerset countryside, Glastonbury, Wells and Bath, many lovely gardens and National Trust properties, from a Georgian farmhouse on a working farm two miles from Castle Cary. Flagstone hall, English oak staircase, old elm floorboards, period furniture and Oriental rugs. Spacious and fully equipped en suite rooms, full heating, a log fire in winter and a heated outdoor pool. Wonderful Aga breakfasts with local produce including our own hens' eggs! See our website for full details and availability.

Mrs Sally Snook, Clanville Manor, Castle Cary, Somerset BA7 7PJ
Tel: +44 1963 350124
Fax: +44 1963 350719

www.clanvillemanor.co.uk • clanvillemanor@aol.com

---

28   Please mention Bed & Breakfast Stops when enquiring

Somerset

ETC ♦♦♦

"MOORLANDS"
Hutton, Near Weston-super-Mare,
Somerset BS24 9QH
Tel and Fax: 01934 812283
e-mail: margaret-holt@hotmail.co.uk
website: www.guestaccom.co.uk/35

Enjoy fine food and warm hospitality at this impressive late Georgian house set in landscaped gardens below the slopes of the Western Mendips. A wonderful touring centre, perfectly placed for visits to beaches, sites of special interest and historic buildings. Families with children particularly welcome; reduced terms and pony rides. Full central heating, open fire in comfortable lounge. Open all year. Bed and Breakfast from £23 per person.

Resident host: Mrs Margaret Holt

'LANA'
Hollow Farm, Westbury-sub-Mendip,
Near Wells, Somerset BA5 1HH
Tel & Fax: 01749 870635
Mrs Sheila Stott
e-mail: Sheila@stott2366.freeserve.co.uk

Modern farmhouse on working farm. Comfortable family home in beautiful gardens with views of Somerset Levels and Mendips. Quiet location. Breakfast room for sole use of guests. Full English breakfast. Meals available at local pub five minutes' walk away. En suite rooms with fridge, hairdryer, tea/coffee making facilities, shaver point, colour TV and central heating. Non-smoking.

Terms £25pppn, reduced rates for 3 nights or more.

Silver Award

The Old Mill
Bishop's Hull, Taunton TA1 5AB
Tel & Fax: 01823 289732

Grade II Listed former Corn Mill, situated on the edge of a conservation village just two miles from Taunton. We have two lovely double bedrooms, The Mill Room with en suite facilities overlooking the weir pool, and The Cottage Suite with its own private bathroom, again with views over the river. Both rooms are centrally heated, with TV, generous beverage tray and thoughtful extras. Guests have their own lounge and dining area overlooking the river, where breakfast may be taken from our extensive breakfast menu amidst machinery of a bygone era. We are a non-smoking establishment.

Double en suite £27.50 pppn, double with private bathroom £25 pppn, single occupancy from £35 pn.

The Gascony Hotel
50 The Avenue, Minehead,
Somerset TA24 5BB
Tel: 01643 705939
Fax: 01643 709926
www.gasconyhotel.co.uk

Well-appointed family-run Victorian house hotel, ideally placed on the level in the lovely tree-lined Avenue, only two minutes' walk from the sea front. Spacious en suite bedrooms, all with colour TV, radio alarm, hot drinks tray and hairdryer. Ground floor bedroom suitable for the disabled. Elegant dining room offering a varied and interesting choice of home-cooked dishes.

Prices £29 to £37.50 pppn;
DB&B £42 to £49 pppn.

Two comfortable lounges; one with a well-stocked cocktail bar • Full gas-fired central heating • Large private car park • Ideal for walkers • Open March to December • Major credit cards accepted.

Bed & Breakfast Stops 2006

Somerset

THATCHED COUNTRY COTTAGE & GARDEN B&B

An old thatched country cottage halfway between Taunton and Honiton, set in the idyllic Blackdown Hills, a designated Area of Outstanding Natural Beauty. Picturesque countryside with plenty of flowers and wildlife. Central for north/south coasts of Somerset, Dorset and Devon. Double/single and family suite with own facilities, TV, tea/coffee. Conservatory/Garden Room. Evening Meals also available. Open all year. B&B from £17.50pppn.

**Mrs Pam Parry, Pear Tree Cottage,
Stapley, Churchstanton, Taunton TA3 7QA
Tel & Fax: 01823 601224
e-mail: colvin.parry@virgin.net
www.SmoothHound.co.uk/hotels/thatch.html** OR **www.best-hotel.com/peartreecottage**

See also advertisement in main section

Imposing country house in Exmoor National Park on the wooded slopes of West Porlock commanding exceptional sea views of Porlock Bay and countryside. Set in five acres of beautiful woodland gardens unique for its variety and size of unusual trees and shrubs and offering a haven of rural tranquillity. The house has large spacious rooms with fine and beautiful furnishings throughout. Two double, two twin and one family bedrooms, all with en suite or private bathrooms, TV, tea/coffee making facilities, radio-alarm clock and shaver point. Non-smoking. Private car park. Bed and Breakfast from £29 to £32 per person. Credit Cards accepted. Sorry, no pets.

**West Porlock House
01643 862880**

Margery and Henry Dyer, West Porlock House,
West Porlock, Near Minehead TA24 8NX
E-mail: westporlockhouse@amserve.com

The Owl's Crest

39 Kewstoke Road, Kewstoke
Weston-Super-Mare
BS22 9YE
Tel: 01934 417672

Situated within the small country village of Kewstoke, just 1¼ miles from Weston and just minutes from the M5. Ideally placed for walks through National Trust countryside or relaxing strolls along the unspoilt beach at Sand Bay. A friendly, personal service is offered with the flexibility to make your stay as enjoyable as possible. Relax in our comfortable guest lounge

or in fine weather enjoy the sheltered sunny garden terrace. All our individually decorated rooms are en suite with TV, radio alarm clock, hairdryer and tea/coffee tray. Recommended restaurant/carvery within village.

Bed and Breakfast from £26.00 per person per night.
Non-smoking throughout.

GOLD COMMENDED AWARD WINNERS - WESTON HOTELS ASSOCIATION.
e-mail: theowlscrest.1@btopenworld.com
website: www.theowlscrest.co.uk

hornsbury mill
Eleighwater, Chard TA20 3AQ
Tel & Fax: 01460 63317
e-mail: hornsburymill@btclick.com
www.hornsburymill.co.uk

Contemporary capability blends effortlessly with tradition in the informal landscaped setting of this charming 19th century working mill, set deep in rural Somerset. The Mill Restaurant serves snacks, lunches and evening meals, with traditional roasts on Sundays. Relax on the sun terrace for morning coffee or enjoy a delightful dinner as the water wheel turns beside you. The cosy en suite bedrooms are furnished with everything needed to ensure a pleasant and relaxing stay. Guests can stroll among swans and wildfowl in the four-acre gardens, which make a romantic backdrop for weddings and all kinds of special occasions.

Somerset/Staffordshire/Suffolk

Hungerford Farm is an attractive 13th century farmhouse on a family-run 350 acre farm with cattle, horses, free range chickens and ducks. We are situated in beautiful countryside on the edge of the Exmoor National Park. Ideal country for walking, riding or cycling. The medieval village of Dunster with its spectacular castle, mentioned in the Domesday Book, and the numerous attractions of Exmoor are a short distance away. There is a good choice of local pubs within easy reach. Double and twin bedrooms with TV. Children welcome. Stabling available for visitors' horses. Dogs by arrangement. From £22 per person. Open February to November.

Hungerford Farm, Washford, Somerset TA23 0JZ
Tel: 01984 640285 • e-mail: sarah.richmond@virgin.net

Bailbrook Lodge Hotel
35/37 London Road West, Bath BA1 7HZ

Bailbrook Lodge is a splendid Georgian country house which has been totally and sympathetically redecorated and refurbished. It has delightful lawned gardens and free car parking. There are 15 en suite bedrooms, including 5 with four-poster beds. There is satellite TV, coffee and tea making facilities, complimentary biscuits and mineral water. Dinner is available in our nearby riverside restaurant.

Price per person including full English breakfast is from £35 to £55.

Tel: 01225 859090 • Fax: 01225 852299
e-mail: hotel@bailbrooklodge.co.uk • www.bailbrooklodge.co.uk

Offley Grove Farm, Adbaston, Eccleshall, Staffs ST20 0QB
Tel/Fax: 01785 280205

You'll consider this a good find! Quality accommodation and excellent breakfasts. Small traditional mixed farm surrounded by beautiful countryside. The house is tastefully furnished and provides all home comforts. Whether you are planning to book here for a break in your journey, stay for a weekend or take your holidays here, you will find something to suit all tastes among the many local attractions. Situated on the Staffordshire/ Shropshire borders we are convenient for Alton Towers, Stoke-on-Trent, Ironbridge, etc. Reductions for children. Play area for children. Open all year. Bed and Breakfast all en suite from £25pp. Many guests return. Self-catering cottages available.
Brochure on request.
e-mail: accomm@offleygrovefarm.freeserve.co.uk
website: www.offleygrovefarm.co.uk

A comfortable modernised Edwardian house set in a large secluded garden located four miles south of Ipswich. Ideally situated to explore the Suffolk heritage coast and countryside, within easy reach of "Constable Country", Lavenham, Kersey, the historic market town of Bury St Edmunds plus many other picturesque locations.

Twin, double and single bedrooms; guests' bathroom with shower and toilet, lounge with TV. Good pub meals available in the village. Double and Twin from £26 per person per night. No smoking.

**Mrs Rosanna Steward, High View,
Back Lane, Washbrook, Ipswich IP8 3JA**
Tel: 01473 730494
e-mail: rosanna3@suffolkholidays.com
www.suffolkholidays.com

Bed & Breakfast Stops 2006

Surrey/East Sussex/West Sussex

Chase Lodge Hotel
An Award Winning Hotel
with style & elegance, set in tranquil surroundings at affordable prices

10 Park Road Hampton Wick Kingston-Upon-Thames KT1 4AS
Tel: 020 8943 1862 . Fax: 020 8943 9363
E-mail: info@chaselodgehotel.com Website:www.chaselodgehotel.com
and
www.surreyhotels.com

*Quality en suite bedrooms
Full English Breakfast
A la carte menu
Licensed bar
Wedding Receptions
Honeymoon suite
available with jacuzzi & steam area
20 minutes from Heathrow Airport
Close to Kingston town centre & all
major transport links.*

AA ◆◆◆◆ Les Routiers RAC ★★★★   All major credit cards accepted

---

Bolebroke Castle

Henry VIII's hunting lodge, Bolebroke Castle is set on a beautiful 30 acre estate with lakes, woodlands and views to Ashdown Forest, where you will find 'Pooh Bridge'. Antiques and beamed ceilings add to the atmosphere. Four-poster suite available. B&B or Self-Catering options. Please call for our brochure.

In the heart of "Winnie the Pooh" country.

Bolebroke Castle, Hartfield, East Sussex TN7 4JJ
Tel: 01892 770061

ETC ◆◆◆◆   www.bolebrokecastle.co.uk

Behind the Georgian facade of the White Hart lies an historic Tudor building which has been substantially extended to create a lively county town hotel.

◆ 53 bedrooms, all en suite with colour TV, telephone, tea-making. Some rooms have views of the Downs; some with disabled access.

◆ Wide range of meals and snacks available daily - à la carte, carvery, bar meals, light snacks, teas and coffees.

◆ Leisure Centre and Health Spa with heated indoor pool, fully equipped gym, sauna, aerobics studio, beauty clinic etc.

White Hart Hotel, High Street, Lewes BN7 1XE • Tel: 01273 476694
Fax: 01273 476295 • info@whitehartlewes.co.uk • www.whitehartlewes.co.uk

---

"Meadowhills"
Stedham, Midhurst, West Sussex GU29 0PT
Tel: 01730 812609 or Mobile: 07776 262147

Built in 1908 this small, comfortable, country estate is set in its own grounds of 25 acres with magnificent views over the South Downs.

Activities include Fishing Rights • Walkers' Paradise • Riding Stables nearby • 20 miles to South Coast • Golf • Polo • Leisure Centres • Horse Racing at Fontwell and Goodwood.

Places of interest include Uppark • The Weald & Downland Open Air Museum • Petworth House and other National Trust Properties • Chichester Festival Theatre.

Call or write for further information and tariff • www.meadowhills.co.uk

Warwickshire/Wiltshire

Holly Tree Cottage
Birmingham Road, Pathlow, Stratford-upon-Avon CV37 0ES
Tel & Fax: 01789 204461

Period cottage dating from 17th Century, with antiques, paintings, collection of porcelain, fresh flowers, tasteful furnishings and friendly atmosphere. Picturesque gardens, orchard, paddock and pasture with wildlife and extensive views over open countryside. Situated 3 miles north of Stratford-upon-Avon towards Henley-in-Arden on A3400. Rooms have television, radio/alarm, hospitality trays and hairdryers. Breakfasts are a speciality. Pubs and restaurants nearby. Ideally located for Theatre, Shakespeare Country, Heart of England, Cotswolds, Warwick Castle, Blenheim Palace and National Trust Properties. Well situated for National Exhibition Centre, Birmingham and National Agricultural Centre, Stoneleigh. Children welcome, pets by arrangement. Non-smoking. Bed and Breakfast from £29 per person.

e-mail: john@hollytree-cottage.co.uk • website: www.hollytree-cottage.co.uk

---

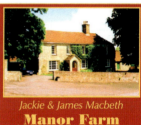

Jackie & James Macbeth
Manor Farm
Collingbourne Kingston,
Marlborough,
Wiltshire SN8 3SD

Tel: 01264 850859
e-mail: stay@manorfm.com
www.manorfm.com

Manor Farm B&B

• Attractive Grade II Listed farmhouse on working family farm, very easy to find, 12 minutes south of Marlborough on the A338 Salisbury Road.
• Our comfortable, spacious and well equipped rooms are all en suite or private, and include double, twin and family (for four).
• Sumptuous traditional, vegetarian, and other special diet breakfasts.
• Beautiful countryside with superb walking and cycling from the farm.
• Pleasure flights by helicopter from our private airstrip.
• Horses and pets welcome • Ample private parking
• Non-smoking • Credit cards welcome

B&B from £27 pppn

WERNHAM FARM
Clench Common, Marlborough, Wiltshire SN8 4DR
Tel: 01672 512236
e-mail: margglvsf@aol.com

This working farm is set in picturesque countryside on Wansdyke, off the A345. It is close to Marlborough, Avebury, Pewsey and the Kennet & Avon Canal.

Accommodation is available in two family bedrooms, one en suite and one with private bathroom.

Terms: £40 single, £55 double.

Five caravan and camping pitches are also available.

Newton Farmhouse
Southampton Road, Whiteparish, Salisbury SP5 2QL

This historic Listed 16th century farmhouse on the borders of the New Forest was formerly part of the Trafalgar Estate and is situated eight miles south of Salisbury, convenient for Stonehenge, Romsey, Winchester, Portsmouth and Bournemouth. All rooms have pretty, en suite facilities and are delightfully decorated, six with genuine period four-poster beds. The beamed diningroom houses a collection of Nelson memorabilia and antiques and has flagstone floors and an inglenook fireplace with an original brick built bread oven. The superb English breakfast is complemented by fresh fruits, preserves and free-range eggs. A swimming pool is idyllically set in the extensive, well stocked gardens and children are most welcome in this non-smoking establishment.

AA ♦♦♦♦
PREMIER SELECTED
SILVER AWARD

Tel: 01794 884416 • e-mail: reservations@newtonfarmhouse.co.uk • www.newtonfarmhouse.co.uk

Bed & Breakfast Stops 2006   33

Worcestershire/North Yorkshire

GABLES BED & BREAKFAST

Gables offers high quality, comfortable accommodation and service. Full English breakfast with free-range eggs in the delightful period diningroom. Excellently fitted en suite facilities. Well-lit parking at rear of premises.

The county cricket ground is a ten-minute walk. Near to Elgar's birthplace and city centre. Ideal for the Cotswolds, Stratford and Malvern and easy access for M5.

We offer a warm welcome to our guests and make their stay as enjoyable as possible.

Janette Ratcliffe,
166 Bromyard Road,
St Johns,
Worcester WR2 5EE
Tel & Fax:
01905 425488

www.gablesbedandbreakfast.co.uk

WELLGARTH HOUSE ETC ♦♦♦
Wetherby Road, Rufforth, York YO23 3QB

A warm welcome awaits you at Wellgarth House.....

Ideally situated in Rufforth (B1224), three miles from York, one mile from the ring road (A1237) and convenient for Park & Ride. Bed & Breakfast from £27pppn. All rooms are en suite and have tea and coffee making facilities and colour TV. Excellent local pub two minutes' walk away. Large private car park.

TEL: 01904 738592
MOBILE: 07711 252577

Banavie is a large semi-detached house set in a quiet part of the picturesque village of Thornton-le-Dale, one of the prettiest villages in Yorkshire with its famous thatched cottage and bubbling stream flowing through the centre. We offer our guests a quiet night's sleep and rest away from the main road, yet only four minutes' walk from the village centre. One large double or twin bedroom and two double bedrooms, all tastefully decorated with en suite facilities, colour TV, hairdryer, shaver point etc. and tea/coffee making facilities. There is a large guest lounge, tea tray on arrival. A real Yorkshire breakfast is served in the dining room. Places to visit include Castle Howard, Eden Camp, North Yorkshire Moors Railway, Goathland ("Heartbeat"), York etc. There are three pubs, a bistro and a fish and chip shop for meals. Children and dogs welcome. Own keys.

B&B from £23 - £27 pppn • SAE please for brochure • Welcome Host • Hygiene Certificate held • No Smoking • Mrs Ella Bowes

BANAVIE, ROXBY ROAD, THORNTON-LE-DALE, PICKERING YO18 7SX
Tel: 01751 474316 • e-mail: info@banavie.co.uk • www.banavie.uk.com

Browson Bank Farmhouse Accommodation

A newly converted granary set in 300 acres of farmland. The accommodation consists of three very tastefully furnished double/twin rooms all en suite, tea and coffee making facilities, colour TV and central heating. A large, comfortable lounge is available to relax in. Full English breakfast served. Situated six miles West of Scotch Corner (A1). Ideal location to explore the scenic countryside of Teesdale and the Yorkshire Dales and close to the scenic towns of Barnard Castle and Richmond. Terms from £20.00 per night.

Browson Bank Farmhouse, Browson Bank, Dalton, Richmond DL11 7HE
Tel: (01325) 718504 or (01325) 718246

North Yorkshire

Oaklands Guest House

351 Strensall Road, Earswick,
York YO32 9SW

A very warm welcome awaits you at our attractive family home set in open countryside, yet only three miles from York. Ideally situated for City, Coast, Dales and Moors.

Our comfortable bedrooms have central heating
• en suite facilities • colour TV • razor point
• tea & coffee tray • radio alarms • hairdryers

Full breakfast is served in a light airy dining room. Discounts available. Open all year. No pets. Smoking in garden only.

Bed and full English Breakfast from £23.

Telephone: 01904 768443
e-mail: mavmo@oaklands5.fsnet.co.uk

Tangalwood

Roxby Road,
Thornton-le-Dale,
Pickering
YO18 7SX

ETC ♦♦♦♦

One twin and one double en suite rooms, one single; all with tea/coffee making facilities and TV; alarm clock/radio and hairdryer also provided; diningroom; central heating.

Very clean and comfortable accommodation with good food. Situated in a quiet part of this picturesque village, which is in a good position for Moors, "Heartbeat" country, coast, North York Moors Railway, Flamingo Park Zoo and forest drives, mountain biking and walking. Good facilities for meals provided in the village. Open Easter to October for Bed and Breakfast from £23 each. Private car park. Secure motorbike and cycle storage.

TELEPHONE: **01751 474688** • WEBSITE: www.accommodation.uk.net/tangalwood

---

Detached 16th century farmhouse in private grounds, one mile east of Skipton, gateway to the Dales. Luxury bed and breakfast with fireside treats in the lounge. All rooms are quiet, spacious, have panoramic views, washbasins, tea facilities and electric overblankets; some en suite. No smoking. No pets and no children under 12 years. Safe parking. Bed and Breakfast from £24-£30pp. Single occupancy from £30-£48. Open all year. Farm cottage (ETC ★★★) sometimes available. Credit cards accepted.

AA ♦♦♦♦
WHICH?

Tel: 07050 207787/01756 793849
www.yorkshirenet.co.uk/accgde/lowskibeden

LOW SKIBEDEN FARMHOUSE, HARROGATE ROAD, SKIPTON BD23 6AB

Mount Grace Farm

A warm welcome awaits you on working farm surrounded by beautiful open countryside with magnificent views. Ideal location for touring or exploring the many walks in the area. Luxury en suite bedrooms with tea/coffee facilities. Spacious guests' lounge with colour TV. Garden. Enjoy delicious, generous helpings of farmhouse fayre cooked in our Aga. Children from 12 years plus. No smoking. No pets. Bed and Breakfast from £30. Open all year except Christmas.

Joyce Ashbridge, Mount Grace Farm,
Cold Kirby, Thirsk YO7 2HL
Tel: 01845 597389 • Fax: 01845 597872
e-mail: joyce@mountgracefarm.com   website: www.mountgracefarm.com

Bed & Breakfast Stops 2006   35

North Yorkshire

Beautiful old farmhouse situated in a lovely valley close to quiet roadside. Set in 120 acres of pastureland and woods. Centre of National Park. Warm and friendly atmosphere. Diningroom/Lounge for guests with TV and books. Close to river, one mile from Glaisdale village and mainline railway, eight miles to Whitby, four miles steam railway and Heartbeat country. Both bedrooms have pretty decor and TV. One double/twin and one family room, both en suite. Full Yorkshire Breakfast. Packed lunches. All diets catered for. B&B from £22-£25.

e-mail: egtonbanksfarm@agriplus.net
website: www.egtonbanksfarm.agriplus.net

EGTON BANKS FARM
♦Glaisdale, Whitby YO21 2QP♦
Tel: 01947 897289

HALL FARM
Gilling East, York YO62 4JW
e-mail: virginia@hallfarmgilling.co.uk
01439 788314

Come and stay with us at Hall Farm

A beautifully situated 400 acre working stock farm with extensive views over Ryedale. We offer a friendly, family welcome with home made scones on arrival. A ground floor double en suite room is available and includes hospitality tray with home made biscuits. Sittingroom with TV and open fire on chilly evenings, diningroom with patio doors to conservatory. You will be the only guests so the breakfast time is up to you. Full English Breakfast includes home made bread and preserves.

Terms from £25 per person.

Excellent eating places in Helmsley and the nearby villages. York, Castle Howard and the North York Moors within half-an-hour drive.

The most beautifully situated accommodation

Five ground floor en suite rooms round a pretty courtyard. All our rooms are full of character - oak beams etc., with modern facilities, all with views of the countryside. Private fishing lake. Terms from £60 to £75.

Details from
Mrs L. Hitchen, St George's Court, Old Home Farm, High Grantley, Ripon HG4 3PJ
Tel: 01765 620618

please note

All the information in this book is given in good faith in the belief that it is correct. However, the publishers cannot guarantee the facts given in these pages, neither are they responsible for changes in policy, ownership or terms that may take place after the date of going to press. Readers should always satisfy themselves that the facilities they require are available and that the terms, if quoted, still apply.

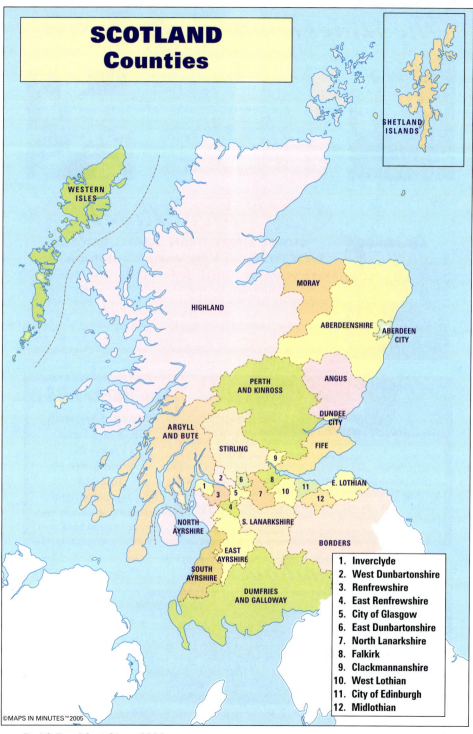

Argyll & Bute/Borders

The Barriemore

Corran Esplanade, Oban PA34 5AQ
Tel: 01631 566356 • Fax: 01631 571604

The Barriemore enjoys a splendid location as the last hotel on the Oban seafront on Corran Esplanade. Built in 1895, the house exudes an opulence in keeping with its late Victorian origins. All bedrooms are beautifully and individually furnished with full en suite facilities. The elegant lounge is an ideal spot for quiet relaxation, while the attractive dining room, overlooking Oban Bay, is the perfect place to enjoy full Scottish breakfasts including locally produced smoked haddock and kippers.

e-mail: reception@barriemore-hotel.co.uk
website: www.barriemore-hotel.co.uk

Palace Hotel

GEORGE STREET, OBAN, ARGYLL PA34 5SB
01631 562294 • www.thepalacehotel.activehotels.com

A small family hotel offering personal supervision situated on Oban's sea front with wonderful views over the Bay, to the Mull Hills beyond. All rooms en suite, with colour TV, tea/coffee making facilities, several non-smoking. The Palace is an ideal base for a real Highland holiday. By boat you can visit the islands of Kerrera, Coll, Tiree, Lismore, Mull and Iona, and by road Glencoe, Ben Nevis and Inveraray. Fishing, golf, horse riding, sailing, tennis and bowls all nearby. Children and pets welcome. Reductions for children. Please write or telephone for brochure. Competitive rates.

The Bantry B&B

Mackays of Eyemouth
20/24 High Street
Eyemouth
Berwickshire
TD14 5EU
Tel & Fax: 018907 51900
info@mackaysofeyemouth.co.uk
www.mackaysofeyemouth.co.uk

The Bantry Bed & Breakfast is situated in the heart of Eyemouth, nestled overlooking the beach and harbour, amongst the fishing cottages and rich history of the town.
The Bantry offers a wide range of comfortable family accommodation from our picturesque location on the shore. Why not sit on our rooftop decking area, sipping an ice-cold drink and relaxing to the sound of the waves breaking gently on the shore as the children play.
The Bantry has four letting rooms, all modern, spacious and well appointed.

Lyne Farmhouse — LYNE FARM, PEEBLES EH45 8NR

Victorian farmhouse with character and spectacular views overlooking Stobo Valley. Tastefully decorated throughout, bedrooms all upstairs, double or twin beds with tea/coffee facilities and TV. Walled garden to sit in, hillwalking, picnic areas, Lyne Roman Fort and site of early Christian graves all on farm. Many sports amenities (The Hub), Glentress Cycling Centre, Icelandic pony trekking, golfing, fishing and swimming. Picturesque Peebles 4 miles with its many restaurants, pubs, museum and Eastgate Theatre, shows and plays every week. B&B from £24 pppn.

'A friendly welcome awaits you.'

Tel & Fax: 01721 740255 • e-mail: lynefarmhouse@btinternet.com • website: www.lynefarm.co.uk

Borders/Dumfries & Galloway

Edwardian country house accommodation offering comfort with spectacular sea views, peaceful gardens and direct access from garden to beach and seashore. Situated on the Berwickshire coast in the historic Scottish Borders, Dunlaverock occupies an elevated position overlooking Coldingham Bay. There are six spacious en suite bedrooms and guests can dine on local seafood overlooking the sea; licensed. Enjoy guided scenic walks along the clifftop nature reserve or a sea fishing trip from St Abbs; 15 golf courses within a half hour drive.
Adjacent to the unspoilt fishing village of St Abbs, this is an ideal base for exploring the historic Scottish Borders, just 45 miles from Edinburgh and 65 miles north of Newcastle.

DUNLAVEROCK HOUSE Coldingham Sands,
Coldingham, Eyemouth TD14 5PA • Tel & Fax: 01890 771450
e-mail: info@dunlaverock.com • www.dunlaverock.com

Allerton House
Oxnam Road, Jedburgh TD8 6QQ
Tel: 01835 869633
e-mail: info@allertonhouse.co.uk
www.allertonhouse.co.uk

Allerton House is a 4-star guest house located in the historic Royal Burgh of Jedburgh. This Georgian home is surrounded by country gardens and provides all the modern amenities of the twenty-first century while preserving the character of its nineteenth century past. Whether you are staying for business or pleasure, the graciously appointed rooms, full range of facilities and warm hospitality will be sure to make your stay a memorable one. Only five minutes' walk from Jedburgh's town centre as well as from a host of lovely Border country walks, Allerton House offers elegant accommodation at competitive prices.

BARRASGATE HOUSE
Millhill, Gretna Green DG16 5HU
Tel: 01461 337577
e-mail: info@barrasgate.co.uk
www.barrasgate.co.uk

Surrounded by broad-leaved woodland and with country views, the accommodation at Barrasgate House is on ground and first floors, with disabled access. Our en suite bathrooms and shower rooms are equipped with soft fluffy towels. To help you relax after a long drive, our Gold Room has a spa shower. Five minutes from the M74 or A7, our central location is ideal for exploring Hadrian's Wall, the Borders, the Lakes and the beautiful Solway Coast. Local produce is used in our menus, and farmhouse baking will appeal to most tastes. Short breaks Spring/Autumn: three nights from £99.

Kirkcroft Guest House

Situated in the heart of Gretna Green, Kirkcroft Guest House, a detached house built in 1836, was once used as the local Post Office, and is now a comfortable and friendly Bed and Breakfast. Gretna Green is well placed for touring. To the south lies the Lake District with all its attractions, and to the west, the lovely Galloway coast towards Stranraer on the Gulf Stream. There is also easy access to the Scottish Border towns, and Kielder Water and Forest in Northumberland.

Double/twin en suite from £49.00 per room
• **DISCOUNTS FOR LONGER STAYS** •
Glasgow Road, Gretna Green DG16 5DU
Tel: 01461 337403
e-mail: info@kirkcroft.co.uk • www.kirkcroft.co.uk

Bed & Breakfast Stops 2006   39

Dumfries & Galloway/Edinburgh & Lothians

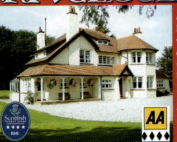

RIVENDELL
105 Edinburgh Rd, Dumfries DG1 1JX
Tel: 01387 252251

A warm welcome is assured at this striking and luxurious Charles Rennie Mackintosh inspired arts and crafts mansion. We are situated within our own extensive mature gardens close to Dumfries town centre and all its amenities. All our bedrooms feature spacious, state of the art en suite facilities and are furnished to the highest standard. All benefit from large screen televisions and full individually controlled Sky Digital packages. We have consistently maintained our four star rating from the Scottish Tourist Board and four diamond rating from the AA. We pride ourselves on our levels of service and customer satisfaction.

e-mail: info@rivendellbnb.co.uk
www.rivendellbnb.co.uk

CASTLE PARK GUEST HOUSE
75 Gilmore Place, Edinburgh EH3 9NU
Tel: 0131 229 1215 or 0131 229 1223
e-mail: castlepark@btconnect.com

A warm and friendly welcome awaits you at Castle Park Guest House, a charming Victorian Guest House ideally situated close to King's Theatre and city centre. Travel along the Royal Mile with Edinburgh Castle at one end and the Palace of Holyrood House, the Official Scottish Residence of the Queen, at the other end.

Centrally heated throughout, colour TV in all rooms, en suite facilities available, tea/coffee hospitality tray, full Scottish/Continental breakfast. Children welcome – special prices. Off-street parking. STB classification.

Inveresk House

Inveresk Village, Musselburgh EH21 7UA

Historic mansion house and award-winning Bed & Breakfast. Family-run "home from home". Situated in three acres of garden and woodland. Built on the site of a Roman settlement from 150 AD, the remains of a bathhouse can be found hidden in the garden. Three comfortable en suite rooms. Original art and antiques adorn the house. Edinburgh's Princes Street seven miles from Inveresk House. Good bus routes. Families welcome. Off-street parking. Telephone first. B&B from £40 per person. Family room £100 to £120.

e-mail: chute.inveresk@btinternet.com
website: http://travel.to/edinburgh

Tel: 0131-665 5855
Fax: 0131-665 0578

A relaxed and friendly base is provided at Cruachan from which to explore central Scotland. The centre of Edinburgh can be reached by train in only 30 minutes from nearby Bathgate, and Glasgow is only 35 minutes by car. All rooms en suite/private facilities, full hospitality tray, fresh towels daily, colour TV and central heating. Hosts Kenneth and Jacqueline ensure you receive the utmost in quality of service, meticulously presented accommodation and of course a full Scottish breakfast. They look forward to having the pleasure of your company.

Bed and Breakfast from £25 per person per night.

Cruachan B&B

78 East Main Street, Blackburn EH47 7QS
Tel: 01506 655221 • Fax: 01506 652395
e-mail: cruachan.bb@virgin.net • www.cruachan.co.uk

Edinburgh & Lothians/Fife/Highlands

THE ALEXANDER GUEST HOUSE
35 Mayfield Gardens, Edinburgh EH9 2BX
Tel: 0131 258 4028 Fax: 0131 258 1247
e-mail: ALEXANDER@guest68.freeserve.co.uk
website: www.SmoothHound.co.uk/hotels/alexand3.html

Classical Edinburgh, the 18th Century 'Athens of the North' conjures a picture of polite and dignified conversation, of elegance, refinement, and of sophistication, but above all of the value of good taste and judgement in the things that matter. At The Alexander we like to think that our guests find these values reflected in the standards we have to offer. Most bedrooms are en suite and all equipped with TV (incl. cable), tea/coffee hospitality tray, hairdryers, iron and ironing board. Private car park.

Usual methods of payment accepted (2% surcharge on credit cards)

With so much to see and do around St Andrews and Fife, we've made where to stay simple.

The University of St Andrews
B&B. 3 Star Hotel or Self-Catering Apartments

To find out more, call 01334 462000 or email holidays@st-andrews.ac.uk

---

This quiet Victorian former rectory provides the ideal location for touring. Ideal base for golf enthusiasts, within easy reach of 46 golf courses and only 14 miles from St Andrews. 40 minutes from Edinburgh Airport, Perth and 30-35 minutes from Dundee.

Mrs Pam MacDonald, Dunclutha Guest House, 16 Victoria Road, Leven KY8 4EX
Tel: 01333 425515 • Fax: 01333 422311
e-mail: pam.leven@blueyonder.co.uk
website: www.dunclutha.myby.co.uk

Facilities include three en suite rooms – one double, one twin, one family (sleeps three to four), one family (sleeps three) with private bathroom. Colour TV and tea/coffee facilities in all rooms, cot available. Visitors' lounge with TV. Most credit cards accepted. Open all year. Terms from £26 pppn. Non-smoking.

Braeburn B&B

Stunning views over Loch Linnhe and the Ardgour Hills. A warm welcome awaits you in this spacious, family-run house with panoramic views of the surrounding area; Ben Nevis only four miles away. Situated in its own private grounds with ample off-road parking and storage for bikes and skiiing equipment. 3 miles from the town centre; local hotels and bars serving good food and drink all within walking distance. Ideally situated for touring the West Highlands of Scotland. Relax in our comfortable residents' lounge or on our sunny patio. Enjoy a hearty breakfast to set you up for the day.

En suite rooms ✤ Colour TV ✤ Hospitality tray ✤ Hairdryer
Prices range from £25.00 to £27.50 per person. Open all year

Badabrie, Fort William PH33 7LX • 01397 772047
e-mail: enquiries@braeburnfortwilliam.co.uk
website: www.braeburnfortwilliam.co.uk

Hosts: John & Julie Mackin

Bed & Breakfast Stops 2006

Highlands/Perth & Kinross

Eriskay

A family-run Bed and Breakfast, situated in a quiet cul-de-sac in the centre of Aviemore

Ideal base for a holiday, whether it is fishing, skiing, sailing, bird watching, climbing or any other outdoor pursuit – we cater for all.
Purpose-built drying room and secure storage to protect vital outdoor equipment.
Pick-up/drop-off service to and from the Ski Centre or local glens.
Packed lunches and dinners by prior arrangement.
Luxurious guest lounge with blazing log fire. Private off-road parking.
All rooms are en suite or have their own private bathroom, with king and queen-size beds, TV, radio, hairdryers, controllable electric heating, and a host of other extras.
Complete No Smoking policy • Pets accepted by prior arrangement.
We hope that you arrive as a guest and leave as a friend

Craig-na-gower Avenue, Aviemore PH22 1RW • Tel: 01479 810717
E-mail: enquiry@eriskay-aviemore.co.uk • Web: www.eriskay-aviemore.co.uk

Moray Park House
Tel: 01463 233528

1 Moray Park, Island Bank Road, Inverness IV2 4SX

Moray Park is a lovely old house overlooking Cavell Gardens and the River Ness, and just a few minutes from the main shopping streets.
The Mathieson Family purchased Moray Park House in August 2003 and have carried out refurbishment during the winter. Seven rooms have en suite facilities and one a private bathroom. All are freshly decorated and all but two have river views. One large ground floor room is designed for use by disabled people, with extra space and suitable en suite facilities. There is a car park for residents.
Moray Park House is ideally positioned for access to the lovely Island Bank Walk, the Eden Court Theatre, the Castle, city parks and numerous restaurants, all of which are within a few minutes' walk. Bed and Breakfast rates vary from £20 to £50.

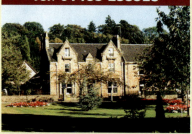

e-mail: MorayParkHouse@aol.com • website: www.MorayParkHotel.co.uk

Tel: 01764 681451

Ideally situated at the gateway to the Highlands, yet only one hour from Edinburgh and Glasgow. Dating from 1700, this charming family-run Inn offers excellent accommodation, an atmospheric dining experience at Willoughby's Restaurant or supper in the Bothy Bar with it s fine range of real ales. We are listed in the Good Beer Guide, Good Pub Guide and Rough Guide to Britain and many more publications.

Tel   - 01764 681451
email - bookings@muthillvillagehotel.com
web   - www.muthillvillagehotel.com

The Log Cabin Hotel

Tel: 01250 881288 Fax: 01250 881206
e-mail: wendy@logcabinhotel.co.uk
website: www.logcabinhotel.co.uk

Kirkmichael, Blairgowrie, Perthshire PH10 7NA

Unique, family-run hotel, set in the picturesque hills of Perthshire, less than half-an-hour from Glenshee, Pitlochry and Blairgowrie. The bar is fully licensed, with a good range of malt whiskies; guests can enjoy panoramic views of Strathardle from the dining room. All bedrooms are en suite.

A good central base for touring Perthshire and beyond; many golf courses are within easy reach; skiing at Glenshee in the winter; ideal for walking holidays.

Pets and children welcome.

Please call for brochure for further information.
Bed and Breakfast from £25 pppn.

42   **Please mention Bed & Breakfast Stops when enquiring**

Perth & Kinross/Renfrewshire/Stirling & The Trossachs

Merlindale is a luxurious Georgian house situated close to the town centre. All bedrooms are en suite (two with sunken bathrooms) and have tea/coffee making facilities. We have a jacuzzi available plus garden, ample parking and satellite television. We also have a Scottish library for the use of our guests. Cordon Bleu cooking is our speciality. A warm welcome awaits you in this non-smoking house.

Terms from: £45 Bed and Breakfast single, £30 double/twin. Dinner from £20. Open February to December.

Mr & Mrs Clifford, Merlindale, Perth Road, Crieff PH7 3EQ • 01764 655205 • Fax: 01764 655205

Ardgowan House
Tel & Fax: 0141-889 4763

David and Gail welcome you to their two adjacent, family-run guesthouses in the heart of Paisley, Scotland's largest town. Enjoy a drink from our licensed bar in the secluded, peaceful gardens or relax in our delightful summer house. We have two levels of accommodation available, so there is something for everyone, from the two-star Ardgowan guest house to the more upmarket Townhouse Hotel. Both have secure storage facilities for cyclists and hikers and free off-street parking. Situated within one mile of Glasgow International Airport, and only ten minutes from Glasgow City Centre, the excellent transport links allow easy access to Loch Lomond, Robert Burns country, Edinburgh and the Highlands and Islands. Please see our website for further details.

92-94 Renfrew Road, Paisley, Renfrewshire PA3 4BJ
website: www.ardgowanhouse.com

Riverview House
Leny Road, Callander FK17 8AL
Tel: 01877 330635 • Fax: 01877 339386

Excellent accommodation in the Trossachs area which forms the most beautiful part of Scotland's first National Park. Ideal centre for walking and cycling holidays, with cycle storage available. In the guest house all rooms are en suite, with TV and tea-making. Private parking. Also available self-catering stone cottages, sleep 3 or 4. Sorry, no smoking and no pets. Call Drew or Kathleen Little for details.

e-mail: drew@visitcallander.co.uk
website: www.visitcallander.co.uk

B&B from £24.
Low season and long stay discounts available.
Self-catering cottages from £150 per week
(STB 4 Stars).

Looking for Holiday Accommodation?

for details of hundreds of properties

throughout the UK including

comprehensive coverage of all areas of Scotland try:

www.holidayguides.com

Bed & Breakfast Stops 2006   43

North Wales/Ceredigion

FRON HEULOG COUNTRY HOUSE
Betws-y-Coed, North Wales LL24 0BL
Tel: 01690 710316
e-mail: jean@fronheulog.co.uk
website: www.fronheulog.co.uk

"The Country House in the Village"

Betws-y-Coed – "Heart of Snowdonia"

You are invited to enjoy real hospitality at Fron Heulog; an elegant Victorian stone-built house with excellent non-smoking accommodation, comfortable bedrooms, all with en suite bathrooms, spacious lounges, a pleasant dining room, and full central heating. Enjoy the friendly atmosphere with hosts' local knowledge and home cooking. Sorry, no small children; no pets. From the centre of Betws-y-Coed turn off busy A5 road over picturesque Pont-y-Pair bridge (B5106), then immediately turn left. Fron Heulog is 150 yards up ahead facing south, in quiet, peaceful, wooded, riverside scenery.

Welcome! – Croeso! Bed & Breakfast £25-£35 pppn
Holiday? Short Break? Pleased to quote.
AA ♦♦♦♦, *Recommended by Which?*
Jean & Peter Whittingham welcome house guests

Fairy Glen Hotel offers you a warm and friendly welcome, comfortable accommodation and excellent home-cooked food, in a relaxed and convivial atmosphere. All our rooms are well equipped with central heating, colour TV, alarm clock-radio, hairdryer and tea/coffee making facilities. We have a TV lounge, and cosy licensed bar for our residents to relax in. Our private car park is for guests only. Evening meals available from £15.00 per person. Bed and Breakfast from £26.00 per person per night.

Brian and Enid Youe, Fairy Glen Hotel, Beaver Bridge, Betws-y-Coed LL24 0SH • 01690 710269
e-mail: fairyglen@youe.fsworld.co.uk
website: www.fairyglenhotel.co.uk

Queensbridge Hotel
The Promenade, Aberystwyth, Ceredigion SY23 2DH
Tel: 01970 612343 • Fax: 01970 617452

Aberystwyth, with its award-winning beach, is one of Wales's favourite traditional seaside towns. With many visitor attractions it is the ideal venue for touring North, Mid and South Wales.

Situated at the quieter end of Aberystwyth's historic Victorian promenade, overlooking the panoramic sweep of Cardigan Bay, the Queensbridge Hotel offers guests superior comfort in fifteen spacious en suite bedrooms, all with colour TV, hospitality tray and telephone. A hearty Welsh breakfast is served in the welcoming Breakfast Room where we pride ourselves on our prompt, efficient service and excellent menu choice.

Established 1972 – "Our reputation for comfort and good service remains steadfast"

Visit the FHG website
www.holidayguides.com
for details of the wide choice of accommodation featured in the full range of FHG titles

44   Please mention Bed & Breakfast Stops when enquiring

Pembrokeshire/Powys

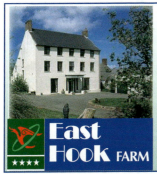

Howard and Jen welcome you to their Georgian Farmhouse surrounded by beautiful countryside, four miles from the coastline and three miles from Haverfordwest. Double, twin and family suite available, all en suite. Ground floor rooms available. Pembrokeshire produce used for dinner and breakfast. Dinner £18pp. Bed and Breakfast from £25 to £30 pp.

Cottage conversion also available from Christmas 2005 — caters for 2 to 8 people.

Mr and Mrs Patrick, East Hook Farm,
Portfield Gate, Haverfordwest, Pembroke SA62 3LN
01437 762211 • www.easthookfarmhouse.co.uk

Caebetran Farm

A warm welcome, a cup of tea and home-made cakes await you when you arrive at Caebetran. Well off the beaten track, where there are breathtaking views of the Brecon Beacons and the Black Mountains, and just across a field is a 400 acre common, ideal for walking, bird-watching or just relaxing. The rooms are all en suite and have colour TV and tea making facilities. The dining room has separate tables, there is also a comfortable lounge with colour TV and video. Caebetran is an ideal base for exploring this beautiful, unspoilt part of the country with pony trekking, walking, birdwatching, wildlife, hang-gliding and so much more. For a brochure and terms please write, telephone or fax.

"Arrive as visitors and leave as our friends".
Winners of the 'FHG Diploma' for Wales 1998/99. Welcome Host.
Gwyn and Hazel Davies Caebetran Farm, Felinfach,
Brecon, Powys LD3 0UL • Tel & Fax: 01874 754460
e-mail: hazelcaebetran@aol.com • www.caebetranfarmhousebedandbreakfastwales.com

---

Other specialised
FHG Guides

Published annually: available in all good bookshops or direct from the publisher.

Recommended **COUNTRY INNS & PUBS** OF BRITAIN

Recommended **COUNTRY HOTELS** OF BRITAIN

Recommended **SHORT BREAK HOLIDAYS** IN BRITAIN

The bestselling **PETS WELCOME!**

FHG Guides • Abbey Mill Business Centre,
Seedhill, Paisley, Renfrewshire PA1 1TJ
Tel: 0141-887 0428 • Fax: 0141-889 7204
e-mail: admin@fhguides.co.uk
website: www.holidayguides.com

Bed & Breakfast Stops 2006

CULTURE SMART! GUIDES
A quick guide to customs and etiquette

·K·U·P·E·R·A·R·D·
www.KUPERARD.co.uk

CULTURE SMART! Guides are the only guides giving essential information on attitudes, beliefs and behaviour in over 30 different countries, turning ignorant tourists into informed travellers.

Suitable for short breaks, long stays or business trips. Ideal for the culturally unaware Brit. These concise guides tell you what to expect, how to behave, and how to establish a rapport with your hosts.

Covers all cultural aspects – customs, traditions, politics, history and religion.

Breaks down cultural barriers without causing offence.

'Full of fascinating tips to help you avoid embarrassing faux pas' *The Observer*

'Culture Smart! has come to the rescue of hapless travellers' *The Sunday Times*

'Perfect introduction to the weird, wonderful and odd quirks and customs of various countries' *Global Travel*

CULTURE SMART! THE SMARTER WAY TO TRAVEL

Regularly featured on:

Price £6.95 each

·K·U·P·E·R·A·R·D·

Publishers and Distributors
59 Hutton Grove, London N12 8DS
Tel: 020 8446 2440 • Fax: 020 8446 2441 • E-mail: culturesmart@kuperard.co.uk

'Order any Culture Smart! guide via the Kuperard website and receive free postage on any quantity of guides. Visit www.kuperard.co.uk to see the full range in the series and type in the following promotional code on the payment page FHG01. Or call us on 0208 446 2440 and quote the same code'

hotels - retreats – haciendas - villas - chalets - spas

chic guides

Price £16.95 each

A vividly illustrated guide to exciting destinations

The modern traveller's companion to the most exciting luxurious and alluring hotels, mountain retreats, beachside villas, spas, exciting shops and choice restaurants.

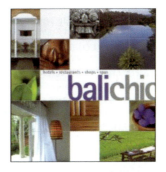

Available from all good bookshops

Stunning illustrated chapters, describe in detail the design and their intimate character and surroundings. Fact panels on each property provide suitable information on local attractions and facilities lying within easy reach.

Stylish paperback style makes this the ideal travel and coffee table guide

Alpine   Bali   Mexico   Morocco   South Africa   Thailand

www.KUPERARD.co.uk

Publishers and Distributors
59 Hutton Grove, London N12 8DS

Tel: 020 8446 2440 • Fax: 020 8446 2441 • E-mail: chic@kuperard.co.uk

47

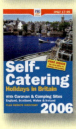

FHG 2006
KUPERARD

Your guides to
Good Holidays

Recommended COUNTRY HOTELS
a quality selection of Britain's best Country Houses and Hotels

Recommended COUNTRY INNS & PUBS
accommodation, food and traditional good cheer

CARAVAN & CAMPING HOLIDAYS
covers every type of caravan and camping facility

BED & BREAKFAST STOPS
ever more popular independent guide with over 1000 entries

THE GOLF GUIDE Where to Play / Where to Stay
a detailed list covering virtually every club and course
in the UK with hotels and other accommodation nearby,
– recommended by golfers, to golfers.

CHILDREN WELCOME!
Family Holiday and Days Out guide

PETS WELCOME!
the pet world's version of the ultimate hotel guide,
over 1000 properties where pets
and their owners are made welcome

Recommended SHORT BREAK HOLIDAYS
approved accommodation all year round for short breaks

BRITAIN'S BEST HOLIDAYS
user-friendly guide to all kinds of holiday opportunities

COAST & COUNTRY HOLIDAYS
holidays for all the family, from traditional farm houses
to inns, guesthouses and small hotels

SELF CATERING HOLIDAYS
one of the best and perhaps the widest selection
of self-catering accommodation

Available from bookshops
or larger newsagents

FHG GUIDES LTD
Abbey Mill Business Centre, Seedhill,
Paisley PAI ITJ
www.holidayguides.com

The best-selling series
of UK Holiday Guides

Porthcurno Beach, Cornwall, looking to Logan Rock

THE FHG DIPLOMA

HELP IMPROVE BRITISH TOURIST STANDARDS

You are choosing holiday accommodation from our very popular FHG Guides.
Whether it be a hotel, guest house, farmhouse or self-catering accommodation, we think you will find it hospitable, comfortable and clean, and your host and hostess friendly and helpful.

Why not write and tell us about it?

As a recognition of the generally well-run and excellent holiday accommodation reviewed in our publications, we at FHG Guides Ltd. present a diploma to proprietors who receive the highest recommendation from their guests who are also readers of our Guides. If you care to write to us praising the holiday you have booked through FHG Guides Ltd. – whether this be board, self-catering accommodation, a sporting or a caravan holiday, what you say will be evaluated and the proprietors who reach our final list will be contacted.

The winning proprietor will receive an attractive framed diploma to display on his premises as recognition of a high standard of comfort, amenity and hospitality. FHG Guides Ltd. offer this diploma as a contribution towards the improvement of standards in tourist accommodation in Britain. Help your excellent host or hostess to win it!

FHG DIPLOMA

We nominate

Because

Name ....

Address ....

....

Telephone No..

Ratings You Can Trust

ENGLAND

The **English Tourism Council** (now **VisitBritain**) has joined with the **AA** and **RAC** to create an easily understood quality rating for serviced accommodation, giving a clear guide of what to expect.

HOTELS are given a rating from One to Five **Stars** – the more Stars, the higher the quality and the greater the range of facilities and level of services provided.

GUEST ACCOMMODATION, which includes guest houses, bed and breakfasts, inns and farmhouses, is rated from One to Five **Diamonds**. Progressively higher levels of quality and customer care must be provided for each one of the One to Five Diamond ratings.

HOLIDAY PARKS, TOURING PARKS and CAMPING PARKS are now also assessed using **Stars**. Standards of quality range from a One Star (acceptable) to a Five Star (exceptional) park.

Look out also for the new **SELF-CATERING** Star ratings. The more **Stars** (from One to Five) awarded to an establishment, the higher the levels of quality you can expect. Establishments at higher rating levels also have to meet some additional requirements for facilities.

VisitBritain has launched a new **Quality Accredited Agency Standard**. Agencies who are awarded the Quality Accredited Agency marque by VisitBritain are recognised as offering good customer service and peace of mind, following an assement of their office polices, practices and procedures.

SCOTLAND

Star Quality Grades will reflect the most important aspects of a visit, such as the warmth of welcome, efficiency and friendliness of service, the quality of the food and the cleanliness and condition of the furnishings, fittings and decor.

THE MORE STARS,

THE HIGHER THE STANDARDS.

The description, such as Hotel, Guest House, Bed and Breakfast, Lodge, Holiday Park, Self-catering etc tells you the type of property and style of operation.

WALES

Places which score highly will have an especially welcoming atmosphere and pleasing ambience, high levels of comfort and guest care, and attractive surroundings enhanced by thoughtful design and attention to detail

STAR QUALITY GUIDE FOR

HOTELS, GUEST HOUSES AND FARMHOUSES
SELF-CATERING ACCOMMODATION
(Cottages, Apartments, Houses)
CARAVAN HOLIDAY HOME PARKS
(Holiday Parks, Touring Parks, Camping Parks)

★★★★★	Exceptional quality
★★★★	Excellent quality
★★★	Very good quality
★★	Good quality
★	Fair to good quality

In England, Scotland and Wales, all graded properties are inspected annually by Tourist Authority trained Assessors.

Foreword

In our entries in **BED & BREAKFAST STOPS**, we have tried to avoid flowery descriptions and lavish praise, and instead have concentrated on hard facts such as the location of the property, what kind of facilities are offered - bedrooms, bathrooms etc - and if they have official approval or other gradings from tourism authorities, or AA etc. Guests can expect a friendly service from our advertisers - we ask them to vouch for this when confirming their entry - and a very warm welcome, whether they plan to stay for a few weeks, a few days, or just overnight.

The following points should help you make the most of the huge selection in this edition of the guide.

ENQUIRIES AND BOOKINGS. Give full details of dates (with an alternative), numbers and any special requirements. Ask about any points in the holiday description which are not clear and make sure that prices and conditions are clearly explained. You should receive confirmation in writing and a receipt for any deposit or advance payment. If you book your holiday well in advance, confirm your arrival details nearer the time. Some proprietors request full payment in advance but a reasonable deposit is more normal.

CANCELLATIONS. A holiday booking is a form of contract with obligations on both sides. If you have to cancel, give as much notice as possible. The longer the notice the better the chance that your host can replace your booking and therefore refund any payments. If the proprietor cancels in such away that causes serious, inconvenience, he may have obligations to you which have not been properly honoured. Take advice if necessary from such organisations as the Citizen's Advice Bureau, Consumer's Association, Trading standards Office, Local Tourist Office, etc., or your own solicitor. It is possible to insure against holiday cancellation. Brokers and insurance companies can advise you about this.

COMPLAINTS. It's best if any problems can be sorted out at the start of your holiday. If the problem is not. solved, you can contact the organisations mentioned above. You can also write to us. We will follow up the complaint with the advertiser – but we cannot act as intermediaries or accept responsibility for holiday arrangements.

FHG Guides Ltd. do not inspect accommodation and an entry in our guides does not imply a recommendation. However our advertisers have signed their agreement to work for the holidaymaker's best interests and as their customer, you have the right to expect appropriate attention and service.

Please mention **BED & BREAKFAST STOPS** when you are making enquiries or bookings and don't forget to use our Readers' Offer Voucher/Coupons if you're near any of the attractions which are kindly participating.

Anne Cuthbertson, Editor

Bed & Breakfast Stops
2006

READERS' OFFER 2006

LEIGHTON BUZZARD RAILWAY
Page's Park Station, Billington Road,
Leighton Buzzard, Bedfordshire LU7 4TN
Tel: 01525 373888
e-mail: info@buzzrail.co.uk
www.buzzrail.co.uk

One FREE adult/child with full-fare adult ticket
Valid 12/3/2006 - 29/10/2006

NOT TO BE USED IN CONJUNCTION WITH ANY OTHER OFFER

READERS' OFFER 2006

BUCKINGHAMSHIRE RAILWAY CENTRE
Quainton Road Station, Quainton,
Aylesbury HP22 4BY
Tel & Fax: 01296 655720
e-mail: bucksrailcentre@btopenworld.com
www.bucksrailcentre.org

One child FREE with each full-paying adult
Not valid for Special Events

NOT TO BE USED IN CONJUNCTION WITH ANY OTHER OFFER

READERS' OFFER 2006

BEKONSCOT MODEL VILLAGE & RAILWAY
Warwick Road, Beaconsfield,
Buckinghamshire HP9 2PL
Tel: 01494 672919
e-mail: info@bekonscot.co.uk
www.bekonscot.com

Bekonscot Model Village & Railway

One child FREE when accompanied by full-paying adult
Valid February to October 2006

NOT TO BE USED IN CONJUNCTION WITH ANY OTHER OFFER

READERS' OFFER 2006

SACREWELL FARM & COUNTRY CENTRE
Sacrewell, Thornhaugh,
Peterborough PE8 6HJ
Tel & Fax: 01780 782254
e-mail: info@sacrewell.fsnet.co.uk
www.sacrewell.org.uk

One child FREE with one full paying adult
Valid from March 1st to October 1st 2006

NOT TO BE USED IN CONJUNCTION WITH ANY OTHER OFFER

A 70-minute journey into the lost world of the English narrow gauge light railway. Features historic steam locomotives from many countries.

PETS MUST BE KEPT UNDER CONTROL AND NOT ALLOWED ON TRACKS

Open: Sundays and Bank Holiday weekends 12 March to 29 October. Additional days in summer.

Directions: on A4146 towards Hemel Hempstead, close to roundabout junction with A505.

FHG GUIDES, ABBEY MILL BUSINESS CENTRE, PAISLEY PA1 1TJ • www.holidayguides.com

---

A working steam railway centre. Steam train rides, miniature railway rides, large collection of historic preserved steam locomotives, carriages and wagons.

Open: Sundays and Bank Holidays April to October, plus Wednesdays in school holidays 10.30am to 5.30pm.

Directions: off A41 Aylesbury to Bicester Road, 6 miles north west of Aylesbury.

FHG GUIDES, ABBEY MILL BUSINESS CENTRE, PAISLEY PA1 1TJ • www.holidayguides.com

---

Be a giant in a magical miniature world of make-believe depicting rural England in the 1930s. "A little piece of history that is forever England."

Open: 10am-5pm daily mid February to end October.

Directions: Junction 16 M25, Junction 2 M40.

FHG GUIDES, ABBEY MILL BUSINESS CENTRE, PAISLEY PA1 1TJ • www.holidayguides.com

---

Farm animals, 18th century watermill and farmhouse, farm artifacts, caravan and camping, children's play areas. Restaurant and gift shop.

Open: all year.
9.30am to 5pm 1st March -30th Sept
10am-4pm 1st Oct to 28th Feb

Directions: signposted off both A47 and A1.

FHG GUIDES, ABBEY MILL BUSINESS CENTRE, PAISLEY PA1 1TJ • www.holidayguides.com

55

READERS' OFFER 2006

GEEVOR TIN MINE
Pendeen, Penzance,
Cornwall TR19 7EW
Tel: 01736 788662 • Fax: 01736 786059
e-mail: bookings@geevor.com
www.geevor.com

TWO for the price of ONE or £3.50 off a family ticket
Valid 02/01/2006 to 20/12/2006

NOT TO BE USED IN CONJUNCTION WITH ANY OTHER OFFER

READERS' OFFER 2006

NATIONAL SEAL SANCTUARY
Gweek, Helston,
Cornwall TR12 6UG
Tel: 01326 221361
e-mail: seals@sealsanctuary.co.uk
www.sealsanctuary.co.uk

TWO for ONE - on purchase of another ticket of
equal or greater value. Valid until December 2006.

NOT TO BE USED IN CONJUNCTION WITH ANY OTHER OFFER

READERS' OFFER 2006

TAMAR VALLEY DONKEY PARK
St Ann's Chapel, Gunnislake,
Cornwall PL18 9HW
Tel: 01822 834072
e-mail: info@donkeypark.com
www.donkeypark.com

50p OFF per person, up to 6 persons
Valid from Easter until end October 2006

NOT TO BE USED IN CONJUNCTION WITH ANY OTHER OFFER

READERS' OFFER 2006

CARS OF THE STARS MOTOR MUSEUM
Standish Street, Keswick,
Cumbria CA12 5HH
Tel: 017687 73757
e-mail: cotsmm@aol.com
www.carsofthestars.com

One child free with two paying adults
Valid during 2006

NOT TO BE USED IN CONJUNCTION WITH ANY OTHER OFFER

Geevor is the largest mining history site in the UK in a spectacular setting on Cornwall's Atlantic coast. Guided underground tour, many surface buildings, museum, cafe, gift shop. Free parking.

Open: daily except Saturdays 10am to 4pm

Directions: 7 miles from Penzance beside the B3306 Land's End to St Ives coast road

FHG GUIDES, ABBEY MILL BUSINESS CENTRE, PAISLEY PA1 1TJ • www.holidayguides.com

---

Britain's leading grey seal rescue centre

Open: daily (except Christmas Day) from 10am

Directions: from A30 follow signs to Helston, then brown tourist signs to Seal Sanctuary.

FHG GUIDES, ABBEY MILL BUSINESS CENTRE, PAISLEY PA1 1TJ • www.holidayguides.com

---

Cornwall's only Donkey Sanctuary set in 14 acres overlooking the beautiful Tamar Valley. Donkey rides, rabbit warren, goat hill, children's playgrounds, cafe and picnic area. New all-weather play barn.

Open: Easter to end Oct and Feb half term: daily 10am to 5.30pm. Nov to March: open weekends. Closed Jan.

Directions: just off A390 between Callington and Gunnislake at St Ann's Chapel.

FHG GUIDES, ABBEY MILL BUSINESS CENTRE, PAISLEY PA1 1TJ • www.holidayguides.com

---

A collection of cars from film and TV, including Chitty Chitty Bang Bang, James Bond's Aston Martin, Del Boy's van, Fab1 and many more.

PETS MUST BE KEPT ON LEAD

Open: daily 10am-5pm. Closed February half term. Weekends only in December.

Directions: in centre of Keswick close to car park.

FHG GUIDES, ABBEY MILL BUSINESS CENTRE, PAISLEY PA1 1TJ • www.holidayguides.com

57

READERS' OFFER 2006

ESKDALE HISTORIC WATER MILL
Mill Cottage, Boot, Eskdale,
Cumbria CA19 1TG
Tel: 019467 23335
e-mail: david.king403@tesco.net
www.eskdale.com

Two children FREE with two adults
Valid during 2006

NOT TO BE USED IN CONJUNCTION WITH ANY OTHER OFFER

READERS' OFFER 2006

CUMBERLAND TOY & MODEL MUSEUM
Banks Court, Market Place,
Cockermouth,
Cumbria CA13 9NG
Tel: 01900 827606
www.toymuseum.co.uk

TWO for the price of ONE (cheaper ticket free)
Valid all year except December and January

NOT TO BE USED IN CONJUNCTION WITH ANY OTHER OFFER

FHG · K·U·P·E·R·A·R·D ·

READERS' OFFER 2006

CRICH TRAMWAY VILLAGE
Crich, Matlock
Derbyshire DE4 5DP
Tel: 01773 854321 • Fax: 01773 854320
e-mail: enquiry@tramway.co.uk
www.tramway.co.uk

One child FREE with every full-paying adult
Valid during 2006

NOT TO BE USED IN CONJUNCTION WITH ANY OTHER OFFER

READERS' OFFER 2006

TREAK CLIFF CAVERN
HOME OF BLUE JOHN STONE
Castleton, Hope Valley, Derbyshire S33 8WP
Tel: 01433 620571
e-mail: treakcliff@bluejohnstone.com
www.bluejohnstone.com

10% discount
Valid during 2006 except on Special Events days)

NOT TO BE USED IN CONJUNCTION WITH ANY OTHER OFFER

The oldest working mill in England with 18th century oatmeal machinery running daily. **DOGS ON LEADS**	**Open:** 11am to 5pm April to September (may be closed Saturdays). **Directions:** near inland terminus of Ravenglass & Eskdale Railway or over Hardknott Pass.

FHG GUIDES, ABBEY MILL BUSINESS CENTRE, PAISLEY PA1 1TJ • www.holidayguides.com

Over 100 years of toys in this national award-winning museum. Many visitor-operated exhibits.	**Open:** daily 10am to 5pm **Directions:** follow brown tourist signs from car parks in Cockermouth

FHG GUIDES, ABBEY MILL BUSINESS CENTRE, PAISLEY PA1 1TJ • www.holidayguides.com

A superb family day out in the atmosphere of a bygone era. Explore the recreated period street and fascinating exhibitions. Unlimited tram rides are free with entry. Play areas, woodland walk and sculpture trail, shops, tea rooms, pub, restaurant and lots more.	**Open:** daily April to October 10 am to 5.30pm, weekends in winter. **Directions:** eight miles from M1 Junction 28, follow brown and white signs for "Tramway Museum".

FHG GUIDES, ABBEY MILL BUSINESS CENTRE, PAISLEY PA1 1TJ • www.holidayguides.com

An underground wonderland of stalactites, stalagmites, rocks, minerals and fossils. Home of the unique Blue John stone – see the largest single piece ever found. Suitable for all ages.	**Open:** opens 10am. Enquire for last tour of day and closed days. **Directions:** half-a-mile west of Castleton on A6187 (old A625)

FHG GUIDES, ABBEY MILL BUSINESS CENTRE, PAISLEY PA1 1TJ • www.holidayguides.com

THE BIG SHEEP
Abbotsham, Bideford,
Devon EX39 5AP
Tel: 01237 472366
e-mail: info@thebigsheep.co.uk
www.thebigsheep.co.uk

READERS' OFFER 2006

Admit one child FREE with each paying adult
Valid during 2006

NOT TO BE USED IN CONJUNCTION WITH ANY OTHER OFFER

DEVONSHIRE COLLECTION OF PERIOD COSTUME
Totnes Costume Museum,
Bogan House, 43 High Street,
Totnes,
Devon TQ9 5NP

Devonshire Collection of Period Costume

READERS' OFFER 2006

FREE child with a paying adult with voucher
Valid from Spring Bank Holiday to end of Sept 2006

NOT TO BE USED IN CONJUNCTION WITH ANY OTHER OFFER

LIVING COASTS
Harbourside, Beacon Quay, Torquay,
Devon TQ1 2BG
Tel: 01803 202470 • Fax: 01803 202471
e-mail: info@livingcoasts.org.uk
www.livingcoasts.org.uk

READERS' OFFER 2006

40p OFF standard ticket price for each person
Valid during 2006

NOT TO BE USED IN CONJUNCTION WITH ANY OTHER OFFER

CREALY ADVENTURE PARK
Sidmouth Road, Clyst St Mary, Exeter,
Devon EX5 1DR
Tel: 0870 116 3333• Fax: 01395 233211
e-mail: fun@crealy.co.uk
www.crealy.co.uk

READERS' OFFER 2006

FREE superkart race or panning for gold.
Height restrictions apply. Valid until 31/10/06.
Photocopies not accepted. One voucher per person.

NOT TO BE USED IN CONJUNCTION WITH ANY OTHER OFFER

"England for Excellence" award-winning family entertainment park. Highlights: hilarious shows including the famous sheep-racing and the duck trials; the awesome Ewetopia indoor adventure playground for adults and children; brewery; mountain boarding; great local food.

Open: daily, 10am to 6pm April - Oct Phone for Winter opening times and details.

Directions: on A39 North Devon link road, two miles west of Bideford Bridge.

FHG GUIDES, ABBEY MILL BUSINESS CENTRE, PAISLEY PA1 1TJ • www.holidayguides.com

---

Themed exhibition, changed annually, based in a Tudor house. Collection contains items of dress for women, men and children from 17th century to 1980s, from high fashion to everyday wear.

Open: Open from Spring Bank Holiday to end September. 11am to 5pm Tuesday to Friday.

Directions: centre of town, opposite Market Square. Mini bus up High Street stops outside.

FHG GUIDES, ABBEY MILL BUSINESS CENTRE, PAISLEY PA1 1TJ • www.holidayguides.com

---

Features a range of fascinating coastal creatures from penguins to fur seals, puffins to sea ducks. Reconstructed beaches, cliff faces and an estuary. A huge meshed aviary allows birds to fly free over your head, while special tunnels give stunning crystal-clear views of the birds and seals underwater.

Open: all year from 10am to 6pm (summer) or dusk (winter)

Directions: follow brown tourist signs from Torquay. Situated right on the harbour front.

FHG GUIDES, ABBEY MILL BUSINESS CENTRE, PAISLEY PA1 1TJ • www.holidayguides.com

---

Maximum fun, magic and adventure. An unforgettable family experience, with Tidal Wave log flume, rollercoaster, Queen Bess pirate ship, techno race karts, bumper boats, Vicorian carousel, animal handling, and huge indoor and outdoor play areas. The South-West's favourite family attraction!

Open: Summer: daily 10am to 5pm High season: daily 10am to 6pm Winter (Nov-March): Wed-Sun 10am -5pm

Directions: minutes from M5 J30 on the A3052 Sidmouth road, near Exeter

FHG GUIDES, ABBEY MILL BUSINESS CENTRE, PAISLEY PA1 1TJ • www.holidayguides.com

61

READERS' OFFER 2006

KILLHOPE LEAD MINING MUSEUM
Cowshill, Upper Weardale,
Co. Durham DL13 1AR
Tel: 01388 537505
e-mail: killhope@durham.gov.uk
www.durham.gov.uk/killhope

One child FREE with full-paying adult
Valid April to October 2006 (not Park Level Mine)

NOT TO BE USED IN CONJUNCTION WITH ANY OTHER OFFER

READERS' OFFER 2006

BARLEYLANDS FARM
Barleylands Road, Billericay,
Essex CM11 2UD
Tel: 01268 290229
e-mail: info@barleylands.co.uk
www.barleylands.co.uk

Barleylands Farm

FREE adult ticket when accompanied by one child
Valid 1st March to 31st October (not Special Event days)

NOT TO BE USED IN CONJUNCTION WITH ANY OTHER OFFER

READERS' OFFER 2006

AVON VALLEY RAILWAY
Bitton Station, Bath Road, Bitton,
Bristol BS30 6HD
Tel: 0117 932 5538
e-mail: info@avonvalleyrailway.org
www.avonvalleyrailway.org

One FREE child with every fare-paying adult
Valid May - Oct 2006 (not 'Day Out with Thomas' events)

NOT TO BE USED IN CONJUNCTION WITH ANY OTHER OFFER

READERS' OFFER 2006

NATIONAL WATERWAYS MUSEUM
Llanthony Warehouse, Gloucester Docks,
Gloucester GL1 2EH
Tel: 01452 318200
e-mail: bookingsnwm@thewaterwaystrust.org
www.nwm.org.uk

NATIONAL WATERWAYS MUSEUM

20% off museum admission (excludes combination tickets)
Valid during 2006

NOT TO BE USED IN CONJUNCTION WITH ANY OTHER OFFER

62

Voted 'Most Family-Friendly Museum 2004', Killhope is Britain's best preserved lead mining site, with lots to see and do. Underground Experience is something not to be missed.

Open: April 1st to October 31st 10.30am to 5pm daily.

Directions: alongside A689, midway between Stanhope and Alston in the heart of the North Pennines.

FHG GUIDES, ABBEY MILL BUSINESS CENTRE, PAISLEY PA1 1TJ • www.holidayguides.com

---

Craft Village with animals, museum, blacksmith, glassblowing, miniature railway (Sundays and August), craft shops, tea room and licensed restaurant.

Open: Craft Village open all year. Farm open 1st March to 31st October.

Directions: M25, A127 towards Southend. Take A176 junction off A127, 3rd exit Wash Road, 2nd left Barleylands Road.

FHG GUIDES, ABBEY MILL BUSINESS CENTRE, PAISLEY PA1 1TJ • www.holidayguides.com

---

The Avon Valley Railway offers a whole new experience for some, and a nostalgic memory for others.

PETS MUST BE KEPT ON LEADS AND OFF TRAIN SEATS

Open: Steam trains operate every Sunday, Easter to October, plus Bank Holidays and Christmas.

Directions: on the A431 midway between Bristol and Bath at Bitton.

FHG GUIDES, ABBEY MILL BUSINESS CENTRE, PAISLEY PA1 1TJ • www.holidayguides.com

---

On three floors of a Listed Victorian warehouse telling 200 years of inland waterway history.• Historic boats • Boat trips available (Easter to October)
• Painted boat gallery • Blacksmith
• Archive film • Hands-on displays
"A great day out"

Open: every day 10am to 5pm (excluding Christmas Day). Last admissions 4pm

Directions: Junction 11A or 12 off M5 – follow brown signs for Historic Docks. Railway and bus station - 15 minute walk. Free coach parking.

FHG GUIDES, ABBEY MILL BUSINESS CENTRE, PAISLEY PA1 1TJ • www.holidayguides.com

63

READERS' OFFER 2006

NOAH'S ARK ZOO FARM
Failand Road, Wraxall,
Bristol BS48 1PG
Tel: 01275 852606 • Fax: 01275 857080
e-mail: info@noahsarkzoofarm.co.uk
www.noahsarkzoofarm.co.uk

One FREE child for each group of 4 or more persons
Valid until October 2006 (closed in winter)

NOT TO BE USED IN CONJUNCTION WITH ANY OTHER OFFER

READERS' OFFER 2006

CIDER MUSEUM & KING OFFA DISTILLERY
21 Ryelands Street,
Hereford HR4 0LW
Tel: 01432 354207 • Fax: 01432 371641
e-mail: enquiries@cidermuseum.co.uk
www.cidermuseum.co.uk

50p reduction on entry fee
Valid during 2006

NOT TO BE USED IN CONJUNCTION WITH ANY OTHER OFFER

READERS' OFFER 2006

VERULAMIUM MUSEUM
St Michael's, St Albans,
Herts AL3 4SW
Tel: 01727 751810
e-mail: museums@stalbans.gov.uk
www.stalbansmuseums.org.uk

"Two for One"
Valid until 31/12/06

NOT TO BE USED IN CONJUNCTION WITH ANY OTHER OFFER

READERS' OFFER 2006

MUSEUM OF KENT LIFE
Lock Lane, Sandling, Maidstone,
Kent ME14 3AU
Tel: 01622 763936 • Fax: 01622 662024
e-mail: enquiries@museum-kentlife.co.uk
www.museum-kentlife.co.uk

Two tickets for the price of one (cheapest ticket FREE)
Valid from March to November 2006

NOT TO BE USED IN CONJUNCTION WITH ANY OTHER OFFER

Fantastic 'hands-on' adventure zoo farm for all ages and all weathers. 80 different species from chicks and lambs to camels and rhinos. New indoor and outdoor mazes (longest in world and educational). Family-friendly cafe and shop.

Open: from February half-term to end October 10.30am to 5pm Mon to Sat (closed Mon + Sun in term time)

Directions: on B3128 between Bristol and Clevedon or Exit 19/20 M5

FHG GUIDES, ABBEY MILL BUSINESS CENTRE, PAISLEY PA1 1TJ • www.holidayguides.com

---

Discover the fascinating history of cider making. There is a programme of temporary exhibitions and events plus free samples of Hereford cider brandy.

Open: April to Oct 10am to 5pm ; Nov to March 12noon to 4pm. Closed Sun and Mon excluding Bank Holidays.

Directions: situated west of Hereford off the A438 Hereford to Brecon road.

FHG GUIDES, ABBEY MILL BUSINESS CENTRE, PAISLEY PA1 1TJ • www.holidayguides.com

---

The museum of everyday life in Roman Britain. An award-winning museum with re-created Roman rooms, hands-on discovery areas, and some of the best mosaics outside the Mediterranean.

Open: Monday to Saturday 10am-5.30pm; Sunday 2pm-5.30pm.

Directions: St Albans.

FHG GUIDES, ABBEY MILL BUSINESS CENTRE, PAISLEY PA1 1TJ • www.holidayguides.com

---

Kent's award-winning open air museum is home to a collection of historic buildings which house interactive exhibitions on life over the last 150 years.

Open: seven days a week from February to start November, 10am to 5pm.

Directions: Junction 6 off M20, follow signs to Aylesford.

FHG GUIDES, ABBEY MILL BUSINESS CENTRE, PAISLEY PA1 1TJ • www.holidayguides.com

65

FHG
·K·U·P·E·R·A·R·D·
READERS' OFFER 2006

CHISLEHURST CAVES
Old Hill, Chislehurst,
Kent BR7 5NB
Tel: 020 8467 3264 • Fax: 020 8295 0407
e-mail: info@chislehurstcaves.co.uk
www.chislehurstcaves.co.uk

One FREE entry with one full-paying adult
Valid until 31st December 2006

NOT TO BE USED IN CONJUNCTION WITH ANY OTHER OFFER

FHG
·K·U·P·E·R·A·R·D·
READERS' OFFER 2006

DOCKER PARK FARM
Arkholme, Carnforth,
Lancashire LA6 1AR
Tel & Fax: 015242 21331
e-mail: info@dockerparkfarm.co.uk
www.dockerparkfarm.co.uk

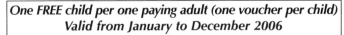

One FREE child per one paying adult (one voucher per child)
Valid from January to December 2006

NOT TO BE USED IN CONJUNCTION WITH ANY OTHER OFFER

FHG
·K·U·P·E·R·A·R·D·
READERS' OFFER 2006

WIGAN PIER
Wall Gate, Wigan
Lancashire WN3 4EU
Tel: 01942 323666
e-mail: wiganpier@wlct.org
www.wiganpier.net

Family Ticket (2 adults, 2 children) £10.50
Valid January-December 2006

NOT TO BE USED IN CONJUNCTION WITH ANY OTHER OFFER

FHG
·K·U·P·E·R·A·R·D·
READERS' OFFER 2006

SNIBSTON DISCOVERY PARK
Ashby Road, Coalville,
Leicestershire LE67 3LN
Tel: 01530 278444 • Fax: 01530 813301
e-mail: snibston@leics.gov.uk
www.leics.gov.uk/museums

SNIBSTON DISCOVERY PARK

One FREE child with every full paying adult
Valid until June 2006

NOT TO BE USED IN CONJUNCTION WITH ANY OTHER OFFER

Miles of mystery and history beneath your feet! Grab a lantern and get ready for an amazing underground adventure. Your whole family can travel back in time as you explore this labyrinth of dark mysterious passageways. See the caves church, Druid altar and more. Under 16s must be accompanied by an adult.

Open: Wed to Sun from 10am. Last tour 4pm. Open daily during local school holidays.

Directions: take A222 between A20 and A21; at Chislehurst railway bridge turn into station approach; turn right at end, then right again.

FHG GUIDES, ABBEY MILL BUSINESS CENTRE, PAISLEY PA1 1TJ • www.holidayguides.com

---

We are a working farm, with lots of animals to see and touch. Enjoy a walk round the Nature Trail or refreshments in the tearoom. Lots of activities during school holidays.

Open: Summer: daily 10.30am to 5pm. Winter: weekends only 10.30am to 4pm.

Directions: Junction 35 off M6, take B6254 towards Kirkby Lonsdale, then follow the brown signs.

FHG GUIDES, ABBEY MILL BUSINESS CENTRE, PAISLEY PA1 1TJ • www.holidayguides.com

---

One of the North West's favourite visitor attractions. Ideal for families and group visitors, Wigan Pier provides an educational and fun-packed day out, transporting visitors back in time to the Victorian period. Must-see attractions include 'The Way We Were' and the Trencherfield Mill Engine.

Open: 10am-5pm Monday to Thursday; 11am to 5pm Sundays. Closed Fridays and Saturdays.

Directions: on the banks of the Leeds-Liverpool canal.

FHG GUIDES, ABBEY MILL BUSINESS CENTRE, PAISLEY PA1 1TJ • www.holidayguides.com

---

Located in 100 acres of landscaped grounds, Snibston is a unique mixture, with historic mine buildings, outdoor science play areas, wildlife habitats and an exhibition hall housing five hands-on galleries, including The Toy Box for under 5s and the Fashion Gallery. Cafe and gift shop.

Open: April-September 10am to 5pm; October-March 10am to 3pm.

Directions: Junction 22 from M1, Junction 13 from M42. Follow brown Heritage signs.

FHG GUIDES, ABBEY MILL BUSINESS CENTRE, PAISLEY PA1 1TJ • www.holidayguides.com

67

SKEGNESS NATURELAND SEAL SANCTUARY
North Parade, Skegness,
Lincolnshire PE25 1DB
Tel: 01754 764345
e-mail: natureland@fsbdial.co.uk
www.skegnessnatureland.co.uk

READERS' OFFER 2006

Free entry for one child when accompanied by full-paying adult. Valid during 2006

NOT TO BE USED IN CONJUNCTION WITH ANY OTHER OFFER

PLEASURELAND
Marine Drive, Southport,
Merseyside PR8 1RX
Tel: 08702 200204 • Fax: 01704 537936
e-mail: mail@pleasurelandltd.freeserve.co.uk
www.pleasureland.uk.com

READERS' OFFER 2006

£5 off an all-day unlimited ride wristband
Valid March-Nov 2006 except Bank Holiday weekends (Sat-Mon)

NOT TO BE USED IN CONJUNCTION WITH ANY OTHER OFFER

THE COLLECTORS WORLD OF ERIC ST JOHN-FOTI
Hermitage Hall, Downham Market,
Norfolk PE38 0AU
Tel: 01366 383185 • Fax: 01366 386519
www.collectors-world.org

READERS' OFFER 2006

50p off adult admission - 25p off child admission
Valid during 2006

NOT TO BE USED IN CONJUNCTION WITH ANY OTHER OFFER

DINOSAUR ADVENTURE PARK
Weston Park, Lenwade, Norwich,
Norfolk NR9 5JW
Tel: 01603 876310 • Fax: 01603 876315
e-mail: info@dinosaurpark.co.uk
www.dinosaurpark.co.uk

READERS' OFFER 2006

50p off standard admission prices for up to six people
Valid until end of October 2006

NOT TO BE USED IN CONJUNCTION WITH ANY OTHER OFFER

Well known for rescuing and rehabilitating orphaned and injured seal pups found washed ashore on Lincolnshire beaches. Also: penguins, aquarium, pets' corner, reptiles, Floral Palace (tropical birds and butterflies etc).

Open: daily from 10am. Closed Christmas/Boxing/New Year's Days.

Directions: at the north end of Skegness seafront.

FHG GUIDES, ABBEY MILL BUSINESS CENTRE, PAISLEY PA1 1TJ • www.holidayguides.com

---

A great family day out for all ages with almost 100 rides and attractions, including the Traumatizer suspended looping coaster, the Lucozade Space Shot, and the Lost Dinosaurs of the Sahara.

Open: March to November, times vary.

Directions: from North: M6 (J31), A59, A565
from South: M6 (J26), M58 (J3), A570.

FHG GUIDES, ABBEY MILL BUSINESS CENTRE, PAISLEY PA1 1TJ • www.holidayguides.com

---

The collections of local eccentric Eric St John-Foti (Mr Norfolk Punch himself!) on view and the Magical Dickens Experience. Two amazing attractions for the price of one. Somewhere totally different, unique and interesting.

Open: 11am to 5pm (last entry 4pm) Open all year.

Directions: one mile from town centre on the A1122 Downham/ Wisbech Road.

FHG GUIDES, ABBEY MILL BUSINESS CENTRE, PAISLEY PA1 1TJ • www.holidayguides.com

---

It's time you came-n-saurus for a monster day out of discovery, adventure and fun. Enjoy the adventure play areas, dinosaur trail, secret animal garden and lots more.

Open: Please call for specific opening times or see our website.

Directions: 9 miles from Norwich, follow the brown signs to Weston Park from the A47 or A1067

FHG GUIDES, ABBEY MILL BUSINESS CENTRE, PAISLEY PA1 1TJ • www.holidayguides.com

READERS' OFFER 2006

NEWARK AIR MUSEUM
The Airfield, Winthorpe, Newark,
Nottinghamshire NG24 2NY
Tel: 01636 707170
e-mail: newarkair@onetel.com
www.newarkairmuseum.co.uk

Party rate discount for every voucher (50p per person off normal admission). Valid during 2006.

NOT TO BE USED IN CONJUNCTION WITH ANY OTHER OFFER

READERS' OFFER 2006

THE TALES OF ROBIN HOOD
30 - 38 Maid Marian Way,
Nottingham NG1 6GF
Tel: 0115 9483284 • Fax: 0115 9501536
e-mail: robinhoodcentre@mail.com
www.robinhood.uk.com

One FREE child with full paying adult per voucher
Valid from January to December 2006

NOT TO BE USED IN CONJUNCTION WITH ANY OTHER OFFER

READERS' OFFER 2006

DIDCOT RAILWAY CENTRE
Didcot,
Oxfordshire OX11 7NJ
Tel: 01235 817200 • Fax: 01235 510621
e-mail: didrlyc@globalnet.co.uk
www.didcotrailwaycentre.org.uk

One child FREE when accompanied by full-paying adult
Valid until end 2006 except during Day Out With Thomas events

NOT TO BE USED IN CONJUNCTION WITH ANY OTHER OFFER

READERS' OFFER 2006

THE HELICOPTER MUSEUM
The Heliport, Locking Moor Road,
Weston-Super-Mare BS24 8PP
Tel: 01934 635227• Fax: 01934 645230
e-mail: office@helimuseum.fsnet.co.uk
www.helicoptermuseum.co.uk

One child FREE with two full-paying adults
Valid from April to October 2006

NOT TO BE USED IN CONJUNCTION WITH ANY OTHER OFFER

A collection of 70 aircraft and cockpit sections from across the history of aviation. Extensive aero engine and artefact displays.

Open: daily from 10am (closed Christmas period and New Year's Day).

Directions: follow brown and white signs from A1, A46, A17 and A1133.

FHG GUIDES, ABBEY MILL BUSINESS CENTRE, PAISLEY PA1 1TJ • www.holidayguides.com

---

Travel back in time to the dark and dangerous world of intrigue and adventure of Medieval England's most endearing outlaw - Robin Hood. Story boards, exhibitions and a film show all add interest to the story.

Open: 10am-5.30pm, last admission 4.30pm.

Directions: follow the brown and white tourist information signs whilst heading towards the city centre.

FHG GUIDES, ABBEY MILL BUSINESS CENTRE, PAISLEY PA1 1TJ • www.holidayguides.com

---

See the steam trains from the golden age of the Great Western Railway. Steam locomotives in the original engine shed, a reconstructed country branch line, and a re-creation of Brunel's original broad gauge railway. On Steam Days there are rides in the 1930s carriages.

Open: Sat/Sun all year; daily 24 June to 3 Sept + school holidays. 10am-5pm weekends and Steam Days, 10am-4pm other days and in winter.

Directions: at Didcot Parkway rail station; on A4130, signposted from M4 (Junction 13) and A34

FHG GUIDES, ABBEY MILL BUSINESS CENTRE, PAISLEY PA1 1TJ • www.holidayguides.com

---

The world's largest helicopter collection - over 70 exhibits, includes two royal helicopters, Russian Gunship and Vietnam veterans plus many award-winning exhibits. Cafe, shop. Flights.

PETS MUST BE KEPT UNDER CONTROL

Open: Wednesday to Sunday 10am to 5.30pm. Daily during school Easter and Summer holidays and Bank Holiday Mondays. November to March: 10am to 4.30pm

Directions: Junction 21 off M5 then follow the propellor signs.

FHG GUIDES, ABBEY MILL BUSINESS CENTRE, PAISLEY PA1 1TJ • www.holidayguides.com

71

**READERS'
OFFER
2006**

FLEET AIR ARM MUSEUM
RNAS Yeovilton, Ilchester,
Somerset BA22 8HT
Tel: 01935 840077
e-mail: enquiries@fleetairarm.com
www.fleetairarm.com

Fleet Air Arm Museum

One child FREE with full paying adult
Valid during 2006 except Bank Holidays

NOT TO BE USED IN CONJUNCTION WITH ANY OTHER OFFER

**READERS'
OFFER
2006**

EXMOOR FALCONRY & ANIMAL FARM
Allerford,
Near Porlock, Minehead,
Somerset TA24 8HJ
Tel: 01643 862816
www.exmoorfalconry.co.uk

10% off entry to Falconry Centre
Valid during 2006

NOT TO BE USED IN CONJUNCTION WITH ANY OTHER OFFER

**READERS'
OFFER
2006**

AMERICAN ADVENTURE GOLF
Fort Fun,
Royal Parade,
Eastbourne,
East Sussex BN22 7LU
Tel: 01323 642833

One FREE game of golf with every full-paying customer
(value £2.50). Valid April-Oct 2006 before 12 noon only

NOT TO BE USED IN CONJUNCTION WITH ANY OTHER OFFER

**READERS'
OFFER
2006**

WILDERNESS WOOD
Hadlow Down, Near Uckfield,
East Sussex TN22 4HJ
Tel: 01825 830509• Fax: 01825 830977
e-mail: enquiries@wildernesswood.co.uk
www.wildernesswood.co.uk

one FREE admission with a full-paying adult
Valid during 2006

NOT TO BE USED IN CONJUNCTION WITH ANY OTHER OFFER

Europe's largest naval aviation collection with over 40 aircraft on display , including Concorde 002 and Ark Royal Aircraft Carrier Experience. Situated on an operational naval air station.

Open: open daily April to October 10am-5.30pm; November to March 10am-4.30pm (closed Mon and Tues).

Directions: just off A303/A37 on B3151 at Ilchester. Yeovil rail station 10 miles.

FHG GUIDES, ABBEY MILL BUSINESS CENTRE, PAISLEY PA1 1TJ • www.holidayguides.com

---

Falconry centre with animals - flying displays, animal handling, feeding and bottle feeding - in 15th century NT farmyard setting on Exmoor. Also falconry and outdoor activities, hawk walks and riding.

Open: 10.30am to 5pm daily

Directions: A39 west of Minehead, turn right at Allerford, half a mile along lane on left.

FHG GUIDES, ABBEY MILL BUSINESS CENTRE, PAISLEY PA1 1TJ • www.holidayguides.com

---

18-hole American Adventure Golf set in ⅓ acre landscaped surroundings. Played on different levels including water features.

Open: April until end October 10am until dusk.

Directions: on the seafront ¼ mile east of Eastbourne Pier.

FHG GUIDES, ABBEY MILL BUSINESS CENTRE, PAISLEY PA1 1TJ • www.holidayguides.com

---

Wilderness Wood is a unique family-run working woodland in the Sussex High Weald. Explore trails and footpaths, enjoy local cakes and ices, try the adventure playground. Many special events and activities. Parties catered for.

Open: daily 10am to 5.30pm or dusk if earlier.

Directions: on the south side of the A272 in the village of Hadlow Down. Signposted with a brown tourist sign.

FHG GUIDES, ABBEY MILL BUSINESS CENTRE, PAISLEY PA1 1TJ • www.holidayguides.com

FHG
·K·U·P·E·R·A·R·D·
**READERS'
OFFER
2006**

YESTERDAY'S WORLD
89-90 High Street, Battle,
East Sussex TN33 0AQ
Tel: 01424 775378
e-mail: info@yesterdaysworld.co.uk
www.yesterdaysworld.co.uk

Yesterday's World

> One child FREE when accompanied by one
> full-paying adult. Valid until end 2006

NOT TO BE USED IN CONJUNCTION WITH ANY OTHER OFFER

FHG
·K·U·P·E·R·A·R·D·
**READERS'
OFFER
2006**

PARADISE PARK & GARDENS
Avis Road, Newhaven,
East Sussex BN9 0DH
Tel: 01273 512123 • Fax: 01273 616000
e-mail: enquiries@paradisepark.co.uk
www.paradisepark.co.uk

PARADISE PARK

> Admit one FREE adult or child with one adult
> paying full entrance price. Valid during 2006

NOT TO BE USED IN CONJUNCTION WITH ANY OTHER OFFER

FHG
·K·U·P·E·R·A·R·D·
**READERS'
OFFER
2006**

WILDFOWL & WETLANDS TRUST
Pattinson, Washington,
Tyne & Wear NE38 8LE
Tel: 0191 416 5454
e-mail: val.pickering@wwt.org.uk
www.wwt.org.uk

Wildfowl & Wetlands Trust

> One FREE admission with full-paying adult
> Valid from 1st Jan to 30th Sept 2006

NOT TO BE USED IN CONJUNCTION WITH ANY OTHER OFFER

FHG
·K·U·P·E·R·A·R·D·
**READERS'
OFFER
2006**

HATTON COUNTRY WORLD FARM VILLAGE
Dark Lane, Hatton, Near Warwick,
Warwickshire CV35 8XA
Tel: 01926 843411
e-mail: hatton@hattonworld.com
www.hattonworld.com

> Admit TWO for the price of ONE into Farm Village.
> Admission into Shopping Village free. Valid during 2006

NOT TO BE USED IN CONJUNCTION WITH ANY OTHER OFFER

74

The past is brought to life at one of the South East's best loved family attractions. 100,000+ nostalgic artefacts on four exciting floors, set in a charming 15th century house and country gardens. **PETS NOT ALLOWED IN CHILDREN'S PLAY AREA**	**Open:** 9.30am to 6pm (last admission 4.45pm, one hour earlier in winter). Closing times may vary – phone or check website. **Directions:** just off A21 in Battle High Street opposite the Abbey.

FHG GUIDES, ABBEY MILL BUSINESS CENTRE, PAISLEY PA1 1TJ • www.holidayguides.com

Discover 'Planet Earth' for an unforgettable experience. A unique Museum of Life, Dinosaur Safari, beautiful Water Gardens with fish and wildfowl, plant houses, themed gardens, Heritage Trail, miniature railway. Playzone includes crazy golf and adventure play area. Garden Centre and Terrace Cafe.	**Open:** open daily, except Christmas Day and Boxing Day. **Directions:** signposted off A26 and A259.

FHG GUIDES, ABBEY MILL BUSINESS CENTRE, PAISLEY PA1 1TJ • www.holidayguides.com

100 acres of parkland, home to hundreds of duck, geese, swans and flamingos. Discovery centre, cafe, gift shop; play area.	**Open:** every day except Christmas Day **Directions:** sgnposted from A19, A195, A1231 and A182.

FHG GUIDES, ABBEY MILL BUSINESS CENTRE, PAISLEY PA1 1TJ • www.holidayguides.com

Two attractions side-by-side. Hatton Farm Village has fun for the whole family, with animals, demonstrations and adventure play. Hatton Shopping Village has 21 craft and gift shops, an antiques centre, a factory-style store, and two restaurants. Free parking.	**Open:** daily 10am to 5pm. Open until 4pm Christmas Eve; 11am-4pm 27 Dec-1st Jan incl; closed Christmas Day & Boxing Day. **Directions:** 5 minutes from M40 (J15), A46 towards Coventry, then just off A4177 (follow brown tourist signs).

FHG GUIDES, ABBEY MILL BUSINESS CENTRE, PAISLEY PA1 1TJ • www.holidayguides.com

75

READERS' OFFER 2006

COVENTRY TRANSPORT MUSEUM
Millennium Place, City Centre
Coventry CV1 1PN
Tel: 024 7623 4270
e-mail: enquiries@transport-museum.com
www.transport-museum.com

10% off all purchases in shop on production of voucher (admission to museum free). Valid until August 2006.

NOT TO BE USED IN CONJUNCTION WITH ANY OTHER OFFER

READERS' OFFER 2006

AVONCROFT MUSEUM
Stoke Heath,
Bromsgrove,
Worcestershire B60 4JR
Tel: 01527 831363 • Fax: 01527 876934
www.avoncroft.org.uk

One FREE child with one full-paying adult
Valid from March to November 2006

NOT TO BE USED IN CONJUNCTION WITH ANY OTHER OFFER

READERS' OFFER 2006

EDEN CAMP MODERN HISTORY THEME MUSEUM
Eden Camp, Malton,
North Yorkshire YO17 6RT
Tel: 01653 697777 • Fax: 01653 698243
e-mail: admin@edencamp.co.uk
www.edencamp.co.uk

One FREE child per paying adult; TWO for ONE Senior Citizen ticket. Valid 9th Jan-23rd Dec 2006 (not Bank Holidays)

NOT TO BE USED IN CONJUNCTION WITH ANY OTHER OFFER

READERS' OFFER 2006

EMBSAY & BOLTON ABBEY STEAM RAILWAY
Bolton Abbey Station, Skipton,
North Yorkshire BD23 6AF
Tel: 01756 710614
e-mail: embsay.steam@btinternet.com
www.embsayboltonabbeyrailway.org.uk

EMBSAY & BOLTON ABBEY STEAM RAILWAY

One adult travels FREE when accompanied by a full fare paying adult (does not include Special Event days). Valid during 2006.

NOT TO BE USED IN CONJUNCTION WITH ANY OTHER OFFER

Over 150 years of unique history, with something different round every corner. The largest collection of British Road Transport in the world with over 230 cars and commercial vehicles, 250 cycles and 90 motorcycles.	**Open:** daily 10am to 5pm **Directions:** Coventry city centre.

FHG GUIDES, ABBEY MILL BUSINESS CENTRE, PAISLEY PA1 1TJ • www.holidayguides.com

A fascinating world of historic buildings covering 7 centuries, rescued and rebuilt on an open-air site in the heart of the Worcestershire countryside. **PETS ON LEADS ONLY**	**Open:** July and August all week. March to November varying times, please telephone for details. **Directions:** A38 south of Bromsgrove, near Junction 1 of M42, Junction 5 of M5.

FHG GUIDES, ABBEY MILL BUSINESS CENTRE, PAISLEY PA1 1TJ • www.holidayguides.com

Housed within the grounds of an original prisoner-of-war camp, a visit to our museum will transport you back in time to WWII. Experience the sights, sounds and even the smells of life on the Home Front and the front line. Both exciting and educational, our museum appeals to all the family.	**Open:** daily, second Monday in January until 23 December. 10am-5pm (last admission 4pm). Allow 4 hours for a full visit. **Directions:** on northern outskirts of Malton, midway between York and Scarborough on junction of A64 and A169

FHG GUIDES, ABBEY MILL BUSINESS CENTRE, PAISLEY PA1 1TJ • www.holidayguides.com

Steam trains operate over a 4½ mile line from Bolton Abbey Station to Embsay Station. Many family events including Thomas the Tank Engine take place during major Bank Holidays.	**Open:** steam trains run every Sunday throughout the year and up to 7 days a week in summer. 10.30am to 4.30pm **Directions:** Embsay Station signposted from the A59 Skipton by-pass; Bolton Abbey Station signposted from the A59 at Bolton Abbey.

FHG GUIDES, ABBEY MILL BUSINESS CENTRE, PAISLEY PA1 1TJ • www.holidayguides.com

77

READERS' OFFER 2006

WORLD OF JAMES HERRIOT
23 Kirkgate, Thirsk,
North Yorkshire YO7 1PL
Tel: 01845 524234
Fax: 01845 525333
www.worldofjamesherriot.org

Admit TWO for the price of ONE (one voucher per transaction only). Valid until October 2006

NOT TO BE USED IN CONJUNCTION WITH ANY OTHER OFFER

READERS' OFFER 2006

YORKSHIRE DALES FALCONRY & WILDLIFE CONSERVATION CENTRE
Crow's Nest, Giggleswick, Near Settle LA2 8AS
Tel: 01729 822832 • Fax: 01729 825160
e-mail: info@falconryandwildlife.com
www.falconryandwildlife.com

One child FREE with two full-paying adults
Valid until end 2006

NOT TO BE USED IN CONJUNCTION WITH ANY OTHER OFFER

READERS' OFFER 2006

MAGNA SCIENCE ADVENTURE CENTRE
Sheffield Road, Templeborough,
Rotherham S60 1DX
Tel: 01709 720002 • Fax: 01709 820092
e-mail: info@magnatrust.co.uk
www.visitmagna.co.uk

One FREE adult or child ticket with each full-paying adult/child (not family tickets). Valid until 31st Dec 2006

NOT TO BE USED IN CONJUNCTION WITH ANY OTHER OFFER

READERS' OFFER 2006

MUSEUM OF RAIL TRAVEL
Ingrow Railway Centre, Near Keighley,
West Yorkshire BD22 8NJ
Tel: 01535 680425
e-mail: vct@museumofrailtravel.co.uk
www.vintagecarriagestrust.org • www.museumofrailtravel.co.uk

"ONE for ONE" free admission
Valid during 2006 except during special events (ring to check)

NOT TO BE USED IN CONJUNCTION WITH ANY OTHER OFFER

Visit James Herriot's original house recreated as it was in the 1940s. Television sets used in the series 'All Creatures Great and Small'. A new children's interactive gallery with life-size model farm animals and three rooms dedicated to the history of veterinary medicine.

Open: daily. April-October 10am-6pm; November-March 11am to 4pm

Directions: follow signs off A1 or A19 to Thirsk, then A168, off Thirsk market place

FHG GUIDES, ABBEY MILL BUSINESS CENTRE, PAISLEY PA1 1TJ • www.holidayguides.com

---

All types of birds of prey exhibited here, from owls and kestrels to eagles and vultures. Special flying displays 12 noon, 1.30pm and 3pm. Bird handling courses arranged for either half or full days.

GUIDE DOGS ONLY

Open: 10am to 4.30pm summer 10am to 4pm winter

Directions: on main A65 trunk road outside Settle. Follow brown direction signs.

FHG GUIDES, ABBEY MILL BUSINESS CENTRE, PAISLEY PA1 1TJ • www.holidayguides.com

---

The UK's first Science Adventure Centre. Explore the elements - Earth, Air, Fire and Water - and have fun firing a giant water cannon, launching rockets, exploding rock faces and working real JCBs. Also Sci Tek, Europe's largest hi-tech adventure playground.

Open: daily 10am to 5pm (closed 24th-27th Dec and Ist Jan)

Directions: from M1 take Junction 33 (from south) or Junction 34 (from north), and follow signs. One mile from Meadowhall Shopping Centre

FHG GUIDES, ABBEY MILL BUSINESS CENTRE, PAISLEY PA1 1TJ • www.holidayguides.com

---

A fascinating display of railway carriages and a wide range of railway items telling the story of rail travel over the years.

ALL PETS MUST BE KEPT ON LEADS

Open: daily 11am to 4.30pm

Directions: approximately one mile from Keighley on A629 Halifax road. Follow brown tourist signs

FHG GUIDES, ABBEY MILL BUSINESS CENTRE, PAISLEY PA1 1TJ • www.holidayguides.com

79

FHG

READERS' OFFER 2006

THE COLOUR MUSEUM
Perkin House, PO Box 244, Providence Street,
Bradford BD1 2PW
Tel: 01274 390955 • Fax: 01274 392888
e-mail: museum@sdc.org.uk
www.colour-experience.org

TWO for ONE
Valid during 2006

NOT TO BE USED IN CONJUNCTION WITH ANY OTHER OFFER

FHG

READERS' OFFER 2006

THACKRAY MUSEUM
Beckett Street, Leeds LS9 7LN
Tel: 0113 244 4343
Fax: 0113 247 0219
e-mail: info@thackraymuseum.org
www.thackraymuseum.org

TWO for ONE on the purchase of a full adult ticket
Valid until July 2006 excluding Bank Holidays

NOT TO BE USED IN CONJUNCTION WITH ANY OTHER OFFER

FHG

READERS' OFFER 2006

EUREKA! THE MUSEUM FOR CHILDREN
Discovery Road, Halifax,
West Yorkshire HX1 2NE
Tel: 01422 330069
e-mail: info@eureka.org.uk
www.eureka.org

243 - £6.50 ticket
244 - £1.95 ticket

One child FREE with one adult paying full price.
Valid Saturdays and Sundays only during 2006

NOT TO BE USED IN CONJUNCTION WITH ANY OTHER OFFER

FHG

Visit the website
www.holidayguides.com
for details of the wide choice of accommodation
featured in the full range of FHG titles

The Colour Museum is unique. Dedicated to the history, development and technology of colour, it is the ONLY museum of its kind in Europe. A truly colourful experience for both kids and adults, it's fun, it's informative and it's well worth a visit.	**Open:** Tuesday to Saturday 10am to 4pm (last admission 3.30pm). **Directions:** just off Westgate on B6144 from the city centre to Haworth.

FHG GUIDES, ABBEY MILL BUSINESS CENTRE, PAISLEY PA1 1TJ • www.holidayguides.com

A fantastic day out for all at the lively and interactive, award-winning Thackray Museum. Experience life as it was in the Victorian slums, discover how medicine has changed our lives and the incredible lotions and potions once offered as cures. Try an empathy belly and explore the interactive bodyworks gallery.	**Open:** daily 10am till 5pm, closed 24th-26th + 31st Dec and 1st Jan. **Directions:** from M621 follow signs for York (A64), then follow brown tourist signs. From the north, take A58 towards city, then follow brown tourist signs.

FHG GUIDES, ABBEY MILL BUSINESS CENTRE, PAISLEY PA1 1TJ • www.holidayguides.com

The UK's first and foremost museum for children under 12, where hundreds of interactive exhibits let them make fascinating discoveries about themselves and the world around them.	**Open:** daily 10am to 5pm (closed 24-26 December) **Directions:** next to Halifax railway station, five minutes from J24 M62

FHG GUIDES, ABBEY MILL BUSINESS CENTRE, PAISLEY PA1 1TJ • www.holidayguides.com

FHG Guides publish a large range of well-known accommodation guides. We will be happy to send you details or you can use the order form at the back of this book.

FHG READERS' OFFER 2006

STORYBOOK GLEN
Maryculter,
Aberdeen
Aberdeenshire AB12 5FT
Tel: 01224 732941
www.storybookglenaberdeen.co.uk

10% discount on all admissions
Valid until end 2006

NOT TO BE USED IN CONJUNCTION WITH ANY OTHER OFFER

FHG READERS' OFFER 2006

THE GRASSIC GIBBON CENTRE
Arbuthnott, Laurencekirk,
Aberdeenshire AB30 1PB
Tel: 01561 361668
e-mail: lgginfo@grassicgibbon.com
www.grassicgibbon.com

TWO for the price of ONE entry to exhibition (based on full adult rate only). Valid during 2006 (not groups)

NOT TO BE USED IN CONJUNCTION WITH ANY OTHER OFFER

FHG READERS' OFFER 2006

INVERARAY JAIL
Church Square, Inveraray,
Argyll PA32 8TX
Tel: 01499 302381 • Fax: 01499 302195
e-mail: inverarayjail@btclick.com
www.inverarayjail.co.uk

One child FREE with one full-paying adult
Valid until end 2006

NOT TO BE USED IN CONJUNCTION WITH ANY OTHER OFFER

FHG READERS' OFFER 2006

OBAN RARE BREEDS FARM PARK
Glencruitten, Oban,
Argyll PA34 4QB
Tel: 01631 770608
e-mail: info@obanrarebreeds.com
www.obanrarebreeds.com

Oban Rare Breeds Farm Park

20% DISCOUNT on all admissions
Valid during 2006

NOT TO BE USED IN CONJUNCTION WITH ANY OTHER OFFER

28-acre theme park with over 100 nursery rhyme characters, set in beautifully landscaped gardens. Shop and restaurant on site.	**Open:** 1st March to 31st October: daily 10am to 6pm; 1st Nov to end Feb: Sat/Sun only 11am to 4pm **Directions:** 6 miles west of Aberdeen off B9077

FHG GUIDES, ABBEY MILL BUSINESS CENTRE, PAISLEY PA1 1TJ • www.holidayguides.com

Visitor Centre dedicated to the much-loved Scottish writer Lewis Grassic Gibbon. Exhibition, cafe, gift shop. Outdoor children's play area. Disabled access throughout.	**Open:** daily April to October 10am to 4.30pm. Groups by appointment including evenings. **Directions:** on the B967, accessible and signposted from both A90 and A92.

FHG GUIDES, ABBEY MILL BUSINESS CENTRE, PAISLEY PA1 1TJ • www.holidayguides.com

19th century prison with fully restored 1820 courtroom and two prisons. Guides in uniform as warders, prisoners and matron. Remember your camera!	**Open:** April to October 9.30am-6pm (last admission 5pm); November to March 10am-5pm (last admission 4pm) **Directions:** A83 to Campbeltown

FHG GUIDES, ABBEY MILL BUSINESS CENTRE, PAISLEY PA1 1TJ • www.holidayguides.com

Rare breeds of farm animals, pets' corner, conservation groups, tea room, woodland walk in beautiful location	**Open:** 10am to 6pm mid-March to end October **Directions:** two-and-a-half miles from Oban along Glencruitten road

FHG GUIDES, ABBEY MILL BUSINESS CENTRE, PAISLEY PA1 1TJ • www.holidayguides.com

83

FHG
·K·U·P·E·R·A·R·D·
READERS'
OFFER
2006

KELBURN CASTLE & COUNTRY CENTRE
Fairlie, Near Largs,
Ayrshire KA29 0BE
Tel: 01475 568685
e-mail: admin@kelburncountrycentre.com
www.kelburncountrycentre.com

One child FREE for each full-paying adult
Valid until October 2006

NOT TO BE USED IN CONJUNCTION WITH ANY OTHER OFFER

FHG
·K·U·P·E·R·A·R·D·
READERS'
OFFER
2006

SCOTTISH MARITIME MUSEUM
Harbourside, Irvine,
Ayrshire KA12 8QE
Tel: 01294 278283 • Fax: 01294 313211
e-mail: info@scottishmaritimemuseum.org
www.scottishmaritimemuseum.org

Scottish Maritime Museum

TWO for the price of ONE
Valid from April to October 2006

NOT TO BE USED IN CONJUNCTION WITH ANY OTHER OFFER

FHG
·K·U·P·E·R·A·R·D·
READERS'
OFFER
2006

JEDFOREST DEER & FARM PARK
Mervinslaw Estate, Camptown, Jedburgh,
Borders TD8 6PL
Tel: 01835 840364
e-mail: mervinslaw@ecosse.net
www.aboutscotland.com/jedforest

One FREE child with two full-paying adults
Valid May/June and Sept/Oct 2006

NOT TO BE USED IN CONJUNCTION WITH ANY OTHER OFFER

FHG
·K·U·P·E·R·A·R·D·
READERS'
OFFER
2006

CREETOWN GEM ROCK MUSEUM
Chain Road, Creetown, Near Newton Stewart,
Kirkcudbrightshire DG8 7HJ
Tel: 01671 820357
e-mail: gem.rock@btinternet.com
www.gemrock.net

GEM ROCK MUSEUM

10% off admission prices
Valid during 2006

NOT TO BE USED IN CONJUNCTION WITH ANY OTHER OFFER

The historic home of the Earls of Glasgow. Waterfalls, gardens, famous Glen, unusual trees. Riding school, stockade, play areas, exhibitions, shop, cafe and The Secret Forest. Falconry Centre, Pottery, indoor playbarn. **PETS MUST BE KEPT ON LEAD**	**Open:** daily 10am to 6pm Easter to October. **Directions:** on A78 between Largs and Fairlie, 45 minutes' drive from Glasgow.

FHG GUIDES, ABBEY MILL BUSINESS CENTRE, PAISLEY PA1 1TJ • www.holidayguides.com

Scotland's seafaring heritage is among the world's richest and you can relive the heyday of Scottish shipping at the Maritime Museum.	**Open:** 1st April to 31st October - 10am-5pm **Directions:** situated on Irvine harbourside and only a 10 minute walk from Irvine train station.

FHG GUIDES, ABBEY MILL BUSINESS CENTRE, PAISLEY PA1 1TJ • www.holidayguides.com

Working farm with visitor centre showing rare breeds, deer herds, ranger-led activities, and walks. Birds of prey displays and tuition. Corporate activities. Shop and cafe.	**Open:** daily. May to August 10am to 5.30pm; Sept/Oct 11am to 4.30pm. **Directions:** 5 miles south of Jedburgh on A68.

FHG GUIDES, ABBEY MILL BUSINESS CENTRE, PAISLEY PA1 1TJ • www.holidayguides.com

Worldwide collection of gems, minerals, crystals and fossils Professor's Study, Prospectors' Pantry, workshop, gift shop.	**Open:** Open daily Easter to 30th November; Dec-Feb: weekends only. **Directions:** 7 miles from Newton Stewart, 11 miles from Gatehouse of Fleet; just off A75 Carlisle to Stranraer.

FHG GUIDES, ABBEY MILL BUSINESS CENTRE, PAISLEY PA1 1TJ • www.holidayguides.com

FHG K·U·P·E·R·A·R·D
READERS' OFFER 2006

SCOTTISH SEABIRD CENTRE
The Harbour, North Berwick,
East Lothian EH39 4SS
Tel: 01620 890202 • Fax: 01620 890222
e-mail: info@seabird.org
www.seabird.org

Any TWO admissions for the price of ONE
Valid until 1st October 2006

NOT TO BE USED IN CONJUNCTION WITH ANY OTHER OFFER

FHG K·U·P·E·R·A·R·D
READERS' OFFER 2006

EDINBURGH BUTTERFLY & INSECT WORLD
Dobbies Garden World, Melville Nursery,
Lasswade EH18 1AZ
Tel: 0131-663 4932 • Fax: 0131 654 2774
info@edinburgh-butterfly-world.co.uk
www.edinburgh-butterfly-world.co.uk

One child FREE with a full-paying adult
Valid from 1st Jan to 30th April 2006

NOT TO BE USED IN CONJUNCTION WITH ANY OTHER OFFER

FHG K·U·P·E·R·A·R·D
READERS' OFFER 2006

THE SCOTTISH MINING MUSEUM
Lady Victoria Colliery, Newtongrange,
Midlothian EH22 4QN
Tel: 0131-663 7519 • Fax: 0131-654 0752
visitorservices@scottishminingmuseum.com
www.scottishminingmuseum.com

One child FREE with full-paying adult
Valid January to December 2006

NOT TO BE USED IN CONJUNCTION WITH ANY OTHER OFFER

FHG K·U·P·E·R·A·R·D
READERS' OFFER 2006

MYRETON MOTOR MUSEUM
Aberlady,
East Lothian
EH32 0PZ
Tel: 01875 870288

MYRETON MOTOR MUSEUM

One child FREE with each paying adult
Valid during 2006

NOT TO BE USED IN CONJUNCTION WITH ANY OTHER OFFER

86

Get close to Nature with a visit to this stunning award-winning Centre. With panoramic views across islands and sandy beaches, the area is a haven for wildlife. Live cameras zoom in close to see wildlife including gannets, puffins and seals. Wildlife boat safaris, new Environmental Zone and Flyway.

Open: daily from 10am

Directions: from A1 take road for North Berwick; near the harbour; Centre signposted.

FHG GUIDES, ABBEY MILL BUSINESS CENTRE, PAISLEY PA1 1TJ • www.holidayguides.com

---

It's Creeping, It's Crawling, It's a Jungle in there! Free-flying exotic butterflies, roaming iguanas, giant pythons, 'glow in the dark' scorpions, and 'Bugs and Beasties' handling and phobia-curing sessions. Incredible leaf-cutting ants.

Open: summer 9.30am to 5.30pm winter 10am to 5pm

Directions: just off Edinburgh City Bypass at Gilmerton exit or Sheriffhall Roundabout

FHG GUIDES, ABBEY MILL BUSINESS CENTRE, PAISLEY PA1 1TJ • www.holidayguides.com

---

visitscotland 5-Star Attraction with two floors of interactive exhibitions and a 'Magic Helmet' tour of the pithead, re-created coal road and coal face. Largest working winding engine in Britain.

Open: daily. Summer: 10am to 5pm (last tour 3.30pm). Winter: 10am to 4pm (last tour 2.30pm)

Directions: 5 minutes from Sherrifhall Roundabout on Edinburgh City Bypass on A7 south

FHG GUIDES, ABBEY MILL BUSINESS CENTRE, PAISLEY PA1 1TJ • www.holidayguides.com

---

On show is a large collection, from 1899, of cars, bicycles, motor cycles and commercials. There is also a large collection of period advertising, posters and enamel signs.

Open: daily April to October 11am to 4pm November to March: weekends 11am to 3pm or by special appointment.

Directions: off A198 near Aberlady. Two miles from A1.

FHG GUIDES, ABBEY MILL BUSINESS CENTRE, PAISLEY PA1 1TJ • www.holidayguides.com

87

SPEYSIDE HEATHER GARDEN & VISITOR CENTRE
Speyside Heather Centre, Dulnain Bridge,
Inverness-shire PH26 3PA
Tel: 01479 851359 • Fax: 01479 851396
e-mail: enquiries@heathercentre.com
www.heathercentre.com

READERS' OFFER 2006

FREE entry to 'Heather Story' exhibition
Valid during 2006

NOT TO BE USED IN CONJUNCTION WITH ANY OTHER OFFER

NEW LANARK WORLD HERITAGE SITE
New Lanark Mills, Lanark,
Lanarkshire ML11 9DB
Tel: 01555 661345• Fax: 01555 665738
e-mail: visit@newlanark.org
www.newlanark.org

READERS' OFFER 2006

One FREE child with one full price adult
Valid until 31st October 2006

NOT TO BE USED IN CONJUNCTION WITH ANY OTHER OFFER

MUSEUM OF CHILDHOOD MEMORIES
1 Castle Street,
Beaumaris,
Anglesey LL58 8AP
Tel: 01248 712498
www.aboutbritain.com/museumofchildhoodmemories.htm

READERS' OFFER 2006

One child FREE with two adults
Valid during 2006

NOT TO BE USED IN CONJUNCTION WITH ANY OTHER OFFER

PILI PALAS - BUTTERFLY PALACE
Menai Bridge
Isle of Anglesey LL59 5RP
Tel: 01248 712474
e-mail: gloyn@pilipalas.co.uk
www.pilipalas.co.uk

READERS' OFFER 2006

One child FREE with two adults paying full entry price
Valid March to October 2006

NOT TO BE USED IN CONJUNCTION WITH ANY OTHER OFFER

Award-winning attraction with unique 'Heather Story' exhibition, gallery, giftshop, large garden centre selling 300 different heathers, antique shop, children's play area and famous Clootie Dumpling restaurant.

Open: all year except Christmas Day.

Directions: just off A95 between Aviemore and Grantown-on-Spey.

FHG GUIDES, ABBEY MILL BUSINESS CENTRE, PAISLEY PA1 1TJ • www.holidayguides.com

---

A beautifully restored cotton mill village close to the Falls of Clyde. Explore the fascinating history of the village, try the 'Millennium Experience', a magical ride which takes you back in time to discover what life used to be like.

Open: 11am-5pm daily. June-August 10.30am-5pm daily. Closed Christmas Day and New Year's Day.

Directions: 25 miles from Glasgow and 35 miles from Edinburgh; well signposted on all major routes.

FHG GUIDES, ABBEY MILL BUSINESS CENTRE, PAISLEY PA1 1TJ • www.holidayguides.com

---

Nine rooms in a Georgian house filled with items illustrating the happier times of family life over the past 150 years. Joyful nostalgia unlimited.

Open: March to end October

Directions: opposite Beaumaris Castle

FHG GUIDES, ABBEY MILL BUSINESS CENTRE, PAISLEY PA1 1TJ • www.holidayguides.com

---

Visit Wales' top Butterfly House, with Bird House, Snake House, Ant Avenue, Tropical Hide, shop, cafe, adventure playground, indoor play area, picnic area, nature trail etc.

Open: March to end Oct: 10am - 5.30pm daily; Nov/Dec 11am-3pm

Directions: follow brown and white signs when crossing to Anglesey; one-and-a- half miles from Bridge

FHG GUIDES, ABBEY MILL BUSINESS CENTRE, PAISLEY PA1 1TJ • www.holidayguides.com

LLANBERIS LAKE RAILWAY
Gilfach Ddu, Llanberis,
Gwynedd LL55 4TY
Tel: 01286 870549
e-mail: info@lake-railway.co.uk
www.lake-railway.co.uk

READERS' OFFER 2006

One pet travels FREE with each full fare paying adult
Valid Easter to October 2006

NOT TO BE USED IN CONJUNCTION WITH ANY OTHER OFFER

FELINWYNT RAINFOREST CENTRE
Felinwynt, Cardigan,
Ceredigion SA43 1RT
Tel: 01239 810882/810250
e-mail: dandjdevereux@btinternet.com
www.butterflycentre.co.uk

READERS' OFFER 2006

TWO for the price of ONE (one voucher per party only)
Valid until end October 2006

NOT TO BE USED IN CONJUNCTION WITH ANY OTHER OFFER

NATIONAL CYCLE COLLECTION
Automobile Palace, Temple Street,
Llandrindod Wells, Powys LD1 5DL
Tel: 01597 825531
e-mail: cycle.museum@care4free.net
www.cyclemuseum.org.uk

READERS' OFFER 2006

TWO for the price of ONE
Valid during 2006 except Special Event days

NOT TO BE USED IN CONJUNCTION WITH ANY OTHER OFFER

RHONDDA HERITAGE PARK
Lewis Merthyr Colliery, Coed Cae Road,
Trehafod, Near Pontypridd CF37 7NP
Tel: 01443 682036
e-mail: info@rhonddaheritagepark.com
www.rhonddaheritagepark.com

READERS' OFFER 2006

Two adults or children for the price of one when accompanied
by a full paying adult. Valid until end 2006 for full tours only.
Not valid on special event days/themed tours.

NOT TO BE USED IN CONJUNCTION WITH ANY OTHER OFFER

A 60-minute ride along the shores of beautiful Padarn Lake behind a quaint historic steam engine. Magnificent views of the mountains from lakeside picnic spots.

DOGS MUST BE KEPT ON LEAD AT ALL TIMES ON TRAIN

Open: most days Easter to October. Free timetable leaflet on request.

Directions: just off A4086 Caernarfon to Capel Curig road at Llanberis; follow 'Country Park' signs.

FHG GUIDES, ABBEY MILL BUSINESS CENTRE, PAISLEY PA1 1TJ • www.holidayguides.com

---

Mini-rainforest full of tropical plants and exotic butterflies. Personal attention of the owner, Mr John Devereux. Gift shop, cafe, video room, exhibition. Suitable for disabled visitors. WTB Quality Assured Visitor Attraction.

PETS NOT ALLOWED IN TROPICAL HOUSE ONLY

Open: daily Easter to end October 10.30am to 5pm

Directions: West Wales, 7 miles north of Cardigan on Aberystwyth road. Follow brown tourist signs on A487.

FHG GUIDES, ABBEY MILL BUSINESS CENTRE, PAISLEY PA1 1TJ • www.holidayguides.com

---

Journey through the lanes of cycle history and see bicycles from Boneshakers and Penny Farthings up to modern Raleigh cycles. Over 250 machines on display

PETS MUST BE KEPT ON LEADS

Open: 1st March to 1st November daily 10am onwards.

Directions: brown signs to car park. Town centre attraction.

FHG GUIDES, ABBEY MILL BUSINESS CENTRE, PAISLEY PA1 1TJ • www.holidayguides.com

---

Make a pit stop whatever the weather! Join an ex-miner on a tour of discovery, ride the cage to pit bottom and take a thrilling ride back to the surface. Multi-media presentations, period village street, children's adventure play area, restaurant and gift shop. Disabled access with assistance.

Open: Open daily 10am to 6pm (last tour 4.30pm). Closed Mondays Oct - Easter, also Dec 25th to 3rd Jan incl.

Directions: Exit Junction 32 M4, signposted from A470 Pontypridd. Trehafod is located between Pontypridd and Porth.

FHG GUIDES, ABBEY MILL BUSINESS CENTRE, PAISLEY PA1 1TJ • www.holidayguides.com

ENGLAND

London (Central & Greater)

BED AND BREAKFAST IN LONDON
IDEAL LONDON LOCATION
Comfortable, centrally located quiet Edwardian home. Great base for sightseeing, close to the river, traditional pubs, lots of local restaurants and antique shops. Excellent transport facilities – easy access to West End, Theatreland, shopping, Harrods, museums, Albert Hall, Earls Court and Olympia Exhibition centres. Direct lines to Eurostar (Waterloo), Airports: Heathrow, Gatwick (Victoria), Stansted (Liverpool Street). Bed and Continental Breakfast Prices: Double/Twin/Triple £24 pppn; Single £34.00; Children's reductions. Smoking only in garden.

Sohel and Anne Armanios
67 Rannoch Road, Hammersmith, London W6 9SS
Tel: 020 7385 4904 • Fax: 020 7610 3235
www.thewaytostay.co.uk

See also Colour Advertisement

CENTRAL LONDON
Manor Court Hotel, 7 Clanricarde Gardens, London W2 4JJ (020 7792 3361 or 020 7727 5407; Fax: 020 7229 2875). Situated off the Bayswater Road, opposite Kensington Palace. Family-run B&B Hotel within walking distance of Hyde Park and Kensington Gardens. Very near to Notting Hill underground and Airbus 2 Stop. All rooms have colour TV and telephone. Terms from £25 to £40 single, £40 to £50 double, £55 to £65 triple and £75 for a quad room. We accept Visa, Mastercard, Diners Club and American Express Cards. Open all year. **ETC** ◆

•••some fun days out in LONDON

BA London Eye • 0870 5000 600 • www.londoneye.com
Thames Barrier Park • 020 7511 4111 • www.thamesbarrierpark.org.uk
Tate Modern • 020 7887 8000 • www.tate.org.uk/modern
The London Dungeon • 020 7403 7221 • www.thedungeons.com

KING'S CROSS
MacDonald Hotel, 45-46 Argyle Square, King's Cross, London WC1H 8AL (020 7837 3552; Fax: 020 7278 9885). Located in central London, just a short walk from Kings Cross and St Pancras main line stations with direct access to Heathrow, Gatwick and Luton airports. With competitive prices, accommodation is provided in a clean and friendly atmosphere. A variety of rooms are available from single to family/quad rooms with both shared and en suite facilities. All rooms are centrally heated, have colour TV, tea/coffee making facilities and wash-hand basins. English breakfast is served between 7am and 9am. Please contact us for further information, our latest rates and for any offers available, or visit our website.
e-mail: enquiries@macdonaldhotel.com
website: www.macdonaldhotel.com

LONDON
Holiday Hosts Accommodation Service (0208 540 7942; Fax: 0208 540 2827). Holiday Hosts London have 18 years experience in providing excellent private home accommodation in central/south/west areas of London, near to public transport for easy access to all London attractions, also Eurostar/airports/main line train stations. Prices start from £16.50 to £45 per person per night. Budget/Standard/Superior. Visit our website for further information.
www.holidayhosts.free-online.co.uk
e-mail: holiday.hosts@btinternet.com

See also Colour Display Advertisement

LONDON
Hotel Columbus, 141 Sussex Gardens, Hyde Park, London W2 2RX (020 7262 0974; Fax: 020 7262 6785). This charming Bed & Breakfast hotel is the ideal choice for individuals and families who seek both value for money and a quality B&B in the "heart of London". Situated in an elegant tree-lined avenue close to Hyde Park and Oxford Street it was a former residence of the aristocracy and has now been converted to provide modern, comfortable accommodation. All rooms now have en suite shower and w.c., telephone, TV, etc. Look no further for London's best B&B!
e-mail: hotelcolumbus@compuserve.com
website: www.delmerehotels.com

LONDON
Europa House Hotel, 151 Sussex Gardens, Hyde Park, London W2 2RY (020 7723 7343; Fax: 020 7224 9331). A small, family-run hotel since 1974, the Europa House Hotel is situated in the heart of London, in the Paddington and Hyde Park area. Personal service of the highest standard. All rooms en suite, double, twin and family rooms available. Special rates for children under 10. Five minutes from Paddington mainline and Underground stations, Heathrow Airport 15 minutes away on the Heathrow to Paddington Railway link. Marble Arch and Oxford Street within walking distance.
e-mail: europahouse@enterprise.net
website: www.europahousehotel.com or
       www.europahousehotel.org.uk

A useful index of towns/counties appears on pages 393-398

London (Central & Greater) 93

LONDON

Barry House Hotel
12 Sussex Place, Hyde Park, London W2 2TP
- Comfortable, family-friendly B&B
- Most rooms with en suite facilities
- Rates include English Breakfast
- Near Hyde Park and Oxford Street
- Paddington Station 4 minutes' walk

www.barryhouse.co.uk
hotel@barryhouse.co.uk
fax: 020 7723 9775

Call us now on: 0207 723 7340

We believe in family-like care

AA
♦♦♦

See also Colour Advertisement

e-mail: info@whitelodgehornsey.co.uk

LONDON
White Lodge Hotel, No. 1 Church Lane, Hornsey, London N8 7BU (020 8348 9765/4259; Fax: 020 8340 7851). White Lodge Hotel is situated in a pleasant North London suburb, with easy access via tube and bus to all parts of London. Alexandra Palace is the closest landmark and buses pass the front door. Prices are kept as low as possible for people on low budget holidays, whilst maintaining a high standard of service and cleanliness. Many guests return year after year which is a good recommendation. Six single, ten double bedrooms, four family bedrooms (eight rooms en suite), all with washbasins; three showers, six toilets; sittingroom; diningroom. Cot, high chair, babysitting and reduced rates for children. No pets, please. Open all year for Bed and Breakfast from £32 single, £42 double.
ETC ♦♦♦
website: www.whitelodgehornsey.co.uk

LONDON
Charlie's House Hotel, 63 Anson Road, London N7 0AR (020 7607 8375; Fax: 020 7697 8019). Single, double, triple and family rooms available. All room en suite, with central heating and TV. Nearest Tube station Tufnell Park.
website: www.charlieshotel.com

LONDON
Mrs B. Merchant, 562 Caledonian Road, Holloway, London N7 9SD (020 7607 0930). Comfortable well furnished rooms in small private home, full central heating. Two double and one single rooms, all non-smoking. Extra single beds for double rooms available. Eight bus routes; one minute for Trafalgar Square, Westminster, St Paul's. Piccadilly Line underground few minutes' walk. Direct Piccadilly and Heathrow. One-and-a-half miles King's Cross, Euston and St Pancras Main Line Stations. Four and a half miles Piccadilly, three miles London Zoo and Hampstead Heath. Two minutes A1. King's Cross for Gatwick. Central for all tourist attractions. Full English Breakfast. Terms: £24.00 per person per night. Children over 10 years. Minimum stay two nights. Unrestricted street parking. SAE, please.

London (Central & Greater)

LONDON

ELIZABETH HOTEL

Quiet, convenient Townhouse overlooking the magnificent gardens of Eccleston Square. Only a short walk from Buckingham Palace and other tourist attractions. Easy access to Knightsbridge, Oxford Street and Regent Street. Extremely reasonable rates in a fantastic location. Visa, Mastercard, Switch, Delta & JCB are all accepted

on-line booking facility   www.elizabethhotel.com

37 Eccleston Square, Victoria,
London SW1V 1PB
info@elizabethhotel.com

15% discount for stays of 7+ nights

AA/ETC ♦♦♦

Tel: 020 7828 6812
Fax: 020 7828 6814

See also Colour Advertisement

LONDON

- Central London
- ★★ B&B Hotel
- Family friendly • Est. 30 years
- Tranquil position
- Set in a garden square
- 2 mins Paddington Station
- Airlines check-ins 15 mins Heathrow on Express Link

FALCON HOTEL

- En-suite facilities
- Very clean and comfortable
- Close to tourist attractions and shops
- Triple and Family rooms
- Full freshly cooked English breakfasts

- e-mail: info@aafalcon.co.uk
- website: www.aafalcon.co.uk
- Tel: +44 (0) 20 7723 8303
- Fax: +44 (0) 20 7402 7009

11 Norfolk Sq., Hyde Park North,
London W2 1RU

Our guests first and always

Affordable prices from: Singles £35, Doubles £55
For latest seasonal prices please call

FALCON HOTEL

See also Colour Advertisement

LONDON

THE ELYSEE HOTEL

25/26 CRAVEN TERRACE, LONDON W2 3EL
Tel: 020 7402 7633 • Fax: 020 7402 4193
E-mail: information@hotelelysee.co.uk
Website: www.hotelelysee.co.uk

Unbeatable value in the *HEART OF LONDON: FACING HYDE PARK*. Near London's famous tourist and shopping areas. Rooms with attached bath/shower and toilets, lifts to all floors. Tea/coffee making facilities, hairdryer, Sky and cable TV; security safes. Rates include Continental breakfast. Three minutes from Lancaster Gate Underground, and six minutes from Paddington Station for Heathrow Express.

Single £49.00; Twin/Double £59.00 (for room); Family (3 persons) £75.00; Family (5 persons) £95.00

See also Colour Advertisement

Visit the FHG website
www.holidayguides.com
for details of the wide choice of accommodation
featured in the full range of FHG titles

London (Central & Greater) 95

LONDON

QUEENS HOTEL

33 Anson Road, Tufnell Park, London N7
Telephone: 0207-607 4725
Fax: 0207-697 9725
E-mail: queens@stavrouhotels.co.uk • Website: www.stavrouhotels.co.uk

The Queens Hotel is a large double-fronted Victorian building standing in its own grounds five minutes' walk from Tufnell Park Station. Quietly situated with ample car parking spaces; 15 minutes to West End and close to London Zoo, Hampstead and Highgate. Two miles from Kings Cross and St Pancras Stations. Many rooms en suite.

Singles from £25-£34 - Double/Twins from £30-£54
Triples and Family Rooms from £18 per person.

All prices include full English Breakfast plus VAT.
Children half price. Discounts on longer stays.

LONDON

LONDON HOTEL

BEST RATES

SINGLES from £30 – £46 pp
DOUBLES from £22 – £36 pp
FAMILIES 3/4/5/6 from £15 – £26 pp

WINDSOR HOUSE HOTEL, 12 PENYWERN ROAD, LONDON SW5 9ST
website:www.windsor-house-hotel.com email:bookings@windsor-house-hotel.com

5 mins to Piccadilly

Tel: 44 (0)20 7373 9087 Fax: 44 (0)20 7385 2417
INCLUDES BIG BREAKFAST, USE OF KITCHEN, GARDEN

CENTRAL LONDON!

ATHENA HOTEL

110-114 SUSSEX GARDENS, HYDE PARK, LONDON W2 1UA
Tel: 0207 706 3866; Fax: 0207 262 6143
E-Mail: athena@stavrouhotels.co.uk   Website: www.stavrouhotels.co.uk

TREAT YOURSELVES TO A QUALITY HOTEL AT AFFORDABLE PRICES

The Athena is a newly completed family-run hotel in a restored Victorian building. Professionally designed, including a lift to all floors, and exquisitely decorated, we offer our clientele the ambience and warm hospitality necessary for a relaxing and enjoyable stay. Ideally located in a beautiful tree-lined avenue, extremely well-positioned for sightseeing London's famous sights and shops; Hyde Park, Madame Tussaud's, Oxford Street, Marble Arch, Knightsbridge, Buckingham Palace and many more are all within walking distance.

Travel connections to all over London are excellent, with Paddington and Lancaster Gate Stations, Heathrow Express, A2 Airbus and buses minutes away.

Our tastefully decorated bedrooms have en suite bath/shower rooms, satellite colour TV, bedside telephones, tea/coffee making facilities. Hairdryers, trouser press, laundry and ironing facilities available on request. Ample car parking.

All prices include a full traditional English Breakfast and VAT
CREDIT CARDS WELCOME

Single Rooms from £50-£65

Double/Twin Rooms from £64-£95

Triple & Family Rooms from £28 per person

WE LOOK FORWARD TO SEEING YOU

London (Central & Greater) 97

LONDON

Lincoln House Hotel
London W1

33 Gloucester Place, London W1U 8HY
Tel: 020-7486 7630 (3 lines), Fax: 020-7486 0166

LONDON
Tourist Board and
Convention Bureau

Built at the end of the 18th century, in the time of King George III, the Lincoln House is a delightfully hospitable bed and breakfast hotel of Georgian townhouse character, in a prime location, close to central London's diverse scenes, activities and theatres; offering en suite rooms with fast internet connection. Near to Marble Arch and Oxford Street shopping.

Our tariff is competitive and includes a superb Full English Breakfast, tax and service. For the last two years running we have been awarded the first prize for our outstanding floral displays. Our hotel is ideal for business, shopping and leisure trips. On airport bus routes. Recommended by reputable guidebooks and motoring organisations.

e-mail: reservations@lincoln-house-hotel.co.uk
website: www.lincoln-house-hotel.co.uk

Modern Comforts and Free Wireless Internet

LONDON

Compton Guest House, 65 Compton Road, Wimbledon SW19 7QA (Fax & Tel: 020 8947 4488 and Tel: 020 8879 3245). Situated approximately six minutes from Wimbledon station and within easy reach of Wimbledon Tennis Courts, Wimbledon Common, golf and squash clubs. Easy access to the West End, central London, all the major motorways, Heathrow Airport, Gatwick Airport, and close to many first class restaurants, theatre and cinemas. All rooms are comfortably furnished with washbasin, colour TV, shaver light points, central heating and tea/coffee making facilities. We have room service, and if you decide to have breakfast it is served in the rooms for your own comfort and privacy. Hairdryers and irons available, free of charge, on request. Please contact **the Manager** for details of competitive prices.

FHG

FHG Guides publish a large range of well-known accommodation guides. We will be happy to send you details or you can use the order form at the back of this book.

Bedfordshire

LUTON
Mr and Mrs Wicks, 19 Wigmore Lane, Stopsley, Luton LU2 8AA (01582 423419). Bed and Breakfast accommodation situated just 10 minutes from Luton Airport, just off the M1 Junction 10 and close to the A505. Near town centre and railway stations (Town Centre and Parkway); 25 minutes' train journey to Central London. Large bungalow with double rooms; tea/coffee making equipment and colour TV. Overnight parking available. Close to local pubs, restaurants and shops. Children welcome. A warm welcome awaits.
e-mail: wicks-bandb@hotmail.co.uk

SANDY
Mrs Anne Franklin, Village Farm, Thorncote Green, Sandy SG19 1PU (01767 627345). Village Farm is a family-run working farm, mixed arable with a flock of 1000 free range laying hens, plus turkeys and geese for Christmas trade. Accommodation comprises one double bedroom, two twin/family rooms, both en suite. Full farmhouse breakfast plus beverages in room. Thorncote Green is a picturesque hamlet within easy reach of many interesting places:- Shuttleworth Collection, Swiss Gardens, RSPB headquarters, Greensand Ridge walk, Woburn Abbey, Wimpole Hall and Cambridge. Bed and Breakfast from £25 per person per night. ETC ◆◆◆

Leighton Buzzard Railway
Leighton Buzzard, Bedfordshire
See our **READERS' OFFER VOUCHER** for details of free or reduced rate entry

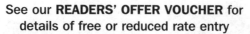

Looking for Holiday Accommodation?
for details of hundreds of properties throughout the UK visit:
www.holidayguides.com

Berkshire

COMPTON

See also Colour Display Advertisement

The Compton Swan Hotel, High Street, Compton, Near Newbury, Berkshire RG20 6NJ (01635 578269; Fax: 01635 578765). Situated in the heart of the Berkshire Downlands. The Hotel has six en suite bedrooms with TV, radio alarms, hairdryers, beverage facilities, telephones and sauna. An extensive menu with traditional, exotic, vegetarian, and special diets catered for. Our home-cooked meals are a speciality. Downlands Healthy Eating Award winner. Large walled garden where we have al fresco eating; BBQs. Near the famous ancient Ridgeway National Trail and is an ideal base for walking, horse-riding, and golf. Stabling and horsebox available. Real ales and bar meals available. Entry in CAMRA Good Beer Guide and Good Pub Guide. A friendly reception by staff and our Jack Russells "Mushy & Bonnie".

e-mail: info@comptonswan.co.uk

website: www.SmoothHound.co.uk

NEWBURY

Mr & Mrs Pocklington, Hilltop, Long Lane, Newbury RG14 2TH (01635 202150). Surrounded by uninterrupted views, in the heart of the countryside yet only three minutes from the town centre of Newbury. Famous for its racecourse and many golf courses, local pubs and fine restaurants. Good walking area within minutes from the property, we are non-smoking and regret no children. Washbasins in all rooms and off-road parking. One well behaved dog welcome. Details available on request.

READING (Three Mile Cross)

Mrs M.S. Erdwin, Orchard House, Church Lane, Three Mile Cross, Reading RG7 1HD (01189 884457). Orchard House is well situated close to M4 Motorway, Heathrow 30 minutes away, Gatwick 45 minutes; Oxford 30 miles and London 35 miles (just 29 minutes by train); five minutes' from Arborfield Garrison. Wealth of holiday interest to suit all tastes in the area. Ideal halt for that long journey to Cornwall or Wales. Accommodation all year round in this modern, large, homely house close to the Chilterns and Berkshire Downs. Babysitting can be arranged. English or Continental Breakfast; Evening Drink/Meal/Light Supper available; Packed Lunches on request. Pets permitted at extra charge. Close to Thames, Kennet and Avon Canal/River for coarse fishing. Also close to M3, Reading Rock Festival, and the new Reading football/rugby stadium. We accept guests returning/arriving very late. Ideal for WOMAD festival or on route to Dover, Portsmouth and Newhaven. Terms from £20.50 for Bed and Breakfast (we accept euros). Taxi service at moderate rates. SAE, please.

100 Berkshire

See also Colour Display Advertisement

WINDSOR
Mr Robert Sousa, Netherton Hotel, 96 St Leonards Road, Windsor SL4 3DA (01753 855508; Fax: 01753 621267). This recently refurbished hotel offers a comfortable and friendly atmosphere. All rooms are en suite, with colour TV, direct-dial telephone, and tea/coffee making facilities. Also available are hairdryers and ironing facilities. There is a TV lounge for guests' use. Full English breakfast. We have a private car park and are easy to find. Walking distance to Windsor Castle, town centre, train stations and Legoland is only one mile away. Central London can be reached in 35 minutes by train. M4 only two miles, Heathrow seven miles. Children welcome. **ETC/AA** ◆◆◆
e-mail: netherton@btconnect.com

WINDSOR
Clarence Hotel, 9 Clarence Road, Windsor SL4 5AE (01753 864436; Fax: 01753 857060). Town centre location. Licensed bar and steam room. High quality accommodation at guest house prices. All rooms have en suite bathrooms, TV, tea/coffee making facilities, radio alarms, hairdryers, free wi-fi and internet. Heathrow Airport 25 minutes by car. Convenient for Legoland. **AA/RAC** ◆◆◆

WINKFIELD (near Windsor)
Bluebell House, Lovel Lane, Winkfield SL4 2DG (01344 886828; Fax: 01344 893256). Charming ex-coaching inn on the outskirts of Windsor and Ascot, and close to Bracknell and Maidenhead. Traditional rooms offering classic accommodation with an added touch of class. All rooms are tastefully furnished and have TV, telephone, hairdryer, trouser press, iron, mini-fridge and toaster/food warmer, one room has a four-poster bed. A very full Continental breakfast is taken in your room. Patio and gardens with swimming pool. Private off-road parking. Well behaved dogs welcome by prior arrangement. **ETC** ◆◆◆◆
e-mail: registrations@bluebellhousehotel.co.uk
website: www.bluebellhousehotel.co.uk

The Golf Guide · 2006
Where to Play, Where to Stay

Available from most booksellers, **The Golf Guide, Where to Play, Where to Stay** covers details of every UK golf course – well over 2800 entries – for holiday or business golf. Hundreds of hotel entries offer convenient accommodation, with accompanying details of the courses – the 'pro', par score, length and more. Including holiday golf in Ireland, France, Portugal, Spain, the USA, South Africa and Thailand.

**Only £9.99 from booksellers or direct from the publishers:
FHG GUIDES, Abbey Mill Business Centre, Seedhill,
Paisley PA1 1TJ** (postage charged outside UK)
e-mail: admin@fhguides.co.uk • www.holidayguides.com

Cambridgeshire 101

Cambridgeshire

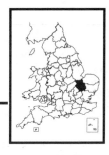

BURWELL
Mrs Marsh, The Meadow House Bed and Breakfast, 2a High Street, Burwell, Cambridge CB5 0HB (01638 741926: Fax: 01638 741861). Magnificent modern house set in two acres of wooded grounds offering superior Bed and Breakfast accommodation in spacious rooms, some with king-size beds. The variety of en suite accommodation endeavours to cater for all requirements; a suite of rooms sleeping six complete with south-facing balcony; a triple room on the ground floor with three single beds, and the Coach House, a spacious annexe with one double and one single bed; also one double and two twins sharing a well equipped bathroom. All rooms have TV, central heating and tea/coffee facilities. Car parking. No smoking. Terms from £25pp. **ETC ♦♦♦♦**

e-mail: hilary@themeadowhouse.co.uk
website: www.themeadowhouse.co.uk

CAMBRIDGE
Victoria Guest House, 57 Arbury Road, Cambridge CB4 2JB (01223 350086). Victoria Guest House is an extremely comfortable Victorian house situated off Milton Road, within walking distance of the City Centre, River Cam and Colleges, with easy access to the M14, M11 and the Cambridge Science Park. Most rooms are en suite or have private facilities. Colour TV, iron, ironing board, hair dryer, tea and coffee making facilities; good parking to the front available. Our guests can enjoy a lovely breakfast served in the dining room, overlooking picturesque gardens to the rear; there we can cater for all your needs. Emma and Duncan strive very hard to offer all their guests a very warm welcome and comfortable stay, which is why guests return to us over and over again. **ETC ♦♦♦**

e-mail: victoriahouse@ntlworld.com
website: www.cambridge-accommodation.com

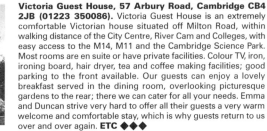

CAMBRIDGE
Paul and Alison Tweddell, Dykelands Guest House, 157 Mowbray Road, Cambridge CB1 7SP (01223 244300; Fax: 01223 566746). Enjoy your visit to Cambridge by staying at our lovely detached guesthouse. Ideally located for city centre and for touring the secrets of the Cambridgeshire countryside. Easy access from M11 Junction 11, but only one-and-a-half miles from the city centre, on a direct bus route. Near Addenbrookes Hospital. All bedrooms have colour TV, clock radio, tea/coffee making facilities; heating and double glazing; seven en suite; ground floor rooms available. Bed and full English Breakfast from £35 singles to £54 doubles. Ample car parking. Most major credit/debit cards welcome. Open all year. Brochure on request. Non-smoking establishment. **ETC/AA ♦♦♦**
website: www.dykelands.com

The FHG Directory of Website Addresses
on pages 339-370 is a useful quick reference guide for holiday accommodation with e-mail and/or website details

CAMBRIDGE

DORSET HOUSE
35 Newton Road, Little Shelford,
Cambridge CB2 5HL • Tel: 01223 844440
E-mail: dorsethouse@msn.com
Website: www.SmoothHound.co.uk

Just three miles from the historic city of Cambridge, *DORSET HOUSE* is situated in its own extensive grounds. The house has open fireplaces and wooden beams, and each luxury bedroom is individually decorated. Some rooms are en suite and all have colour TV and tea/coffee facilities. Breakfast is served in our lovely dining room.

If you are looking for the best:
Bed & Breakfast £38-£48 Single, £55-£65 Double, £69-£85 Family.

ELY

Jeff and Linda Peck, Sharps Farm, Twentypence Road, Wilburton, Ely CB6 3PU (01353 740810). A charming tranquil setting awaits you along with friendly hospitality in our family home. Situated in open countryside and ideally placed to visit the surrounding historic sites of Cambridge, Ely and Newmarket. Our two en suite ground floor rooms, and one double on the first floor with private bathroom, all have TV, radio alarm, tea/coffee making facilities and hairdryers. A delicious English breakfast is served in our garden room using eggs from our own free range chickens. Evening meal by arrangement. Special diets catered for. Disabled facilities. Non-smoking. Ample parking. B&B from £27 per person.
e-mail: sharpsfarm@yahoo.com
website: www.sharpsfarm.co.uk

HORSEHEATH

Chequer Cottage, Streetly End, Horseheath CB1 6RP (01223 891522). Set in a quiet hamlet of 15th Century thatched properties; our cottage offers a comfortable, peaceful stay in the countryside. Annexed, spacious accommodation with a king sized bed and en suite facilities - loads of luxury and a warm welcome awaits you. **ETC ♦♦♦♦**
e-mail: stay@chequercottage.com
website: www.chequercottage.com

WICKEN

Mrs Valerie Fuller, Spinney Abbey, Wicken, Ely CB7 5XQ (01353 720971). Working farm. Spinney Abbey is an attractive Grade II Listed Georgian stone farmhouse with views across pasture fields. It stands in a large garden with tennis court next to our farm which borders the National Trust Nature Reserve Wicken Fen. One double and one family room, both en suite, and twin-bedded room with private bathroom, all with TV, hospitality tray, etc. Full central heating, guests' sittingroom. Regret no pets and no smoking. Situated just off A1123, half a mile west of Wicken. Open all year. Bed and Breakfast from £28 per person. **ETC ♦♦♦♦**
e-mail: spinney.abbey@tesco.net
website: www.spinneyabbey.co.uk

Cheshire

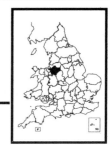

BALTERLEY (near Crewe)

Mrs Joanne Hollins, Balterley Green Farm, Deans Lane, Balterley, Near Crewe CW2 5QJ (01270 820214). Working farm, join in. Jo and Pete Hollins offer guests a friendly welcome to their home on a 145-acre dairy farm in quiet and peaceful surroundings. Green Farm is situated on the Cheshire/Staffordshire border and is within easy reach of Junction 16 on the M6. An excellent stop-over place for travellers journeying between north and south of the country. One family room en suite, one single and one twin-bedded room on ground floor suitable for disabled guests. Tea-making facilities and TV in all rooms. Children welcome, cot provided. Pets welcome. This area offers many attractions; we are within easy reach of historic Chester, Alton Towers and the famous Potteries of Staffordshire. Open all year. Caravans and tents welcome. Bed and Breakfast from £25 per person.

See also Colour Display Advertisement

CHESTER

Stafford Hotel, City Road, Chester CH1 3AE (01244 326052/320695 ; Fax: 01244 311403). Friendly, medium sized, family-run hotel near Chester Railway Station and City Centre. Ground floor, family, non-smoking and four poster bedrooms available. All of the en suite bedrooms have direct dial telephone, satellite TV, tea making facilities and hairdryer. There is a comfortable residents' lounge bar where you are able to enjoy drinks and snacks, or alternatively you can dine in our pleasant restaurant which serves freshly prepared English fayre. The ancient city of Chester is world famous for its walls, parts of which date back to Roman times. Chester is the ideal location from which to tour the North West and North Wales resorts. Short breaks available. Closed Christmas and New Year. ETC ★★

e-mail: enquiries@staffordhotel.com
website: www.staffordhotel.com

CHESTER

Mitchell's of Chester Guest House, 28 Hough Green, Chester CH4 8JQ (01244 679004; Fax: 01244 659567). This elegantly restored Victorian family home is set on the south side of Chester, on a bus route to the city centre. Guest bedrooms have been furnished in period style, with fully equipped shower room and toilet, central heating, TV, refreshment tray and other thoughtful extras. An extensive breakfast menu is served in the elegant dining room, and the guest lounge overlooks the well-maintained garden. The historic city of Chester is ideally placed for touring Wales and the many attractions of the North West of England. ETC/AA ♦♦♦♦♦
e-mail: mitoches@dialstart.net
website: www.mitchellsofchester.com

**FREE or REDUCED RATE entry to Holiday Visits and Attractions
– see our READERS' OFFER VOUCHERS on pages 53-90**

CHESTER

Brian and Hilary Devenport, White Walls, Village Road, Christleton, Chester CH3 7AS (Tel & Fax: 01244 336033). White Walls, a 100 year old converted stables, in the heart of award-winning village Christleton, two miles Chester, off the A41, close to A55, M53 and North Wales. Walking distance to village pub and two canalside pub/restaurants, church, Post Office, hairdresser and bus stop. Half-hourly bus service to Chester. The village pond is home to swans, mallards, Aylesbury ducks and moorhens. En suite double bedroom, twin-bedded room with washbasin, all including English Breakfast. Minimum rates from £30 single, £50 double. Colour TV, tea/coffee making facilities, central heating, overlooking garden. Non-smoking. Sorry, no children or pets.

e-mail: hilary-devenport@supanet.com

CHESTER CITY

Frank and Maureen Brady, Holly House, 41 Liverpool Road, Chester CH2 1AB (01244 383484). Holly House is a Victorian townhouse on the A5116, offering a friendly welcome in quiet, elegant surroundings. Comfort and high standards are our priority. Only five minutes' walk from the famous Roman walls which encircle this historic city with its 11th century Cathedral, castle, museum of Roman artifacts, buildings of architectural interest, Amphitheatre, walks by the river, shopping in "The Rows". Spacious accommodation comprises two double/family rooms fully en suite and a double with full private facilities. TV, tea/coffee facilities, own keys. Parking. Bed and Breakfast from £46 for two sharing, or as family rooms at £14 per additional person supplement. Vegetarians catered for. Non-smoking. A warm welcome from Frank and Maureen Brady. ETC ◆◆◆

CHESTER (near)

See also Colour Display Advertisement

Beryl and John Milner, Green Cottage, The Green, Higher Kinnerton, Chester CH4 9BZ (Tel & Fax: 01244 660137). A homely, friendly, peaceful and comfortable country retreat just over the Welsh border, ideally situated for exploring the historic City of Chester under seven miles away. Easy access to all routes (five minutes from the A55) makes this an ideal base for touring North Wales, West Cheshire and North Shropshire. Beryl and John, previous winners of a Prince of Wales' Award, will offer you warm hospitality and invite you into their home, which has recently been renovated and furnished to a high standard. A double room and a twin room are available, overlooking open countryside. Tea/coffee making facilities, TV, shared private bathroom with bath and shower, central heating, off-road parking, pleasant gardens. There are two pubs within the village offering excellent cuisine. Non-smoking. Bed and Full English Breakfast from £25 per person, with reductions for weekly stays. Please send or telephone for our brochure.
★★★ *GUEST HOUSE*

•••some fun days out in CHESHIRE

Cholmondeley Castle Gardens, Malpas • 01829 720583 • www.gardens-guide.com
Blue Planet Aquarium, Ellesmere Port • 0151 357 8800 • www.blueplanetaquarium.com
Chester Zoo, Upton-by-Chester • 01244 380280 • www.chesterzoo.org

Cheshire 105

CHURCH MINSHULL
Brian and Mary Charlesworth, Higher Elms Farm, Minshull Vernon, Crewe CW1 4RG (01270 522252). A 400-year-old farmhouse on working farm. Oak-beamed comfort in dining and sittingrooms, overlooking Shropshire Union Canal. No dinners served but four pubs within two miles. Interesting wildlife around. Convenient for M6 but tucked away in the countryside; from M6 Junction 18, off A530 towards Nantwich. Family room, double, twin and single rooms are all en suite, with colour TV and tea/coffee facilities. Well behaved pets welcome. Within 15 miles of Jodrell Bank, Oulton Park, Bridgemere Garden World, Stapeley Water Gardens, Nantwich and Chester. Bed and Breakfast from £26. Half price for children under 12 years.

MALPAS
Chris and Angela Smith, Mill House, Higher Wych, Malpas SY14 7JR (01948 780362); Fax: 01948 780566). Modernised mill house on the Cheshire/Clwyd border in a quiet valley, convenient for visiting Chester, Shrewsbury and North Wales. The house is centrally heated and has an open log fire in the lounge. Bedrooms have washbasins, TV and radio and tea-making facilities. Two bedrooms have en suite shower and WC. Reductions for children and Senior Citizens. Open January to November. Bed and Breakfast from £25. Evening Meal from £10.
WTB ★★★ GUEST HOUSE.

NANTWICH
Lea Farm, Wrinehill Road, Wybunbury, Nantwich CW5 7NS (01270 841429 Fax: 01270 841030) Charming farmhouse set in landscaped gardens, where peacocks roam, on 150 acre family farm. Working farm, join in. Spacious bedrooms, colour TVs, electric blankets, radio alarm and tea/coffee making facilities. Centrally heated throughout. Family, double and twin bedrooms, en suite facilities. Luxury lounge, dining room overlooking gardens. Pool/snooker; fishing in well stocked pool in beautiful surroundings. Bird watching. Children welcome, also dogs if kept under control. Help feed the birds, animals and cows. Near to Stapeley Water Gardens, Bridgemere Garden World. Also Nantwich, Crewe, Chester, the Potteries and Alton Towers. B&B from £25 per person, children half price, weekly terms available.
AA ◆◆◆
e-mail: contactus@leafarm.freeserve.co.uk   website: www.leafarm.co.uk

please note

All the information in this book is given in good faith in the belief that it is correct. However, the publishers cannot guarantee the facts given in these pages, neither are they responsible for changes in policy, ownership or terms that may take place after the date of going to press. Readers should always satisfy themselves that the facilities they require are available and that the terms, if quoted, still apply.

Cornwall

BODMIN

Mrs Joy Rackham, High Cross Farm, Lanivet, Near Bodmin PL30 5JR (01208 831341). Traditional Victorian granite farmhouse surrounded by fields on this working farm. Lanivet is the geographical centre of Cornwall and thereby central for touring the moor and the north and south coasts. The exciting Eden Project, Lost Gardens at Heligan and Lanhydrock House are close by. Fishing, cycling, golf and horse riding are available within the area. High Cross offers ample off-road parking and modern facilities for guests. Rooms have hot/cold, shaver points and tea and coffee making facilities. One room is en suite. Separate dining room and sitting room for guests. Full English breakfast, optional evening meal. Open all year except Christmas. Bed and Breakfast from £20.

•••some fun days out in CORNWALL

Caerhays Castle Gardens, St Austell • 01872 501310 • www.caerhays.co.uk
National Maritime Museum, Falmouth • 01326 313388 • www.nmmc.co.uk
The Monkey Sanctuary, Looe • 01503 262532 • www.monkeysanctuary.org
Pendennis Castle, St Mawes • 0870 333 1181 • www.english-heritage.org.uk
Land's End, Sennen • 0870 458 0099 • www.landsend-landmark.co.uk
Goonhilly Satellite Earth Station, Lizard Peninsula • 0800 679593 • www.goonhilly.bt.com
King Arthur's Great Halls, Tintagel • 01840 770526 • www.kingarthursgreathalls.com
The Eden Project, St Austell • 01726 811911 • www.edenproject.com

Cornwall 107

BOSCASTLE
Mrs P. E. Perfili, Trefoil Farm, Camelford Road, Boscastle PL35 0AD (01840 250606). Set in its own tranquil grounds with ample parking. Trefoil offers non-smoking, centrally heated, en suite accommodation with tea and coffee making facilities and colour TV. Overlooking Boscastle village, with views of the coast and Lundy Island, Trefoil is ideally positioned to explore Cornwall. Two minutes' walk leads you to a local 16th century Inn with real ales and good food. Terms from £24 per person per night. **ETC ♦♦♦**
e-mail: trefoil.farm@tiscali.co.uk
website: www.thisisnorthcornwall.com

BOSCASTLE
Ruth and Michael Parsons, The Old Coach House, Tintagel Road, Boscastle PL35 0AS (01840 250398; Fax: 01840 250346). Relax in a 300 year old former coach house now tastefully equipped to meet the needs of the new millennium with all rooms en suite, colour TVs, radios, tea/coffee makers and central heating. Accessible for disabled guests. Good cooking. This picturesque village is a haven for walkers with its dramatic coastal scenery, a photographer's dream, and an ideal base to tour both the north and south coasts. The area is famed for its sandy beaches and surfing whilst King Arthur's Tintagel is only three miles away. Come and enjoy a friendly holiday with people who care. Brochure on request. Bed and Breakfast from £20 to £28. Non-smoking. **AA ♦♦♦♦**

e-mail: parsons@old-coach.demon.co.uk   website: www.old-coach.co.uk

BUDE
Margaret and Richard Heard, Trencreek Farmhouse, St Gennys, Bude EX23 0AY (01840 230219). Comfortable farmhouse which offers a homely and relaxed family atmosphere. Situated in quiet and peaceful surroundings yet within easy reach of Crackington Haven. Well placed for easy access to coastal and countryside walks. Family, double and twin-bedded rooms, most en suite, all with tea and coffee making facilities. Two comfortable lounges. Games room. Separate diningroom. Generous portions of home-cooked farmhouse food are always freshly prepared. Children welcome, special rates for under twelves. Spring and Autumn breaks available. Non-smoking. Sunday lunches and midday lunches optional.

BUDE
Mrs Christine Nancekivell, Dolsdon Farm, Boyton, Launceston PL15 8NT (01288 341264). Dolsdon was once a 17th century coaching inn, now modernised, situated on the Launceston to Bude road within easy reach of sandy beaches, surfing, Tamar Otter Park, leisure centre with heated swimming pool, golf courses, fishing, tennis and horse riding and is ideal for touring Cornwall and Devon. Guests are welcome to wander around the 260 acre working farm. All bedrooms en suite with TV and tea making facilities. Comfortably furnished lounge has colour TV. Plenty of good home cooking assured - full English breakfast. Parking. Bed and Breakfast from £20; reductions for children. Brochure available.

108 Cornwall

BUDE
Mrs Pearl Hopper, West Nethercott Farm, Whitstone, Holsworthy (Devon) EX22 6LD (01288 341394). Personal attention and a warm welcome await you on this dairy and sheep farm. Watch the cows being milked, scenic farm walks. Short distance from sandy beaches, surfing and the rugged North Cornwall coast. Ideal base for visiting any part of Devon or Cornwall. We are located in Cornwall though our postal address is Devon. The traditional farmhouse has four bedrooms, two en suite; diningroom and separate lounge with TV. Plenty of excellent home cooking. Access to the house at anytime. Bed and Breakfast from £20, Evening Meal and packed lunches available. Children under 12 years reduced rates. Weekly terms available.
e-mail: pearl@westnethercott.fsnet.co.uk

BUDE
Margaret Short, Langaton Farm, Whitstone, Holsworthy EX22 6TS (01288 341215). Traditional working farm set in the quiet countryside, eight miles from the market town of Holsworthy and six miles from the coast at Bude, with its sandy beaches. Help to feed the calves and chickens and make friends with the farm dogs and cats. Play area for children. Close to local 18-hole golf course, swimming pool, horse riding, local park and bowling green and Tamar Lakes for birdwatching. Two bedrooms, one suitable for a family, with an en suite shower room, the other has a double bed and en suite shower. Both rooms have a TV and hospitality tray; cot and high chair available. Central heating and log fires. Bed and Breakfast from £24pppn, children under 12 half price. Weekly rate from £150. ETC ◆◆◆◆

e-mail: langatonfarm@hotmail.com
website: www.langaton-farm-holidays.co.uk

CUBERT (near)
Ron and Brenda Franks, Willowmeade, Trevail, Cubert, Near Newquay, Cornwall TR8 5HP (01637 830393). Willowmeade is a large detached house in the small peaceful hamlet of Trevail, with picturesque village of Crantock and Cubert village nearby. Five miles from Newquay. Close to beaches, pubs and restaurants, coastal footpath and lovely walks. Ideal for touring, sightseeing, walking, fishing, sailing or just relaxing. Two first floor en suite double rooms and one ground floor twin room. All rooms have TV, hospitality tray, clock and hairdryer. Non-smoking. We offer a variety of freshly cooked breakfasts. Bed & Breakfast from £26 per person per night.

DELABOLE
John and Sue Theobald, Tolcarne, Trebarwith Road, Delabole PL33 9DB. Quiet, comfortable bungalow with private bathroom and shower, TV lounge, double or twin rooms. Pets always welcome in the house. We also have a large kennel and run for dogs left at home during the day. Delabole is situated between Padstow and Bude, with access to many footpaths. Britain's first wind farm and Delabole Slate Quarry have interesting visitor centres. Ample parking. For free brochure please telephone **01840 213558.**

Tamar Valley Donkey Park
Gunnislake, Cornwall
See our **READERS' OFFER VOUCHER** for details of free or reduced rate entry

Cornwall 109

FALMOUTH
Heritage House, 1 Clifton Terrace, Falmouth TR11 3QG (01326 317834). We offer visitors a warm, friendly welcome at our comfortable family-run guesthouse. Centrally located for town and beaches. All bedrooms are tastefully decorated with colour TV, free tea/coffee, vanity basins and central heating, with access available at all times throughout the day. Children are welcome, with cot and highchair available. Bed and full English or vegetarian breakfast from £19 per person nightly. Reduced rates for longer stays. Accommodation includes single, twin, double and family bedrooms. On-street parking available with no restrictions. Open all year (except Christmas). Resident proprietors: **Lynn and Ken Grimes.**
e-mail: heritagehouse@tinyonline.co.uk
website: www.heritagehousefalmouth.co.uk

FALMOUTH
"Wickham", 21 Gyllyngvase Terrace, Falmouth TR11 4DL (01326 311140). A small, friendly, non-smoking guest house situated between the harbour and beach with views over Falmouth Bay. We are close to the railway station and within easy reach of the town. Wickham is the ideal base for exploring Falmouth and South Cornwall's gardens, castles, harbour, coastal footpath and much more. All rooms have television and beverage facilities, some have sea views. Bed and Breakfast from £24 nightly, £161 weekly. Discount for children. Single overnight stays subject to availability.
e-mail: enquiries@wickhamhotel.freeserve.co.uk

FALMOUTH
Rosemullion Hotel, Gyllyngvase Hill, Falmouth TR11 4DF (01326 314690; Fax: 01326 210098). Built as a gentleman's residence in the latter part of the 19th century, Rosemullion Hotel offers you a holiday that is every bit as distinctive as its Tudor appearance. Rosemullion is a house of great character and charm, appealing strongly to the discerning guest. The emphasis is very much on that rarest of commodities in today's world – peace. That is why we do not cater for children and do not have a bar of our own. A family-owned hotel continually being refurbished and updated to first class accommodation. Fully centrally heated with 13 bedrooms, some with glorious views over the bay. Large parking area. Non-smoking. B&B £27.50 to £29.50pppn inclusive of VAT.
e-mail: gail@rosemullionhotel.demon.co.uk
website: www.SmoothHound.co.uk/hotels/rosemullion.html

HAYLE
Mrs Anne Cooper, 54 Penpol Terrace, Hayle TR27 4BQ (01736 752855). Central for beaches and Land's End Peninsula. All rooms with colour TV, beverage making facilities, handbasins and shaver points. Non-smoking establishment. Private parking.
e-mail: annejohn@cooper827.fsnet.co.uk

HELSTON
Mrs P. Roberts, Hendra Farm, Wendron, Helston TR13 0NR (01326 340470). Hendra Farm, just off the main Helston/Falmouth road, is an ideal centre for touring Cornwall; three miles to Helston, eight to both Redruth and Falmouth. Safe sandy beaches within easy reach – five miles to the sea. Two double, one single, and one family bedrooms with washbasins and tea-making facilities; bathroom and toilets; sittingroom and two diningrooms. Cot, babysitting and reduced rates offered for children. No objection to pets. Car necessary, parking space. Enjoy good cooking with roast beef, pork, lamb, chicken, genuine Cornish pasties, fish and delicious sweets and cream. Open all year except Christmas. Evening Dinner, Bed and Breakfast from £150 per week which includes cooked breakfast, three course evening dinner, tea and homemade cake before bed. Bed and Breakfast only from £17 per night also available.

110 Cornwall

See also Colour Display Advertisement

HELSTON (near)
Mrs D. J. Hill, Rocklands, Pentreath Road, The Lizard, Near Helston TR12 7NX (01326 290339). "Rocklands" is situated overlooking part of Cornwall's superb coastline and enjoys uninterrupted sea views. The Lizard is well known for its lovely picturesque scenery, coastal walks and enchanting coves and beaches, as well as the famous Serpentine Stone which is quarried and sold locally. Open Easter to October. Generations of the Hill family have been catering for visitors on the Lizard since the 1850s. Three bedrooms with sea views, two en suite, tea/coffee making facilities and electric heaters; sittingroom with TV and video; sun lounge; diningroom with separate tables. Children and well trained pets welcome. Bed and Breakfast £23pppn, en suite £25pppn; reductions for children under 10 years.

LISKEARD
Mrs Rowe, Trewint Farm, Menheniot, Liskeard PL14 3RE (01579 347155). A Cornish Cream tea awaits your arrival; enjoy the peace and tranquillity of the countryside. Trewint is a working farm, well known for its prize-winning cattle. Enjoy walks around the area, or make use of the games and fitness rooms. All rooms are en suite, with matching decor, and TV and tea/coffee facilities. Have breakfast overlooking the garden, and watch the birds while you enjoy the farmhouse fare. Ideal for National Trust properties; Looe six miles. Also available - self catering properties, sleep four/five. Ideal for winter breaks. Bed and Breakfast £25-£30. Self-catering from £150. **ETC ◆◆◆◆** *SILVER AWARD*.
e-mail: holidays@trewintfarm.co.uk
website: www.trewintfarm.co.uk

LISKEARD
Hotel Nebula, 27 Higher Lux Street, Liskeard PL14 3JU (01579 343989). Relax in your home from home friendly hotel. Old English atmosphere in a Grade II Listed building. Unwind by our large granite fireplace in the lounge area where we have a licensed bar. Evening meals are home cooked. The Nebula has six spacious comfortable en suite rooms, single, double, twin and family, all with TV and tea/coffee facilities. Large car park. Liskeard is ideally placed to tour Cornwall and Plymouth. Near the moors, coast, gardens, golf courses, Eden Project and museums. Enjoy! Book the whole hotel (sleeps 15) and use it as your home in a relaxing atmosphere. Terms from £28. **ETC ◆◆◆**, *SECTA, CORNWALL TOURIST BOARD*.
e-mail: info@nebula-hotel.com
website: www.nebula-hotel.com

LOOE
Mrs D. Eastley, Bake Farm, Pelynt, Looe PL13 2QQ (Tel & Fax: 01503 220244). Working farm. This is an old farmhouse, bearing the Trelawney Coat of Arms (1610), situated midway between Looe and Fowey. The two double bedrooms and the family room, all en suite, are decorated to a high standard and have tea/coffee making facilities and TV. Sorry, no pets. No smoking. Open from March to October. A car is essential for touring the area, ample parking. There is much to see and do here – horse riding, coastal walks, golf, National Trust properties, the Eden Project and Heligan Gardens within easy reach. The sea is only four miles away and there is shark fishing at Looe. Bed and Breakfast from £23 to £27. Brochure available on request. **ETC ◆◆◆◆**

A useful index of towns/counties appears on pages 393-398

LOOE

Mr & Mrs R. S. Blanks, Kantana Guest House, 7 Trelawney Terrace, West Looe, Looe PL13 2AG (01503 262093). Ideally positioned for all the attractions Cornwall has to offer yet only five minutes' walk to the historic main street of Looe with its restaurants, pubs and shops. Stroll past medieval buildings and fishermen's cottages to a stretch of golden sand or take a fishing trip from the bustling Quay. As hosts, we are always glad to pass on any local knowledge that will maximise your enjoyment during your stay with us. All rooms are en suite or with full private bathrooms, including colour TV, coffee/tea facilities etc. Bed and Breakfast from £20-£30pppn subject to season.
e-mail: enquiries@kantana.co.uk
website: www.kantana.co.uk

MEVAGISSEY

Mrs Dawn Rundle, Lancallan Farm, Mevagissey, St Austell PL26 6EW (Tel & Fax: 01726 842284). Lancallan is a large 17th century farmhouse on a working 700 acre dairy and beef farm in a beautiful rural setting, one mile from Mevagissey. We are close to Heligan Gardens, lovely coastal walks and sandy beaches, and are well situated for day trips throughout Cornwall. Also six to eight miles from the Eden Project (20 minutes' drive). Enjoy a traditional farmhouse breakfast in a warm and friendly atmosphere. Accommodation comprises one twin room and two double en suite rooms (all with colour TV and tea/coffee facilities); bathroom, lounge and diningroom.Terms and brochure available on request. SAE please.
e-mail: dawn@lancallan.fsnet.co.uk
website: www.lancallanfarm.co.uk

MEVAGISSEY

Tregorran, Cliff Street, Mevagissey PL26 6QW (01726 842319). Bed and Breakfast accommodation with magnificent views over the village and harbour. Just a short two minute walk the the harbour itself. All rooms are en suite or have private facilities with colour TV/tea and coffee making facilities. All centrally heated and double glazed. There is also a sauna and a south facing sun deck. Private off-road parking. An ideal touring base. Special promotion for Heligan Gardens or Eden Project tickets (ring for details). For further information telephone **Helen Blamey.**
e-mail: patricia@parsloep.freeserve.co.uk
website: www.tregorran.homestead.com/home.html

NEWQUAY

Jean & Rob Boston, Highfield Lodge Hotel, Halwyn Road, Crantock, Newquay TR8 5TR (01637 830744). Detached 9 bedroomed licensed hotel situated in one of Cornwall's most beautiful villages. Rooms have panoramic views of sea or countryside and most are en suite. Four-poster bedroom available. Colour TV and tea/coffee facilities in all rooms. Licensed bar. Short walk to one of Cornwall's finest beaches. Highfield Lodge is a no smoking Hotel. Private car park. Open all year. Mid-week bookings and short breaks early and late season. Bed and Breakfast from £20 to £30 per night. Special rates for children. Bar meals available. Ring for free brochure. Self-catering flat also available. **ETC ♦♦♦**

National Seal Sanctuary
Helston, Cornwall

See our **READERS' OFFER VOUCHER** for
details of free or reduced rate entry

NEWQUAY
Karen and John, Pensalda Guest House, 98 Henver Road, Newquay TR7 3BL (Tel & Fax: 01637 874601). Take a break in the heart of Cornwall. A warm and friendly welcome awaits you at Pensalda. Situated on the main A3068 road, an ideal location from which to explore the finest coastline in Europe. Close to airport and the Eden Project. Single, double and family rooms available, most en suite, all with TV, tea/coffee making facilities, including two chalets set in a lovely garden. Fire certificate, large car park, licensed, central heating. Non-smoking. Bed and Breakfast from £18, special offer breaks November to March (excluding Christmas and New Year).
e-mail: karen_pensalda@yahoo.co.uk
website: www.pensalda-guesthouse.co.uk

NEWQUAY
Terri and Dave Clark, Trewerry Mill, Trerice, St Newlyn East TR8 5GS (01872 510345). A 17th Century watermill which ground corn for the nearby Trerice Manor, now National Trust. Four miles from the north coast in the peaceful Gannel valley; very central for exploring Cornwall, convenient for Eden Project. In seven acres of beautiful grounds with river and wildlife pond. Enjoy Cornish cream teas in the tranquil gardens. The large, beamed mill-room is now the residents' lounge, with TV and bar. Non-smoking throughout. Comfortable bedrooms: two double, one triple, one twin and two single. Some are en suite and all have washbasin and tea making facilities. Large car park. Bed and full Breakfast from £24. Self-catering cottages also available. Please phone for colour brochure or view our website.
e-mail: trewerry.mill@which.net
website: www.trewerrymill.co.uk

NEWQUAY
Mike and Alison Limer, Alicia, 136 Henver Road, Newquay TR7 3EQ (01637 874328). A warm welcome from your hosts Mike and Alison, who offer you a relaxed and friendly atmosphere in the comfort of their home.Traditional full English breakfast. Four en suite bedrooms, all tastefully furnished, with TV, clock/radio, hairdryer and refreshment tray; one standard with private facilities; iron provided. Relax in the conservatory or spacious lounge. Choose between the golden beaches along Newquay's coastline or a breathtaking coastal walk to Watergate Bay. The Eden Project, quaint fishing villages and the spectacular Cornish coastline, are all within 30 minutes' car ride. Open all year and fully centrally heated. Bed and Breakfast from £25 per person daily. Please telephone or write for brochure. **ETC ♦♦♦♦**
e-mail: aliciaguesthouse@mlimer.fsnet.co.uk
website: www.cornishlight.freeserve.co.uk/alicia.htm

NEWQUAY
Meryl and Mark Dewolfreys, Dewolf Guest House, 100 Henver Road, Newquay TR7 3BL (01637 874746). Dewolf Guest House is situated on the A3058 into Newquay town centre. All the amenities of Newquay are close at hand with Porth Beach only a short walk from the guest house. We have double or family rooms including two chalets situated in the rear garden. All rooms are non-smoking and offer en suite facilities, colour TV and tea/coffee making facilities. Prices are from £22 per person. Special Christmas/ New Year Breaks. Off-road car parking available, some pets welcome by arrangement. Licensed Bar. Open all year. **RAC ♦♦♦**, *N.A.T.C. APPROVED, NATIONAL ACCESSIBLE SCHEME M1.*
e-mail: holidays@dewolfguesthouse.com
website: www.dewolfguesthouse.com

Cornwall 113

NEWQUAY
Mr and Mrs A Slater, St George's Hotel, 71 Mount Wise, Newquay TR7 2BP (01637 873010). The small hotel with a lot to offer. Fabulous sea views. Quality food and service. BIG BREAKFAST. Clean comfortable accommodation - en suite available. Colour TVs. Licensed bar and pool table. Two minutes from town centre and beaches. Large car park. Personal attention. Warm welcome awaits friends old and new. B&B from £168 per person per week.
e-mail: enquiries@stgeorgeshotel.free-online.co.uk
website: www.st-georges-newquay.co.uk

NEWQUAY
Hotel Victoria, East Street, Newquay TR7 1DB (01637 872255; Fax: 01637 859295). One of Newquay's finest hotels. 113 en suite rooms; 7 luxury suites. Unique lift through cliff to beach. Victoria Health Club with gym, indoor pool, spa bath, sauna and sunbeds. Short drive to Eden Project and Maritime Museum. Take a virtual tour on our website. Off-peak midweek special breaks available. **ETC ★★★**
website: www.hotel-victoria.co.uk

PADSTOW
Mrs Sandra May, Trewithen Farm, St Merryn, Near Padstow PL28 8JZ (01841 520420). Trewithen farmhouse is a renovated Cornish Roundhouse, set in a large garden and situated on a working farm enjoying country and coastal views. The picturesque town of Padstow with its pretty harbour and narrow streets with famous fish restaurants is only three miles away. St Merryn Parish boasts seven beautiful sandy beaches and bays. Also coastal walks, golf, fishing and horse riding on neighbouring farm. Hire a bike or walk along the Camel Trail cycle and footpath - winding for 18 miles along the River Camel. Eden Project 20 miles. The accommodation has been tastefully decorated to complement the exposed beams and original features. All bedrooms are en suite or have private bathrooms, TVs and hot drink facilities. Parking. Full English breakfast. TV lounge. Bed and Breakfast from £25 to £30 per person per night. Winter weekend breaks available. Non-smoking. **ETC ♦♦♦♦** *SILVER AWARD.*
website: www.trewithenfarmhouse.co.uk

PENPILLICK
Round House Mill, Penpillick Hill, Near Par PL24 2RT (01726 813585). A great location, stunning views and superb rooms make the Round House Mill an ideal base. Features include ground level access to all rooms; guests' own entrance, secure parking and lounge; fresh fruit and yoghurt served at breakfast; heated swimming pool on upper terrace with stunning views; hospitality tray, TV, mini fridge, hairdryer and clock radio in rooms. Double and twin rooms available, all en suite. Non-smoking accommodation. Eden two miles, Lost Gardens of Heligan 15 minutes. Tariff: £30 to £40 pppn. Your hosts, **Bertie and Beth Pardoe** look forward to welcoming you into their home for a relaxing, refreshing stay.
e-mail: beth.pardoe@tesco.net
website: www.roundhousemill.co.uk

PENRYN
Brian and Penny Ward, 62 St Thomas Street, Penryn TR10 8JP (01326 374473). Bed and Breakfast run by husband and wife Brian and Penny, Number 62 is a Grade II Listed house, reputed to be over 250 years old, which offers a friendly welcome. Full English breakfast that can be served early if required. Free tea and coffee and your flasks filled free of charge. Accommodation comprises family, double, twin and single rooms. Situated three minutes' walk from the bus route and a 10 minute walk from the train station, and within easy reach of some of the finest beaches in Cornwall. Open March - October. Bed and Breakfast £14 - £16, children half price.

PENZANCE
Martin & Diane Miller, Beechwood, Alexandra Place, Penzance TR18 4NE (01736 360380) Martin and Diane Miller offer the warmest welcome at Beechwood, a spacious and elegant Victorian villa ideally situated with easy access to both the sea and Penzance town centre. A short walk through the lovely Morrab gardens brings you within yards of the best pubs and restaurants in the area; set off in the other direction and the promenade is only a five minute walk away. Beechwood offers three luxury en suite rooms on the first floor, one double, one family room and one twin bedded. All are freshly decorated with colour TV and tea and coffee making facilities. Your hosts have recently moved to Penzance after thirty years in the hospitality business, and so you can be sure your stay at Beechwood will be pretty special.

e-mail:dianemillera@aol.com

website: www.beechwoodpenzance.co.uk

See also Colour Display Advertisement

PENZANCE
Boscean Country Hotel, St Just, Penzance TR19 7QP (Tel & Fax: 01736 788748). This country house offers a wonderful combination of oak panelled walls, a magnificent oak staircase and open log fires. The natural gardens, extending to nearly three acres, are a haven for wildlife including foxes and badgers. Situated on the Heritage Coast in an Area of Outstanding Natural Beauty close to Cape Cornwall and the Coastal Footpath, this is an ideal base from which to explore the Land's End Peninsula. Penzance, St Michael's Mount, St Ives, Land's End and the Minack Theatre are all a short distance away. 12 en suite rooms, centrally heated throughout, licensed bar. Excellent home cooking using fresh local produce. Unlimited Desserts!! Open all year. Bed & Breakfast £23, Dinner, Bed & Breakfast £36. **ETC** ◆◆◆

e-mail: Boscean@aol.com

website: www.bosceancountryhotel.co.uk

PENZANCE
Mrs G. Owen, Penalva Private Hotel, Alexandra Road, Penzance TR18 4LZ (01736 369060). The hotel is TOTALLY NON-SMOKING, offering full central heating, fresh immaculate interior, en suite facilities, excellent food and a real welcome with courteous service. Penalva is a well positioned, imposing, late Victorian hotel set in a wide tree-lined boulevard with ample parking, close to promenade and shops. Perfect centre for enjoying the wealth of beautiful sandy coves, historical remains and magnificent walks. Colour TV and tea/coffee making facilities in bedrooms. Open all year. Special diets by prior arrangement. Sorry, no pets. Bed and Breakfast from £18 to £30. Weekly reductions. Children 6 to 12 half-price if sharing family rooms. Highly recommended. SAE, please, for brochure. **AA** ◆◆◆

PENZANCE
"Tradewinds", 21 Regent Terrace, Penzance TR18 4DW (01736 330990). Family-run guest house (non-smoking). Seafront location, convenient for Isle of Scilly boat and parking. TV, tea/coffee making facilities. All rooms en suite. Family room for five. Full English breakfast, vegetarians welcome. Terms from £25 per person. Reductions for children. Proprietor: **Mrs L. Matthews.**

PENZANCE (near)
Mrs M. D. Olds, Mulfra Farm, Newmill, Penzance TR20 8XP (01736 363940). Near Mulfra Quoit, this hill farm, with cows and calves, high on the edge of the Penwith moors, offers superb accommodation which attracts many of our guests to return year after year. The 17th century, stone-built, beamed farmhouse, with far-reaching views, offers two double en suite bedrooms with beverage trays and T.V. There is a comfortable guests' lounge, with inglenook fireplace and Cornish bread oven, dining room and sun lounge. Car essential, ample parking, friendly atmosphere, good food, beautiful walking country. We even have our own Iron Age settlement! Ideal centre for exploring West Cornwall. Bed and Breakfast £25. *CORNWALL TOURIST BOARD HIGHLY COMMENDED.*
website: www.mulfrafarm.co.uk

PENZANCE (near Porthcurno)
Mrs P. M. Hall, Treen Farmhouse, Treen, St Levan, Penzance TR19 6LF (01736 810253). Just off the South West Coastal Footpath, Treen Farm is a family-run, organic dairy farm set in 80 acres of pasture land on the cliffs beside the famous Minack Theatre and the historic Logan Rock. Land's End four miles. Visitors are welcome to use the gardens, walk around the farm and watch milking (children supervised please). Pub, shop, cafe, bus stop and beaches nearby. Ideal for walking, relaxing and sightseeing. Comfortable farmhouse Bed and Breakfast accommodation - twin and double (en suite) rooms with tea/coffee making facilities, garden/sea views; some with TV. Traditional English Breakfast. Guests' lounge with open fire and television. Private parking. Pets welcome. Child reductions. Sorry, no smoking. Bed and Breakfast from £15. Self-catering for two from £120 to £350 per week.
e-mail: paulachrishall@treenfarm.fsnet.co.uk

PERRANPORTH
Chy an Kerensa, Cliff Road, Perranporth TR6 0DR (01872 572470). Licensed Guest House situated by Coastal Path, directly overlooking miles of rolling surf, golden sands, rocks and heathland. Only 200 metres from beach and village centre, which has various restaurants, shops and pubs to suit all tastes and ages. Also tennis, bowls, wetsuit and surfboard hire, with golf and horse riding nearby. Our comfortable bedrooms, most en suite, have colour TV, central heating and tea/coffee making facilities. Many have panoramic sea views, as do our lounge/bar and dining room. Room only from £20 pppn, Bed and Breakfast from £24 to £30 pppn. A warm welcome from **Wendy Woodcock** all year. Please write or telephone for further details. **ETC** ♦♦♦

POLZEATH
Mrs P. White, Seaways, Polzeath PL27 6SU (01208 862382). Seaways is a small family guest house, 250 yards from safe, sandy beach. Surfing, riding, sailing, tennis, squash, golf all nearby. All bedrooms with en suite or private bathrooms, comprising one family, two double, two twin and a single room. Sittingroom; dining room. Children welcome (reduced price for under 10s). Cot, high chair available. Comfortable family holiday assured with plenty of good home cooking. Lovely cliff walks nearby. Padstow a short distance by ferry. Other places of interest include Tintagel, Boscastle and Port Isaac. Non-smoking establishment. Open all year round. Bed and Breakfast from £27.50. **AA** ♦♦♦
e-mail: pauline@seaways99.freeserve.co.uk
website: www.seawaysguesthouse.com

PORTHLEVEN
Mrs Neal, Tamarind, Shrubberies Hill, Porthleven, Helston TR13 9EA (01326 574303). Situated on the Looe Bar side of Porthleven on Lizard Peninsula. Sea views from bedrooms. Continental and English breakfast served with panoramic views over Mounts Bay. 264 yards from beach and coastal path. Five minutes' walk from harbour, shops, restaurants and inns. Guests are welcome to use the garden. Off-road parking on the property. B&B from £22, double en suite £25 per person. Smoking in sun lounge only.

See also Colour Display Advertisement

PORT ISAAC
Long Cross Hotel & Victorian Gardens, Trelights, Port Isaac PL29 3TF (01208 880243). Stay in one of Cornwall's most unusual hotels. Set in our own magnificent gardens in an Area of Outstanding Natural Beauty, and visited by thousands of garden lovers every year. Restaurant, Bar and Terraces with panoramic views. Spacious, newly refurbished, en suite rooms. Children's adventure play area.
e-mail: **longcross@portisaac.com**
website: **www.portisaac.com**

e-mail: alison.merchant@virgin.net

RILLA MILL (near Liskeard)
Woodpeckers, Rilla Mill, Callington PL17 7NT (01579 363717). Woodpeckers is set in a beautiful conservation village, local for hikers to Bodmin Moor (which is only five minutes away), Sterts Theatre and famous Cornish Yarg cheese farm. Central for Eden Project, Looe and Trago Mills. Come and try our candlelit three-course evening meals (£18) with complimentary bottle of wine, served in the conservatory overlooking the countryside and babbling brook. All rooms are fully en suite; the Lilac Haven room also contains a four-poster antique pine bed. Our prices are from £25pppn. Woodpeckers' high standards, reflected in the RAC Four Diamond rating, coupled with Sparkling Diamond award and Highly Commended Cornwall Tourism awards, will ensure an enjoyable stay. **RAC ♦♦♦♦**, *SPARKLING DIAMOND AWARD.*
website: **www.woodpeckersguesthouse.co.uk**

ST AGNES
Ted and Jeanie Ellis, Cleaderscroft Hotel, 16 British Road, St Agnes TR5 0TZ (01872 552349). This small, detached, family-run Victorian hotel stands in the heart of the picturesque village of St Agnes, convenient for many outstanding country and coastal walks. Set in mature gardens and having a separate children's play area we can offer peace and relaxation after the beach, which is approximately half-a-mile away. Accommodation is provided in generous sized rooms, mostly en suite and all with colour TV. Public rooms comprise lounge, bar, dining rooms and small games room. Private parking. Non-smoking. Regret no pets. Bed and Breakfast from £28 per person per night (sharing). Evening set menu. Self-catering annexe available.
e-mail: **tedellis@cchotel.fsnet.co.uk**

Cornwall 117

ST AGNES

Dorothy Gill-Carey, Penkerris, Penwinnick Road, St Agnes TR5 0PA (Tel & Fax: 01872 552262). A creeper-clad B&B hotel/guest house with lawned garden in unspoilt Cornish village. A home from home offering real food, comfortable bedrooms with facilities (TV, radio, kettle, H&C). Dining room serving breakfast, with dinner available by arrangement. Bright cosy lounge with a log fire in winter - colour TV, video and piano. Licensed. Ample parking. Dramatic cliff walks and beaches with good surfing available nearby. Easy to find on the B3277 road from big roundabout on the A30 and just by the village sign. Bed and Breakfast from £17.50 to £25.00 per night; Dinner available from £12.50. Open all year. ETC/AA/RAC ◆◆
e-mail: info@penkerris.co.uk
website: www.penkerris.co.uk

ST AUSTELL

The Elms, 14 Penwinnick Road, St Austell PL25 5DW (Tel & Fax: 01726 74981). The Elms Guest House is a 1920s Georgian style house within walking distance of the town centre. The Eden Project and the Lost Gardens of Heligan are approximately five miles away. Ideally situated for visiting the numerous other attractions in Cornwall and close to sandy beaches. Traditional English breakfast is offered; three-course evening dinners are available; licensed, three double en suite bedrooms, all completed to a very high standard for guests' comfort and enjoyment. Prices from £30 to £35 pppn. Open all year. ETC/AA ◆◆◆◆
e-mail: sue@edenbb.co.uk
website: www.edenbb.co.uk

ST AUSTELL

Mrs Liz Berryman, Polgreen Farm, London Apprentice, St Austell PL26 7AP (01726 75151). Polgreen is a family-run dairy farm nestling in the Pentewan Valley in an Area of Outstanding Natural Beauty. One mile from the coast and four miles from the picturesque fishing village of Mevagissey. A perfect location for a relaxing holiday in the glorious Cornish countryside. Centrally situated, Polgreen is ideally placed for touring all of Cornwall's many attractions. Cornish Way Leisure Trail adjoining farm. Within a few minutes' drive of the spectacular Eden Project and Heligan Gardens. All rooms with private facilities, colour TV, tea/coffee making facilities. Guest lounge. Children welcome. Terms from £24 per person per night. AA ◆◆◆◆
e-mail: polgreen.farm@btclick.com
website: www.polgreenfarm.co.uk

ST IVES

Angela Walker, Rivendell, 7 Porthminster Terrace, St Ives TR26 2DQ (Tel & Fax: 01736 794923). Our family-run, non-smoking guest house is in a superb location, with a reputation for excellent meals prepared by resident chef. Homely atmosphere. Close to town, beaches and all amenities. Full central heating, en suite rooms. Colour TV and beverage facilities in all rooms. Television and video in lounge. Fire certificate. Parking available. Open all year (including Christmas and New Year). Phone or send SAE to Angela Walker for brochure. Reduced rates for children and off-peak discounts for over 60s and Countdown cardholders. RAC ◆◆◆◆, *SPARKLING DIAMOND AWARD, DINING AWARD*.
e-mail: rivendellstives@aol.com
website: www.rivendell-stives.co.uk

**FREE or REDUCED RATE entry to Holiday Visits and Attractions
- see our READERS' OFFER VOUCHERS on pages 53-90**

ST IVES

Julie Fitzgerald, Horizon Guest House, 5 Carthew Terrace, St Ives TR26 1EB (01736 798069). Do you want a holiday with first-class accommodation, and to feel at home instantly? With beautiful sea view rooms overlooking Porthmeor Surf beach. We are close to the Coastal Footpath to Zennor, yet only five minutes from the Tate Gallery, Town Centre and beaches, and have some private parking. There is access to your rooms at any time; guests' lounge with colour TV, separate tables for dining and option of home-cooked dinner. Three-night breaks, early and late season £90. All rooms en suite. Private parking. Brochure and colour postcard available.

ST IVES

Mrs N.I. Mann, Trewey Farm, Zennor, St Ives TR26 3DA (01736 796936). Working farm. On the main St Ives to Land's End road, this attractive granite-built farmhouse stands among gorse and heather-clad hills, half-a-mile from the sea and five miles from St Ives. The mixed farm covers 300 acres, with Guernsey cattle and fine views of the sea; lovely cliff and hill walks. Guests will be warmly welcomed and find a friendly atmosphere. Five double, one single and three family bedrooms (all with washbasin); bathroom, toilets; sittingroom, dining room. Cot, high chair and babysitting available. Pets allowed. Car essential, parking. Open all year. Electric heating. Bed and Breakfast only. SAE for terms, please.

ST IVES

Linda & Bob Gale, Fairfield House, Porthrepta Road, Carbis Bay, St Ives TR26 2NZ (01736 793771). Linda and Bob welcome you to their homely Edwardian Guest House with fabulous sea views. Ideally situated close to Carbis Bay beach in St Ives Bay, voted one of the most beautiful bays in the world. Two minutes' walk to the Coastal Path, beach and rail line (branch line to St Ives takes three minutes) or walk the beautiful Coastal Path to St Ives. Visit the galleries including the famous Tate, the cobbled streets and harbour, with its many restaurants/pubs. Fairfield House has been recently refurbished with new en suite rooms added in 2003. Lovely rooms, most with sea views across the bay to St Ives. Non-smoking guest house with emphasis on comfort, cleanliness and personal service. Cream teas served in our lovely garden. Bed and Breakfast with varied menus from £27.00 per person per night. AA ◆◆◆◆
e-mail: info@fairfieldhouse.net   website: www.fairfieldhouse.net

TINTAGEL

Cate West, Chilcotts, Bossiney, Tintagel PL34 0AY (Tel & Fax: 01840 770324). Without stepping onto a road, slip through the side gate of this 16th Century listed cottage into a landscape owned by the National Trust and designated as an Area of Outstanding Natural Beauty. Closest cottage to nearby Bossiney beach for rock pools, surfing, safe swimming and caves to explore. Walk the airy cliff path north to nearby Rocky Valley or on to picturesque Boscastle Harbour. Southwards takes you to the ruins of King Arthur's Castle and onwards to busy Trebarwith Strand. Notice you have not stepped onto a road yet? Detached traditional country cottage ideal for a small number of guests. Home cooking, warm informal atmosphere, large bright double/family bedrooms with beamed ceilings and olde worlde feel. All rooms have TV, tea/coffee makers. Self-catering annexe available. May I send you a brochure? Bed and Breakfast from £20. Directions: Bossiney adjoins Tintagel on the B3263 (coast road), Chilcotts adjoins large lay-by with telephone box.

Cornwall 119

See also Colour Display Advertisement

e-mail: info@trurotownhouse.com

TRURO
The Townhouse Rooms, 20 Falmouth Road, Truro TR1 2HX (01872 277374; Fax: 01872 241666). The Townhouse is different - relaxed, friendly, flexible - and our guests seem to love it! We are not a hotel or a traditional bed and breakfast. We aim to give you lovely rooms, real value for money, and the flexibility you need to enjoy your stay. You have your own key - come and go as you please. There is an all day breakfast/dining room - use it whenever you want. And if you fancy a night in - grab a takeaway and a bottle of wine and chill out. We are just five minutes from restaurants, bars, shops and the theatre. And within a short drive, you can be sunning yourself on the beach, walking the Coastal Path, or checking out the Eden Project. Please ring for brochure. **RAC ♦♦♦♦** *WARM WELCOME AWARD.*
website: www.trurotownhouse.com

WADEBRIDGE
Mrs E. Hodge, Pengelly Farm, Burlawn, Wadebridge PL27 7LA (01208 814217). A Listed Georgian farmhouse on a working dairy farm, in a quiet location overlooking wooded valleys. Tastefully decorated and centrally heated throughout, offering one double and one twin room, both en suite with TV, radio, hairdryer and beverage trays. Full English breakfast, using mainly local produce, is served in the traditional style diningroom. Special diets by prior arrangement. Comfortable lounge with TV/video. Large garden with outstanding views for relaxing. An ideal walking, touring and cycling base, only six miles from the coast, with sailing, surfing, golf, riding and coastal walks; Camel Trail, the Saints' Way and Pencarrow House nearby. The Eden Project 35 minutes' drive, Padstow 20 minutes, Wadebridge one

and a half miles, with shopping, pubs, restaurants, leisure facilities and The Camel Trail. Static caravan (new 2004) also available. **ETC ♦♦♦♦** *SILVER AWARD.*
e-mail: hodgepete@hotmail.com   website: www.pengellyfarm.co.uk

FHG
·K·U·P·E·R·A·R·D·

Other specialised
FHG Guides
Published annually: available in all good bookshops or direct from the publisher.

Recommended **COUNTRY INNS & PUBS** OF BRITAIN

Recommended **COUNTRY HOTELS** OF BRITAIN

Recommended **SHORT BREAK HOLIDAYS** IN BRITAIN

The bestselling **PETS WELCOME!**

FHG Guides • Abbey Mill Business Centre,
Seedhill, Paisley, Renfrewshire PA1 ITJ
Tel: 0141-887 0428 • Fax: 0141-889 7204
e-mail: admin@fhguides.co.uk
www.holidayguides.com

Cumbria

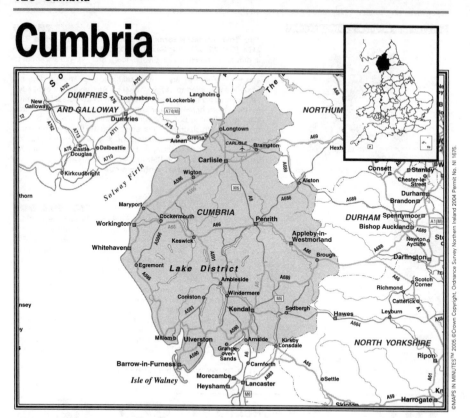

AMBLESIDE
Mr D. Sowerbutts, 2 Swiss Villas, Vicarage Road, Ambleside LA22 9AE (015394 32691). A small Victorian terrace house set just off the main road in the centre of Ambleside, near the church, in a slightly elevated position overlooking Wansfell. There is immediate access to the cinemas and shops and the wide variety of restaurants and cafes in the town. There are three double bedrooms (one with twin beds) recently refurbished in the traditional style. Each room has central heating, tea-making facilities and colour TV. A full English Breakfast or vegetarian meal available. We are open all year round and you are sure of a friendly welcome and good home cooking. Parking permit supplied. Bed and Breakfast from £26 to £27.50 per person. Self-catering accommodation is also available in house next door. See website for details.

e-mail: sowerbutts@swissvillas.plus.com
website: www.swissvillas.co.uk

•••some fun days out in CUMBRIA

Museum of Lakeland Life, Kendal • 01539 722464 • www.lakelandmuseum.org.uk
Dove Cottage, Grasmere • 015394 35544 • www.wordsworth.org.uk
World of Beatrix Potter, Bowness-on-Windermere • 015394 88444 • www.hop-skip-jump.com
Honister Slate Mine, Borrowdale • 017687 77530 • www.honister-slate-mine.co.uk
Cumberland Pencil Museum, Keswick • 017687 73626 • www.pencils.co.uk
Trotters World of Animals, Bassenthwaite • 017687 76239 • www.trottersworld.com

AMBLESIDE

The Old Vicarage
at Ambleside ❖

is a charming detached Lakeland house set in its own wooded gardens. Tucked quietly away from traffic, it is an ideal base for exploring the surrounding fells or boating on the lovely lakes. Fishing, riding, golfing and sailing are just a few of the facilities available nearby.

All bedrooms are furnished to a high standard; there are four-poster rooms, rooms with king-size beds, some rooms with spa baths and some on the ground floor. Spacious and comfortable lounge for guests' use. Ample free parking

Quality Bed & Breakfast Accommodation

- ❖ *Quiet, central location* ❖ *Car Park* ❖ *Log Fire*
- ❖ *Superb English Breakfasts* ❖ *Lovely views*
- ❖ *Heated Indoor Swimming Pool* ❖ *Sauna* ❖ *Hot Tub*
- ❖ *Sun Lounge* ❖ *Roof Top Terrace* ❖ *Holiday plans and guidance* ❖ *Dogs welcome*
- ❖ *No smoking in bedrooms* ❖ *Sensible prices* ❖ *Value for money*

Vicarage Road, Ambleside, Cumbria LA22 9DH
Tel: 015394 33364 Fax: 015394 34734
www.oldvicarageambleside.co.uk
E-mail: the.old.vicarage@kencomp.net

AMBLESIDE
Mrs Maureen Rushby, Fern Cottage, 6 Waterhead Terrace, Ambleside LA22 0HA (015394 33007). Homely Lakeland stone terraced house situated on the edge of Ambleside only two minutes' walk from the head of Lake Windermere and the Steamer Piers and one mile from the village. Ideal base for touring the Lakes. Kendal approximately 12 miles, Bowness-on-Windermere five miles, Hawkshead and Grasmere about 20 minutes' drive away. The accommodation comprises two double rooms and one twin room, all with tea/coffee making facilities and vanity unit; shared bathroom, lounge/diner with TV. Brochure available. Bed and Breakfast £19 – £21 per person sharing, £22 - £24 single.

AMBLESIDE
Mrs Parsons, Wynford, Nook Lane, Ambleside LA22 9BJ (015394 32294). Peace, comfort and stunning views in a quiet corner of Ambleside. Three double rooms, all en suite; central heating, TV. Lots of lovely walks from the door. Open all year. Non-smoking. No pets or children. Bed and Breakfast £35 per person per night. *NATIONAL ACCESSIBLE SCHEME LEVEL 1.*
e-mail: wynfordgh@aol.com
web: amblesideonline.co.uk/display/wynford/main.html

AMBLESIDE

Ambleside Lodge

Elegant Lakeland home built circa 1875, offering a high standard of accommodation to suit both the discerning traveller or to provide an anchor location while you discover the Lake District. All bedrooms are en suite and our premier suites and king-size four-poster rooms offer total relaxation and indulgence and have jacuzzi spa baths. Leisure facilities at a private club just five minutes' drive away include swimming pool, sauna, steam room, squash, gymnasium and beauty salon. Free parking.

Rothay Road, Ambleside LA22 0EJ
Tel: 015394 31681 • Fax: 015394 34547
e-mail: enquiries@ambleside-lodge.com • website: www.ambleside-lodge.com

See also Colour Advertisement

AMBLESIDE

The Dower House

**Wray Castle, Ambleside
Cumbria LA22 0JA
Tel: 015394 33211**

Lovely old house, quiet and peaceful, stands on an elevation overlooking Lake Windermere, with one of the most beautiful views in all Lakeland. Its setting within the 100-acre Wray Castle estate (National Trust), with direct access to the Lake, makes it an ideal base for walking and touring. Hawkshead and Ambleside are about ten minutes' drive and have numerous old inns and restaurants. Ample car parking; prefer dogs to sleep in the car. Children over five years welcome.

Bed and Breakfast from £30.00
Optional Evening Meal from £15.00
Open all year round

See also Colour Advertisement

See also Colour Display Advertisement

AMBLESIDE

Ferndale Lodge, Lake Road, Ambleside LA22 0DB (015394 32207). Ferndale Lodge is a small, family-run guesthouse where you will find a warm, friendly welcome and personal attention at all times. Offering excellent accommodation with good home cooked English or Vegetarian breakfast. Our ten attractive bedrooms have all been individually decorated and furnished, each with full en suite facilities, colour TV and tea/coffee making tray. Full central heating throughout; several rooms have views of the fells, including ground floor bedrooms. Open all year round with car park, offering packed lunches, hair dryer, clothes/boot drying and ironing facilities. A wide choice of places to dine within minutes' walking distance, ranging from excellent pub food to superb restaurants of many varied cuisines will complete your day.
Bed and Breakfast £28 to £30 per person per night. Weekly £182 to £196. Please phone for brochure. **ETC ♦♦♦**
e-mail: stay@ferndalelodge.co.uk
website: www.ferndalelodge.co.uk

 Cars of the Stars Motor Museum
Keswick, Cumbria
See our **READERS' OFFER VOUCHER** for
details of free or reduced rate entry

Cumbria

AMBLESIDE

Rothay House, Rothay Road, Ambleside LA22 0EE (Tel & Fax: 015394 32434). Rothay House is an attractive modern detached guest house set in pleasant gardens with views of the surrounding fells. All bedrooms are comfortable and well furnished with en suite facilities, colour TV, tea and coffee trays. Robin and Margaret combine 20 years quality hotel experience with a friendly atmosphere in clean, attractive surroundings. The house is within easy walking distance of the village centre. Ambleside has a variety of interesting shops and restaurants and makes an ideal base for walking, touring or enjoying sailing, watersports and angling on Lake Windermere. Car not essential, but ample parking. Open all year. Children welcome; sorry, no pets. Strictly non-smoking. Bed and Breakfast from £28 to £32; Winter Weekend Breaks available.

e-mail: email@rothay-house.com
website: www.rothay-house.com

APPLEBY

Mrs K.M. Coward, Limnerslease, Bongate, Appleby CA16 6UE (Tel & Fax: 017683 51578). Limnerslease is a family-run guest house five minutes' walk from the town centre. A good halfway stopping place on the way to Scotland. There is a good golf course and an indoor heated swimming pool. Many lovely walks are all part of the charm of Appleby. Two double and one twin bedrooms, all with washbasin, colour TV, tea/coffee making facilities at no extra charge; bathroom, toilet; dining room. Open January to November with gas heating. Ample parking. Bed and Breakfast from £20 to £23.

e-mail: kathleen@limnerslease63.fsnet.co.uk
website: http://mysite.freeserve.com/limnerslease

APPLEBY

Mrs Diana Dakin, Morningside, Morland, Penrith CA10 3AZ (01931 714393) Morningside is idyllically situated in the pretty village of Morland, midway between Appleby and Penrith, in the beautiful Eden Valley. Convenient for touring all of Cumbria and only 10 miles from Ullswater, it is perfect for a relaxing break. Friendly, personal service is assured in the beautifully appointed, ground floor twin-bedded room with en suite shower room, colour TV, hot drinks facilities plus the advantage of own entrance from private patio. A delicious breakfast is served in the bedroom overlooking the garden and village views. Central heating. Parking. Bed and Breakfast £25 per person. No smoking please.

APPLEBY

Barbara and Derick Cotton, Glebe House, Bolton, Appleby-in-Westmorland CA16 6AW (017683 61125). Our 17th century former farmhouse is ideally located for exploring the Eden Valley, an area waiting to be discovered by those who seek tranquillity in an Area of Outstanding Natural Beauty. Very quiet location with outstanding views of the Pennines. Approximately one mile from the A66 and four miles west of Appleby, and very convenient for visits to the Lake District, Yorkshire Dales and Scottish Borders. Centrally heated accommodation includes two double (one en suite) and one twin room all with tea-making facilities. Hearty breakfasts are served, with special diets catered for. Children welcome. Non-smoking. Bed and Breakfast from £25 to £30; Evening Meal from £15 to £17.50. Please send SAE for brochure. **ETC ♦♦♦♦**

e-mail: derick.cotton@btinternet.com
website: www.glebeholidays.co.uk

Readers are requested to mention this FHG publication when seeking accommodation

124 Cumbria

BOWNESS-ON-WINDERMERE
Annisgarth B&B, 48 Craig Walk, Bowness-on-Windermere LA23 2JT (015394 43866). Sharron Moore welcomes you to her friendly and relaxed Victorian home, quietly situated only minutes' walk from Lake Windermere and all the cafes, pubs, restaurants, shops and attractions of Bowness village. Three double bedrooms, one twin, one family room and a deluxe room with a jacuzzi bath and lake view. All rooms have TV with DVD and a collection of movies and books to read. All diets are catered for including vegetarian and vegan. All produce is local with free range eggs. There is a real coal fire for those winter mornings. Terms £20 to £35 pppn. Exclusively non-smoking.
website: www.annisgarth.co.uk

BOWNESS-ON-WINDERMERE
Holly Cottages Guest House, 2 Holly Cottages, Rayrigg Road, Bowness-on-Windermere LA23 3BZ (015394 44250). Guest House in the centre of Bowness-on-Windermere, offering four double en suite rooms with colour TV and tea making facilities. Centrally situated to all shops and restaurants. Lake Windermere and boat trips five minutes away. Excellent position for exploring the Lake District. If you enjoy walking, cycling, shopping, steam power, visiting houses and gardens, viewing wonderful scenery or simply pottering about, there is something here for any age or ability. We look forward to welcoming you soon. Sorry, no smoking in house. Private parking and access at all times. Dogs by arrangement. Contact: **Jan or Jim Bebbington (015394 44250)**.
website: www.hollycottageguesthouse.co.uk

BOWNESS-ON-WINDERMERE
Mrs Stones, Belsfield House, 4 Kendal Road, Bowness-on Windermere LA23 3EQ (015394 45823; Fax: 015394 46913). Janet and John extend a warm welcome to all who stay at their charming Victorian house, located only a minute's walk from the lake front of beautiful Lake Windermere. All guests have access to Parklands Country Club leisure complex which is a five minute stroll away. We offer eight well appointed en suite bedrooms, some with lake views, on two floors, all of which have central heating, tea/coffee making facilities,colour TV, alarm clock radios, hair dryers, ironing facilities and of course, an outstanding full English breakfast, using local produce. Special dietary needs are catered for. We also have a ground floor room suitable for the less physically able. Children welcome as are assistance dogs. Bed and Breakfast from £25 pppn. ETC/AA ♦♦♦♦
e-mail: enquiries@belsfieldhouse.co.uk
website: www.belsfieldhouse.co.uk

BRAMPTON
Mrs Annabel Forster, High Nook Farm, Low Row, Brampton CA8 2LU (016977 46273). Friendly farmhouse with relaxing atmosphere and good home cooking. Situated one mile from Low Row village and four miles from Brampton in peaceful Irthing Valley. Beef cattle, sheep, goats and poultry are kept and visitors are allowed to wander around the farm. Conveniently situated for touring Northumberland, Lake District and Scottish Borders and only a few miles from Roman Wall, Lanercost Priory and Talkin Tarn. Accommodation comprises one double and one family room, lounge, TV, diningroom. Bed and Breakfast from £18 single, £35 double; reductions for children under 12 years. Light snacks and packed lunches available. Well-controlled dogs accepted.

BUTTERMERE
Dalegarth Guest House, Hassness Estate, Buttermere CA13 9XA (017687 70233). Close to the Lake shore, one and a quarter miles south of village. Bed and Breakfast from £20 including VAT.
website: www.dalegarthguesthouse.co.uk

Cumbria 125

CALDBECK

Mr and Mrs A. Savage, Swaledale Watch, Whelpo, Caldbeck CA7 8HQ (Tel & Fax: 016974 78409). Ours is a mixed farm of 300 acres situated in beautiful countryside within the Lake District National Park. Central for Scottish Borders, Roman Wall, Eden Valley and the Lakes. Primarily a sheep farm (everyone loves lambing time). Visitors are welcome to see farm animals and activities. Many interesting walks nearby or roam the peaceful Northern fells. Enjoyed by many Cumbrian Way walkers. Very comfortable accommodation with excellent breakfasts. All rooms have private facilities. Central heating. Tea making facilities. We are a friendly Cumbrian family and make you very welcome. Bed and Breakfast from £20 to £27. **AA/ETC ♦♦♦♦**
e-mail: nan.savage@talk21.com
website: www.swaledale-watch.co.uk

See also Colour Display Advertisement

CARLISLE

Mrs Dorothy Nicholson, Gill Farm, Blackford, Carlisle CA6 4EL (01228 675326; mobile: 07808 571586). In a delightful setting on a beef and sheep farm, this Georgian-style farmhouse, dated 1740, offers a friendly welcome to all guests breaking journeys to or from Scotland or having a holiday in our beautiful countryside. Near Hadrian's Wall, Gretna Green and Lake District. Golf, fishing, swimming and large agricultural auction markets all nearby; also cycle path passes our entrance. Accommodation is in one double room en suite, one family and one twin/single bedrooms. All rooms have washbasins, shaver points and tea/coffee making facilities. Two bathrooms, shower; lounge with colour TV; separate diningroom. Open all year. Reductions for children; cot provided. Central heating. Car essential, good parking. Bed and Breakfast from £21 to £25. Telephone for further details or directions.

CARLISLE

Mr G. Shipp, Abberley House, 33 Victoria Place, Carlisle CA1 1HP (01228 521645). An imposing town house offering informal, comfortable high standard en suite rooms with TV, tea and coffee facilities and private parking. We are only a short walk from the excellent town centre with its fine variety of shops, restaurants, pubs and of course the cathedral, castle and award-winning Tullie House museum. Also close by are Stoney Holme and Swift golf courses, the Sands sports and leisure centre and the splendid River Eden. A short drive takes you to historic Hadrian's Wall, the magnificent Lake District and romantic Gretna Green. Our rates start from only £19 per person which includes English breakfast and taxes. **ETC ♦♦♦♦**
e-mail: bbs@abberleyhouse.co.uk
website: www.abberleyhouse.co.uk

See also Colour Display Advertisement

COCKERMOUTH

Mr & Mrs R. Mortimer, The Manor House, Oughterside, Aspatria CA7 2PT (Tel & Fax: 016973 22420). Our lovely manor farmhouse dates from the 18th century and retains many original features as well as several acres of land. Rooms are spacious with large en suite bathrooms, tea and coffee making facilities, full size TVs, views and lots of little extras. Our double rooms have kingsize beds and our twin room has double beds. The grounds are home to many species of birds, including barn owls. Set in peaceful surroundings we enjoy easy access to the magnificent scenery of the Western Lakes and Solway Coast. Pets and children welcome. Bed & Breakfast from £25. Evening meals by arrangement.
e-mail: richardandjudy@themanorhouse.net
website: www.themanorhouse.net

126 Cumbria

See also Colour Display Advertisement

COCKERMOUTH
Amanda Vickers, Mosser Heights, Mosser, Cockermouth CA13 0SS (01900 822644). Expect a warm welcome at our family-run farm, just off the beaten track, yet near to the fells and lakes of Loweswater (two miles) and Cockermouth (four miles). Comfortable spacious en suite bedroom, cosy lounge and dining room with log fires. A hearty breakfast to set you up for the day. An ideal base for walking, cycling, touring and bird watching. Arrive as guests and leave as friends. We are a hidden jewel awaiting your discovery.
e-mail: AmandaVickers1@aol.com

See also Colour Display Advertisement

COCKERMOUTH
Shepherds Hotel and Restaurant, Egremont Road, Cockermouth CA13 0QX (Tel & Fax: 01900 822673). 26 en suite rooms, single, double, twin and some family rooms, all furnished to a high standard and are fully equipped with direct dial telephone, trouser press, colour TV with satellite channels, plus facilities for making tea and coffee. One room has disabled facilities. Each bedroom includes an additional BT socket and work area to accommodate personal computers and portable fax machines. Small conference room and a large auditorium. The restaurant is open throughout the day serving a selection of bar meals and snacks. An extensive evening menu is freshly and skilfully prepared by our chef. Full English breakfast. An ideal base to explore this breathtaking part of the Lake District. B&B £24.50 to £49.
e-mail: reception@shepherdshotel.co.uk   website: www.shepherdshotel.co.uk

COCKERMOUTH
The Allerdale Court Hotel, Market Place, Cockermouth CA13 9NQ (01900 823 645; Fax: 01900 823 033). Situated in the old Market Place of Cockermouth, this Listed building dates back to the 17th century. Original oak beams and open fire help to retain the warm relaxing atmosphere found here. Family-owned and run, we pride ourselves on warm hospitality, good food in our restaurants, and constant attention to detail. The hotel has 24 en suite bedrooms, individually furnished and tastefully equipped to complement the character of the building, all with hospitality trays, TV, radio and phone. Family rooms are available, dogs are welcome. Our concern is your comfort and relaxation throughout your stay.
e-mail: info@allerdalecourthotel.co.uk
website: www.allerdalecourthotel.co.uk

COCKERMOUTH
Mrs V. A. Waters, The Rook Guesthouse, 9 Castlegate, Cockermouth CA13 9EU (01900 828496). Interesting 17th century town house, adjacent to historic castle, we offer comfortable accommodation with full English, vegetarian or Continental breakfast. Rooms are equipped with washbasin, colour TV, tea/coffee facilities and central heating. En suite and standard rooms available. Cockermouth is an unspoilt market town located at the North Western edge of the Lake District within easy reach of the Lakes, Cumbrian Coast and Border country. We are ideally situated as a base for walkers, cyclists and holidaymakers. Bed and Breakfast from £17 - £19 per person sharing room, single occupancy £20 - £22. Open all year, except Christmas.
website: www.therookguesthouse.gbr.cc/

A useful index of towns/counties appears on pages 393-398

Cumbria 127

COCKERMOUTH (near)

Mrs Nicholson, Swinside End Farm, Scales, High Lorton, Near Cockermouth CA13 9VA (01900 85134; mobile: 07913 337556; Fax: 01900 85410). Working farm situated in a peaceful part of Lorton Valley, the perfect base for your Lakeland holiday. Ideal for hill walking and touring around the Lake District. All rooms are en suite with central heating, tea/coffee making facilities and hairdryer. TV lounge with open fire. Magnificent views. Packed lunches available. A warm welcome awaits you. Open all year. No dogs in the house. Bed and Breakfast from £21 to £25 per person per night, single £23 to £26. ETC ♦♦♦♦
e-mail: swinside@supernet.com

ESKDALE GREEN

Mr & Mrs J. D. Bromage, Forest How Guest House, Eskdale Green CA19 1TR (019467 23201). Tucked away at the end of a quiet country lane lies Forest How. It is a very special place surrounded by gardens and natural fellside. There is an amazing abundance of wildlife and excellent walks all from the doorstep. The views across the lovely Eskdale Valley are spectacular. All rooms, some en suite, have TV, tea/coffee making facilities and are warm and cosy. We are renowned for our hearty breakfasts and personal caring attention. Good eating places locally. Ample car parking. Narrow gauge steam railway five minutes' walk. Brochure available. **ETC ♦♦♦, WELCOME HOST.**

HAWKSHEAD (near)

Paul and Fran Townsend, Pepper House, Satterthwaite LA12 8LS (01229 860206, Fax: 01229 860306). A warm welcome awaits in 16th century farmhouse with elevated position in tranquil valley on edge of Grizedale Forest, four miles from Hawkshead. Red and roe deer and other wildlife abound. Trout fishing nearby. Excellent, peaceful base for exploring the Lakes, close to Beatrix Potter's farm and Ruskin's Brantwood. Miles of forest trails for walking and cycling. Sympathetically updated, all bedrooms have en suite facilities. Two comfortable lounges, one with TV. Central heating, log fires; dining room and terraces with wonderful views. Licensed bar, generous home cooking. Non-smoking. Bed and Breakfast from £26 to £30; three-course Dinner £15 per person. Weekly rates and special winter rates available.
website: www.pepper-house.co.uk

KENDAL

Mrs A. Taylor, Russell Farm, Burton-in-Kendal, Carnforth, Lancs. LA6 1NN (01524 781334; Fax: 01524 782511). Why not spend a few days at Russell Farm? The proprietors pride themselves on trying to give guests an enjoyable holiday with good food, friendly atmosphere, relaxing surroundings away from the hustle and bustle. The 150-acre dairy farm is set in a quiet hamlet one mile from the village of Burton-in-Kendal, and five miles from the old market town of Kirkby Lonsdale. An ideal centre for touring Lakes and Yorkshire Dales, or going to the coast. Ideal stopover for people travelling south or to Scotland, only five minutes from M6 Motorway. One double, one single and one family bedrooms; bathroom, toilet; sittingroom and diningroom. Children welcome; cot, high chair and babysitting offered. Pets accepted, if well-behaved. Evening Dinner, Bed and Breakfast or Bed and Breakfast. Reductions for children. Car essential, parking. Send large SAE, please, for terms and brochure.

The FHG Directory of Website Addresses
on pages 339-370 is a useful quick reference guide for holiday accommodation with e-mail and/or website details

Cumbria

KENDAL
Hollin Root Farm, Garth Row, Skelsmergh, Kendal LA8 9AW (01539 823638). Dating from 1844 Hollin Root Farm is a typical Lakeland farmhouse set in beautiful open countryside. Tranquil settings and large gardens make this an ideal place for longer stays and a good base from which to explore the Lake District. Ideal as a stopover between England and Scotland. Accommodation consists of two en suite rooms, both with colour TV and tea/coffee making facilities, one ground floor en suite room available. Excellent breakfasts. Packed lunches available. Private car park, safe cycle storage. Children and vegetarians welcome. Open all year. Non-smoking establishment. B&B from £25 to £30 pppn. **ETC** ◆◆◆◆
e-mail: b-and-b@hollin-root-farm.freeserve.co.uk
website: www.hollinrootfarm.co.uk

KESWICK
Glencoe Guest House, 21 Helvellyn Street, Keswick CA12 4EN (017687 71016). Cycling, walking or touring, a warm, friendly welcome is guaranteed at our Victorian guest house, situated in a quiet area of town and yet only five minutes' stroll from the centre of Keswick and all its amenities. Glencoe offers spacious en suite and standard rooms, all decorated and furnished to a high standard. Each provides colour TV, hospitality tray and radio alarm; double, twin and single rooms available. Local knowledge and maps are at hand. Here at Glencoe we also provide a drying room, cycle storage and free flask filling. Non-smoking. B&B from £20pp. An enjoyable and comfortable stay awaits.
e-mail: enquiries@glencoeguesthouse.co.uk
website: www.glencoeguesthouse.co.uk

KESWICK
Mrs Burns, Lindisfarne Guest House, 21 Church Street, Keswick CA12 4DX (017687 73218). A cosy, friendly guest house with home cooking and hearty breakfasts. Situated within a residential area close to the town centre of Keswick and within easy walking distance of Lake Derwentwater and Fitz Park. We have some en suite rooms and all bedrooms have colour TV, tea/coffee facilities, central heating and washbasin. Bed and Breakfast from £23; Evening Meal optional. Chris and Alison Burns look forward to welcoming you. **ETC** ◆◆◆◆
e-mail: alison@burns1067.freeserve.co.uk
website: www.lindisfarnehouse.com

KESWICK
Springs Farm Guesthouse, Springs Farm, Springs Road, Keswick CA12 4AN (mobile: 07816 824253, Tel: 017687 72144/72546; Fax: 017687 72546). This charming family-run farm guesthouse offers warm comfortable accommodation with good food and friendly atmosphere as standard. Three en suite rooms with wonderful views of surrounding meadows and mountains make this working dairy farm the ideal location for families and a perfect base for walkers and cyclists; secure lock up area for bikes, drying facilities and packed lunches are available. The peaceful location is only a 10-minute walk from town. Disabled access. Stair lift available. Our small farm shop offers locally produced goods and gifts, ice cream and hot and cold drinks. Contact: **Mrs A Hutton or Ms H.C. Hutton.**
e-mail: info@springsfarmcumbria.co.uk
website: www.springsfarmcumbria.co.uk

KESWICK

See also Colour Display Advertisement

Mrs S. Park, Langdale, 14 Leonard Street, Keswick CA12 4EL (017687 73977). Victorian town house, quietly situated, yet close to town, park, lake and fells. All rooms furnished to a very high standard, having quality en suite facilities, central heating, colour TV, tea/coffee making facilities throughout. Family, double or twin available. Enjoy a good home cooked English or vegetarian breakfast or our popular Continental breakfast. We have a non-smoking policy throughout the house. We will ensure your stay is a pleasant one. Bed and Breakfast from £25; Theatre Breaks.
ETC ♦♦♦
website: www.langdaleguesthouse.co.uk

KESWICK

Ann & Norman Pretswell, Woodside, Penrith Road, Keswick CA12 4LJ (017687 73522). Late 19th century property set in almost an acre of mature grounds with views of Grizedale Pike and surrounding hills. Ideally situated away from the busy town centre yet only a short walk down the C2C bridle path to the town. The property has been extensively refurbished and has larger than average rooms with good-sized en suites. We have a large private car park, and for those using cycles, secure storage, hosepipe, repair stand and associated tools for your use. Being a family-run establishment you are guaranteed a friendly reception and sound advice on anything, from where to go to do extreme rock climbs, to gentle strolls and ferry cruises. After a good night's sleep you will be ready for a hearty English breakfast together with cereal, fruit and yoghurt. We will cater for special needs on request. Credit cards accepted. Dogs welcome by arrangement. Bed and Breakfast from £27.
e-mail: ann@pretswell.freeserve.co.uk   website: www.woodside.uk.net

KESWICK/BORROWDALE

Mrs S. Bland, Thorneythwaite Farm, Borrowdale, Keswick CA12 5XQ (017687 77237). Thorneythwaite Farm has a beautiful, peaceful position in the Borrowdale Valley standing half-a-mile off the road. The 220 acre sheep farm is seven miles from Keswick and half-a-mile from Seatoller. The 18th century farmhouse has great character inside and out, several rooms having oak beams and panelling and being furnished to suit. Two double and one family bedrooms, all with tea/coffee making facilities; sittingroom with open or electric fire; diningroom; bathroom and toilet. Cot, high chair and reduced rates for children. Sorry no pets. Open from April to November, mid-week bookings accepted. A perfect base for fell walking; Scafell, Great Gable, Glaramara are all within walking distance from the farm. Bed and Breakfast from £19.

KIRKBY LONSDALE

Pat & Brian Bradley, Wyck House, 4 Main Street, Kirkby Lonsdale, Carnforth LA6 2AE (Tel & Fax: 015242 71953). Quality accommodation in a Victorian town house, close to local pubs and restaurants. Our double and twin rooms have en suite facilities, all rooms have TV and hospitality trays. The famous Ruskin's View and Devil's Bridge, are only a short walk away, with several lovely walks taking one to three hours. Cyclists can find us on the Cumbrian cycle way and the Lancashire cycle way and Land's End to John o' Groats. We have safe storage for cycles. Want to visit the Lake District and the Yorkshire Dales? Then come and stay with Pat and Brian at Wyck House in Kirkby Lonsdale. No smoking. B&B from £25-£35 pppn. *WHICH? GUIDE RECOMMENDED, GOOD B&B GUIDE.*

e-mail: wyckhouse@studioarts.co.uk   website: www.studioarts.co.uk/wyckhouse.htm

Cumbria

KIRKBY STEPHEN
Cocklake House, Mallerstang CA17 4JT (017683 72080). Charming, High Pennine country house Bed and Breakfast in unique position above Pendragon Castle in Upper Mallerstang Dale offering good food and exceptional comfort to a small number of guests. Ample Dales breakfast served in the farmhouse-style kitchen. Comfortable sitting room with cosy fire. Two double rooms with large private bathrooms. Three acres of riverside grounds bordering on the North Yorkshire National park. Easy access to Herriot Country and the Eden Valley; Lake District 30 minutes. Dogs welcome.

LAKE DISTRICT/HAWKSHEAD
Grizedale Lodge, Hawkshead, Ambleside LA22 0QL (015394 36532; Fax: 015394 36572). Set in the heart of Grizedale Forest National Park, Grizedale Lodge is one of the most beautiful Bed and Breakfast locations. Within easy reach are the famous sculpture trails, sailing on Windermere or Coniston, Brantwood, Beatrix Potter country, trout fishing, and other attractions; Hawkshead five minutes. All rooms are en suite, centrally heated, and have colour TV, tea and coffee making facilities and hairdryers. Some have the added luxury of four-poster beds. Ample parking, TV lounge and sun terrace. Residential licence. Open all year, rates start from £30 per person per night.

e-mail: enquiries@grizedale-lodge.com   website: www.grizedale-lodge.com

See also Colour Display Advertisement

LANGDALE
The Britannia Inn, Elterwater, Langdale LA22 9HP (015394 37210). A 500 year-old quintessential Lakeland Inn nestled in the centre of the picturesque village of Elterwater amidst the imposing fells of the Langdale Valley. Comfortable, newly refurbished en suite double and twin-bedded rooms. Dogs welcome. Enquire about our Winter Mid-Week Special Offer of three nights B&B for the price of two. Relax in the oak-beamed Bars or Dining Room whilst sampling local real ales and dishes from our extensive menu of fresh, home-cooked food using lots of Cumbrian produce. **ETC ★★★**.
e-mail: info@britinn.co.uk
website: www.britinn.co.uk

 Eskdale Historic Water Mill
Eskdale, Cumbria
See our **READERS' OFFER VOUCHER** for details of free or reduced rate entry

---

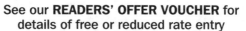

Visit the  website
www.holidayguides.com
for details of the wide choice of accommodation featured in the full range of FHG titles

LOWESWATER

Mrs Vickers, Askhill Farm, Loweswater, Cockermouth CA13 0SU (01946 861640). Askhill is a family-run farm which has beef and sheep. Situated on the hillside overlooking Loweswater Lake. The area is ideal for fell-walkers; there are plenty of walks (high fells or low walks) to suit everyone's level of ability; we are handy for all the western lakes, Crummock Water, Buttermere, Ennerdale (with lots of woodland walks), Wast Water (the deepest lake). Loweswater is handy for Keswick (10 miles approximately), Cockermouth (eight miles), the city of Carlisle with Roman connections (30 miles approximately), Maryport, steeped in Roman history (12 miles), and we are roughly 12 miles from the Solway coast. B & B from £23 per person; Dinner, B & B from £38 per person. Also 6 berth, self-catering caravan to let from £230 per week. Telephone for a brochure. **ETC ♦♦♦♦**

e-mail: askhillfarm@aol.com
website: www.countrycaravans.co.uk/askhillfarm

MARYPORT

Riverside B&B, 10 Selby Terrace, Maryport CA15 6NF (01900 813595). Clean, welcoming Victorian townhouse, family-run. Many original features including stained glass entrance, staircase, fireplaces, coving etc. No smoking. Ideal base for the Lake District and Coastal Route. Cyclists and Walkers Welcome. Fishing available (sea and river). Delicious full English breakfast and towels provided. Colour TV and tea/coffee facilities in all rooms. Packed lunch available. Standard rooms: one single, one double and one family (double and two single beds - also used as a twin/double/triple), from £18pppn. One double en suite room available from £22pppn. Contact: **Mrs L. Renac.**

MARYPORT

Ms Yvonne Hetherington-Tunstall, Curzon Grill, 64/66 Curzon Street, Maryport CA15 6DA (01900 819265). A family-run B&B providing excellent en suite accommodation. Spacious rooms with tea/coffee facilities and colour TV. Home of the biggest breakfast - often copied, never beaten. Licensed restaurant on premises, meals served all day. Evening meal available by request (try Yvonne's world famous steak pie!). Maryport is located on the fringe of the Lake District, and is ideal for walking, sailing, cycling, golfing or just relaxing. We have a beautiful harbour/marina, and for the children, the Lakeland Aquarium, all within a five minute walk. Maryport is famous for its Blues Festivals, Annual Carnival, Sea-Shanty weekends, and more!

NEAR SAWREY

Mrs Elizabeth Mallett, Esthwaite How Farmhouse, Near Sawrey, Ambleside LA22 0LB (015394 36450). A warm and friendly welcome awaits you at Esthwaite How Farmhouse, situated in this lovely village where Beatrix Potter wrote her books. Beautiful views of the countryside and the lake (where part of the television film about her life was made) can be seen from bedrooms and the diningroom. Ideal for walking, fishing and touring. Accommodation comprises two double rooms, one en suite, and one twin bedded room. Dining/sitting room with open log fire, central heating. Children welcome; babysitting can be arranged. Open all year. Car essential, parking for three cars. Bed and Breakfast from £17; Bed, Breakfast and Evening Meal from £27.

FHG *Cumberland Toy & Model Museum*
Cockermouth, Cumbria
See our **READERS' OFFER VOUCHER** for
details of free or reduced rate entry

132 Cumbria

See also Colour Display Advertisement

e-mail: info@brackenbank.co.uk

PENRITH
Bracken Bank Lodge, Lazonby, Penrith CA10 1AX (01768 898241; Fax: 01768 898221). This beautifully appointed famous shooting lodge stands in its own private 700 acre estate. It is traditionally furnished with antiques, oil paintings, sporting trophies and log fires. Amenities include a wonderful traditional English bar, a gun room and snooker room. All bedrooms are individually styled, each double and single room has a four poster bed. The Lodge is well known for its professionally run activities, weddings, corporate entertainments and Country House weekends. Guests may enjoy a wide range of sports including clay pigeon shooting, fishing and falconry on the estate. Locally there is riding and sailing in the Lake District. Boarding Kennels on site. Single, double and twin rooms. B&B £35 per person per night.
website: www.brackenbank.co.uk

PENRITH
Mrs Brenda Preston, Pallet Hill Farm, Penrith CA11 0BY (017684 83247). Pallet Hill Farm is pleasantly situated two miles from Penrith on the Penrith-Greystoke-Keswick road (B5288). It is four miles from Ullswater and has easy access to the Lake District, Scottish Borders and Yorkshire Dales. There are several sports facilities in the area - golf club, swimming pool, pony trekking. Good farmhouse food and hospitality with personal attention. An ideal place to spend a relaxing break. Double, single and family rooms; TV lounge and dining room. Children welcome, cot, high chair. Sorry no pets. Car essential, parking. Open Easter to November. Bed and Breakfast £15 (reduced weekly rates). Reduced rates for children.

PENRITH
Little Blencowe Farm, Blencowe, Penrith CA11 0DG (017684 83338; mobile: 07745 460186). A warm welcome awaits you on our dairy and sheep farm. Situated in a small, quiet village within easy reach of the Lakes, Scotland, the Pennines and Hadrian's Wall, ten minutes from the M6/A66. Two spacious rooms with private facilities, comfortable chairs, TV and hospitality tray. Farmhouse breakfast using local produce. Homemade bread and jams. Dinner available by prior arrangement, otherwise there is a very nice, small pub serving good food within walking distance.

PENRITH
Peter & Cynthia Barry, Blue Swallow Guest House, 11 Victoria Road, Penrith CA11 8HR (01768 866335) A comfortable Victorian house set in the attractive market town of Penrith, ideally situated to explore the delightful Eden Valley, the wonderful scenery of the Lake District and the Yorkshire Dales National Parks. For golfing enthusiasts, Penrith boasts an 18 hole golf course and there are several more within easy driving distance. The resident proprietors look forward to welcoming you whether you are on holiday, just breaking a long journey or in the area for business - you'll be made to feel at home. Seven rooms, twin/double or family (four en suite), one private bathroom; two single en suite rooms. All rooms have colour TV, tea tray and central heating. Full English breakfast using local produce.Non-smoking throughout.Bed and Breakfast from £27 to £35 pppn.
e-mail: blueswallow@tiscali.co.uk
website: www.blueswallow.co.uk

A list of contents appears on pages 2 and 3.

Cumbria 133

PENRITH
Mrs Bell, Albany House, 5 Portland Place, Penrith CA11 7QN (01768 863072). Close to the town centre, Albany House is a lovely mid-Victorian terraced property. Fine, spacious rooms (two double, two multi, one family), en suite facilities, central heating, colour TV, tea/coffee. Situated close to M6, A6 and A66, an ideal base for touring the Lake District, Eden Valley, Hadrian's Wall and Scottish Borders. An excellent stopover, with the warmest welcome and hearty breakfasts. B&B from £23pp. **ETC ♦♦♦, RAC ♦♦♦**
e-mail: info@albany-house.org.uk
website: www.albany-house.org.uk

PENRITH
Leon and Debbie Kirk, Brooklands Guest House, 2 Portland Place, Penrith CA11 7QN (01768 863395). Charming, elegant surroundings await any visitor to Brooklands, conveniently situated in the heart of historic Penrith. This beautifully restored Victorian town house provides an excellent base for exploring the many and varied delights of the English Lakes. Luxury en suite rooms, with all facilities. Four-poster and deluxe rooms also available. Debbie and Leon will make it their business to ensure that your stay is as enjoyable as possible and that you will want to return to repeat the experience time and again. Bed and Breakfast from £30pppn. Credit cards accepted. **AA/RAC ♦♦♦♦, RAC** *SPARKLING DIAMOND AWARD, AWARD FOR CLEANLINESS.*

e-mail: enquiries@brooklandsguesthouse.com   website: www.brooklandsguesthouse.com

PENRITH
Mrs Ann Toppin, Gale Hall, Melmerby, Penrith CA10 1HN (01768 881254). Working farm. Mrs Ann Toppin welcomes guests to her home on a working beef/sheep farm 10 miles east of Penrith and the M6, a mile-and-a-half from the peaceful village of Melmerby. Beautiful setting at the foot of the Pennines and with extensive views of the Lakeland Fells. Ideal for walking, convenient for the Lake District. Single, double, twin or family rooms available; cot and babysitting. Residents' lounge. Pets welcome by arrangement. Bed and Breakfast from £18; reduction for children under 12 years. Special diets catered for. Full English or Vegetarian Breakfast served. Excellent bar meals available locally.

ST BEES
John and Susan Carr, Fairladies Barn, Main Street, St Bees CA22 0AD (01946 822718; Fax: 01946 825838). Fairladies is a 17th century sandstone barn situated on the main street in the coastal village of St Bees. The barn was initially converted in the 1980s into a large guest house and self-contained flats and has been recently refurbished throughout. St Bees, Cumbria's most westerly point, is a small village which was built around an 11th century priory. It has a superb sandy beach, tennis courts and a nine hole golf course. There are plenty of public houses offering excellent local pub food and a restaurant serving French cuisine. Family, double and twin rooms, all with colour TV and tea/coffee making facilities; non-smoking. En suite rooms available. Large private car park and attractive gardens. **ETC ♦♦♦♦**

e-mail: info@fairladiesbarn.co.uk
website: www.fairladiesbarn.co.uk

SHAP
Mr and Mrs D. L. and M. Brunskill, Brookfield, Shap, Penrith CA10 3PZ (01931 716397). Situated one mile from M6 motorway (turn off at Shap interchange No. 39), first accommodation off motorway. Excellent position for touring Lakeland, or overnight accommodation for travelling north or south. Central heating throughout, renowned for good food, comfort and personal attention. All bedrooms are well appointed and have en suite facilities, remote-control colour TV, hospitality tray and hairdryer. Diningroom where delicious home cooking is a speciality. Well stocked bar. Residents' lounge. Sorry, no pets. Open from January to December. Terms sent on request, ample parking. Full Fire Certificate. AA ♦♦♦♦

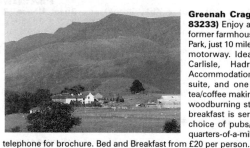

TROUTBECK (Penrith)
Greenah Crag, Troutbeck, Penrith CA11 0SQ (017684 83233) Enjoy a relaxing break at Greenah Crag, a 17th century former farmhouse peacefully located in the Lake District National Park, just 10 miles from Keswick and only eight miles from the M6 motorway. Ideal for exploring Northern Lakes, Eden Valley, Carlisle, Hadrian's Wall and the Western Pennines. Accommodation is in two double bedrooms with bathroom en suite, and one twin-bedded room with washbasin, all with tea/coffee making facilities. The guests' sittingroom with TV and woodburning stove is a cosy place on the coldest days! A full breakfast is served in the oak-beamed diningroom. Excellent choice of pubs/restaurants within three miles, nearest three-quarters-of-a-mile. Regret no pets or smoking in the house. Please telephone for brochure. Bed and Breakfast from £20 per person.
e-mail: greenahcrag@lineone.net   **website: www.greenahcrag.co.uk**

ULLSWATER
Knotts Mill Country Lodge, Watermillock, Penrith CA11 0JN (017684 86699). Spacious guesthouse close to magical Ullswater, in peaceful, scenic surroundings. Ideal for walking, boating or touring the Lake District. Nine en suite bedrooms with stunning views, including family rooms and facilities for the disabled. Our large dining room and lounge have picture windows that overlook the fells. Big breakfasts; fully licensed for wines, beer etc. 10 minutes from Junction 40 M6 with private grounds and parking. When the Lake District is at its most beautiful, with snow on the peaks, you can relax at Knotts Mill Country Lodge. ETC ♦♦♦
website: www.knottsmill.com

WINDERMERE
Mr and Mrs G. Simpson, Lingmoor, 7 High Street, Windermere LA23 1AF (015394 44947). There is nowhere to visit that comes close to the breathtaking scenery of the Lake District. Stay at Lingmoor, where a warm and hospitable welcome is assured in this small, family-run guest house. Close to all amenities, it is perfect if you just want to relax, maybe take a lake cruise or, for the more energetic, walk, cycle or sail on or around the lake. A two-minute walk from the train station, we are situated in the very heart of the village, a good base from which to explore the surrounding district. Large family room where children over five years of age are welcome, three double rooms, one twin, all en suite, and one standard twin. All rooms have colour TV, hospitality trays and central heating. Hairdryers and iron available on request. The house is strictly no smoking and we cannot accommodate pets. Tariff from £28 single, £40 double.
website: www.lingmoor-guesthouse.co.uk

Cumbria 135

WINDERMERE

The Firgarth
Ambleseide Road, Windermere LA23 1EU

Elegant Victorian house on Windermere to Ambleside Road with a Lake viewpoint nearby. The front rooms overlook a tree-lined paddock, the rear rooms overlook Wynlass Beck where ducks, rabbits and the occasional deer can be seen. We have a private lounge for guests to relax in. All bedrooms have colour TV and tea/coffee making facilities. Non-smoking establishment. Ample private parking. A good selection of restaurants available nearby. Rooms are available from £20.00 per person, all with en suite facilities. Ring Gillian who will be happy to discuss your requirements.

Tel: 015394 46974 • Fax: 015394 42384
e-mail: thefirgarth@ktdinternet.com
website: www.firgarth.com

WINDERMERE

Mr and Mrs D. Lennon, Meadow Cottage, Ratherheath Lane, Crook LA8 8JX (015398 21269). Sandra and David Lennon extend a warm welcome to guests who stay at Meadow Cottage. Set in one and a half acres, this old Lakeland cottage has spectacular views and is the ideal location when visiting this beautiful region. All bedrooms are en suite, have tea and coffee facilities and colour TV. We provide Aga-cooked vegetarian or English breakfasts. Some five miles from Lake Windermere, the popular heart of the Lake District, we are conveniently placed for touring, walking or cycling exploration. A flexible service is provided in this non-smoking guesthouse. Please enquire for details. Prices from £28 per person per night.
website: www.meadow-cottage.net.co.uk

WINDERMERE

Fir Trees Guest House, Lake Road, Windermere LA23 2EQ (015394 42272; Fax: 015394 42512). Situated mid-way between Windermere village and the lake, built in the traditional Lakeland style, Fir Trees offers delightful accommodation of exceptional quality and charm. Our bedrooms are lovely, all furnished and decorated to a very high standard and all have private en suite facilities, tea/coffee making and television. Breakfasts are traditionally English in style and cooked to perfection.
e-mail: enquiries@fir-trees.com
website: www.fir-trees.co.uk

publisher's note

While every effort is made to ensure accuracy, we regret that FHG Guides cannot accept responsibility for errors, misrepresentations or omissions in our entries or any consequences thereof. Prices in particular should be checked. We will follow up complaints but cannot act as arbiters or agents for either party

FHG
K·U·P·E·R·A·R·D

136 Cumbria

See also Colour Display Advertisement

WINDERMERE
St John's Lodge, Lake Road, Windermere LA23 2EQ (015394 43078; Fax: 015394 88054). This pretty Lakeland B&B is ideally situated between Windermere village and the lake (10 minutes' walk) and close to all amenities. The guesthouse caters exclusively for non-smokers and has been awarded 3 AA Red Diamonds for excellence. The choice of breakfast menu is probably the largest in the area. From a touring visitor's point of view, or if you prefer healthier alternatives, this is a refreshing change. There is the usual choice of cereals and fresh fruit and a good selection of traditional English breakfasts, but there are also over 20 other tasty dishes, including vegetarian/vegan, fresh fish, and a number of house specialities. All guests are offered free access to a nearby local luxury leisure club (about 2 minutes by car). Free internet access is provided via a dedicated computer. For laptop owners, radio connectivity is available, or you can simply plug in and use ASDL technology. **AA** *THREE RED DIAMONDS*.
e-mail: mail@st-johns-lodge.co.uk
website: www.st-johns-lodge.co.uk

See also Colour Display Advertisement

WINDERMERE
Carole Vernon and Alex Tchumak, Green Gables, 37 Broad Street, Windermere LA23 2AB (015394 43886). A family-owned and run licensed guesthouse in Windermere. One minute's walk from village centre with shops, banks and pubs and only five minutes from the station or bus stop. Accommodation comprises two doubles, one family triple/twin and one single room, all en suite; one family (four) and two family triple/twin rooms with private facilities; all with central heating, colour TV, hairdryers, kettles, tea & coffee. Comfortable lounge bar on the ground floor. No smoking in bedrooms. We can book tours and trips for guests and can advise on activities and special interests. B&B from £20 to £30 pppn. Special Winter offers available. Open just about all year round. **AA ♦♦♦**.
e-mail: greengables@FSBdial.co.uk
info@greengablesguesthouse.co.uk

WINDERMERE
Autumn Leaves Guest House, 29 Broad Street, Windermere LA23 2AB (015394 48410). A comfortable Victorian Guest House located in the heart of Windermere, five minutes' walk from the train/bus station. Autumn Leaves has a variety of rooms accommodating the single traveller, couples and families/small groups. Some rooms are en suite and all have central heating, colour TV, radio alarms and tea/coffee making facilities. Autumn Leaves is an ideal base from which to explore the Lake District. We have plenty of maps and information for guests to borrow and are happy to share our extensive knowledge of the area. Pets welcome. Non-smoking throughout. B&B from £19-£25 pppn. **ETC ♦♦♦**
e-mail: autumnleaves@nascr.net
website: www.autumnleaves.gbr.cc

WINDERMERE
Mrs Dorothy Heighton, Beckmead House, 5 Park Avenue, Windermere LA23 2AR (Tel & Fax: 015394 42757). A small family-run guest house with quality accommodation, delicious breakfasts and a relaxed friendly atmosphere. Single, double or family rooms, with en suite or private showers, all decorated to a high standard with central heating, electric blankets, tea/coffee making facilities, colour TV, hairdryers and clean towels daily. Comfortable residents' lounge. Walking, climbing, sailing, water skiing, pony trekking, golf nearby, or visit historic houses, gardens and museums. **ETC ♦♦♦♦**
e-mail: beckmead_house@yahoo.com
website: www.beckmead.co.uk

Cumbria 137

WINDERMERE

Mrs J. Seal, Brook House, 30 Ellerthwaite Road, Windermere LA23 2AH (015394 44932). A friendly welcome awaits you at Brook House which is convenient for village and lake. Ideal touring centre. We offer personal service, together with excellent English cooking, under the personal supervision of the proprietors. All rooms are decorated to a high standard; residents' lounge with colour TV; full central heating. All bedrooms have private showers/baths, colour TV, tea/coffee making facilities, and most have private toilets. Access to rooms at all times. Guests' parking. Full Fire Certificate. Open all year. Bed and Breakfast from £18.50 to £27. **ETC** ◆◆◆

WINDERMERE

Meadfoot Guest House, New Road, Windermere LA23 2LA (015394 42610). A warm welcome and a memorable holiday experience await you at Meadfoot, with your hosts, Sandra and Tim Shaw. Meadfoot is a detached house set in its own grounds on the edge of Windermere village. There is a large garden with patio for guests' use. The bedrooms, all en suite, are tastefully furnished with pine furniture - some are on the ground floor, some are four-poster and one is a self-contained family suite with two separate rooms and direct access to the garden. Private car park. Free Leisure Club facilities available nearby.
website: www.meadfoot-guesthouse.co.uk

Useful Guidance for Guests and Hosts

Every year literally thousands of holidays, short breaks and overnight stops are arranged through our guides, the vast majority without any problems at all. In a handful of cases, however, difficulties do arise about bookings, which often could have been prevented from the outset.
It is important to remember that when accommodation has been booked, both parties – guests and hosts – have entered into a form of contract. We hope that the following points will provide helpful guidance.

- When enquiring about accommodation, be as precise as possible. Give exact dates, numbers in your party and the ages of any children.
- State the number and type of rooms wanted and also what catering you require – bed and breakfast, full board etc. Make sure that the position about evening meals is clear – and about pets, reductions for children or any other special points.
- Read our reviews carefully to ensure that the proprietors you are going to contact can supply what you want. Ask for a letter confirming all arrangements, if possible.
- If you have to cancel, do so as soon as possible. Proprietors do have the right to retain deposits and under certain circumstances to charge for cancelled holidays if adequate notice is not given and they cannot re-let the accommodation.
- Give details about your facilities and about any special conditions. Explain your deposit system clearly and arrangements for cancellations, charges etc. and whether or not your terms include VAT.
- If for any reason you are unable to fulfil an agreed booking without adequate notice, you may be under an obligation to arrange suitable alternative accommodation or to make some form of compensation.

Derbyshire

See also Colour Display Advertisement

ASHBOURNE
Mrs A.M. Whittle, Stone Cottage, Green Lane, Clifton, Ashbourne DE6 2BL (01335 343377; Fax: 01335 347117). A charming cottage in the quiet village of Clifton, one mile from the Georgian market town of Ashbourne. Ideal for visiting Chatsworth House, Haddon Hall, Dovedale, Carsington Water and the theme park of Alton Towers. Each bedroom is furnished to a high standard; all rooms en suite with four-poster beds, TV and coffee making facilities. Large garden to relax in. A warm welcome is assured and a hearty breakfast in our delightful cottage. Nearby good country pubs serving evening meals. Bed and Breakfast from £22.50 per person. Please write or telephone for further details. ETC/AA ♦♦♦
e-mail: info@stone-cottage.fsnet.co.uk

ASHBOURNE
The Courtyard, Dairy House Farm, Alkmonton, Longford, Ashbourne DE6 3DG (Tel & Fax: 01335 330187). Grazing farm. Victorian cowshed tastefully converted and furnished to a very high standard. Tranquil location, yet within easy reach of Alton Towers (eight miles), Chatsworth House, Calke Abbey and many other historic houses. The Potteries are close to hand, as is the American Adventure Theme Park. We are surrounded by beautiful countryside which includes Dovedale and the many other lovely Dales which make up the Derbyshire Dales. A newly opened 18 hole, par-three golf course is only four miles away. Good farmhouse fare served on our 18 acre farm. Stay in one of our seven rooms – five double, one twin and a family suite, all with en suite facilities. Level 3 Wheelchair Access. Children welcome. Regret, no pets. Bed and Breakfast from £26 double/twin, £35 single. Winter breaks from October 20th till March 20th: Dinner, Bed and Breakfast £48 per person per night, minimum two nights. AA/RAC ♦♦♦♦, **RAC** *SPARKLING DIAMOND AWARD AND WARM WELCOME AWARD, CLA BUILDING AWARD WINNER, NATIONAL ACCESSIBLE SCHEME LEVEL 3.*
e-mail: michael@dairyhousefarm.org.uk   website: www.dairyhousefarm.org.uk

ASHBOURNE
Compton House, 27-31 Compton, Ashbourne DE6 1BX (01335 343100). Situated in the charming market town of Ashbourne, we are a small family-run guest house with accent on good food, locally produced where possible, and quality accommodation in a warm and friendly atmosphere. Originally three terraced cottages, now converted into one rather individual house which has been our home since 1986. As well as a comfortable sitting room, we have five en suite bedrooms, all with colour TV and well-stocked tea tray. We have safe parking in our delightful garden at the rear of the house. Bed and Breakfast from £23 per person. AA ♦♦♦♦
e-mail: jane@comptonhouse.co.uk
website: www.comptonhouse.co.uk

Derbyshire 139

ASHBOURNE (near)

Mr J. Parker, Mona Villas, Church Lane, Middle Mayfield, Mayfield, Near Ashbourne DE6 2JS (01335 343773). A warm, friendly welcome to our home with purpose-built en suite accommodation. Beautiful views over open countryside. A local pub serves excellent food within a five minute walk. Situated near Alton Towers, Dove Dale, etc. Bed and Breakfast from £22.50 to £25.00 per night. Three en suite rooms available, single supplement applies. Family rooms available. Parking. **ETC/AA** ♦♦♦♦
e-mail: info@mona-villas.fsnet.co.uk
website: www.mona-villas.fsnet.co.uk

BAKEWELL

Mrs Julia Finney, Mandale House, Haddon Grove, Bakewell DE45 1JF (01629 812416). Relax in the warm and friendly atmosphere of our peaceful farmhouse situated on the edge of Lathkill Dale. Conveniently located for visiting the many attractions of the area. All rooms are en suite, colour TV and tea making facilities. Ground floor rooms available. A varied breakfast menu is offered, and packed lunches by arrangement. Excellent local inns and restaurants a short drive away. Bed and Breakfast £25 - £27 per person sharing double/twin room. Single occupancy £35 per night. Discount for 3-night stays mid-week. No smoking in house. **ETC** ♦♦♦♦
e-mail: julia.finney@virgin.net
website: www.mandalehouse.co.uk

BUXTON

Roger and Maria Hyde, Braemar, 10 Compton Road, Buxton SK17 9DN (01298 78050). Guests are warmly welcomed into the friendly atmosphere of Braemar, situated in a quiet residential part of this famous spa town. Within five minutes' walk of all the town's many and varied attractions i.e., Pavilion Gardens, Opera House, swimming pool; golf courses, horse riding, walking, fishing, etc are all within easy reach in this area renowned for its scenic beauty. Many of the Peak District's famous beauty spots including Chatsworth, Haddon Hall, Bakewell, Matlock, Dovedale and Castleton are nearby. Accommodation comprises comfortable double and twin bedded rooms fully en suite with colour TV and hospitality trays, etc. Full English Breakfast served and diets catered for. Non-smokers preferred. Terms from £24.50 inclusive for Bed and Breakfast. Weekly terms available. **ETC** ♦♦♦♦
e-mail: buxtonbraemar@supanet.com   website: www.cressbrook.co.uk/buxton/braemar

See also Colour Display Advertisement

CASTLETON

Ye Olde Cheshire Cheese Inn, How Lane, Castleton, Hope Valley S33 8WJ (01433 620330; Fax: 01433 621847). This delightful 17th century free house is situated in the heart of the Peak District and is an ideal base for walkers and climbers; other local attractions include cycling, swimming, gliding, horse riding and fishing. All bedrooms are en suite with colour TV and tea/coffee making facilities. A "Village Fayre" menu is available all day, all dishes home cooked in the traditional manner; there is also a selection of daily specials. Large car park. Full Fire Certificate. B&B from £25. All credit cards accepted. Special golf packages arranged. Personal training instructor and gym available on premises. **ETC** ♦♦♦♦
e-mail: kslack@btconnect.com
website: www.cheshirecheeseinn.co.uk

Derbyshire

DERBY

Mrs Catherine Dicken, Bonehill Farm, Etwall Road, Mickleover DE3 5DN (01332 513553). This 120 acre mixed farm with Georgian farmhouse is set in peaceful rural surroundings, yet offers all the convenience of being only three miles west of Derby, on the A516 between Mickleover and Etwall. Within 10 miles there is a choice of historic houses to visit; Calke Abbey, Kedleston Hall, Sudbury Hall. Peak District 20 miles, Alton Towers 20 miles. Accommodation in three bedrooms (one twin, one double en suite, one family room with en suite facilities), all with tea/coffee making facilities. Cot and high chair provided. Open all year. Bed and Breakfast from £25. Croquet available. A warm and friendly welcome awaits you.

MATLOCK

Mrs S. Elliott, "Glendon", Knowleston Place, Matlock DE4 3BU (01629 584732). Warm hospitality and comfortable accommodation in this Grade II Listed building. Conveniently situated by the Hall Leys Park and River Derwent, it is only a short level walk to Matlock town centre. Large private car park. Rooms are centrally heated and have washbasin, colour TV and tea/coffee making facilities. En suite available. No smoking. An ideal base for exploring the beautiful Peak District of Derbyshire, with easy access to many places of interest including Chatsworth House, Haddon Hall, Crich Tramway Village and Heights of Abraham cable car. Bed and Breakfast from £24.50 per person.
AA ♦♦♦♦

MELBOURNE (near)

Mrs Mary Kidd, Ivy House Farm, Stanton-by-Bridge, Near Melbourne DE73 1HT (Tel & Fax: 01332 863152). Working farm, join in. Ivy House Farm is a 400 acre arable farm. The farmhouse, converted in 2000, has three en suite double rooms and we have also converted some cowsheds into chalets, all of which are en suite with tea/coffee making facilities and TV. Each chalet has a theme – Cowshed, Sheep Pen, Stable and Pigsty. The area has lots to do and see, such as Calke Abbey, ski slopes, Alton Towers, motor racing at Donington Park. There are also lots of places to eat. Children are welcome, but we are strictly non-smoking. Ample off-road parking. Bed and Breakfast from £32.
ETC ♦♦♦♦ *SILVER AWARD.*
e-mail: mary@guesthouse.fsbusiness.co.uk
website: www.ivy-house-farm.com

WINSTER

Mrs Jane Ball, Brae Cottage, East Bank, Winster DE4 2DT (01629 650375). In one of the most picturesque villages in the Peak District National Park this 300-year-old cottage offers independent accommodation across the paved courtyard. Breakfast is served in the cottage. Rooms are furnished and equipped to a high standard; both having en suite shower rooms, tea/coffee making facilities, TV and heating. The village has two traditional pubs which provide food. Local attractions include village (National Trust) Market House, Chatsworth, Haddon Hall and many walks from the village in the hills and dales. Ample private parking. Non-smoking throughout. Bed and Breakfast from £23 per person (reduced rates for children). **ETC ♦♦♦♦** *SILVER AWARD, 'WHICH?' GOOD BED & BREAKFAST GUIDE, 'WHICH?' GUIDE TO GOOD HOTELS.*

Crich Tramway Village
Matlock, Derbyshire

See our **READERS' OFFER VOUCHER** for details of free or reduced rate entry

Devon

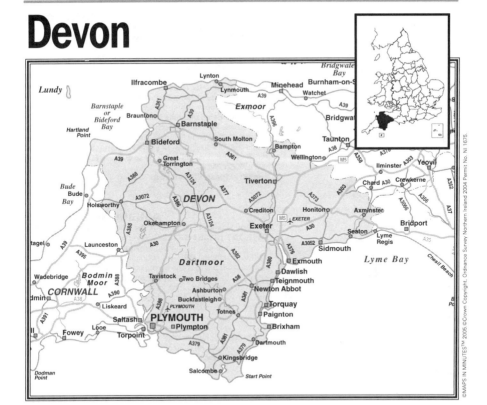

ASHBURTON

Roborough House   Tel: 01364 654614
85 East Street, Ashburton, Devon TQ9 6PA

Ideally located within easy walking distance of this popular Dartmoor town and perfect for exploring the nearby moors.
Nicky and her family offer guests a really welcoming atmosphere in their lovely Georgian town house, together with excellent breakfasts to start the day. The spacious and comfortable bedrooms are fully en suite and include bathroom toiletries, hot drink makers, colour TVs and DVD players with free films. There is easy access for the disabled and off road parking for all guests.

e-mail: roborough@onetel.com
www.roboroughhouse.co.uk

The Big Sheep
Bideford, Devon
See our **READERS' OFFER VOUCHER** for details of free or reduced rate entry

ASHBURTON

Lynda Richards, Gages Mill, Buckfastleigh Road, Ashburton TQ13 7JW (Tel & Fax: 01364 652391). Relax in the warm and friendly atmosphere of our lovely 14th century former wool mill, set in over an acre of gardens on the edge of the Dartmoor National Park. Seven delightful en suite rooms, one on the ground floor; all with tea and coffee making facilities, central heating, hairdryers, radio and alarm clocks. We have a large comfortable dining room with corner bar and granite archways leading to the cosy sittingroom with colour TV. Licensed. Ample car parking. Being one mile from the centre of Ashburton, this is an ideal base for touring South Devon or visiting Exeter, Plymouth, Dartmouth, the many National Trust properties and other places of interest. Children over 12 years welcome. Sorry no pets. Bed and Breakfast only. ETC/AA ♦♦♦♦, ETC *SILVER AWARD FOR EXCELLENCE.*
e-mail: gagesmill@aol.com

ASHBURTON (Dartmoor)

Mrs Joy Hasler, Riversmead, Newbridge, Near Ashburton TQ13 7NT (01364 631224). Riversmead, a detached country house, is situated in the picturesque River Dart valley in the Dartmoor National Park, yet is only three miles from Ashburton and the A38. Set in a one acre garden with stream and spinney, we offer quality en suite accommodation, two double and one twin room, with stunning views from all aspects. Ideally located for river walks, only two minutes from the house. There is a guests' sittingroom with TV, full central heating, tea/coffee making facilities, comfortable dining room and ample parking. A drying room is available if required. Bed and Breakfast from £26 per person per night. Restricted smoking. Children over 12. Dogs by arrangement. Open all year.
website: www.riversmead.net

ASHPRINGTON

The Durant Arms, Ashprington TQ9 7UP (01803 732240/732471; Fax: 01803 732471). Nestling amidst the verdant beauty of the Dart Valley in a picturesque and well-preserved South Hams village, this attractive inn has all the virtues of a traditional English country inn, with the comforts of the contemporary holiday-maker in mind. With many footpaths and bridleways nearby leading to the leafy shores of the River Dart, this lovely hostelry will repay a casual or even longer visit. The cuisine is worthy of special mention, with a wide range of main courses catering for all tastes, plus an interesting selection of imaginative desserts. Just three miles past the Elizabethan town of Totnes, this is a fine overnight stop and several beautifully appointed en suite bedrooms suit the purpose admirably.

AA ♦♦♦♦♦ *ROSETTE FOR FOOD.*
e-mail: info@thedurantarms.com

website: www.thedurantarms.com

BARNSTAPLE

C & M. Hartnoll, Little Bray House, Brayford, Near Barnstaple EX32 7QG (Tel & Fax: 01598 710295). Situated nine miles east of Barnstaple, Little Bray House is ideally placed for day trips to East Devon, Somerset and Cornwall, the lovely sandy surfing beaches at Saunton Sands and Woolacombe, and many places of interest both coastal and inland. Exmoor also has great charm out of season! Come and share the pace of life and fresh air straight from the open Atlantic, and be sustained by a good healthy breakfast. One twin-bedded flatlet with bathroom, one double en suite with shower. Also a cottage for four if available. B&B rate £25 pppn, £30 pppn for a one-night stopover.

Devon 143

BARNSTAPLE

Mrs V.M. Chugg, "Valley View", Guineaford, Marwood, Barnstaple EX31 4EA (01271 343458). Working farm. "Valley View" is a bungalow set in 320 acres of farmland which visitors are free to enjoy. The farm produces lamb, and is home of the Helenbrie Miniature Shetland ponies, all under 34 inches, and of different colours. It is near Marwood Hill Gardens and Arlington Court, properties renowned for their beauty, and which are open from March to December. Situated three-and-a-half miles from Barnstaple, the market town. Accommodation comprises two bedrooms each containing a double and single bed. Dining/sittingroom with colour TV and video. Bathroom/toilet. Good English Breakfast. Bed and Breakfast from £20. Children are welcomed, half-price for those under 12 years. Babysitting free of charge. Pets by arrangement. Car essential – parking. Open all year.
website: www.helenbriestud.co.uk

BARNSTAPLE

Mrs Sheelagh Darling, Lee House, Marwood, Barnstaple EX31 4DZ (01271 374345). Stone-built Elizabethan Manor House dating back to 1256, standing in its own secluded gardens and grounds with magnificent views over rolling Devon countryside. James II ceilings, an Adam fireplace, antiques and the work of resident artist add interest. Easy access to coast and moor. Family-run, friendly and relaxing atmosphere. Walking distance to local pub with excellent food. Marwood Gardens one mile. Open April to October. One double, one twin room and one four-poster room, all en suite with colour TV and tea/coffee making facilities. Bed and Breakfast from £23. No children under 12 years. Well-behaved pets welcome.

BARNSTAPLE (near)

Mrs J. Ley, West Barton, Alverdiscott, Near Barnstaple EX31 3PT (Tel & Fax: 01271 858230). Our family-run working farm of 240 acres, with a pedigree herd of suckler cows and sheep, is situated in a small rural village between Barnstaple and Torrington on the B3232. It is an ideal base for your holiday, within easy reach of Exmoor and many sandy beaches on our rugged coastline; also near RHS Rosemoor Gardens, Dartington Glass, the Tarka Trail, golf courses and many beauty spots. Comfortable accommodation with family room, twin beds, single and double rooms; private bathroom with shower; double room en suite. Guest lounge with TV and tea/coffee making facilities. Good farmhouse cooking including a variety of our own produce when available. Ample parking. Sorry, no pets. Non-smoking. B&B from £20, Evening Meal optional. Reduced rates for children under 12; weekly terms on request.

BIDEFORD

Iris and Brian Chapple, Meadow Park, Buckland Brewer, Bideford EX39 5NY (01237 451511). Offering homely accommodation and traditional farmhouse fare that will help to make a memorable stay, Meadow Park is spacious, centrally heated and provides panoramic views to the distant hills of Dartmoor and Exmoor. We can accommodate up to six guests in all ground floor, en suite rooms with tea/coffee facilities and colour TV. A full English breakfast is offered, using local produce whenever possible. Good food served at the 13th century thatched Inn within walking distance. Ideal location for visiting North Devon/Cornwall coast, RHS Rosemoor Gardens, Tarka Trail, and world famous Clovelly, with its cobbled street and harbour. Non-smoking and sorry, no pets. Off-road parking. Brochure on request. Open all year except Christmas. Bed and Breakfast from £23pppn. Reductions for weekly bookings and short winter breaks.
e-mail: iris.chapple@meadow-park.co.uk   website: www.meadow-park.co.uk

144 Devon

BIDEFORD
Sunset, Landcross, Bideford EX39 5JA (Tel & Fax: 01237 472962). 'Somewhere Special' in North Devon. A country house in quiet, peaceful location, overlooking spectacular scenery in an Area of Outstanding Natural Beauty, one and a half miles from Bideford town. Beautifully decorated and spotlessly clean, offering highly recommended quality accommodation, all en suite with colour TV and tea/coffee facilities. We have an excellent reputation, so book with confidence in our non-smoking establishment. Private parking. Resident proprietors for 35 years.
e-mail: HazelLamb@hotmail.com

BIDEFORD
The Mount, Northdown Road, Bideford EX39 3LP (01237 473748). A warm welcome awaits you at The Mount in the historic riverside town of Bideford. This small, interesting Georgian building is full of character and charm and is set in its own semi-walled garden, with a beautiful Copper Beech, making it a peaceful haven so close to the town. Within five minutes easy walking, you can be in the centre of the Old Town, with its narrow streets, quay, medieval bridge and park. The Mount is also an ideal centre for exploring the coast, countryside, towns and villages of North Devon. The quiet, restful bedrooms, (single, double, twin and family) are all en suite. Tea and coffee making facilities are available. All rooms have TV. Non-smoking. Bed and Breakfast £30 to £33 per person per night. Golfing breaks – discounted green fees.
ETC/AA♦♦♦♦

BIDEFORD (near)
Mr and Mrs C Ridd, Bakers Farm, Torrington EX38 7ES (01805 623260). Colin and June Ridd welcome you to Bakers Farm, a 16th Century farmhouse set in 250 acres of glorious Devon countryside. Both the food and accommodation is highly recommended by previous guests. Delicious meals prepared from fresh farm produce. Accommodation comprises one family, one double, one twin bedroom, with two bathrooms both having bath and shower. Tea/coffee facilities and TV in rooms. Comfortable lounge with colour TV. Fishing on the farm's private lake. Great Torrington (one mile) local amenities include indoor swimming pool, golf course, sports centre and the famous Tarka Trail for walking and cycling. Other attractions include the 1646 Civil War centre and Dartington Glass. Within easy reach of the coastline, Exmoor and Dartmoor. Full fire certificate.

BIDEFORD (near)
Graham and Liz White, Bulworthy Cottage, Stoney Cross, Alverdiscott, Near Bideford EX39 4PY (01271 858441). Once three 17th century miner's cottages, Bulworthy has been sympathetically renovated to modern standards whilst retaining many original features. Our twin and double guest rooms both offer en suite accommodation, with central heating, colour TV, and many other extras. Standing in quiet countryside, Bulworthy is within easy reach of the moors, Tarka Trail, South West Coastal Path, Rosemoor and numerous National Trust properties. We offer a choice of breakfasts and evening meals, using home grown and local produce whenever possible, with a wine list chosen to complement your meal. ETC ♦♦♦♦ *SILVER AWARD*
e-mail: bulworthy@aol.com
website: www.bulworthycottage.co.uk

Devon 145

BIDEFORD (near)

Mrs Yvonne Heard, West Titchberry Farm, Hartland Point, Near Bideford EX39 6AU (Tel & Fax: 01237 441 287). Situated on the rugged North Devon coast, West Titchberry is a traditionally run stock farm, half a mile from Hartland Point. The South West Coast Path skirts around the farm, making it an ideal base for walkers. The three guest rooms comprise an en suite family room; one double and one twin room both having wash basins. All rooms have colour TV, radio, hairdryer, tea/coffee making facilities; bathroom/toilet and separate shower room on the same floor. Outside, guests may take advantage of a sheltered walled garden and a games room for the children. Hartland village is three miles away, Clovelly six miles, Bideford and Westward Ho! 16 miles and Bude 18 miles. Bed and Breakfast from £20 to £25 per person per night. Evening meal £12. Children welcome at reduced rates for under 12s. Open all year except Christmas. Sorry, no pets.

BISHOPSTEIGNTON

Mrs Nicky Dykes, Whidborne Manor, Ashill, Bishopsteignton, Teignmouth TQ14 9PY (01626 870177). Dating back to 1450, Whidborne Manor retains an abundance of 'olde worlde' charm, yet offers attractive and spacious accommodation with modern day comforts. Situated three miles from the popular seaside town of Teignmouth, this is an ideal place from which to explore the South Devon coast and Dartmoor National Park, along with many other places of beauty and interest. Exeter and Plymouth are easily accessible via main road links/train. Accommodation consists of a twin room and two double rooms, all with en suite or private facilities, tea/coffee trays and colour TV. Children welcome. Sorry, no pets or smoking. Prices from £20 per person per night Bed and Breakfast. ETC ♦♦♦♦ SILVER AWARD.

e-mail: nicola.dykes@ntlworld.com
website: www.whidbornemanor.co.uk

See also Colour Display Advertisement

BRIXHAM

Brookside Guest House, 160 New Road, Brixham TQ5 8DA (01803 858858). Tess and Joan Harris, the resident proprietors, will be pleased to welcome you to Brookside, a small, friendly guest house situated on a level position on the main approach road into Brixham. All accommodation offers the best in comfort, with tea and coffee making facilities, remote-control colour TV and refrigerators in all rooms. There is ample off-road parking, both at the front and rear of the property. To add further to your comfort, Brookside is a no smoking establishment. After a hard day's sightseeing relax on our large outside terrace. B&B (standard) from £22pppn; B&B (en suite) from £25pppn; B&B (superior) from £30pppn. Credit cards accepted.

•••some fun days out in DEVON

Chambercombe Manor, Ilfracombe • 01271 862624 • www.chambercombemanor.co.uk
Devon Railway Centre, Bickleigh • 01884 855671 • www.devonrailwaycentre.co.uk
National Marine Aquarium, Plymouth • 01752 600301 • www.national-aquarium.co.uk
Fursdon House & Gardens, Thorverton • 01392 860860 • www.fursdon.co.uk
Babbacombe Model Village, Torquay • 01803 315315 • www.babbacombemodelvillage.co.uk
Paignton Zoo, Paignton • 01803 697500 • www.paigntonzoo.org.uk
Quince Honey Farm, South Molton • 01769 572501 • www.quincehoney.co.uk
Watermouth Castle, Ilfracombe • 01271 867467 • www.watermouthcastle.com

BRIXHAM

Devon • The English Riviera
WOODLANDS GUEST HOUSE
Parkham Road, Brixham, South Devon TQ5 9BU

Overlooking the beautiful Brixham Harbour

Victorian House with large car park at rear and unrestricted on-road parking to the front. All bedrooms en suite, with colour TV, tea/coffee making facilities, mini fridges etc. Four-Poster bedroom with panoramic views over Brixham Harbour and Torbay. Just a short walk away from the picturesque harbour, ancient fishing port with its quaint streets full of varied shops, pubs and restaurants. Ideal holiday base from which to explore the glorious South-West, romantic Dartmoor, boat trips, Paignton and Dartmouth Steam Railway.

Walkers can explore the marvellous Devon countryside. Fishing trips available from the harbour. Bed and Breakfast from £20pppn.
We hope to see you soon and make your stay a memorable one.

Phone 01803 852040, Paul and Rita Pope for free colour brochure and details, or fax 01803 850011
www.woodlandsdevon.co.uk • e-mail: woodlandsbrixham@btinternet.com

See also Colour Advertisement

CHAGFORD
Mr I Satow, Week Brook, Chagford TQ13 8JQ (01647 433345). Escape the tumult of the world and spend some time at Week Brook, a lovely ancient thatched house set in a large garden. It is one mile from the centre of the highly regarded, unspoilt little town of Chagford on the edge of Dartmoor. It is a good centre from which to explore Devon's many places of interest and the beautiful countryside. Pets welcome. Bed and Breakfast up to £18.00.

CHUDLEIGH
Jill Shears, Glen Cottage, Rock Road, Chudleigh TQ13 0JJ (01626 852209). 17th century thatched cottage idyllically set in secluded garden, with stream surrounded by woods. Adjoining a beauty spot with rocks, caves and waterfall. A haven for wildlife and birds; kingfishers and buzzards are a common sight. Outdoor swimming pool. Central for touring the moors or sea. Bed and Breakfast from £20. Tea/coffee all rooms.

Devon 147

COLEBROOKE

Pearl Hockridge, The Oyster, Colebrooke, Crediton EX17 5JQ (01363 84576). The Oyster is a modern bungalow in the pretty, peaceful village of Colebrooke in the heart of Mid Devon. There is a spacious garden for children to play around or sit on the patio. Comfortable accommodation with tea/coffee making facilities, with TV in bedroom and lounge. Bedrooms en suite or with private bathroom - two double and one twin. Walking distance to the New Inn, Coleford, a lovely 13th century free house. Dartmoor and Exmoor are only a short drive away. Central heating. Open all year. Ample parking. Terms from £20 per person for Bed and Breakfast. Children and pets welcome. Smoking accepted. To find us take the Barnstaple road (A377)out of Crediton, turn left after one-and-a-half miles at sign for Colebrooke and Coleford. In Coleford village turn left at the crossroads, then in Colebrooke village take the left hand turning before the church, the Oyster is the second on the right.

COLYTON

Mrs Norma Rich, Sunnyacre, Rockerhayne Farm, Northleigh, Colyton EX24 6DA (01404 871422). Working farm, join in. A warm and friendly welcome awaits you. Come and enjoy a relaxing holiday in our bungalow on our working farm, which is set in an Area of Outstanding Natural Beauty amongst the rolling hills of East Devon. Enjoy the views whilst dining and relaxing. Local attractions include the fishing village of Beer and picturesque Branscombe. If you enjoy walking, there are plenty of easily accessible country walks and we are close to the coastal footpaths. There is a full English Breakfast. Fresh and mainly homegrown produce is used to make excellent and varied Evening Meals. Sweets are all homemade. Early morning tea, evening drinks. Three bedrooms with washbasin, separate WC. TV in lounge, sun room. Children welcome. Please enquire for reasonable rates.

CREDITON

Mrs M Reed, Hayne Farm, Cheriton Fitzpaine, Crediton EX17 4HR (01363 866392). Guests are welcome to our 17th century working beef and sheep farm, situated between Cadeleigh and Cheriton Fitzpaine. Exeter nine miles, Tiverton eight miles. South and North coast, Exmoor and Dartmoor within easy reach. Three local pubs nearby. Good farm fayre. Fishing lake; summer house overlooking duck pond. Bed and Breakfast from £22, reduction for children.

CROYDE

Crowborough B&B, Georgeham, Braunton EX33 1JZ (01271 891005). OPEN ALL YEAR. Peaceful farmhouse only two miles from Croyde. Ideal location close to the sandy beaches of Croyde, Putsborough, Woolacombe, Saunton, the South West Coastal Path, Braunton Burrows Biosphere Reserve and Saunton Championship golf course. Five minutes' walk to the village and its two friendly Inns. Exmoor National Park is only 45 minutes' drive and other places of interest include: Lundy Island; Arlington Court (National Trust); Clovelly; RHS Rosemoor Gardens, etc. Accommodation consists of two double and one twin rooms; breakfast/sitting room with TV, tea/coffee facilities, and wood burner in winter. Ideal for a family or group. Bed and Breakfast from £25 pppn. For more information please telephone **Audrey Isaac**. website: www.crowboroughfarm.co.uk

---

The FHG Directory of Website Addresses
on pages 339-370 is a useful quick reference guide for holiday accommodation with e-mail and/or website details

148 Devon

DAWLISH
Mrs Henley, Ocean's Guest House, 9 Marine Parade, Dawlish EX7 9DJ (01626 888139). Sea front location, enjoy the sea views from our balcony. All rooms en suite with tea/coffee facilities and colour TV. Ground floor rooms available with wheelchair access for people with walking disabilities. Partially non-smoking. Bed and Breakfast from £20 per person per night. Children under 14 years old sharing, £14 per night (minimum cost of £40 per room with one parent and one child). 10% discount for Senior Citizens in October. No smoking.

DUNSFORD
The Royal Oak Inn, Dunsford, Near Exeter EX6 7DA (01647 252256). Enjoy a friendly welcome in our traditional Country Pub in the picturesque thatched village of Dunsford. Quiet en suite bedrooms are available in the tastefully converted cob barn. An ideal base for touring Dartmoor, Exeter and the coast, and the beautiful Teign Valley. Real ale and home-made meals are served. Well behaved children and dogs are welcome. The accommodation is suitable for disabled guests and non-smokers. Please ring **Mark or Judy Harrison** for further details. *CAMRA, GOOD PUB GUIDE.*

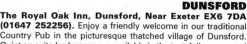

See also Colour Display Advertisement

EXETER
Mrs Dudley, Culm Vale Guest House, Stoke Canon, Exeter EX5 4EG (Tel & Fax: 01392 841615). A fine old country house of great charm and character, giving the best of both worlds as we are only three miles to the north of the Cathedral city of Exeter, with its antique shops, yet situated in the heart of Devon's beautiful countryside on the edge of the pretty village of Stoke Canon. An ideal touring centre. Our spacious comfortable Bed and Breakfast accommodation includes full English breakfast, colour TV, tea/coffee facilities, washbasin and razor point in both rooms. Full central heating. Ample free parking. Bed and Breakfast £20 to £27.50 pppn according to room and season. Credit cards accepted. ETC ♦♦♦, **AA** *THREE RED DIAMONDS.*
e-mail: culmvale@hotmail.com
website: www.SmoothHound.co.uk/hotels/culm-vale.html

EXETER
Mrs Gillian Howard, Ebford Court, Ebford, Exeter EX3 0RA (01392 875353; Fax: 01392 876776). 15th century thatched farmhouse set in quiet surroundings yet only five minutes from Junction 30, M5. The house stands in pleasant gardens and is one mile from the attractive Exe Estuary. The coast and moors are a short drive away and it is an ideal centre for touring and birdwatching. The two double bedrooms have washbasins and tea/coffee facilities; sitting/diningroom with colour TV. Non-smoking accommodation. Open all year. Ample parking. Bed and Breakfast from £22 per night; £140 weekly.
e-mail: beegeehoward@aol.com

EXMOOR
Mr and Mrs P. Carr, Greenhills Farm, Yeo Mill, West Anstey, South Molton EX36 3NU (01398 341300; mobile: 07974 806099). A warm friendly atmosphere awaits you at Greenhills. Our charming farmhouse on a working farm, situated in the southern foothills of Exmoor, offers an exceptionally high standard of accommodation. Delicious food using home-grown and local produce. Warm, comfortable private suite of rooms, one twin and one double en suite. Separate dining room and lounge, both with beams, inglenooks and log fires. On the Two Moors Way, it's a country-lovers' paradise. Bed and Breakfast £24. Evening Meal £10. ETC ♦♦♦♦ *SILVER AWARD*

Devon 149

See also Colour Display Advertisement

EXMOUTH
Devoncourt Hotel, Douglas Avenue, Exmouth EX8 2EX (01395 272277; Fax: 01395 269315). Standing in four acres of mature subtropical gardens, overlooking two miles of sandy beach, yet within easy reach of Dartmoor and Exeter, Devoncourt provides an ideal base for a family holiday. Single, double and family suites, all en suite, well furnished and well equipped; attractive lounge bar and restaurant. Recreational facilities include indoor and outdoor heated pools, sauna, steam room, spa and solarium; snooker room; putting, tennis and croquet; golf, sea fishing and horse riding nearby. Bed and Breakfast from £75 single, £115 double; self-catering /room only from £60 single, £90 double. Weekly rates available.

EXMOUTH
Pound House, Pound Lane, Exmouth EX8 4NP (01395 222684). Large Georgian house. All rooms are tastefully furnished and decorated, with private bathroom, colour TV, tea/coffee making facilities. Beautiful sandy beaches and natural beauty of Woodbury Common five minutes by car. Attractions in area include golf, riding, hiking, swimming, National Trust and Heritage properties, Dartmoor and Exmoor National Parks and coastal walks, etc. Large traditional English breakfast. Visitors welcome to use garden. Children and pets welcome. Ample private parking. Details on request.

HARTLAND
Mrs A. Heard, Greenlake Farm, Hartland, Bideford EX39 6DN (01237 441251). Greenlake is a mixed farm set in approximately 250 acres of unspoilt countryside, just two miles from Hartland on the North Devon coast. While the farmhouse retains its original character with features such as oak beams in some of the rooms, it also offers every facility for your comfort. Some accommodation offers en suite facilities, while all rooms have fitted carpets, TV and tea/coffee equipment. There is a television lounge and a separate dining room. Guests are welcome to watch the farm work in progress. Ideally situated for touring North Devon and North Cornwall; the popular sandy beaches of Bude and Westward Ho! are only a 30 minute drive away, as are the market towns of Bideford and Holsworthy.

 Crealy Adventure Park
Exeter, Devon
See our **READERS' OFFER VOUCHER** for details of free or reduced rate entry

---

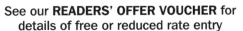

FHG *Devonshire Collection of Period Costume*
Totnes, Devon
See our **READERS' OFFER VOUCHER** for details of free or reduced rate entry

Devonshire Collection of Period Costume

150 Devon

See also Colour Display Advertisement

HONITON
Mrs June Tucker, Yard Farm, Upottery, Honiton EX14 9QP (01404 861680). A most attractively situated working farm. The house is a very old traditional Devon farmhouse located just three miles east of Honiton and enjoying a superb outlook across the Otter Valley. Enjoy a stroll down by the River Otter which runs through the farmland. Try a spot of trout fishing. Children will love to make friends with our two horses. Lovely seaside resorts 12 miles, swimming pool, adventure park and garden near by. Traditional English breakfast, colour TV, washbasin, heating, tea/coffee facilities in all rooms. Bed and Breakfast £17.50 to £20. Reductions for children.

See also Colour Display Advertisement

ILFRACOMBE
Geoff and Sharon Burkinshaw, Wentworth House, 2 Belmont Road, Ilfracombe EX34 8DR (Tel & Fax: 01271 863048). Wentworth House, a friendly family-run private hotel built as a gentleman's residence in 1857, standing in lovely gardens only a stone's throw from the town and minutes from the sea, harbour and Torrs Walks. En suite rooms with colour TV and tea/coffee making facilities. Family rooms sleeping up to four persons. Home-cooked food with packed lunches on request. Spacious bar/lounge. Secure storage for bicycles etc. Private parking in grounds. Open all year. Bed & Breakfast from £19.50. Bed, Breakfast and Evening Meal from £28. Discounted rates for weekly bookings. Stay a few days or a week, we will make your visit a pleasant one.
e-mail: wentworthhouse@tiscali.co.uk

IVYBRIDGE
Mrs P. Stephens, Venn Farm, Ugborough, Ivybridge PL21 0PE (01364 73240). Working farm. Enjoy a rural retreat at Venn, yet only three miles from dual carriageway. We are 20 minutes from beaches and South Dartmoor is visible from the farm. We have two family bedrooms, and a separate garden cottage which has two twin ground floor bedrooms overlooking a large pond. We also have self-catering for eight, four and two persons, again with ground floor bedrooms. Brochure on request from: **Pat Stephens (01364 73240). ETC ♦♦♦ (★★★★** SELF-CATERING), NATIONAL ACCESSIBLE SCHEME LEVEL 2.
website: www.SmoothHound.co.uk/hotels/vennfarm

KINGSBRIDGE
Mrs Angela Foale, Higher Kellaton Farm, Kellaton, Kingsbridge TQ7 2ES (Tel & Fax: 01548 511514). Working farm. Smell the fresh sea air and enjoy the delicious Aga-cooked breakfast in the comfort of this lovely old farmhouse. Nestled in a valley, our farm with friendly animals welcomes you. Spacious, well-furnished rooms, en suite, colour TVs, tea/coffee making facilities, own lounge, central heating and log fires. Flexible meal times. Attractive walled garden. Safe car parking. Situated between Kingsbridge and Dartmouth. Visit Salcombe by ferry. One-and-a-half miles to the lost village of Hallsands and Lannacombe Beach. Beautiful, peaceful, unspoilt coastline with many sandy beaches, paths, wild flowers and wildlife. Ramblers' haven. Good pubs and wet-weather family attractions. Open Easter to October. Non-smoking. Bed and Breakfast from £20. **ETC ♦♦♦**
e-mail: higherkellatonfarm@agriplus.net   website: www.welcome.to/higherkellaton

Devon 151

KINGSBRIDGE

Mrs B. Kelly, Blackwell Park, Loddiswell, Kingsbridge TQ7 4EA (01548 821230). Bed and Breakfast and optional Evening Meal is offered at Blackwell Park, a 17th century farmhouse situated five miles from Kingsbridge. Seven bedrooms, some en suite, and all with washbasins and tea-making facilities. Games room; large garden, also adjoining 54 acres of woodland/nature reserve. Ample food with a choice of menu. CHILDREN AND PETS ESPECIALLY WELCOME; babysitting, DOGSITTING. Pets welcome FREE of charge. Dartmoor, Plymouth, Torbay, Dartmouth and many beaches lie within easy reach.

KINGSBRIDGE

Anne Rossiter, Burton Farm, Galmpton, Kingsbridge TQ7 3EY (01548 561210). Working farm in South Huish Valley, one mile from the fishing village of Hope Cove, three miles from famous sailing haunt of Salcombe. Walking, beaches, sailing, windsurfing, bathing, diving, fishing, horse-riding – facilities for all in this area. We have a dairy herd and two flocks of pedigree sheep. Guests are welcome to take part in farm activities when appropriate. Traditional farm house cooking and home produce. Country restaurant on site serving freshly cooked meals using local produce. Lunches, cream teas, dinner, children's meals. Access to rooms at all times. Tea/ coffee making facilities and TV in rooms, all of which are en suite. Games room. Non-smoking. Open all year, except Christmas. Warm welcome assured. Self-catering cottages also available. Dogs by arrangement. Details and terms on request. Bed and Breakfast from £30 to £42.50 per person. **ETC** ♦♦♦♦ *SILVER AWARD.*
e-mail: anne@burtonfarm.co.uk   **website: www.burtonfarm.co.uk**

LYDFORD

The Castle Inn Hotel & Restaurant, Lydford, Okehampton EX20 4BH (01822 820241; Fax: 01822 820454). One of the finest traditional wayside inns in the West Country, this romantic Elizabethan, family-run hotel simply oozes character. Featured in Conan Doyle's 'The Hound of the Baskervilles', it nestles on the western slopes of Dartmoor, offering first-class food in a bar and restaurant with slate floors, bowed ceilings, low, lamp-lit beams and fascinating antiques; dining by candlelight from imaginative à la carte menus is a memorable experience. Close by is Lydford Castle, built in 1195, and picturesque Lydford Gorge. Guest rooms, decorated in individual style, are beautifully furnished and equipped. This is a wonderful place to shake off the cobwebs of urban existence and appreciate the really worthwhile things of life.
e-mail: info@castleinnlydford.co.uk
website: www.castleinnlydford.co.uk

LYNMOUTH

Tricia and Alan Francis, Glenville House, 2 Tors Road, Lynmouth EX35 6ET (01598 752202). Idyllic riverside setting for our delightful Victorian house built in local stone, full of character and lovingly refurbished, at the entrance to the Watersmeet Valley. Award-winning garden. Picturesque village, enchanting harbour and unique water-powered cliff railway nestled amidst wooded valleys. Beautiful area where Exmoor meets the sea. Breathtaking scenery, riverside, woodland and magnificent coastal walks with spectacular views to the heather-clad moorland. Peaceful, tranquil, romantic - a very special place. Tastefully decorated bedrooms, most with pretty en suite facilities. Elegant lounge overlooking river. Enjoy a four-course breakfast in our attractive dining room. Non-smoking. Licensed. Bed and Breakfast from £27 per person per night. **AA** ♦♦♦♦
e-mail: tricia@glenvillelynmouth.co.uk   **website: www.glenvillelynmouth.co.uk**

152 Devon

See also Colour Display Advertisement

LYNTON
Cliff Bench, Valley House, Lynbridge Road, Lynton EX35 6BD (01598 752285). A secluded Victorian country house, five minutes' walk from Lynton. Set into the rock face high above the West Lyn River, with magnificent views of the National Trust Woodland and sea. All rooms are stylishly decorated, en suite with tea/coffee making facilities, hairdryer, colour TV and beautiful views. Interesting breakfast menu; scrumptious evening meals most days; packed lunches available. Relax in the bar/lounge, the new conservatory room or the front terrace. A walkers' paradise, with some of the best horse riding in the country; also golf and surfing. Rates from £27.50 pppn. **RAC** ♦♦♦♦
e-mail: info@valley-house.co.uk
website: www.valley-house.co.uk

LYNTON
Longmead House, Longmead, Lynton EX35 6DQ (01598 752523) One of Lynton's best kept secrets, with a Silver Award for standards of comfort, hospitality and food. Longmead is a small, friendly, family-run hotel providing old-fashioned hospitality and attention to detail in a relaxed and informal atmosphere, with well equipped, en suite rooms. This delightful house is quietly situated in beautiful surroundings towards the Valley of Rocks, yet close to the village centre, with ample car parking. Imaginative evening menu. Licensed. Bed and Breakfast from £23 to £27 pppn. Special short break terms. Details from **Jacqueline and Nigel Poole.** No smoking or pets. **ETC** ♦♦♦♦ *SILVER AWARD,* **AA** ♦♦♦♦
e-mail: info@longmeadhouse.co.uk
website: www.longmeadhouse.co.uk

LYNTON
Anne and Dave Wilford, Gable Lodge, 35 Lee Road, Lynton EX35 6BS (Tel & Fax: 01598 752367). Gable Lodge is a non-smoking family-run guest house offering family friendly Bed and Breakfast accommodation (evening meals can be arranged). Gable Lodge is situated in a level part of Lynton, with views over Countisbury Hill, the East Lyn Valley and Exmoor National Park. All our rooms have en suite facilities and central heating, with clock radio, TV, tea/coffee making facilities and hairdryer. An ideal spot for a relaxing holiday. Sorry, but we are unable to accept pets other than Assistance Dogs. All meals freshly prepared using local produce where possible. Private car park. B&B from £19. Please contact us for a brochure.
website: www.gablelodgelynton.co.uk

LYNTON
Croft House, Lydiate Lane, Lynton EX35 6HE (01598 752391). A small and charming licensed bed and breakfast establishment where you will be able to relax. A beautiful Listed building with much style and character. Situated in the heart of the old town of Lynton on Devon's dramatic coastline within Exmoor National Park. Relax in our sumptuous sitting room, enjoy our unique secluded walled garden - a little haven in Devon. A choice of comfortable character en suite bedrooms including standard or deluxe twin/doubles to a delightful four-poster with own sitting room. B&B from £27 to £38 per person per night. Special rates for group bookings and discounts for stays of three and six nights. Please phone to book or request a brochure.
e-mail: relax@crofthotel.uk.com
website: www.smoothhound.co.uk/hotels/crofthou.html

Devon 153

LYNTON

The Sandrock Hotel & Bar, Longmead, Lynton EX35 6DH (01598 753307). A fine example of Edwardian architecture, retaining its original character. Located in a sunny, south-facing tranquil setting on the village edge close to the Valley of Rocks and the South West Coastal Path. Ideal for walkers and hikers or for those who just want to admire the beautiful scenery. Nine fully equipped large, en suite double/twin/family bedrooms. Also singles with private facilities. The Sandrock fully licensed bar and restaurant is also open to non-residents. There is a large car park for the use of residents and for bar/restaurant customers. This non-smoking hotel is open all year. Bed and Breakfast £28 to £30pppn. Half board terms available. See website for details. ETC ◆◆◆

e-mail: enquiries@sandrockhotel.co.uk
website: www.sandrockhotel.co.uk

LYNTON

Mark and Christine Channing, Alford House Hotel, Alford Terrace, Lynton EX35 6AT (Tel & Fax: 01598 752359). Mark and Christine extend a warm welcome to you at Alford House, a beautiful Georgian-style Grade II Listed private hotel, nestling on the slopes of Lynton, with stunning views of the sea and coastline. We have individually decorated and furnished en suite rooms, elegant four-posters, all with colour TV and beverage making facilities. We serve candlelight dinners cooked from freshly prepared produce, with menu choice. Relax in our licensed bar, or quiet TV lounge with beautiful coastal views. Five minutes' walk to Lynton and the cliff railway to Lynmouth. You will enjoy a peaceful and relaxed holiday at Alford House, good food on the table and a genuine warm welcome, whatever the weather!! B&B from £23 to £30 per person. **AA** ◆◆◆◆

e-mail: enquiries@alfordhouse.co.uk
website: www.alfordhouse.co.uk

LYNTON

Pine Lodge, Lynway, Lynton EX35 6AX (01598 753230). A sunny, sheltered, traffic-free location set in landscaped gardens with uninterrupted views of the Watersmeet Estate. A short stroll along the Lynway takes you to Lynton village where you can ride the famous Cliff Railway to Lynmouth. We have spacious en suite rooms and comfortable lounge. All rooms with TV, hairdryer, hospitality tray and central heating. Ground floor bedrooms, level private car park. Children over 12 welcome. Non-smoking. Licensed. Bed and Breakfast from £24 to £27. **ETC** ◆◆◆◆ *SILVER AWARD*, **AA** *FOUR RED DIAMOND AWARD 2003-2006*.
e-mail: info@pinelodgelynton.co.uk
website: www.pinelodgelynton.co.uk

LYNTON (near)

Moorlands, Woody Bay, Parracombe EX31 4RA (01598 763224). Moorlands, formerly the Woody Bay Station Hotel, is a family run establishment in a most beautiful part of North Devon, surrounded by Exmoor countryside and within two miles of the spectacular coastline. Very comfortable and quite single, double or family suite accommodation, all en suite with bath or shower, colour TV and beverage making facilities. Moorlands has a licensed dining room and residents' lounge with open fire, a private outdoor swimming pool, all set in six acres of gardens. Open all year except Christmas. A perfect retreat for the country lover to relax in. Dinner, Bed and Breakfast from £42, three nights Dinner, Bed & Breakfast £126 per person. Bed & Breakfast from £30 per person. Some ground floor rooms and self catering apartments available. Please see our website for special offers.
website: www.moorlandshotel.co.uk

MORETONHAMPSTEAD

Mrs T. M. Merchant, Great Sloncombe Farm, Moretonhampstead TQ13 8QF (01647 440595). Working farm. Share the magic of Dartmoor all year round while staying in our lovely 13th century farmhouse full of interesting historical features. A working mixed farm set amongst peaceful meadows and woodland abundant in wild flowers and animals, including badgers, foxes, deer and buzzards. A welcoming and informal place to relax and explore the moors and Devon countryside. Comfortable double and twin rooms with en suite facilities, TV, central heating and coffee/tea making facilities. Delicious Devonshire breakfasts with new baked bread. Open all year. No smoking. ETC ◆◆◆◆ *SILVER AWARD*, AA ◆◆◆◆, *FARM STAY UK MEMBER*.
e-mail: hmerchant@sloncombe.freeserve.co.uk
website: www.greatsloncombefarm.co.uk

NEWTON ABBOT

Mrs L. Westcott, Chipley Farm, Bickington, Newton Abbot TQ12 6JW (01626 821486). Near sandy beaches, rugged Dartmoor, historic towns, pretty villages and numerous tourist attractions, this delightful modern farmhouse, with its large gardens and wonderful views, nestles into the southern slope of a beautiful Devon valley. Louisa, an artist, and Fred, a farmer, have been awarded a major hospitality award by the AA for their friendly welcome and relaxed family atmosphere as well as for their delicious breakfasts, farmhouse suppers and attention to detail. Accommodation consists of one double, one twin and one family room (the latter being en suite with four-poster bed and sliding doors opening onto a private garden area). No smoking please. Bed and Breakfast from £27.50; Dinner £17.50. Brochure available. AA ◆◆◆◆
e-mail: louisa@chipleyfarmholidays.co.uk
website: www.chipleyfarmholidays.co.uk

NORTH TAWTON

Stephen and Elizabeth Parker, Kayden House Hotel, High Street, North Tawton EX20 2HF (01837 82242). A character building in the heart of an historic market town. Located in the centre of Devon, we are ideally situated for exploring the real Devon. Easy reach of South Devon or North Cornwall coasts. We offer a comfortable, relaxing lounge, and a bar and restaurant open to non-residents. Bar meals or à la carte menu available to suit all palates. Bedrooms are en suite and offer tea/coffee making facilities and colour TV. Family-run, Stephen and Elizabeth look forward to welcoming you and hope your stay with us will be a memorable one.
e-mail: Kaydenhouse@fsmail.net
website: www.parkerholidays.co.uk

See also Colour Display Advertisement

OKEHAMPTON

Higher Cadham Farm, Jacobstowe, Okehampton EX20 3RB (01837 851647). Just off the A3072, five miles from Dartmoor, this 16th century farmhouse with barn conversions offers a total of twelve rooms, all en suite, family suites available. There is a non-smoking lounge with TV, games and books, to meet friends or to relax in, as well as a separate bar with a residential licence. You are assured of plenty of hearty Devonshire food and a warm welcome. Babies and well-behaved dogs are welcome by arrangement. We have farm walks, ponies, goats, rabbits, plus a working sheep flock and suckler cow herd. Walkers and cyclists on the Tarka Trail are catered for, with cycle sheds and packed lunches etc. B&B from £27.50, Dinner from £12.50. AA ◆◆◆◆
website: www.highercadham.co.uk

Devon 155

See also Colour Display Advertisement

OTTERY ST MARY
Mrs Forth, Fluxton Farm, Ottery St Mary EX11 1RJ (01404 812818) Cat lovers' paradise in charming 16th century farmhouse set in beautiful Otter Valley with two acre gardens including stream and pond. Only four miles from beach at Sidmouth. Central heating. All rooms en suite. Dogs welcome free of charge. Lovely touring and walking country. Terms: Bed and Breakfast from £25 per person per day. AA ◆◆
website: www.fluxtonfarm.co.uk

PAIGNTON
Steve and Freda Bamford Dwane, The No Smoking Clifton Hotel Paignton, 9-10 Kernou Road, Paignton TQ4 6BA (Tel & Fax: 01803 556545). A licensed, "green" home from home in the heart of the English Riviera. Ideal level location just off the sea front and close to shops and stations. On the SW Coastal Path. All rooms en suite with TV and beverages. Superb evening meals available using mostly organic produce - special diets catered for. Good public transport system for exploring locally and further afield - Exeter, Plymouth, Dartmoor, etc. Open Easter to October. From £26 per person Bed and Breakfast.
e-mail: b&b@cliftonhotelpaignton.co.uk
website: www.cliftonhotelpaignton.co.uk

PLYMOUTH
Mayflower Guest House, 209 Citadel Road East, The Hoe, Plymouth PL1 2JF (01752 667496; Fax: 01752 202727). Your hosts, Mary and Dave, welcome you to this small, family-run guest house, joint winner of 2004 Plymouth Guest Houses in Bloom. The location is very central, with the historic Barbican and the famous Plymouth Hoe, where Sir Francis Drake played bowls, close by. A 10-minute stroll will take you to the heart of the city where you will find a traffic-free shopping centre. ETC ◆◆◆
e-mail: info@mayflowerguesthouse.co.uk
website: www.mayflowerguesthouse.co.uk

PLYMOUTH
Cranbourne Hotel, 278/282 Citadel Road, The Hoe, Plymouth PL1 2PZ (01752 263858/661400/224646; Fax: 01752 263858). The Cranbourne Hotel is situated just 200 yards from the Hoe Promenade, and a few minutes' walk from train, ferry and bus links. All bedrooms are beautifully decorated, heated, with colour TV and tea/coffee facilities. Keys for access at all times. Licensed Bar. Pets by prior arrangement (no charge). Large secure car park. Under the personal supervision of The Williams Family.
AA/RAC ◆◆◆◆
e-mail: cran.hotel@virgin.net
website: www.cranbournehotel.co.uk

SEATON
Tony and Jane Hill, Beaumont, Castle Hill, Seaton EX12 2QW (01297 20832). Spacious and gracious Victorian, seafront guesthouse in a quiet East Devon town on England's only World Heritage coastline. Shopping, restaurants and leisure facilities nearby. Unrivalled views over Lyme Bay and Beer Cliffs. Half-mile promenade just yards away. All five rooms en suite with TV, tea and coffee making facilities. Parking available. Bed and Breakfast from £27 per person per night. Special weekly rate. A warm welcome is assured. ETC/AA ◆◆◆◆
e-mail: tony@lymebay.demon.co.uk
website: www.s-h-systems.co.uk/hotels/beaumon1.html

156 Devon

SHALDON
Glenside House, Ringmore Road, Shaldon TQ14 0EP (01626 872448). Built originally as a private residence in 1820 and in use more recently as a private school, Glenside now offers seven charming en suite rooms, two with their own lounges, and all with armchairs, TV and beverage trays. Being situated on the southern bank of the Teign estuary, it is an easy level riverside walk into the heart of the village with its numerous pubs, restaurants and tearooms, some by the beach. We have a sunny garden; car park. Dogs welcome; children over eight years. No smoking. B&B from £26. Proprietors **Keith and Tricia Underwood.** ETC ◆◆◆
e-mail: glensidehouse@amserve.com
website: www.smoothhound.co.uk/hotels/glensideho.html

See also Colour Display Advertisement

SIDMOUTH
Mrs Elizabeth Tancock, Lower Pinn Farm, Peak Hill, Sidmouth EX10 0NN (01395 513733). Working farm. 19th century built farmhouse on the World Heritage Jurassic Coast, two miles west of the unspoilt coastal resort of Sidmouth and one mile to the east of the pretty village of Otterton. Ideally situated for visiting many places and walking with access to coastal path. Comfortable centrally heated en suite rooms with colour television and hot drink making facilities. Guests have their own keys and may return at all times throughout the day. Good hearty breakfast served in the dining room. Ample off-road parking. Children and pets welcome. Lower Pinn is a no smoking establishment. Open all year. Bed and Breakfast from £24 to £28. ETC ◆◆◆◆
e-mail: liz@lowerpinnfarm.co.uk
website: www.lowerpinnfarm.co.uk

SOUTH MOLTON
Mrs J.M. Bray, West Bowden Farm, Knowstone, Near South Molton EX36 4RP (01398 341224). West Bowden is a working farm, mainly beef and sheep. It is situated just north of the A361 about a mile from Knowstone village which has a thatched pub. The house, which is thatched and has inglenook fireplaces, is thought to date from the 17th century. It is spacious and comfortable and has a lounge with colour TV and a separate dining room. Accommodation comprises five en suite bedrooms and others with washbasins; all have tea-making facilities. Guests receive hospitality in the real Devon tradition, plus good home cooking, fresh vegetables and clotted cream. Pets welcome. B & B from £25, evening meal extra. ETC ◆◆◆

SOUTH MOLTON (near)
Hazel Milton, Partridge Arms Farm, Yeo Mill, West Anstey, Near South Molton EX36 3NU (01398 341217; Fax: 01398 341569). Now a working farm of over 200 acres, four miles west of Dulverton, "Partridge Arms Farm" was once a coaching inn and has been in the same family since 1906. Genuine hospitality and traditional farmhouse fare await you. Comfortable accommodation in double, twin and single rooms, some of which have en suite facilities. There is also an original four-poster bedroom. Children welcome. Animals by arrangement. Residential licence. Open all year. Fishing and riding available nearby. Bed and Breakfast from £22 to £27; Evening Meal from £11. *FARM HOLIDAY GUIDE DIPLOMA WINNER.*
e-mail: bangermilton@hotmail.com

FREE or REDUCED RATE entry to Holiday Visits and Attractions

– see our READERS' OFFER VOUCHERS on pages 53-90

Devon 157

TIVERTON

Mrs L. Arnold, The Mill, Lower Washfield, Tiverton EX16 9PD (01884 255297). A warm welcome awaits you at our converted mill, beautifully situated on the banks of the picturesque River Exe. Close to the National Trust's Knightshayes Court and on the route of the Exe Valley Way. Easy access to both the north and south coasts, Exmoor and Dartmoor. Only two miles from Tiverton. Relaxing and friendly atmosphere with delicious farmhouse fare. En suite bedrooms with TV and tea/coffee making facilities. Bed and Breakfast from £26.
e-mail: arnold5@washfield.freeserve.co.uk
website: www.washfield.freeserve.co.uk

See also Colour Display Advertisement

TORQUAY

Heathcliff House Hotel, 16 Newton Road, Torquay TQ2 5BZ (01803 211580). This former vicarage is now a superbly appointed, family-run hotel equipped for today yet retaining its Victorian charm. All the bedrooms have full en suite facilities, colour TV and drink making facilities. The elegant licensed bar boasts an extensive menu and unlike many hotels, the car park has sufficient space to accommodate all vehicles to eliminate roadside parking. Torquay's main beach, high street shops, entertainment and restaurants are all nearby and with full English breakfast included it is easy to see why guests return time after time. Tariff for B&B ranges between £21 and £32 pppn. Family rooms available. So, be it main holiday, touring or business, make the Heathcliff your first choice. **ETC ♦♦♦♦**
e-mail: heathcliffhouse@btconnect.com   website: www.heathcliffhousehotel.co.uk

See also Colour Display Advertisement

TORQUAY

Aveland Hotel, Aveland Road, Babbacombe, Torquay TQ1 3PT (01803 326622). A family-run licensed non-smoking hotel, in a quiet level location near Cary Park and Babbacombe Downs. Close to beaches and South West Coastal Path. Situated within easy reach of harbour and town, the ideal base for many attractions in the area. All rooms en suite. Full central heating. Car park; gardens. Children welcome. Rates from £25 to £30 per person per night B&B, evening meal optional. All major debit and credit cards accepted. Sign Language OCSL stage one.
AA ♦♦♦♦, *WELCOME HOST AND COMMITMENT TO QUALITY AWARDS.*
e-mail: avelandhotel@aol.com
website: www.avelandhotel.co.uk

See also Colour Display Advertisement

TORQUAY

Fairmount House Hotel, Herbert Road, Chelston, Torquay TQ2 6RW (01803 605446). Enjoy a taste of somewhere special in the tranquillity, warmth and informal atmosphere of our small hotel of character. Set above the picturesque Cockington Valley, Fairmount House, with its mature gardens and sun-filled terraces, is a haven for the discerning visitor seeking a peaceful setting for their holiday or short break. All our bedrooms are tastefully furnished, clean and comfortable, with en suite bathroom or shower, remote-control TV, tea and coffee making facilities. Relax with a drink in our conservatory bar, or choose from an extensive menu in our fully licensed restaurant. Bed and Breakfast from £24.
ETC ♦♦♦♦, *SILVER AWARD.*
e-mail: stay@fairmounthousehotel.co.uk
website: www.fairmounthousehotel.co.uk

A useful index of towns/counties appears on pages 393-398

See also Colour Display Advertisement

TORQUAY

David and Pam Skelly, Glenorleigh Hotel, 26 Cleveland Road, Torquay TQ2 5BE (01803 292135; Fax: 01803 213717). Situated in a quiet residential area, Glenorleigh is 10 minutes' walk from both the sea front and the town centre. Delightful en suite rooms, with your comfort in mind. Good home cooking, both English and Continental, plenty of choice, with vegetarian options available daily. Bar leading onto terrace overlooking Mediterranean-style garden with feature palms and heated swimming pool. Discounts for children and Senior Citizens. Featured on BBC Holiday programme. Brochures and menus available on request. B&B £30-£40; Dinner £14. **AA** ◆◆◆◆
e-mail: glenorleighhotel@btinternet.com
website: www.glenorleigh.co.uk

TORQUAY

Dave & Kim Heaslewood, Sea Point Hotel, Old Torwood Road, Torquay, TQ1 1PR (Tel & Fax: 01803 211808). The Seapoint Hotel is a lovely Grade II Listed building ideally situated in a quiet location just 10 minutes' walk to the harbour and the town's many other attractions. Our family-run hotel is open all year and benefits from having en suite rooms equipped with colour TVs and beverage making facilities. Comfortable TV lounge, cosy residents' bar, outside decking area. Off-road parking and evening meals available. Children and pets welcome. B&B from £17 to £25pppn; DB&B £35 to £45pppn. Children under 13 half price, under 2s free. 10% discount on weekly bookings. Please ring Dave or Kim for a brochure. **ETC** ◆◆◆
e-mail: seapointhotel@hotmail.com
website: www.seapointhotel.co.uk

See also Colour Display Advertisement

YELVERTON

Mrs Linda Landick, Eggworthy Farm, Sampford Spiney, Yelverton PL20 6LJ (01822 852142). Holiday on Dartmoor! In the beautiful Walkham Valley. Moorland and valley walking within yards of the accommodation or just relax in the garden and adjoining woodland. Many local attractions. Comfortable rooms, one double en suite, one family suite with private bathroom. Both rooms have colour TV, tea/coffee facilities and fridge. Full English breakfast. Non-smoking. Pets welcome. Open all year except Christmas. Brochure available. Terms from £22 to £28. We look forward to seeing you. **ETC** ◆◆◆
e-mail: eggworthyfarm@aol.com
website; www.eggworthyfarm.co.uk

Visit the FHG website
www.holidayguides.com
for details of the wide choice of
accommodation featured in
the full range of FHG titles

Living Coasts
Torquay, Devon
See our **READERS' OFFER VOUCHER** for
details of free or reduced rate entry

Dorset

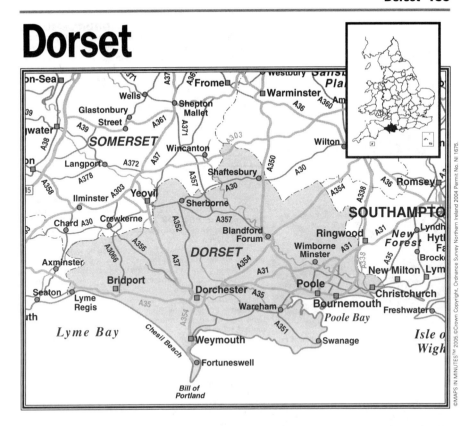

BEAMINSTER

Caroline and Vincent Pielesz, The Walnuts, 2 Prout Bridge, Beaminster DT8 3AY (01308 862211). The property is very well situated in this medieval town in the heart of the beautiful Hardy countryside. Just off the main square with private parking and short walk to local inns, restaurants and tasteful little shops. Ideal for the person who enjoys coastal walks, exploring the countryside and visiting large country houses and gardens. The house has been very tastefully refurbished with en suite rooms, tea and coffee making facilities, all the comforts of home. Bed and full English breakfast from £40 per person. Totally non-smoking. ETC ♦♦♦♦ *SILVER AWARD*.
e-mail: caroline@thewalnuts.co.uk

BOURNEMOUTH

East Cliff Cottage Hotel, 57 Grove Road, Bournemouth BH1 3AT (Tel & Fax: 01202 552788). Situated only a few hundred yards from the East Cliff Promenade, sea and sands. There is parking and a garden for guests, and the hotel is in close proximity to the town centre, shops and all amenities. Bedrooms have en suite facilities, satellite TV, hostess tray, central heating and some with sea views. An impressive guest lounge with colour TV, and the elegant dining room bring out the real quality of East Cliff Cottage. The licensed restaurant offers good home cooking for breakfast and dinner at very moderate prices. Pets and children welcome; large family rooms available at special rates, accommodating up to two adults and three children. Special midweek breaks at any time off season on a 'two for one' basis, fully inclusive of full English breakfast. Please ring for details. ETC/AA ♦♦♦
e-mail: info@eastcliffcottage.com   website: www.eastcliffcottage.com

160 Dorset

BOURNEMOUTH
Tiffany's Bed & Breakfast, Chine Crescent, West Cliff, Bournemouth BH2 5LB (01202 551424; Fax: 01202 318559). Set in its own spacious grounds with ample parking, Tiffany's is centrally situated within minutes' walk of the town centre with unrivalled shopping, fine restaurants and lively nightlife. A leisurely stroll will take you to the promenade and miles of clean, safe beaches. Relax in the hotel's elegant Breakfast Room and enjoy an English breakfast. The 15 beautifully appointed en suite bedrooms have colour TV, hairdryer and tea/coffee making facilities. Family rooms and non-smoking rooms available. An excellent base for exploring the New Forest and the South Coast. **AA ♦♦♦**
e-mail: tiffanyshotel@aol.com
website: www.tiffanysbb.co.uk

BOURNEMOUTH
Southernhay Hotel, 42 Alum Chine Rd, Westbourne, Bournemouth BH4 8DX (Tel & Fax: 01202 761251). The Southernhay Hotel provides warm, friendly, high standard accommodation with a large car park. All rooms have colour TV, tea/coffee making facilities, hairdryer and radio alarm clock. The hotel is ideally situated at the head of Alum Chine (a wooded ravine) leading down to the sea and miles of safe sandy beaches. The Bournemouth International Centre, cinemas, theatres, restaurants, clubs and pubs are all within easy reach; minutes by car or the frequent bus service. Two for one golf available. Seven bedrooms, five en suite. Open all year. Details from Tom and Lynn Derby. Bed and Breakfast from £20 to £30 per adult per night. **ETC ♦♦♦**

e-mail: enquiries@southernhayhotel.co.uk   website: www.southernhayhotel.co.uk

BOURNEMOUTH
Mr S. Goodwin, Cransley Hotel, 11 Knyveton Road, East Cliff, Bournemouth BH1 3QG (01202 290067). A licensed hotel for non-smokers. This comfortable, elegant Edwardian house set in a quiet tree-lined avenue in the East Cliff area of Bournemouth is situated in its own attractive grounds. Close to the heart of Bournemouth and a short stroll from the beach, the hotel is conveniently placed for all major road and rail links. Rooms are en suite with colour television and hospitality tray. Open all year. Bed and Breakfast from £25. Car park. Ground floor accommodation for the less mobile guest. Evening Meals available. Sorry no children and no pets. **ETC/AA ♦♦♦♦**
e-mail: info@cransley.com
website: www.cransley.com

BOURNEMOUTH
Mrs S. Barling, Mayfield, 46 Frances Road, Knyveton Gardens, Bournemouth BH1 3SA (Tel & Fax: 01202 551839). Sandra and Mike Barling make your comfort, food and relaxation their concern, offering a high standard of catering and comfort. Ideally situated overlooking Knyveton Gardens with bowls, petanque, tennis and sensory garden. Handy for sea, shops, shows, rail and coach stations. Residential licence. All rooms are en suite, with colour TV, teamaking, central heating, hairdryer, trouser press, fridge and radio alarm. Own keys. Parking, evening refreshments. Bed and Breakfast from £25 to £28 daily. Bed, Breakfast and Evening Dinner from £155 to £180 weekly per person. Bargain Breaks October/April. **ETC ♦♦♦** *SILVER AWARD.*
website: www.hotelmayfield.co.uk

Readers are requested to mention FHG GUIDES when enquiring about accommodation featured in these pages

Dorset 161

BOURNEMOUTH
Hazel & Keith Ingram, Woodside Hotel, 29 Southern Road, Southbourne, Bournemouth BH6 3SR (01202 427213). A small, friendly, family-run, licensed, NON-SMOKING hotel, situated in one of the most pleasant parts of Southbourne, in a quiet tree-lined road. We are within two minutes of European award 'Blue Flag' beach, offering seven miles of sandy beaches and safe bathing. The promenade can be reached by either a zig-zag path or the popular cliff lift. The Woodside is in a wonderful position for cliff top walks, with panoramic views over the Isle of Wight and the Purbeck Hills. All rooms are en suite, with tea/coffee making facilities, colour TV and shaver points. ETC ♦♦♦♦.
e-mail: woodsidehotel@btinternet.com
website: www.woodsidehotel.co.uk

BOURNEMOUTH
Alan Sibthorpe, Denewood Hotel, 40 Sea Road, Bournemouth BH5 1BQ (01202 309913; Fax: 01202 391155). Warm, friendly hotel in excellent central location, just 500 yards from the beach and close to the shops. Good parking. Single, twin, double and family rooms available, all en suite. Residential and Restaurant licence. TV, tea/coffee and biscuits in rooms. Health salon and spa on site. Open all year. Children and pets welcome. Bed and Breakfast from £22.50 to £25. Special weekly rates available and short break discounts. Please check out our website. ETC ♦♦♦
website: www.denewood.co.uk

BOURNEMOUTH
Tony and Veronica Bulpitt, Sun Haven Guest House, 39 Southern Road, Southbourne, Bournemouth BH6 3SS (01202 427560). The Sun Haven is in a superb position being only 150 yards from the cliff top, near the cliff lift and zigzag path to a beautiful sandy beach which is regularly awarded the European Blue Flag for superior water quality. Southbourne shopping area with its variety of cafes and restaurants is only a few minutes' walk away. A short drive or bus ride takes you to Bournemouth centre or Christchurch. All day access to rooms. All bedrooms have colour TV, shaver point, washbasin, tea/coffee making facilities and central heating. En suite available. Bed and Breakfast from £20 per person per night. A friendly welcome awaits you. No smoking. ETC ♦♦♦

BRIDPORT
Jane Greening, New House Farm, Mangerton Lane, Bradpole, Bridport DT6 3SF (Tel & Fax: 01308 422884). Stay in a modern, comfortable farmhouse on a small farm set in the rural Dorset hills and become one of the family. A large wild garden where you are welcome to sit or stroll round. Two large rooms available, both en suite, both with lovely views over the surrounding countryside, both with television, fridge and tea/coffee making facilities. We are near to Bridport and the seaside, golf courses, fossil hunting, beautiful gardens, wonderful walking, coarse fishing lake – lots to do. Bed and Breakfast from £25. ETC ♦♦♦ *FARM STAY UK MEMBER, WELCOME HOST.*
e-mail: jane@mangertonlake.freeserve.co.uk
website: www.mangertonlake.co.uk

•••some fun days out in DORSET

Tank Museum, Bovington • 01929 405096 • www.tankmuseum.org
Alice in Wonderland Park, Christchurch • 01202 483444 • www.aliceinwonderlandpark.co.uk
Abbotsbury Swannery, Abbotsbury • 01305 871858 • www.abbotsbury-tourism.co.uk
Mapperton Gardens, Beaminster • 01308 862645 • www.mapperton.com

162 Dorset

BRIDPORT
Britmead House Hotel, West Bay Road, Bridport DT6 4EG (01308 422941; Fax: 01308 422516). An elegant Edwardian house, family-run and ideally situated between Bridport and West Bay Harbour, with its beaches, golf course, Chesil Beach and Dorset Coastal Path. We offer full en suite rooms (two ground floor), all with TV, tea/coffee making facilities, and hairdryer. South facing lounge and dining room overlooking the garden. Private parking. Non-smoking.
e-mail: britmead@talk21.com
website: www.britmeadhouse.co.uk

BRIDPORT
Mrs Sally Long, Old Dairy House, Walditch, Bridport DT6 4LB (01308 458021). Relax in an Area of Outstanding Natural Beauty, one mile from Bridport town centre. One twin, one double (non-smoking) bedrooms. Tea/coffee facilities. Guests' shared bathroom, also downstairs shower/cloakroom. Central heating throughout. Guests' TV lounge with open log fire. Hearty full English breakfast with home-made preserves. Gardens abundant with birds and wildlife. Off-road parking. Rural and coastal walks. Real tennis within short walk; 18 hole golf course two miles. Good selection of restaurants and pubs nearby. Open all year for adults only. You will find an informal, friendly atmosphere and warm welcome.

BRIDPORT
Mrs K.E. Parsons, 179 St Andrews Road, Bridport (01308 422038). Situated two miles from the beautiful Jurassic coastline, 10 miles from Lyme Regis and 20 miles from Weymouth. Bedrooms with TV, tea making facilities and washbasins. Parking space available.

BRIDPORT (near)
Mrs Sue Norman, Frogmore Farm, Chideock, Bridport DT6 6HT (01308 456159). Working farm. Set in the rolling hills of West Dorset, enjoying splendid sea views, our delightful 17th century farmhouse offers comfortable, friendly and relaxing accommodation. An ideal base from which to ramble the many coastal and country footpaths of the area (nearest beach Seatown one-and-a-half miles) or tour by car the interesting places of Dorset and Devon. Bedrooms with en suite shower rooms, TV and tea making facilities. Guests' dining room and cosy lounge with woodburner. Well behaved dogs welcome. Open all year; car essential. Bed and Breakfast from £24. Brochure and terms free on request.

FHG Guides publish a large range of well-known accommodation guides. We will be happy to send you details or you can use the order form at the back of this book.

Dorset 163

See also Colour Display Advertisement

CHARMOUTH
Mr & Mrs Derham, Kingfishers, Newlands Bridge, Charmouth DT6 6QZ (01297 560232). Come to Kingfishers and relax on your large sunny balcony overlooking the river and garden. Set in beautiful surroundings on the banks of the River Char, Kingfishers offers a secluded setting yet it is only a short stroll to the beach and village amenities. You are assured of a warm welcome, great food and a friendly atmosphere. We offer a full selection of breakfasts including vegetarian. All rooms are en suite or with private bathroom, balcony, drink making facilities, colour TV and central heating. Home-baked food and clotted cream teas available throughout the day in our lovely Garden Room or outside in the garden. Free access and ample parking. We are open for B&B all year round and now offer Sunday roasts.

DORCHESTER
Mrs V.A. Bradbeer, Nethercroft, Winterbourne Abbas, Dorchester DT2 9LU (01305 889337). This country house with its friendly and homely atmosphere welcomes you to the heart of Hardy's Wessex. Central for touring the many places of interest that Dorset has to offer, including Corfe Castle, Lyme Regis, Dorchester, Weymouth, Lulworth Cove, etc. Lovely country walks and many local attractions. Two double rooms, one single, en suite or separate bathroom. TV lounge, dining room. Large garden. Open all year. Central heating. Car essential, ample parking. Bed and Breakfast from £20. Take A35 from Dorchester, we are the last house at the western edge of the village.
e-mail: v.bradbeer@ukonline.co.uk

e-mail: stay@churchview.co.uk

DORCHESTER (near)
Michael and Jane Deller, Churchview Guest House, Winterbourne Abbas, Near Dorchester DT2 9LS (Tel & Fax: 01305 889296). Our 17th century Guest House, noted for warm hospitality and delicious breakfasts and evening meals, makes an ideal base for touring beautiful West Dorset. Our character bedrooms are all comfortable and well appointed. Meals, served in our beautiful diningroom, feature local produce, with relaxation provided by two attractive lounges and licensed bar. Your hosts Jane and Michael Deller are pleased to give every assistance with local information to ensure a memorable stay. NON SMOKING. Terms: Dinner, Bed and Breakfast £42 to £54; Bed and Breakfast £28-£38. Short Breaks available, please call for further details. ETC/AA ♦♦♦♦
website: www.churchview.co.uk

LULWORTH COVE
John and Jenny Aldridge, Applegrove, West Road, West Lulworth, Wareham BH20 5RY (01929 400592). Comfortable home offering accommodation in central yet quiet off-main road position in old vicarage orchard. Two double rooms and one twin/super king (with balcony). All have en suite shower rooms, beverage trays and colour TVs. Parking in spacious walled garden with mature fruit trees, lawns and garden furniture for guests' use. Generous traditional English, Vegetarian or Vegan breakfast using home grown produce and eggs. 10 minute stroll from Lulworth Cove. Coast path for other beaches, Durdle Door and Fossil Forest nearby. Central for South Dorset Coast. Bed and Breakfast from £23 per person per night. Open all year except Christmas and New year. ETC ♦♦♦
e-mail: jennyandjohn@applegrove-lulworth.co.uk
website: www.applegrove-lulworth.co.uk

164 Dorset

See also Colour Display Advertisement

LULWORTH COVE
Cromwell House Hotel, Lulworth Cove BH20 5RJ (01929 400253/400332; Fax: 01929 400566). Catriona and Alistair Miller welcome guests to their comfortable family-run hotel, set in secluded gardens with spectacular sea views. Situated 200 yards from Lulworth Cove, with direct access to the Jurassic Coast. A heated swimming pool is available for guests' use from May to October. Accommodation is in 17 en suite bedrooms, with TV, direct-dial telephone, and tea/coffee making facilities; most have spectacular sea views. Restaurant, bar wine list. Two nights dinner, bed and breakfast (fully en suite) from £90 per person. Off-peak mid week breaks available. Open all year except Christmas. **ETC/AA/RAC ★★**

LYME REGIS
Mrs L. Brown, Providence House, Lyme Road, Uplyme DT7 3TH (01297 445704). Comfortable accommodation on the edge of historic Lyme Regis in 200 year old character house with open beamed fireplace, raised gallery area and roof garden. 25 minutes' walk from the sea. Ideal for artists, fossil hunting, walking etc. Easy access by road. Axminster five miles with main line connection to Waterloo. Accommodation comprises one single, one double, one double en suite; all with TV and tea/coffee making facilities. Full English Breakfast and vegetarian option. Rooms available from £20 to £22 per person per night. Secure courtyard area available for bikes/motor bikes, etc.

MOSTERTON
Mrs Caroline Osmond, Yeabridge Farm, Whetley Cross, Mosterton, Near Beaminster DT8 3HE (Tel & Fax: 01308 868944). Caroline and family are looking to give all guests a warm welcome to this modern spacious thatched farmhouse with panoramic views of the West Dorset Downs. Accommodation available in one twin, one double, one family room en suite, all with tea/coffee making facilities. Large residents' lounge with colour TV. Children welcome. Ideal base for exploring - there are country footpaths within 100 yards. Coastal town and harbour eight miles away, and a golf course four miles. Post office, shop half-a-mile, various inns and public houses in the immediate area. A303 15 minutes, M5 30 minutes, A35 10 minutes. Prices from £25 per person per night. (reduced rates for children). Evening Meals are available on request. Ample parking. Open all year. Non-smoking. **ETC ◆◆◆◆**
e-mail: Crlnosmnd@aol.com
website: www.yeabridge.co.uk

POOLE
Mrs Stephenson, Holly Hedge Farm, Bulbury Lane, Lytchett Matravers, Poole BH16 6EP (01929 459688). Built in 1892, Holly Hedge Farm is situated next to Bulbury Woods Golf Course, set in 11 acres of wood and grassland adjacent to lake. We are just 15 minutes away from the Purbecks, the beach and the forest. The area is ideal for walking or cycling and Poole Quay and Harbour are also nearby. Accommodation comprises two double/family rooms, one twin and one single, all with en suite showers, colour TV, tea/coffee making facilities, radio alarms and central heating. Prices for a single room £30 to £32, double £52 to £55, per night. Open all year round for summer or winter breaks. Full English or Continental breakfast served.

Dorset 165

PORTLAND
Alessandria Hotel, 71 Wakeham, Easton, Portland DT5 1HW (01305 822270/820108; Fax: 01305 820561). This former 18th century inn is situated in a quiet location. Comfortable accommodation; most rooms en suite, some with sea view; colour TV; tea/coffee; free parking. Ground floor rooms. Children welcome. Bed and Breakfast at reasonable prices. Warm and friendly hospitality. **ETC/AA/RAC ♦♦♦**
website: www.s-h-systems.co.uk/hotels/alessand.html

STURMINSTER NEWTON
Mrs Jill. Miller, Lower Fifehead Farm, Fifehead, St Quinton, Sturminster Newton DT10 2AP (01258 817335). Come and have a relaxing holiday at Lower Fifehead Farm. Stay in our lovely listed 17th century farmhouse mentioned in Dorset books for its architectural interest, or Honeysuckle House, actually on the farm, and with outstanding views. Both offer excellent breakfasts and tea and coffee making. Honeysuckle House offers evening meals. We are within easy reach of all of Dorset's beauty spots. Excellent walking, and both riding and fishing can be arranged. Lower Fifehead Farm pictured here. Or contact **Mrs Jessie Miller, Honeysuckle House (01258 817896)** ETC ♦♦♦♦.

SWANAGE
Janet Foran, Sandhaven Guest House, 5 Ulwell Road, Swanage BH19 1LE (01929 422322). You can be sure of a warm welcome with good home-cooking whenever you stay at Sandhaven. We wish to make sure your stay is as relaxing and enjoyable as possible. All bedrooms are en suite, non-smoking and equipped with tea and coffee making facilities; all have colour TV. There is a residents' lounge, diningroom and conservatory for your comfort. The Purbeck Hills are visible from the guest house, as is the beach, which is only 100 metres away. Sandhaven is open all year except Christmas and Bed and Breakfast is available from £26 to £31.
e-mail: mail@sandhaven-guest-house.co.uk

TOLPUDDLE
Paul Wright, Tolpuddle Hall, Tolpuddle, Near Dorchester DT2 7EW (01305 848986). An historic house in village centre in an Area of Outstanding Natural Beauty, not far from the coast. Convenient for Bournemouth, Poole, Dorchester, Weymouth, Isle of Purbeck and many small market towns and villages. Centre for local interests e.g. bird-watching, walking, local history, Thomas Hardy, the Tolpuddle Martyrs, etc. Two double, one twin, one family and two single bedrooms. Full English breakfast. Tea/coffee making, TV sitting room. Pets welcome except high season. From £20 per person. Weekly rate available. Open all year.

Visit the FHG website
www.holidayguides.com
for details of the wide choice of accommodation
featured in the full range of FHG titles

166 Dorset

WEST LULWORTH
Val and Barry Burrill, Graybank Bed and Breakfast, Main Road, West Lulworth BH20 5RL (01929 400256). Built in 1871 of "local" Purbeck limestone, Graybank sits in a beautiful, quiet location five minutes' stroll from the spectacular Lulworth Cove and the South West Coastal Path. All rooms have wash basins, colour TV and tea/coffee making facilities. We have a breakfast menu offering a choice of traditional or lighter fare. In addition, there is a good choice of cafes and restaurants within walking distance of Graybank. Free parking for all guests. Fire Certificate held. We are non-smoking throughout the house and open from February to November. We do not accept pets. Bed and Breakfast from £20 per person per night. Please telephone for our brochure.

WEYMOUTH
Mark and Jean Mitchell, Ferndown Guest House, 47 Walpole Street, Weymouth DT4 7HQ (01305 775228). A friendly welcome awaits you at Ferndown Guest House. A welcoming place to stay, it is family-run by Mark and Jean. Situated just two minutes' walk to the seafront and five minutes into town, it is the ideal place to stay in Weymouth. All rooms have washbasins, colour TV and tea and coffee making facilities; some en suite available. Visitors are welcome to use the lounge with colour TV. Open from April to October. Bed and Breakfast from £18pppn. AA ◆◆
e-mail: jeanmitchel@amserve.com

WEYMOUTH
Anna and Peter Vincent, Old Harbour View, 12 Trinity Road, Weymouth DT4 8TJ (01305 774633; Fax: 01305 750828). Anna and Peter welcome you to their idyllic Georgian harbourside townhouse, offering two charming double bedrooms, both en suite. Old Harbour View enjoys Weymouth's historic harbour right outside the door, with harbourside restaurants, the ferries to Jersey, Guernsey and France, Weymouth beach and town centre just over the town bridge. From its position on the Jurassic Coastal Path, Old Harbour View gives you the base to explore the amazing prehistoric coast. Both rooms are beautifully decorated with deliciously comfortable beds, colour televisions with teletext and full tea/coffee facilities. A luxurious breakfast awaits you before you head out for the surrounding area. Bed and Breakfast from £35 to £40 pppn.

Pets Welcome!

"THE PET WORLD'S VERSION OF THE ULTIMATE HOTEL GUIDE!" (The Times)

Now bigger than ever and with full colour throughout,
Pets Welcome! is used every year by thousands of discriminating owners who simply refuse to leave their pets "home alone".
Published twice a year in Autumn and Spring.

Only £8.99 from booksellers or direct from the publishers:
FHG Guides, Abbey Mill Business Centre, Seedhill, Paisley PA1 1TJ *(postage charged outside UK)*
e-mail: admin@fhguides.co.uk • www.holidayguides.com

Durham

CORNFORTH/DURHAM
Mrs D. Slack, Ash House, 24 The Green, Cornforth DL17 9JH (01740 654654; mobile: 07711 133547). Built in the mid-19th Century, Ash House is a beautifully appointed period home combining a delicate mixture of homeliness and Victorian flair. Elegant rooms, individually and tastefully decorated, combining antique furnishings, beautiful fabrics, carved four-posters and modern fittings. Spacious and graceful, filled with character, Ash House offers a warm welcome to both the road-weary traveller and those wishing merely to unwind in the quiet elegance of this charming home on a quiet village green. Private parking. 10 minutes from historic Durham city, and adjacent A1(M) motorway. Well-placed between York and Edinburgh. Excellent value. Terms from £25 per person per night.
e-mail: delden@btopenworld.com

FROSTERLEY IN WEARDALE
Newlands Hall, Frosterley in Weardale, Bishop Auckland DL13 2SH (01388 529233). Working farm. A warm welcome awaits you on our beef and sheep farm surrounded by beautiful open countryside with its magnificent views of Weardale - an Area of Outstanding Natural Beauty. Rich in wildlife, the farm is at the centre of a network of local footpaths. The area has much to offer visitors, ranging from the high wild fells of Weardale and Teesdale to pretty villages, market towns and the University City of Durham, with its cathedral, castle and medieval streets. Accommodation comprises a family room with en suite bathroom and a family room with en suite shower. Both rooms have stunning views, tea/coffee making facilities, TV, hairdryer, radio alarm and central heating. Sorry no pets and no smoking indoors. Full English breakfast is served with homemade bread, our own free range eggs and other local produce. Bed and Breakfast from £25 per person per night, reduced rates for children under 10 years old sharing. Open Easter to October.
e-mail: carol@newlandshall.co.uk   website: www.newlandshall.co.uk

See also Colour Display Advertisement

STANLEY
Mrs P. Gibson, Bushblades Farm, Harperley, Stanley DH9 9UA (01207 232722). Ideal stop-over when travelling north or south. Only 10 minutes from A1(M), Chester-le-Street. Durham City 20 minutes, Beamish Museum two miles, Metro Centre 15 minutes, Hadrian's Wall and Northumberland coast under an hour. Comfortable Georgian farmhouse set in large garden. Twin ground floor en suite room and double first floor en suite bedrooms. All rooms have tea/coffee making facilities, colour TV and easy chairs. Ample parking. Children over 12 years welcome. Sorry, no pets. Bed and Breakfast from £25 to £30 single, £48 double. Self-catering accommodation also available. Leave A1(M) at Chester-le-Street for Stanley on the A693, then follow sign for Consett. Half-a-mile after Stanley follow signs for Harperley. Farm on right, half-a-mile up from crossroads. ETC ♦♦♦

Essex

COLCHESTER

Mrs Jill Tod, Seven Arches Farm, Chitts Hill, Lexden, Colchester CO3 9SX (01206 574896). Working farm. Georgian farmhouse set in large garden close to the ancient town of Colchester. The farm extends to 100 acres and supports both arable crops and cattle. Private fishing rights on the River Colne, which runs past the farmhouse. This is a good location for visits to North Essex, Dedham and the Stour Valley which have been immortalised in the works of John Constable, the landscape painter. Children and pets welcome. Open all year. Bed and Breakfast from £30; Evening Meal from £5. Twin room £50; family room en suite. Static caravan on caravan site also available.

COLCHESTER

Mrs Wendy Anderson, The Old Manse, 15 Roman Road, Colchester CO1 1UR (01206 545154). Award-winning spacious Victorian family home situated in a quiet square beside the Castle Park. Only three minutes' walk from bus/coach station or through the Park to town centre. We promise a warm welcome and a friendly, informal atmosphere. All rooms have central heating, TV and tea/coffee making facilities. Ground floor double room has private facilities; two twin-bedded rooms on first floor, one en suite. Full, varied English Breakfast. Bed and Breakfast from £35 single, £57 double. Only 30 minutes' drive from Harwich and Felixstowe. Within easy reach of Constable country and one hour's train journey from London. Sorry, no smoking.
e-mail: wendyanderson15@hotmail.com
website: www.doveuk.com/oldmanse

**Visit the FHG website
www.holidayguides.com**
for details of the wide choice of
accommodation featured in
the full range of FHG titles

Barleylands Farm
Billericay, Essex
See our **READERS' OFFER VOUCHER** for
details of free or reduced rate entry

Barleylands Farm

Essex 169

COLCHESTER

Peveril Hotel, 51 North Hill, Colchester CO1 1PY (Tel & Fax: 01206 574001). Town centre hotel with unrestricted parking all weekend and evenings (6pm to 8.30am). Comfortable lounge bar and excellent restaurant providing a comprehensive range of English, Continental and Asian foods, all home cooking. Our hotel is within easy reach of all amenities and only seven miles from Constable Country and six miles from the North Sea. ETC ◆◆

KELVEDON

Mr and Mrs R. Bunting, Highfields Farm, Highfields Lane, Kelvedon CO5 9BJ (Tel & Fax: 01376 570334). Highfields Farm is set in a quiet area on a 700 acre working farm. This makes a peaceful overnight stop on the way to Harwich or a base to visit historic Colchester and Constable country. Convenient for Harwich, Felixstowe and Stansted Airport. Easy access to A12 and main line trains to London. The accommodation comprises one twin room with private bathroom, one twin room en suite and one double en suite, all with TV and tea/coffee making facilities. Residents' lounge. Good English breakfast is served in the oak beamed dining room. Ample parking. Bed and Breakfast from £32 single and £52 twin or double. ETC ◆◆◆
e-mail: HighfieldsFarm@farmersweekly.net   website: www.highfieldsfarm.co.uk

See also Colour Display Advertisement

WESTCLIFF-ON-SEA

Mr Ian Bartholomew, Retreat Guest House, 12 Canewdon Road, Westcliff-on-Sea SS0 7NE (01702 348217/337413; Fax: 01702 391179). Quality accommodation ideally situated in the quieter more picturesque side of Southend. Close to the Cliffs Pavilion and beautiful gardens. Conveniently by Westcliff station and near to the seafront leading to Southend's main attractions. Most bedrooms en suite, some on ground floor. En suite rooms also available with own kitchen. All rooms have remote-controlled colour TV (some rooms with video), tea/coffee making facilities. Choice of English Breakfast. Private secure parking. Bed and Breakfast from £25 per person. Major debit/credit cards accepted. ETC ◆◆◆
e-mail: retreatguesthouse.co.uk@tinyworld.co.uk

please note All the information in this book is given in good faith in the belief that it is correct. However, the publishers cannot guarantee the facts given in these pages, neither are they responsible for changes in policy, ownership or terms that may take place after the date of going to press. Readers should always satisfy themselves that the facilities they require are available and that the terms, if quoted, still apply.

FHG
K·U·P·E·R·A·R·D

Gloucestershire

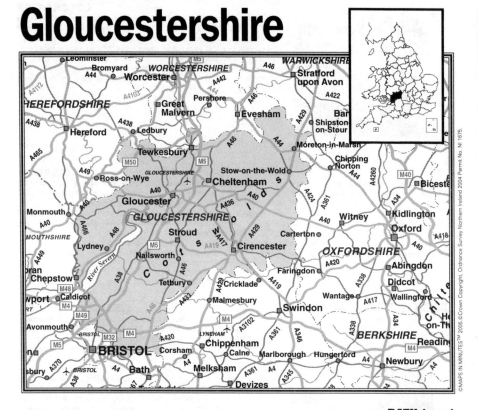

BATH (near)
Mrs Pam Wilmott, Pool Farm, Bath Road, Wick, Bristol BS30 5RL (0117 937 2284). Welcome to our 350 year old Grade II Listed farmhouse on a working farm. On A420 between Bath and Bristol and a few miles from Exit 18 of M4, we are on the edge of the village, overlooking fields, but within easy reach of pub, shops and golf club. We offer traditional Bed and Breakast in one family and one twin room with tea/coffee facilities and TV. Guest lounge. Central heating. Ample parking. Open all year except Christmas. Terms from £22 per person per night.

•••some fun days out in GLOUCESTERSHIRE

Cinderbury Iron Age Experience, Coleford • 0870 609 3219 • www.cinderbury.co.uk
Woodchester Mansion, Stonehouse • 01453 861541 • www.woodchestermansion.org.uk
Berkeley Castle, Berkeley • 01453 810332 • www.berkeley-castle.com

Avon Valley Railway
Bristol, South Gloucestershire
See our **READERS' OFFER VOUCHER** for
details of free or reduced rate entry

Gloucestershire

BRISTOL

WHEN IN BRISTOL COME AND STAY WITH US

11 bedrooms, all en suite • Satellite TV in each room
Bar & Restaurant open all day
36 holes of Golf • 25 Bay Driving Range
Stay and Play Deals available on request

Call: 01454 281144

Thornbury Golf Centre, Bristol Road, Thornbury, Bristol BS35 3XL
www.thornburygc.co.uk
Located just 10 minutes from Junction 16 of the M5 on the A38

Room prices start from £51.95 per room per night.
Weekend rate £45 room only

AA ★★

BRISTOL
Marilyn and Bob Downes, Box Hedge Farm, Coalpit Heath, Bristol BS36 2UW (01454 250786). Box Hedge Farm is set in 200 acres of beautiful rural countryside on the edge of the Cotswolds. Local to M4/M5, central for Bristol and Bath and the many tourist attractions in this area. An ideal stopping point for the South West and Wales. We offer a warm, friendly atmosphere with traditional farmhouse cooking. All bedrooms have colour TV and tea/coffee making facilities. Bed and Breakfast from £25 single standard, £30 single en suite, £40 double standard, £46 double en suite. Family rooms - prices on application. All prices include VAT. Self-catering accommodation also available. Full details on our website.
website: www.bed-breakfast-bristol.com

See also Colour Display Advertisement

BRISTOL
Jane Roper, Roylands Farm Cottage Bed & Breakfast, Fernhill, Almondsbury, Bristol BS32 4LU (07791 221102; 07768 286924). Roylands Farm Cottage is a comfortable home from home situated within a working farm, with classic styling to blend in with its rural surroundings. Rooms are spacious, bright and welcoming with all usual en suite and private facilities, lounge and kitchen. One single, one twin and a double bedroom, all with full English breakfast, towels, TV and tea and coffee making facilities. Uniquely guests can take advantage of their own lounge, or relax and take in the beautiful views of the Severn estuary and the surrounding countryside from the adjoining conservatory or large country garden. Ample secure and secluded off road parking.
e-mail: jane@roylandfarmcottage.co.uk
website: www.roylandfarmcottage.co.uk

CHELTENHAM
Dove House, 128 Cheltenham Road, Bishops Cleeve, Cheltenham GL52 4LZ (01242 679452/679600; Fax: 01242 679600; Mobile: 07973 424358). Dove House is situated on the outskirts of Cheltenham, close to the Racecourse and is ideal as a base for touring/walking the Cotswolds, Forest of Dean, Tewkesbury, Evesham. Golf courses and private fishing lakes close by. All rooms are furnished to a high standard and have central heating, colour TV and tea/coffee making facilities. Ample parking and garden for guests' use. Bed and Breakfast from £20 per person per night; en suite available. Open all year.
e-mail: eric.jenny@lineone.net

172 Gloucestershire

See also Colour Display Advertisement

CHIPPING CAMPDEN

Mrs Gené Jeffrey, Brymbo, Honeybourne Lane, Mickleton, Chipping Campden GL55 6PU (01386 438890; Fax: 01386 438113). A warm and welcoming farm building conversion with large garden in beautiful Cotswold countryside, ideal for walking and touring. Close to Stratford-upon-Avon, Broadway, Chipping Campden and with easy access to Oxford and Cheltenham. All rooms are on the ground floor, with full central heating. The comfortable bedrooms all have colour television and tea/coffee making facilities. Sitting room with open log fire. Breakfast room. Children and dogs welcome. Parking. Maps and guides to borrow. Sample menus from local hostelries for your information. Homemade bread and preserves a speciality. FREE countryside tour of area offered to three-night guests. Rooms: two double, two twin, one family. Bathrooms: three en suite, two private or shared. Bed and Breakfast: single £25 to £40; double £40 to £55. Brochure available. Credit Cards accepted. **ETC ♦♦♦♦**

e-mail: enquiries@brymbo.com
website: www.brymbo.com

CHIPPING CAMPDEN

Mrs C. Hutsby, Holly House, Ebrington, Chipping Campden GL55 6NL (01386 593213; Fax: 01386 593181). Holly House is set in the centre of the picturesque thatched Cotswold village of Ebrington. Ideally situated for touring the Cotswolds and Shakespeare's country. Two miles Chipping Campden and Hidcote Gardens, five miles Broadway, 11 miles Stratford-upon-Avon, 19 miles Warwick. Double, twin and family rooms available, all beautifully appointed with en suite facilities, TV and tea and coffee. Laundry facility available. Private parking. Lovely garden room at guests' disposal. Village pub serves meals. Bike hire available locally. Directions: from Chipping Campden take B4035 towards Shipston on Stour, after half-a-mile turn left to Ebrington, we are in the centre of the village. Double/Twin: £27.50 - £32.50; Single: £45 - £60, Family: £70-£90. Child reductions. Non- smoking. **AA ♦♦♦♦**

e-mail: hutsbybandb@aol.com
website: www.hollyhousebandb.co.uk

COTSWOLDS

Alison Lane, Hill Barn, Clapton Road, Bourton-on-the-Water GL54 2LF (01451 810472). Spacious en suite accommodation in a converted barn in the middle of the countryside. Friendly and tranquil with beautiful views across the Cotswold hills, yet only five minutes from picturesque Bourton-on-the-Water with its many attractions. Single rooms from £30 per night, double/twin £22 per person per night and family room £22 per adult/£10 for children under 10. Self-catering also available. Sorry, no smoking or pets. For photos and extra information please visit our website.

e-mail: ali.lane@ukonline.co.uk
website: www.hillbarnholidays.co.uk

FAIRFORD (near)

Mrs Z.I. Williamson, Kempsford Manor, Near Fairford GL7 4EQ (Tel & Fax: 01285 810131). 17th century private manor house set in peaceful gardens. Fine reception rooms, lovely garden, home-grown vegetables, excellent home cooking. Ideal setting for weddings, receptions, long or short stays. Three miles from Fairford, Cirencester nine miles. Easy access to M4 and M5. Two double bedrooms, one en suite, one with private facilities. Terms from £35 single, £60 double, children up to 14 years £15. Open all year. **ETC ♦♦♦**

e-mail: ipek@kempsfordmanor.co.uk
website: www.kempsfordmanor.co.uk

Gloucestershire

See also Colour Display Advertisement

GLOUCESTER (near)

S.J. Barnfield, "Kilmorie Smallholding", Gloucester Road, Corse, Staunton, Gloucester GL19 3RQ (Tel & Fax: 01452 840224). Quality all ground floor accommodation. "Kilmorie" is Grade II Listed (c1848) within conservation area in a lovely part of Gloucestershire, deceptively spacious yet cosy, and tastefully furnished. Double, twin, family or single bedrooms, all having tea tray, colour TV, radio, mostly en suite. Very comfortable guests' lounge, traditional home cooking is served in the separate diningroom overlooking large garden where there are seats to relax, watch our free range hens (who provide excellent eggs for breakfast!) or the wild birds and butterflies we encourage to visit. Perhaps walk waymarked farmland footpaths which start here. Children may "help" with our retired pony, and free range hens. Rural yet perfectly situated to visit Cotswolds, Royal Forest of Dean, Wye Valley and Malvern Hills. Children over five years. No smoking, please. Bed, full English Breakfast and Evening Dinner from £31; Bed and Breakfast from £21. Ample parking. **ETC** ◆◆◆◆
e-mail: sheila-barnfield@supanet.com

LECHLADE ON THAMES

Mr and Mrs J. Titchener, Cambrai Lodge, Oak Street, Lechlade on Thames GL7 3AY (01367 253173; mobile: 07860 150467). Situated in an attractive village on the River Thames, this family-run guest house is only eight miles from Burford and 12 miles from Swindon. Ideal base for touring the Cotswolds, with Kemscott Manor and Buscot House and Gardens nearby. We are close to the river and guests can make use of our lovely garden. One family, two double (en suite), one twin (en suite) and two single rooms available. One room has a Victorian four-poster bed and one room is on the ground floor. Breakfast is served in our airy conservatory overlooking the garden. Non-smoking. Pets by arrangement. Open all year. Bed and Breakfast from £30 to £40 single; £50 to £65 double. A warm and friendly welcome is assured at Cambrai Lodge. **ETC** ◆◆◆◆ *SILVER AWARD*, **AA** ◆◆◆◆
e-mail: cambrailodge@btconnect.com

See also Colour Display Advertisement

MINCHINHAMPTON (near Stroud)

Mrs Margaret Helm, Hunters Lodge, Dr Brown's Road, Minchinhampton Common, Near Stroud GL6 9BT (01453 883588). Hunters Lodge is a beautiful stone-built Cotswold country house set in a large secluded garden adjoining 600 acres of National Trust common land at Minchinhampton. Accommodation available - one double room en suite; two twin/double-bedded rooms both with private bathrooms. All have tea/coffee making facilities, dressing gowns, central heating and colour TV and are furnished and decorated to a high standard. Private lounge with TV and a delightful new conservatory. Car essential, ample parking space. Ideal centre for touring the Cotswolds, Bath, Cheltenham, Cirencester, with many delightful pubs and hotels in the area for meals. You are sure of a warm welcome, comfort, and help in planning excursions to local places of interest. Bed and Breakfast from £25 to £30pp; single from £40. Non-smoking. Children over 10. No dogs. SAE please, or telephone. **AA** ◆◆◆◆◆ *PREMIER COLLECTION*.
e-mail: hunterslodge@hotmail.com   website: www.cotswoldsbandb.co.uk

---

Noah's Ark Zoo Farm
Bristol, South Gloucestershire
See our **READERS' OFFER VOUCHER** for
details of free or reduced rate entry

STONEHOUSE

Mrs D.A. Hodge, Merton Lodge, 8 Ebley Road, Stonehouse GL10 2LQ (01453 822018). A former gentleman's residence situated about three miles from Stroudwater interchange on the M5 (Junction 13), on B4008 (keep going on old road) just outside Stonehouse towards Stroud. Opposite side to Wyevale Garden Centre, 300 yards from the Cotswold Way. Full central heating and washbasins in all bedrooms; one en suite. Only cotton or linen sheets used. Two bathrooms with showers. Large sittingroom with panoramic views of Selsey Common. Well placed for Cotswold villages, Wildfowl Trust, Berkeley Castle, Westonbirt Arboretum, Bath/Bristol, Cheltenham and Gloucester ski slope and Forest of Dean. Satisfaction guaranteed. Excellent cuisine. Carvery/pub 200 yards away. Bed and Breakfast from £21 per person, en suite from £23 per person. Children half price. Friendly welcome. Sorry, no smoking or dogs. **ETC ♦♦**

See also Colour Display Advertisement

STOW-ON-THE-WOLD

Mrs F.J. Adams, Aston House, Broadwell, Moreton-in-Marsh GL56 0TJ (01451 830475). Aston House is in the peaceful village of Broadwell, one-and-a-half miles from Stow-on-the-Wold, four miles from Moreton-in-Marsh. It is centrally situated for all the Cotswold villages, while Blenheim Palace, Warwick Castle, Oxford, Stratford-upon-Avon, Cheltenham and Gloucester are within easy reach. Accommodation comprises a twin-bedded and a double room, both en suite (first floor), and a double room with private bathroom (ground floor). All rooms have tea/coffee making facilities, radio, colour TV, hairdryer, electric blankets for the colder nights and fans for hot weather. Bedtime drinks and biscuits are provided. Open March to October. No smoking. Car essential, parking. Pub within walking distance. PC and internet access available. Bed and good English breakfast from £27 to £29 per person daily; weekly from £195 per person.
ETC ♦♦♦♦ *SILVER AWARD*, RAC ♦♦♦♦ *WARM WELCOME AWARD AND SPARKLING DIAMOND AWARD*.
e-mail: fja@netcomuk.co.uk
website: www.astonhouse.net

STOW-ON-THE-WOLD

South Hill Farmhouse, Fosseway, Stow-on-the-Wold, GL54 1JU (01451 831888; Fax: 01451 832255). Siân and Mark Cassie welcome you to South Hill Farmhouse. The house is a Listed Cotswold stone farmhouse (no longer a working farm) situated on the ancient Roman Fosse Way on the outskirts of Stow-on-the-Wold. There is ample parking for guests, and it is only 10 minutes' walk to the pubs, restaurants and shops of Stow-on-the-Wold. 2006 prices: single £35 to £42, double/twin £50 to £58, family (three/four) £63 to £94 per room per night, including generous breakfast. See our website for special winter rates. Non-smoking house. **ETC ♦♦♦♦**
e-mail: info@southhill.co.uk
website: www.southhill.co.uk

---

publisher's note

While every effort is made to ensure accuracy, we regret that FHG Guides cannot accept responsibility for errors, misrepresentations or omissions in our entries or any consequences thereof. Prices in particular should be checked. We will follow up complaints but cannot act as arbiters or agents for either party

Gloucestershire 175

STOW-ON-THE-WOLD

Robert Smith and Julie-Anne, Corsham Field Farmhouse, Bledington Road, Stow-on-the-Wold GL54 1JH (01451 831750; Fax: 01451 832247). A traditional farmhouse with spectacular views of Cotswold countryside. Quiet location one mile from Stow, ideally situated for exploring all Cotswold villages including Bourton-on-the-Water, Broadway, Burford and Chipping Campden. Within easy reach of Cheltenham, Oxford and Stratford-upon-Avon; also places of interest such as Blenheim Palace, Warwick Castle and many National Trust houses and gardens. Family, twin and double bedrooms, mostly en suite. TV, tea tray and hairdryer in all rooms. Relaxing guest lounge/dining room. Open all year for Bed and Breakfast from £24 (reductions for children). Excellent pub food five minutes' walk away. **ETC/AA** ◆◆◆
e-mail: farmhouse@corshamfield.co.uk   website: www.corshamfield.co.uk

TEWKESBURY

Mrs Bernadette Williams, Abbots Court, Church End, Twyning, Tewkesbury GL20 6DA (Tel & Fax: 01684 292515). Working farm. A large, quiet farmhouse set in 350 acres, built on the site of monastery between the Malverns and Cotswolds, half a mile M5-M50 junction. Six en suite bedrooms with colour TV and tea making facilities. Centrally heated. Open all year except Christmas. Large lounge with open fire and colour TV. Licensed bar. Good home cooked food in large quantities, home produced where possible. Lawn. Cot and high chair available. Laundry facilities. Ideally situated for touring with numerous places to visit. Swimming, tennis, sauna, golf within three miles. Coarse fishing available on the farm. Bed and Breakfast from £21 to £25. Reduced rates for children and Senior Citizens. **ETC** ◆◆◆
e-mail: abbotscourt@aol.com

WINCHCOMBE

Mrs Margaret Warmington, Ireley Farm, Broadway Road, Winchcombe GL54 5PA (01242 602445). Ireley is an 18th century farmhouse located in the heart of gentle countryside, one-and-a-half miles from Winchcombe and within easy reach of Cheltenham, Gloucester, Stratford-upon-Avon and Worcester. The cosy yet spacious guest rooms (one double and two twin) offer either en suite or private bathroom. Relax in the evening beside a traditional open fire and in the morning enjoy a delicious English breakfast. Families are welcomed to enjoy the unique atmosphere of this working farm. B&B from £25 per person.
e-mail: warmingtonmaggot@aol.com

WOODCHESTER

Mrs Wendy Swait, Inschdene, Atcombe Road, South Woodchester, Stroud GL5 5EW (01453 873254). Inschdene is a comfortable family house with magnificent views across the valley, set in an acre of garden near the centre of a quiet village. A double room with private bathroom and a twin-bedded room are available, both being spacious with washbasin and tea/coffee making facilities. Colour TV available in the rooms. Woodchester is an attractive village with excellent local pubs renowned for their food, and all within easy walking distance. An ideal centre for the Cotswolds and close to Slimbridge, Berkeley Castle and Westonbirt Arboretum and more, including Badminton and Gatcombe Horse Trials. Guests are requested not to smoke in the house. Bed and Breakfast from £22.50 per person.

Hampshire

BARTON-ON-SEA
Lee & Melanie Snook, Laurel Lodge, 48 Western Avenue, Barton-on-Sea, New Milton BH25 7PZ (01425 618309).

Ideally situated for the delights of the New Forest, scenic cliff top walks, local beaches, pleasure cruises to the Isle of Wight, the Needles and historic Hurst Castle, horse riding, cycling, golf and a whole host of indoor and outdoor pursuits. Laurel Lodge is a comfortable, centrally heated, converted bungalow, offering twin, double & family rooms. All rooms are fully en suite with tea and coffee making facilities, comfortable chairs, colour TV and alarm clock radio. Ground floor rooms available. Breakfast is served in our conservatory / diningroom with views over the garden. Bed and Breakfast from £25 per person. Special deals for longer breaks. Children welcome, cot and high chair supplied by prior arrangement. Off-road parking for all rooms. Strictly no smoking. Open all year. Please phone for further details.
ETC ♦♦♦♦ *SILVER AWARD.*

•••some fun days out in HAMPSHIRE

The Spinnaker Tower, Portsmouth • 023 9285 7520 • www.spinnakertower.co.uk
Broadlands, Romsey • 01794 505010/505020 • www.broadlands.net
Blue Reef Aquarium, Portsmouth • 023 9287 5222 • www.bluereefaquarium.co.uk
Exbury Gardens & Steam Railway, Beaulieu • 023 8089 1203 • www.exbury.co.uk
New Forest Museum, Lyndhurst • 023 8028 3444 • www.newforestmuseum.org.uk

Hampshire 177

BEAULIEU (near)
Langley Village Restaurant, Lepe Road, Langley, Near Beaulieu, Southampton SO45 1XR (Tel & Fax: 023 8089 1667; Mobile: 07989 781616). A friendly family atmosphere will greet you in this large detached property on the edge of the beautiful New Forest. Ample off-road parking. Each day begins with a hearty full English breakfast. Accommodation comprises one twin, one double and two single rooms, all tastefully decorated and having washbasins, central heating, colour TV and tea-making facilities. A restaurant is attached offering meals all day. Conveniently situated for golf, fishing, horse riding and walking. Close to Exbury Gardens, Lepe Country Park and Beaulieu Motor Museum. Open all year. Bed and Breakfast from £25. Special diets catered for by arrangement.
website: www.langley-hampshire.co.uk

BROCKENHURST (New Forest)
Hilden, Southampton Road, Boldre, Brockenhurst (New Forest) SO41 8PT (01590 623682; Fax: 01590 624444). Hilden is a friendly Edwardian home in two-and-a-half acres of gardens and paddock, 50 yards from the open New Forest, offering wonderful cycling, riding and walking. Both the pretty Georgian sailing town of Lymington and the New Forest village of Brockenhurst (80 minutes to Waterloo by train) are about two miles away. There are numerous very good pubs and restaurants nearby, including The Hobler Inn, which serves excellent food, under 200 yards away. Children and dogs welcome, stabling can be arranged, as can cycle hire, and riding from various local stables within five minutes' drive.
website: www.newforestbandb-hilden.co.uk

See also Colour Display Advertisement

CADNAM (New Forest)
Simon and Elaine Wright, Bushfriers, Winsor Road, Winsor, New Forest, Southampton SO40 2HF (02380 812552). A special B&B experience in the rural village of Winsor, the quieter northern side of New Forest. Bushfriers is an individual forest cottage having wonderful countryside views; full of character and charm with delightful accommodation, comfy double bed and spacious en suite, TV, hair dryer and hospitality tray. A restful sitting room with log fire and timbered ceiling reflect the warm and friendly atmosphere, or relax in the secluded pretty garden. We care what you eat: an excellent breakfast is cooked to suit the individual tastes of guests. Local farm fresh produce, home-made organic bread, preserves from our organically grown fruit. The traditional village pub serves good food. Wander through the New Forest, hire a bike, ride a horse or visit the coast. B&B from £26.50 per person. Discount three nights.
e-mail: bushfriers@waitrose.com
website: www.newforest-uk.com/bushfriers.htm

CHANDLER'S FORD
Mrs A Barr, Pinehurst Guest House, 287 Hursley Road, Chandler's Ford SO53 5PJ (02380 270303). Pinehurst is a charming, cottage-style home with a large garden offering a calm, friendly and welcoming atmosphere to the stressed business person or to anyone wishing to explore the area. This family-run house has spacious, comfortable rooms with beautifully fitted en suite facilities; softened water, toiletries, colour TV, tea/coffee making facilities and a wide choice of breakfast provided for guests. There is ample off-road parking. Pinehurst is close to J12 of the M3 and convenient for Southampton, Winchester, Romsey, Eastleigh Station and Airport, also M27 and New Forest. We operate a no smoking policy.
e-mail: info@pinehurstguesthouse.co.uk
website: www.pinehurstguesthouse.co.uk

178 Hampshire

HAYLING ISLAND
Jane & Phil Taylor, Ravensdale, 19 St Catherines Road, Hayling Island PO11 0HF (Tel & Fax: 023 9246 3203; Mobile: 07802 188259). Jane and Phil welcome you to their home, which is comfortably fitted and in a quiet location within a short walk of the beach and golf course. Two double rooms with en suite facilities, triple room with three single beds, one small double bedroom with use of main bathroom. Central heating, television, tea/coffee making facilities. A full English Breakfast is included and Evening Meal is optional. Car parking. No smoking, and no pets please. Double room from £48-£56, single room from £36, triple room from £58. AA ♦♦♦♦

See also Colour Display Advertisement

HOOK
Oaklea Guest House, London Road, Hook RG27 9LA (01256 762673; Fax: 01256 762150). Friendly, family-run Guest House. All bedrooms en suite and non-smoking. Guest lounge with SKY TV, licensed bar. Evening meals available on request. Easy access from Junction 5 M3, London 55 minutes by train. Many excellent golf courses within 10-mile radius. Horse racing at Sandown, Ascot and Goodwood. Shopping at The Oracle, Reading and Festival Place, Basingstoke. Days out: Thorpe Park, Chessington, Legoland, Windsor Castle, Hampton Court, RHS Wisley, Milestones. AA ♦♦♦

LYMINGTON
The Rowans, 76 Southampton Road, Lymington SO41 3GZ (01590 672276; Fax: 01590 688610). Set in its own grounds in a quiet location, this delightful 1912 period house offers a friendly and relaxed atmosphere, a high standard of accommodation and ample parking. A delicious choice of breakfasts is served in the spacious residents' dining room. Only five minutes' walk from the High Street and Quay area, ideal for mariners and for travellers catching Isle of Wight ferries. Delightful forest and coastal walks. Open all year.
e-mail: therowans@totalise.co.uk

LYMINGTON
Mrs R. Sque, Harts Lodge, 242 Everton Road, Lymington SO41 0HE (01590 645902). Bungalow (non-smoking) set in three acres. Large garden with small lake and an abundance of bird life. Quiet location. Three miles west of Lymington. Friendly welcome and high standard. Accommodation comprises double, twin and family en suite rooms, each with tea/coffee making facilities and colour TV. Delicious four-course English breakfast. The sea and forest are five minutes away by car. Horse riding, golf and fishing are nearby. The village pub, serving excellent home-made meals, is half a mile away. Children and pets welcome. Bed and Breakfast from £27.50pp. AA ♦♦♦♦

FHG
Free or reduced rate entry to Holiday Visits and Attractions
see our READERS' OFFER VOUCHERS
on pages 53-90

Hampshire 179

LYMINGTON

"The home of Mrs Tee's Wild Mushrooms"

This restored Edwardian family residence, furnished in its period, but with modern conveniences, stands on an elevated site a mile-and-a-half from Lymington and a mile from the New Forest. On the first floor, three double/twin family rooms, all en suite; easy assisted wheelchair access to ground floor double en suite and double room with sitting room (bed/settee) and en suite shower and toilet. TV/tea/coffee facilities in all rooms. Gardens, barbecue area, and paddocks for guests' horses. Mushroom seminars held. Fluent in French and German. Bed and full English Breakfast from £40pppn; Evening Meal from £25 inclusive of wine. **ETC ♦♦♦**

Gorse Meadow Guest House
Sway Road, Lymington SO41 8LR
Tel: (01590) 673354 • Fax: (01590) 673336 • Mobile: 07774 139731
e-mail: gorse.meadow.guesthouse@wildmushrooms.co.uk • website: www.wildmushrooms.co.uk

LYNDHURST

Mrs E.M. Rowland, Forest Cottage, High Street, Lyndhurst SO43 7BH (023 802 83461). Charming 300-year-old cottage. Guests' sitting room with TV and a library of natural history, reference books, maps and local literature; tea/coffee always available. Warm, pretty bedrooms: one double, one twin and one single. A lovely garden contains an interesting collection of plants. Lyndhurst is the centre of the New Forest, convenient for many inland and coastal attractions. Horse riding and bicycle hire nearby. Private parking. No smoking please. Bed and Breakfast from £26pppn. **VisitBritain ♦♦♦♦** *SILVER AWARD.*
website: www.forestcottage.co.uk

LYNDHURST

Penny Farthing Hotel, Romsey Road, Lyndhurst SO43 7AA (023 802 84422; Fax: 023 802 84488). The Penny Farthing is a cheerful small Hotel ideally situated in Lyndhurst village centre, the capital of "The New Forest". The Hotel offers en suite single, twin, double and family rooms with direct-dial telephone, tea/coffee tray, colour TV and clock radio. We also have some neighbouring cottages available as Hotel annexe rooms or on a self-catering basis. These have been totally refitted, much with "Laura Ashley" decor, and offer quieter, more exclusive accommodation. The hotel has a licensed bar, private car park and bicycle store. Lyndhurst has a charming variety of shops restaurants, pubs and bistros and "The New Forest Information Centre and Museum". All major credit cards accepted. **AA/RAC/ETC ♦♦♦**
website: www.pennyfarthinghotel.co.uk

MILFORD-ON-SEA (New Forest)

Carolyn and Roy Plummer, Ha'penny House, 16 Whitby Road, Milford-on-Sea, Lymington SO41 0ND (01590 641210). Ha'penny House is a delightful character house with a warm, friendly atmosphere. Set in a quiet area of the unspoilt village of Milford-on-Sea and just a few minutes' walk to both sea and village, it is ideally situated for visiting the New Forest, Bournemouth, Salisbury and the Isle of Wight. The comfortable bedrooms are all en suite and beautifully decorated, with TV, hospitality tray and many extra touches. Award-winning breakfast menu with many choices. Large sunny diningroom and cosy guest lounge. Attractive gardens and summer house. Ample private parking. Three double, one twin. Non-smoking. Bed and Breakfast from £28 to £32.50 per person per night. Three-night short breaks for two people sharing, including breakfast from £168. Self-catering apartment also available. Open all year. **ETC ♦♦♦♦♦** *SILVER AWARD,* **AA ♦♦♦♦♦** *BREAKFAST AWARD.*
e-mail: info@hapennyhouse.co.uk   website: www.hapennyhouse.co.uk

180 Hampshire

NEW FOREST
Mrs J. Pearce, "St Ursula", 30 Hobart Road, New Milton BH25 6EG (01425 613515). Large detached family home offering every comfort in a friendly relaxed atmosphere. Off Old Milton Road, New Milton. Ideal base for visiting New Forest with its ponies and beautiful walks; Salisbury, Bournemouth easily accessible. Sea one mile. Leisure centre with swimming pool etc, town centre and mainline railway to London minutes away. Twin (en suite), double, family, single rooms, all with handbasin, TV and tea-making facilities. High standards maintained throughout; excellent beds. Two bathrooms/showers, four toilets. Downstairs twin bedroom suitable for disabled persons. Children and pets welcome. Cot etc, available. Pretty garden with barbecue which guests are welcome to use. Lounge with large colour TV. Two diningrooms. Smoke detectors installed. Full central heating. Open all year. Bed and Breakfast from £25. ETC ♦♦♦♦, *NATIONAL ACCESSIBLE SCHEME LEVEL 1.*

PETERSFIELD
Mrs Mary Bray, Nursted Farm, Buriton, Petersfield GU31 5RW (01730 264278). Working farm. This late 17th century farmhouse, with its large garden, is open to guests throughout most of the year. Located quarter-of-a-mile west of the B2146 Petersfield to Chichester road, one-and-a-half-miles south of Petersfield, the house makes an ideal base for touring the scenic Hampshire and West Sussex countryside. Queen Elizabeth Country Park two miles adjoining picturesque village of Buriton at the western end of South Downs Way. Accommodation consists of three twin-bedded rooms (two with washbasin), two bathrooms/toilets; sittingroom/breakfast room. Full central heating. Children welcome, cot provided. Sorry, no pets. Car essential, ample parking adjoining the house. Non-smoking. Bed and Breakfast only from £22 per adult, reductions for children under 12 years. Open all year except Christmas, March and April.

PORTSMOUTH
Graham and Sandra Tubb, "Hamilton House", 95 Victoria Road North, Southsea, Portsmouth PO5 1PS (Tel & Fax: 023 928 23502). Delightful Victorian townhouse B&B, centrally located five minutes by car from Continental and Isle of Wight Ferry Terminals, M27/A27, Stations, City Centres, University, Seafront, Historic Ships/Museums and all the tourist attractions that Portsmouth, and its resort of Southsea, has to offer. Bright, modern, centrally heated rooms with remote-control colour TV, hairdryer, clock, cooler fan and generous tea/coffee making facilities. Some rooms have en suite facilities. Ideal touring base for southern England. Full English, vegetarian and Continental breakfasts are served in lovely Spanish style dining room. Also Continental breakfasts served from 6am (for early morning travellers). Nightly/weekly stays welcome all year. Bed and Breakfast £25 to £28 per person nightly in standard rooms and £28 to £31 per person in en suite rooms. TOTALLY NON-SMOKING. ETC/AA ♦♦♦♦
e-mail: sandra@hamiltonhouse.co.uk
website: www.hamiltonhouse.co.uk

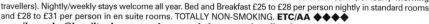

RINGWOOD (New Forest)
Mr and Mrs M. Burt, Fraser House, Salisbury Road, Blashford, Ringwood BH24 3PB (01425 473958). Fraser House is situated one mile from the market town of Ringwood, overlooking the Avon Valley. This comfortable family house is on the edge of the New Forest, famous for its ponies, deer and pleasant walks. It is ten miles from Bournemouth and the South Coast, and is convenient for visiting Southampton, Stonehenge and the cathedral city of Salisbury. All rooms have en suite bath or shower facilities, central heating, comfortable beds, colour TV, tea/coffee making facilities. Guest lounge with colour TV. Fishing and water sports available nearby. Non-smokers preferred. Ample parking space. Open all year. Most major credit cards accepted. Bed and Breakfast from £29 per person per night. ETC ♦♦♦♦
e-mail: mail@fraserhouse.net
website: www.fraserhouse.net

Hampshire 181

ROMSEY/NEW FOREST
Mrs J. Hayter, Woodlands, Bunny Lane, Sherfield English, Romsey SO51 6FT (01794 884840; Fax: 01794 885858). Woodlands is a small family-run guest house close to the New Forest and situated in a quiet country lane. Our bedrooms – double, twin and family en suite – overlook dairy fields and have washbasin, colour TV and tea/coffee making facilities. Guests' lounge. Close to the Isle of Wight ferry, Southampton, Salisbury, Winchester, Romsey, Florence Nightingale Country, Broadlands, Hillier Arboretum. Hearty breakfast and home-cooked evening meals available. Local village pubs. Roy and Jenny offer a warm welcome to all guests. Bed and Breakfast from £19.50 per person. Evening Meal from £6.50. Weekly bookings also. Open all year.
e-mail: woodlandsbb@amserve.com

SOUTHAMPTON
Mrs Rose Pell, Verulam House, 181 Wilton Road, Shirley, Southampton SO15 5HY (023 8077 3293 or 07790 537729). Guests are warmly welcomed to this comfortable, warm, roomy Edwardian establishment, in a nice residential area. Good cuisine. Two twin and one double room (used as singles when necessary) all with TV and tea/coffee making facilities; two bathrooms - plenty of hot water. Car parking space. Five minutes by car to historic Southampton city noted for its parks; railway station 10 minutes. Airport, Cross Channel ferries and Isle of Wight within easy reach and not far from M27, M3, Portsmouth, Winchester, Bournemouth, New Forest and coast. Bed and Breakfast from £24 per person per night. Non-smokers only.

SOUTHAMPTON
Dormy House Hotel, 21 Barnes Lane, Sarisbury Green/Warsash, Southampton SO31 7DA (01489 572626; Fax: 01489 573370). The Dormy House Hotel is a tranquil Victorian House, set in a quiet residential area, fully modernised and located within half a mile of the River Hamble and Warsash, perfect for all activities on the river. Accommodation consists of a charming dining room, comfortable lounge, twelve tastefully decorated, en suite bedrooms, each with tea/coffee making facilities, direct-dial telephones and remote-control TV. Ground floor bedrooms have access to the attractive and peaceful garden. Fully licensed. Local restaurants offer a broad range of traditional, light or ethnic menus. Easy access to the many attractions along the South Coast, Isle of Wight and the New Forest and within easy reach of Business Parks at Whitely, Segensworth and Hedge End.
AA ♦♦♦♦
e-mail: dormyhousehotel@warsash.globalnet.co.uk   website: www.dormyhousehotel.net

STOCKBRIDGE
Mr and Mrs A.P. Hooper, Carbery Guest House, Stockbridge SO20 6EZ (01264 810771). Ann and Philip Hooper welcome you to Carbery Guest House situated on the A30, just outside the village of Stockbridge, overlooking the famous trout fishing River Test. This fine old Georgian House has one acre of landscaped gardens, with swimming pool. Stonehenge and numerous places of interest nearby; sporting and recreational facilities close at hand. Accommodation includes double, twin, family and single rooms, available with private facilities. Centrally heated with colour TV, tea and coffee making equipment, hair dryers, radio alarms. Cots, high chairs. Car essential, parking. Open January to December for Evening Dinner, Bed and Breakfast or Bed and Breakfast only. Terms on application. **ETC/AA/RAC ♦♦♦**

182 Hampshire

WICKHAM
Mrs Patricia Toogood, 23 School Road, Wickham, Fareham PO17 5AA (01329 832457). Comfortable and friendly B&B close to picturesque 13th century village with shops, pubs and restaurants. We are four miles from Fareham, 20 minutes from Portsmouth Ferry Port and historic ships. Ideal overnight stop. Accommodation comprises family, double, twin and single rooms; guests' TV lounge. Excellent breakfast which can be served early if required. Free tea and coffee, flasks filled free of charge. No smoking anywhere in the house. Cooling fans in all rooms. Parking available. Deposit required for all bookings. Bed and Breakfast £20 per person per night. No hidden extras.

WINCHESTER
Lang House, 27 Chilbolton Avenue, Winchester SO22 5HE (Tel & Fax: 01962 860620). Winchester is one of the most beautiful cities in Britain and somewhere that demands exploration. Good accommodation is a must, and that is to be found at Lang House. Built at the beginning of the 20th century it has all the graciousness of buildings of that time. You will be warm in winter and enjoy the cool airy rooms in summer. Ample parking in the grounds and the house overlooks the Royal Winchester Golf Course. All bedrooms have en suite facilities and are comfortable and well furnished with colour TV and tea/coffee making facilities. You can be assured of a warm and friendly welcome and Winchester has a plethora of good eateries. Single from £45, double from £60.
website: www.langhouse.co.uk

WINCHESTER
Mrs S. Buchanan, "Acacia", 44 Kilham Lane, Winchester SO22 5PT (01962 852259; Mobile: 07801 537703). First class Tourist Board inspected accommodation in a peaceful location on the edge of the countryside, yet only a five minute drive from Winchester city centre. Excellent and easy access to road and rail communications to many tourist areas, all within one hour including London (by rail), Portsmouth, the New Forest, Salisbury, Stonehenge, etc. The accommodation consists of two doubles and one twin bedroom, all of which have en suite or private bathroom and tea/coffee making facilities. Charming sitting room with satellite TV. Excellent choice of breakfast. Non-smokers only. Off-street parking. Leave Winchester by the Romsey road, Kilham Lane is right at the second set of traffic lights. "Acacia" is 200 metres on the right. Bed and Breakfast from £60 to £65 double; single £46 to £48. **ETC/AA ♦♦♦♦** *SILVER AWARD*.
e-mail: ericbuchanan@btinternet.com   website: www.btinternet.com/~eric.buchanan

See also Colour Display Advertisement

WINCHESTER (near)
Mays Farm, Longwood Dean, Near Winchester SO21 1JS (01962 777486; Fax 01962 777747). Twelve minutes' drive from Winchester, (the eleventh century capital city of England), Mays Farm is set in rolling countryside on a lane which leads from nowhere to nowhere. The house is timber framed, originally built in the sixteenth century, and has been thoroughly renovated and extended by its present owners, James and Rosalie Ashby. There are three guest bedrooms, (one double, one twin and one either), each with a private bathroom or shower room. A sitting room with log fire is usually available for guests' use. Ducks, geese, chickens and goats make up the two acre "farm". Prices from £25 per person per night for Bed and Breakfast. Booking is essential. Please telephone or fax for details.

A useful index of towns/counties appears on pages 393-398

Herefordshire

HEREFORD
Hedley Lodge, Belmont Abbey, Hereford HR2 9RZ (01432 374747; Fax: 01432 374754). Hedley Lodge lies two miles to the south of the City of Hereford and is superbly located for visiting this wonderful Marches City or for touring the beautiful towns and villages of Herefordshire and the Wye Valley. Set within the grounds of historic Belmont Abbey, this modern, comfortable venue offers a warm, friendly welcome to all visitors and is ideal for short stays, holidays, conferences, retreats and wedding receptions. 17 en suite bedrooms with tea and coffee making facilities, colour TV and direct-dial telephone. Fully licensed restaurant is surrounded by beautiful gardens. B&B from £40 per room. **ETC ♦♦♦♦**
e-mail: hedleylodge@aol.com
website: www.hedleylodge.com

HEREFORD
Heron House, Canon Pyon Road, Portway, Burghill, Hereford HR4 8NG (01432 761111; Fax: 01432 760603). Heron House, with its panoramic views of the Malvern Hills, provides friendly and spacious Bed and Breakfast services. Facilities include en suite, family room, vanity units, colour TV, tea making equipment, breakfast room/lounge with stone fireplace and real log fire. Situated four miles north of Hereford in a rural location, this is an ideal base for walking, fishing, golf, cycling and bird-watching. Business facilities available on site. Secure off-road parking. Non-smoking. Bed and full English Breakfast from £20 per person per night. Evening meal by arrangement.
ETC ♦♦♦
e-mail: info@theheronhouse.com
website: www.theheronhouse.com

HEREFORD
David Jones, Sink Green Farm, Rotherwas, Hereford HR2 6LE (01432 870223). Working farm. A friendly welcome awaits you at our 16th century farmhouse overlooking the picturesque Wye Valley, yet only three miles from Hereford. Our individually decorated en suite rooms, one four-poster, all have tea/coffee facilities, colour TV and central heating. Relax in our extensive garden, complete with summer house and hot tub, or enjoy a stroll by the river. Fishing by arrangement. Pets by arrangement; children welcome. Terms from £25 per person.
AA ♦♦♦♦
e-mail: enquiries@sinkgreenfarm.co.uk
website: www.sinkgreenfarm.co.uk

•••some fun days out in HEREFORDSHIRE

Eastnor Castle, Ledbury • 01531 633410 • www.eastnorcastle.co.uk
Goodrich Castle, Ross-on-Wye • 01600 890538 • www.english-heritage.org.uk

184 Herefordshire

LEDBURY
Mrs C. Gladwin, Hill Farm, Eastnor, Ledbury HR8 1EF (01531 632827). HILL FARM is a 300-year-old stone and brick farmhouse surrounded by woodland at the foot of the Malvern Hills, one mile from Ledbury and one mile from Eastnor Castle. Accommodation comprises one twin room and two family rooms also used as twin/double rooms, all with washbasin, TV and tea/coffee making facilities. Guests' own sittingroom with log fire and the dining room look out onto a large garden and rural views. Bed and Breakfast from £19. Evening Meal by arrangement from £12.

The Coach House

LEDBURY
Mrs S.W. Born, The Coach House, Putley, Near Ledbury HR8 2QP (01531 670684; Fax: 01531 670992). The Coach House is an 18th century coaching stable set in gorgeous Herefordshire. It lies six miles west of historic Ledbury, home of the famous Poetry Festival. The spectacular Wye Valley National Footpath is only five miles away, browse the "Black and White Trail", Malvern Hills or Brecon Beacons. The accommodation comprises double, twin and single rooms all en suite. Guests have their own private lounge with TV, video, radio and woodburning stove, also the use of an adjacent kitchen. A hearty, full English breakfast is served in the stable dining room. Tariffs are £24pppn double and twin, £29 per night single, reduced by £1.50 pppn for three nights and more.
e-mail: wendyborn@putley-coachhouse.co.uk   website: www.putley-coachhouse.co.uk

LEOMINSTER
Mrs A. Pritchard, Eaton Court Farm, Stoke Prior Road, Leominster, Hereford HR6 0NA (01568 612095). B&B NON-SMOKING accommodation in a Listed Georgian farmhouse, in countryside, yet on the outskirts of Leominster town (five minutes by car) with many interesting shops including antique markets. An excellent point for just stopping off or as a base for local pursuits of interest of which there are many! Kingsize, double and twin rooms with bath/shower room en suite. Lounge with TV. Full English Breakfast. Terms from £22 pppn including cup of tea on arrival if required. Car parking on site. We are approached by a short minor road linking the A44 east of its junction with the A49. Children of 10 years and over are welcome. Sorry, no pets. Open from April to end October. Also small caravan and camping site on the farm.

LEOMINSTER
Rossendale House, 46 Broad Street, Leominster HR6 8BS (01568 612464). Rossendale House is a 17th century town house in the centre of historic Leominster. Restaurants, taverns and places of interest are on our doorstep. Railway and bus stations are conveniently close. A perfect base for visiting Hereford, Ludlow, Bromyard, Kington, The Marches, Black & White villages and the glorious surrounding countryside. Our en suite double rooms are each unique and extremely comfortable, they are exceptional value at £50 per night (£35 single occupancy). Room rates include breakfast and we are delighted to offer vegetarian and special diet options. We have secure private parking facilities for all guest vehicles and covered overnight storage for cycles, fishing tackle, etc. The house has spacious secluded gardens. ROSSENDALE HOUSE IS A NO SMOKING ESTABLISHMENT.
e-mail: enquiries@rossendalehouse.co.uk   website: www.rossendalehouse.co.uk

Cider Museum
Hereford, Herefordshire
See our **READERS' OFFER VOUCHER** for details of free or reduced rate entry

Herefordshire 185

ROSS-ON-WYE
Mrs Maggie Adams, Brookfield House, Over Ross Street, Ross-on-Wye HR9 7AT (01989 562188). A Grade II Listed building, part Georgian, part Queen Ann house, which has been refurbished to a high standard by the present owners. Accommodation comprises large, tastefully decorated en suite rooms with king-size beds, colour TV and hospitality trays. All rooms are non-smoking. Within an easy stroll of the centre of Ross-on-Wye but with the advantage of a large private car park. Price includes Full English Breakfast with a Vegetarian option. Bed and Breakfast £27 to £32pppn (double or twin). Please visit our website.
website: www.brookfield-house.co.uk

ROSS-ON-WYE
Lea House, Lea, Ross-on-Wye HR9 7JZ (01989 750652). A 16th century former coaching inn, Lea House has been beautifully refurbished, with exposed oak beams, an inglenook fireplace, antiques and imaginative decor. The spacious bedrooms have kingsize or twin beds and full en suite or private bathrooms. AA award-winning breakfasts are a real treat, with home-made breads and jams, fresh fruit and juice, local butcher's sausages and locally smoked fish. Dinner is also available on request. On the Hereford/Gloucester border, adjacent to the Royal Forest of Dean and the spectacular Wye Valley, there is a wealth of activities and wonderful walking. We accept dogs and children. Non-smoking. Bed and Breakfast from £25 - £30 pppn. **AA ♦♦♦♦ EGG CUP AWARD.**

e-mail: enquiries@leahouse.co.uk
website: www.leahouse.co.uk

ROSS-ON-WYE
Mrs H. Smith, Old Kilns, Howle Hill, Ross-on-Wye HR9 5SP (Tel & Fax 01989 562051). A high quality bed and breakfast establishment in picturesque, quiet village location. Centrally heated, private parking. Some rooms with super king-size bed plus en suite shower, toilet; also brass king-size four-poster bed with private bathroom and jacuzzi. Colour TV and tea/coffee making facilities in bedrooms. Lounge with log fire. Full English breakfast. Central for touring Cotswolds, Malvern, Stratford-upon-Avon, Wye Valley and Royal Forest of Dean. Open all year. Bed and Breakfast from £20 per person. Children and pets welcome (high chair, cots and babysitting service provided). Please telephone for free brochure. **AA/RAC ♦♦♦♦, SPARKLING DIAMOND AWARD.** Self-catering cottages also available sleeping 2-14 with four-poster beds and jacuzzi.

ROSS-ON-WYE
Mrs M.E. Drzymalski, Thatch Close, Llangrove, Ross-on-Wye HR9 6EL (01989 770300). Secluded, peaceful, comfortable Georgian farmhouse, yet convenient for A40, M4 and M50. Our three lovely bedrooms, each with its own bathroom (two en suite), have magnificent views over the unspoilt countryside. Relax in the visitors' lounge or sit in the shade of mature trees in our garden. You may be greeted by our dog or free flying parrot. Terms £25 to £30 per person (sharing). Please telephone or e-mail for brochure. **ETC ♦♦♦♦**
e-mail: info@thatchclose.co.uk
website: www.thatchclose.co.uk

The FHG Directory of Website Addresses
on pages 339-370 is a useful quick reference guide for holiday accommodation with e-mail and/or website details

Hertfordshire

RICKMANSWORTH
Mrs Elizabeth Childerhouse, Tall Trees, 6 Swallow Close, Nightingale Road, Rickmansworth WD3 7DZ (01923 720069). Large detached house situated in a quiet cul-de-sac with the centre of Rickmansworth only a short walk away. It is a small picturesque old town where there are many places to eat. We are five minutes' walk from the Underground station, half-an-hour to central London. Full breakfast served with homemade bread and preserves. Vegetarians and coeliacs catered for. Tea and coffee making facilities in rooms. Off-street parking. Convenient for M25 and Watford. No pets. This is a non-smoking household. Bed and Breakfast from £28.

Isle of Wight

See also Colour Display Advertisement

SANDOWN
Sandhill Hotel, 6 Hill Street, Sandown PO36 9DB (01983 403635; Fax: 01983 403695). Trevor Sawtell and family welcome you to a friendly family hotel five minutes' walk from the beach and train station. All rooms are en suite, with colour TV, tea/coffee making facilities and telephone with internet ports. We have a reputation for quality food served in our comfortable dining room, and after dinner, why not take a stroll in nearby Los Altos Park. Bed and Breakfast from £22. Bed, Breakfast and Evening Meal (five courses) from £32 per night. Special rates for children. Disabled friendly. Please call for brochure.
ETC ♦♦♦♦
e-mail: sandhillhotel@btconnect.com
website: www.sandhill-hotel.com

•••some fun days out in THE ISLE OF WIGHT

Calbourne Water Mill, Calbourne • 01983 531227 • www.calbournewatermill.co.uk
Fort Victoria, Yarmouth • 01983 760283 • www.fortvictoria.co.uk
Dinosaur Farm Museum, Brighstone • 01983 740544 • www.dinosaur-farm.co.uk
The Needles Park, Alum Bay • 0870 458 0022 • www.theneedles.co.uk

Isle of Wight 187

SANDOWN

FERNSIDE HOTEL
30 Station Avenue, Sandown, Isle of Wight PO36 9BW
Tel: 01983 402356 •• Fax: 01983 403647
e-mail: enquiries@fernsidehotel.co.uk •• www.fernsidehotel.co.uk

This family-run hotel is ideally situated within walking distance of sandy beaches, town centre and visitor attractions - the perfect location for a relaxing and enjoyable holiday or short break.

* Bed & Breakfast accommodation
* 11 comfortable en suite rooms (all non-smoking). Ground floor and family rooms (cots available).
* Remote-control colour TV and tea/coffee in all rooms, comfortable lounge with books, magazines and games
* Traditional full English breakfasts served in our dining room

See also Colour Advertisement

TOTLAND

Frenchman's Cove
ALUM BAY OLD ROAD, TOTLAND, ISLE OF WIGHT PO39 0HZ

Our delightful family-run guesthouse is set amongst National Trust downland, not far from the Needles and safe sandy beaches. Ideal for ramblers, birdwatchers, cyclists and those who enjoy the countryside. We have almost an acre of grounds. Cots and high chairs are available. All rooms are en suite, with colour TV and tea/coffee making facilities. Guests can relax in the attractive lounges.
Also available is the Coach House (**ETC ★★★**), a delightfully appointed apartment for two adults and two children.
Please contact Sue or Chris Boatfield for details.
Tel: 01983 752227 • www.frenchmanscove.co.uk

See also Colour Advertisement

The Golf Guide • 2006
Where to Play, Where to Stay

Available from most booksellers, **The Golf Guide, Where to Play, Where to Stay** covers details of every UK golf course – well over 2800 entries – for holiday or business golf. Hundreds of hotel entries offer convenient accommodation, with accompanying details of the courses – the 'pro', par score, length and more. Including holiday golf in Ireland, France, Portugal, Spain, the USA, South Africa and Thailand.

Only £9.99 from booksellers or direct from the publishers:
**FHG GUIDES, Abbey Mill Business Centre, Seedhill,
Paisley PA1 1TJ** *(postage charged outside UK)*
e-mail: admin@fhguides.co.uk • www.holidayguides.com

Visit the FHG website
www.holidayguides.com
for details of the wide choice of accommodation featured in the full range of FHG titles

Kent

ASHFORD

Mrs Janet Feakins, Old Farm House, Soakham Farm, Whitehill, Bilting, Ashford TN25 4HB (01233 813509). Soakham is a working farm situated on the North Downs Way between Boughton Aluph and Chilham and adjoining Challock Forest. It is ideally located both for walking and visiting many places in the South East area. Canterbury and Ashford are ten miles and five miles respectively. The farmhouse was originally a Hall House and Grade II Listed with much exposed woodwork. It offers the following accommodation; two double rooms including one with a four-poster bed and a twin-bedded room. Prices are from £25 per person for Bed and Breakfast. Ample parking is available and we are open all year round.

BROADSTAIRS

Keston Court Hotel, 14 Ramsgate Road, Broadstairs CT10 1PS (01843 862401). The Keston Court is a small hotel of charm and character, with friendly service and a homely atmosphere. It is only five minutes' walk to the shops and beach. Parking is free, and our licensed bar will cater for all your needs. All rooms have tea/coffee making appliances, also colour TV. The hotel holds a full fire certificate. Central heating in all rooms. Adults only. Closed during winter months. Room tariff (per night): single £20, standard double or twin £40, twin with shower £44, en suite double £46.
e-mail: kestoncourt@tinyonline.co.uk
website: www.SmoothHound.co.uk/hotels.html

Kent 189

See also Colour Display Advertisement

CANTERBURY

Mrs Lewana Castle, Great Field Farm, Stelling Minnis, Canterbury CT4 6DE (01227 709223). Situated in beautiful countryside, our spacious farmhouse is about eight miles from Canterbury and Folkestone, 12 miles from Dover and Ashford. We are an arable farm with soft fruit and chickens. We provide friendly, comfortable accommodation with full central heating and double glazing, traditional breakfasts cooked on the Aga, courtesy tray and colour TV in each of our suites/bedrooms. Our cottage suite has its own entrance, stairs, lounge, bathroom and twin-bedded room. Our large double bedroom has en suite bathroom and airbath. Our annexe suite has lounge/dining room, kitchen, double bedroom and bathroom, ideal for B&B and self-catering as is our new detached ground floor "Sunset Lodge", which sleeps 4 in two en suite bedrooms. There is ample off-road parking and good pub food nearby. Bed and Breakfast from £25 per person; reductions for children. Non-smoking establishment. ETC ♦♦♦♦ *SILVER AWARD.*
website: www.great-field-farm.co.uk

CANTERBURY

Mrs Prudence Latham, Tenterden House, The Street, Boughton, Faversham ME13 9BL (01227 751593). Stay in one of the en suite bedrooms (one double, one twin) in this delightful gardener's cottage and stroll through the shrubbery to the 16th century diningroom, in the main house, for a traditional English breakfast, beneath the Dragon Beam. Close to Canterbury, Whitstable and the Channel Ports. It makes an ideal base for exploring Kent, then walk to one of the historic inns in the village for your evening meal. Tea/coffee making facilities. Off-road parking. Open all year. Bed and Breakfast from £23 per person.

CANTERBURY

Maria and Alistair Wilson, Chaucer Lodge Guest House, 62 New Dover Road, Canterbury CT1 3DT (01227 459141). A highly recommended friendly guest house which is elegantly decorated and immaculately clean. Fully double glazed and centrally heated. Secure parking. Seven bedrooms en suite, including family rooms, with colour TV, tea/coffee making facilities, radio/alarm and hairdryer. Open all year round. 10 minutes' walk to city centre, cathedral, bus and rail stations. Hospital and cricket ground only five minutes' walk. Ideal base for touring Kent and for trips to the Continent. Bed and Breakfast from £18 per person.

CANTERBURY

Mr and Mrs R. Linch, Upper Ansdore, Duckpit Lane, Petham, Canterbury CT4 5QB (01227 700672; Fax: 01227 700840). Beautiful secluded Listed Tudor farmhouse with various livestock, situated in an elevated position with far-reaching views of the wooded countryside of the North Downs. The property overlooks a Kent Trust Nature Reserve, is five miles south of the cathedral city of Canterbury and only 30 minutes' drive to the ports of Dover and Folkestone. The accommodation comprises one family, three double and one twin-bedded rooms. All have shower and WC en suite and tea making facilities. Dining/sitting room, heavily beamed with large inglenook. Pets welcome. Car essential. Bed and Breakfast from £25 per person. Credit cards accepted. ETC ♦♦♦
e-mail: roger@ansdore.fsnet.co.uk   website: www.SmoothHound.co.uk/hotels/upperans.html

Museum of Kent Life
Maidstone, Kent

See our **READERS' OFFER VOUCHER** for details of free or reduced rate entry

MUSEUM OF KENT LIFE

190 Kent

CANTERBURY
Frances Mount, South Wootton House, Capel Road, Petham, Canterbury CT4 5RG (01227 700643; Fax: 01227 700613). A beautiful farmhouse with conservatory set in extensive garden, surrounded by fields and woodland. Fully co-ordinated bedroom with private bathroom. Tea/coffee facilities, colour TV. Children welcome. Canterbury four miles. Non-smoking. Bed and Breakfast from £25. Open all year. ETC ♦♦♦

DEAL
Sutherland House Hotel, 186 London Road, Deal CT14 9PT (01304 362853; Fax: 01304 381146). Situated on the A258 Deal to Sandwich Road, 200 yards from the Deal Hospital. This stylish hotel offers charming bedrooms which are decorated and furnished with great style and taste. The yellow and blue dining room provides a charming venue for home cooked dinners and breakfasts and guests have the use of a comfortable lounge well stocked with books and magazines. Four en suite non-smoking bedrooms. No smoking area in diningroom. TV, tea/coffee facilities and direct dial telephone in bedrooms. Licensed. Central heating. Sorry, no children under five years. Parking. Bed and Breakfast from £45 to £50 per night single occupancy of a double room, £55 to £60 per night double. Major Credit Cards accepted. AA ♦♦♦♦♦

e-mail: info@sutherlandhouse.fsnet.co.uk
website: www.sutherlandhousehotel.co.uk

DOVER
Bleriot's, 47 Park Avenue, Dover CT16 1HE (01304 211394). A Victorian residence set in a tree-lined avenue, in the lee of Dover Castle. Within easy reach of trains, bus station, town centre, hoverport and docks. Channel Tunnel approximately 10 minutes' drive. Off-road parking. We specialise in one night 'stop-overs' and mini-breaks. Single, double, twin and family rooms with full en suite. All rooms have colour TV, tea and coffee making facilities, and are fully centrally heated. Full English breakfast served from 7am. Reduced rates for room only. Open all year. Bed and Breakfast £23 to £27 per person per night. Mini-Breaks January to April and October to December £20 per person per night. MasterCard and Visa accepted. ETC ♦♦♦

DOVER
Penny Farthing Guest House, 109 Maison Dieu Road, Dover CT16 1RT (01304 205563; Fax: 01304 204439).
• Totally non-smoking Victorian residence. • All rooms are spacious en suite with many comfortable touches. • Town centre location with off-street forecourt parking. • Convenient for Ferry/Cruise terminals, Bus/Train station and Channel Tunnel. • Selection of breakfasts from 7.30am/ early morning departures catered for. • Room rate quoted. • Credit cards accepted.
e-mail: pennyfarthingdover@btinternet.com
website: www.pennyfarthingdover.com

FHG

Chislehurst Caves
Chislehurst, Kent
See our **READERS' OFFER VOUCHER** for details of free or reduced rate entry

·K·U·P·E·R·A·R·D·

Kent 191

DOVER
St Mark's Guest House, 23 Castle Street, Dover CT16 1PT (01304 201894). St Mark's Guest House in White Cliffs country is within sight of the famous Dover Castle and in walking distance of the ferry port and town centre with all its shops and cosmopolitan restaurants. Fifteen minutes' drive from the Channel Tunnel. We offer a comprehensive range of facilities. Most rooms are en suite and all have showers and washbasins. All rooms have tea/coffee making facilities, TV and are clean, comfortable and centrally heated. We offer an excellent English breakfast and cater for vegetarians. Bed and Breakfast from £18 to £27 pppn. Family rooms available.

See also Colour Display Advertisement

FOLKESTONE
Jim and Alison Taylor, Bolden's Wood, Fiddling Lane, Stowting, Near Ashford TN25 6AP (Tel & Fax: 01303 812011). Between Ashford/Folkestone. Friendly atmosphere, modern accommodation (one double, two singles) on our smallholding, set in unspoilt countryside. Non-smoking throughout. Log-burning stove in TV lounge. Full English breakfast. Country pubs (meals) nearby. Children love the old-fashioned farmyard, free range chickens, friendly sheep and...Llamas, Alpacas and Rheas! Treat yourself to a Llama-led picnic trek to our private secluded woodland and downland, and enjoy watching the bird life, rabbits, foxes, badgers and occasionally deer. Easy access to Channel Tunnel and Ferry Ports. Bed and Breakfast £25 per person.
e-mail: StayoverNight@aol.com
website: www.countrypicnics.com

FOLKESTONE
Mr and Mrs M. Sapsford, Wycliffe Hotel, 63 Bouverie Road West, Folkestone CT20 2RN (Tel & Fax: 01303 252186). However long, or short, your stay, a warm welcome is guaranteed at our friendly, family hotel offering clean, comfortable and affordable accommodation. We are based centrally and are close to all amenities. Our menu is interesting and varied, and guests have their own keys for freedom of access at all times. If you are travelling to or from the Continent we can offer an ideal stopover as we are conveniently situated just a short distance from the Channel Tunnel and Folkestone is an easy drive from the port of Dover. Off-street parking. Pets and children welcome - family rooms available. All major credit cards accepted. Bed and Breakfast from £25, Evening Meal £14. Discount for four or more nights. Please write or call for our brochure.

e-mail: sapsford@wycliffhotel.freeserve.co.uk   website: www.wycliffehotel.com

HEADCORN
Mrs Dorothy Burbridge, Waterkant Guest House, Moat Road, Headcorn, Ashford TN27 9NT (01622 890154). Waterkant is a small guest house situated in tranquil Wealdon Village of olde worlde charm. A warm and friendly welcome is assured and the relaxed and informal atmosphere is complemented by fine cuisine, excellent service and comfortable surroundings. Bedrooms have private or en suite bathrooms, four-poster beds, tea/coffee making facilities, colour TV and are centrally heated and double glazed. Lounge with colour TV. The beautifully landscaped secluded garden bounded by a stream provides a large pond, summerhouse for visitors' use and ample parking. Fast trains to London and a wealth of historic places to visit nearby. Open all year. Visitors return year after year. Bed and Breakfast from £20, with reduced rates for children, Senior Citizens, mid-week and winter season bookings, and referrals from FHG. Participants in ETC's Quality Assurance schemes.

e-mail: colin@waterkant.freeserve.co.uk

192 Kent

LENHAM

The Harrow Hill Hotel, Warren Street, Lenham, Maidstone ME17 2ED (01622 858727; Fax: 01622 850026). This 17th century inn is situated high on the North Downs of Kent amidst lush farmland in the hamlet of Warren Street. The Harrow houses 14 en suite, fully equipped bedrooms including two special occasion suites - one with a romantic four-poster and the other with an en suite jacuzzi. Featuring a lounge bar and fine dining restaurant, The Harrow makes the perfect venue for business or leisure trips. Fully licensed to perform Civil Marriage ceremonies. Located close to several tourist attractions including Leeds Castle, Chilston Park and the historic city of Canterbury.
website: www.activehotels.com

MAIDSTONE

Mrs Clifford, Langley Oast, Langley Park, Langley, Maidstone ME17 3NQ (01622 863523). Langley Oast was built in 1873 as part of Langley Park Farm, which was owned at that time by "Fremlins", the local brewery. The farm was a working farm until 1985 when the farm buildings were sold for conversion to homes. Langley Park, as it is now known, forms a secluded hamlet of about twelve homes, a quarter of a mile from the main road, the A274, about two miles from the centre of Maidstone and two miles from Leeds Castle. The Oast is set in the heart of Kentish countryside with fields as far as the eye can see, with a lake at the bottom of the nearest field. Maidstone is the county town of Kent and an ideal touring base for London or to visit the many tourist attractions in Kent. Or as a 'Stop Over' to or from the Continent, we are only 35 minutes from Folkestone and Dover. The Oast has been luxuriously converted by its present owners, Peter and Margaret Clifford. Bedrooms are either in the large Roundel rooms (24 ft across), one with jacuzzi en suite, or in twin rooms with Half Tester Canopies. Peter and Margaret look forward to welcoming you and will do everything in their power to ensure that your stay will be a happy and enjoyable one. Single room from £35, twin room from £50, Double round room from £50 to £85. **AA ♦♦♦♦, MEMBER SOUTH EAST ENGLAND TOURIST BOARD.**

See also Colour Display Advertisement

TENTERDEN

The White Lion, High Street, Tenterden, Kent TN30 6BD (01580 765077; Fax: 01580 764157). Taking its place proudly amongst Tenterden's attractive Tudor buildings, this fine 15th century hostelry, once a favoured staging post, retains its convivial character, the bar invariably buzzing with animated conversation between locals and visitors to this neat little town of tree-lined streets and interesting shops. All around is a peaceful and verdant countryside and the coast may be reached in little over half-an-hour. A spacious bar restaurant offers excellent home-cooked fare with both traditional and modern influences. The temptation to stay here for a few days is heightened by the offer of a tranquil night in a delightfully appointed en suite bedroom with the option of a luxury four-poster bed. Children and pets welcome. **ETC/AA ♦♦♦♦**

e-mail: whitelion@cetlicinnspubs.co.uk
website: www.whitelion/tenterden.co.uk

TENTERDEN/BIDDENDEN

Mrs Susan Twort, Heron Cottage, Biddenden, Ashford TN27 8HH (01580 291358). Peacefully situated in own grounds of six acres amidst acres of arable farmland, boasting many wild animals and birds, a stream and pond for coarse fishing. Within easy reach of Leeds Castle and many National Trust Properties including Sissinghurst Castle. You can choose between five tastefully furnished rooms with en suite and TV, or two rooms with separate bathroom. All rooms are centrally heated and have tea/coffee making facilities. There is a residents' lounge with log fire. Evening meals by arrangement. Bed and Breakfast from £22.50 to £27.50 per person per night.

Lancashire 193

Lancashire

See also Colour Display Advertisement

BLACKPOOL
Elsie and Ron Platt, Sunnyside and Holmsdale Hotel, 25-27 High Street, North Shore, Blackpool FY1 2BN (01253 623781). Two minutes from North Station, five minutes from Promenade, all shows and amenities. Colour TV lounge. Full central heating. No smoking. Children welcome; cots available. Reductions for children sharing. Senior Citizens' reductions May and June, always welcome. Special diets catered for, good food and warm friendly atmosphere awaits you. Bed and Breakfast from £18. Morning tea available. Overnight guests welcome when available. Small parties catered for.
e-mail: elsieandron@amserve.net

•••some fun days out in LANCASHIRE

Leighton Hall, Carnforth • 01524 734474 • www.leightonhall.co.uk
RSPB Leighton Moss, Near Carnforth • 01524 701601 • www.rspb.org.uk
Sea Life, Blackpool • 01253 622445 • www.sealifeeurope.com
Blackpool Zoo, Blackpool • 01253 830830 • www.blackpoolzoo.org.uk
National Football Museum, Preston • 01772 908400 • www.nationalfootballmuseum.com
British Commercial Vehicle Museum • 01772 451011 • www.commercialvehiclemuseum.co.uk

Lancashire

CHORLEY
Mrs Val Hilton, Jepsons Farm, Moor Road, Anglezarke, Chorley PR6 9DQ (01257 481691). Jepsons Farm, formerly a 17th century inn, is a stone built farmhouse with oak beams and wood burning stoves and is situated in Anglezarke, next to Rivington in the West Pennine Moors. Non-working farm apart from horses. It boasts excellent views and is surrounded by beautiful countryside for all outdoor activities including riding, walking, climbing, abseiling, cycling and fishing or simply relaxing. Good food assured and bedrooms have colour TV and tea/coffee trays; en suite facilities. Places of interest include Wigan Pier, Martin Mere, Astley Hall, Camelot and coastal resorts of Blackpool and Southport. Bed and Breakfast from £30; Evening Meal from £10. Reductions for children. Special rates for longer stays.

e-mail: enquiries@jepsonsfarm.co.uk website: www.jepsonsfarm.co.uk

See also Colour Display Advertisement

CLITHEROE
Rakefoot Farm, Chaigley, Near Clitheroe BB7 3LY (Chipping 01995 61332; mobile: 07889 279063; Fax: 01995 61296). Family farm in the beautiful countryside of the Ribble Valley in the peaceful Forest of Bowland, with panoramic views. Ideally placed for touring Coast, Dales and Lakes. Nine miles from M6 Junction 31a. Superb walks, golf and horse riding nearby, or visit pretty villages and factory shops. Warm welcome whether on holiday or business, refreshments on arrival. Bed and Breakfast or Self Catering in 17th century farmhouse and traditional stone barn conversion. Wood-burning stoves, central heating, exposed beams and stonework. Most bedrooms en suite, some ground floor. Excellent home-cooked meals, laundry; pubs/restaurants nearby. Indoor games room, garden and patios. Dogs by arrangement. Bed and Breakfast £20 to £30pppn sharing double/twin room, £20 to £35pn single. Four self-catering properties, three can be internally interlinked. £90 to £570 per property per week. Short breaks available. ETC ♦♦♦♦ *GUEST ACCOMMODATION*; ETC ★★★/★★★★. *PAST WINNER OF NWTB SILVER AWARD FOR SELF CATERING HOLIDAY OF THE YEAR.*
e-mail: info@rakefootfarm.co.uk website: www.rakefootfarm.co.uk

LANCASTER
Roy and Helen Domville, Three Gables, Chapel Lane, Galgate, Lancaster LA2 0PN (01524 752222). A large detached bungalow, three miles south of Lancaster and 400 yards from Lancaster University. Access from M6 Junction 33 and A6 in Galgate village. Two double bedrooms each with shower, toilet, colour TV and tea/coffee making facilities. One bedroom also has a private TV lounge. Open all year with full central heating. Spacious parking. A good location for visiting Blackpool, Morecambe, the Lake District and Yorkshire Dales. You will be sure of a friendly welcome and a homely atmosphere. Sorry, no pets. Non-smokers only please. Bed and Breakfast from £25 per person.

LANCASTER/KENDAL
Mrs Jean Scrase, The Old Police Station, 6 Dykes Lane, Yealand Conyers, Carnforth LA5 9SP (01524 735142). Bed and Breakfast in a genuine Victorian Police Station in a small village on the North Lancashire/Cumbria borders. The house has magnificent views onto the Lakeland Fells and Pennine Hills. It is ideally situated for the RSPB at Leighton Moss, Silverdale. The Lake District and Yorkshire Dales are a short drive away. The village has ancient woods, hills and the Lancaster Canal on its doorstep. Two miles from Junction 35 on M6, off A6. En suite twin room, central heating, tea/coffee facilities and parking. English breakfast with home made bread and preserves. Vegetarian food, packed lunches available on request. Why not stop over en route to or from Scotland! From £22 per person. Regret no pets.

Lancashire / Leicestershire & Rutland 195

MORECAMBE

Mrs R. Holdsworth, Broadwater Hotel, 356 Marine Road, East Promenade, Morecambe LA4 5AQ (01524 411333). The Broadwater is a small friendly hotel, situated on the select East Promenade with glorious views of Morecambe Bay and Lakeland Mountains. Only five minutes' walk from the town centre, shops and amusements. We offer every comfort and the very best of foods, varied and plentiful with choice of menu. All rooms en suite with heating, colour TV and tea making facilities. A perfect base for touring, the Broadwater is only 45 minutes' drive away from Blackpool, Yorkshire Dales and the Lake District, and 10 minutes from the historic city of Lancaster. Dinner available. Bed and Breakfast from £21. **ETC** ◆◆◆

Leicestershire & Rutland

BELTON-IN-RUTLAND (near Uppingham)

The Old Rectory, Belton-in-Rutland, Oakham LE15 9LE (01572 717279; Fax: 01572 717343). Victorian country house and guest annexe in charming village overlooking Eyebrook valley and rolling Rutland countryside. Comfortable and varied selection of rooms, mostly en suite, with direct outside access. Prices from £24 per person per night including breakfast. Small farm environment (horses and sheep) with excellent farmhouse breakfast. Public house 100 yards. Lots to see and do: Rutland Water, castles, stately homes, country parks, forestry and Barnsdale Gardens. Non-smoking. Self-catering also available. **RAC** ◆◆◆
e-mail: bb@iepuk.com
website: www.theoldrectorybelton.co.uk

MELTON MOWBRAY

Hillside House, 27 Melton Road, Burton Lazars, Melton Mowbray LE14 2UR (01664 566312; Fax: 01664 501819). Situated on the edge of the village with views over rolling countryside, Hillside House is a comfortable, converted old farm building, offering one double and one twin room both en suite, and one twin with private bathroom. All have colour TV and tea/coffee making facilities. There is a guests' lounge; Rutland Water, Geoff Hamilton's Garden and Belvoir Castle are close by. Melton Mowbray with its bustling market is one and a half miles away. Bed and Breakfast from £22 to £24.50; 10% reduction for 3-night stay (except during special events). Children over ten only. Closed Christmas and New Year. **ETC** ◆◆◆◆
e-mail: hillhs27@aol.com
website: www.hillside-house.co.uk

Lincolnshire

ALFORD

Westbrook House, Gayton Le Marsh, Alford LN13 ONW (01507 450624). At Westbrook House we offer carefully designed, thoughtfully equipped, quality en suite accommodation in a tranquil village location, between superb beaches and the Lincolnshire Wolds. Breakfasts and optional evening meals are served in the conservatory overlooking the patio garden and feature "Tastes of Lincolnshire". There is a galleried TV/sitting area with tourist information. Ideal base for local market towns, countryside, walking, cycling etc. (bikes available). Discover the "Real Lincolnshire". Open all year. Bed & Breakfast from £22.50. **ETC** ♦♦♦♦ *"WHICH?" GOOD B&B GUIDE.*
e-mail: westbrook_house@hotmail.com
website: www.bestbookwestbrook.co.uk

CONINGSBY

Mrs C. Whittington, High House Farm, Tumby Moorside, Near Coningsby, Boston PE22 7ST (01526 345408). An early 18th century Listed farmhouse with spacious en suite bedrooms and original beamed ceilings. Enjoy a generous farmhouse breakfast using fresh local produce. Centrally located for five 'Bomber Country' museums, championship golf at Woodhall Spa, antiques at Horncastle and local fishing. Historic pubs nearby serving excellent evening meals. Within easy reach of the east coast and the Lincolnshire Wolds. One double and one twin bedroom. Central heating, tea and coffee facilities and colour TV. Open all year except Christmas. No smoking. Children welcome. B&B from £20pp; reductions for three days or more.
e-mail: HighHousefarm@aol.com

GAINSBOROUGH

See also Colour Display Advertisement

The Black Swan Guest House, 21 High Street, Marton, Gainsborough DN21 5AH (Tel & Fax: 01427 718878). We offer a warm and friendly stay at our delightfully converted 18th century coaching inn, so get away from the 'hurly burly' of modern life, and escape to the peace and quiet, although Lincoln is only 12 miles away and many other attractions are nearby. All our rooms are en suite, with full facilities; we also have a comfortable guest lounge with ample reading matter. Our breakfasts are made with the best quality local produce and should set you up for the day. We are a non-smoking establishment. Single from £35, double/twin from £58. **AA** ♦♦♦♦
e-mail: info@blackswan-marton.co.uk
website: www.blackswan-marton.co.uk

•••some fun days out in LINCOLNSHIRE

Rand Farm Park, Near Wragby • 01673 858904 • www.randfarmpark.com
National Fishing Heritage Centre, Grimsby • 01472 323345 • www.nelincs.gov.uk

Lincolnshire 197

See also Colour Display Advertisement

HORNCASTLE

Mrs C.E. Harrison, Baumber Park, Baumber, Near Horncastle LN9 5NE (01507 578235; Fax: 01507 578417; mobile: 07977 722776). Spacious elegant farmhouse of character in quiet parkland setting, on a mixed farm. Large plantsman's garden, wildlife pond and grass tennis court. Fine bedrooms with lovely views, period furniture, log fires and books. Central in the county and close to the Lincolnshire Wolds, this rolling countryside is little known, quite unspoilt, and ideal for walking, cycling or riding. Championship golf courses at Woodhall Spa. Well located for historic Lincoln, interesting market towns and many antique shops. Enjoy a relaxing break, excellent breakfasts, and a comfortable, homely atmosphere. Double, twin, single/family suite. All en suite or private bathroom. Bed and Breakfast from £26.
website: http://uk.geocities.com/baumberpark/thehouse

LOUTH

Tony and Beverly Moss, Keddington House Host Home, 5 Keddington Road, Louth LN11 0AA (01507 603973). Tony and Beverly offer personal accommodation in our beautiful Victorian house, set back 100 yards from the road, in our quiet grounds with ample parking. Just 10 minutes from the 'capital of the wolds', Louth town centre and Cadwell Park; and half-an-hour from Humberside airport. Also convenient for Lincoln, Skegness, Cleethorpes, etc. Tea/coffee served in lounge. Excellent food. TV in all rooms, en suite available. Heated outdoor swimming pool in summer months. 'A Hidden Oasis'.
e-mail: keddingtonhouse@btinternet.com
website: www.keddingtonhouse.co.uk

LOUTH

The Priory Hotel, Eastgate, Louth LN11 9AJ (01507 602930; Fax: 01507 609767). The Priory is a Grade II Listed building dating from 1818. With its stunning Victorian-Gothic style architecture, set in beautiful tranquil surroundings, it is the ideal location for those seeking a relaxing break – business or social. The hotel is set in three acres with mature trees, a lake with a natural spring, old folly and a ruined mausoleum. Ten en suite bedrooms, recently refurbished. Restaurant, marquee facilities, wedding receptions, private parties, weekend breaks, modern English cuisine, degustation menu, car parking. Our friendly and caring staff are just as impressive as the setting. Please telephone for further information.
website: www.theprioryhotel.com

MARKET RASEN

Mrs Vivienne Klockner, Redhurst, Holton-cum-Beckering, Market Rasen LN8 5NG (Tel & Fax: 01673 857927). A warm welcome awaits guests at Redhurst B&B, set in gardens, orchard and copse in a small village nestling on the edge of the Lincolnshire Wolds. Enjoy swimming in the heated outdoor pool in summer and warmth from a crackling log fire in winter. An ideal centre from which to explore the many and varied attractions of Lincolnshire. Two twin rooms en suite (one ground floor); one single room with private facilities. From £22 per person per night. Self-catering also available. Non-smoking; sorry, no pets. Open all year. Details on request. **ETC ♦♦♦**

Natureland Seal Sanctuary
Skegness, Lincolnshire
See our **READERS' OFFER VOUCHER** for details of free or reduced rate entry

198 Lincolnshire

See also Colour Display Advertisement

PETERBOROUGH
Bed & Breakfast at No. 19 West Street, Kings Cliffe, Near Stamford, Peterborough PE8 6XB (01780 470365; Fax 01780 470623). A beautifully restored 500-year-old Listed stone house, reputedly one of King John's Hunting Lodges, situated in the heart of the stone village of Kings Cliffe on the edge of Rockingham Forest. Both the double and twin rooms have their own private bathrooms, and there is colour TV and a welcome tray in each. In the summer breakfast can be served on the terrace overlooking a beautiful walled garden. Off-street parking is behind secure gates. Within 10 miles there are seven stately homes, including Burghley House, famous for the Horse Trials, Rutland Water, and the beautiful old towns of Stamford and Oundle. Imaginative evening meals are available on request and prices range from £12 to £18. Open all year. A non-smoking house. Bed and Breakfast from £22.50 per person. Proprietor: **Jenny Dixon**.
e-mail: kjhl_dixon@hotmail.com
website: www.kingjohnhuntinglodge.co.uk

SCUNTHORPE
The Beverley Hotel, 55 Old Brumby Street, Scunthorpe DN16 2AJ (01724 282212; Fax: 01724 270422). Situated between Scunthorpe and Ashby in a quiet residential area in one of the oldest parts of town, with easy access to all main routes; nine miles from Humberside airport and within easy reach of five golf courses, the Humber Bridge, Beverley, Hull, York and Doncaster. Comfortable residents' lounge with colour TV, where you can sit and relax; charmingly decorated dining room for both evening meals and breakfasts; well-stocked bar. Double rooms are tastefully decorated with all modern fittings, colour TV, tea/coffee making facilities and all are en suite with shower; some also with bath. Executive rooms are available for that extra comfort with luxury fittings and bedding. Please contact us for more information.
website: www.beverleyhotelscunthorpe.co.uk

See also Colour Display Advertisement

THORPE FENDYKES
Mrs S. Evans, Willow Farm, Thorpe Fendykes, Wainfleet, Skegness PE24 4QH (01754 830316). In the heart of the Lincolnshire Fens, Willow Farm is a working smallholding with free range hens, goats, horses and ponies. Situated in a peaceful hamlet with abundant wildlife, ideal for a quiet retreat – yet only 15 minutes from the Skegness coast, shops, amusements and beaches. Bed and Breakfast is provided in comfortable en suite rooms from £20 per person per night, reductions for children (suppers and sandwiches can be provided in the evening on request). Rooms have tea and coffee making facilities and a colour TV and are accessible to disabled guests. Horse riding available. Friendly hosts! Ring for brochure.
e-mail: willowfarmhols@aol.com
website: www.willowfarmholidays.co.uk

WOODHALL SPA
Barbara and Tony Hodgkinson, Kirkstead Old Mill Cottage, Tattershall Road, Woodhall Spa LN10 6UQ (01526 353637; mobile: 07970 040401). A warm welcome awaits you at this peaceful, sunny, detached non-smoking house, which is set beside the River Witham on the outskirts of Woodhall Spa, a village which is noted for its 'old world' charm, park with open-air heated swimming pool, Kinema in the woods and championship golf course. A new garden, three-acre woodland garden, rowing boat, riverbank walks and membership of a local leisure club are also yours to enjoy, plus seasonal coarse fishing. There are numerous pubs and restaurants locally, or you are welcome to bring back a takeaway. We have a telephone, e-mail, fridge, iron and hairdryer for guests to use, and each of our three guest bedrooms (two en suite) has a TV, clock radio and hot drinks tray. A video, piano and open fire help to make the lounge a relaxing area. From £27 per person, a cooked, typical English breakfast is served or you can choose a lighter, healthy option.
website: www.woodhallspa.com

WOODHALL SPA

Mrs Claire Brennan, Claremont Guest House, 9-11 Witham Road, Woodhall Spa LN10 6RW (01526 352000). Homely Bed and Breakfast in a traditional, unspoilt Victorian guest house in the centre of Woodhall Spa, Lincolnshire's unique resort. Off-street parking. Good food close by. Excellent centre for touring, walking and cycling. En suite rooms. Golf locally. Tea and coffee making facilities and TV in rooms. Special rates for short breaks. Prices from £15 per person. **ETC/AA ◆◆**

Merseyside

BEBINGTON

The Bebington Hotel, 24 Town Lane, Bebington, Wirral CH63 5JG (0151-645 0608). A family business which guarantees a warm and friendly welcome within a professional atmosphere. Close to Bebington station and within easy reach of Birkenhead, Liverpool and Chester. All rooms en suite, colour TV, tea/coffee facilities. Car park. Residents' licence. Family rooms available.
e-mail: vaghena@aol.com

See also Colour Display Advertisement

LIVERPOOL

Holme Leigh Guest House, 93 Woodcroft Road, Wavertree, Liverpool L15 2HG (0151-734 2216). Situated close to Sefton Park and two-and-a-half miles from Liverpool city centre, Holme Leigh Guest House has been family-run for over 35 years. Recently fully refurbished, all rooms are comfortably furnished complete with TV, tea and coffee, en suite facilities with full central heating and the award-winning breakfast room. Just two miles from the M62 and 20 minutes from the airport, all of Merseyside is accessible from our convenient position. Single rooms available from £22 per night, doubles and twins from £44. Family rooms also available. All rates include VAT and Continental breakfast. **ETC ◆◆◆**
e-mail: info@holmeleigh.com
website: www.holmeleigh.com

Norfolk

ATTLEBOROUGH

Mrs Liz Rivett, Manor Farm, Hingham Road, Great Ellingham, Attleborough NR17 1JE (Tel & Fax: 01953 453388). Manor Farm is situated in a rural location only five minutes from the A11 (20 minutes from Norwich). We are within easy reach of the many and varied places of interest East Anglia has to offer. Set in a large garden backing on to a young woodland, the farmhouse offers a peaceful, relaxing environment. The house has great character with inglenook fireplace and exposed beams. Every effort is made to ensure guests' comfort and the rooms are spacious and well appointed. Further details and terms on request.
e-mail: rivett.and.son@farmline.com

ATTLEBOROUGH

Hill House Farm, Deopham Road, Great Ellingham, Attleborough NR17 1AQ (Tel & Fax: 01953 453113). A working farm in quiet rural setting situated within easy reach of all local attractions. We offer our guests a warm welcome, children welcome, pets by arrangement only. Attractions include Banham Zoo, Snetterton Racing Circuit and fishing lakes are close by; seaside resorts and Norfolk Broads are approximately 40 miles distant. Comfortable rooms with washbasins, tea/coffee facilities and colour TV; central heating. Ample off-road parking. Open all year. Awarded Good Food Hygiene Certificate. Walkers and cyclists welcome, clothes drying facilities. Special diets and packed lunches available. Cot available. Non-smoking. Terms from £22.50pppn, reduced rates for children under ten years.
e-mail: beales@hillhousefarm.fslife.co.uk

AYLSHAM

The Old Pump House, Holman Road, Aylsham, Norwich NR11 6BY (01263 733789). This comfortable 1750s house, facing the thatched pump a minute from Aylsham's church and historic marketplace, has six bedrooms, four en suite (including one four-poster), with colour TV and tea/coffee facilities. English Breakfast with free-range eggs and local produce (or vegetarian breakfast) is served in the pine-shuttered sitting room overlooking the peaceful garden. Aylsham is central for Norwich, the coast, the Broads, National Trust houses, steam railways and unspoilt countryside. Well-behaved children are very welcome. Bed and Breakfast from £27 to £37. Dinner by prior arrangement from October to May. Non-smoking. Off-road parking for six cars. ETC ♦♦♦♦ *SILVER AWARD*.
e-mail: tonyandlynda@oldpumphouse.fsworld.co.uk
web: www.smoothhound.co.uk/hotels/oldpumphouse.html

BEETLEY

Mrs Jenny Bell, Peacock House, Peacock Lane, Old Beetley, Dereham NR20 4DG (01362 860371). Old farmhouse. Lovely countryside with good walks three and a half miles from Dereham, close for Norwich, National Trust houses, Sandringham, beaches. All rooms en suite, tea/coffee facilities, TV. Own lounge, no smoking. Very warm welcome. B&B from £26 per person. Open all year. Children and dogs welcome. ETC ♦♦♦♦ *GOLD AWARD, WHICH? GOOD B&B GUIDE*.
e-mail: PeackH@aol.com
website: www.SmoothHound.co.uk/hotels/peacockh.html

See also Colour Display Advertisement

CROMER

Mrs Ann Youngman, Shrublands Farm, Northrepps, Cromer NR27 0AA (Tel & Fax: 01263 579297). Shrublands Farm is an arable farm set in the village of Northrepps, two-and-a-half miles south east of Cromer and 20 miles north of Norwich. This is the ideal situation for exploring the wonderful coast of Norfolk, National Trust properties and the Norfolk Broads. The Victorian/Edwardian house has three bedrooms all with private facilities, colour TV and tea/coffee facilities. There is full central heating and plenty of parking space. This is a no smoking house. Children over 12 years welcome. Sorry, no pets. Prices from £27-£29pppn; single supplement £10. Recommended by "Which?" Magazine. ETC/AA ♦♦♦♦

e-mail: youngman@farming.co.uk
website: www.broadland.com/shrublands

GREAT YARMOUTH

Mrs E. Dack, `Dacona', 120 Wellesley Road, Great Yarmouth NR30 2AP (01493 856863 or 855305). Homely guest house with own keys and access at all times. Centrally situated, it is only two/three minutes from the seafront and five minutes from shopping centre. Every amenity provided - tea making facilities in all rooms, comfortable accommodation and an ideal location. Bed and Breakfast terms from £15 to £17 nightly, room only available. Children catered for (half-price rates sharing with two adults). Dogs accepted on enquiry.

Dinosaur Adventure Park
Norwich, Norfolk
See our **READERS' OFFER VOUCHER** for details of free or reduced rate entry

202 Norfolk

See also Colour Display Advertisement

HUNSTANTON
Marine Bar, 10 St Edmunds Terrace, Hunstanton, Norfolk PE36 5EH (01485 533310). Pets are very welcome at a small charge of £1 per night. We do not have en suite rooms but every room has its own basin. Bar meals available all day. Colour TV in all bedrooms. Most rooms have a view. £22.50pppn, including breakfast. Town centre location. Open all year.

KING LYNN (near Spalding)
Harbour View Barns, Eastbank Farm, Garners Lane, Sutton Bridge, Spalding, Lincs PE12 9YP (01406 351333). Beautifully restored, turn-of-the-century, traditional barns, adjacent to traditional farmhouse on the borders of Lincolnshire, Norfolk and Cambridgeshire. Within a short distance of the coast, with enjoyable walks and birdwatching. Situated beside the river, and close to good inland fishing rivers. Close to market towns in the direction of both King's Lynn and Spalding. 10 rooms, all en suite and finished to a high standard. Themed breakfast and evening restaurant area, lounge area, ample parking, relaxing garden with large pond. B&B from £30 per person per night.

LONG STRATTON (near Norwich)
Mrs Joanna Douglas, Greenacres Farmhouse, Woodgreen, Long Stratton, Norwich NR15 2RR (01508 530261). Period 17th century farmhouse on 30 acre common with ponds and natural wildlife, 10 miles south of Norwich (A140). The beamed sittingroom with inglenook fireplace invites you to relax. A large sunny dining room encourages you to enjoy a leisurely traditional breakfast. All en suite bedrooms (two double/twin) are tastefully furnished to complement the oak beams and period furniture, with tea/coffee facilities and TV. Full size snooker table and all-weather tennis court for guests' use. Jo is trained in therapeutic massage, aromatherapy and reflexology and is able to offer this to guests who feel it would be of benefit. Come and enjoy the peace and tranquillity of our home. Bed and Breakfast from £25. Reductions for two nights or more. Non-smoking. **ETC ♦♦♦♦**
website: www.abreakwithtradition.co.uk

MUNDESLEY
Mrs Christine Thrower, Whincliff Bed & Breakfast, Cromer Road, Mundesley NR11 8DU (01263 721554). Situated upon the picturesque 'whin gorse' covered cliffs, overlooking the sea. Near beautiful unspoilt beaches, with the lively entertainment centre of Great Yarmouth also close by. Ideal for exploring the Norfolk Broads, with its wealth of wildlife or for visiting the historic city of Norwich. Family, twin and single rooms available, some en suite, all with colour TV and tea/coffee making facilities. Off-road parking available. Non-smoking. Pets welcome at no extra charge.
e-mail: whincliff@freeuk.com
website: www.whincliff.freeuk.com

Readers are requested to mention this FHG publication when seeking accommodation

Norfolk 203

See also Colour Display Advertisement

NORTH WALSHAM
Mrs G. Faulkner, Dolphin Lodge, 3 Knapton Road, Trunch, North Walsham NR28 0QE (01263 720961). Friendly welcome from the proprietors of this bungalow accommodation. Bed and Breakfast in a village setting just two-and-a-half miles from beaches. Many rural walks locally; within easy reach of all Norfolk's attractions including the Norfolk Broads. All rooms en suite, with tea/coffee making facilities, TV, hairdryer. **ETC ◆◆◆◆**

See also Colour Display Advertisement

NORWICH
Simon and Heather Moss, Oakbrook Guest House, Frith Way, Great Moulton, Norwich NR15 2HE (01379 677359; mobile: 07885 351212). Simon and Heather welcome you to this former village school, fully refurbished in 2005, with views over the quiet Tas Valley, south of Norwich. Oakbrook House is an excellent touring base for East Anglia, centrally situated in the region. Nine warm comfortable rooms of various sizes and prices to match individual budget and comfort, each with en suite wc and basin, colour TV, clock radio and hospitality tray, en suite or private shower. All diets catered for, central heating, smoke-free, pets by arrangement. Evening meals and daytime use of the facilities available. Contact us for brochure. Long stay discounts. B&B from £19 pppn.
**e-mail: simonandheather@btopenworld.com
website: www.oakbrookhouse.co.uk**

NORWICH
Mr Brian and Mrs Diane Curtis, Rosedale Guest House, 145 Earlham Road, Norwich NR2 3RG (01603 453743; Fax: 01603 259887). Friendly, family-run Victorian Guest House pleasantly situated within short walking distance of city centre and University, on the B1108. All rooms have colour TV, tea/coffee making facilities and own keys for your convenience. A full English breakfast is served in the diningroom and vegetarians are made very welcome. There are several good eating places nearby and once you have parked your car you can relax and enjoy Norwich. The Norfolk Broads are just seven miles away and the coast 20 miles. Full central heating. Bed and Breakfast from £20 per person. Completely no smoking. All major credit cards accepted. **ETC ◆◆**

SEA PALLING
Tony and Liza Etheridge, The Old Hall Inn, Sea Palling NR12 0TZ (01692 598323; Fax: 01692 598822). The Old Hall Inn is an old world character freehouse/restaurant situated on the coast road between Cromer and Great Yarmouth. It is in the middle of the village and just five minutes' walk from one of the best beaches along the Norfolk coast. There are six letting rooms, three of which are en suite, all have tea/coffee making facilities and TV. There is a non-smoking à la carte restaurant and bar meals are also available. Well behaved children and pets are welcome. Wireless internet available. Prices start at £35 for a single room, inclusive of full English breakfast, and £50 for a double room (two persons) per night.

Collectors World of Eric St John Foti
Downham Market, Norfolk
See our **READERS' OFFER VOUCHER** for
details of free or reduced rate entry

WELLS-NEXT-THE-SEA

Mrs Dorothy MacCallum, Machrimore, Burnt Street, Wells-next-the-Sea NR23 1HS (01328 711653). A warm welcome awaits you at this attractive barn conversion. Set in quarter-of-an-acre in quiet location close to the shops and picturesque harbour of Wells. Three en suite guest bedrooms (two twin and one double) at ground floor level overlook their own patio and garden area. Ample car parking. Sorry no smoking in the bedrooms. Ideal for the bird watching sanctuaries at Cley, Salthouse and Titchwell. Close to Sandringham, Holkham and the Shrines at Walsingham. Prices from £30 to £34 daily; £190 to £215 weekly. 10% reduction three nights or more. **ETC** *SILVER AWARD.*
e-mail: dottiemac39@hotmail.com
website: www.machrimore.co.uk

WOODTON

Mrs J. Read, George's House, The Nurseries, Woodton, Near Bungay NR35 2LZ (01508 482214). A charming 17th century cottage with a six acre free-range egg unit and working forge/ blacksmith's showroom, situated in the centre of the village, just off the main Norwich to Bungay road. Wonderful holiday area, ideal for touring Norfolk and Suffolk. Within 10 miles is historic Norwich, with its castle, cathedral, theatre and excellent shops. Coast 18 miles. Guest accommodation comprises three double bedrooms with washbasins. Bathroom, shower, toilet, dining room, lounge/TV, sun room. Ample parking. Bed and Breakfast £23 per person per night. Excellent pub meals available 100 yards.
e-mail: julietandpeter@aol.com
website: www.rossmag.com/georges/

WROXHAM

Wroxham Park Lodge, 142 Norwich Road, Wroxham NR12 8SA (01603 782991). Friendly Bed and Breakfast in an elegant Victorian house, in Wroxham 'Capital of Norfolk Broads'. Ideal for touring, day boats and boat trips on the beautiful Broads, fishing, steam railways, National Trust Houses, Wroxham Barns. Near north Norfolk coast, Great Yarmouth and Norwich. Good local restaurants and pubs. Guests arriving by train will be met. Open all year. All rooms en suite, tea/coffee, non-smoking, colour TV. Hearty breakfasts. Conservatory, garden, car park, ground floor room, central heating and public telephone. Pets by arrangement. Bed and Breakfast from £24 per person. Ring for brochure. **ETC** ♦♦♦♦

WYMONDHAM

Mrs Joy Morter, Home Farm, Morley, Wymondham NR18 9SU (01953 602581). Comfortable accommodation set in four acres, quiet location, secluded garden. Conveniently situated off A11 between Attleborough and Wymondham, an excellent location for Snetterton and only 20 minutes from Norwich and 45 minutes from the Norfolk Broads. Accommodation comprises two double rooms and one twin-bedded room, all with TV, tea/coffee facilities and central heating. Children over five years old welcome, but sorry no animals and no smoking. Bed and Breakfast from £25 to £28 per person per night.

FHG

Visit the FHG website
www.holidayguides.com
for details of the wide choice of accommodation
featured in the full range of FHG titles

·K·U·P·E·R·A·R·D·

Northamptonshire

DAVENTRY
Carrie Hart, Murcott Mill, Long Buckby NN6 7QR (01327 842236; Fax: 01327 844524). Murcott Mill is an imposing Georgian mill house set within a working farm. It has a large garden and lovely outlook over open countryside. All rooms are en suite with colour TV. Central heating throughout and visitors have their own lounge and dining room with open log fires. An ideal stopover, close to M1 and good location for touring the area. Children and pets welcome. Bed and Breakfast from £28 single; double £50. Open all year.
e-mail: carrie.murcottmill@virgin.net
website: www.murcottmill.com

KETTERING
Mrs A. Clarke, Dairy Farm, Cranford St Andrew, Kettering NN14 4AQ (01536 330273). Enjoy a holiday in our comfortable 17th century farmhouse with oak beams and inglenook fireplaces. Four-poster bed now available. Peaceful surroundings, large garden containing ancient circular dovecote. Dairy Farm is a working farm situated in a beautiful Northamptonshire village just off the A14, within easy reach of many places of interest or ideal for a restful holiday. Good farmhouse food and friendly atmosphere. Open all year, except Christmas. Bed and Breakfast from £25 to £35 (children under 10 half price); Evening Meal £17. **ETC** ♦♦♦ *SILVER AWARD.*

---

publisher's note
While every effort is made to ensure accuracy, we regret that FHG Guides cannot accept responsibility for errors, misrepresentations or omissions in our entries or any consequences thereof. Prices in particular should be checked. We will follow up complaints but cannot act as arbiters or agents for either party

FHG
·K·U·P·E·R·A·R·D·

The FHG Directory of Website Addresses
on pages 339-370 is a useful quick reference guide for holiday accommodation with e-mail and/or website details

Northumberland

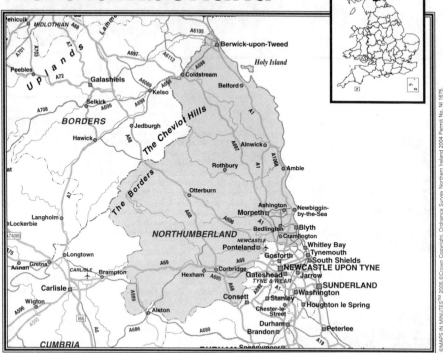

ALLENDALE

Mrs Eileen Ross Finn, Thornley House, Allendale NE47 9NH (01434 683255). Beautiful country house in spacious grounds surrounded by field and woodland, one mile out of Allendale, 10 miles south of Hexham, near Hadrian's Wall. Two large beautifully furnished lounges, one with TV, one with Steinway Grand Piano; three bedrooms all with private facilities, tea maker and radio. Marvellous walking country where you don't see anybody. Golf course nearby. Home baking. Bring your own wine. Packed lunches, vegetarians catered for. Ample parking. Bed and Breakfast from £26. Dinner £16. Bed and Breakfast weekly from £160. Cat lovers' delight – resident Manx and Maine Coon; wonderful feline art collection. A no smoking house.
ETC ◆◆◆◆

e-mail: e.finn@ukonline.co.uk

website: web.ukonline.co.uk/e.finn

ALNWICK

K. and J. Bateman, Charlton House, 2 Aydon Gardens, South Road, Alnwick NE66 2NT (01665 605185). Charlton House is a very special guest house, where our guests are always welcomed in a friendly, relaxed atmosphere. All rooms are beautifully decorated, some with original fireplaces and patchwork quilts. All bedrooms have private facilities, alarm clock radio, hair dryer, hospitality trays and colour TV. There is also a comfortable guest lounge. Choose from Traditional English, vegetarian or Continental breakfasts. Private and off-street parking. Tariff from £27 per person per night (includes Breakfast). We think you will remember Charlton House fondly, long after your stay has ended.
ETC ◆◆◆◆. WHICH?' 'GOOD BED AND BREAKFAST' GUIDE, PRIDE OF NORTHUMBRIA FOOD HYGIENE AWARD.

website: www.SmoothHound.co.uk/hotels/charlt2.html

Northumberland 207

See also Colour Display Advertisement

ALNWICK
Sheila Dodds, South Hazelrigg, Chatton, Alnwick NE66 5RZ (01668 215216; mobile: 07710 346076). South Hazelrigg is situated between the market town of Wooler and the coastal village of Belford, approximately ten minutes off the A1 road, ideally placed for trips to the beach, Farne Islands, Holy Island, the Cheviot Hills and the many castles. Rooms are spacious and comfortable with hospitality trays and colour TV. Breakfast is served in the elegant dining room and the local village inns provide an extensive menu. Local activities include birdwatching, fishing, horse riding and golf, Bamburgh being the most scenic English course. ETC ♦♦♦♦ *SILVER AWARD*
e-mail: sed@hazelrigg.fsnet.co.uk
website: www.farmhousebandb.co.uk

ALNWICK (near)
Mrs Celia Curry, Howick Scar Farm House, Craster, Alnwick NE66 3SU (Tel & Fax: 01665 576765). Comfortable farmhouse accommodation on working mixed farm situated on the Heritage Coast between the villages of Craster and Howick. Ideal base for walking, golfing, bird-watching or exploring the coast, moors and historic castles. The Farne Islands, famous for their colonies of seals and seabirds, and Lindisfarne (Holy Island) are within easy driving distance. Accommodation is in two double rooms with washbasins. Guests have their own TV lounge/dining room with full central heating. Non-smoking. Bed and Breakfast from £22. Open April to October. ETC ♦♦♦, *FARM STAY UK*.
e-mail: stay@howickscar.co.uk
website: www.howickscar.co.uk

BERWICK-UPON-TWEED
Alannah House, 84 Church Street, Berwick-upon-Tweed TD15 1DU (01289 307252). A Georgian townhouse situated in the centre of the historic walled town of Berwick-upon-Tweed, once used as officers' married quarters by the nearby Berwick barracks (now a museum and regimental home to the King's Own Scottish Borderers). Ideally situated, this 300 year-old house offers easy access to all local amenities and places of historic interest in the region. All rooms are centrally heated, with en suite shower and toilet, have colour TV, ironing and tea/coffee making facilities. Large private garden for residents' use. Residential parking available, strictly non-smoking. ETC ♦♦♦♦ *SILVER AWARD*.

CORBRIDGE
Mrs L. Adamson, Low Fotherley Farm, Riding Mill, Corbridge NE44 6BB (Tel & Fax: 01434 682277). Low Fotherley is an impressive Victorian farmhouse built around 1895 situated on the A68 south of Riding Mill in the beautiful Northumbrian countryside with outstanding views. The market towns of Hexham and Corbridge are nearby. Explore Hadrian's Wall, Durham, Beamish, Kielder, the Scottish Borders, Northumberland's coastline, Bamburgh and the Farne Islands. The farmhouse has lots of character, with open fireplaces and beams. The house is spacious and comfortable. Our rooms are of a high standard. One twin en suite, one double en suite and one double with private facilities, all with full central heating, TV, tea/coffee making facilities, hairdryer and radio. Farmhouse breakfast is cooked on the Aga with toast, home-made jams and marmalade. Families welcome. No smoking. £25 per person, discounts for children. ETC ♦♦♦♦, *FARM STAY UK MEMBER*.
e-mail: hugh@lowfotherley.fsnet.co.uk   website: www.westfarm.freeserve.co.uk

---

A useful index of towns/counties appears on pages 393-398

HEXHAM
Mrs Ruby Keenleyside, Struthers Farm, Catton, Allendale, Hexham NE47 9LP (01434 683580). Struthers Farm offers a warm welcome in the heart of England, with many splendid local walks from the farm itself. Panoramic views. Situated in an area of outstanding beauty. Double/twin rooms, en suite, central heating. Good farmhouse cooking. Ample safe parking. Come and share our home and enjoy beautiful countryside. Children welcome, pets by prior arrangement. Open all year. Near Hadrian's Wall (half an hour's drive). Bed and Breakfast from £25; Optional Evening Meal from £12.50.

HEXHAM
Ros Johnson, West Wharmley, Hexham NE46 2PL (Tel & Fax: 01434 674227). Set on a 550 acre working farm. We offer a warm welcome to our well appointed accommodation which has outstanding views over the South Tyne Valley. The 18th century farmhouse has a self-contained wing, decorated to a high standard with full central heating. A large private sittingroom, complete with fire, oak beams and colour TV, provides a homely retreat for the evenings. Two large bedrooms, both en suite, have colour TVs and tea/coffee making facilities. Ideal for families (children from 5 years). Close to Hadrian's Wall and very accessible to Northumberland's many attractions. Bed and Breakfast from £30 to £40. ETC ♦♦♦

MARSKE-BY-THE-SEA
Ship Inn, High Street, Marske-by-the-Sea TS11 7LL (Tel & Fax: 01642 482640). The Ship Inn has a warm, friendly atmosphere and is situated close to the beach (100 yards). Grade II Listed with impressive exterior; good home cooked food, ales and wines. Accommodation consists of four double bedrooms and one family room, en suite available. B&B per person from £31.50 to £41.50 single, £20.75 to £22.50 double. Evening meals available. Children welcome. All major credit cards accepted. Open all year. ETC ♦♦♦
e-mail: shipmates@supanet.com

ROTHBURY
Katerina's Guest House, High Street, Rothbury NE65 7TQ (01669 620691). Charming old guest house, ideally situated for the amenities of pretty Rothbury village, and to explore Northumberland's hills, coast, castles, Hadrian's Wall. Beautiful bedrooms, each decorated and colour co-ordinated to enhance its individual character; some with original stone fireplaces/beamed ceilings, all en suite, with four-poster beds, TV, and superbly stocked tea tray (with home-made scones!). Wide, interesting choice of breakfasts; licensed evening meals also available – sample Cath's bread, 'whisky porridge', vegetarian nutballs, or Steak Katerina. Bed and Breakfast from £26.
e-mail: cath@katerinasguesthouse.co.uk
website: www.katerinasguesthouse.co.uk

•••some fun days out in NORTHUMBERLAND
Alnwick Castle, Alnwick • 01665 510777 • www.alnwick.com
Grace Darling Museum, Bamburgh • 01668 214465 • www.rnli.org.uk

Northumberland 209

See also Colour Display Advertisement

STAMFORDHAM

Stamfordham Bay Horse Inn, South Side, Stamfordham NE18 0PB (01661 886244). Family-run 16th century village inn serving lunches and evening meals; real ales, pool and darts. Four double, one twin/family and one single en suite rooms with TV and hot drinks facilities; central heating. Newcastle Airport six miles. Children and pets welcome. Parking available. Open January to December. B&B from £33 single, £58 double and £68 to £78 (for four) family room.
e-mail: stay@stamfordham-bay.co.uk
website: www.stamfordham-bay.co.uk

WARKWORTH

Beck'N'Call, Birling West Cottage, Warkworth NE65 0XS (01665 711653). This traditional country cottage is set in beautiful terraced gardens with a stream, and is only five minutes' walk from the village, castle, river walks and sandy beaches. The accommodation is comfortably furnished and includes two double rooms and one family room. All on ground floor with washbasins, shaver points, colour TV, tea/coffee making facilities and heating; en suite available. Residents' lounge. Warkworth makes an ideal base from which to explore rural Northumberland and the Borders with their unspoilt beauty and historic interest. Children welcome, reduced rates. Non-smokers. Private parking. Colour brochure available. Open all year. Terms from £25pppn; en suite from £27pppn. ETC ◆◆◆◆

e-mail: beck-n-call@lineone.net
website: www.beck-n-call.co.uk

WARKWORTH

Sue and Geoff Lillico, Aulden, 9 Watershaugh Road, Warkworth NE65 0TT (Tel & Fax: 01665 711583). Enjoy a high standard of care and hospitality, as you relax in an Area of Outstanding Natural Beauty. With Warkworth as a base, you can explore the coastline, hills and castles from Berwick in the north to Hadrian's Wall in the west. Situated in a quiet part of the village, off the main road, we provide one double en suite and one twin-bedded room with private facilities. Each room has TV, hospitality tray and hairdryer. Extensive breakfast menu. Bed and Breakfast from £23. Weekly rates available. Non-smoking.
e-mail: auldenbandb@hotmail.com
website: www.northumberland-bed-breakfast.co.uk

Pets Welcome!

"THE PET WORLD'S VERSION OF THE ULTIMATE HOTEL GUIDE!" (The Times)

Now bigger than ever and with full colour throughout,
Pets Welcome! is used every year by thousands of discriminating owners who simply refuse to leave their pets "home alone".
Published twice a year in Autumn and Spring.

Only £8.99 from booksellers or direct from the publishers:
**FHG Guides, Abbey Mill Business Centre, Seedhill,
Paisley PA1 1TJ** *(postage charged outside UK)*
e-mail: admin@fhguides.co.uk • www.holidayguides.com

Nottinghamshire

BURTON JOYCE

Mrs V. Baker, Willow House, 12 Willow Wong, Burton Joyce, Nottingham NG14 5FD (0115 931 2070). A large period house (1857) in quiet village location yet only four miles from city. Attractive, interesting accommodation with authentic Victorian ambience. Bright, clean rooms with tea/coffee facilities, TVs. Walking distance of beautiful stretch of River Trent (fishing). Ideally situated for Holme Pierrepont International Watersports Centre; golf course; National Ice Centre; Trent Bridge (cricket); Sherwood Forest (Robin Hood Centre) and the unspoiled historic town of Southwell with its Minster and Racecourse. Good local eating. Parking. From £21 per person per night. Reduced rates for children. Dogs welcome. Please phone first for directions.

EDWINSTOWE (near Mansfield)

Robin Hood Farmhouse B&B, Rufford Road, Edwinstowe NG21 9JA (Tel & Fax: 01623 824367). Traditional Olde English farmhouse in Robin Hood's village in the middle of Sherwood Forest. We are in close proximity of Clumber and Rufford Country Parks and adjacent to Center Parcs and South Forest Leisure Complex. Easy access to Nottingham and Lincoln. The farmhouse, which is set in extensive gardens, is open and centrally heated all year round. Accommodation comprises double/family and twin room, colour TV, tea/coffee making facilities in all rooms. Tariff from £22.50 per person per night. Reductions for children and extra nights. Pets and special requirements available on request. Ample secure parking.
e-mail: robinhoodfarm@aol.com

NOTTINGHAM

Peter and Josephine Howat, Andrews Private Hotel, 310 Queens Road, Beeston, Nottingham NG9 1JA (0115 9254902; Fax: 0115 178839). Everything at Andrews Hotel is done with a view to making your stay enjoyable and relaxing. Friendly atmosphere and a sense of home-from-home. All rooms have colour TV, tea/coffee and washbasins, some are en suite. We are within easy reach of the Derbyshire Dales and Robin Hood country. We are situated on the west side of Nottingham, 10 minutes from the city centre. Also close by is Nottingham Tennis Centre and University. Prices start at £28 basic single, and £25 per person for a twin/double room including breakfast.
ETC/AA ♦♦♦

The Tales of Robin Hood
Nottingham, Notts

See our **READERS' OFFER VOUCHER** for details of free or reduced rate entry

Nottinghamshire / Oxfordshire 211

SUTTON-IN-ASHFIELD
Mr P. Jordan, Dalestorth Guest House, Skegby Lane, Skegby, Sutton-in-Ashfield NG17 3DH (01623 551110). Dalestorth Guest House is an 18th century Georgian family home converted in the 19th century to become a school for young ladies of the local gentry and a boarding school until the 1930s. In 1976 it was bought by the present owners and has been modernised and converted into a comfortable, clean and pleasant guest house serving the areas of Mansfield and Sutton-in-Ashfield, offering overnight accommodation of Bed and Breakfast or longer stays to businessmen, holidaymakers or friends and relations visiting the area. Please send for further information.

Oxfordshire

BANBURY
Mrs Rosemary Cannon, High Acres Farm, Great Bourton, Banbury OX17 1RL (Tel & Fax: 01295 750217). New Farmhouse situated on edge of village off A423 Southam Road, three miles north of Banbury overlooking the beautiful Cherwell Valley. Ideally situated for touring Cotswolds, Stratford, Warwick, Oxford, Blenheim Palace. Local pubs serving evening meals Tuesdays to Saturdays. Very comfortable accommodation comprising one twin room, one family room (one double and one single bed). Tea/coffee making facilities, hair dryers; central heating; shower room with electric shower; guests' sittingroom with colour TV. All rooms fully carpeted. Non-smoking. Parking. Bed and Breakfast from £20. Child under 10 sharing family room £10. Sorry, no pets. A warm welcome awaits you.

BURFORD (near)
Mrs Karen Stanley, Potters Hill Farm, Leafield, Near Burford OX29 9QB (Tel & Fax: 01993 878018; Mobile: 07711 045207). Set in 15 acres of peaceful, mature parkland, supporting diverse bird and wildlife, on a large mixed, family farm. Accommodation in a sympathetically converted former coach house adjacent to the main house comprises three comfortable en suite rooms – one family, one double and one twin. There is a guest sitting room, and all rooms enjoy views over the parkland and farm. All Cotswold attractions are within half an hour's drive, and there are several inns nearby serving excellent evening meals. Lambing time is March to May, and harvest is July to September. Non-smoking. **AA ♦♦♦♦**

e-mail: potterabout@freenet.co.uk
website: www.country-accom.co.uk/potters-hill-farm

212 Oxfordshire

HENLEY-ON-THAMES

The Old Bakery, Skirmett, Near Henley-on-Thames RG9 6TD (01491 638309; office: 01491 410716; Fax: 01491 638086). This welcoming family house is situated on the site of an old bakery, seven miles from Henley-on-Thames and Marlow; half-an-hour from Heathrow and Oxford; one hour from London. It is in the Hambleden Valley in the beautiful Chilterns, with many excellent pubs selling good food nearby. Excellent village pub in Skirmett within easy walking distance. One double en suite, one twin-bedded room and one double with use of own bathroom. All with TV and tea making facilities. Open all year. Parking for five cars (car essential). Children and pets welcome. Bed and Breakfast from £30 single; £60 double, £75 en suite. ETC ♦♦♦♦
e-mail: lizzroach@aol.com

See also Colour Display Advertisement

LONG HANBOROUGH

Mrs I.J. Warwick, The Close Guest House, Witney Road, Long Hanborough OX29 8HF (01993 882485). We offer comfortable accommodation in house set in own grounds of one-and-a-half acres. Three family rooms, four double rooms, all are en suite; one double and one single. All have colour TV and tea/coffee making facilities. Full central heating. Use of garden and car parking for eight cars. Close to Woodstock, Oxford and the Cotswolds. Open all year except Christmas. Bed and Breakfast from £20. Please mention FHG when booking. ETC ♦♦♦

OXFORD

D. J. Underwood, Conifer Lodge, 159 Eynsham Road, Botley OX2 9NE (01865 862280; Fax: 01865 865135). Luxury stone house on the outskirts of Oxford city, only two miles. Frequent bus route to the city centre, yet in the peace and quiet of the countryside. Very accessible to all tourist areas. Central heating in all rooms, double glazed throughout, colour television, large garden and patio, plenty of parking space. Bed and Breakfast, business persons welcome, reasonable rates. ETC ♦♦♦
website: www.smoothhound.co.uk/oxford

OXFORD

Mr Stratford, The Bungalow, Cherwell Farm, Mill Lane, Old Marston, Oxford OX3 0QF (01865 557171). Modern bungalow on five acres set in countryside but only three miles from the city centre. Offering comfortable accommodation and serving traditional breakfast. Colour TV, tea/coffee facilities in all rooms. Private parking. Non-smoking. Not on bus route. Bed and Breakfast from £24 to £28 per person. ETC ♦♦♦
e-mail: ros.bungalowbb@btinternet.com
website: www.cherwellfarm-oxford-accom.co.uk

OXFORD

Mr and Mrs L. Price, Arden Lodge, 34 Sunderland Avenue (off Banbury Road), Oxford OX2 8DX (01865 552076; Fax: 01865 512265; mobile: 07702 068697). Modern detached house in select part of Oxford, within easy reach of Oxford Centre. Excellent position for Blenheim Palace and for touring Cotswolds, Stratford, Warwick etc. Close to river, parks, country inns and golf course. Easy access to London. All rooms have tea/coffee making and private facilities. Parking. Bed and Breakfast from £24 per person per night.

Oxfordshire 213

TETSWORTH (near Thame)

Mrs Julia Tanner, Little Acre, Tetsworth, Thame, Oxford OX9 7AT (01844 281423; mobile: 07798 625252). Charming country retreat with pretty landscaped gardens and paddocks to walk the dog. Quiet location but only two miles from J6 M40. Near Chilterns, Oxford, Cotswolds, Heathrow Airport. Comfy beds, hearty breakfasts, 'olde worlde' style dining room. Open all year with friendly, relaxed atmosphere. En suite rooms; ground floor bedrooms. Tea/coffee making facilities and TV in rooms. Pets welcome. Highly recommended by previous guests. Bed and Breakfast from £25 pppn twin en suite, £27.50 pppn king-size double en suite, family room (3 persons) £75 per night. All prices include a full English breakfast. Dogs welcome - £1.50 per night. **AA** ◆◆◆

WITNEY

Mrs Elizabeth Simpson, Field View, Wood Green, Witney OX28 1DE (01993 705485; Mobile: 07768 614347). Witney is famous for blankets, made here for over 300 years. Our house was built in 1959, of Cotswold stone. Set in two acres and situated on picturesque Wood Green, with football and cricket pitches to the rear, yet only 10 minutes' walk from the centre of this lively, bustling market town. An ideal touring centre for Oxford University (12 miles), Blenheim Palace (eight miles), Cotswold Wildlife Park (eight miles) and country walks. Ample parking. Three delightful en suite bedrooms with central heating, tea/coffee making facilities and colour TV. Non- smoking. A peaceful setting and a warm, friendly atmosphere await you. Bed and full English Breakfast from £27. **ETC** ◆◆◆ *SILVER AWARD*.

e-mail: bandb@fieldview-witney.co.uk   website: www.fieldview-witney.co.uk

WOODSTOCK

Mrs Kay Bradford, Hamilton House, 43 Hill Rise, Old Woodstock OX20 1AB (01993 812206; Mobile: 07778 705568). Highly recommended Bed and Breakfast establishment with parking, overlooking Blenheim Park, Blenheim Palace and the town centre with good selection of restaurants, pubs and shops within walking distance. Accommodation offered - one twin-bedded room and two double rooms, all en suite with colour TV and tea making facilities. Excellent selection of Continental and full English breakfast. Comfortable and relaxed atmosphere with informative and very hospitable hostess. Ideal base for Blenheim Palace, Bladon, the Cotswolds, Stratford-upon-Avon, Oxford and major airports. Access off A44 northern end of Woodstock, one-third-of-a-mile up the hill from the Black Prince Pub. Children and pets welcome. Double room (single occupancy) £40-£60, double/twin room £50-£65; triple room £60-£75.

e-mail: kay@hamiltonhousewoodstock.co.uk   website: www.hamiltonhousewoodstock.co.uk

Looking for Holiday Accommodation?

for details of hundreds of properties throughout the UK visit:

www.holidayguides.com

214 Oxfordshire

WOODSTOCK

The Leather Bottel, East End, North Leigh, Near Witney OX8 6PY (01993 882174). Joe and Nena Purcell invite you to The Leather Bottel guest house situated in the quiet hamlet of East End near North Leigh, convenient for Blenheim Palace, Woodstock, Roman Villa, Oxford and the Cotswolds. Breathtaking countryside walks. Two double en suite bedrooms, one family room with own bathroom, one single bedroom, all with colour TV and tea/coffee making facilities. Bed and Breakfast £35 per night for single room, from £50 for double. Children welcome. Open all year. Directions: follow signs to Roman Villa off A4095.
ETC ♦♦♦

WOODSTOCK (near)

Carol Ellis, Wynford House, 79 Main Road, Long Hanborough OX29 8JX (01993 881402). Wynford House is situated in the village of Long Hanborough a mile from the Bladon burial place of Sir Winston Churchill, three miles from Woodstock and Blenheim Palace. Oxford is twelve miles away and the Cotswolds are close by. Comfortable non-smoking accommodation. Family, double and twin rooms with colour TV, tea/coffee making facilities. All rooms en suite. Pubs serving good food within walking distance. Bed and Breakfast from £35.

The Golf Guide 2006
Where to Play, Where to Stay

Available from most booksellers, **The Golf Guide, Where to Play, Where to Stay** covers details of every UK golf course. Bigger and brighter than ever, with over 650 pages packed with comprehensive details of over 2800 clubs and courses in Britain and Ireland – the 'pro', par score, length and more. Including holiday golf in Ireland, France, Portugal, Spain, the USA, South Africa and Thailand. Hundreds of hotel entries offer convenient accommodation for golfers, their families, friends and colleagues.

Pets Welcome!

"THE PET WORLD'S VERSION OF THE ULTIMATE HOTEL GUIDE!" (The Times)

Now bigger than ever and with full colour throughout, **Pets Welcome!** is used every year by thousands of discriminating owners who simply refuse to leave their pets "home alone". Published twice a year in Autumn and Spring.

Available from booksellers or direct from the publishers:

FHG GUIDES
Abbey Mill Business Centre, Seedhill,
Paisley PA1 1TJ *(postage charged outside UK)*
www.holidayguides.com • e-mail: admin@fhguides.co.uk

Shropshire 215

Shropshire

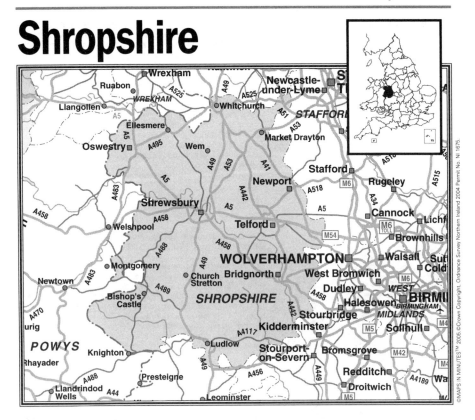

BISHOP'S CASTLE
Mrs Ann Williams, Shuttocks Wood, Norbury, Bishop's Castle SY9 5EA (01588 650433; Fax: 01588 650492).
Shuttocks Wood is a Scandinavian house in woodland setting situated within easy travelling distance of the Long Mynd and Stiperstones Hills. Accommodation consists of one double and two twin-bedded rooms, all en suite and with tea/coffee facilities and colour TV. Good walks and horse riding nearby and a badger set just 20 yards from the door! Ample parking. Non-smoking establishment. Children over 12 years welcome. Sorry, no pets. Open all year. Bed and Breakfast from £25 per person per night. Credit cards accepted.

FHG Guides publish a large range of well-known accommodation guides. We will be happy to send you details or you can use the order form at the back of this book.

A useful index of towns/counties appears at the back of this book

216 Shropshire

See also Colour Display Advertisement

CHURCH STRETTON
Mrs Mary Jones, Acton Scott Farm, Acton Scott, Church Stretton SY6 6QN (01694 781260; Fax: 0870-129 4591). Lovely 17th century farmhouse in peaceful village amidst the beautiful South Shropshire Hills, an Area of Outstanding Natural Beauty. The farmhouse is full of character and all rooms have heating and are comfortable and spacious. The bedrooms are either en suite or private bathroom with hairdryers, tea/coffee making facilities, patchwork quilts and colour TV. There is a lounge with colour TV and inglenook fireplace. Children welcome. We are a working farm, centrally situated for visiting Ironbridge, Shrewsbury and Ludlow, each easily reached within half an hour. Touring and walking information is available for visitors. Bed and full English Breakfast from £23pppn. Non- smoking. Open all year excluding November, December and January. **ETC ♦♦♦**, *FARM STAY UK.*

e-mail: fhg@actonscottfarm.co.uk
website: www.actonscottfarm.co.uk

CHURCH STRETTON
Mrs Chris Brandon-Lodge, North Hill Farm, Cardington, Church Stretton SY6 7LL (01694 771532). Farmhouse Bed and Breakfast accommodation in the beautiful Shropshire hills, one mile from Cardington village, itself a conservation gem. Quiet, rural setting with plenty of wildlife, an ideal base for walking and riding. Central for Ludlow, Shrewsbury and Ironbridge. Rooms have lovely views of the valley with TV and hot drinks tray. Well-behaved dogs and horses welcome. Bed and full English breakfast from £24 per person. En suite courtyard room from £28 per person. Non-smoking. **AA ♦♦♦♦**

e-mail: cbrandon@btinternet.com
website: www.virtual-shropshire.co.uk/northhill/

CLUN
Mrs M. Jones, Llanhedric, Clun, Craven Arms SY7 8NG (01588 640203). Working farm. Put your feet up and relax in the recliners as the beauty of the garden, the trickle of the pond, and the views of Clun and its surrounding hills provide solace from the stress of modern day life. Receive a warm welcome at this traditional oak-beamed farmhouse set back from the working farm. Three bedrooms, double en suite, tea/coffee facilities and good home cooking. Visitors' lounge with inglenook fireplace; separate dining room. Walks, history and attractions all close by. Bed and Breakfast from £25. Reductions for children. Non-smoking household. Regret no dogs in house. Open April to October. *FARM STAY UK MEMBER.* **ETC ♦♦♦♦**

DORRINGTON
Ron and Jenny Repath, Meadowlands, Lodge Lane, Frodesley, Dorrington SY5 7HD (Tel & Fax: 01694 731350). Former farmhouse, set in eight acres of gardens, paddocks and woodland, with pleasant woodland trail for guests' use. Quiet location in a delightful hamlet seven miles south of Shrewsbury. The guest house lies on a no-through road to a forested hill rising to 1000ft. Meadowlands features panoramic views over open countryside to the Stretton Hills. Guest accommodation includes en suite facilities and every bedroom has a colour TV, drink-making facilities and a silent fridge. Guests' lounge with maps and guides for loan. Central heating. Plenty of parking space. Strictly no smoking. Bed and Breakfast from £25. Brochure available. **ETC ♦♦♦**

e-mail: meadowlands@talk21.com
website: www.meadowlands.co.uk

Shropshire 217

LUDLOW

M.A. and E. Purnell, Ravenscourt Manor, Woofferton, Ludlow SY8 4AL (Tel & Fax: 01584 711905). Ravenscourt is a superb, recently renovated Tudor Manor set in two acres of lovely gardens. Beautifully furnished and equipped bedrooms. Wonderful area for walking or touring. Two miles from Ludlow, famous for its restaurants and architecture, eight miles from Leominster, famous for antiques, and 15 miles from Hereford and Worcester with their historic cathedrals. Close to National Trust properties and only 40 minutes from Ironbridge and Stratford. Excellent home cooked food. All rooms are en suite with remote-control colour TV, tea/coffee facilities and central heating. Bed and Breakfast from £32.50 per person based on two sharing; £5 per night discount for three nights or more. Warm welcome assured. Also self-catering cottages available, £140 to £330 per week, 10% discount for two weeks. **ETC** ◆◆◆◆◆ *GOLD AWARD.*
e-mail: ravenscourtmanor@amserve.com   website: www.smoothhound.co.uk or www.cottagesdirect.com

LUDLOW

Southcot Guesthouse, Livesey Road, Ludlow SY8 1EZ (01584 879655; mobile: 07787 533718; Fax: 01584 878372). Gill and John welcome you to our high quality Bed and Breakfast with comfortable spacious en suite rooms, off-road parking and only a 10-minute walk from Ludlow town centre and railway station. We are ideally located as a centre for touring Shropshire and the Welsh Borders. Nearby are the Ironbridge Gorge Museums, many National Trust and English Heritage properties, the Severn Valley Steam Railway and many other attractions. Dine out in the evening and let us spoil you in the morning, using only fresh produce from our local butchers, bakers, greengrocers and fishmongers. All you have to do is relax and enjoy. **AA** ◆◆◆◆
e-mail: gillandjohn@southcotbandb.co.uk   website: www.southcotbandb.co.uk

MARKET DRAYTON

See also Colour Display Advertisement

The Four Alls Inn & Motel, Newport Road, Woodeaves, Market Drayton TF9 2AG (01630 652995; Fax: 01630 653930). A warm welcome is assured at the Four Alls, situated in a quiet location of Woodeaves yet only a mile from Market Drayton, and within easy reach of Shropshire's premier attractions. Relax in our spacious bar, sample our home-cooked food and excellent traditional beers, then enjoy a good night's sleep in one of our nine en suite chalet-style rooms with central heating, TV, tea/coffee making facilities and own entrance. The function room is available for weddings, celebrations or as a conference venue and can accommodate 50-100. Large car park. Children welcome. **AA** ◆◆◆
e-mail: inn@thefouralls.com   website: www.thefouralls.com

OSWESTRY (near)

Pam Morrissey, Top Farm House, Knockin, Near Oswestry SY10 8HN (01691 682582). Full of charm and character, this beautiful 16th century Grade 1 Listed black and white house is set in the delightful village of Knockin. Enjoy the relaxed atmosphere and elegant surroundings of this special house with its abundance of beams. Sit in the comfortable drawing room where you can read, listen to music, or just relax with a glass of wine (please feel free to bring your own tipple). Hearty breakfasts from our extensive menu are served in the lovely dining room which looks out over the garden. The large bedrooms are all en suite, attractively decorated and furnished. All have tea/coffee making facilities, colour TV, etc. Convenient for the Welsh Border, Shrewsbury, Chester and Oswestry. Friendly hosts and great atmosphere. Bed and Breakfast from £27.50 to £35. **ETC** ◆◆◆◆ *SILVER AWARD*, **AA** *FOUR RED DIAMONDS*.
e-mail: p.a.m@knockin.freeserve.co.uk

218 Shropshire

SHREWSBURY (near)
Mrs Gwen Frost, Oakfields, Baschurch Road, Myddle, Shrewsbury SY4 3RX (01939 290823; mobile: 07952 058945). Visiting Shropshire? Why not enjoy the warm welcome and home-from-home atmosphere at Oakfields, which is in a quiet, idyllic setting located in the picturesque village of Myddle made famous by Gough's "History of Myddle" written in 1700. All ground floor bedrooms, each tastefully decorated and equipped with colour TV, tea-making facilities, washbasin, hairdryer and shaver point; cot and high chair also available; guests' TV lounge. Central heating throughout. Large and pleasant garden for guests to enjoy. 15 minutes from Shrewsbury and Hawkstone Park and convenient for Ironbridge, Wales, Chester, etc. Golf and riding nearby. Extensive car park. Non-smoking. Bed and Breakfast from £22.50 pppn. Nearest main road A528, also straight road from A5. **ETC ♦♦♦**

TELFORD
Mrs Judy Yates, The Mill House, Shrewsbury Road, High Ercall, Telford TF6 6BE (01952 770394). Judy and Chris Yates welcome you to The Mill House, an 18th century converted water mill situated beside the River Roden on a 9 acre working small holding. Located in the village of High Ercall, halfway between the historic county town of Shrewsbury and the new town of Telford. Luxury bed and breakfast accommodation in three beautifully decorated, en suite bedrooms. Perfect for exploring Shropshire and the Welsh borderlands. A short distance from the World Heritage Site of the Ironbridge Gorge and the surrounding area offers a wide range of attractions and activities to suit all tastes. Children welcome. Dogs by prior arrangement. Non-smoking. Single £33 pppn, Double/Twin £28 pppn, Family room (sleeps 4) from £22 pppn.

e-mail: cjpy@lineone.net
website: www.ercallmill.co.uk

FHG Guides
2006
October Edition

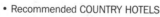
- Recommended COUNTRY HOTELS

- Recommended COUNTRY INNS & PUBS

- BED & BREAKFAST STOPS • CHILDREN WELCOME!
- The Original FHG Guide to COAST & COUNTRY HOLIDAYS
- CARAVAN & CAMPING HOLIDAYS, England, Scotland, Wales & Ireland
- BRITAIN'S BEST HOLIDAYS
- THE GOLF GUIDE Where to Play / Where to Stay
- PETS WELCOME!
- Recommended SHORT BREAK HOLIDAYS in Britain
- SELF CATERING HOLIDAYS in Britain

April Edition

Available from bookshops or larger newsagents

FHG GUIDES LTD
Abbey Mill Business Centre,
Seedhill, Paisley PA1 ITJ
www.holidayguides.com

Somerset

ASHBRITTLE

Mrs Ann Heard, Lower Westcott Farm, Ashbrittle, Wellington TA21 0HZ (01398 361296). On Devon/Somerset borders, 230 acre family-run farm with cattle, sheep, poultry and horses. Ideal for walking, touring Exmoor, Quantocks, both coasts and many National Trust properties. Pleasant farmhouse, tastefully modernised but with olde worlde charm, inglenook fireplaces and antique furniture, set in large gardens with lawns and flower beds in peaceful, scenic countryside. Two family bedrooms with private facilities and tea/coffee making. Large lounge, separate dining room offering guests every comfort. Noted for relaxed, friendly atmosphere and good home-cooking. Brochure by request. Bed and Breakfast from £22; Dinner £10 per person. Reductions for children. ETC ♦♦♦♦
e-mail: lowerwestcott@aol.com

BATH

Mr Wynne, The White Guest House, 23 Pulteney Gardens, Bath BA2 4HG (01225 426075). Steve and Anna welcome you to their guest house. Very conveniently located five minutes' walk to the city and all of Bath's famous attractions. Close to the Kennet and Avon canal. (Bath in Bloom winners.) All rooms en suite, with central heating, TV, tea/coffee facilitie. Traditional cooked breakfast or Continental breakfasts. Bed & Breakfast single from £30, double/twin from £25pp. Sorry, no pets and no smoking. AA ♦♦♦
e-mail: thewhiteguesthouse@zoom.co.uk
website: www.thewhiteguesthouse.co.uk

BATH

Mary Cooper, Flaxley Villa, 9 Newbridge Hill, Bath BA1 3PW (01225 313237). Enjoy the friendly atmosphere of this delightful Victorian House. Each bedroom is individually furnished. All have colour TV, complimentary beverages, radio alarm clock and en suite shower. All rooms are non smoking. Traditional English breakfast isserved in the breakfast room. There is ample off road car parkingand a baby listening service is available. There is a pleasant river walk into Bath, or alternatively, through the Royal Victoria Park, past the world famous Royal Crescent and Circus. Prices start from £25 per person per night. **ETC** ◆◆◆
e-mail: Flaxleyvilla@fsmail.net

BATH

Margaret and Vic Gentle, Ellsworth House, Fosseway, Midsomer Norton BA3 4AU (01761 412305). Homely accommodation situated on the A367 Bath/Shepton Mallet road, we are eight miles from Bath and within easy reach of Bristol, Wells, Glastonbury, Cheddar Gorge, Longleat and the Bath and West show ground, in the heart of the west country. We have an attractive garden for relaxing. Ample off-street parking. We have three double rooms, two family rooms (one double and two single beds) and two twin rooms, all en suite with shower, colour TV, shaver point, hairdryer, tea/coffee making and central heating. Good English breakfast served. Open all year. No smoking. A good selection of eating places nearby. Bed and Breakfast from £26 per person per night.
e-mail: accommodation@ellsworth.fsbusiness.co.uk   website: www.ellsworth.fsbusiness.co.uk

BATH

Mrs Chrissie Besley, The Old Red House, 37 Newbridge Road, Bath BA1 3HE (01225 330464; Fax: 01225 331661). Welcome to our romantic Victorian "Gingerbread" house which is colourful, comfortable and warm; full of unexpected touches and intriguing little curiosities. The leaded and stained glass windows are now double glazed to ensure a peaceful night's stay. Each bedroom is individually furnished, some with antiques and a king-size bed. All have colour TV, complimentary beverages, radio alarm clock, hairdryer and either en suite shower or private bathroom. Generous four-course breakfasts are served. Waffles, pancakes or kippers are just a few alternatives to our famous hearty English grill. Dinner is available at the local riverside pub, just a short stroll away. We are non-smoking and have private parking. Prices range from £27.50 to £35 per person in double rooms. **ETC** ◆◆◆
e-mail: orh@amserve.com   website: www.oldredhouse.co.uk

BATH

Mrs Judith Goddard, Cherry Tree Villa, 7 Newbridge Hill, Bath BA1 3PW (01225 331671). Friendly Victorian home approximately one mile from centre of Bath, at the start of the A431. Very frequent bus service, or for those who enjoy walking, a stroll through Victoria Park will take you comfortably into the city. Bright comfortable bedrooms, all with washbasin, colour TV and tea/coffee making facilities. Full central heating and off-street parking. Bed and full English Breakfast from £20 per person per night. Children welcome. From city centre take main A4 Upper Bristol road, at Weston Pub take A431 and Cherry Tree Villa lies on the left hand side. Winner of an FHG Diploma awarded by readers. **ETC** ◆◆◆

Somerset 221

See also Colour Display Advertisement

BATH
Bailbrook Lodge Hotel, 35/37 London Road West, Bath BA1 7HZ (01225 859090; Fax: 01225 852299). Bailbrook Lodge is a splendid Georgian country house which has been totally and sympathetically redectorated and refurbished. It has delightful lawned gardens and free car parking. There are 15 en suite bedrooms, including five with four-poster beds. There is satellite TV, coffee and tea making facilities, complimentary biscuits and mineral water. Dinner is available in our nearby riverside restaurant. Price per person including full English breakfast is from £35 to £55. **ETC/AA ♦♦♦♦** *SILVER AWARD*.
e-mail: hotel@bailbrooklodge.co.uk
website: www.bailbrooklodge.co.uk

BATH
Mrs June E. A. Coward, Box Road Gardens, Box Road, Bathford, Bath BA1 7LR (01225 852071). Homely, comfortable country house in two acres, situated on A4 road three miles east of Bath City Centre. Easy access to M4, local beauty spots. Accommodation in twin, double and family rooms with central heating, tea/coffee making facilities; TV. Shower en suite. Ample parking and good local "pub food". Open all year for Bed and Breakfast from £20 per person. This is a non-smoking house. Sorry, no pets. Phone June on **01225 852071** for further details.

BATH
Michael and Carole Bryson, Walton Villa, 3 Newbridge Hill, Bath BA1 3PW (01225 482792; Fax: 01225 313093). Our immaculate Victorian family-run B&B offers non-smoking accommodation in a relaxed and friendly atmosphere. Just a short bus journey or 25 minute stroll to town centre, via the beautiful gardens of the Royal Victoria Park. Our three en suite bedrooms are delightfully decorated and furnished for your comfort, with colour TV, hairdryer and hospitality tray. Enjoy a delicious Full English or Continental breakfast served in our gracious dining room. Sorry, no pets. Off-street parking. Bed and Breakfast from £30. **ETC ♦♦♦**
e-mail: walton.villa@virgin.net   website: www.walton.izest.com

BATH (near)
Mrs Barbara Keevil, Eden Vale Farm, Mill Lane, Beckington, Near Frome BA11 6SN (01373 830371). Eden Vale Farm nestles down in a valley by the River Frome. Enjoying a picturesque location, this old watermill offers a selection of rooms including en suite facilities, complemented by an excellent choice of full English or Continental breakfasts. Beckington is an ideal centre for visiting Bath, Longleat, Salisbury, Cheddar, Stourhead and many National Trust Houses including Lacock Village. Only a ten minute walk to the village pub, three-quarters of a mile of river fishing. Local golf courses and lovely walks. Very friendly animals. Dogs welcome. Open all year. **ETC ♦♦♦**
e-mail: bandb@edenvalefarm.co.uk
website: www.edenvalefarm.co.uk

•••some fun days out in SOMERSET

Jane Austen Centre, Bath • 01225 443000 • www.janeausten.co.uk
Tropiquaria, Watchet • 01984 640688 • www.tropiquaria.co.uk
West Somerset Railway, Minehead • 01643 704996 • www.west-somerset-railway.co.uk
Westonbirt Arboretum, Tetbury • 01666 880220 • www.forestry.gov.uk/westonbirt
Wookey Hole, Wells • 01749 672243 • www.wookey.co.uk
Dyrham Park, Near Bath • 01179 372501 • www.nationaltrust.org.uk
Cheddar Caves & Gorge, Cheddar • 01934 742343 • www.cheddarcaves.co.uk

BRIDGWATER

The Cottage
Fordgate, Bridgwater, Somerset TA7 0AP
Beverley Jenkins • Tel: 01278 691908

A charming country cottage set in two acres of garden in an Area of Outstanding Natural Beauty and special interest, close to rivers and canal where birds and wildlife flourish.
A centre for the famous Somerset Levels and all of this historic county.
We offer you privacy, comfort and tranquillity, staying in en suite rooms with king-size antique four-poster beds, TV, heating and hospitality trays.
Easy access, with all rooms at ground level opening directly onto the gardens.
English country cooking at its best, using fresh vegetables, fruit, honey and free range eggs.
Bed and Breakfast from £21pppn. Easy access Junction 24 M5.
Ample secure parking.
A delightful place to stay especially for that special short break.
No smoking in house please. Phone or write for brochure and map.

Open all year.
HIGHLY RECOMMENDED
E-mail: victor@victorjenkins.wanadoo.co.uk

BRISTOL
Downs View Guest House, 38 Upper Belgrave Road, Clifton, Bristol BS8 2XN (0117 9737046; Fax: 0117 9738169). A well established, family-run Victorian guest house situated on the edge of Durdham Downs. All rooms have panoramic views over the city or the Downs. We are one-and-a-half miles north of the city centre, just off Whiteladies Road where there are plenty of restaurants, shops and buses. We are within walking distance of Bristol Zoo and Clifton Suspension Bridge. All rooms have tea/coffee making facilities, washbasin, colour TV and central heating. There are nine en suite rooms, all non-smoking. Full English breakfast. Bed and Breakfast from £40 single, £55 double. **ETC** ◆◆◆

BRISTOL
Mrs M. Hasell, The Model Farm, Norton Hawkfield, Pensford, Bristol BS39 4HA (01275 832144). Working farm. Model Farm is situated two miles off the A37 in a peaceful hamlet, nestling under the Dundry Hills. A working arable and beef farm in easy reach of Bristol, Bath, Cheddar and many other interesting places. The spacious accommodation is in two en suite rooms, one family and one double, with tea/coffee facilities. Separate dining room and lounge with colour TV for visitors. Private parking. Open all year (except Christmas and New Year). Bed and Breakfast from £20. **ETC** ◆◆◆

Somerset 223

BRISTOL (near)
Leigh Farm, Pensford, Near Bristol BS39 4BA (Tel & Fax: 01761 490281). 200-year old comfy, warm, centrally heated, natural stone-built farmhouse, with open log fire in the guest lounge during the winter months. TV, video. Bedrooms with TV and beverage trays. Keys for access at all times. Double en suite, family room with cot and private bathroom. Extra bedrooms can be facilitated (subject to availability) at short notice on empty self-catering properties with private facilities. Menu available and breakfasts freshly cooked to order. We are a working livestock farm with cows, calves and growing stock. We also have a few free-range pigs and chickens. Credit cards accepted. Regret no pets. B&B from £25 pp.

BURNHAM-ON-SEA
Mrs F. Alexander, Priors Mead, 23 Rectory Road TA8 2BZ (Tel & Fax: 01278 782116). Peter and Fizz welcome guests to enjoy their enchanting Edwardian home set in half-an-acre of beautiful gardens with weeping willows, croquet and swimming pool. All three rooms have either twin or king-size beds, en suite/private facilities, washbasins, hospitality trays, colour TVs, etc. Peaceful location, walk to the sea, town, golf and tennis clubs. Ideal touring base for Bristol, Bath, Wells, Glastonbury, Wookey Hole, Cheddar and Dunster. A no-smoking home. Parking. Easy access to Junction 22 M5 for Wales, Devon and Cornwall. Bed and Breakfast from £22.50. Reductions for three nights. *"WHICH?" RECOMMENDED.*
e-mail: priorsmead@aol.com
website: www.priorsmead.co.uk

e-mail: Dyerfarm@aol.com

CANNINGTON
Blackmore Farm, Cannington, Bridgwater TA5 2NE (01278 653442; Fax: 01278 653427). Blackmore Farm is a 15th Century, Grade I Listed Manor House with views to the Quantock Hills and within easy reach of the West Somerset coast and Exmoor. The house retains many of its period features including stone archways, oak beams, open fireplaces and its own private chapel. Spacious and comfortable accommodation includes a four-poster bedroom and the gallery bedroom with its own private sitting room. Ground floor bedrooms are also available in the Courtyard, a barn conversion with access for disabled guests. All bedrooms have en suite bath or shower, colour TV and tea/coffee making facilities. 2006 prices: £60 - £75 per room per night, £40 - £45 per person single occupancy.
website: www.dyerfarm.co.uk

See also Colour Display Advertisement

CASTLE CARY
Mrs Sally Snook, Clanville Manor, Castle Cary BA7 7PJ (01963 350124; Fax: 01963 350719). 18th century elegance: 21st Century comfort! Stay for a few days and really explore the Somerset countryside, Glastonbury, Wells and Bath, many lovely gardens and National Trust properties, from a Georgian farmhouse on a working farm two miles from Castle Cary. Flagstone hall, English oak staircase, old elm floorboards, period furniture and Oriental rugs. Spacious and fully equipped en suite rooms, fully heating, a log fire in winter and a heated outdoor pool. Wonderful Aga breakfasts with local produce including our own hens' eggs! **ETC/AA ♦♦♦♦**
SILVER AWARD.
e-mail: clanvillemanor@aol.com
website: www.clanvillemanor.co.uk

A useful index of towns/counties appears on pages 393-398

224 Somerset

See also Colour Display Advertisement

CHARD
Hornsbury Mill, Eleighwater, Chard TA20 3AQ (Tel & Fax: 01460 63317). Contemporary capability blends effortlessly with tradition in the informal landscaped setting of this charming 19th century working mill, set deep in rural Somerset. The Mill Restaurant serves snacks, lunches and evening meals, with traditional roasts on Sundays. Relax on the sun terrace for morning coffee or enjoy a delightful dinner as the water wheel turns beside you. The cosy en suite bedrooms are furnished with everything needed to ensure a pleasant and relaxing stay. Guests can stroll among swans and wildfowl in the four-acre gardens, which make a romantic backdrop for weddings and all kinds of special occasions. **ETC ♦♦♦♦** *SILVER AWARD.*
e-mail: hornsburymill@btclick.com
website: www.hornsburymill.co.uk

CHARD
Mrs Jean Watkis, Keymer Cottage, Buckland St Mary, Chard TA20 3JF (01460 234226 or 07940 051439). Keymer Cottage is a stone-built Victorian farmhouse, with inglenook, attractively furnished, offering friendly and comfortable hospitality. Good local eating venues and many places of interest in the area, including National Trust properties, cider mills, museums, gardens etc. It is one mile from the A303, five miles from Chard and Ilminster, and nine miles from Taunton, the county town. Exmoor, Dartmoor and the North Somerset coast are within easy reach and Lyme Regis is only 19 miles away. There is a guest sittingroom with colour TV and three bedrooms, either en suite or with private bathroom; tea making facilities. Non-smoking. Sorry, no children. Bed and full English Breakfast from £22.50 per person per night.
e-mail: keymercottage@tiscali.co.uk

CHURCHILL
Winston Manor Hotel, Bristol Road, Churchill, Winscombe BS25 5NL (01934 852348; Fax: 01934 852033). This newly refurbished, well-appointed Victorian manor house sits in its own secluded walled garden overlooking the Mendip Hills. The hotel is privately owned and offers personal service in traditional style. The 14 bedrooms, all with private bathroom, are equipped with modern comforts. There is a small friendly bar with warming log fires in winter. Close to the M5 (Junctions 21 or 22), Churchill is centrally located for Bath, Bristol, Glastonbury or Wells, and is only four miles from Cheddar Gorge. Bristol Airport is just five miles away, making Winston Manor the ideal country retreat for small business meetings. Children welcome. Residential licence. No smoking accommodation.
e-mail: info@winstonmanorhotel.co.uk   **website: www.winstonmanorhotel.co.uk**

Exmoor Falconry & Animal Farm
Porlock, Somerset
See our **READERS' OFFER VOUCHER** for details of free or reduced rate entry

The Helicopter Museum
Weston-Super-Mare, Somerset
See our **READERS' OFFER VOUCHER** for details of free or reduced rate entry

Somerset 225

CONGRESBURY

Brinsea Green Farm

Brinsea Green is a Period farmhouse surrounded by open countryside. Set in 500 acres of farmland, it has easy access from the M5, (J21), A38 and Bristol Airport. Close to the Mendip Hills, the historic towns of Bath, Bristol and Wells, plus the wonders of Cheddar Gorge and Wookey Hole. Beautifully furnished en suite/shower bedrooms offer lovely views, comfortable beds, complimentary hot drinks and biscuits, radio, alarm, toiletries, sewing kit and hairdryer for your convenience. Both guest lounge (with TV) and dining room have inglenook fireplaces providing a warm, home from home atmosphere. Choose from our wide range of books and enjoy real peace and tranquillity.

SINGLE FROM £24 -£30   DOUBLE FROM £38 - £48

**Mrs Delia Edwards, Brinsea Green Farm
Brinsea Lane, Congresbury, Near Bristol BS49 5JN
Tel: Churchill (01934) 852278; Fax: (01934) 852861**
e-mail: delia@brinseagreenfarm.co.uk
website: www.brinseagreenfarm.co.uk

CREWKERNE

Mrs Catherine Bacon, Honeydown Farm, Seaborough Hill, Crewkerne TA18 8PL (Tel & Fax: 01460 72665). Situated in quiet countryside one-and-a-half miles from Crewkerne, we offer friendly and comfortable accommodation in our modern farmhouse on a working dairy farm with panoramic views. Ideal for a short break or holiday, with many National Trust properties and private gardens locally. The Dorset coast is only 14 miles. One double en suite, one double and one twin both with washbasin, hospitality trays and TV in rooms. Enjoy the patio and garden or relax in the lounge or conservatory. Non-smoking. Bed and Breakfast from £52 double, £31 single. Brochure available.
e-mail: c.bacon@honeydown.co.uk
website: www.honeydown.co.uk

DULVERTON

Mrs Carole Nurcombe, Marsh Bridge Cottage, Dulverton TA22 9QG (01398 323197). This superb accommodation has been made possible by the refurbishment of this Victorian former ex-gamekeeper's cottage on the banks of the River Barle. The friendly welcome, lovely rooms, delicious (optional) evening meals using local produce, and clotted cream sweets are hard to resist! Open all year, and in autumn the trees that line the river either side of Marsh Bridge turn to a beautiful golden backdrop. Just off the B3223 Dulverton to Exford road, it is easy to find and, once discovered, rarely forgotten. From outside the front door footpaths lead in both directions alongside the river. Fishing available. Terms from £20 per person Bed and Breakfast or £35.50 per person Dinner, Bed and Breakfast.

226 Somerset

DULVERTON
Mrs Gill Summers, Higher Langridge Farm, Exbridge, Dulverton TA22 9RR (01398 323999). Find our 17th century farmhouse hidden amid picturesque countryside two miles southwest of Dulverton - off the beaten track. Guests' accommodation is a private wing of the farmhouse; relax in our cosy guests' lounge with TV and inglenook fireplace with woodburner for winter months. Guests' bedrooms are furnished with country pine furniture, decorated in pastel colours and pretty linen; one double with shower en suite, one family room to sleep two to four with private bathroom. Full English breakfast cooked on the Aga is served with farm eggs and local sausages. Wonderful views over fields and woodland with resident wildlife. Prices from £25 to £30 based on two sharing.
e-mail: info@langridgefarm.co.uk
website: www.langridgefarm.co.uk

DULVERTON
Mrs M. Rawle, Winsbere House, Dulverton TA22 9HU (01398 323278). Attractive private house set in pretty gardens on the edge of Dulverton, 10 minute walk from the centre and a short drive to Tarr Steps and the moors. Comfortable, tastefully decorated rooms with lovely country views and a friendly informal atmosphere. One double, one twin both with luxury en suite plus one double/single with private bathroom. Superb full English breakfast. Cyclists welcome. Route Three West Country Way on doorstep. Ample private parking and lockup cycle shed. No dogs. Non-smoking. Children welcome aged 8 or over. Excellent location for touring Exmoor, West Somerset and North Devon. Open all year (except Christmas and New Year). Terms: £20 to £25 per person per night (single £25). **ETC ♦♦♦**
e-mail: info@winsbere.co.uk
website: www.winsbere.co.uk

EXFORD

Marc Watts, late of Trevaunance Point Hotel at St Agnes in Cornwall has moved with his menagerie of horses, ponies, dogs, ducks and cats to the charismatic Edgcott House in the horseman's mecca of Exford, slap bang in the centre of the Exmoor National Park, yet only a few miles from his beloved ocean.
It is an age-old house with immense charm, mixed with modern standards yet retaining features like roaring log fires and 'the other' Long Room after Lords. Seven recently rejuvenated, fully en suite bedrooms, big gardens, woodlands, green pastures, a lake with wild fowl and even a cascading brook.
Unlicensed for alcohol, but guests may bring their own, we provide Bed and those memorable Breakfasts still cooked by Marc, and on request traditional 'suppers' as well. Children and pets welcome OF COURSE.
Also for 2006 we have our newly restored and delightful CASCADE COTTAGE, separate but close to the great house, and available all year round for Self-Catering Holidays.

Tel: 01643 831495 • E-mail: enquiries@edgcotthouse.co.uk • www.edgcotthouse.co.uk
Exford on Exmoor • Somerset TA24 7QG

Somerset 227

GLASTONBURY

Mrs J.M. Gillam, Wood Lane House, Butleigh, Glastonbury BA6 8TG (01458 850354). Charming old AA Listed house with lovely views over open countryside and woods. Quiet yet not isolated and only 200 yards from excellent village "local". Ideal touring centre for Cheddar, Wells, Bath and many beauty spots and only 20 miles from coast. Attractions include Butterfly Farm, Fleet Air Arm Museum, Rural Life Museum, cheese making, steam engines and many places of historic interest. Accommodation comprises three double rooms with well equipped en suite facilities, tea/coffee and TV. Comfortable and warm sitting/dining room. Open all year round except Christmas and New Year. Car essential. Parking. Bed and Breakfast from £25.50pp sharing twin room; single £35. Half price for children.

e-mail: info@mearemanor.com

GLASTONBURY (near)

Sue Chapman, Meare Manor, 60 St Mary's Road, Meare, Glastonbury BA6 9SR (Tel & Fax: 01458 860449). 200 year old Manor House set in own grounds with beautiful gardens and views over Mendip Hills. Peaceful setting in the heart of King Arthur country. Ideal base for tourist attractions including Glastonbury Abbey, Chalice Well, Wells Cathedral, Cheddar Gorge and Clarks Shopping Village. Warm welcome assured with friendly help and advice. Family rooms and suite available. Hospitality trays, colour TV. Some rooms suitable for disabled guests. Ample car parking. Open all year. From M5, Junction 23 follow A39 Glastonbury - Street, take B3151 Glastonbury to Wedmore, approximately three miles from Glastonbury. Bed and Breakfast from £40 per person per night. ETC ◆◆◆◆
website: www.mearemanor.com

MARK VILLAGE (near Highbridge)

Mrs B. M. Puddy, Laurel Farm, Mark Causeway, Near Highbridge TA9 4PZ (01278 641216; Fax: 01278 641447). Laurel Farm is on the Wells to Burnham-on-Sea B3139 road; M5 Junction 22 two miles; 12 miles from the cathedral city of Wells, five miles from Burnham-on-Sea; Highbridge two miles. Ideal for overnight or short breaks to tour our lovely area. Nicely furnished and decorated, with a large well kept lawn and flower garden at the back. Doubles, singles and family rooms available. All en suite with tea/coffee facilities. Large sitting room, colour TV. Central heating, electric blanket and log fires for cooler evenings. Bed and Breakfast from £21.50. ETC ◆◆◆

See also Colour Display Advertisement

MINEHEAD

The Gascony Hotel, 50 The Avenue, Minehead TA24 5BB (01643 705939; Fax: 01643 709926). Well appointed family-run Victorian House Hotel, ideally placed on the level in the lovely tree-lined Avenue, only two minutes walk from the sea front. Spacious en suite bedrooms all with colour TV, radio alarm, hot drinks tray and hairdryer. Ground floor bedroom suitable for the disabled. Elegant dining room offering a varied and interesting choice of home-cooked dishes. Two comfortable and tastefully furnished lounges, one with well-stocked cocktail bar. Full gas fired central heating. Large private car park. Ideal for walkers. Open March to December. Major credit cards accepted. B&B £29 to £37.50 pppn, DB&B £42 to £49 pppn. ETC ◆◆◆◆
website: www.gasconyhotel.co.uk

228 Somerset

> See also Colour Display Advertisement

PORLOCK
Margery and Henry Dyer, West Porlock House, West Porlock, Near Minehead TA24 8NX (01643 862880). Imposing country house in Exmoor National Park on the wooded slopes of West Porlock commanding exceptional sea views of Porlock Bay and countryside. Set in five acres of beautiful woodland gardens unique for its variety and size of unusual trees and shrubs and offering a haven of rural tranquillity. The house has large spacious rooms with fine and beautiful furnishings throughout. Two double, two twin and one family bedrooms, all with en suite or private bathrooms, TV, tea/coffee making facilities, radio-alarm clock and shaver point. Non-smoking. Private car park. Bed and Breakfast from £29 to £32 per person. Credit Cards accepted. Sorry, no pets. **ETC** ◆◆◆
e-mail: westporlockhouse@amserve.com

PORLOCK
Mrs A.J. Richards, Ash Farm, Porlock, near Minehead TA24 8JN (01643 862414). Ash Farm is situated two miles off the main Porlock to Lynmouth road (A39) and overlooks the sea. It is two-and-a-half miles from Porlock Weir, and eleven from Minehead and Lynmouth. Only 10 minutes to the tiny church of "Culbone", and Coleridge is reputed to have used the farmhouse which is 200 to 300 years old. The house has double, single and family bedrooms, all with washbasins; toilet and separate bathroom; large sittingroom and diningroom. Open from Easter to October. Oare Church, Valley of Rocks, County Gate, Horner Valley and Dunkery Beacon are all within easy reach. Bed and Breakfast from £20 which includes bedtime drink. SAE please.

TAUNTON
James and Katie Hawthorne, Pound Farm, Bishops Lydeard, Taunton TA4 3DN (01823 433443). Set at the foot of the Quantock Hills, Pound Farm offers a warm family welcome. A working farm of sheep, horses and arable, we will offer you a peaceful and friendly stay. Home-made cake and tea on arrival, pleasantly decorated bedrooms with bath and shower en suite facilities in all rooms. Guests have their own sitting room where breakfast is served in front of an open log fire. We are five minutes' drive from the West Somerset Railway and half an hour from Exmoor and the West Somerset coast. We are open all year round and look forward to welcoming you to our home. **ETC** ◆◆◆
e-mail: hawthorne@poundfarmsomerset.wanadoo.co.uk
website: www.poundfarm.co.uk

TAUNTON
John and Ann Bartlett, The Spinney, Curland, Taunton TA3 5SE (Tel & Fax: 01460 234362). Six miles from Taunton, convenient for A303 and M5. Ann and John welcome you to their home on the slopes of the Blackdown Hills. Nestling in a designated Area of Outstanding Natural Beauty, The Spinney is an ideal base for holidays, day excursions, walking or visiting places of interest. The double, twin or family bedrooms all have colour TV, beverage tray and central heating with quality en suite facilities. Ground floor rooms available. Evening meals are recommended. Non-smokers only please. Open all year. Bed and Breakfast: double/twin £28 per person per night, single £40 per person per night. **AA** *FOUR RED DIAMONDS*
e-mail: bartlett.spinney@zetnet.co.uk
website: www.somerweb.co.uk/spinney-bb

FHG

Fleet Air Arm Museum
Ilchester, Somerset

See our **READERS' OFFER VOUCHER** for details of free or reduced rate entry

K·U·P·E·R·A·R·D

Somerset 229

TAUNTON

The Falcon Hotel, Henlade, Taunton TA3 5DH (01823 442502; Fax: 01823 442670). You can always expect a warm welcome at this historic villa, with just the right blend of comfortable, spacious accommodation, friendly efficient staff and the personal attention of its family owners. Located one mile from the M5 motorway, it makes an ideal base for business stays, or as a touring centre for this attractive corner of the West Country. Facilities include ten en suite bedrooms with colour TV, tea/coffee making facilities, direct dial telephone, etc. Honeymoon suite, conference facilities, restaurant and ample parking. Superbly accessible to Quantock, Blackdown Hills, Exmoor, North and South Devon coasts. Our tariff is inclusive of a Full English Breakfast. **ETC/AA ★★**

See also Colour Display Advertisement

TAUNTON

Bill Slipper, The Old Mill, Bishop's Hull, Taunton TA1 5AB (Tel & Fax: 01823 289732). Relax and enjoy the hospitality in this Grade II Listed former Corn Mill, situated on the edge of a conservation village just two miles from Taunton. We have two lovely double bedrooms, The Mill Room with en suite facilities overlooking the weir pool, and The Cottage Suite with its own private bathroom, again with views over the river. Both rooms are centrally heated, with TV, generous beverage tray and thoughtful extras. Guests have their own lounge and dining area overlooking the river, where breakfast may be taken from our extensive breakfast menu amidst machinery of a bygone era. We are a non-smoking establishment. Double en suite £27.50 pppn, double with private bathroom £25 pppn, single occupancy from £35 per night. **ETC ◆◆◆◆◆** *SILVER AWARD.*

TAUNTON

Mrs Hayes, Hall Farm Guest House, Stogumber, Taunton TA4 3TQ (01984 656321). Nestled in the centre of Stogumber, a pretty character village surrounded by the Quantocks and Exmoor and within easy reach of the sea at Minehead, Blue Anchor, Watchet and St Audries Bay. We have three double, one family, one twin room, and one single room, all with full en suite facilities. Breakfast is served from 8am. For the energetic there is walking, riding and fishing all available nearby and the West Somerset Steam Railway stops at the station, a short walk away. A car is essential and there is ample parking available. Children and well-behaved dogs are welcome. Bed and Breakfast from £22.50. Please telephone for further details.

TAUNTON

Mr and Mrs P.J. Painter, Blorenge House, 57 Staplegrove Road, Taunton TA1 1DG (Tel & Fax: 01823 283005). Spacious Victorian residence set in large gardens with a swimming pool and large car park. Situated just five minutes' walking distance from Taunton town centre, railway, bus station and Records Office. 24 comfortable bedrooms with washbasin, central heating, colour TV and tea making facilities. Five of the bedrooms have traditional four-poster beds, ideal for weekends away and honeymoon couples. Family and twin rooms are available. The majority of rooms have en suite facilities. Large dining room traditionally furnished; full English breakfast/ Continental breakfast included in the price. Please send for our colour brochure. **ETC/AA ◆◆◆◆**
website: www.blorengehouse.co.uk

230 Somerset

See also Colour Display Advertisement

TAUNTON (near)
Thatched Country Cottage & Garden B&B, Mrs Pam Parry, Pear Tree Cottage, Stapley, Churchstanton, Taunton TA3 7QA (Tel & Fax: 01823 601224). An old thatched country cottage halfway between Taunton and Honiton, set in the idyllic Blackdown Hills, designated an Area of Outstanding Natural Beauty. Picturesque countryside laced with winding lanes full of natural flora and fauna. Wildlife abounds. Three-quarters of an acre traditional cottage garden leading off to two-and-a-half acres of meadow garden planted with specimen trees. Central for north/south coasts of Somerset, Dorset and Devon. Exmoor, Dartmoor, Bristol, Bath, etc within little more than an hour's drive. Many gardens and National Trust properties encompassed in a day's outing. Double/ single and family suite with own facilities, TV, tea/coffee. Conservatory/Garden Room. Evening Meals available. Bed and Breakfast from £17.50pppn. Open all year. ETC ◆◆◆
e-mail: colvin.parry@virgin.net
www.SmoothHound.co.uk/hotels/thatch.html   or   www.best-hotel.com/peartreecottage

THEALE
Gilly & Vern Clark, Yew Tree Farm, Theale, Near Wedmore BS28 4SN (01934 712475). This 17th century farmhouse is equidistant between Wells and Cheddar both approximately ten minutes away by car. The seaside towns of Weston, Burnham and Brean are close by and the cities of Bath and Bristol, both served with park and ride facilities, are approx. 40 minutes' drive. There is a very warm welcome awaiting you at this farm, which has been in the Clark family for over 120 years. Lovely accommodation with en suite facilities, colour TV (one room with video) and full coffee and tea making facilities. Two and three-course meals available. Children welcome; occasional pets at discretion of the owners. From £21 per person per night. Please telephone for brochure.
e-mail: enquiries@yewtreefarmbandb.co.uk

See also Colour Display Advertisement

WASHFORD
Roger and Sarah Richmond, Hungerford Farm, Washford, Watchet TA23 0JZ (01984 640285). Hungerford Farm is an attractive 13th century farmhouse on a family-run, 350 acre farm with cattle, horses, free range chickens and ducks, situated in beautiful countryside on the edge of the Exmoor National Park, two-and-a-half miles from the coast, beaches and the Quantock Hills. Ideal country for walking, riding or cycling. Enjoy a traditional farmhouse breakfast before visiting 12th century Cleeve Abbey, Washford Mill, a local cider farm, or take a ride on the West Somerset Steam Railway - all within walking distance. The medieval village of Dunster with its spectacular castle, mentioned in the Domesday Book and the numerous attractions of Exmoor are a short distance away. Good choice of local pubs within easy reach. Double and twin bedrooms with TV. Children welcome. Stabling available for visitors' horses. Dogs by arrangement. From £22 per person. Open February to November.
e-mail: sarah.richmond@virgin.net

WATCHET
Ann and Kevin Morgan, "Green Bay", Washford TA23 0NN (01984 640303). Small guest house on the A39 provides a friendly welcome, good home cooking, relaxing atmosphere and comfortable en suite rooms, all with TV, drinks tray, radio/alarm, hairdryer and washing accoutrements. It is close to Exmoor, Quantocks, coast and W.S. Railway and an ideal base for touring, cycling, walking, fishing and sightseeing. Evening meals and pets by arrangement. Adjacent parking for cars, motorcycles and secure store for bicycles. Open all year. ETC ◆◆◆
e-mail: green_bay@btinternet.com
website: www.greenbaybedandbreakfast.co.uk

Somerset 231

See also Colour Display Advertisement

WELLS
Mrs Sheila Stott, Lana, Hollow Farm, The Hollow, Westbury-sub-Mendip, Near Wells BA5 1HH (Tel & Fax: 01749 870635). Modern farmhouse on working farm. Comfortable family home in beautiful gardens with views of Somerset Levels and the Mendip Hills. Quiet location. Breakfast room for sole use of guests. Full English breakfast (meals available at local pub five minutes' walk away). En suite rooms including fridge, hairdryer, tea/coffee facilities, shaver point, colour TV and central heating. Non-smoking. Terms from £25 per person per night. Reduced rates for three nights or more.
e-mail: Sheila@stott2366.freeserve.co.uk

WELLS
Mrs Sue Crane, Birdwood House, Bath Road, Wells BA5 3EW (01749 679250). Imposing Victorian house situated on the edge of the Mendip Hills but only one and a half miles from Wells town centre. Accommodation consists of one double en suite room, one double and two single rooms, all with TV and tea/coffee making facilities. Off-road secure parking. Pub nearby. Located close to a walking trail and cycling route - facilities available for cycle storage. Children welcome. Pets by arrangement. Groups and parties welcome. No smoking. Open all year. Bed and Breakfast from £25 per person. AA ♦♦♦

e-mail: fletcherels@yahoo.co.uk

WELLS
Cadgwith House B&B, Hawkers Lane, Wells BA5 3JH (01749 677799). Ideally situated for touring the Mendip Hills, the Somerset Levels, Glastonbury, Cheddar Gorge and Wookey Hole, yet only a few minutes' walk from the centre of Wells with its beautiful cathedral, historic buildings, museum, restaurants and the picturesque market place. The cities of Bath and Bristol are only 20 miles away. There are three double bedrooms offering double, twin or family accommodation. All have spacious en suite facilities or private bathroom and each has remote-control colour TV, radio alarm, hairdryer and tea/coffee making facilities. Folding bed and cot available. Choice of breakfasts available in our dining room, special diets catered for. No smoking. Terms from £26 ppppn double, single occupancy from £30. ETC ♦♦♦
website: www.cadgwithhouse.co.uk

See also Colour Display Advertisement

WESTON-SUPER-MARE
Mrs Margaret Holt, Moorlands, Hutton, Weston-super-Mare BS24 9QH (Tel & Fax: 01934 812283). Enjoy fine food and warm hospitality at this impressive late Georgian house set in landscaped gardens below the slopes of the Western Mendips. A wonderful touring centre, perfectly placed for visits to beaches, sites of special interest and historic buildings. Families with children particularly welcome; reduced terms and pony rides. Full central heating, open fire in comfortable lounge. Open all year. Bed and Breakfast from £23 per person. ETC ♦♦♦
e-mail: margaret-holt@hotmail.com
website: www.guestaccom.co.uk/35

Free or reduced rate entry to Holiday Visits and Attractions – see our READERS' OFFER VOUCHERS on pages 53-90

232 Somerset

See also Colour Display Advertisement

WESTON-SUPER-MARE

John and Katie Nelson, The Owl's Crest, 39 Kewstoke Road, Kewstoke, Weston-super-Mare BS22 9YE (01934 417672). Situated within the small country village of Kewstoke, just one and three quarter miles from Weston and just minutes from the M5. Ideally placed for walks through National Trust countryside or relaxing strolls along the unspoilt beach at Sand Bay. A friendly, personal service is offered with the flexibility to make your stay as enjoyable as possible. Relax in our comfortable guest lounge or in fine weather enjoy the sheltered sunny garden terrace. All our individually decorated rooms are en suite with TV, radio alarm clock, hairdryer and tea/coffee tray. Recommended restaurant/carvery within village. Bed and Breakfast from £26 per person per night. Non-smoking throughout. *WELCOME HOST AWARD. GOLD COMMENDED AWARD WINNERS – WESTON HOTELS ASSOCIATION.*
e-mail: theowlscrest.1@btopenworld.com
website: www.theowlscrest.co.uk

WESTON-SUPER-MARE

Sunset Bay Hotel, 53 Beach Road, Weston-Super-Mare BS23 1BH (01934 623519). Sunset Bay Hotel is a non-smoking, small, family-run hotel enjoying an unrivalled position on the seafront, with superb views to Weston Bay and the Welsh coastline. A guest lounge on the first floor overlooks the bay, with games and books for the enjoyment of our guests. Breakfast is served in the dining room/bar overlooking the beach and lawns, and though we do not provide evening meals, there is a menu of hot and cold snacks. Packed lunches can be supplied on request. All rooms are en suite, or with a private bathroom, and TV, tea/coffee making facilities, hairdryers and towels are supplied in all rooms. On arrival we would like to welcome you with a complimentary tray of tea and cakes. Sunset Bay is ideal for family holidays, weekend breaks, short breaks and holidays at any time of year.
e-mail: relax@sunsetbayhotel.co.uk

WIVELISCOMBE

Jenny Cope, North Down Farm, Pyncombe Lane, Wiveliscombe, Taunton TA4 2BL (Tel & Fax: 01984 623730). In tranquil, secluded surroundings on the Somerset/Devon Border. Traditional working farm set in 150 acres of natural beauty with panoramic views of over 40 miles. M5 motorway seven miles and Taunton ten miles. All rooms tastefully furnished to high standard include en suite, TV, and tea/coffee facilities. Double, twin or single rooms available. Dining room and lounge with log fires for our guests' comfort; centrally heated and double glazed. Drying facilities. Delicious home produced food a speciality. Fishing, golf, horse riding and country sports nearby. Dogs welcome. Bed and Breakfast from £29 pppn, B&B and Evening Meal £225 weekly. North Down Break: three nights Bed and Breakfast and Evening Meal £109 per person. **ETC** ♦♦♦♦ *SILVER AWARD.*
e-mail: jennycope@tiscali.co.uk
website: www.north-down-farm.co.uk

publisher's note

While every effort is made to ensure accuracy, we regret that FHG Guides cannot accept responsibility for errors, misrepresentations or omissions in our entries or any consequences thereof. Prices in particular should be checked. We will follow up complaints but cannot act as arbiters or agents for either party

Staffordshire

ECCLESHALL
Mrs Sue Pimble, Cobbler's Cottage, Kerry Lane, Eccleshall ST21 6EJ (Tel & Fax: 01785 850116). A five minute walk from the centre of historic Eccleshall and just past the 12th century church is Cobbler's Cottage, in a lane within the conservation area. We offer two bedrooms: one double and one twin, both with en suite shower, colour TV, tea/coffee making facilities and central heating. Eccleshall has seven pubs, five with restaurants for your evening meal. Ideally situated midway between Junctions 14 and 15 of the M6; the Potteries, Wedgwood, Ironbridge, Alton Towers and other attractions are within easy reach. Pets welcome. Non-smoking. Terms from £22.50 per person per night including full English breakfast; £32 for single occupancy. **ETC ♦♦♦♦**
e-mail: cobblerscottage@tinyonline.co.uk

See also Colour Display Advertisement

ECCLESHALL
M. Hiscoe-James, Offley Grove Farm, Adbaston, Eccleshall ST20 0QB (Tel & Fax: 01785 280205). You'll consider this a good find! Quality accommodation and excellent breakfasts. Small traditional mixed farm surrounded by beautiful countryside. The house is tastefully furnished and provides all home comforts. Whether you are planning to book here for a break in your journey, stay for a weekend or take your holidays here, you will find something to suit all tastes among the many local attractions. Situated on the Staffordshire/Shropshire borders we are convenient for Alton Towers, Stoke-on-Trent, Ironbridge, etc. Just 15 minutes from M6 and M54; midway between Eccleshall and Newport, four miles from the A519. Reductions for children. Play area for children. Open all year. Bed and Breakfast all en suite from £25. Many guests return. Self-catering cottages available. Brochure on request. **RAC ♦♦♦♦** *WARM WELCOME AWARD AND SPARKLING DIAMOND AWARD.*
e-mail: accomm@offleygrovefarm.freeserve.co.uk   website: www.offleygrovefarm.co.uk

STOKE-ON-TRENT
Hollinhurst Farm Bed & Breakfast, Park Lane, Endon, Stoke-on-Trent ST9 9JB (01782 502633). Sam and Joan would like to invite you to stay in their 17th century stone-built farmhouse nestling in the Staffordshire Moorlands. Hollinhurst Farm is a working farm offering our visitors the opportunity of seeing a variety of free-ranging animals in a beautiful location. A high standard of facilities is available for the discerning traveller - we offer a selection of rooms to cater to your needs including ground floor accommodation. Twin, double and family rooms available, all equipped with TV and tea/coffee making facilities, most of our rooms are en suite and have panoramic views. Within easy reach of the M6 and A50. **ETC ♦♦♦**
e-mail: joan.hollinhurst@btconnect.com
website: www.smoothhound.co.uk/hotels/hollinhurst

FHG FHG Guides Ltd publish a wide range of holiday accommodation guides – for details see the back of this book

234 Staffordshire / Suffolk

TAMWORTH
Mrs Jane Davies, Middleton House Farm, Middleton, Near Tamworth B78 2BD (01827 873474; Fax: 01827 872246). Middleton House Farm is a family-run arable farm of 400 acres. The farmhouse dates back to the 18th century and, after extensive refurbishment, consists of six bedrooms, all individually and tastefully furnished to a very high standard with locally crafted old pine furniture. Situated just two miles from J9 of M42 opposite the Belfry Golf Course, 15 minutes from Birmingham and NEC, 10 minutes from Tamworth (Castle, Snowdome and Drayton Manor). Guests' own lounge and diningroom with individual tables. Bedrooms all with colour TV, hospitality tray, hairdryer and extras; full central heating. Bed and Breakfast from £30 per person. Non-smoking. Ample car parking. ETC ♦♦♦♦ *SILVER AWARD.*
e-mail: rob.jane@tinyonline.co.uk
website: www.middletonhousefarm.co.uk

Suffolk

BURY ST EDMUNDS
Ann & Roy Dakin, Dunston Guest House/Hotel, 8 Springfield Road, Bury St. Edmunds IP33 3AN (01284 767981; Fax: 01284 764574). Dunston Guest House is a delightful Victorian house, five minutes from the town centre, situated in a quiet, tree-lined road. Seventeen individually decorated rooms, many en suite, all with colour TV, tea/coffee tray. Ground floor rooms available in the Coach House. Well furnished guests' lounge with colour TV. No smoking in downstairs area. Car Parking. Garden. **AA/ETC ♦♦♦**
website: www.dunstonguesthouse.co.uk

BURY ST EDMUNDS
Kay Dewsbury, Manorhouse, The Green, Beyton, Near Bury St Edmunds IP30 9AF (01359 270960). You will find a welcoming and relaxed atmosphere at this lovely timbered 15th century farmhouse, set in large gardens overlooking village green. Pretty, spacious, en suite bedrooms – two twin and two king-size, with sofas; all with colour TV, tea-making, radio and hairdryer. Choice of breakfasts at individual tables. A non-smoking house. Parking. Good local inns. Terms from £28 per person per night. Beyton signposted off A14. **ETC ♦♦♦♦♦** *GOLD AWARD, WHICH? GUIDE RECOMMENDED.*
e-mail: manorhouse@beyton.com
website: www.beyton.com

•••some fun days out in SUFFOLK

Melford Hall, Long Melford • 01787 379228 • www.nationaltrust.org.uk
Kentwell Hall, Long Melford • 01787 310207 • www.kentwell.co.uk
Suffolk Wildlife Park, Kessingland • 01502 740291 • www.suffolkwildlifepark.co.uk
National Horse Racing Museum, Newmarket • 01638 667333 • www.nhrm.co.uk

Suffolk 235

CLARE

Alastair and Woolfy Tuffill, "Cobbles", 26 Nethergate Street, Clare, Near Sudbury CO10 8NP (01787 277539; Fax: 01787 278252). Situated in one of the loveliest parts of East Anglia, a friendly welcome awaits you at Cobbles - this Grade II Listed beamed house dates back to the 14th century. Clare is an historic market town and the area abounds in history and ancient buildings, with many antique shops and places of interest to visit. The house is within easy walking distance of the ancient castle and country park, and the town centre with pubs and restaurants which provide excellent food. Accommodation is provided in one twin and one single bedroom in the house with bathroom. Within the pretty walled garden is the charming beamed twin-bedded en suite cottage with private access. All rooms have central heating, colour TV, handbasins and tea/coffee making facilities. Bed and Breakfast from £35 per person per night. Easy parking. We are strictly non-smoking.

FELIXSTOWE

Geoffrey and Elizabeth Harvey, The Grafton Guest House, 13 Sea Road, Felixstowe IP11 2BB (01394 284881; Fax: 01394 279101). Situated by the sea front, the Grafton offers quality Bed and Breakfast accommodation. All en suite and standard rooms have colour TV, clock radio, hairdryer and tea/coffee making facilities. Owners Geoffrey and Elizabeth are committed to providing a first class service and extend a warm welcome to all guests. Non-smoking throughout. Single rooms from £25, double from £43, per night, including breakfast. **ETC/RAC ♦♦♦** *SPARKLING DIAMOND, WARM WELCOME AWARD.*
e-mail: info@grafton-house.com
website: www.grafton-house.com

FRAMLINGHAM

Mr & Mrs Jones, Bantry, Chapel Road, Saxtead, Woodbridge IP13 9RB (01728 685578). Bantry is situated in the picturesque village of Saxtead close to the historic castle town of Framlingham. Saxtead is best known for its working windmill beside the village green. Bantry is set in half an acre of gardens overlooking open countryside and three-quarters-of-a-mile along Tannington Road on right-hand side from Saxtead Windmill. We offer you accommodation in one of three purpose-built self-contained en suite apartments (one ground floor), separate from the house. For secluded comfort each comprises an en suite bedroom leading through to its own private lounge/diningroom with TV and drink-making facilities. Bed and Breakfast from £22 per person per night. Non-smoking.
e-mail: cheryl.jones@sleepysuffolk.co.uk   website: www.sleepysuffolk.co.uk

FRAMLINGHAM

Mrs Jennie Mann, Fiddlers Hall, Cransford, Near Framlingham, Woodbridge IP13 9PQ (01728 663729). Working farm, join in. Signposted on B1119, Fiddlers Hall is a 14th century, moated, oak-beamed farmhouse set in a beautiful and secluded position. It is two miles from Framlingham Castle, 20 minutes' drive from Aldeburgh, Snape Maltings, Woodbridge and Southwold. A Grade II Listed building, it has lots of history and character. The bedrooms are spacious; one has en suite shower room, the other has a private bathroom. Use of lounge and colour TV. Plenty of parking space. Lots of farm animals kept. Traditional farmhouse cooking. Bed and Breakfast terms from £60 per room.

236 Suffolk

| See also Colour Display Advertisement |

e-mail: rosanna3@suffolkholidays.com

IPSWICH
Mrs Rosanna Steward, High View, Back Lane, Washbrook, Ipswich IP8 3JA (01473 730494). A comfortable modernised Edwardian house set in a large secluded garden located four miles south of Ipswich, the county town of Suffolk. Ideally situated to explore the Suffolk heritage coast and countryside, we are within easy reach of "Constable Country", Lavenham, Kersey, the historic market town of Bury St Edmunds plus many other picturesque locations. There is a maze of public footpaths in and around the village providing a good variety of walks through woodland and open countryside. Twin, double and single bedrooms; guests' bathroom with shower and toilet, lounge with TV. Good pub meals available in the village. Double and Twin from £26 per person per night. No smoking. ETC ♦♦♦♦

website: www.suffolkholidays.com

STOWMARKET
Mrs Mary Noy, Red House Farm, Station Road, Haughley, Near Stowmarket IP14 3QP (01449 673323; Fax: 01449 675413). A warm welcome and homely atmosphere awaits you at our attractive farmhouse set in the beautiful surroundings of mid-Suffolk. Comfortably furnished bedrooms with en suite shower rooms, tea/coffee making facilities. One double, one twin and two single rooms. Central heating. Guests' own lounge with TV; dining room. Ideal location for exploring, walking, cycling and birdwatching. Bed and Breakfast from £30 to £35 per person; Single room £35 to £45. Open all year. No smoking or pets. ETC ♦♦♦♦

e-mail: mary@noy1.fsnet.co.uk
website: www.farmstayanglia.co.uk

WOODBRIDGE/FRAMLINGHAM
Grange Farm, Dennington, Woodbridge IP13 8BT (01986 798388; mobile: 07774 182835). A warm welcome awaits you at our exceptional moated farmhouse dating from the 13th Century, and set in extensive grounds including Ace all weather tennis court, in a superb spot two and a half miles north of Dennington, 13 miles from Woodbridge. A comfortable base with log fires in winter and plenty of beams. Close to Snape Maltings, the coast, Minsmere and many places of interest. Accommodation comprises one single, one double, two twin bedrooms, guests' own bathroom and sitting room. Good pubs nearby. Bread and marmalade home made. Parking available. Children welcome. Non-smoking. B&B from £25 single, £50 double/twin. ETC ♦♦♦

website: www.grangefarm.biz

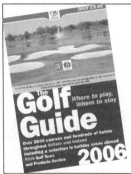

The Golf Guide · 2006
Where to Play, Where to Stay

Available from most booksellers, **The Golf Guide, Where to Play, Where to Stay** covers details of every UK golf course – well over 2800 entries – for holiday or business golf. Hundreds of hotel entries offer convenient accommodation, with accompanying details of the courses – the 'pro', par score, length and more. Including holiday golf in Ireland, France, Portugal, Spain, the USA, South Africa and Thailand.

**Only £9.99 from booksellers or direct from the publishers:
FHG GUIDES, Abbey Mill Business Centre, Seedhill,
Paisley PA1 1TJ** *(postage charged outside UK)*
e-mail: admin@fhguides.co.uk • www.holidayguides.com

Surrey 237

Surrey

GATWICK
Carole and Adrian Grinsted, The Lawn Guest House, 30 Massetts Road, Horley RH6 7DF (01293 775751; Fax: 01293 821803). The Lawn, a totally non-smoking establishment, is a lovely Victorian house in a pleasant garden, two minutes from the centre of Horley and one-and-a-half miles from Gatwick. All rooms are en suite with colour TV, hairdryers, tea/coffee/chocolate trays and direct dial telephones. Horley, with its restaurants, shops and pubs is 150 yards away. The mainline railway station (300 yards) has services to London (Victoria 40 minutes) and Brighton (45 minutes). The Lawn is ideal for those 'overnighting' before or after a flight from Gatwick Airport. On site holiday parking by arrangement. Bed and Breakfast from £58 per en suite double/twin room. **ETC/AA/RAC ♦♦♦♦**, *ETC SILVER AWARD, RAC SPARKLING DIAMOND AWARD.*
e-mail: info@lawnguesthouse.co.uk   website: www.lawnguesthouse.co.uk

HASLEMERE (near)
Mrs Langdale, Heath Hall Farm, Bowlhead Green, Godalming GU8 6NW (01428 682808). Converted stable courtyard surrounded by its own farmland on edge of village of Bowlhead Green. Countryside charming with outstanding walking. Ideal base for many famous historic attractions - Losely House, Petworth House, Wisley RHS Garden, Arundel Castle, Midhurst (Cowdray Castle), historic Portsmouth. Plenty in locality to visit with children. Central for golf courses; polo at Midhurst. Close to South and North Downs. Relaxed atmosphere in house, domestic pets, cattle, sheep, ducks and chooks. All rooms have en suite bathrooms, TV, tea/coffee making facilities. Three rooms on ground floor. Ample car parking. Warm welcome with friendly help and advice. Dogs welcome if kept under control and with prior arrangement. £30 per person per night, £10 per child (up to 14 years). Cot provided on application (£10 per night). Open all year.
e-mail: heathhallfarm@btinternet.co.uk   website: www.heathhallfarm.co.uk

HORLEY (near Gatwick)
Mrs G. McLean, Gorse Cottage, 66 Balcombe Road, Horley RH6 9AY (01293 784402). Friendly, welcoming accommodation, two miles from Gatwick Airport in residential area with pubs and restaurants within walking distance. Five minutes from railway station serving London (45 minutes) and the South East. Early breakfast catered for, light breakfast served after 7.30am - cereal, scrambled eggs (free-range), toast, coffee, tea and juice. Centrally heated, pleasant room with tea and coffee making facilities. Terms £40 double/twin, £30 single. Short term single accommodation offered for business people.

238 Surrey

See also Colour Display Advertisement

KINGSTON-UPON-THAMES
Chase Lodge Hotel, 10 Park Road, Hampton Wick, Kingston-upon-Thames KT1 4AS (020 8943 1862; Fax: 020 8943 9363). An award-winning hotel with style and elegance, set in tranquil surroundings at affordable prices. Quality en suite bedrooms. Full English breakfast. À la carte menu. Licensed bar. Wedding receptions catered for. Honeymoon suite available with jacuzzi and steam area. Only 20 minutes from Heathrow Airport. Close to Kingston town centre and all major transport links. All Major credit cards accepted. **AA ♦♦♦♦, RAC ★★★★, LES ROUTIERS.**
e-mail: info@chaselodgehotel.com
websites: www.chaselodgehotel.com
www.surreyhotels.com

LINGFIELD
Mrs V. Manwill, Stantons Hall Farm, Eastbourne Road, Blindley Heath, Lingfield RH7 6LG (01342 832401). Stantons Hall Farm is an 18th century farmhouse, set in 18 acres of farmland and adjacent to Blindley Heath Common. Family, double and single rooms, most with WC, shower and wash-hand basins en suite. Separate bathroom. All rooms have colour TV, tea/coffee facilities and are centrally heated. There are plenty of parking spaces. We are conveniently situated within easy reach of M25 (London Orbital), Gatwick Airport (car parking for travellers) and Lingfield Park racecourse. Enjoy a traditional English breakfast in our large farmhouse kitchen. Bed and Breakfast from £25 per person, reductions for children sharing. Cot and high chair available. Well behaved dogs welcome by prior arrangement.

LINGFIELD
Mrs Vivienne Bundy, Oaklands, Felcourt Road, Lingfield RH7 6NF (01342 834705). Oaklands is a spacious country house of considerable charm dating from the 17th century. It is set in its own grounds of one acre and is about one mile from the small town of Lingfield and three miles from East Grinstead, both with rail connections to London. It is convenient to Gatwick Airport and is ideal as a "stop-over" or as a base to visit many places of interest in south-east England. Dover and the Channel Ports are two hours' drive away whilst the major towns of London and Brighton are about one hour distant. One family room en suite, one double and one single bedrooms with washbasins; three bathrooms, two toilets; sittingroom; diningroom. Cot, high chair, babysitting and reduced rates for children. Gas central heating. Open all year. Parking. Bed and Breakfast from £23.
e-mail: oaklands@ukonline.co.uk

OXTED
Pinehurst Grange Guest House, East Hill (A25), Oxted RH8 9AE (01883 716413). Victorian ex-farmhouse offers one double, one twin and one single bedroom. All with washbasin, tea/coffee making facilities, colour TV; residents' dining room. Private parking. Close to all local amenities. Only 20 minutes' drive from Gatwick Airport and seven minutes' walk to the station with good trains to London/Croydon. Also close to local bus and taxi service. There are many famous historic houses nearby including "Chartwell", "Knole", "Hever Castle", and "Penshurst Place". Very handy for Lingfield Park racecourse. WALKERS NOTE: only one mile from North Downs Way. No smoking.

SURBITON
Mrs Menzies, Villiers Lodge, 1 Cranes Park, Surbiton KT5 8AB (020 8399 6000). Excellent accommodation in small Guest House. Every comfort, tea/coffee making facilities in all rooms. Close to trains and buses for London, Hampton Court, Kew, Windsor and coast. Ham House is a favourite visiting place and Merton Abbey Mills is a wonderful place for a day shopping and exploring. Reasonable terms.

Sussex

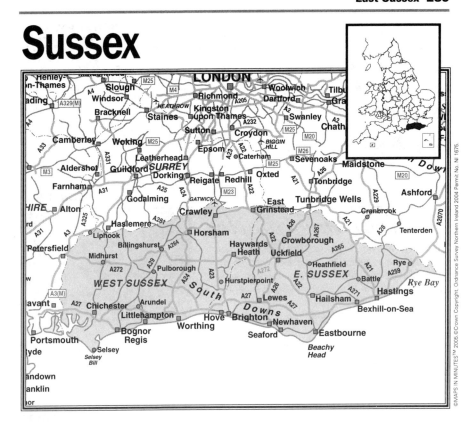

East Sussex

EASTBOURNE
Tim and Karen Camp, Far End Private Hotel, 139 Royal Parade, Eastbourne BN22 7LH (01323 725666). From the moment you arrive you are assured of a warm welcome and real "home from home" atmosphere. Our centrally heated bedrooms with colour TV and tea/coffee making facilities are tastefully decorated, most have en suite facilities and sea views. Residents have their own lounge and private car park. Enjoy freshly prepared traditional home cooking. Special diets can be catered for. We are adjacent to the popular Princes Park with boating lake, lawns, bowling greens and pitch'n'putt, close by you can enjoy sailing, fishing, bowling, tennis and swimming. We are in easy reach of Beachy Head, the South Downs and Newhaven. We will be delighted to provide information on the many local attractions and services, and shall do our best to make your stay as memorable and pleasant as possible. Credit cards accepted. Bed and Breakfast from £22; Evening Meal available. Low season short breaks. Please call or write for our colour brochure. **AA ♦♦♦**
website: www.farendhotel.co.uk

•••some fun days out in EAST SUSSEX

Drusillas Park, Alfriston • 01323 874100 • www.drusillas.co.uk
Michelham Priory, Hailsham • 01323 844224 • www.sussexpast.co.uk
Ashdown Forest Llama Park, Forest Row • 01825 712040 • www.llamapark.co.uk

240 East Sussex

HAILSHAM (near)
David and Jill Hook, Longleys Farm Cottage, Harebeating Lane, Hailsham BN27 1ER (Tel & Fax: 01323 841227). Situated in quiet private country lane one mile north of the market town of Hailsham with its excellent amenities including modern sports centre and leisure pool, surrounded by footpaths across open farmland. Ideal for country lovers. Dogs and children welcome. The coast at Eastbourne, South Downs, Ashdown Forest and 1066 country are all within easy access. The non-smoking accommodation comprises one twin room, double room en suite; family room en suite and tea/coffee making facilities. Bed and Breakfast from £22. Reductions for children. ETC ◆◆◆

HARTFIELD

Bolebroke Castle

Henry VIII's hunting lodge, Bolebroke Castle is set on a beautiful 30 acre estate with lakes, woodlands and views to Ashdown Forest, where you will find 'Pooh Bridge'. Antiques and beamed ceilings add to the atmosphere. Four-poster suite available. B&B or Self-Catering options. Please call for our brochure.

In the heart of "Winnie the Pooh" country.

ETC ◆◆◆◆ www.bolebrokecastle.co.uk

Bolebroke Castle, Hartfield, East Sussex TN7 4JJ
Tel: 01892 770061

See also Colour Advertisement.

HASTINGS
Peter Mann, Grand Hotel, Grand Parade, St Leonards, Hastings TN38 0DD (Tel & Fax: 01424 428510 or 0870 2257025). Seafront family-run hotel, half-a-mile west of Hastings Pier. Spacious lounge, licensed bar, central heating throughout. Radio/room-call/baby-listening. En suite rooms with TV also available. Free access at all times. Unrestricted/disabled parking. Non-smoking throughout hotel. In the heart of 1066 country close to Battle Abbey, Bodiam and Hever Castles, Kipling's Bateman and historic Cinque Ports plus Hastings Castle, Caves, Sealife Aquarium, local golf courses and leisure centres. Open all year. Bed and Breakfast from £15; Evening Meal from £15. Children welcome, half price when sharing room. SAE for further information. ETC ◆◆◆

e-mail: petermann@grandhotelhastings.co.uk
website: www.grandhotelhastings.co.uk

HASTINGS
Dale and Jo Turner, Seaspray Guest House, 54 Eversfield Place, St Leonards-on-Sea, Hastings TN37 6DB (01424 436583). Recently refurbished family-run B&B, ideally situated on Hastings seafront. Near pier and White Rock Theatre; five minutes' level walk to the town centre, station and tourist attractions. Family, double and twin rooms are all en suite; one single en suite and one with private bathroom. All rooms have tea/coffee making, colour TV, radio alarm, double glazing and central heating; access at all times. Ground floor room available. Extensive breakfast menu. Children welcome. No smoking. Short breaks available October to April (excluding Christmas, New Year and Easter) – details on request. ETC ◆◆◆◆

e-mail: jo@seaspray.freeserve.co.uk
website: www.seaspraybb.co.uk

East Sussex 241

See also Colour Display Advertisement

LEWES

White Hart Hotel, High Street, Lewes BN7 1XE (01273 476694; Fax: 01273 476695). Behind the Georgian facade of the White Hart lies an historic Tudor building which has been substantially extended to create a lively county town hotel. 53 bedrooms, all en suite with colour TV, telephone, tea-making. Some rooms have views of the Downs; some with disabled access. Wide range of meals and snacks available daily, à la carte, carvery, bar meals, light snacks, teas and coffees. Leisure Centre and Health Spa with heated indoor pool, fully equipped gym, sauna, aerobics studio, beauty clinic etc.
e-mail: info@whitehartlewes.co.uk
website: www.whitehartlewes.co.uk

RYE

Barbara and Denys Martin, Little Saltcote, 22 Military Road, Rye TN31 7NY (01797 223210; Fax: 01797 224474). Situated in a quiet road, just ten minutes' walk from the centre of medieval Rye, Little Saltcote is an Edwardian family home which offers off-road parking and five comfortable rooms (one at ground floor), all with TV, radio and beverage tray. With a 'nothing is too much trouble' philosophy we aim to ensure our guests leave relaxed and refreshed. We welcome families and are pleased to offer tourist advice or arrange bike hire. Ideally located for touring Sussex and Kent's varied attractions, including everything from sandy beaches to castles, historic houses and gardens. Rates, including acclaimed full English or vegetarian breakfast, start from £20 per person. Special offer available from November to February. Pets welcome by arrangement. **AA ♦♦♦**
e-mail: littlesaltcote.rye@virgin.net

WINCHELSEA

Mrs Wendy Hysted, Orchard Spot, Broad Street, Icklesham, Winchelsea TN36 4AS (01424 814681). A very private detached room in a garden setting with own patio and ample parking. Freedom to come and go as you please. Picturesque area, near to the historic towns of Winchelsea, Rye and Battle. Good walking and cycling and within close proximity of many seaside resorts. Many good local pubs serving a vast variety of excellent food. Twin bedded non-smoking room, with colour TV, tea/coffee making facilities and private en suite. Friendly atmosphere and a good English breakfast is served. Bed and Breakfast from £58 per room. Open April to October. Home-made cakes available.

American Adventure Golf
Eastbourne, East Sussex
See our **READERS' OFFER VOUCHER** for details of free or reduced rate entry

Yesterday's World
Battle, East Sussex
See our **READERS' OFFER VOUCHER** for details of free or reduced rate entry

West Sussex

HAYWARDS HEATH
Broxmead Paddock, Broxmead Lane, Bolney, Haywards Heath RH17 5RG (01444 881458; Fax: 01444 881491). A warm welcome awaits you at this country-style B&B set in two-and-a-half acres of land in an Area of Outstanding Natural Beauty in the Sussex Downs. Relax in our garden with a cream tea, listen to the birds, walk through the woods and along the numerous footpaths and take time out to recharge your batteries. Alternatively we are close to several National Trust properties, only 15 minutes from Brighton, 20 minutes from Gatwick Airport and only 50 minutes from London. Single, twin, double and family rooms available, all rooms have private bathroom, TV, tea/coffee facilities and central heating. Children welcome - cot and high chair available. Open all year with the exception of Christmas and New Year. Bed and full English breakfast from £20. **ETC ♦♦♦♦**
e-mail: broxmeadpaddock@hotmail.com   website: www.broxmeadpaddock.eclipse.co.uk

HENFIELD
Mrs J. Forbes, Little Oreham Farm, off Horne Lane, Near Woodsmill, Henfield BN5 9SB (01273 492931). Delightful old Sussex farmhouse situated in rural position down lane, adjacent to footpaths and nature reserve. One mile from Henfield village, eight miles from Brighton, convenient for Gatwick and Hickstead. Excellent base for visiting many gardens and places of interest in the area. The farmhouse is a Listed building of great character; oak-beamed sittingroom with inglenook fireplace (log fires), and a pretty diningroom. Two comfortable attractive bedrooms with en suite or private facilities, colour TV; tea making facilities. Central heating throughout. Lovely garden with views of the Downs. Situated off Horne Lane, one minute from Woodsmill Countryside Centre. You will enjoy a friendly welcome and pleasant holiday. Sorry, no children under 10. Bed and Breakfast from £23 per person. Also available charming two-bedroomed self-catering cottage in village. Available weekly or for short breaks. Non-smoking. Open all year.

See also Colour Display Advertisement

MIDHURST
Mrs R.M. Reeves-Fisher, Meadowhills, Stedham, Midhurst GU29 0PT (01730 812609; mobile: 07776 262147). This small, comfortable, homely country estate, dating from 1908, is set in grounds of 25 acres with magnificent views over the South Downs. Amenities include fishing rights, and the area is a walker's paradise; riding stables nearby. Local attractions include leisure centres at Midhurst and Petersfield, Cowdray Park with golf and polo, horse racing at Fontwell and Goodwood; the South Coast is 20 miles away. Places of interest include Uppark, the Weald and Downland Museum, National Trust properties and Chichester Festival Theatre.
website: www.meadowhills.co.uk

Free or reduced rate entry to Holiday Visits and Attractions – see our READERS' OFFER VOUCHERS on pages 53-90

•••some fun days out in WEST SUSSEX

Weald & Downland Museum, Chichester • 01243 811348 • www.wealddown.co.uk
Arundel Castle, Arundel • 01903 883136 • www.arundelcastle.org
Knockhatch Adventure Park, Hailsham • 01323 442051 • www.knockhatch.com

Tyne & Wear

NEWCASTLE-UPON-TYNE

New Kent Hotel, 127 Osborne Road, Jesmond, Newcastle-upon-Tyne NE2 2TB (0191-281 7711; Fax: 0191-281 3369). This privately owned hotel is situated in a quiet location, but only minutes from the city centre. It has built up a reputation for good food and friendly, efficient service in a warm and congenial atmosphere. All bedrooms are en suite, with hospitality tray, direct-dial telephone, colour TV with satellite, and radio. There is a spacious cocktail lounge and a restaurant serving the best of modern and classic cuisine. Local attractions include the Metro Centre, Northumbria National Park, Holy Island and Bamburgh Castle. Single from £52.50, double from £79.50.
AA ★★★

FHG Guides
2006 October Edition

- Recommended COUNTRY HOTELS
- Recommended COUNTRY INNS & PUBS
- BED & BREAKFAST STOPS • CHILDREN WELCOME!
- The Original FHG Guide to COAST & COUNTRY HOLIDAYS
- CARAVAN & CAMPING HOLIDAYS, England, Scotland, Wales & Ireland
- BRITAIN'S BEST HOLIDAYS
- THE GOLF GUIDE Where to Play / Where to Stay
- PETS WELCOME!
- Recommended SHORT BREAK HOLIDAYS in Britain
- SELF CATERING HOLIDAYS in Britain

Available from bookshops or larger newsagents

FHG GUIDES LTD
Abbey Mill Business Centre,
Seedhill, Paisley PA1 ITJ
www.holidayguides.com

Warwickshire

ALCESTER
Mrs Hammersley, Sambourne Hall Farm, Sambourne, Alcester B96 6NZ (01527 852151). Beautiful 16th Century Farmhouse set in 500 acres of farmland in picturesque village. Large comfortable bedrooms, own sitting room. Walled garden. Excellent local pubs nearby. Coughton Court one mile. Ragley Hall five miles and Stratford-upon-Avon 10 miles. Ideal for business or vacation. National Exhibition Centre and Cotswolds easy access. Terms from £40 single, £50 to £55 double.

ALCESTER
The Globe Hotel, 54 Birmingham Road, Alcester B49 5EG (Tel & Fax: 01789 763287). A warm and friendly hotel in the historic market town of Alcester (seven miles from Stratford-upon-Avon). Stylish and spacious en suite bedrooms with remote-control TV, radio alarm clock, direct dial telephones, modem connection and hospitality trays. Ideally placed for Stratford-upon-Avon, motorways M40/42 and M5, Airport/NEC (30 minutes) and touring the Cotswolds. Rooms from £35 to £65. Totally refurbished in 2000. **ETC/AA** ♦♦♦♦

Warwickshire 245

COVENTRY (near)

BOURNE BROOK LODGE

Barbara Chamberlain,
Bourne Brook Lodge,
Mill Lane, Fillongley,
Near Coventry CV7 8EE
Tel: 01676 541898
www.bournebrooklodge.co.uk

Experience the peace and tranquillity of our country house offering high standards of comfort and cleanliness in picturesque surroundings. En suite in stone-built chalet rooms having colour TV and hostess tray. Private car park and gardens. Prices include full English breakfast.

Double/twin en suite	£60 per room
single en suite	£35
single with shared facilities	£27

A no smoking establishment. Telephone bookings only.
Convenient for N.E.C., Forest of Arden and Belfry golf courses, Birmingham, Coventry and Stratford.

FILLONGLEY (near Coventry)
Mary Smith, Grooms Cottage, Manor House Farm, Green End Road, Fillongley, Coventry CV7 8DS (01676 540256). Situated on a working mixed farm. The Grooms Cottage is a self-contained, twin-bedded room with en suite facilities, TV, radio, hairdryer and tea and coffee making facilities. Close to the M6 and M42. 15 minutes from National Exhibition Centre, Birmingham International Airport and Coventry railway station. Golf close by at the Forest of Arden. ETC ♦♦♦♦ *SILVER AWARD.*

KENILWORTH
Trudi and Ken Wheat, The Hollyhurst Guest House, 47 Priory Road, Kenilworth CV8 1LL (01926 853882; Fax: 01926 855211). A comfortable Victorian house close to the town centre and a pleasant stroll from Kenilworth Castle. A market town with excellent restaurants, located in the heart of the Warwickshire countryside, Kenilworth is well connected by road and convenient for the NEC, Stoneleigh Park and the University of Warwick. You'll find the Hollyhurst perfect as a business base or holiday stopover. In either case we offer real hospitality and home comforts in our seven-bedroom guest house. Four rooms have en suite/private facilities and there is private parking for up to seven vehicles. No smoking. No pets. Bed and Breakfast from £24 per person. AA ♦♦♦

e-mail: admin@hollyhurstguesthouse.co.uk   website: www.hollyhurstguesthouse.co.uk

246 Warwickshire

LEAMINGTON SPA

Mrs R. Gibbs, Hill Farm, Lewis Road, Radford Semele, Leamington Spa CV31 1UX (01926 337571). Working farm. Guests are welcome all year round to this comfortable, centrally heated farmhouse on a 350 acre mixed farm. Ideally situated for Warwick, Coventry, Stratford-upon-Avon, Leamington Spa, Royal Showground, Birmingham, NEC and the Cotswolds. Three pretty double bedrooms and two twin rooms with washbasins, tea and coffee facilities and TV. Some are en suite. Guests' sittingroom with colour TV; lovely conservatory for breakfast dining and excellent Breakfast Menu. Car preferable, ample parking. Farm Holiday Bureau member. FHG past Diploma Winner. Bed and Breakfast from £25-£30 per person. **AA/ETC** ♦♦♦♦

See also Colour Display Advertisement

STRATFORD-UPON-AVON

Mrs Julia Downie, Holly Tree Cottage, Birmingham Road, Pathlow, Stratford-upon-Avon CV37 0ES (Tel & Fax: 01789 204461). Period cottage dating from 17th Century, with antiques, paintings, collection of porcelain, fresh flowers, tasteful furnishings and friendly atmosphere. Picturesque gardens, orchard, paddock and pasture with wildlife and extensive views over open countryside. Situated three miles north of Stratford-upon-Avon towards Henley-in-Arden on A3400. Rooms have television, radio/alarm, hospitality trays and hairdryers. Breakfasts are a speciality. Pubs and restaurants nearby. Ideally located for Theatre, Shakespeare Country, Heart of England, Cotswolds, Warwick Castle, Blenheim Palace and National Trust Properties. Well situated for National Exhibition Centre, Birmingham and National Agricultural Centre, Stoneleigh. Children welcome, pets by arrangement. Non-smoking. Bed & Breakfast from £29.
e-mail: john@hollytree-cottage.co.uk   website: www.hollytree-cottage.co.uk

STRATFORD-UPON-AVON

Mrs M. Turney, Cadle Pool Farm, The Ridgeway, Stratford-upon-Avon CV37 9RE (01789 292494). Working farm. Situated in picturesque grounds, this charming oak-panelled and beamed family home is part of a 450-acre farm. It is two miles from Stratford-upon-Avon, between Anne Hathaway's Cottage and Mary Arden's House. Only eight minutes by car from the Royal Shakespeare Theatre and the race course. Ideal touring centre for Warwick and the Cotswolds. Accommodation comprises one family and one double room en suite, with TV and one double room with private bathroom. All have central heating, tea/coffee facilities, hairdryers. There is an antique oak dining room and guest sitting room. The gardens and ornamental pool are particularly attractive with peacocks and ducks roaming freely. Children over ten welcome. Sorry, no pets. Non-smoking accommodation available. Bed and Breakfast from £28.50 per person, £27.50 if stay two nights or more. **AA** ♦♦♦♦

WARWICK

Mr and Mrs D. Clapp, The Croft, Haseley Knob, Warwick CV35 7NL (Tel & Fax: 01926 484447). Join David and Pat and share the friendly family atmosphere, the picturesque rural surroundings, home cooking and very comfortable accommodation. Bedrooms, all en suite/private bathroom, have colour TV, tea/coffee making equipment. Ground floor en suite bedrooms available. Bed and Full English Breakfast from £28 per person sharing a double/twin room. Centrally located for touring Warwick (Castle), Stratford (Shakespeare), Coventry (Cathedral), and Birmingham. Also ideal for the businessman visiting the National Exhibition Centre or Birmingham Airport, both about 15 minutes. No smoking inside. Ample parking. Mobile home available, also caravan park. Large gardens. Open all year. French spoken. **ETC/AA** ♦♦♦♦
e-mail: david@croftguesthouse.co.uk   website: www.croftguesthouse.co.uk

Wiltshire

CORSHAM
Kate Waldron, Park Farm Barn, Westrop, Corsham SN13 9QF (01249 715911; mobile: 07976 827083; Fax: 01249 701107). Recently converted 18th century tithe barn with newly constructed Cotswold style Bed and Breakfast accommodation close by. Park Farm Barn has three en suite bedrooms which are light and spacious with apex ceilings and beams. Colour TV and tea/coffee making facilities in each room. Central heating throughout. Breakfast is served in the dining room. Park Farm Barn is an ideal base for the many interesting and historic places in and around Corsham, situated in the delightful hamlet of Westrop, one mile from Corsham and seven miles from Junction 17 on the M4. The National Trust village of Lacock is only a short drive away with a number of excellent pubs for evening meals. Castle Combe and Bradford-upon-Avon only 20 minutes, Bath ten miles. Children welcome, cot and highchair available. No smoking. Parking. Terms from £30 pppn single, £22.50 pppn double/twin. **ETC ♦♦♦♦**, *FARM STAY UK MEMBER.*
e-mail: thewaldrons@lineone.net   website: www.parkfarmbarn.co.uk

---

•••some fun days out in WILTSHIRE

Abbey House & Gardens, Malmesbury • 01666 822212 • www.abbeyhousegardens.co.uk
Fox Talbot Museum, Lacock • 01249 730459 • www.nationaltrust.org.uk
STEAM - Museum of GWR, Swindon • 01793 466650 • www.steam-museum.org.uk

DEVIZES

Littleton Lodge, Littleton Panell (A360), West Lavington, Devizes SN10 4ES (01380 813131). Superb Victorian family house set in one acre of private grounds, overlooking vineyard within pretty conservation village. Five minutes' drive from historic Devizes. All rooms en suite with beverage tray, TV and radio/alarms. Choice of scrumptious breakfast. Excellent meals are available at two pubs within five/ten minutes' walk. Stonehenge is only 15 minutes' drive and Littleton Lodge is an ideal base to explore the Wiltshire White Horses, prehistoric Avebury, Georgian Bath (40 mins), Salisbury (20 mins), the National Trust village of Lacock, as well as numerous country houses and gardens, including Longleat. Private parking. Mastercard, Visa and Switch accepted. Single occupancy from £45, Double from £60. **AA ♦♦♦♦**

e-mail: stay@littletonlodge.co.uk
website: www.littletonlodge.co.uk

MALMESBURY

Mrs Susan Barnes, Lovett Farm, Little Somerford, Near Malmesbury SN15 5BP (Tel & Fax: 01666 823268; mobile: 07808 858612). Working farm. Enjoy traditional hospitality at our delightful farmhouse just three miles from the historic town of Malmesbury with its wonderful Norman abbey and gardens and central for Cotswolds, Bath, Stratford, Avebury and Stonehenge. Two attractive en suite bedrooms with delightful views, each with tea/coffee making facilities, colour TV and radio. Delicious full English breakfast served in our cosy dining room/lounge. Central heating throughout. Bed and Breakfast from £25. Credit cards accepted. Non-smoking accommodation. Open all year. **ETC/AA ♦♦♦♦, *FARM STAY UK MEMBER*.**
e-mail: lovettfarm@btinternet.com
website: www.lovettfarm.co.uk

MARLBOROUGH

Mrs Maggie Vigar-Smith, Wernham Farm, Clench Common, Marlborough SN8 4DR (01672 512236). This working farm is set in picturesque countryside on Wansdyke, off the A345. It is close to Marlborough, Avebury, Pewsey and the Kennet & Avon Canal. Accommodation is available in two family bedrooms, one en suite and one with private bathroom. Terms: £40 single, £55 double. **ETC ♦♦♦**. Five caravan and camping pitches are also available.
e-mail: margglvsf@aol.com

MARLBOROUGH

Jackie and James Macbeth, Manor Farm, Collingbourne Kingston, Marlborough SN8 3SD (01264 850859). Attractive Grade II Listed farmhouse on a working family farm, very easy to find, 12 minutes south of Marlborough on the A338 Salisbury Road. We are opposite the church in the centre of the pretty village of Collingbourne Kingston. Ample private parking. Our comfortable, spacious and well equipped rooms are all en suite or private, and include double, twin and family (for four). Sumptuous traditional, vegetarian, gluten-free and other special diet breakfasts. Beautiful countryside with superb walking and cycling from the farm. Horses and pets welcome. Pleasure flights by helicopter from our private airstrip. Non-smoking. Credit cards welcome. B&B from £27 pppn. **ETC ♦♦♦, *FARM STAY MEMBER*.**
e-mail: stay@manorfm.com
website: www.manorfm.com

Wiltshire 249

MERE
Mrs Jean Smith, The Beeches, Chetcombe Road, Mere BA12 6AU (01747 860687). A comfortable, old Toll House with interesting carved stairway and gallery, standing in beautiful garden at entrance to early English village. Centrally situated for Bath, Wells, Salisbury, Bournemouth, New Forest and Sherborne. In close proximity to the famous Stourhead Gardens and Longleat House and Wildlife Park. We have one double, one family and one single room. The house is furnished to a very high standard, is centrally heated with TV, tea/coffee making facilities, washbasin and shaver point in all rooms, one room having en suite shower. Large lounge. Enclosed car park. Open all year. Bed and Breakfast from £20. Reductions for children.

SALISBURY
Scotland Lodge Farm, Winterbourne Stoke, Salisbury SP3 4TF (01980 621199; Fax: 01980 621188). Warm welcome at family-run competition yard set in 46 acres of grassland. Lovely views and walks. Stonehenge and Salisbury nearby. Conservatory and garden for guests' use. Dogs by arrangement. French, Italian and German spoken. Easy access off A303 with entry through automatic gate. Excellent local pubs. Salisbury Stars Award for Customer Care. **ETC/AA** ◆◆◆◆
e-mail: william.lockwood@bigwig.net
website: www.smoothhound.co.uk/hotels/scotlandl

See also Colour Display Advertisement

SALISBURY
Lizzie and David Guild, Newton Farmhouse, Southampton Road, Whiteparish, Salisbury SP5 2QL (01794 884416). This historic Listed 16th century farmhouse on the borders of the New Forest was formerly part of the Trafalgar Estate and is situated eight miles south of Salisbury, convenient for Stonehenge, Romsey, Winchester, Portsmouth and Bournemouth. All rooms have pretty, en suite facilities and are delightfully decorated, six with genuine period four-poster beds. The beamed diningroom houses a collection of Nelson memorabilia and antiques and has flagstone floors and an inglenook fireplace with an original brick built bread oven. The superb English breakfast is complemented by fresh fruits, preserves and free-range eggs. A swimming pool is idyllically set in the extensive, well stocked gardens and children are most welcome in this non-smoking establishment. *SILVER AWARD*, **AA** ◆◆◆◆ *PREMIER SELECTED.*
e-mail: reservations@newtonfarmhouse.co.uk   website: www.newtonfarmhouse.co.uk

SALISBURY
Dawn and Alan Curnow, Hayburn Wyke Guest House, 72 Castle Road, Salisbury SP1 3RL (Tel & Fax: 01722 412627). Hayburn Wyke is a Victorian house, situated adjacent to Victoria Park, and a ten minute riverside walk from the city centre. Salisbury and surrounding area have many places of interest to visit, including Salisbury Cathedral, Old Sarum, Wilton House and Stonehenge. Most bedrooms have en suite facilities, all have washbasin, television, and tea/coffee making equipment. Children are welcome at reduced rates. Sorry, no pets (guide dogs an exception). Private car parking for guests. Open all year. Bed and full English Breakfast from £23. Credit cards and Switch accepted. **AA/RAC** ◆◆◆
e-mail: hayburn.wyke@tinyonline.co.uk
website: www.hayburnwykeguesthouse.co.uk

SWINDON

Mrs Mary Richards, Little Cotmarsh Farm, Broad Town, Wootton Bassett, Swindon SN4 7RA (01793 731322). Little Cotmarsh Farm is a lovely 17th Century farmhouse nestling quietly in the hamlet of Cotmarsh. Enjoy the relaxed atmosphere of our home, the attractive bedrooms are spacious and well equipped – two en suite, one with private bathroom. We are just seven miles from Avebury, one of the largest monuments in Britain. Hungerford, Tetbury and Bradford-on-Avon are full of glorious antique shops or visit Swindon's new Great Western Designer Outlet Village. Best of all, borrow "100 Walks in Wiltshire" and explore our wonderful countryside. Good local pub food. M4 Junction 16 approximately four miles. Bed and Breakfast from £25 to £33 per person. No smoking. AA ♦♦♦♦
website: www.littlecotmarshfarm.co.uk

WARMINSTER

Mrs M. Hoskins, Spinney Farmhouse, Chapmanslade, Westbury BA13 4AQ (01373 832412). Off A36, three miles west of Warminster; 16 miles from historic city of Bath. Close to Longleat, Cheddar and Stourhead. Reasonable driving distance to Bristol, Stonehenge, Glastonbury and the cathedral cities of Wells and Salisbury. Pony trekking and fishing available locally. Washbasins, tea/coffee-making facilities and shaver points in all rooms. Family room available. Guests' lounge with colour TV. Central heating. Children and pets welcome. Ample parking. Open all year. Enjoy farm fresh food in a warm, friendly family atmosphere. Bed and Breakfast from £22 per night. Reduction after two nights. Evening Meal £12.

Worcestershire

DROITWICH

Mrs Salli Harrison, Middleton Grange, Salwarpe, Droitwich Spa WR9 0AH (01905 451678; Fax: 01905 453978). Enjoy high quality accommodation and hospitality in this traditional 18th century country house surrounded by peaceful and picturesque gardens. All rooms have en suite with colour TV, generous beverage tray, hairdryer, radio alarm and more. Excellent breakfast. Wedding nights catered for. Children welcome. Babysitting service. Dogs and cats by arrangement. Superbly situated for exploring the Heart of England. Stratford-upon-Avon, Warwick, Cotswolds, Birmingham and Wales all within one hour. M5 motorway six minutes. Many traditional eating establishments close by. Single from £35, double from £55. **ETC** ♦♦♦ *SILVER AWARD*.

e-mail: salli@middletongrange.com   website: www.middletongrange.com

Worcestershire 251

DROITWICH SPA
David and Tricia Havard, Phepson Farm, Himbleton, Droitwich Spa WR9 7JZ (01905 391205). Working farm.
In our 17th century oak beamed farmhouse and converted buildings, we offer a warm welcome, good food and a relaxed and informal atmosphere. All rooms en suite with colour TV, hairdryers and tea/coffee facilities. Situated on a small sheep farm with scenic fishing lake; walking on Wychavon Way. Convenient for touring the beautiful Heart of England. Five miles from motorway network. Featured on 'Wish You Were Here'. Self-catering also available. Credit cards accepted. Bed & Breakfast from £27.50 to £35 pppn. **ETC ♦♦♦♦, WINNER OF BEST WORCESTERSHIRE BREAKFAST AWARD.**
website: www.phepsonfarm.co.uk

MALVERN
Phil and Em Butler, Copper Beech House, 32 Avenue Road, Great Malvern WR14 3BJ (01684 565013). Great Malvern is renowned for its porcelain, annual music festivals, prestigious theatres, mineral water and Morgan Cars. The area offers a haven of elegant landscapes, open spaces and fantastic walks. Copper Beech House is conveniently located just five minutes' walk from Malvern Station, a short distance from the town centre, and just over two miles from the Three Counties Showground. All seven non-smoking bedrooms offer a relaxed environment, with en suite bath or shower rooms, hairdryers, colour television and hot drink facilities. Guest lounge with widescreen TV. Bed and Breakfast from £46 single room, £76 double/ twin room, £95 family room.

e-mail: enquiries@copperbeechhouse.co.uk   website: www.copperbeechhouse.co.uk

MALVERN (near)
Ann and Brian Porter, Croft Guest House, Bransford, Worcester WR6 5JD (01886 832227; Fax: 01886 830037). 16th-18th century part black-and-white cottage-style country house situated in the Teme Valley, four miles from Worcester and Malvern. Croft House is central for visiting numerous attractions in Worcester, Hereford, the Severn Valley and surrounding countryside. River and lake fishing are close by, and an 18-hole golf course is opposite. Three en suite guest rooms (two double, one family) and two with washbasins are available. All bedrooms are non-smoking. Rooms are double glazed and have colour TV, radio alarm and courtesy tray. TV lounge, residential licence. Dogs welcome by arrangement. Full English breakfast and evening meals are prepared from home-grown/made or locally sourced produce. Bed and Breakfast from £26 to £35 single, £44 to £60 double. **AA ♦♦♦**
e-mail: hols@crofthousewr6.fsnet.co.uk   website: www.croftguesthouse.com

MALVERN WELLS
Mrs J.L. Morris, Brickbarns Farm, Hanley Road, Malvern Wells WR14 4HY (016845 61775). Working farm. Brickbarns, a 200-year-old mixed farm, is situated two miles from Great Malvern at the foot of the Malvern Hills, 300 yards from the bus service and one-and-a-half miles from the train. The house, which is 300 years old, commands excellent views of the Malvern Hills and guests are accommodated in one double, one single and one family bedrooms with washbasins; two bathrooms, shower room, two toilets; sitting room and dining room. Children welcome and cot and babysitting offered. Central heating. Car essential, parking. Open Easter to October for Bed and Breakfast from £20 nightly per person. Reductions for children and Senior Citizens. Birmingham 40 miles, Hereford 20, Gloucester 17, Stratford 35 and the Wye Valley is just 30 miles.

A useful index of towns/counties appears on pages 393-398

252 Worcestershire

NEWNHAM BRIDGE
Deepcroft Farm House, Newnham Bridge, Tenbury Wells WR15 8JA (01584 781412). Set in the Teme Valley, off the A456, on the borders of Worcestershire, Herefordshire and Shropshire, this secluded old farmhouse, with five acres of garden and orchard, offers easy access to the Severn Valley Railway, the historic towns of Ludlow and Worcester, as well as to the Welsh Marches and the Shropshire Hills. Ideal for fishermen, cyclists and tourists, the accommodation comprises two twin-bedded and one single room, all with hand basins, shaver points, and tea/coffee making facilities. A comfortable sitting room with colour TV is also available for guests. Bed and full English Breakfast from £25.

See also Colour Display Advertisement

WORCESTER
Janette Ratcliffe, Gables Bed & Breakfast, 166 Bromyard Road, St Johns, Worcester WR2 5EE (Tel & Fax: 01905 425488). Gables offers high quality, comfortable accommodation and service. Full English breakfast with free-range eggs in the delightful period diningroom. Excellently fitted en suite facilities. Well-lit parking at rear. Ten minutes walk to the county cricket ground. Near to Elgar's birthplace and city centre. Ideal for the Cotswolds, Stratford, Malvern and easy access for M5. We offer a warm welcome to our guests and make their stay as enjoyable as possible. **ETC** ♦♦♦♦
website: www.gablesbedandbreakfast.co.uk

Useful Guidance for Guests and Hosts

Every year literally thousands of holidays, short breaks and overnight stops are arranged through our guides, the vast majority without any problems at all. In a handful of cases, however, difficulties do arise about bookings, which often could have been prevented from the outset.
It is important to remember that when accommodation has been booked, both parties – guests and hosts – have entered into a form of contract. We hope that the following points will provide helpful guidance.

- When enquiring about accommodation, be as precise as possible. Give exact dates, numbers in your party and the ages of any children.
- State the number and type of rooms wanted and also what catering you require – bed and breakfast, full board etc. Make sure that the position about evening meals is clear – and about pets, reductions for children or any other special points.
- Read our reviews carefully to ensure that the proprietors you are going to contact can supply what you want. Ask for a letter confirming all arrangements, if possible.
- If you have to cancel, do so as soon as possible. Proprietors do have the right to retain deposits and under certain circumstances to charge for cancelled holidays if adequate notice is not given and they cannot re-let the accommodation.
- Give details about your facilities and about any special conditions. Explain your deposit system clearly and arrangements for cancellations, charges etc. and whether or not your terms include VAT.
- If for any reason you are unable to fulfil an agreed booking without adequate notice, you may be under an obligation to arrange suitable alternative accommodation or to make some form of compensation.

Yorkshire 253

Yorkshire

Visit the FHG website
www.holidayguides.com
for details of the wide choice of accommodation featured in the full range of FHG titles

Free or reduced rate entry to Holiday Visits and Attractions – see our **READERS' OFFER VOUCHERS** on pages 53-90

East Yorkshire

BRIDLINGTON

Christine and Peter Young, The White Rose, 123 Cardigan Road, Bridlington YO15 3LP (01262 673245). We are a small hotel situated in a quiet residential area close to the South Beach and within walking distance of the Spa and Harbour. We offer comfortable accommodation with most bedrooms en suite with colour TV, hospitality tray and gas heating. We have a non-smoking bedroom and dining room. We offer choice of menus at all meals; choice of early or late evening dinner. Open all year including Christmas. Bed and Breakfast from £24 per person. Weekend winter breaks with two nights Bed and Breakfast £82 per couple; mid-week winter breaks of four nights Monday to Friday Bed and Breakfast, one adult pays full price £96, second adult pays £60 when sharing double/twin room. Available October to February inclusive, except during Christmas and New Year. **ETC** ♦♦♦

BRIDLINGTON

The Seacourt Hotel and Annabel's Restaurant, 76 South Marine Drive, Bridlington YO15 3NS (01262 400872). This large Edwardian house standing quietly in a prime position overlooking the beautiful South Bay, with panoramic views of the Old Harbour, town and Flamborough Head, has been refurbished and transformed into a delightful, small hotel of distinction. Luxuriously appointed. 12 standard and de luxe bedrooms, some with stunning sea views, all en suite with colour TV, direct-dial telephones, hospitality trays, toiletries and central heating. Annabel's Restaurant situated within the hotel. Miles of safe sandy beaches, 18 hole golf course, bowling green all within walking distance.
e-mail: seacourt.hotel@tiscali.co.uk
website: www.seacourt-hotel.co.uk

BRIDLINGTON

John and Helen Gallagher, Rosebery House, 1 Belle Vue, Tennyson Avenue, Bridlington YO15 2ET (01262 670336; Fax: 01262 608381). Grade II Listed Georgian house with character. It has a long sunny garden and superb views of the gardens and sea. Amenities are close by making it an ideal centre for walking, bird-watching, golfing, wind and sailboarding or touring the historic, rolling Wolds. A high standard of comfort, friendliness and satisfaction guaranteed. All rooms are en suite, centrally heated, have colour TV and tea/coffee facilities. Vegetarians are most welcome. Some car parking available. Open all year except Christmas and New Year. Bed and Breakfast from £22 per person. **ETC** ♦♦♦♦
e-mail: info@zexus.co.uk
website: www.roseberyhouse.biz

DRIFFIELD

Mrs Tiffy Hopper, Kelleythorpe Farm, Driffield YO25 9DW (01377 252297). Lovely Georgian farmhouse with large garden in idyllic setting overlooking a small lake, the source of the River Hull. Friendly atmosphere, attractive bedrooms with pretty chintzes. 200 acre farm with pedigree Aberdeen Angus herd. Beef for sale in shop. Centrally situated for York, the coast or the moors. Bed and Breakfast from £22, Evening Meal £14 by prior arrangement. Children welcome.

East Yorkshire / North Yorkshire 255

DRIFFIELD
Mrs Katrina Gray, The Wold Cottage, Wold Newton, Driffield YO25 3HL (Tel & Fax: 01262 470696). The Wold Cottage is a spacious Georgian farmhouse, set in its own grounds. We can offer you peace and tranquillity with views of new and mature woodlands and continuous Wold Land. So come and relax and forget the pressures of everyday life, stroll around and observe the wildlife and history, or explore the wonders of the East Coast, York and Moors. We have a twin, double, and four-poster room with air spa bath, all en suite and tastefully furnished and decorated. There are beverage making facilities in each room. We pride ourselves on our cleanliness and do not allow any smoking or pets in the house. A warm friendly, family atmosphere awaits you. Bed and Breakfast £40 to £55 per person per night. Evening Meal £17.50. **ETC/AA ◆◆◆◆** *GOLD AWARD.*
website: www.woldcottage.com

HORNSEA
Mrs H. Hooton, Admiralty Guest House, 7 Marine Drive, Hornsea HU18 1NJ (01964 536414). This friendly, family-run guest house is situated on the promenade in the picturesque town of Hornsea which offers all the pleasures of a seaside resort whilst providing a convenient base for touring. Hornsea Mere, Yorkshire's largest freshwater lake is nearby, with rowing, sailing, fishing, motor boat trips and pitch and putt. At Hornsea Freeport there is a vast array of shops and attractions including a model village and butterfly world. The historic town of Beverley with its 'Gothic' Minster is just 20 minutes by car, as is the North Sea Ferry Terminal at Hull. York is one hour's drive. Double, twin and family rooms with tea/coffee making facilities and TV; 13 rooms are en suite. Full central heating. Parking. Children welcome. Bed and Breakfast from £21 per night. Weekly rates available. Fully licensed.

North Yorkshire

BEDALE
Mrs M. Keighley, Southfield, 96 South End, Bedale DL8 2DS (01677 423510). This is a quiet country town only five minutes from A1, so is ideal for breaking journey from South to Scotland. With the Dales immediate and the Lakes only one hour away, it is a good base for touring. Area attractions include Fountains Abbey, Ripon Cathedral, Harewood House, Bolton Castle, Lightwater Valley (as on TV) and many more. Four 18-hole golf courses and swimming, to keep husband and children happy. Free off-road parking for four/five cars. Two double en suite bedrooms, one twin and one single both with washbasins and tea/coffee making facilities and sittingroom. SAE please. Now open all year. Established 1977. **AA/RAC ◆◆◆**, *"WHICH?" RECOMMENDED.*

• • • some fun days out in NORTH YORKSHIRE

RHS Garden - Harlow Carr, Harrogate • 01423 565418 • www.rhs.org.uk
Ripley Castle & Gardens, Harrogate • 01423 770152 • www.ripleycastle.co.uk
Yorkshire Air Museum, Elvington • 01904 608595 • www.yorkshireairmuseum.co.uk
Ingleton Waterfalls Walk, Ingleton • 015242 41930 • www.ingletonwaterfallswalk.co.uk
Kinderland Fun, Play & Activity Park, Scarborough • 01723 354555 • www.kinderland.co.uk

DANBY
Mrs L. Tindall, Rowantree Farm, Ainthorpe, Whitby YO21 2LE (01287 660396). Rowantree Farm is a family-run dairy and sheep farm situated in the heart of the North York Moors. Ideal walking and mountain biking area, with panoramic moorland views. Our non-smoking home comprises one family room and one twin-bedded room, with private bathroom and shower room respectively, also full central heating, tea and coffee tray, clock radio and hairdryer. Relax in our residents' lounge with colour TV and video. Children welcome; cot available. Good home cooking, vegetarians catered for, served in our separate dining room. B&B from £21; Evening Meal by prior arrangement. Packed lunches available. Ample car parking. ETC ◆◆◆
e-mail: krbsatindall@aol.com
website: www.rowantreefarm.co.uk

GLAISDALE
Tom and Sandra Spashett, Red House Farm, Glaisdale, Near Whitby YO21 2PZ (Tel & Fax: 01947 897242). Listed Georgian farmhouse featured in "Houses of the North York Moors". Completely refurbished to the highest standards, retaining all original features. Bedrooms have bath/shower/toilet, central heating, TV and tea making facilities. Excellent walks straight from the doorstep. Friendly farm animals – a few cows, horses, geese and pretty free-roaming hens. One-and-a-half acres of gardens, sitting-out areas. Magnificent views. Interesting buildings – Listed barns now converted to two holiday cottages. Games room with snooker table. Eight miles from seaside/Whitby. Village pubs within walking distance. Stabling available for horses/dogs. Non-smoking. Please phone Tom or Sandra for more information.
e-mail: spashettredhouse@aol.com
website: www.redhousefarm.net

GLAISDALE
Mr & Mrs Mortimer, Hollins Farm, Glaisdale, Whitby YO21 2PZ (01947 897516). Comfortable accommodation in 16th century farmhouse, one large double/or family room sleeps four, a further en suite family/double/or twin room sleeps three. Each has TV, tea/coffee facilities amd wash basins. Sitting/dining room with TV; conservatory. The house is fully heated. Guests have access at all times, attractive gardens. Situated in the centre of the National Park, in the beautiful Esk Valley, surrounded by moorland; five miles to steam railway, six miles Heartbeat country, lovely walking area. Nine miles from historic Whitby and coastal villages. Farmhouse breakfast, all diets catered for. Camping facilities available, send SAE for details.

HARROGATE
Mrs M. Banks, Azalea Court Hotel, 56/58 Kings Road, Harrogate (01423 560424; Fax: 01423 505662). Superb position directly opposite the Conference Centre on Kings Road. 100 yards from the town centre. Bargain breaks available on request. With fourteen rooms, all with en suite facilities, the Azalea offers comfortable accommodation and an excellent position for the Conference / Exhibition Centres and the town centre. All rooms have TV, hospitality trays and you will be served a full English breakfast. There is a large floodlit private car park at the rear. Teppanyaki Japanese restaurant open (can accommodate 100 people).
e-mail: astonhotel@btinternet.com
website: www.hotel-harrogate.com

World of James Herriot
Thirsk, North Yorkshire

See our **READERS' OFFER VOUCHER** for
details of free or reduced rate entry

North Yorkshire 257

e-mail: neil.clarke@virgin.net

HARROGATE

Mrs Sue Clarke, Brimham Lodge, Brimham Rocks Road, Burnt Yates, Harrogate HG3 3HE (01423 771770; Fax: 01423 770370). Working farm, join in. The Lodge, built in 1661, was extensively refurbished in 1999 but the farmhouse retains all its original character. Our accommodation offers two twin/double rooms with private facilities. All rooms have central heating, beverage tray, hairdryer, colour TV and clock radio. There is a large sitting room with a blazing fire set in a large inglenook, with television, video and games available. A hearty farmhouse breakfast is served in the oak panelled dining room. Brimham Lodge Farm is situated in the heart of Nidderdale, with many sites of interest within a short walk or car journey. Bed and Breakfast from £20 to £25 per person. ETC ◆◆◆◆
website: www.brimhamlodge.co.uk

HARROGATE

Mrs C.E. Nelson, Nidderdale Lodge Farm, Fellbeck, Pateley Bridge, Harrogate HG3 5DR (01423 711677). Working farm. Homely, comfortable, Christian accommodation. Spacious stone built bungalow in beautiful Nidderdale which is very central for touring the Yorkshire Dales; Pateley Bridge two miles, Harrogate 14 miles, Ripon nine miles. Museums, rocks, caves, fishing, bird watching, beautiful quiet walks, etc all nearby. En suite rooms (one twin, two double), TV. Private lounge. Tea making facilities available. Choice of breakfast. Evening meals available one mile away. Ample parking space on this working farm. Open Easter to end of October. ETC ◆◆◆

HARROGATE

Mr & Mrs C. Richardson, The Coppice 9 Studley Road, Harrogate HG1 5JU (01423 569626; Fax: 01423 569005). A high standard of comfortable accommodation awaits you at The Coppice, with a reputation for excellent food and a warm friendly welcome. All rooms en suite with telephones. Quietly located off Kings Road, five minutes' walk from the elegant shops and gardens of the town centre. Just three minutes' walk from the Conference Centre. Ideal location to explore the natural beauty of the Yorkshire Dales. Midway stop Edinburgh–London. Free Yorkshire touring map - ask for details. Bed and Breakfast £38 single, £58 double, twin from £60, family from £68; Evening Meal £18.50. ETC ◆◆◆◆
e-mail: coppice@harrogate.com.
website: www.harrogate.com/coppice

See also Colour Display Advertisement

HELMSLEY

Virginia Collinson, Hall Farm, Gilling East, York YO62 4JW (01439 788314). Come and stay with us at Hall Farm. A beautifully situated 400 acre working stock farm with extensive views over Ryedale. Completely away from all the traffic, we are half-a-mile away from the road, as you drive up to the farm you may see cows with their calves and in the spring and early summer ewes with their lambs. We offer a friendly, family welcome with home made scones on arrival. A ground floor double en suite room is available and includes hospitality tray with home made biscuits. Sittingroom with TV and open fire on chilly evenings, diningroom with patio doors to conservatory. You will be the only guests so the breakfast time is up to you. Full English Breakfast includes home made bread and preserves. There are lots of excellent places to eat in the evenings in the historic market town of Helmsley and nearby villages. York, Castle Howard and the North York Moors within half-an-hour drive. Terms from £25 per person.
e-mail: virginia@hallfarmgilling.co.uk

258 North Yorkshire

HELMSLEY
Mrs J. Milburn, Barn Close Farm, Rievaulx, Helmsley YO62 5LH (01439 798321). Barn Close Farm is nicely situated in the North York Moors National Park. This family offers homely accommodation to holidaymakers all year round. The farmhouse is in beautiful surroundings. Within easy reach of Rievaulx Abbey, and many other places of interest. It is an ideal centre for tourists. Pony trekking nearby. Good walking terrain! Highly commended for good food. En suite double and one family bedroom; bathroom; toilets; sitting room and dining room. Children are welcome. Cot, high chair and babysitting available. Bed and Breakfast from £22 to £30, Evening Dinner £15. **ETC ◆◆◆** *"WHICH?" RECOMMENDED. "DAILY TELEGRAPH" RECOMMENDED.*

HIGH BENTHAM
Mrs Metcalfe, Fowgill Park Farm, High Bentham, Lancaster LA2 7AH (015242 61630). A Georgian farmhouse with panoramic views, quietly situated, but only a few miles from Ingleton Waterfall and Caves, and the Three Peaks; ideal for touring the Dales, Lake District and coast. Peaceful riverside walks a short distance from the front door. Two tastefully decorated en suite beamed bedrooms, with colour TV, radio and beverage tray. Comfortable guests' lounge; beamed dining room where hearty breakfasts are served. **ETC ◆◆◆**
e-mail: info@fowgillpark.co.uk
website: www.fowgillpark.co.uk

KIRKBYMOORSIDE
Mr Chris Tinkler, The Cornmill Luxury Guest House, Kirby Mills, Kirkbymoorside, York YO62 6NP (01751 432000). This sympathetically restored 18th century watermill and Victorian farmhouse provide a warm and friendly welcome and tranquil, well-appointed accommodation on the River Dove. The large (no smoking) bedrooms with en suite baths and/or powerful showers, fluffy towels, kingsize or twin beds, themed four-poster rooms, guest lounge with self-service honesty bar and wood-burning stove, plus boot room, are in the farmhouse. Our sumptuous breakfasts and pre-booked dinners are served in the Mill, with glass-floored viewing panel over the millrace. Wheelchair friendly. Golf and horse riding nearby. On site parking. Open all year round. Self-catering accommodation also available.
e-mail: cornmill@kirbymills.demon.co.uk
website: www.kirbymills.demon.co.uk

LEYBURN
Mrs Hilary Richardson, Sunnyridge, Argill Farm, Harmby, Leyburn DL8 5HQ (01969 622478). Situated on a small sheep farm in Wensleydale, Sunnyridge is a spacious bungalow in an outstanding position. Magnificent views are enjoyed from every room. In the heart of the Yorkshire Dales and the midst of Herriot country, it is an ideal centre for exploring the wide variety of activities and attractions; or a restful stop-over for travellers. Sample Yorkshire hospitality and relax in comfortable ground floor accommodation comprising one double or twin bedroom and one family/double/twin-bedded room, both en suite, each with colour TV and tea/coffee facilities. Non-smoking. Guest lounge. Children welcome. Pets by arrangement. Bed and Breakfast from £23. **VisitBritain ◆◆◆**
e-mail: richah@freenet.co.uk

North Yorkshire 259

NORTHALLERTON

Ann Saxby, Hallikeld House, Stokesley Road, Brompton, Northallerton DL6 2UE (01609 773613; Fax: 01609 770262; mobile: 077300 58807). Two miles east of Northallerton in open countryside, ideal for travelling from coast to Dales. Easy access to A19 and A1. Central heating, lounge. Bed and Breakfast from £18 per person per night.
e-mail: asaxby@supanet.com

See also Colour Display Advertisement

PICKERING

Mrs S. Wardell, Tangalwood, Roxby Road, Thornton-le-Dale, Pickering YO18 7SX (01751 474688). Tangalwood provides a warm welcome. Very clean and comfortable accommodation with good food. Situated in a quiet part of this picturesque village, which is in a good central position for Moors, "Heartbeat" country, coast, North York Moors Railway, Flamingo Park Zoo and forest drives, mountain biking and walking. Good facilities for meals provided in the village. Accommodation in one twin and one double en suite rooms, one single; all with tea/coffee making facilities and TV; alarm clock/radio and hairdryer also provided; diningroom; central heating. Open Easter to October for Bed and Breakfast from £23 each. Private car park. Secure motorbike and cycle storage. ETC ◆◆◆◆
website: www.accommodation.uk.net/tangalwood

See also Colour Display Advertisement

PICKERING

Mrs Ella Bowes, Banavie, Roxby Road, Thornton-le-Dale, Pickering YO18 7SX (01751 474616). Banavie is a large semi-detached house set in a quiet part of the picturesque village of Thornton-le-Dale, one of the prettiest villages in Yorkshire with its famous thatched cottage and bubbling stream flowing through the centre. We offer our guests a quiet night's sleep and rest away from the main road, yet only four minutes' walk from the village centre. One large double or twin bedroom and two double bedrooms, all tastefully decorated with en suite facilities, colour TV, hairdryer, shaver point etc. and tea/coffee making facilities. There is a large guest lounge, tea tray on arrival. A real Yorkshire breakfast is served in the dining room. Places to visit include Castle Howard, Eden Camp, North Yorkshire Moors Railway, Goathland ("Heartbeat"), York etc. There are three pubs, a bistro and a fish and chip shop for meals. Children and dogs welcome. Own keys. B&B from £23-£27 pppn. Welcome Host. Hygiene Certificate held. No Smoking. SAE please for brochure. ETC ◆◆◆◆
e-mail: info@banavie.co.uk   website: www.banavie.uk.com

See also Colour Display Advertisement

RICHMOND

Browson Bank Farmhouse Accommodation, Browson Bank Farmhouse, Browson Bank, Dalton, Richmond DL11 7HE (01325 718504 or 01325 718246). A newly converted granary set in 300 acres of farmland. The accommodation consists of three very tastefully furnished double/twin rooms all en suite, tea and coffee making facilities, colour TV and central heating. A large, comfortable lounge is available to relax in. Full English breakfast served. Situated six miles west of Scotch Corner (A1). Ideal location to explore the scenic countryside of Teesdale and the Yorkshire Dales and close to the scenic towns of Barnard Castle and Richmond. Terms from £20 per night.

FHG
·K·U·P·E·R·A·R·D·

Yorkshire Dales Falconry
Settle, North Yorkshire

See our **READERS' OFFER VOUCHER** for details of free or reduced rate entry

YORKSHIRE DALES FALCONRY & WILDLIFE CONSERVATION CENTRE

RICHMOND
Mrs L. Brooks, Holmedale, Dalton, Richmond DL11 7HX (Tel & Fax: 01833 621236). Holmedale is a Georgian house set in a quiet village midway between Richmond and Barnard Castle. Seven miles from Scotch Corner and ideally situated for touring Swaledale, Wensleydale and Teesdale. One double en suite and one twin with bathroom, both with central heating. Comfortable sittingroom with open fire when necessary. Personal attention with good home cooking. Tea/coffee making facilities available. Bed and Breakfast from £20 per person.

RICHMOND
Mrs S. Lawson, Stonesthrow, Dalton, Near Richmond DL11 7HS (01833 621493). With a welcoming fire, private garden and conservatory, Stonesthrow offers you a friendly, family atmosphere. Unmistakable Yorkshire hospitality from the moment you arrive – we greet you with a tea or coffee and home made cakes. Situated midway between the towns of Richmond and Barnard Castle, it offers you an ideal base for exploring the Yorkshire Dales, Teesdale, and York. Stonesthrow, a non-smoking Bed and Breakfast, has well appointed bedrooms with TV, tea/coffee facilities and full central heating. Off-road parking. Children eight and over are welcome. Sorry, no pets. B&B £18pppn, £20 single.

See also Colour Display Advertisement

RIPON
Mrs L. Hitchen, St George's Court, Old Home Farm, High Grantley, Ripon HG4 3PJ (01765 620618). The most beautifully situated accommodation. Five ground floor en suite rooms round a pretty courtyard. All our rooms are full of character - oak beams etc with modern facilities, all with views of the countryside. Private fishing lake. Terms from £60 to £75. **AA** ♦♦♦♦

ROBIN HOOD'S BAY
Mrs B. Reynolds, 'South View', Sledgates, Fylingthorpe, Whitby YO22 4TZ (01947 880025). Pleasantly situated, comfortable accommodation in own garden with sea and country views. Ideal for walking and touring. Close to the moors, within easy reach of Whitby, Scarborough and many more places of interest. There are two double rooms, lounge and diningroom. Bed and Breakfast from £20, including bedtime drink. Parking spaces. Phone for further details.

FHG
·K·U·P·E·R·A·R·D·

Eden Camp Museum
Malton, North Yorkshire
See our **READERS' OFFER VOUCHER** for details of free or reduced rate entry

North Yorkshire 261

ROBIN HOOD'S BAY (near)
David and Angela Pattinson, Hogarth Hall, Boggle Hole Road, Near Robin Hood's Bay, Whitby YO22 4QQ (01947 880547; mobile: 07966 915352). Hogarth Hall is set in 145 acres of habitat attracting a variety of wildlife. Wonderful views over ancient woodlands, heather-covered moorland and down the valley to the sea. Enjoy wonderful sunsets and sunrises. All rooms are en suite with TV. Tea/coffee making facilities are available. Scarborough 12 miles, Whitby nine miles, York 40 miles, Rievaulx Abbey 30 miles. Walks around the farm and further afield. Robin Hood's Bay is an 80 minute walk along the road, unused railway, cliff path or beach. Use your car to visit points of interest listed on our tour. New fishing lake available shortly. Bed and Breakfast from £25 per person per night, and from £100 per person from one week's stay.

SCARBOROUGH
Simon and Val Green, Killerby Cottage Farm, Killerby Lane, Cayton, Scarborough YO11 3TP (01723 581236; Fax: 01723 585465). Simon and Val extend a warm Yorkshire welcome and invite you to share their charming farmhouse in the pleasant countryside between Scarborough and Filey. All our bedrooms are tastefully decorated and have en suite facilities, colour TV, and well-stocked beverage trays. Hearty breakfasts that will keep you going all day are served in the conservatory overlooking the lovely garden. Our 350-acre farm has diversified and we now have the Stained Glass Centre and tearoom which are open to visitors. Cayton offers easy access to Scarborough, Filey, Whitby, the North York Moors, and York. **ETC ♦♦♦♦**
e-mail: val@stained-glass.demon.co.uk
website: www.smoothhound.co.uk/hotels/killerby

SCARBOROUGH
Angela and Roland Thompson, The Windmill Hotel, Mill Street, Off Victoria Road, Scarborough YO11 1SZ (01723 372735). 18th century windmill. Built around the windmill is The Old Mill Hotel, comprising 12 attractively decorated en suite rooms surrounding the mill courtyard. All are tastefully furnished with tea/coffee making facilities, colour TV and central heating. Four-poster beds available. Breakfast is served on the ground floor of the Mill itself. There is private parking in the courtyard. Within the Mill is the contemporary Toy Museum, tea rooms and play area for children. The Mill is a few minutes' walk from the town centre, rail and bus stations. Pets welcome by arrangement. Bed and Breakfast from £26. Children aged 2 to 14 years £10; children aged under 2 £5. **ETC ♦♦♦**

e-mail: info@windmill-hotel.co.uk
website: www.windmill-hotel.co.uk

SCARBOROUGH
Sylvia and Chris Kirk, The Terrace Hotel, 69 Westborough, Scarborough YO11 1TS (01723 374937). A small family-run Hotel situated between North and South Bays, close to all Scarborough's many attractions and only a short walk from the town centre, rail and bus stations. Private car park. Three double bedrooms (one en suite), three family rooms (one en suite) and one single bedroom, all with colour TV and tea making facilities. Full Fire Certificate. Non-smoking accommodation available. Bed and full English Breakfast from £18. En suite facilities £3 extra per person per night. Children (sharing room with adults) under four years FREE, four to 11 years half price.
websites: www.4hotels.co.uk/uk/hotels/theterrace.html
www.s-h-systems.co.uk/hotel/theterrace.html

SCARBOROUGH

Michael and Angela Saville, The Leeway Hotel, 71 Queen's Parade, Scarborough YO12 7HT (01723 374371). The Leeway is a family-run Guest House which is ideally situated close to the North Bay beach, and yet near to the local amenities. A superb base from which to explore the North York Moors, York, Whitby, etc. All double rooms are en suite and have tea/coffee making facilities, TV and radio. Sea views are available. Car parking for six cars, and on-street parking is available outside the hotel. For your comfort and safety, bedrooms are non-smoking. Bed and Breakfast from £18 to £22.
website: www.leewayhotel.co.uk

SCARBOROUGH

Mrs V. Henson, Brinka House, 2 Station Square, Ravenscar, Scarborough YO13 0LU (01723 871470). Brinka House Bed & Breakfast is situated in Ravenscar midway between Scarborough and Whitby, with stunning views across to Robin Hood's Bay and is surrounded by the moors. The village boasts a variety of walks, cycle tracks, golf course, pony and llama trekking, and a bus service from the front door to town. A warm welcome and tasty breakfast awaits, vegetarians and special diets catered for. We have a romantic double room with a large corner bath en suite and a twin/family room en suite. All rooms have TV, drinks facilities and sea views. Terms from £20 per person per night, £25 single.
website: www.brinkahousebedandbreakfast.co.uk

SCARBOROUGH

Mrs L.M. Coates, Howdale Hotel, 121 Queens Parade, Scarborough YO12 7HU (Freephone: 0800 056 6622; Tel & Fax: 01723 372696). Overlooks beautiful North Bay. Close to town. Licensed. Excellent food. Clean, comfortable rooms with colour TV, tea/coffee making facilities and hairdryer. Most en suite. Terms from £22 per person. ETC ♦♦♦♦
e-mail: mail@howdalehotel.co.uk
website: www.howdalehotel.co.uk

SCARBOROUGH

Sue and Tony Hewitt, Harmony Country Lodge, Limestone Road, Burniston, Scarborough YO13 0DG (0800 2985840; Tel & Fax: 01723 870276). DISTINCTIVELY DIFFERENT. Peaceful and relaxing retreat, octagonal in design and set in two acres of private grounds with 360° panoramic views of the National Park and sea. An ideal centre for walking or touring. Two miles from Scarborough and within easy reach of Whitby, York and the beautiful North Yorkshire countryside. Tastefully decorated en suite centrally heated rooms with colour TV and all with superb views. Attractive dining room, guest lounge and relaxing conservatory. Traditional English breakfast, including vegetarian. Fragrant massage available. Bed and Breakfast from £25 to £32.50. Non-smoking, licensed, private parking facilities. Personal service and warm, friendly Yorkshire hospitality. Spacious five-berth caravan also available for self-catering holidays. Children over seven years welcome. Christmas packages. ETC ♦♦♦♦
e-mail: tony@harmonylodge.net
website: www.harmonylodge.net

Free or reduced rate entry to Holiday Visits and Attractions – see our READERS' OFFER VOUCHERS on pages 53-90

North Yorkshire 263

See also Colour Display Advertisement

SKIPTON

Mrs Heather Simpson, Low Skibeden Farmhouse, Harrogate Road, Skipton BD23 6AB (07050 207787/01756 793849). Detached 16th century farmhouse in private grounds one mile east of Skipton (five minutes from town centre) off the A59/A65 gateway to the Dales, eg Bolton Abbey - Malham, Settle. Luxury bed and breakfast with fireside treats in the lounge. All rooms are quiet, spacious, have panoramic views, washbasins, tea facilities and electric overblankets; some en suite. Central heating October to May. All guests are warmly welcomed and served tea/coffee and cakes on arrival, bedtime beverages are served from 9.30pm. Breakfast is served from 7am to 8.45am in the dining room. No smoking. No pets and no children under 12 years. Safe parking. New arrivals before 10pm. Quality and value guaranteed. Bed and Breakfast from £24 per person per night for standard room with washbasin, shared facilities, two-piece en suite from £26 per person per night shared; single occupancy from £30-£48. Full en suite from £30 per person per night. Farm cottage sometimes available (**ETC ★★★**). A deposit secures a room. Open all year. Credit cards accepted. **AA ♦♦♦♦**, *"WELCOME HOST", "WHICH?"*
website: www.yorkshirenet.co.uk/accgde/lowskibeden

STOKESLEY

Sue & Mike Barnfather, Four Wynds, Whorl Hill, Faceby, Stokesley TS9 7BZ (01642 701315). A warm and friendly welcome awaits you at 'Four Wynds', a smallholding set in beautiful, quiet and tranquil countryside on the edge of the North Yorkshire Moors and within easy commuting distance of Teeside (15 minutes) and only five minutes from the A19. We are the perfect location for visiting York and Whitby, or for touring Herriot, Captain Cook and Heartbeat Country, and an ideal stopover for 'Coast to Coast', 'Cleveland Way' and 'Lykewake' walkers – transport can be arranged from a pick-up point. All bedrooms have tea/coffee making facilities, colour TV and radio alarm, some en suite. Traditional hearty breakfast served at a time to suit and evening meal on request. Ample free and safe parking. Bed & Breakfast from £24 to £27 en suite per person per night. Sorry no dogs. **ETC ♦♦♦**

THIRSK

Fern Bank Bed & Breakfast, Dishforth, Thirsk YO7 3JX (01845 577460). Hilary and David welcome you to their 19th century home, set in large grounds, offering comfortable rooms in a restful atmosphere with modern facilities. Situated half way between London and Edinburgh, just off the A1, Fern Bank is centrally located for touring, an ideal base from which to explore the Yorkshire dales, moors, forests, coasts, stately homes, abbeys, gardens and much, much more. All rooms have double glazing, cental heating, colour TV/video, hairdryer, bathrobes, sewing kit and hospitality tray, some en suite available. Lounge and sunroom for guests use. Choice of breakfasts. Terms from £25 pppn. Pets welcome. Parking. No smoking.
e-mail: hilaryanddavid@fernbankbb.freeserve.co.uk
website: http://mysite.wanadoo-members.co.uk/fernbankbb

See also Colour Display Advertisement

THIRSK

Joyce Ashbridge, Mount Grace Farm, Cold Kirby, YO7 2HL (01845 597389; Fax: 01845 597872). A warm welcome awaits you on working farm surrounded by beautiful open countryside with magnificent views. Ideal location for touring or exploring the many walks in the area. Luxury en suite bedrooms with tea/coffee facilities. Spacious guests' lounge with colour TV. Garden. Enjoy delicious, generous helpings of farmhouse fayre cooked in our Aga. Children from 12 years plus. No smoking. No pets. Bed and Breakfast from £30. Open all year except Christmas.
e-mail: joyce@mountgracefarm.com
website: www.mountgracefarm.com

264 North Yorkshire

THIRSK
Mrs Julie Bailes, Glen Free, Holme-on-Swale, Sinderby, Near Thirsk YO7 4JE (01845 567331). Glen Free is an old Lodge Bungalow set in a very peaceful situation, but still only one mile from A1 motorway (off the B6267 Masham/Thirsk road). Approximately seven miles from Ripon, Thirsk, Bedale. York and Harrogate 40 minutes approximately. One double room and one double with single bed with washbasin. Central heating, tea making facilities and TV. All rooms ground floor. Golf, fishing, swimming and riding available locally. Ideal for touring the Dales and Herriot country. Bed and Breakfast from £18 per person.

See also Colour Display Advertisement

WHITBY
Mr and Mrs Richardson, Egton Banks Farm, Glaisdale, Whitby YO21 2QP (01947 897289). Beautiful old farmhouse situated in a lovely valley close to quiet roadside. Set in 120 acres of pastureland and woods. Centre of National Park. Warm and friendly atmosphere. Diningroom/Lounge for guests with TV and books. Close to river, one mile from Glaisdale village and mainline railway, eight miles to Whitby, four miles steam railway and Heartbeat country. Both bedrooms have pretty decor and TV. One double/twin and one family room, both en suite. Full Yorkshire Breakfast. Packed lunches. All diets catered for. B&B from £22-£26. ETC ◆◆◆◆
e-mail: egtonbanksfarm@agriplus.net
website: www.egtonbanksfarm.agriplus.net

WHITBY
Janice and Donna Hillier, Ashford Non-Smoking Guest House, 8 Royal Crescent, Whitby YO21 3EJ (01947 602138). "Come as a Guest - Leave as a Friend". The Ashford is a family-run guest house providing a relaxed, informal atmosphere and friendly service. Situated on Whitby's West Cliff, the Ashford occupies a superb position in Royal Crescent, overlooking Crescent Gardens and the sea. It is ideally situated for coastal and country walks, and makes an excellent base for exploring the North York Moors. Take a short drive inland and visit "Heartbeat Country", the North York Moors Railway, Rievaulx Abbey, Pickering and a myriad of pretty moorland villages, or take the coast road to discover the attractions of Scarborough, Bridlington and Filey. A little further afield you will find the historic city of York and Harrogate. Full central heating. Comfortable lounge. All bedrooms have en suite facilities, courtesy tray and colour TV. Good home cooking. Access at all times. Bed and Breakfast from £23.50. ETC ◆◆◆
e-mail: info@ashfordguesthouse.co.uk   website: www.ashfordguesthouse.co.uk

WHITBY
Heather and John Hall, Endeavour B&B, 28 Upgang Lane, Whitby YO21 3EA (01947 821110). Situated in the historic town of Whitby, this luxuriously appointed detached residence is on the West Cliff, with sea views yet close to the centre of town. Recently refurbished, this lovely home offers top class accommodation with three en suite bedrooms, two with fabulous sea views and all having hospitality trays, colour TVs and central heating. Full English breakfasts are served in the lovely dining room, which has separate tables. Parking for three cars. Heather and John offer friendly and personal service to ensure guests are comfortable and content during their stay. Bed & Breakfast from £25 pppn; special rate midweek short breaks available. Non-smoking.
e-mail: hhall49@hotmail.com
website: www.endeavourbedandbreakfast.co.uk

North Yorkshire 265

WHITBY (near)
Mrs Pat Beale, Ryedale House, Coach Road, Sleights, Near Whitby YO22 5EQ (Tel & Fax: 01947 810534). Exclusive to non-smokers, welcoming Yorkshire house of character at the foot of the moors, National Park "Heartbeat" country. Three-and-a-half-miles from Whitby. Magnificent scenery, moors, dales, picturesque harbours, cliffs, beaches, scenic railways, superb walking - it's all here! Highly commended, beautifully appointed rooms with private facilities, many extras. Guest lounge; breakfast room with views over Esk Valley. Enjoy the large south-facing terrace and landscaped gardens. Extensive traditional and vegetarian breakfast choice. Local inns and restaurants - two within a short walk. Parking available, also public transport. Bed and Breakfast double £24 to £26, single £26 to £28, minimum stay two nights. Weekly reductions and Monday-Friday four-night offers available (not high season). Regret, no pets or children. ETC ♦♦♦
website: www.ryedalehouse.co.uk

See also Colour Display Advertisement

YORK
Mrs Helen Butterworth, Wellgarth House, Wetherby Road, Rufforth, York YO23 3QB (01904 738592; mobile: 07711 252577). A warm welcome awaits you at Wellgarth House, ideally situated in Rufforth (B1224) three miles from York, one mile from the Ring Road (A1237) and convenient for "Park and Ride" into York City. This country guest house offers a high standard of accommodation with en suite facilities. Bed and Breakfast from £27pppn. All rooms have complimentary tea/coffee making facilities, colour TV. Excellent local pub just two minutes' walk away which serves lunches and dinners. Large private car park. ETC ♦♦♦

YORK
Cumbria House, 2 Vyner Street, Haxby Road, York YO31 8HS (01904 636817). A warm and friendly welcome awaits you at Cumbria House - an elegant, tastefully decorated Victorian guest house, where comfort and quality are assured. We are convenient for the city, being only 15 minutes' walk from York's historic Minster and yet within minutes of the northern by-pass (A1237). A launderette, post office and children's park are close by. All rooms have colour TV, radio alarms and tea/coffee facilities. Most are en suite and all are non-smoking. Central heating. Fire Certificate. Guests' car park. Full English breakfast or vegetarian alternative. £25 to £30 per person. AA ♦♦♦
e-mail: candj@cumbriahouse.freeserve.co.uk
website: www.cumbriahouse.com

YORK
Mr and Mrs G. Steel, Alder Carr House, York Road, Barmby Moor, York YO42 4HT (Tel & Fax: 01759 380566; mobile: 07885 277740). A Georgian-style house in 10 acres with a large garden for guests to relax in. Rooms are spacious with good views over countryside. The nearby market town of Pocklington has a National Water Lily collection and a Gliding Club. A wide range of local restaurants and country pubs offer an excellent choice for evening meals. Within easy reach of the York 'Park and Ride', Yorkshire Coast, Moors and Wolds. Closed Christmas and New Year. Twin, double/family rooms, all en suite or private facilities. Children welcome. Restricted smoking. Prices from £35 single, £48 double.

YORK
Newton House, Neville Street, Haxby Road, York YO31 8NP (01904 635627). Diana and John offer all their guests a friendly and warm welcome to their Victorian end town house a few minutes' walk from the city centre, York's beautiful Minster, medieval walls and museums. We are only a 40 mile drive from coastal resorts, the lovely Yorkshire Moors and Dales. Three double/twin en suite rooms, colour TV, tea/coffee tray, central heating. Breakfast menu. Car park. Non-smoking. Fire Certificate. Terms from £25pp.

YORK
Church View, Stockton-on-the-Forest, York YO32 9UP (01904 400403; Fax: 01904 400325; mobile: 0775 2273371). Enjoy a short stay in any season in our pretty village three miles east of York. Our 200-year-old cottage offers real fires in our cosy visitors' lounge (candlelit dinner if required). Four-poster room available. Music, TV available; games room with full-size snooker table; pub over the road. There is a golf course in the village and the area is perfect for visiting the North York Moors (location of Heartbeat), Castle Howard (location of Brideshead Revisited), the East Coast, and of course, the beautiful city of York. We can provide cycle hire. Please ring for further information. Bed and Breakfast from £20 per person per night.

See also Colour Display Advertisement

YORK
Mav and Maureen Davidson, "Oaklands" Guest House, 351 Strensall Road, Old Earswick, York YO32 9SW (01904 768443). A very warm welcome awaits you at our attractive family home set in open countryside, yet only three miles from York with close access to the York ring road (A1237), A64, A1 and A19. Ideally situated for City, Coast, Dales and Moors. Our comfortable bedrooms are centrally heated with colour TV, razor point, tea and coffee tray, radio alarms and hairdryers. En suite facilities available. A more than ample full breakfast is served in a light airy diningroom. Your hosts, Maureen and Mav, very much look forward to seeing you. Bed and full English Breakfast from £23. Discounts available. Open all year. No pets. Smoking in garden only. **ETC** ♦♦♦♦

e-mail: mavmo@oaklands5.fsnet.co.uk

YORK
Ascot House, 80 East Parade, York YO31 7YH (01904 426826; Fax: 01904 431077). An attractive Victorian villa built in 1869 with easy access to the historic city centre by walking or by public transport. All bedrooms have central heating, colour TV and complimentary tea/coffee making facilities while the family and double rooms are en suite. Most rooms have four-poster or canopy beds. Comfortable residents' lounge with TV; attractive dining room. There is also a sauna which can be hired by the hour. York has much to offer with its ancient narrow streets, medieval churches, Roman, Viking and National Railway museums and the Minster. Private parking. Single from £30 to £60 per room per night, double £60 to £75 per room per night, including Traditional English Breakfast and VAT. Contact: **June, Keith or Rob Wood.** **ETC/AA/RAC** ♦♦♦♦, ETC *SILVER AWARD.*

e-mail: admin@ascothouseyork.com

website: www.ascothouseyork.com

North Yorkshire / West Yorkshire 267

YORK
Mrs J. Woodland, Cavalier Hotel, 39 Monkgate, York YO31 7PB (Tel & Fax: 01904 636615). The Cavalier is an early Georgian Listed building, recently refurbished to provide very comfortable accommodation. It is ideally located close to the city centre and yards from the ancient city walls and most of the historic sites. Also convenient for touring North York Moors, Dales and East Coast resorts. Most rooms are en suite, and all have washbasins, colour TV, shaver points, radio alarms, and tea/coffee making facilities. Hairdryer and ironing facilities are available on request. Bed and full English breakfast with vegetarian options. Amenities include sauna, pay phone, garage parking, full central heating. Full Fire Certificate. Open all year. Winter/Spring mini-breaks available, details on request. **ETC ♦♦♦**

YORK
Mr and Mrs G. Hudson, Orillia House, 89 The Village, Stockton on Forest, York YO3 9UP (01904 400600). A warm welcome awaits you at Orillia House, conveniently situated in the centre of the village, three miles north east of York, one mile from A64. The house dates back to the 17th century and has been restored to offer a high standard of comfort with modern facilities yet retaining its original charm and character. All rooms have private facilities, colour TV and tea/coffee making facilities. Our local pub provides excellent evening meals. We also have our own private car park. Bed and Breakfast from £25. Telephone for our brochure. **ETC ♦♦♦♦**
e-mail: info@orilliahouse.co.uk
website: www.orilliahouse.co.uk

YORK
David and Katherine Leedham, York House, 62 Heworth Green, York YO31 7TQ (Tel & Fax: 01904 427070). Receive a warm welcome at this family-run guesthouse. Enjoy breakfast in our attractive conservatory or outside on our beautiful patio. York House is approximately 10 minutes' walk from York Minster and is the perfect base for a visit to York or the surrounding areas. Rooms offer all the conveniences you could need for a relaxing and enjoyable stay. Some of the facilities offered: en suite shower or bath facilities, four-poster, double, twin, family and single rooms, tea/coffee making facilities, off-street parking, full English/vegetarian breakfast. No smoking establishment. Prices from £27.50pppn. Children welcome. **ETC ♦♦♦♦**
e-mail: yorkhouse.bandb@tiscali.co.uk
website: www.yorkhouseyork.com

West Yorkshire

HALIFAX
Mrs L. White, Staups House, Staups Lane, Shibden, Halifax HX3 7AB (01422 362866). Staups House is a beautiful Grade II* Listed manor house built in 1684 by John Crowther. The house has a facinating history and boasts many original features such as the magnificent oak staircase and inglenook fireplaces. The whole house is furnished to a very high standard. Set in peaceful surroundings, but handy for Leeds, Bradford and Haworth (Brontë country). M62 only five minutes away. A generous breakfast to suit your times and needs. One double en suite, one family suite, comprising double with four-poster, one single and private bathroom. Terms from £25 to £35 per person.
e-mail: rikki.white@lineone.net
website: www.staupshouse.co.uk

THE FHG DIPLOMA

HELP IMPROVE BRITISH TOURIST STANDARDS

You are choosing holiday accommodation from our very popular FHG Guides.
Whether it be a hotel, guest house, farmhouse or self-catering accommodation, we think you will find it hospitable, comfortable and clean, and your host and hostess friendly and helpful.
Why not write and tell us about it?

As a recognition of the generally well-run and excellent holiday accommodation reviewed in our publications, we at FHG Guides Ltd. present a diploma to proprietors who receive the highest recommendation from their guests who are also readers of our Guides. If you care to write to us praising the holiday you have booked through FHG Guides Ltd. – whether this be board, self-catering accommodation, a sporting or a caravan holiday, what you say will be evaluated and the proprietors who reach our final list will be contacted.

The winning proprietor will receive an attractive framed diploma to display on his premises as recognition of a high standard of comfort, amenity and hospitality. FHG Guides Ltd. offer this diploma as a contribution towards the improvement of standards in tourist accommodation in Britain. Help your excellent host or hostess to win it!

FHG DIPLOMA

We nominate

Because

Name ....

Address...

....

Telephone No..

Scotland

Castle Grant, Morayshire

Ratings You Can Trust

ENGLAND

  The *English Tourism Council* (now *VisitBritain*) has joined with the AA and RAC to create an easily understood quality rating for serviced accommodation, giving a clear guide of what to expect.

HOTELS are given a rating from One to Five *Stars* – the more Stars, the higher the quality and the greater the range of facilities and level of services provided.

  GUEST ACCOMMODATION, which includes guest houses, bed and breakfasts, inns and farmhouses, is rated from One to Five *Diamonds*. Progressively higher levels of quality and customer care must be provided for each one of the One to Five Diamond ratings.

HOLIDAY PARKS, TOURING PARKS and CAMPING PARKS are now also assessed using *Stars*. Standards of quality range from a One Star (acceptable) to a Five Star (exceptional) park.

Look out also for the new *SELF-CATERING* Star ratings. The more *Stars* (from One to Five) awarded to an establishment, the higher the levels of quality you can expect. Establishments at higher rating levels also have to meet some additional requirements for facilities.

 VisitBritain has launched a new *Quality Accredited Agency Standard*. Agencies who are awarded the Quality Accredited Agency marque by VisitBritain are recognised as offering good customer service and peace of mind, following an assement of their office polices, practices and procedures.

SCOTLAND

Star Quality Grades will reflect the most important aspects of a visit, such as the warmth of welcome, efficiency and friendliness of service, the quality of the food and the cleanliness and condition of the furnishings, fittings and decor.

THE MORE STARS,

THE HIGHER THE STANDARDS.

The description, such as Hotel, Guest House, Bed and Breakfast, Lodge, Holiday Park, Self-catering etc tells you the type of property and style of operation.

WALES

Places which score highly will have an especially welcoming atmosphere and pleasing ambience, high levels of comfort and guest care, and attractive surroundings enhanced by thoughtful design and attention to detail

STAR QUALITY GUIDE FOR

HOTELS, GUEST HOUSES AND FARMHOUSES
SELF-CATERING ACCOMMODATION
(Cottages, Apartments, Houses)
CARAVAN HOLIDAY HOME PARKS
(Holiday Parks, Touring Parks, Camping Parks)

★★★★★	Exceptional quality
★★★★	Excellent quality
★★★	Very good quality
★★	Good quality
★	Fair to good quality

In England, Scotland and Wales, all graded properties are inspected annually by Tourist Authority trained Assessors.

SCOTLAND

Aberdeen, Banff & Moray

ABERDEEN

Balvenie Guest House, 9 St Swithin Street, Aberdeen AB10 6XB (01224 322559). Isobel and Edward welcome you to their comfortable, family-run guest house in a quiet location in Aberdeen's West End. The house is within easy walking distance of the city centre and is also adjacent to major bus routes to the beach, city centre, airport, railway station and universities. All five rooms have central heating and double glazing, beverage facilities, washbasin and colour TV. Prices include full Scottish or Continental breakfast; evening meals are available on request. For further information, please telephone or see our website. Terms from £18 per night single, double/twin from £34; four nights or more negotiable.
e-mail: balveniegh@aol.com
website: www.balvenieguesthouse.co.uk

ABERDEEN

University of Aberdeen, Conference & Event Office, King's College, Aberdeen AB24 3FX (+44 (0)1224 272660; Fax: +44 (0)1224 276246). Situated in the heart of historic Old Aberdeen, the University of Aberdeen has a wide variety of Bed & Breakfast accommodation available. Modern, hotel-style, en suite rooms are available year round at King's Hall. Facilities include TV, trouser press, hairdryer, telephone, tea and coffee. During the summer vacations additional B&B accommodation is available in the student residences at very attractive rates. En suite, standard and self catered flats are available. **STB ★/★★** *B&B.*
e-mail: accommodation@abdn.ac.uk
website: www.abdn.ac.uk/confevents

ABERDEEN

Aberdeen Springbank Guest House, 6 Springbank Terrace AB11 6LS (Tel & Fax: 01224 592048). A warm welcome awaits you at our comfortable family-run Victorian Guest House, well located five minutes from the city centre, rail, bus and ferry terminals. All rooms are en suite, with TV, tea/coffee making facilities, hairdryer and clock radio. Special diets and vegetarians catered for. Close to pubs, restaurants and nightlife. Other amenities include riding, swimming, and fishing nearby, with easy access to a region of historic interest and scenic beauty. Children welcome. Non-smoking. Car park available. Bed and Breakfast from £20.
e-mail: betty@springbank6.fsnet.co.uk
website: www.aberdeen-guesthouse.co.uk

272 Aberdeen, Banff & Moray

BANCHORY
Mrs Jean Robb, Ardconnel, 6 Kinneskie Road, Banchory AB31 5TA (01330 822478). Home from home bungalow in a quiet location, yet just a three minute walk from the high street and all amenities. Ideal base for walking, fishing, golfing and sightseeing or exploring the Castle and Whisky Trails nearby. All guest accommodation overlooks Banchory Golf Course and to the hills beyond. One double/twin room en suite, one double/twin with private bathroom. Guest lounge and sun lounge. Bed & Breakfast from £22pppn (sharing), singles from £30. Open March - October. STB ★★★★ B&B

DUFFTOWN

DAVAAR B&B
Church Street, Dufftown AB55 4AR • Tel & Fax: 01340 820464
e-mail: Davaar@ClunieCameron.co.uk • website: www.davaardufftown.co.uk

Davaar is a traditional stone Scottish villa. It is situated adjacent to the main square in Dufftown, which although only a village, is the Malt Whisky capital of Scotland, with seven distilleries. All bedrooms are en suite, and have TV and tea/coffee facilities. For the energetic we have two mountain cycles for hire to explore the local cycleways. Details from Mrs Susan Cameron. Double or twin-bedded rooms from £22.50 to £24 per person per night, family room £60 per night for the room.

FORRES
Sherston House, Hillhead, Forres IV36 2QT (01309 671087; Fax: 01343 850535). Tastefully restored stone built house one mile from Forres and beside main A96. Large, comfortable, en suite rooms with TV, tea/coffee making facilities, hairdryers and trouser press. Garden area available. Home cooked dinners available "highly recommended". Wonderful gardens in Forres and Findhorn Village and Foundation also nearby. Excellent location for golf, pony trekking, walking and fishing. B&B from £25-£30 pppn. STB ★★★★ *GUEST HOUSE*

FORRES
Mrs Hilda Massie, Milton of Grange Farm, By Forres IV36 2TR (01309 676360). A warm welcome to our family farm, situated close to Forres, Findhorn and Kinloss. En suite rooms are tastefully furnished to a high standard, with TV and tea/coffee facilities; delicious Scottish cuisine is offered. The farm adjoins the Findhorn Nature Reserve which is popular with birdwatchers. Findhorn village has watersports and a lovely sandy beach. Nearby Findhorn Foundation, with its Eco Village, is world famous, or spend the day touring the coastline dolphin spotting. To the east is Elgin, with Johnston's cashmere outlet. This is an excellent base for golf; Coastal, Castle and Malt Whisky Trails; places of historic interest including the Pictish Stone (Sueno) at Forres; to the west Culloden Battlefield and Fort George. Inverness, Gateway to the Highlands, is 30 miles (also airport). Rates - single from £25 per person to £38 (high season) double from £22.50 per person to £30.00 (high season). No smoking, no pets. STB ★★★★ *B&B. WELCOME HOST.*

e-mail: hildamassie@aol.com   **website: www.forres-accommodation.co.uk**

Argyll & Bute

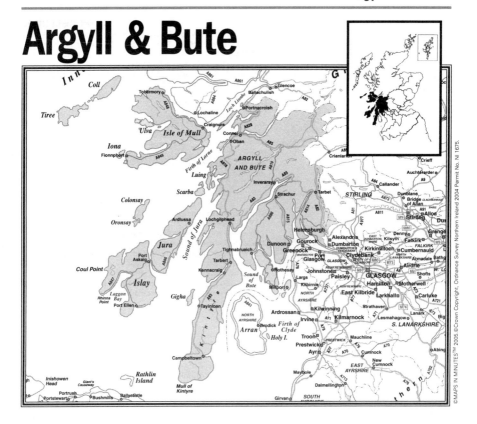

BALLACHULISH (near Glencoe)

Mr & Mrs J.A. MacLeod, Lyn-Leven Guest House, Ballachulish PA39 4JW (01855 811392; Fax: 01855 811600). Lyn-Leven, a superior award-winning licensed guest house overlooking Loch Leven, with every comfort, in the beautiful Highlands of Scotland, is situated one mile from historic Glencoe village. Four double, two twin and two family bedrooms, all rooms en suite; sittingroom and diningroom. Central heating. Excellent and varied home cooking served daily. Children welcome at reduced rates. An ideal location for touring. Fishing, walking and climbing in the vicinity. The house, open all year, is suitable for disabled guests. Car not essential but private car park provided. Bed and Breakfast from £22. Dinner, Bed and Breakfast from £210 to £240 per person per week. Credit and debit cards accepted. **STB ★★★★** *GUEST HOUSE*, **AA/RAC ♦♦♦♦**
website: **www.Lynleven.co.uk**

•••some fun days out in ARGYLL & BUTE

Scottish Sea Life Sanctuary, Oban • 01631 720386 • www.sealsanctuary.co.uk
Oban Rare Breeds Park, Oban • 01631 770608 • www.obanrarebreeds.com
Inveraray Castle, Inveraray • 01499 302203 • www.inveraray-castle.com

274 Argyll & Bute

CAMPBELTOWN
Mrs Lesley Cowan, Oatfield House, Southend Road, Campbeltown PA28 6PH (01586 551551; Fax: 01586 551855). Oatfield is a Listed Georgian laird's house set well away from the main road in its own small country estate. Enjoying a beautiful and peaceful setting on the edge of the wilds, it has numerous walks and wonderful views, yet is only a few minutes from Campbeltown and the airport and half way between the two golf courses of Machrihanish and Dunaverty. A welcoming family home, Oatfield has many period features, including an important Iron Age Hill Fort. Aga-cooked breakfasts are served in the panelled dining room and the guest sitting room offers both an open fire and a wide screen television. Non-smoking. Sheer tranquillity! Prices from £25 per person per night.
e-mail: visit@oatfield.org
website: www.oatfield.org

HELENSBURGH
Mrs Elizabeth Howie, Drumfork Farm, Helensburgh G84 7JY (01436 672329). Traditional sandstone farmhouse, extensively refurbished; all rooms en suite, some with sea views. The Victorian seaside town of Helensburgh, with its wide streets and stylish architecture, is port of call for the paddle steamer, 'Waverley', and the site of the Hill House by Charles Rennie Mackintosh. Open all year. Babysitting available. Bed and Breakfast from £22.50 pppn. Non-smoking. **STB ★★★** *B&B*.
e-mail: drumfork@supanet.com

INVERARAY
Mrs Semple, Killean Farmhouse, Inveraray PA32 8XT (01499 302474). Killean Farmhouse is located just a few miles outside Inveraray. Ideally situated for walking, climbing, pony trekking or just touring. There is fishing for trout, pike or salmon, and opportunities to enjoy boating, water skiing or windsurfing. The whole area is steeped in history and the town of Inveraray itself is a classic example of 18th century Scottish town planning. With all this in mind, the cottages provide high quality accommodation for family holidays.

INVERARAY
Mr R. Gayre, Minard Castle, Minard PA32 8YB (Tel & Fax: 01546 886272). Stay in style in our 19th Century Scottish castle which stands in its own grounds in beautiful countryside beside Loch Fyne, three-quarters-of-a-mile from the A83 Inveraray to Lochgilphead road. A peaceful location for a quiet break, you can stroll in the grounds, walk by the loch, explore the woods, or use Minard Castle as your base for touring this beautiful area with its lochs, hills, gardens, castles and historic sites. Breakfast in the Morning Room and relax in the Drawing Room. The comfortable bedrooms have colour television, tea/coffee making facilities and en suite bathrooms. No smoking in the house. Evening Meals available within five miles. Bed and Breakfast £55 per person, children half price. Open April to October. We offer a warm welcome in a family home. Self-catering properties also available, £120 to £370 per week. **STB ★★★★** *B&B*.
STB ★★/★★★ *SELF-CATERING*.
e-mail: reinoldgayre@minardcastle.com   website: www.minardcastle.com

---

A useful index of towns/counties appears on pages 393-398

Argyll & Bute 275

See also Colour Display Advertisement

OBAN
Nic and Sarah Jones, The Barriemore Hotel, Corran Esplanade, Oban PA34 5AQ (01631 566356; Fax: 01631 571084). The Barriemore enjoys a splendid location as the last hotel on the Oban seafront on Corran Esplanade. Built in 1895, the house exudes an opulence in keeping with its late Victorian origins. All bedrooms are beautifully and individually furnished with full en suite facilities. The elegant lounge is an ideal spot for quiet relaxation, while the attractive dining room, overlooking Oban Bay, is the perfect place to enjoy full Scottish breakfasts including locally produced smoked haddock and kippers. **STB ★★★★** *GUEST HOUSE.*
e-mail: reception@barriemore-hotel.co.uk
website: www.barriemore-hotel.co.uk

OBAN
Mrs J. Currie, Hawthorn, 5 Keil Crofts, Benderloch, Oban PA37 1QS (01631 720452). A warm welcome awaits you in this delightful bungalow set in 20 acres of farmland where we breed our own Highland cattle which graze at the front. It is a peaceful location as we are set back from the road, and an ideal spot for touring, with the main ferry terminal at Oban just 10 minutes away. Our luxurious rooms have their own special sitting room attached where you can enjoy your coffee or a glass of wine in peace.
e-mail: june@hawthorncottages.com
website: www.hawthorncottages.com

See also Colour Display Advertisement

OBAN
Mr and Mrs I. Donn, Palace Hotel, Oban PA34 5SB (01631 562294). A small family hotel offering personal supervision situated on Oban's sea front with wonderful views over the Bay, to the Mull Hills beyond. All rooms en suite, with colour TV, tea/coffee making facilities, several non-smoking. The Palace is an ideal base for a real Highland holiday. By boat you can visit the islands of Kerrera, Coll, Tiree, Lismore, Mull and Iona, and by road Glencoe, Ben Nevis and Inveraray. Fishing, golf, horse riding, sailing, tennis and bowls all nearby. Children and pets welcome. Reductions for children. Please write or telephone for brochure. Competitive rates.
website: www.thepalacehotel.activehotels.com

OBAN
Margaret and Archie MacDonald, Kings Knoll Hotel, Dunollie Road, Oban PA34 5JH (01631 562536; Fax: 01631 566101). The hotel enjoys magnificent views standing in its own grounds overlooking Oban Bay and is the first hotel that visitors meet when entering on the A85. Most bedrooms are en suite with colour TV and hospitality tray. The elegant Kings Rest lounge bar has a Highland theme and is ideal for a cosy dram before dinner in the Knoll restaurant, which specialises in fresh local produce. Oban is ideally located for visiting the Western Isles and exploring the spectacular local scenery. **STB ★★★** *HOTEL.*
e-mail: enquiries@kingsknollhotel.co.uk
website: www.kingsknollhotel.co.uk

Inveraray Jail
Inveraray, Argyll
See our **READERS' OFFER VOUCHER** for
details of free or reduced rate entry

276 Argyll & Bute

OBAN

Mrs C. MacDonald, Bracker, Polvinister Road, Oban PA34 5TN (01631 564302; Fax: 01631 571167). Bracker is a modern bungalow built in 1975 and extended recently to cater for visitors. We have three guest rooms, two double and one twin-bedded, all en suite with TV and tea/coffee making facilities. Small TV lounge and diningroom. Private parking. The house is situated in a beautiful quiet residential area of Oban and is within walking distance of the town (approximately eight to 10 minutes) and the golf course. Friendly hospitality and comfortable accommodation. Bed and Breakfast from £20. Non-smoking. **STB ★★★** *GUEST HOUSE.*
website: www.bracker.co.uk

TARBERT

Mrs Linda Whyatt, Rhu House, Tarbert PA29 6YF (Tel & Fax: 01880 820231). Rhu House is found in a quiet rural location, set in mature gardens, on the shore of West Loch Tarbert. Situated four miles south of Tarbert on the Campbeltown Road, close to Kennacraig Ferry Terminal. Ideal base for exploring the Kintyre Peninsula or making day trips to the Southerly Hebrides. This is a non-smoking establishment. En suite facilities available, all rooms have scenic views, tea/coffee making facilities and TV. There is a spacious residents' lounge with television. Ample parking, but sorry no dogs in the house. Prices from £25 per person. **STB ★★★** *B&B.*
e-mail: rhuhouse@ukonline.co.uk

Other specialised FHG Guides

Published annually: available in all good bookshops or direct from the publisher.

Recommended **COUNTRY INNS & PUBS** OF BRITAIN

Recommended **COUNTRY HOTELS** OF BRITAIN

Recommended **SHORT BREAK HOLIDAYS** IN BRITAIN

The bestselling **PETS WELCOME!**

FHG Guides • Abbey Mill Business Centre,
Seedhill, Paisley, Renfrewshire PA1 1TJ
Tel: 0141-887 0428 • Fax: 0141-889 7204
e-mail: admin@fhguides.co.uk
www.holidayguides.com

Ayrshire & Arran

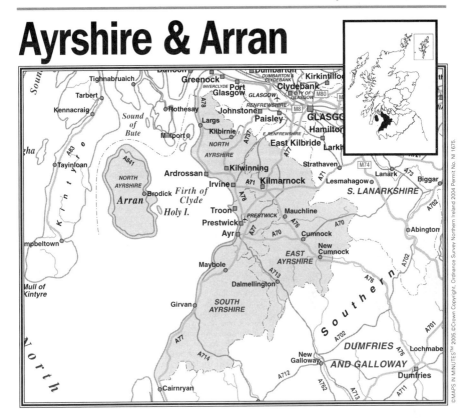

AYR

Mrs Wilcox, Fisherton Farm, Dunure, Ayr KA7 4LF (Tel & Fax: 01292 500223). Traditional stone-built farmhouse on working mixed farm with extensive sea views to Arran. Convenient for golf, walking and Burns Country. Also convenient for Culzean Castle and Prestwick Airport. From Ayr take A719 coast road past Haven Craig Tara; farm is five miles south of Ayr. Accommodation comprises one double and one twin en suite, ground floor bedrooms with TV and tea/coffee making facilities. Central heating throughout. Children welcome. Pets by arrangement. Please write, telephone or fax for further information. Prices from £20 to £25. Also self catering. STB ★★★ B&B. WELCOME HOST.

website: www.fishertonfarm.homestead.com/webpage.html

AYR

Peter and Julia Clark, Eglinton Guest House, 23 Eglinton Terrace, Ayr KA7 1JJ (01292 264623). In Welcome Host Scheme. Situated within a part of Ayr steeped in history, within a few minutes' walk of the beach, town centre and many other amenities and entertainment for which Ayr is popular. There are sea and fishing trips available from Ayr Harbour, or a cruise "Doon the Water" on the "Waverley"; golf, swimming pool, cycling, tennis, sailing, windsurfing, walking, etc all available nearby; Prestwick Airport only three miles away. We have family, double and single rooms, all with washbasins, colour TV and tea/coffee making facilities. En suite facilities and cots available on request. We are open all year round. Bed and Breakfast from £20. Please send for our brochure for further information.

e-mail: eglintonguesthouse@yahoo.co.uk

website: www.eglinton-guesthouse-ayr.com   or   www.ayrshire-guest-house.com

AYR

e-mail: gemmelldunduff@aol.com

Mrs Agnes Gemmell, Dunduff Farm, Dunure, Ayr KA7 4LH (01292 500225; Fax: 01292 500222). Welcome to Dunduff Farm where a warm, friendly atmosphere awaits you. Situated just south of Ayr at the coastal village of Dunure, this family-run beef and sheep unit of 600 acres is only 15 minutes from the shore providing good walks and sea fishing and enjoying close proximity to Dunure Castle and Park. Accommodation is of a high standard yet homely and comfortable. Bedrooms have washbasins, radio alarm, tea/coffee making facilities, central heating, TV, hair dryer and en suite facilities (the twin room has private bathroom). There is also a small farm cottage available sleeping two/four people. Bed and Breakfast from £25 per person; weekly rate £170. Cottage from £250 per week. Colour brochure available. **STB ★★★★ B&B, AA/RAC ♦♦♦♦♦**
website: www.gemmelldunduff.co.uk

BEITH

Mrs Jane Gillan, Shotts Farm, Beith KA15 1LB (Tel & Fax: 01505 502273). Comfortable friendly accommodation is offered on this 200 acre dairy farm well situated for the A736 Glasgow to Irvine road and for the A737; well placed to visit golf courses, country parks, or leisure centre, also ideal for the ferry to Arran or Millport and for many good shopping centres all around. A high standard of cleanliness is assured by Mrs Gillan who is a first class cook holding many awards, food being served in the diningroom with its beautiful picture windows. Three comfortable bedrooms (double en suite, family and twin), all with tea-making facilities, central heating and electric blankets. Two bathrooms with shower; sittingroom with colour TV. Children welcome. Bed and Breakfast from £18 double room; en-suite from £23. Dinner can be arranged. **STB ★★★ B&B, AA ★★★**.
e-mail: shotts.farm@btinternet.com

KILMARNOCK

Mrs M. Howie, Hill House Farm, Grassyards Road, Kilmarnock KA3 6HG (Tel & Fax: 01563 523370). Enjoy a peaceful holiday on a working dairy farm two miles east of Kilmarnock. We offer a warm welcome with home baking for supper, choice of farmhouse breakfasts with own preserves. Four large comfortable bedrooms with lovely views over Ayrshire countryside, en suite facilities, tea/coffee, electric blankets, central heating; TV lounge, sun porch, diningroom and garden. Excellent touring base with trips to coast, Arran, Burns Country and Glasgow nearby. Easy access to A77 and numerous golf courses. Children very welcome. Bed and Breakfast from £21 (including supper). Self-catering cottage also available. **STB ★★★★ B&B**.

Scottish Maritime Museum
Irvine, Ayrshire
See our **READERS' OFFER VOUCHER** for details of free or reduced rate entry

---

Kelburn Castle
Largs, Ayrshire
See our **READERS' OFFER VOUCHER** for details of free or reduced rate entry

Ayrshire & Arran 279

KILMARNOCK
Mrs Nancy Cuthbertson, West Tannacrieff, Fenwick, Kilmarnock KA3 6AZ (01560 600258; mobile: 07773 226332; Fax: 01560 600914). A warm welcome awaits all guests to our dairy farm, situated in the peaceful Ayrshire countryside. Relax in spacious, well furnished, en suite rooms with all modern amenities, colour TV and tea/coffee making facilities. Large parking area and garden. Situated off the A77 (M77) on the B751 road to Kilmaurs, so easily accessible from Glasgow, Prestwick Airport, and the south. An ideal base for exploring Ayrshire's many tourist attractions. Enjoy a hearty breakfast with homemade breads and preserves and home baking for supper. Children welcome. Non-smoking. Terms from £20 per person. Brochure available. **STB ★★★★ B&B.**

e-mail: westtannacrieff@btopenworld.com
website: www.SmoothHound.co.uk/hotels/westtannacrieff.html

LARGS
South Whittlieburn Farm, Brisbane Glen, Largs KA30 8SN (01475 675881; Fax: 01475 675080). Why not try our superb farmhouse accommodation with lovely scenic views on our working sheep farm in peaceful Brisbane Glen? Ample parking. Only five minutes' drive from the popular tourist resort of Largs and near the ferries to the islands. 40 minutes from Glasgow and Prestwick airports. Warm friendly hospitality, enormous delicious breakfasts. All rooms ensuite. Chosen by "WHICH? TOP TEN BEST BED & BREAKFAST", WELCOME HOST. Nominated for AA LANDLADY OF THE YEAR 2005. Bed & Breakfast from £26.50pppn. **STB ★★★★ B&B, AA ◆◆◆◆** Caravan and camping site on our farm two and a half miles north east of Largs with electric hook-ups, toilet and shower, from £9 per night. Caravan for hire. Also self-catering flat available at Dunoon. Open all year except Christmas. A warm welcome from **Mary Watson**. Enjoy a great holiday at South Whittlieburn Farm, for a holiday you will want to repeat where guests become friends.

e-mail: largsbandb@southwhittlieburnfarm.freeserve.co.uk
website: www.SmoothHound.co.uk/hotels/whittlie.html

MAUCHLINE
Mrs J. Clark, Auchenlongford, Sorn, Mauchline KA5 6JF (01290 550761). Working farm. The farm is situated in the hills above the picturesque village of Sorn, with its castle set on a promontory above the River Ayr, and its 17th century church nearby. It is only 19 miles east of the A74 and 20 miles inland from the town of Ayr. Accommodation comprises three attractive, furnished bedrooms and a large, well appointed residents' lounge. Full Scottish breakfast is served with home-made jams and marmalade; traditional High Tea and/or Dinners are also available on request. Bed and Breakfast £18; Bed, Breakfast and Evening Meal £28. Brochure available.

PATNA
Mrs Joyce Bothwell, Smithston Farm, Patna, By Ayr KA6 7EZ (01292 531211). Working farm. A warm welcome awaits you at our family farm situated in the beautiful Doon valley. An ideal base for touring Galloway or Ayrshire on the (A713) Galloway tourist route, six miles south of Ayr. Our spacious, well appointed farmhouse offers twin/double and family bedrooms with king-sized beds and all facilities, guest lounge, dining room and large garden. We serve a delicious varied farmhouse breakfast, with homebaking and farm produce in season. At bedtime relax with a tea/coffee or hot chocolate with a homebaked cookie. Prestwick airport guests welcome (whatever the time!). Children and pets welcome. Non-smoking. £20pppn, children £10.

e-mail: bothwellfarming@onetel.com

Borders

BIGGAR

Mrs Rosemary Harper, South Mains Farm, Biggar ML12 6HF (01899 860226). Working farm. South Mains Farm is a working family farm, situated in an elevated position with good views, on the B7016 between Biggar and Broughton. An ideal place to take a break on a North/South journey. Edinburgh 29 miles, Peebles 11 miles. Well situated for touring the Border regions in general. A comfortable bed and excellent breakfast provided in this centrally heated and well furnished farmhouse. The lounge has a log fire and the bedrooms, two double and one single, have hand-basins, electric blankets and tea/coffee making facilities; guests' bathroom. Open all year. Car essential, parking. Terms £18 per night. If you are interested just ring, write or call in. Warm welcome assured.

See also Colour Display Advertisement

EYEMOUTH

The Bantry B&B, Mackays of Eyemouth, 20/24 High Street, Eyemouth TD14 5EU (Tel & Fax: 018907 51800). The Bantry Bed & Breakfast is situated in the heart of Eyemouth, nestled overlooking the beach and harbour, amongst the fishing cottages and rich history of the town. The Bantry offers a wide range of comfortable family accommodation from our picturesque location on the shore. Why not sit on our rooftop decking area, sipping an ice-cold drink and relaxing to the sound of the waves breaking gently on the shore as the children play. The Bantry has four letting rooms, all modern, spacious and well appointed.
e-mail: info@mackaysofeyemouth.co.uk
website: www.mackaysofeyemouth.co.uk

Borders 281

See also Colour Display Advertisement

e-mail: info@dunlaverock.com

EYEMOUTH
Dunlaverock House, Coldingham Sands, Coldingham, Eyemouth TD14 5PA (Tel & Fax: 01890 771450). Edwardian country house accommodation offering comfort with spectacular sea views, peaceful gardens and direct access from garden to beach and seashore. Situated on the Berwickshire coast in the historic Scottish Borders, Dunlaverock occupies an elevated position overlooking Coldingham Bay. There are six spacious en suite bedrooms and guests can dine on local seafood overlooking the sea; licensed. Enjoy guided scenic walks along the clifftop nature reserve or a sea fishing trip from St Abbs; 15 golf courses within a half hour drive. Adjacent to the unspoilt fishing village of St Abbs, this is an ideal base for exploring the historic Scottish Borders, just 45 miles from Edinburgh and 65 miles north of Newcastle. STB ★★★ *HOTEL.*
website: www.dunlaverock.com

JEDBURGH
Sheila Whittaker, Hundalee House, Jedburgh TD8 6PA (Tel & Fax: 01835 863011). Large historic Manor House set in 15 acres of secluded gardens and woodland. The house is decorated in a charming Victorian style. All rooms are en suite, two with four-posters, and all with the expected luxuries including TV, tea/coffee making facilities, hairdryer, central heating etc. We would be delighted to welcome you to Hundalee House; we love the place and firmly believe that it should be shared with others. We hope by our efforts we have created a warm and welcoming atmosphere and that you take away with you many happy memories. Bed and Breakfast from £22 to £27 per person per night. Single £28 to £40.
e-mail: sheila.whittaker@btinternet.com

See also Colour Display Advertisement

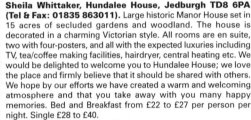

JEDBURGH
Mr Brian Leask, Allerton House, Oxnam Road, Jedburgh TD8 6QQ (01835 869633). Allerton House is a 4-star guest house located in the historic Royal Burgh of Jedburgh. This Georgian home is surrounded by country gardens and provides all the modern amenities of the twenty-first century while preserving the character of its nineteenth century past. Whether you are staying for business or pleasure, the graciously appointed rooms, full range of facilities and warm hospitality will be sure to make your stay a memorable one. Only five minutes' walk from Jedburgh's town centre as well as from a host of lovely Border country walks, Allerton House offers elegant accommodation at competitive prices. STB ★★★★ *GUEST HOUSE,* AA ◆◆◆◆
e-mail: info@allertonhouse.co.uk
website: www.allertonhouse.co.uk

JEDBURGH
Mrs Jean Lyle, Edgerston Mill, Jedburgh TD8 6NF (01835 840343; Fax: 01835 840387). Early 19th century converted sawmill in one acre of garden, 500 metres off A68 and eight miles south of the border town of Jedburgh. Owned by Jean and Robert Lyle and their little dog Millie, the mill was converted in 1990 into a charming house in a very peaceful and tranquil setting and furnished in a rustic style. Jedburgh has many historical features, as have Melrose, Kelso and Dryburgh, all close at hand. The mill has one double room en suite and a twin en suite. It lies within the foothills of the Cheviot Hills with many lovely walks with Roman remains all within easy distance. It is also a very handy stopping off point en route to Edinburgh and the Highlands. There is fishing to be had on the Tweed,Teviot and Jed Waters, and shooting in season, by prior arrangement. Double en suite £25.00, twin en suite £25, or £30 single.
e-mail: jean@edgerstonmill@co.uk   website: www.edgerstonmill.co.uk

JEDBURGH
The Glenbank House Hotel, Castlegate, Jedburgh TD8 6RD (01835 862258; Fax: 01835 863697). Glenbank is set in its own grounds with ample private car parking. Guests can relax in one of the en suite bedrooms, all comfortably furnished with central heating, television and tea/coffee making facilities. We have a cosy, well-stocked lounge bar with a wide selection of malt whiskies, wines, liqueurs, spirits, beers and soft drinks. Bar lunches and evening meals are served in our 30-seater à la carte restaurant, where the extensive menus use local produce according to season. Jedburgh offers an attractive setting for a well-deserved break. With town trails, riverside walks, renovated buildings, Mill shops, Visitor Centres as well as numerous castles and abbeys nearby – there is plenty to keep you occupied!

e-mail: enquiries@glenbankhotel.co.uk   website: www.glenbankhotel.co.uk

MELROSE
Mike & Helen Dalgetty, Braidwood, Buccleuch Street, Melrose TD6 9LD (01896 822488; Fax: 01896 822148). Elegant townhouse built within original grounds of Melrose Abbey, with an excellent reputation for its high standards and excellent facilities. The four guest bedrooms with their own individual charm have been tastefully modernised. The family room and twin room are both en suite, two double rooms have their own spacious bathrooms, just a few steps away. All rooms have TV, hairdryer and tea/coffee facilities. Breakfast is served in the well furnished dining room, with all tastes catered for, special dietary requirements by arrangement. Ideally situated for touring, walking or cycling holidays being convenient for many beauty spots and places of interest. No smoking. Special golf and Short Break offers.

STB ★★★ *GUEST HOUSE.* RAC ◆◆◆◆ *WALKERS & CYCLISTS WELCOME. GREEN TOURISM AWARD.*
e-mail: enquiries@braidwoodmelrose.co.uk   website: www.braidwoodmelrose.co.uk

MELROSE
Mrs Ann O'Neill, Old Abbey School, Waverley Road, Melrose TD6 9SH (01896 823432). This comfortable family home in a 150-year-old converted school house is situated within easy walking distance of the town centre and River Tweed. Ideal as a centre for visiting the abbeys, castles and museums in the Scottish Borders, and close to Abbotsford House, the home of Sir Walter Scott. Also a good centre for walking holidays. Two double rooms, one with private bathroom, and one twin en suite. All with TV and tea-making facilities. Non-smoking. Private parking. Open from March to November. B&B single £30, double £25. STB ★★★ *B&B.*
e-mail: oneill@abbeyschool.fsnet.co.uk

PEEBLES
Mrs Haydock, Winkston Farmhouse, Peebles EH45 8PH (01721 721264). Well established, welcoming and comfortably furnished Georgian country house. Situated close to Peebles in the centre of lovely Borders countryside. Very central for all local amenities. Mountain biking, golfing, fishing, walking and much more. Central situation 23 miles from Edinburgh on the bus route. Three rooms: one double/twin en suite, one double and one twin. Prices from £20 per person per night. Non-smoking. Selection of self-catering cottages also available. STB ★★★ *B&B*
e-mail: holidayatwinkston@btinternet.com
website: www.winkstonholidays.co.uk

Free or reduced rate entry to Holiday Visits and Attractions – see our *READERS' OFFER VOUCHERS* on pages 53-90

Borders 283

See also Colour Display Advertisement

e-mail: lynefarmhouse@btinternet.com

PEEBLES
Arran Waddell, Lyne Farmhouse, Lyne Farm, Peebles EH45 8NR (Tel & Fax: 01721 740255). Victorian farmhouse with character and spectacular views overlooking Stobo Valley. Tastefully decorated throughout, bedrooms all upstairs, double or twin beds with tea/coffee facilities and TV. Walled garden to sit in, hillwalking, picnic areas, Lyne Roman Fort and site of early Christian graves all on farm. Great walk along old railway line via Neidpath Castle viaduct to Peebles. Excellent location for border towns, historic houses and castles. Many sports amenities (The Hub), Glentress Cycling Centre, Icelandic pony trekking, golfing, fishing and swimming. Picturesque Peebles four miles with its many restaurants, pubs, museum and Eastgate Theatre, shows and plays every week. B&B from £24 pppn.
website: www.lynefarm.co.uk

PEEBLES
Mrs Mary Sweeney, The Steading, Venlaw Castle Road, Peebles EH45 8QG (01721 720293). Tastefully converted steading with spacious rooms peacefully situated on an elevated position with panoramic views over Peebles. Surrounded by countryside, yet only a short distance from the town centre. Two double and one twin room, all en suite, with hairdryer, TV and tea/coffee making facilities. Large garden and cobbled courtyard. Ideal base for touring. Ample parking. Pets welcome. Non-smoking. **STB ★★★★** *B&B.*
e-mail: marysweeney@wanadoo.co.uk

WEST LINTON
Mrs M. Thain, The Meadows Bed and Breakfast, 4 Robinsland Drive, West Linton EH46 7JD (01968 661798). The Meadows is a modern four bedroom detached house located in a quiet situation near the centre of the conservation village of West Linton, which is on the A702, the main Edinburgh to Carlisle road, with handy access to Edinburgh and central Scotland. All bedrooms have tea/coffee making facilities, TV and hairdryer. Full range of quality breakfasts available including traditional English or scrambled egg with smoked salmon and oatcakes. Evening meals available by prior arrangement. Pets welcome. Parking. Terms from £20pppn twin, £22.50pppn single, £22.50pppn double en suite. **STB ★★★** *B&B.*
e-mail: mbthain@ntlworld.com
website: www.themeadowsbandb.co.uk

FHG *Jedforest Deer & Farm Park*
Jedburgh, Borders
See our **READERS' OFFER VOUCHER** for details of free or reduced rate entry

•••some fun days out in THE BORDERS

Hirsel Country Park, Coldstream • 01890 882834 • www.hirselcountrypark.co.uk
Halliwell's House Museum, Selkirk • 01750 20096 • www.scotborders.gov.uk
Manderston, Duns • 01361 882636 • www.manderston.co.uk
Floors Castle, Kelso • 01573 223333 • www.floorscastle.com

Dumfries & Galloway

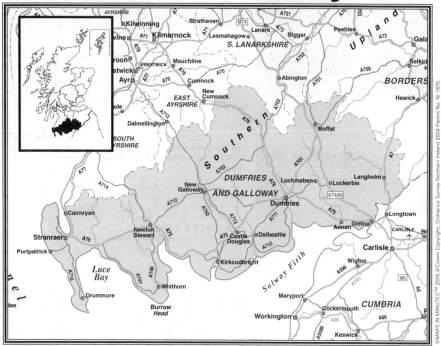

DUMFRIES

Mr Bruce Harper, Rivendell, 105 Edinburgh Rd, Dumfries DG1 1JX (01387 252251). A warm welcome is assured at this striking and luxurious Charles Rennie Mackintosh inspired arts and crafts mansion. We are situated within our own extensive mature gardens close to Dumfries town centre and all its amenities. All our bedrooms feature spacious, state of the art en suite facilities and are furnished to the highest standard. All benefit from large screen televisions and full individually controlled Sky Digital packages. We have consistently maintained our four star rating from the Scottish Tourist Board and four diamond rating from the AA. We pride ourselves on our levels of service and customer satisfaction. **STB ★★★★ B&B, AA ♦♦♦♦**
e-mail: info@rivendellbnb.co.uk
website: www.rivendellbnb.co.uk

•••some fun days out in DUMFRIES & GALLOWAY

Mabie Farm Park, Near Dumfries • 01387 259666 • www.mabiefarm.co.uk
Threave Gardens & Estate, Castle Douglas • 01556 502196 • www.nts.org.uk
Gem Rock Museum, Creetown • 01671 82357 • www.gemrock.net

DUMFRIES

Mrs D Beattie, Langlands Guest House, 8 Edinburgh Road, Dumfries DG1 1JQ (01387 266549). Langlands has been open for guests since February 2004, and Donna and Jeff would have great pleasure in welcoming you to this newly refurbished house. We are a member of the Scottish Tourist Board and have been inspected. Langlands is situated less than five minutes from the railway station and town centre and we also overlook the River Nith. Rooms are either en suite or standard, all with coffee and tea making facilities and television. We also have our own website, please feel free to have a look around it! STB ★★★
website: www.langlands.info

DUMFRIES

Mr & Mrs G. Hood, Wallamhill House, Kirkton, Dumfries DG1 1SL (Tel & Fax: 01387 248249). A charming country house, tastefully furnished, with a warm, friendly, welcoming atmosphere. The spacious en suite bedrooms - two double/family and one twin, have lovely views over garden and countryside. Beautifully appointed, each room has colour and satellite TV plus video, tea/coffee making facilities, shower and toilet and full central heating. Small health suite, steam room and sauna available for guests' use. Situated in peaceful countryside only three miles from Dumfries town centre with excellent shopping, swimming pool, ice bowl for curling, green bowling, fishing and golf. Hill and forest walks, birdwatching, cycling and mountain bike trails all nearby. Bed and Breakfast from £25 per person. Evening meal by arrangement. STB ★★★★ B&B, AA ◆◆◆◆◆

e-mail: wallamhill@aol.com
website: www.wallamhill.co.uk

GATEHOUSE OF FLEET

Stephen and Frances, Green, The Bobbin Guest House, 36 High Street, Gatehouse of Fleet, Castle Douglas DG7 2HP (01557 814229). The family-run Bobbin Guest House is located on the High Street within easy walking distance of pubs, cafes and restaurants. Spacious en suite bedrooms equipped with bath/shower, tea/coffee making facilities and colour TV. Guest lounge and dining room. Front door keys allow you to come and go as you please, with private off-road parking to the rear. Two king-size double en suite bedrooms available at £27 per person per night, one double/twin en suite £25 pppn and one family room £55 per night.

See also Colour Display Advertisement

GRETNA GREEN

Keith and Margaret Torrington, Kirkcroft Guest House, Glasgow Road, Gretna Green DG16 5DU (01461 337403). Situated in the heart of Gretna Green, Kirkcroft Guest House is a detached house built in 1836, was once used as the Post Office for Gretna Green. It is now a comfortable and friendly Bed and Breakfast. Gretna Green is well placed for touring, it offers the Lake District to the South with all its attractions, to the west is the lovely Galloway coast travelling towards Stranraer. If these do not appeal, there is the Scottish Borders with the town of Hawick. To the east is Kielder Water and forest. Double/twin en suite from £49 per room. Discounts for longer stays. STB ★★ *GUEST HOUSE*.
e-mail: info@kirkcroft.co.uk
website: www.kirkcroft.co.uk

A useful index of towns/counties appears on pages 393-398

286 Dumfries & Galloway

See also Colour Display Advertisement

GRETNA GREEN

Joan & Alan Graham, Barrasgate House, Millhill, Gretna Green DG16 5HU (01461 337577). Surrounded by broad-leaved woodland and with country views, the accommodation at Barrasgate House is on ground and first floors, with disabled access. Our en suite bathrooms and shower rooms are equipped with soft fluffy towels. To help you relax after a long drive, our Gold Room has a spa shower. Five minutes from the M74 or A7, our central location is ideal for exploring Hadrian's Wall, the Borders, the Lakes and the beautiful Solway Coast. Local produce is used in our menus, and farmhouse baking will appeal to most tastes. Short breaks Spring/Autumn: three nights from £99. **STB** ★★★ *B&B*, **AA** ♦♦♦
e-mail: info@barrasgate.co.uk
website: www.barrasgate.co.uk

LOCKERBIE

Mrs D Dempster, Castlehill Farm, Tundergarth, Lockerbie DG11 2PX (01576 710223). We are a farming family and make everyone welcome. Large bedrooms, one family and one twin or double. A TV lounge and separate dining room, tea or coffee served at anytime, and we enjoy a chat with our guests over a bedtime cuppa with biscuits. Gretna Green and Gretna Outlet Village are close by. Moffat is another favourite trip. We are just one and a half hours from Glasgow and Edinburgh or Hadrian's Wall. Traditional meals and home baking. We are situated just three and a half miles from Lockerbie town. So come and enjoy the countryside, and stop over on our farm. Bed & Breakfast £24, B&B and evening meal £34. Children special rates.

MOFFAT

Rob and Mhairi Ashkuri, Hartfell House, Hartfell Crescent, Moffat DG10 9AL (01683 220153). Only two miles from the M74 (Junction 15), this 'B' Listed property is a stunning example of Victorian architecture set in a designated 'Outstanding Conservation Area'. The house boasts breathtaking views of the surrounding hills, yet is only a four minute walk from the attractive town centre. Rob and Mhairi will make every effort to use their combined 20 years experience of five star hotels to make your stay in this licensed guest house as comfortable and enjoyable as possible. Eight spacious bedrooms, single, double, twin and family, all en suite and equipped with TV, radio alarm, hairdryer and tea/coffee making facilities. A residents' lounge with stunning views of the Moffat hills can be found on the first floor. B&B from £27.50 pp. Children £15.

Strictly non-smoking. Pets welcome. **AA** ♦♦♦♦
e-mail: enquiries@hartfellhouse.co.uk
website: www.hartfellhouse.co.uk

MOFFAT

Mrs Deakins, Annandale House, Moffat DG10 9SA (01683 221460). Situated just five minutes' walk from Moffat town centre and one mile off the M74, Annandale House is a haven of peace, surrounded by mature gardens with private parking and storage for cycles. The three well appointed spacious bedrooms all have central heating, tea/coffee making facilities hairdryers and colour TVs. There is one en suite double with king-size bed, one twin and one family room. Well behaved pets welcome. Open all year. An ideal base for exploring south west Scotland and the Scottish Borders. Bed and Breakfast from £19.50 per person per night (reduced rates for children). No smoking policy in house. Short Breaks available.
e-mail: june@annandalehouse.com
website: www.annandalehouse.com

Dumfries & Galloway 287

MOFFAT

Stag Hotel, 21-23 High Street, Moffat DG10 9HL (01683 220343; Fax: 01683 220914). Situated in the picturesque conservation town of Moffat, only one mile from the M74 and surrounded by some of the most beautiful scenery in Scotland, the hotel has recently been completely refurbished. Public rooms offer a bar/lounge and restaurant, and a games room with pool table and dart board. All eight bedrooms are furnished to a high standard with comfortable beds, en suite shower and toilet, colour TV, tea and coffee facilities and hairdryer; all non-smoking. B&B - single room £38, double/twin room £64. Proprietors: **Linda and David Bullock.**
website: www.staghotelmoffat.co.uk

MOFFAT

Mr and Mrs W. Gray, Barnhill Springs Country Guest House, Moffat DG10 9QS (01683 220580). Barnhill Springs is an early Victorian country mansion standing in its own grounds overlooking Upper Annandale. Situated half-a-mile from the A74/M, the house and its surroundings retain an air of remote peacefulness. Internally it has been decorated and furnished to an exceptionally high standard of comfort. Open fire in lounge. Accommodation includes family, double, twin and single rooms, some en suite. Children welcome. Pets welcome free of charge. Open all year. Bed and Breakfast from £24. STB ★★ GUEST HOUSE, AA ♦♦♦

MOFFAT

Buchan Guest House, Beechgrove, Moffat DG10 9RS (01683 220378). Are you looking to break a long journey without straying far from the Motorway, or spend a relaxing few days exploring the Borders? Moffat's wide main street with specialist shops and choice of restaurants makes it the ideal location. Chris and Brenda Wallace welcome you to the freedom of Buchan House, an 1830 Listed building where we strive to make everyone's stay memorable for all the right reasons. Double, twin, triple and family rooms, two on the ground floor. Most bedrooms en suite, others have private bathrooms. Breakfast choices include vegetarian. Illuminated car park. STB ★★★
website: www.buchanguesthouse.co.uk

STRANRAER

Barnhills Farmhouse, Kirkcolm, Stranraer DG9 0QG (01776 853236). Large elegant farmhouse set in the midst of 436 acres of peaceful dairy farmland with spectacular sea views from most rooms. The bedrooms are spacious, comfortable and tastefully decorated, all en suite with TV, tea/coffee facilities and clock alarms. Large comfortable sitting room for guests' use with TV, video, DVD and books to read. Full Scottish or Continental breakfast served in our bright and spacious dining room. Ample secure parking. No smoking. There are many restaurants and bars within a short drive serving high quality food and drink. Activities in the area include golf, fishing, pony trekking, bowling, wind surfing and sailing. Stranraer offers shopping and sports facilities, or why not take the ferry to Northern Ireland? STB ★★★★ B&B. Proprietors: **Horace and Caroline Watt.**
e-mail: info@barnhillsfarmhouse.co.uk   website: www.barnhillsfarmhouse.co.uk

---

FHG *Creetown Gem Rock Museum*
Newton Stewart, Kirkcudbrightshire
See our **READERS' OFFER VOUCHER** for details of free or reduced rate entry

GEM ROCK MUSEUM

STRANRAER
The George Metro Hotel, 49 George Street, Stranraer DG1 7RJ (01776 702487; Fax: 01776 702488). The George Metro is a new style of hotel with only suites and apartments instead of the more traditional bedrooms. Each suite can accommodate 1-4, and apartments 1-6, for a set price, depending on size of suite and length of stay. Breakfast can be served in your room if required, and food and drink packs can be installed prior to your arrival. We have full conference facilities, including internet access, and can accommodate up to 16 people on a residential basis, or 20 people for a daytime conference. There are many restaurants locally offering a wide range of international cuisine, and transport can be arranged to and from restaurants outwith the town. Leisure facilities locally include four golf courses, a pool and sauna, Leisure Centre and sea and loch angling. Short Break details available on request.
website: www.georgehotelstranraer.co.uk

WHITHORN (near)
Mike and Helen Alexander, Craiglemine Cottage B&B, Glasserton, Near Whithorn DG8 8NE (01988 500594). With a rural location and peaceful atmosphere it's a wonderful place to unwind for a short break or a longer holiday. We have one double/family room, one single/twin room and dining room/lounge. Prices from £22. Evening meals available on request, including vegetarian or other dietary needs. Non-smoking. Off-road parking. Children welcome (under six years free). Pets welcome. An ideal base for walkers, cyclists, golf or touring. We also cater for amateur astronomers - call for details. Whether exploring the history, countryside or unspoilt beaches there is something for everyone. You can be sure of a friendly welcome all year round. Contact us for more details, or visit our website. **STB ★★**

e-mail: cottage@fireflyuk.net

website: www.startravel.fireflyinternet.co.uk

Dundee & Angus

BRECHIN
Rosemary Beatty, Brathinch Farm, By Brechin DD9 7QX (01356 648292; Fax: 01356 648003). Working farm. Brathinch is an 18th century farmhouse on a family-run working arable farm, with a large garden, situated off the B966 between Brechin and Edzell. Rooms have private or en suite bathroom, TV and tea/coffee making facilities. Shooting, fishing, golf, castles, stately homes, wildlife, swimming and other attractions are all located nearby. Easy access to Angus Glens and other country walks. Double £21, twin £22, single £25 - £26. Open all year. We look forward to welcoming you.
STB ★★★ *B&B.*
e-mail: adam.brathinch@btinternet.com

Edinburgh & Lothians

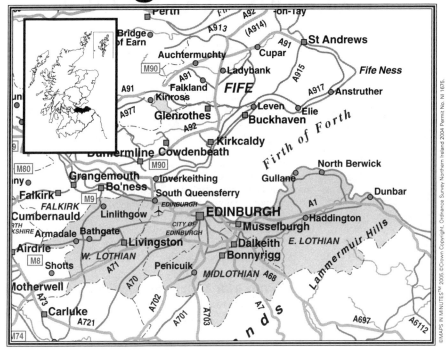

BATHGATE (near)

Mrs F. Gibb, Tarrareoch Farm, Station Road, Armadale, Near Bathgate EH48 3BJ (01501 730404). This 17th century farmhouse is situated two miles from M8 Junction 4, which is midway between Glasgow and Edinburgh. This peaceful location overlooks panoramic views of the countryside. All rooms are on the ground floor, ideal for disabled visitors, and have central heating, colour TV and tea/coffee making facilities. We are within easy reach of golf, fishing, cycling (15 mile cycle track runs along back of property). Ample security parking. Open January to December. Terms from £18 to £25 per person per night, single £25 to £30. **STB ★★★** *B&B.*

See also Colour Display Advertisement

BLACKBURN

Cruachan B&B, 78 East Main Street, Blackburn EH47 7QS (01506 655221; Fax: 01506 652395). A relaxed and friendly base is provided at Cruachan from which to explore central Scotland. The centre of Edinburgh can be reached by train in only 30 minutes from nearby Bathgate, and Glasgow is only 35 minutes by car. All rooms en suite/private facilities, full hospitality tray, fresh towels daily, colour TV and central heating. Hosts Kenneth and Jacqueline ensure you receive the utmost in quality of service, meticulously presented accommodation and of course a full Scottish breakfast. They look forward to having the pleasure of your company. Bed and Breakfast from £25 per person per night. **STB ★★★** *B&B.* **AA ♦♦♦**
e-mail: cruachan.bb@virgin.net
website: www.cruachan.co.uk

EDINBURGH

INTERNATIONAL GUEST HOUSE

AA ♦♦♦♦   37 Mayfield Gardens, Edinburgh EH9 2BX   **STB ★★★★**
Tel: 0131 667 2511   Fax: 0131 667 1112   Mrs Niven
E-mail: intergh1@yahoo.co.uk
Internet: www.accommodation-edinburgh.com

The **International** is an attractive, stone-built Victorian terrace house conveniently situated one-and-a-half-miles south of Princes Street on the main A701 and only four miles from the Straiton junction on the Edinburgh city by-pass. Lying on the main bus route, access to the city centre is easy. The **International** has ample private parking. Visitors who require a touch of luxury a little out of the ordinary can do no better than visit **The International**. All bedrooms have en suite, direct dial telephone, colour television and tea/coffee making facilities. The decor is outstanding, with ornate plasterwork on the ceilings as fine as in 'The New Town.' Some rooms enjoy magnificent views across to the extinct volcano of Arthur's Seat. The full Scottish breakfasts served on the finest bone china are a delight.

B&B from £30 to £65 single; £50 to £120 double
19th century setting with 21st century facilities!
In *Britain* magazine has rated **The International** as their 'find' in all Edinburgh.

EDINBURGH
Aeon-Kirklands Guest House, 128 Old Dalkeith Road, Edinburgh EH16 4SD (0131 664 2755; Fax: 0131 468 1736). Aeon-Kirklands is a 200 year-old former coach house which has been extensively modernised. All rooms are fully en suite, having colour TV, hairdryer, radio alarm and hospitality tray. There is also a large private car park for residents. On bus route with an abundance of local buses for city centre. Good selection of pubs serving reasonably priced food nearby. We are ideally placed for visiting attractions such as Holyrood Palace, the Castle and the Commonwealth swimming pool; twelve golf courses within ten minutes. A traditional Scottish breakfast is served each morning in our attractive, airy dining room; we also cater for vegetarians and those with special diets. **STB ★★★** *GUEST HOUSE.*
e-mail: enquiries@aeon-kirklands.co.uk
website: www.aeon-kirklands.co.uk

See also Colour Display Advertisement

EDINBURGH
Ms Heather El-Ghamri, The Alexander Guest House, 35 Mayfield Gardens, Edinburgh EH9 2BX (0131-258 4028). "A place of refreshment and peace." The Alexander lies just one-and-a-quarter miles from the city centre with all its attractions and three miles from the Straiton Junction on the City By-Pass. Most bedrooms have en suite bathrooms, and all are fully equipped with colour television including cable, tea/coffee hospitality tray, hairdryer, iron and ironing board; and if there is anything else you would like, don't hesitate to ask. Varied breakfast menu. Private car park. Credit cards accepted. **STB ★★★★** *GUEST HOUSE.*
e-mail: alexander@guest68.freeserve.co.uk
website: www.SmoothHound.co.uk/hotels/alexand3.html

Edinburgh & Lothians 291

EDINBURGH
Mrs Ritchie, Ingleneuk, 31 Drum Brae North, Edinburgh EH4 8AT (0131-317 1743). Comfortable detached bungalow approximately four miles west of city centre and three miles from airport. Close to Forth Road Bridge and City bypass. Good bus service. Ample car parking. No smoking. Our self-contained family unit comprises a twin-bedded room with seating and breakfasting area, a double bedroom and a shower room. All bedrooms have private entrance and look onto landscaped gardens with birds and squirrels. All rooms are en suite with hospitality trays, colour TV, iron, hairdryer, etc. and the family unit has a fridge. Breakfast is served to your room. Bed and Breakfast from £23 per person. Stuart and Lynda look forward to welcoming you to their home.
e-mail: ingleneukbnb@btinternet.com
website: www.ingleneukbandb.co.uk

EDINBURGH
The Ivy Guest House, 7 Mayfield Gardens, Edinburgh EH9 2AX (0131-667 3411; Fax: 0131-620 1422). Bed and Breakfast in a comfortable Victorian villa. Open all year round. Private car park. Close to city centre and all its cultural attractions with excellent public transport and taxi services available on the door step. Many local sports facilities (booking assistance available). All rooms have central heating, washbasins, colour TV and tea/coffee making facilities. Choice of en suite or standard rooms, all power showers. Public phone. Large selection of eating establishments nearby. A substantial Scottish breakfast and warm welcome is assured, courtesy of Dolly Green. Terms from £20 per person per night. STB ★★★ *GUEST HOUSE*. AA ♦♦♦♦, RAC ♦♦♦♦

e-mail: dolly@ivyguesthouse.com
website: www.ivyguesthouse.com

EDINBURGH
David Martin, Spylaw Bank House, 2 Spylaw Avenue, Colinton, Edinburgh EH13 0LR (0131-441 5022; mobile: 07981 923017). Elegant Georgian Country House built around 1790, situated within the city of Edinburgh. It has a secluded position in walled gardens close to Colinton village and three miles from the city centre. Luxuriously appointed en suite bedrooms with many personal touches. Relax in the original drawing room with its open fire and antique furnishings and take breakfast in the period dining room. Ideally situated for sightseeing in Edinburgh and touring the Borders, Fife and Perthshire. Five miles from airport, one from city by-pass. Ample parking. Frequent buses to city centre - a 15 minute journey. Bed and Breakfast from £30 per person. STB ★★★★ *B&B*.

e-mail: davidsmartin@blueyonder.co.uk
website: www.spylawbankhouse.com

See also Colour Display Advertisement

EDINBURGH
Castle Park Guest House, 75 Gilmore Place, Edinburgh EH3 9NU (0131-229 1215 or 0131-229 1223). A warm welcome awaits you at our family-run guest house, close to the King's Theatre, conference centre and city centre. Travel along the Royal Mile with Edinburgh Castle at one end and the Palace of Holyrood, the Queen's official Scottish residence, at the other. All rooms are tastefully decorated with colour TV and tea/coffee making facilities and are centrally heated throughout. Twin, single and en suite rooms available. Pleasant dining room where guests can enjoy a hearty breakfast. Children welcome; special prices. Off-street parking. Full Scottish/Continental breakfast. Bed and Breakfast from £17.50 to £25 per person.
e-mail: castlepark@btconnect.com

e-mail: blossom_house@hotmail.com

EDINBURGH

Mrs Kay, Blossom House, 8 Minto Street, Edinburgh EH9 1RG (0131-667 5353; Fax: 0131-667 2813). Blossom House is a traditional stone-built town house attractively situated within the Newington district of Edinburgh, less than one mile from the City Centre and on a main bus route. All bedrooms are tastefully furnished, with colour TV and tea/coffee hospitality tray; most with en suite facilities. Some rooms enjoy attractive views towards the extinct volcano of Arthur's Seat. Full Scottish breakfasts are served in the spacious dining room. Many fine restaurants are situated nearby, providing a wide range of cuisine to suit everyone's taste and pocket. Central heating. Private car park. B&B from £20 per person per night. STB ★★ *GUEST HOUSE.*

website: www.blossomguesthouse.co.uk

e-mail: mccraes.bandb@lineone.net

EDINBURGH

Mr Ian McCrae, 44 East Claremont Street, Edinburgh EH7 4JR (Tel & Fax: 0131-556 2610). Situated in the Victorian part of Edinburgh's New Town, McCrae's is only 15 minutes' walk from the city centre giving easy access to all attractions. The comfortable accommodation comprises three twin/double rooms, all at ground level. All rooms have en suite facilities, central heating, colour TV, radio/alarm, fridge, hairdryer and tea/coffee trays. Iron available on request. A full traditional breakfast is served using fresh local produce. Unrestricted on-street parking immediately outside. Rates from £24.50 per person per night sharing or from £28.50 for single occupation. Reductions available for long stays. Visa/Mastercard accepted. Open all year. STB ★★★ *B&B.*

website: http://website.lineone.net/~mccraes.bandb

EDINBURGH

Mr and Mrs Derek Mowat, Dunstane House Hotel, 4 West Coates, Haymarket, Edinburgh EH12 5JQ (Tel & Fax: 0131 337 6169). Impressive Victorian mansion, dating back to the 1850s and retaining its spectacular original features. All rooms have been luxuriously refurbished; four-poster bed available. We offer fine dining in our unique 'Skerries' restaurant, and more informal meals in the Stane bar. Only fresh produce from the Orkney Isles is used. City centre location only minutes from Princes Street and the castle. Private parking. Bed and Breakfast from £49 to £69 per person per night. STB ★★★★ *HOTEL*, AA ◆◆◆◆◆

e-mail: reservations@dunstanehousehotel.co.uk
website: www.dunstane-hotel-edinburgh.co.uk

GULLANE

Mrs Mary Chase, Jadini Garden, Goose Green, Gullane, East Lothian EH31 2BA (01620 843343). Comfortable family home in a delightful secluded walled garden, which guests are welcome to use. Private parking for up to eight cars. Gullane is a charming coastal village, well-known for its famous golf courses. Gullane Golf Club is just a few minutes' walk from Jadini Garden, and Muirfield is at the other end of the village. Nearby also are the beautiful sandy beaches bordered by cliffs and dunes, providing spectacular walks and seabird nature trails. Edinburgh is only 30 minutes by car, four miles from North Berwick. French, German and Spanish spoken. Bed and Breakfast from £22 to £32 per person. STB ★★★ *B&B.*

e-mail: marychase@jadini.com
website: www.jadini.com

Edinburgh & Lothians 293

LINLITHGOW

Mr & Mrs J Caddle, Strawberry Bank House, 13 Avon Place, Strawberry Bank, Linlithgow EH49 6BL (Tel & Fax: 01506 848 372). A large Victorian villa with modern spacious accommodation overlooking historic Linlithgow Palace - centrally located for easy access to all local amenities. With the Town Centre only a few minutes' walk away the house is within easy reach of the Canal Basin, the main bus and rail terminals, and the motorway network to Glasgow, Edinburgh and Stirling. Open all year. Credit Cards accepted. B&B available from £30 per night. **STB ★★★★ B&B.**
e-mail: gillian@strawberrybank-scotland.co.uk
website: www.strawberrybank-scotland.co.uk

LINLITHGOW

Mr and Mrs R. Inglis, Thornton, Edinburgh Road, Linlithgow EH49 6AA (01506 844693). Comfortable family-run Victorian house with original features retained. Central situation in a peaceful location near the Union Canal in historic Linlithgow - only five minutes' walk from the town centre, Linlithgow Palace and railway station. This is a real home from home offering quality accommodation in a friendly and relaxing atmosphere. Open March to November inclusive. Excellent base for visiting Edinburgh, Stirling, Glasgow and the Falkirk Wheel. Early booking advisable. Credit cards accepted. Terms from £28 per person. **STB ★★★★ B&B, AA ♦♦♦♦, WINNER AA 'BEST BREAKFAST' SCOTLAND AWARD, RECOMMENDED BY "WHICH?" B&B GUIDE.**
e-mail: inglisthornton@hotmail.com
website: www.thornton-scotland.co.uk

See also Colour Display Advertisement

MUSSELBURGH

Inveresk House, Inveresk Village, Musselburgh EH21 7UA (0131-665 5855; Fax: 0131-665 0578). Historic mansion house and award-winning Bed & Breakfast. Family-run "home from home". Situated in three acres of garden and woodland. Built on the site of a Roman settlement from 150 AD, the remains of a bathhouse can be found hidden in the garden. Three comfortable en suite rooms. Original art and antiques adorn the house. Edinburgh's Princes Street seven miles from Inveresk House. Good bus routes. Families welcome. Off-street parking. Telephone first. B&B from £40 per person. Family room £100 to £120.
e-mail: chute.inveresk@btinternet.com
website: http://travel.to/edinburgh

FAIRSHIELS

PATHHEAD

Mrs Anne Gordon, "Fairshiels", Blackshiels, Pathhead EH37 5SX (01875 833665). We are situated on the A68, three miles south of Pathhead at the picturesque village of Fala. The house is an 18th century coaching inn (Listed building). All bedrooms have washbasins and tea/coffee making facilities; one is en suite. All the rooms are comfortably furnished. We are within easy reach of Edinburgh and the Scottish Borders. A warm welcome is extended to all our guests – our aim is to make your stay a pleasant one. Cost is from £20 per person; children under 12 years £13.
e-mail: anne@fairshiels.fsnet.co.uk

The FHG Directory of Website Addresses
on pages 339-370 is a useful quick reference guide for holiday accommodation with e-mail and/or website details

ROSLIN
Mrs Rosemary Noble, Glenlea House, Hawthornden, Lasswade EH18 1EJ (0131-440 2079). Glenlea is one mile from the picturesque village of Roslin. Large 150-year-old family house standing in one acre of garden, overlooking historic Rosslyn Chapel and the Pentland Hills. Plenty of good eating places in the area, also walking and riding, but within easy reach of Edinburgh which is seven miles away. Accommodation comprises one large family room, two double and one single. One of the double rooms is on the ground floor with bathroom adjacent. Full Scottish breakfast. Fully centrally heated. Ample parking. Bed and Breakfast from £25.

Fife

CRAIL
Mrs Margaret Carstairs, Selcraig House, 47 Nethergate, Crail KY10 3TX (01333 450697; Fax: 01333 451113). Selcraig is a 200-year old house with original period features and antique furniture. We are situated in a quiet street near the sea, in a conservation area; ample parking. All rooms are en suite or have private facilities, colour TV, clock radios and heating. From Crail High Street turn right at the Golf Hotel, right again, house is on right opposite Marine Hotel. B&B from £20 to £30.
e-mail: margaret@selcraighouse.co.uk
website: www.selcraighouse.co.uk

CULROSS
Judith Jackson, St Mungo's B&B, Low Causeway, Culross KY12 8HJ (01383 882102). 17th century Listed building on the outskirts of the best preserved medieval village in Scotland. Culross has a range of National Trust buildings and an historic abbey. It is an ideal location for touring central Scotland – Edinburgh, Glasgow, Stirling, Perth, St Andrews and the Trossachs are all within easy reach. All rooms have views over the Forth Estuary and have TV, hairdryer etc. One family room (sleeps two or three) and one double room, both with en suite. One twin room with private bathroom. Full central heating. Extensive mature gardens. Off-street parking. All rooms non-smoking. Bed and Breakfast from £25pp.
e-mail: martinpjackson@hotmail.com
website: www.milford.co.uk/scotland/accom/h-a1763.html

Fife 295

KIRKCALDY

Mrs A. Crawford, Crawford Hall, 2 Kinghorn Road, Kirkcaldy KY1 1SU (01592 262658). Crawford Hall is a large rambling old house over 100 years old and was once the local vicarage. Spacious rooms and some sea views. Teasmaid and colour TV in all rooms. Guests have use of hairdryer and iron on request. Pay phone. Ample private parking. Lovely walled gardens. Five minutes' walk to town centre. Handy for golf course, cinema, theatre and ice rinks. Kirkcaldy also boasts two beautiful parks. Evening meal by arrangement. Double and twin rooms £19 per person, single room £25 per person.

See also Colour Display Advertisement

LEVEN

Mrs Pam MacDonald, Dunclutha Guest House, 16 Victoria Road, Leven KY8 4EX (01333 425515; Fax: 01333 422311). This quiet Victorian former rectory provides the ideal location for touring. Ideal base for golf enthusiasts, within easy reach of 46 golf courses and only 14 miles from St Andrews. Forty minutes from Edinburgh Airport, Perth and 30-35 minutes from Dundee. Facilities include three en suite rooms - one double, one twin, one family (sleeps three to four), one family (sleeps three) with private bathroom. Colour TV and tea/coffee facilities in all rooms, cot available. Visitors' lounge with TV. Most credit cards accepted. Open all year. Terms from £26 pppn. Non-smoking.
STB ★★★★ *GUEST HOUSE,* **AA ♦♦♦♦**.

e-mail: pam.leven@blueyonder.co.uk
website: www.dunclutha.myby.co.uk

See also Colour Display Advertisement

ST ANDREWS

The University of St Andrews. B&B, 3 Star hotel or self-catering apartments. To find out more e-mail or call **01334 462000. STB ★★★.**
e-mail: holidays@st-andrews.ac.uk

---

publisher's note

While every effort is made to ensure accuracy, we regret that FHG Guides cannot accept responsibility for errors, misrepresentations or omissions in our entries or any consequences thereof. Prices in particular should be checked. We will follow up complaints but cannot act as arbiters or agents for either party

FHG
·K·U·P·E·R·A·R·D·

•••some fun days out in FIFE

Deep Sea World, North Queensferry • 01383 411880 • www.deepseaworld.com
Scottish Fisheries Museum, Anstruther • 01333 310528 • www.scottishmuseum.org
British Golf Museum, St Andrews • 01334 460046 • www.britishgolfmuseum.co.uk
Scottish Deer Centre, Cupar • 01337 810391 • www.thedeercentre.com

Glasgow & District

GLASGOW

Mrs P. Wells, "Avenue End" B&B, 21 West Avenue, Stepps, Glasgow G33 6ES (0141-779 1990; Fax: 0141-779 1951). Stepps village is situated north-east of Glasgow just off the A80. This self-built family home nestles down a quiet leafy lane offering the ideal location for an overnight stay or touring base with the main routes to Edinburgh, Stirling and the North on our doorstep. Easy commuting to Loch Lomond, the Trossachs or Clyde Valley. M8 exit 12 from the south, or A80 Cumbernauld Road from the north. Glasgow only ten minutes away, Glasgow Airport 12 miles. Ample parking. All rooms offer colour TV, compliments tray and en suite or private facilities. Home from Home – warm welcome assured! All from £22.50 per person per night. Self-catering also available. **STB ★★★** *B&B*.

e-mail: avenueEnd@aol.com
website: www.hometown.aol.co.uk/avenueend/myhomepage/business.html

KILSYTH

Libby MacGregor, Allanfauld Farm, Kilsyth, Glasgow G65 9DF (Tel & Fax: 01236 822155). A working family farm situated close to the town of Kilsyth at the foot of the Kilsyth Hills, a great base to explore central Scotland. Glasgow, Stirling 20 minutes. Croy Station is just five minutes' drive away, where a short train journey will take you into the centre of Edinburgh. Golf, fishing, hill walking and a swimming pool are all within half a mile plus Cumbernauld and Kirkintilloch five minutes away. One twin/family room, one single room, both with TV and tea/coffee facilities. B&B from £22. Open all year. **STB ★★★** *B&B*
e-mail: allanfauld@hotmail.com

Pets Welcome!

"THE PET WORLD'S VERSION OF THE ULTIMATE HOTEL GUIDE!" (The Times)

Now bigger than ever and with full colour throughout,
Pets Welcome! is used every year by thousands of discriminating owners who simply refuse to leave their pets "home alone".
Published twice a year in Autumn and Spring.

Only £8.99 from booksellers or direct from the publishers:
**FHG Guides, Abbey Mill Business Centre, Seedhill,
Paisley PA1 1TJ** *(postage charged outside UK)*
e-mail: admin@fhguides.co.uk • www.holidayguides.com

Highlands

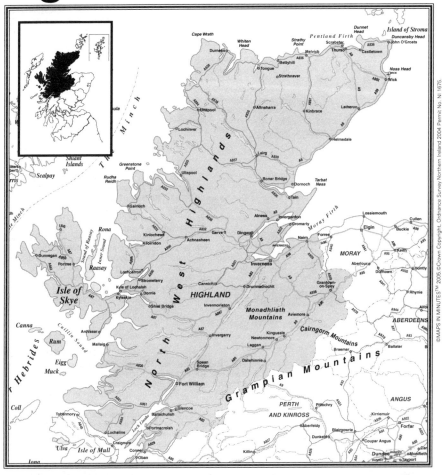

Visit the

ORKNEY ISLANDS

Daily from John O'Groats and Inverness.

Fascinating full Day Tours of the beautiful Orkney Islands leave Inverness at 7.30am and from John O'Groats at 9am and 10.30am.
Every Day All Summer

DAY TRIPS

Phone Now For Full Details

Tel: 01955 611353
Website: www.jogferry.co.uk

John O'Groats Ferries, Ferry Office, John O'Groats, Caithness, Scotland KW1 4YR   Fax: 01955 611301

Highlands North

DORNOCH
Amalfi Bed and Breakfast, River Street, Dornoch IV25 3LY (01862 810015). A friendly, family-run B&B located alongside Royal Dornoch's Struie Course, close to the beach and all other attractions. All bedrooms are on the ground floor, are comfortably furnished and have en suite shower rooms with washbasin and wc, colour TV, hairdryer and complimentary hostess tray. One room is twin-bedded and the other has a double and single bed. There is private off-street parking and a garden for your enjoyment. Reductions on Royal Dornoch's green fees for our guests. Rates from £23 pppn.
e-mail: EMackayAmalfi@aol.com
website: www.amalfidornoch.com

JOHN O' GROATS
Mrs Sina Houston, Mill House, John O' Groats, By Wick, Caithness KW1 4YR (01955 611239). Situated one mile from John O'Groats passenger ferry and two miles from the Gills Bay car ferry to South Ronaldsay on the main A836 Thurso road, with excellent views over the Pentland Firth and Orkney Islands. Beautiful walks by the Stocks of Duncansby. Accommodation consists of three bedrooms, one twin and two double, private bathroom. All rooms have tea making facilities and washbasin. Bright, comfortable TV lounge. Non-smoking. Ample parking. Open May to October. Terms from £20 to £25 per person.
e-mail: s.m.houston@talk21.com

KINLOCHBERVIE
The Kinlochbervie Hotel, Kinlochbervie, By Lairg, Sutherland IV27 4RP (01971 521275; Fax: 01971 521438). In one of the most stunning locations on the North West coast of Scotland. Wide open seas, majestic hills and unforgettable sunsets – these views can be yours when you stay in one of our supremely comfortable guest rooms. Each room has en suite bathroom, colour TV, telephone and tea/coffee making facilities. Standard and Premier rooms available, also one suite. All public rooms are relaxing and comfortable and we take special pride in our cuisine, with fresh fish and seafood, hill lamb and venison. The Garbet Bistro offers a more informal atmosphere for an excellent selection of lunches and snacks. STB ★★★
e-mail: klbhotel@aol.com
website: www.kinlochberviehotel.com

LAIRG
Caroline Snow, Carnbren, Station Road, Lairg IV27 4AY (01549 402259). This peaceful village is the perfect base from which to tour the northern Highlands. Our home overlooks Loch Shin and is ten minutes' walk from the shops, pub etc. It's perfect for walkers, wildlife enthusiasts, cyclists, bikers and those who just need a break! All three rooms have private bathrooms and TVs. No smoking indoors. Please call for prices (from £18pppn depending upon time of year, length of stay, two sharing room etc.)
e-mail: highlandvegan@aol
website: www.carnbren-vegan.highland-guesthouse.co.uk

LOCHINVER
Arthur and Meryl Quigley, Ardglas Guest House, Inver, Lochinver IV27 4LJ (01571 844257 or 01571 844632). The guest house gives panoramic views of Lochinver village, the loch, the harbour and the mountains around, including Suilven, in an area distinguished for its walking and angling. We can advise on local walks and attractions. Accommodation comprises one single, five double/twin rooms and two family rooms with shared facilities. Guest lounge. Ample parking. Terms from £21 per person, children under four years free, age four to 11 half price. Open all year. STB ★★★ *GUEST HOUSE.*
e-mail: art@ardglas.co.uk
website: www.ardglas.co.uk

LOCHINVER
Mr C. MacLeod, Polcraig Guest House, Lochinver IV27 4LD (Tel & Fax: 01571 844429). Polcraig Guest House nestles on the hillside, centrally in Lochinver village. Family-run, with six very comfortable en suite bedrooms, three twin and three double. Each room is equipped with tea/coffee tray, colour TV, hairdryer and shaving point. Enjoy hearty breakfasts in our dining room, with local produce used whenever possible. Generous helpings of fresh salmon, smoked haddock, sausage, bacon, eggs and black pudding will set you up nicely for the day ahead. The area is a paradise for anglers (permits available), climbers, walkers, birdwatchers and photographers. Drying area. Car park. STB ★★★★ *GUEST HOUSE.*
e-mail: cathelmac@aol.com
website: www.smoothhound.co.uk/hotels/polcraig.html

Highlands Mid

GAIRLOCH
Miss I. Mackenzie, Duisary, Strath, Gairloch IV21 2DA (01445 712252). Enjoy the warmth of true West Coast hospitality in this modernised crofthouse on the outskirts of the remote village of Gairloch, with its superb views over the sea to the Western Isles and across the beautiful Torridon Mountains. Gairloch makes a perfect holiday base, and is an ideal spot for hill walking, birdwatching, fishing or just relaxing; nine-hole golf course, safe sandy beaches and close to the National Trust garden at Inverewe. Boats can be chartered at the harbour, or you can take a fishing trip or wildlife safari to look for seals and porpoises in the loch. Pony trekking and swimming pool nearby. Warm and comfortable twin, family and double en suite rooms with TV and tea/coffee making facilities. Open from April to October. Children welcome. Tariff £20 to £25 per night, including breakfast.
e-mail: isabel@duisary.freeserve.co.uk   website: www.duisary.freeserve.co.uk

GAIRLOCH
Mrs A. MacIver, Heatherdale, Charleston, Gairloch IV21 2AH (01445 712388). A warm welcome awaits at Heatherdale, situated on the outskirts of Gairloch, overlooking the harbour and bay beyond. Within easy walking distance of the golf course and sandy beaches. Ideal base for hill walking. All rooms have en suite facilities, some with sea view. Excellent eating out facilities nearby. Ample parking. Residents' lounge with open fire. Bed and Breakfast prices from £22 per person per night. STB ★★★★ *B&B.*
e-mail: BrochoD1@aol.com

PLOCKTON
Mrs Mackenzie, Seann Bhruthach, Duirinish, by Plockton IV40 8BE (01599 544204). A very warm welcome in our comfortable modern home in a picturesque crofting township with outstanding views over the Inner Hebrides. Situated on a working croft with Highland cattle midway between Kyle of Lochalsh and the village of Plockton. Two double rooms en suite, one twin with private facilities. Non-smoking. Open all year except Christmas/New Year. Bed and Breakfast from £22 per person.
STB ★★★ *B&B*
e-mail: info@highlandhideaway.co.uk
website: www.highlandhideaway.co.uk

PLOCKTON
Mrs Janet MacKenzie Jones, "Tomacs", Frithard Road, Plockton IV52 8TQ (Tel & Fax: 01599 544321). Fine views overlooking Loch Carron and Applecross Hills. Double and twin bedrooms. One room has en suite facilities and one has private facilities; all have washbasin, central heating, TV and tea/coffee making facilities. Bed and Breakfast from £20. STB ★★★ *GUEST HOUSE.*
e-mail: janet@tomacs.freeserve.co.uk

PLOCKTON
Margaret and Gerry Arscott, Soluis Mu Thuath Guest House, Braeintra, by Achmore, Lochalsh IV53 8UP (01599 577219). A warm welcome awaits guests at this family-run, non-smoking guesthouse. All rooms are spacious with lovely views over mountain and forest, en suite facilities, central heating, televisions and hospitality trays. Two of the ground floor rooms are suitable for disabled visitors. Situated about ten miles north of Kyle of Lochalsh, we offer traditional Scottish hospitality. Whether you are touring, biking, walking or just soaking up the atmosphere, Soluis Mu Thuath is in the ideal location for exploring some of the most dramatic scenery in the Western Highlands. Visit Skye, Plockton, Torridon, Applecross and Glenelg or enjoy some of the many challenging (and less challenging) walks. Prices from £23. STB ★★ *GUEST HOUSE.*

e-mail: soluismuthuath@btopenworld.com   website: www.highlandsaccommodation.co.uk

STRATHPEFFER
Dunraven Lodge, Golf Course Road, Strathpeffer IV14 9AS (01997 421210). Beautiful Listed period house with all rooms en suite; recently refurbished to a very high standard of comfort and design. Guest lounge, dining room, full-size snooker room and lovely gardens provide an excellent base for your holiday or business trip. Open all year with many seasonal specials. Golf course, restaurants, bars and shops are just a short distance away, and we are ideally situated for exploring both the East and West coasts of the Highlands, Aviemore, Ullapool, Dornoch, Inverness, the Isle of Skye and Loch Ness. Bed and Breakfast from £28 to £33 pppn. STB ★★★★ *B&B*
e-mail: sandraiddon@aol.com
website: www.dunravenlodge.com

Free or reduced rate entry to Holiday Visits and Attractions – see our READERS' OFFER VOUCHERS on pages 53-90

Highlands South

ARISAIG

Mr & Mrs Murray, The Old Library Lodge, Arisaig PH39 4NH (01687 450651; Fax: 01687 450219). The Old Library is a family-run business in a converted 18th century stable, located on the famous 'Road to the Isles', overlooking the sea loch, Nan Ceall, with views to Eigg, Rum and the Inner Hebrides. Our six bedrooms (four garden and two sea view), are all en suite, with colour TV, telephone and tea/coffee making facilities. The fully licensed restaurant takes pride in serving the best in fresh local fish and meat dishes in a relaxed atmosphere. **STB ★★★** e - mail: reception@oldlibrary.co.uk
website: www.oldlibrary.co.uk

AVIEMORE

Jill and Jonathan Gatenby, Ravenscraig Guest House, 141 Grampian Road, Aviemore PH22 1RP (01479 810278; Fax: 01479 810210). A 12 bedroomed Victorian house situated on the main street in Aviemore, right in the centre of Cairngorm National Park. An ideal base for exploring the Highlands. Six en suite rooms available in the main house, some with views towards the Cairngorm Mountains and ski area, others overlook Craigellachie Nature Reserve. Six en suite rooms available in the newly-built garden annexe; large, spacious rooms, each with its own porch and front door onto the garden and parking area. Traditional Scottish breakfast served using locally produced ingredients. Bed and Breakfast £25 to £30. **STB ★★★** *GUEST HOUSE,* **AA/RAC** ◆◆◆◆

e-mail: info@aviemoreonline.com
website: www.aviemoreonline.com

AVIEMORE

See also Colour Display Advertisement

Eriskay, Craig-na-gower Avenue, Aviemore PH22 1RW (01479 810717). A family-run Bed and Breakfast, situated in a quiet cul-de-sac in the centre of Aviemore. Ideal base for a holiday, whether it is fishing, skiing, sailing, bird watching, climbing or any other outdoor pursuit – we cater for all. Purpose-built drying room and secure storage to protect vital outdoor equipment. Pick-up/drop-off service to and from the Ski Centre or local glens. Packed lunches and dinners by prior arrangement. Luxurious guest lounge with blazing log fire. Private off-road parking. All rooms are en suite or have their own private bathroom, with king and queen-size beds, television, radio, hairdryers, controllable electric heating, and a host of other extras. Complete No Smoking policy. Pets accepted by prior arrangement. **STB ★★★** *B&B,*

CYCLISTS & WALKERS WELCOME.
e-mail: enquiry@eriskay-aviemore.co.uk
Website: www.eriskay-aviemore.co.uk

CARRBRIDGE

Dudleston Family, Craigellachie House, Main Street, Carrbridge PH23 3AS (01479 841641). In the very heart of Carrbridge, Craigellachie House has off-road parking, locked storage for bicycles, motorbikes etc., plus a drying room for wet clothes. In our comfortable guest lounge, with open fire, you can read, enjoy games, watch TV or relax with a drink. Special dietary needs for breakfast can be catered for given reasonable notice. All our bedrooms are either en suite or have private shower rooms. Craigellachie House is within walking distance of all village amenities and eating places, and is ideally situated for exploring the Highland region. Non-smoking. Licensed. B&B from £21pppn. **STB ★★★** *GUEST HOUSE.*

e-mail: craigellachiehouse@fsmail.net
website: www.carrbridge.com

DRUMNADROCHIT
Roy and Alison Pankhurst, Woodlands Guest House, East Lewiston, Drumnadrochit IV63 6UJ (01456 450356). Peacefully located in the heart of 'Nessie' country and with panoramic views of the surrounding hills, Woodlands provides a perfect base from which to explore the history and romance of the beautiful Highlands and Islands. Offering a wide range of tastefully appointed accommodation, comprising two superior en suite rooms (one king/twin suite with private lounge, one large ground floor king/twin equipped to suit the disabled) and three luxury double rooms (two en suite one with private facilities). The STB awards we have received reflect the standard of service and facilities provided. Children over six years welcome. No smoking. Bed and Breakfast tariffs from £20 per person per night, evening meal by arrangement. **STB ★★★★, STB** CAT-2 *ASSISTED WHEELCHAIR ACCESS AWARD.*
e-mail: woodlands2004@btinternet.com
website: www.woodlands-drumnadrochit.co.uk

DRUMNADROCHIT
Carol and Ewan Macleod, Glenurquhart House Hotel, Balnain, Drumnadrochit IV63 6TJ (01456 476234). Escape to the Scottish Highlands for peace and tranquillity and stay in our comfortable, friendly hotel with fantastic views of Loch Meiklie and Glen Urquhart. The hotel nestles in six acres of wooded grounds close to Loch Ness and Glen Affric nature reserve and is ideally suited for touring the Highlands. Most rooms are en suite and all have tea/coffee making facilities, hairdryer, colour TV, plus video in family rooms. There is a residents' lounge warmed by a log fire, restaurant serving freshly cooked meals and a cosy bar with ample supply of malt whiskies. Bikes can be hired and there is fishing available. **STB ★★★** *SMALL HOTEL.*
e-mail: info@glenurquhart-house-hotel.co.uk
website: www.glenurquhart-house-hotel.co.uk

FORT WILLIAM
Toby and Bev Richardson, Mansefield House, Corpach, Fort William PH33 7LT (01397 772262). Mansefield House offers Dinner, Bed and Breakfast in comfortable accommodation, at affordable prices. Home dining in a warm, friendly atmosphere. Situated at the heart of Scotland's most dramatic scenery, this historic building, formerly a church manse, is set in mature gardens with mountain views. Ideal touring base for the West Highlands. Private, off- street parking. Non-smoking. **STB ★★★** *GUEST HOUSE.* **AA ♦♦♦♦,** *WELCOME HOST.*
e-mail: mansefield@btopenworld.com
website: www.fortwilliamaccommodation.com

FORT WILLIAM
Nether Lochaber Hotel, Onich, Fort William, Inverness-shire PH33 6SE (01855 821235; Fax: 01855 821545). An ideal centre from which to explore Lochaber, the Ardnamurchan Peninsula and Glencoe. Traditional home cooking goes hand in hand with homely service, comfortable accommodation and private facilities. The inn stands on the shores of beautiful Loch Linnhe at Corran Ferry, eight miles south of Fort William. Terms from £30-£40 per person Bed and Breakfast. Children and pets welcome!

Highlands South

See also Colour Display Advertisement

FORT WILLIAM
John and Julie Mackin, Braeburn B&B, Badabrie, Fort William PH33 7LX (01397 772047). A warm welcome awaits you at Braeburn, a spacious family-run house with panoramic views of the surrounding area; Ben Nevis four miles. Situated in its own private grounds with ample off-road parking and storage for bikes and skiing equipment. Three miles from the town centre; local hotels and bars serving good food and drink all within walking distance. Ideally situated for touring the West Highlands of Scotland. All rooms are en suite with colour TV, hairdryer and hospitality tray, relax in the residents' lounge or on our sunny patio. Enjoy a hearty breakfast to set you up for the day. Prices range from £25.00 to £27.50 per person. **STB ★★★ B&B.**
e-mail: enquiries@braeburnfortwilliam.co.uk
website: www.braeburnfortwilliam.co.uk

FORT WILLIAM
Mrs Mary MacLean, Innishfree, Lochyside, Fort William PH33 7NX (01397 705471). Set against the background of Ben Nevis, this spacious Bed and Breakfast house offers a high level of service. Just two miles from the town centre and three miles from Glen Nevis. Visitors are guaranteed a warm friendly welcome and excellent accommodation. All rooms have en suite facilities and also offer remote-control colour TV and tea/coffee making facilities. Breakfast is served in the conservatory, which is overlooked by panoramic views. Enthusiastic advice on pursuits and activities are given. Access to private car park is available. This house has a non-smoking policy and pets are not allowed. Open all year. Prices from £24 per person per night. **STB ★★★★ B&B.**

e-mail: mburnsmaclean@aol.com
website: www.innishfree.co.uk

FORT WILLIAM
Stuart and Mandy McLean, Distillery Guest House & Cottages, North Road, Nevis Bridge, Fort William PH33 6LR (01397 700103; Fax: 01397 702980). Set in the extensive grounds of the former Glenlochy Distillery with its fine distinctive distillery buildings forming a backdrop to one of the most attractive areas in Fort William. The house is situated on the banks of the River Nevis, at the entrance to Glen Nevis and the West Highland Way, but only five minutes' walk from the town centre, railway and bus stations. Seven very well equipped guest rooms, all with en suite facilities, TV, central heating, tea/coffee facilities and hairdryer. Lovely home cooked traditional breakfast. Full fire certificate. Non-smoking policy in bedrooms. Car parking. Open all year. We look forward to welcoming you. Self-catering accommodation also available. Terms from £22.50 to £38.00 per person per night. **STB ★★★★ GUEST HOUSE, AA ♦♦♦♦, RAC ♦♦♦♦** *SPARKLING DIAMOND AWARD. WALKERS AND CYCLISTS WELCOME*
e-mail: DistHouse@aol.com
website: www.stayinfortwilliam.co.uk

FORT WILLIAM
Mrs Wallace, Ossian's Hotel, High Street, Fort William PH33 6DH (01397 700857). Ossian's can provide the traveller to the Scottish Highlands a comfortable, friendly and informal hotel, right in the centre of town. Shops, pubs and entertainment are just outside our front door. Relax and enjoy some of our good home cooking. All rooms are en suite. Budget/family rooms available. Some rooms have loch views. Lift access to all floors. Well-behaved pets and children are welcome. We are only a four minute walk from train or bus stations. Fort William makes an excellent base for touring the West Highlands, and with some of the best climbing in Britain, walkers and climbers are very welcome here. Bed and Breakfast from £18 to £32.

Speyside Heather Garden
Dulnain Bridge, Inverness-shire
See our **READERS' OFFER VOUCHER** for details of free or reduced rate entry

304 Highlands South

FORT WILLIAM
Mr Neilson, Glenshiel, Achintore Road, Fort William PH33 6RW (01397 702271). Modern purpose-built guest house situated near the shore of Loch Linnhe with panoramic views of the surrounding mountains. Accommodation comprises three en suite double bedrooms and one twin-bedded en suite, all with colour TV and tea making facilities. Non-smoking. Large car park. Garden. Directions: on the A82 one-and-a-half-miles south of Fort William. Bed and Breakfast from £18 to £25.
e-mail: glenshielguesthous@amserve.com

e-mail: bennevisview@amserve.net

FORT WILLIAM
John and Jeanette Mooney, Ben Nevis View Bed and Breakfast, Station Road, Corpach, Fort William PH33 7JH (01397 772131). Bed and Breakfast establishment located adjacent to the Caledonian Canal basin on the outskirts of Fort William, affording superb views across the water to Ben Nevis. Providing all the modern comforts for today's traveller, Ben Nevis View is open from February to October and caters for two to six people in one double and one family room (one double and two single beds), both en suite with colour TV, hairdryer and tea/coffee making facilities. Enjoy a hearty cooked breakfast in our bright, cheery dining room in true Scottish style. Tariff from £20 to £22.50 per person per night, subject to season. Family room prices available on request. Non-smoking; sorry, no dogs. **STB ★★★** *B&B*.
website: www.bennevisview.co.uk

FORT WILLIAM
Mrs Catriona Morrison, Torlinnhe, Achintore Road, Fort William PH33 6RN (Tel & Fax: 01397 702583). Friendly family-run Bed and Breakfast with ample parking. Five rooms all en suite. All with colour TV and hospitality trays. One family, two double, one twin and one single room, most have views over Loch Linnhe and the hills beyond. Full fire certificate. Torlinnhe is situated one mile south of the town on the main A82 and is an excellent base for touring or enjoying a pleasant walk into town. New and return guests always welcome. Prices range from £20 to £27. **STB ★★★** *B&B*.

e-mail: info@strathassynt.com

GLENCOE
Mike and Christine Richardson, Strathassynt Guest House, Loanfern, Ballachulish, Near Glencoe PH49 4JB (01855 811261; Fax: 01855 811914). We are a family-run, licensed Guest House in the beautiful village of Ballachulish, right next to the spectacular scenery of Glencoe and situated ideally for exploring the Scottish Highlands and Islands. All of our rooms have en suite facilities, colour TV, DVD player, hospitality tray and individually controlled room heaters. We have a comfortable guest lounge, mini bar facilities, separate diningroom, drying room, bike store and large car park. We can also offer our guests access to leisure facilities including a swimming pool, jacuzzi, sauna and gym. Easy to find, next door to the Tourist Information Centre. Bed and Breakfast from £18.
website: www.strathassynt.com

The FHG Directory of Website Addresses
on pages 339-370 is a useful quick reference guide for holiday accommodation with e-mail and/or website details

GRANTOWN-ON-SPEY

Mrs Val Dickinson, An Cala Guest House, Woodlands Terrace, Grantown-on-Spey PH26 3JU (01479 873293). An Cala is a lovely Victorian granite house set in half an acre and offers comfort in a friendly and cosy atmosphere, only a ten minute walk from the town centre. Four delightful en suite guest bedrooms with tea/coffee tray and colour TV, hairdryers. Doubles have king-size beds. Ideally situated for Spey walks, Munros, RSPB Reserves at Boat of Garten and Loch Insh, the Whisky Trail and as a base for visiting castles and most places in the Highlands. Excellent local golf and tennis clubs. Non-smoking. On-site parking. Terms from £26 to £28 per person. STB ★★★★ *GUEST HOUSE.* AA ◆◆◆◆◆
e-mail: ancala@globalnet.co.uk
website: ancala.info

INVERNESS

See also Colour Display Advertisement

Moray Park House, 1 Moray Park, Island Bank Road, Inverness IV2 4SX (01463 233528). Moray Park is a lovely old house overlooking Cavell Gardens and the River Ness, and just a few minutes from the main shopping streets. The Mathieson Family purchased Moray Park House in August 2003 and have carried out refurbishment during the winter. Seven rooms have en suite facilities and one a private bathroom. All are freshly decorated and all but two have river views. One large ground floor room is designed for use by disabled people, with extra space and suitable en suite facilities. There is a car park for residents. Moray Park House is ideally positioned for access to the lovely Island Bank Walk, the Eden Court Theatre, the Castle, city parks and numerous restaurants, all of which are within a few minutes' walk. Bed and Breakfast rates vary from £20 to £50.

e-mail: MorayParkHotel@aol.com
website: www.MorayParkHotel.co.uk

INVERNESS

Mrs C. White, Aberfeldy Lodge Guest House, 11 Southside Road, Inverness IV2 3BG (01463 231120). Beautifully presented Victorian detached villa situated in a most desirable residential area of Inverness. All rooms are en suite and provide hospitality tray, TV, clock/radio alarm and hairdryer. The guest house is within a five minute walk of the city centre and only ten minutes from bus and rail terminals. Free off-street parking. Excellent restaurants and bars located within a two minute walk and a variety of entertainment is available within the city centre, from traditional Scottish ceilidh music to clubbing. Inverness is the ideal base for exploring the Highlands. STB ★★★ *GUEST HOUSE.*
e-mail: admin@aberfeldylodge.com
website: www.aberfeldylodge.com

INVERNESS

Mr J. Munro, Castle View Guesthouse, 2a Ness Walk, Inverness IV3 5NE (Tel & Fax: 01463 241443). A late 19th century Victorian house situated on the bank of the River Ness, ideally situated in the centre of Inverness. The High Street and station are only five minutes' walk away and the guest house is in close proximity to good restaurants. The rooms are spacious, warm and comfortable with high ceilings and central heating. All with shower, family room en suite. The dining room is particularly well appointed with large windows overlooking the river. All rooms have tea/coffee making facilities, remote-control video/colour TV. Daily newspapers are supplied free and hairdryers, ironing facilities, drying room and trouser presssing can be arranged.Traditional Scottish, vegetarian and Continental-style breakfast can be provided. STB ★★ *GUEST HOUSE.*

e-mail: jmunro4161@aol.com
website: www.castleviewinverness.co.uk

INVERNESS

Mrs Margaret Campbell, Bay View, Westhill, By Inverness IV2 5BP (01463 790386). Bay View is set in a rural area on famous Culloden Moor, offering comfortable homely accommodation in one twin-bedded room with en suite shower, one double room with en suite bathroom, and one double room with private bathroom. An excellent touring base for the Highlands of Scotland and many famous historic sites. All home made food, local produce used. Bed and Breakfast from £20. **STB** ★★★ *B&B*.
website: www.bayviewguest.com

INVERNESS

Mrs E. MacKenzie, The Whins, 114 Kenneth Street, Inverness IV3 5QG (01463 236215). Comfortable, small homely non-smoking accommodation. 10 minutes bus and railway stations, with easy access to many golf courses, walking and cycling areas, and a great base for touring North, East and West by car, rail or bus. Bedrooms have TV, tea making, washbasins and heating off season. Bathroom, shared toilet and shower; £17 per person. Write or phone for full details.

KINGUSSIE

Valerie J. Johnston, Ardselma, The Crescent, Kingussie PH21 1JZ (mobile: 07786 696384). An imposing Victorian villa situated in an elevated position within two acres of private grounds, Ardselma commands magnificent views of the Cairngorm Mountains. Accommodation comprises two family and one double en suite rooms, one twin room with private facilities, and one single and one twin room with shared facilities. TV lounge available with tea/coffee making facilities; central heating. A three minute walk to the high street or to the golf course. Evening meals by prior arrangement, fresh local produce and game our speciality. Packed lunches available. Groups catered for, discounts available. Children and pets welcome. Smoking. Safe cycle storage. Bed and Breakfast from £16 pppn.
e-mail: valeriedunmhor@aol.com

KINGUSSIE

Balcraggan House, Feshiebridge, By Kingussie PH21 1NG (01540 651488). Set in the heart of Cairngorms National Park, Balcraggan House offers a unique setting for a relaxing holiday. Nature lovers can walk through ancient pine woods straight from the front door, with the chance of seeing deer, red squirrel, ospreys and eagles; for mountain bikers there are miles of off-road cycle routes or you can participate in golfing, fishing, sailing, canoeing, skiing, the list is endless. For the less energetic there are lovely car routes to nearby castles, whisky distilleries, wildlife park, Glenmore Forest Park and the reindeer herd for example. Balcraggan has a large double and a twin bedded rooms, both en suite with TV. No smoking, no neighbours. Sorry, no pets. Terms from £27 pppn sharing, £35 pppn single.
e-mail: balcraggan@kincraig.com
website: www.kincraig.com/balcraggan

Highlands South / Lanarkshire **307**

SPEAN BRIDGE

Mr & Mrs P. de Billot, The Braes Guest House, Tirindrish, Spean Bridge PH34 4EU (01397 712437). Panoramic mountain views, hearty home-cooked food and genuine hospitality await you at The Braes, your home away from home. Situated in its own peaceful gardens on the edge of Spean Bridge, The Braes provides an ideal base from which to explore the magnificent Highland countryside, enjoy a variety of outdoor activities, or simply relax and unwind at any time of year. Your hosts, Philippe and Teresa se Billot, pride themselves on offering a friendly and relaxing atmosphere and delicious, varied meals using local Highland produce. Five double and one single room, all en suite, one twin with private facilities. Rates from £24 per night, discounts for stays of three days or more. Early breakfast, packed lunches and dinner by arrangement, special diets catered for. Guests' lounge. Drying facilities. Major credit cards accepted. See our website for more details and photos! We look forward to welcoming you. COMPLETELY NON-SMOKING. **STB** ★★★ *GUEST HOUSE, WALKERS AND CYCLISTS WELCOME.*
e-mail: enquiry@thebraes.co.uk   website: www.thebraes.co.uk

TOMATIN

Robert Coupar and Lesley Smithers, Glenan Lodge (Licensed), Tomatin IV13 7YT (0845 6445793; Fax: 0845 6445794). The Glenan Lodge is a typical Scottish Lodge situated in the midst of the Monadhliath Mountains in the valley of the Findhorn River, yet only one mile from the A9. It offers typical Scottish hospitality, home cooking, warmth and comfort. The seven bedrooms, including two family rooms, are all en suite, with central heating, tea-making facilities and colour TV. There is a large comfortable lounge and a homely dining room. The licensed bar is well stocked with local malts for the guests. Glenan Lodge caters for the angler, birdwatcher, hillwalker, stalker and tourist alike whether passing through or using as a base. Open all year round. Bed and Breakfast; Dinner optional. Non-smoking. Credit cards accepted. **AA** ♦♦♦
e-mail: glenanlodgecouk@hotmail.com   website: www.glenanlodge.co.uk

Lanarkshire

AIRDRIE

The Knight's Rest, 150 Clark Street, Airdrie ML6 6DZ (01236 606193). A recently renovated Victorian villa comprising four double and one twin bedroom, all en suite, with tea/coffee making facilities, shaver points and TV; hairdryer available. The Knight's Rest is the closest B&B to Airdrie town centre and is a mere stroll from shops, pubs and various restaurants. Situated only two miles from the M8 and five minutes' walk to a direct rail link to the many and varied attractions in Glasgow. Perfectly positioned for both business visitors and tourists exploring the Clyde Valley or revisiting their roots. Your hostess, Jess, fully understands the travellers' needs and you can be assured of a traditional warm Scottish welcome and the heartiest of breakfasts. Central heating throughout. Private parking. Non-smoking. *WELCOME HOST.*
e-mail: knightsinairdrie@aol.com

Lanarkshire

HAMILTON
Avonbridge Hotel, Carlisle Road, Hamilton ML3 7DB (01698 420525; Fax: 01698 427326). The Avonbridge Hotel is family-owned, and we try to make our guests feel at home from the moment they arrive. Bedrooms are furnished to the highest standards, with satellite TV, hairdryers etc. La Gran Sala Restaurant offers a choice of à la carte or table d'hôte menus; Bar Milano and The Conservatory are sophisticated settings in which to enjoy fine food and wines. Wedding and other functions expertly catered for. Conveniently located just outside Glasgow, and only 30 minutes' drive from Edinburgh. **STB/AA/RAC ★★★**
e-mail: enquiries@avonbridge-hotel.com
website: www.avonbridge-hotel.com

LANARK
Mrs Margaret Findlater, Jerviswood Mains, Cleghorn Road, Lanark ML11 7RL (01555 663987). Warm hospitality is offered in this early 19th century farmhouse. Jerviswood Mains Farm is located only one mile from Lanark on the A706, heading northwards. We combine old world charm with modern amenities and provide good food in a relaxed atmosphere. The unique 1758 industrial village of New Lanark (World Heritage Site) and many other places of historic interest are located nearby. An equal distance to Edinburgh and Glasgow, both only 30 minutes drive. This four-star Bed and Breakfast is an excellent touring base. We look forward to your visit. Bed and Breakfast from £25 per person per night double/twin, from £30 single occupancy.
STB ★★★★ *B&B*.
e-mail: jerviswoodmains@aol.com
website: www.jerviswoodmains.co.uk

LESMAHAGOW
Mrs I.H. McInally, Dykecroft Farm, Kirkmuirhill, Lesmahagow ML11 0JQ (Tel & Fax: 01555 892226). A modern farmhouse bungalow on Dykecroft Farm, set in lovely surroundings in a rural area on the B7086 (old A726) and within easy reach of the M74, making it the ideal stop between north and south; also convenient for Glasgow and Prestwick airports. Centrally situated for touring Glasgow, Edinburgh, Ayr, Stirling and New Lanark - all within one hour's drive. Nearby is Strathclyde Country Park with all watersports activities; other sporting facilities within two miles include sports centre, golf, fishing, quad bikes, rifle and clay pigeon shooting, and swimming. Guests will enjoy the open fires in our TV lounge and the good breakfasts; tea making facilities in all rooms. A warm and friendly welcome awaits all guests. Directions: from south leave M74 at Junction 10, from north leave M74 at Junction 9, then take B7078 onto B7086 for one and a half miles, bungalow is on the left past Boghead. **STB ★★** *B&B*, **AA ♦♦♦**
e-mail: Dykecroft.bandb@tiscali.co.uk   website: www.Dykecroftfarm.co.uk

---

FHG
·K·U·P·E·R·A·R·D·

Looking for Holiday Accommodation?
for details of hundreds of properties throughout the UK visit:
www.holidayguides.com

Perth & Kinross

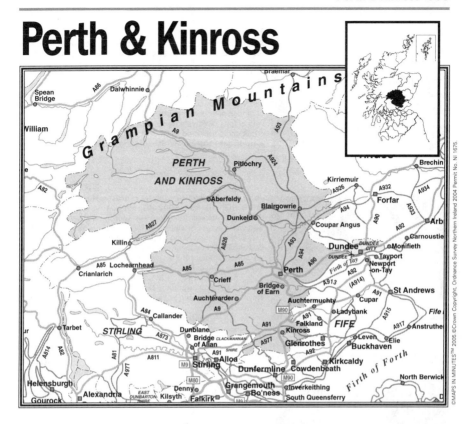

BLAIRGOWRIE

Mrs Morag Houstoun, Glenkilrie, Blacklunans, Blairgowrie PH10 7LR (Tel & Fax:01250 882241). Set in its own grounds on a working hill farm 13 miles north of Blairgowrie on the main A93. Glenkilrie is an ideal touring base wwith Perth, Pitlochry, Braemar, Kirriemuir and the Angus Glens all within easy reach. Outdoor activities in the area include hill walking, fishing, pony trekking, hang gliding, skiing and golfing. Accommodation comprises two double rooms, one twin room. All en suite. Terms from £25. **STB ★★★** *B&B*
e-mail: info@glenkilrie.co.uk
website: www.glenkilrie.co.uk

Free or reduced rate entry to Holiday Visits and Attractions
see our READERS' OFFER VOUCHERS
on pages 53-90

A useful index of towns/counties appears at the back of this book

CALLANDER

Annfield Guest House, North Church Street, Callander FK17 8EG (01877 330204; Fax: 01877 330674). Annfield is situated in a quiet spot a few minutes' walk from shops and restaurants. Ideal as an overnight stop or as a centre for visiting the surrounding Scottish Highlands. You will receive the warmest of welcomes from your hosts, Janet and Mike Greenfield, to their fine Victorian family home. All bedrooms have en suite facilities or private bathroom, hospitality tray and hairdryer. Guests' lounge with colour TV. Private parking. Open all year. No smoking. Major credit cards accepted. **STB ★★★** *B&B*. **AA ♦♦♦♦**
e-mail: janet-greenfield@amserve.com

CRIANLARICH

John and Janice Christie, Inverardran House, Crianlarich FK20 8QS (01838 300240). Set just outside the village of Crianlarich, Inverardran House is sited in an elevated position with views across Strathfillan to Ben Challum. This property offers excellent fishing, walking and touring prospects. We can offer you Bed and Breakfast accommodation for up to eight people in three en suite double rooms and one twin room with a private bathroom. Tea/coffee making facilities in the rooms. Open all year. Prices from £18 to £22 per person per night based on two sharing, £8 surcharge for a single person. Discounts for longer stays. Evening meals and packed lunches on request. **STB ★★★** *GUEST HOUSE.*

e-mail: janice@inverardran.demon.co.uk   website: www.inverardran.demon.co.uk

See also Colour Display Advertisement

CRIEFF

Mr and Mrs Clifford, Merlindale, Perth Road, Crieff PH7 3EQ (Tel & Fax: 01764 655205). Merlindale is a luxurious Georgian house situated close to the town centre. All bedrooms are en suite (two with sunken bathrooms) and have tea/coffee making facilities. We have a jacuzzi available plus garden, ample parking and satellite television. We also have a Scottish library for the use of our guests. Cordon Bleu cooking is our speciality. A warm welcome awaits you in this non-smoking house. Terms from £45 Bed and Breakfast single, £30 double/twin. Dinner from £20. Open February to December. **STB ★★★★** *B&B*, **AA ♦♦♦♦**

CRIEFF

Glenearn House, Perth Road, Crieff PH7 3EQ (01764 650000). A warm welcome awaits visitors to this beautifully kept Victorian house situated within half a mile of Crieff town centre, the Hydro Hotel and Crieff Golf Club. The house offers spacious, finely furnished accommodation with TV, video recorder, tea/coffee trays, trouser press and radio alarm in all bedrooms. Video and book libraries are available to guests. For further comfort a guest lounge is provided. Glenearn is set back from the road and provides generous private car parking and well maintained gardens. Terms from £40 Bed and Breakfast single, £30 double/twin. Open all year. **STB ★★★★** *GUEST HOUSE.*
e-mail: bookings@glenearnhouse.f9.co.uk
website: www.glenearnhouse.com

FHG Guides Ltd publish a wide range of holiday accommodation guides – for details see the back of this book

Perth & Kinross 311

DUNKELD

Birnam Guest House, 4 Murthly Terrace, Birnam, Dunkeld PH8 0BG (Tel & Fax: 01350 727201). A warm Scottish welcome awaits you at the Birnam Guest House, situated in the heart of beautiful Perthshire. Owned and run by Linda and Donald Morton, the guest house forms part of a terraced Victorian villa and has been upgraded to accommodation of a very high standard, including delightful en suite bedrooms, cosy dining room and conservatory lounge overlooking the gardens and private car park. Within easy reach of Glasgow, Edinburgh, Inverness, Aberdeen and Dundee, Birnam Guest House is surrounded by some of Scotland's most beautiful scenery and is the ideal base for those looking for a relaxing short break; golf breaks arranged. Bed and Breakfast from £26 per person per night, £35 single occupancy. **VisitScotland ★★★**

e-mail: birnamguesthouse@hotmail.com   website: www.birnamguesthouse.co.uk

KIRKMICHAEL

See also Colour Display Advertisement

Log Cabin Hotel, Kirkmichael PH10 7NA (01250 881288; Fax: 01250 881206). Unique, family-run hotel, set in the picturesque hills of Perthshire, less than half-an-hour from Glenshee, Pitlochry and Blairgowrie. The bar is fully licensed, with a good range of malt whiskies; guests can enjoy panoramic views of Strathardle from the dining room. All bedrooms are en suite. A good central base for touring Perthshire and beyond; many golf courses are within easy reach; skiing at Glenshee in the winter; ideal for walking holidays. Please call for brochure or further information. Pets and children welcome. Bed and Breakfast from £25 pppn. **STB ★★** *HOTEL.*
e-mail: wendy@logcabinhotel.co.uk
website: www.logcabinhotel.co.uk

MUTHILL

See also Colour Display Advertisement

Muthill Village Hotel, 6 Willoughby Street, Muthill PH5 2AB (01764 681451). Ideally situated at the Gateway to the Highlands, yet only one hour from Glasgow or Edinburgh, and three miles south of Crieff, ideal for walking, golf and fishing. Dating from 1700, this charming family-run Inn offers excellent accommodation, an atmospheric dining experience at Willoughby's Restaurant or supper in the Bothy Bar with its fine range of real ales. We are listed in the Good Beer Guide, Good Pub Guide and Rough Guide to Britain and many more publications. **STB ★★★** *INN.*
e-mail: bookings@muthillvillagehotel.com
website: www.muthillvillagehotel.com

STANLEY

Mrs Ann Guthrie, Newmill Farm, Stanley PH1 4QD (01738 828281). This 330 acre farm is situated on the A9, six miles north of Perth. Accommodation comprises twin and double en suite rooms and a family room with private bathroom; lounge, sittingroom, diningroom; bathroom, shower room and toilet. Bed and Breakfast from £22; Evening Meal on request. The warm welcome and supper of excellent home baking is inclusive. Reductions and facilities for children. Pets accepted. The numerous castles and historic ruins around Perth are testimony to Scotland's turbulent past. Situated in the area known as "The Gateway to the Highlands" the farm is ideally placed for those seeking some of the best unspoilt scenery in Western Europe. Many famous golf courses and trout rivers in the Perth area. **STB ★★★** *B&B.*

e-mail: guthrienewmill@sol.co.uk   website: www.newmillfarm.co.uk

Renfrewshire

See also Colour Display Advertisement

PAISLEY

Ardgowan House, 92-94 Renfrew Road, Paisley PA3 4BJ (Tel & Fax: 0141-889 4763). David and Gail are pleased to welcome you to our two adjacent, family-run guesthouses in the heart of Paisley, Scotland's largest town. Enjoy a drink from our licensed bar in the secluded, peaceful gardens or relax in our delightful summer house. We have two levels of accommodation available, so there is something for everyone, from the two-star Ardgowan guesthouse to the more upmarket Townhouse Hotel. Both have secure storage facilities for cyclists and hikers and free off-street parking. Situated within one mile of Glasgow International Airport, and only ten minutes from Glasgow City Centre, the excellent transport links allow easy access to Loch Lomond, Robert Burns country, Edinburgh and the Highlands and Islands. Please see our website for further details.
website: www.ardgowanhouse.com

Useful Guidance for Guests and Hosts

Every year literally thousands of holidays, short breaks and overnight stops are arranged through our guides, the vast majority without any problems at all. In a handful of cases, however, difficulties do arise about bookings, which often could have been prevented from the outset.

It is important to remember that when accommodation has been booked, both parties – guests and hosts – have entered into a form of contract. We hope that the following points will provide helpful guidance.

- When enquiring about accommodation, be as precise as possible. Give exact dates, numbers in your party and the ages of any children.
- State the number and type of rooms wanted and also what catering you require – bed and breakfast, full board etc. Make sure that the position about evening meals is clear – and about pets, reductions for children or any other special points.
- Read our reviews carefully to ensure that the proprietors you are going to contact can supply what you want. Ask for a letter confirming all arrangements, if possible.
- If you have to cancel, do so as soon as possible. Proprietors do have the right to retain deposits and under certain circumstances to charge for cancelled holidays if adequate notice is not given and they cannot re-let the accommodation.
- Give details about your facilities and about any special conditions. Explain your deposit system clearly and arrangements for cancellations, charges etc. and whether or not your terms include VAT.
- If for any reason you are unable to fulfil an agreed booking without adequate notice, you may be under an obligation to arrange suitable alternative accommodation or to make some form of compensation.

Stirling & The Trossachs

BLAIRLOGIE

Mrs Margaret Logan, Blairmains Farm, Manor Loan, Blairlogie, Stirling FK9 5QA (01259 761338). Working farm. Charming, traditional stone farmhouse set in attractive gardens on a working farm. Adjacent to a picturesque conservation village and close to the Wallace Monument and Stirling University. Three-and-a-half miles from Stirling. Edinburgh airport is 30 minutes' drive and Glasgow airport 45 minutes. Ideal base for touring and walking. Accommodation is in one double and two twin rooms with shared bathroom. Very comfortable TV lounge. Ample private parking at this non-smoking establishment. Children welcome. Sorry no pets. Bed and Breakfast terms – double or twin £22; single £22 to £25. Room only £18. A warm Scottish welcome awaits you.

See also Colour Display Advertisement

CALLANDER

Riverview Guest House, Leny Road, Callander FK17 8AL (01877 330635; Fax: 01877 339386). Excellent accommodation in the Trossachs area which forms the most beautiful part of Scotland's first National Park. Ideal centre for walking and cycling holidays with cycle storage being available. GUEST HOUSE - all rooms en suite, TV and tea making facilities. Bed and Breakfast from £24. Low season and long stay discounts available. Private parking. SELF CATERING - stone cottages sleep three or four from £150 per week. Call Drew or Kathleen Little for details. Sorry no smoking and no pets. **STB ★★★ B&B, STB ★★★★ SELF-CATERING.**
e-mail: drew@visitcallander.co.uk
website: www.visitcallander.co.uk

FALKIRK

Betty and Bede Ward, Ashbank Bed & Breakfast, 105 Main Street, Redding, Falkirk FK2 9UQ (01324 716649; Fax: 01324 712431). On the east side of the town, Ashbank is a detached stone house (100 years old), situated within pleasant gardens on all sides. Off-road parking and good views to Braveheart Country, together with Scottish hospitality await you at Ashbank. Accommodation includes two double en suite rooms and two twin en suite rooms. Each room has TV with four channels, remote-control; tea/coffee facilities. No smoking or pets. Golf, tennis, swimming, hillwalking, restaurants, etc. all nearby. Near trains and motorway. Visit the Falkirk Wheel, Calendar House and Linlithgow Palace. We will endeavour to make your stay at Ashbank as comfortable as possible. **STB ★★★★ B&B. AA ♦♦♦♦**
e-mail: ashbank@guest-house.freeserve.co.uk
website: www.bandbfalkirk.com

•••some fun days out in STIRLING & THE TROSSACHS

The Falkirk Wheel, Falkirk • 01324 619888 / 08700 500208 • www.thefalkirkwheel.co.uk
Barbara Davidson Pottery, Larbert • 01324 554430 • www.barbara-davidson.com
Bannockburn Heritage Centre, Stirling • 01786 812664 • www.nts.org.uk
Motormania, Tillicoultry • 01259 755183 • www.sterlingmotormania.co.uk

Scottish Islands

Barra

NORTHBAY

Airds Guest House, 244 Bruernish, Northbay, Isle of Barra HS9 5UY (01871 890720). A warm welcome awaits you at Airds, a spacious, family-run house, purpose built in 2003. Airds is situated at the north end of the island of Barra, close to the new ferry terminal at Ardmhor, and near Barra's unique airport, where the plane lands on the cockle strand. Accommodation comprises two twin rooms and one double/family room, all en suite; oil central heating, tea/coffee making facilities, and colour TV. Large TV lounge with conservatory (dining area) overlooking Loch na h-Obe. B&B £25pp; packed lunches available. Open all year round. Car parking available. **STB ★★★** B&B, STB DISABLED AWARD, CATEGORY 3.
e-mail: airdsbarra@aol.com
website: www.airdsbarra.co.uk

Orkney Islands

KIRKWALL

John D. Webster, Lav'rockha Guest House, Inganess Road, Kirkwall KW15 1SP (Tel & Fax: 01856 876103). Situated a short walk from the Highland Park Distillery and Visitor Centre, and within reach of all local amenities. Lav'rockha is the perfect base for exploring and discovering Orkney. We offer high quality accommodation at affordable rates. All our rooms have en suite WC and power shower, tea/coffee tray, hairdryer, radio alarm clock and remote-control colour TV. Those with young children will appreciate our family room with reduced children's rates, children's meals and child minding service. We also have facilities for the disabled, with full unassisted wheelchair access from our private car park. All our meals are prepared to a high standard using fresh, local produce as much as possible. Bed and Breakfast from £22 per person. Special winter break prices available. **STB ★★★★** GUEST HOUSE, WINNER OF BEST B&B ORKNEY; FOOD AWARDS, TASTE OF SCOTLAND ACCREDITED.
e-mail: lavrockha@orkney.com   **website: www.lavrockha.co.uk**

Skye

PORTREE

The Royal Hotel, Portree IV51 9BU (01478 612525; Fax: 01478 613198). Set overlooking the picturesque harbour of Portree, The Royal Hotel offers you a quiet, relaxing retreat during your stay on Skye. Recently refurbished, offering new standards in comfort and style. Accommodation consists of 21 well appointed rooms, some equipped to accommodate families, most overlooking the harbour and featuring private bathroom facilities and colour TV. Room service is available as well as a fitness centre and sauna for guests to use. The Royal Hotel offers a wide and varied menu serving sea food, lamb, venison and tender Highland beef. Vegetarians are also catered for. There is something for everyone; from walking, climbing and watersports. Special minimum 2-day Short Break package. **STB ★★★** HOTEL, **RAC ★★**
e-mail: info@royal-hotel-skye.com
website: www.royal-hotel-skye.com

Wales

Bodnant Gardens, North Wales

Ratings You Can Trust

ENGLAND

The **English Tourism Council** (now **VisitBritain**) has joined with the **AA** and **RAC** to create an easily understood quality rating for serviced accommodation, giving a clear guide of what to expect.

HOTELS are given a rating from One to Five **Stars** – the more Stars, the higher the quality and the greater the range of facilities and level of services provided.

GUEST ACCOMMODATION, which includes guest houses, bed and breakfasts, inns and farmhouses, is rated from One to Five **Diamonds**. Progressively higher levels of quality and customer care must be provided for each one of the One to Five Diamond ratings.

HOLIDAY PARKS, TOURING PARKS and CAMPING PARKS are now also assessed using **Stars**. Standards of quality range from a One Star (acceptable) to a Five Star (exceptional) park.

Look out also for the new **SELF-CATERING** Star ratings. The more **Stars** (from One to Five) awarded to an establishment, the higher the levels of quality you can expect. Establishments at higher rating levels also have to meet some additional requirements for facilities.

VisitBritain has launched a new **Quality Accredited Agency Standard**. Agencies who are awarded the Quality Accredited Agency marque by VisitBritain are recognised as offering good customer service and peace of mind, following an assement of their office polices, practices and procedures.

SCOTLAND

Star Quality Grades will reflect the most important aspects of a visit, such as the warmth of welcome, efficiency and friendliness of service, the quality of the food and the cleanliness and condition of the furnishings, fittings and decor.

THE MORE STARS,

THE HIGHER THE STANDARDS.

The description, such as Hotel, Guest House, Bed and Breakfast, Lodge, Holiday Park, Self-catering etc tells you the type of property and style of operation.

WALES

Places which score highly will have an especially welcoming atmosphere and pleasing ambience, high levels of comfort and guest care, and attractive surroundings enhanced by thoughtful design and attention to detail

STAR QUALITY GUIDE FOR

HOTELS, GUEST HOUSES AND FARMHOUSES
SELF-CATERING ACCOMMODATION
(Cottages, Apartments, Houses)
CARAVAN HOLIDAY HOME PARKS
(Holiday Parks, Touring Parks, Camping Parks)

★★★★★	*Exceptional quality*
★★★★	*Excellent quality*
★★★	*Very good quality*
★★	*Good quality*
★	*Fair to good quality*

In England, Scotland and Wales, all graded properties are inspected annually by Tourist Authority trained Assessors.

WALES
Anglesey & Gwynedd

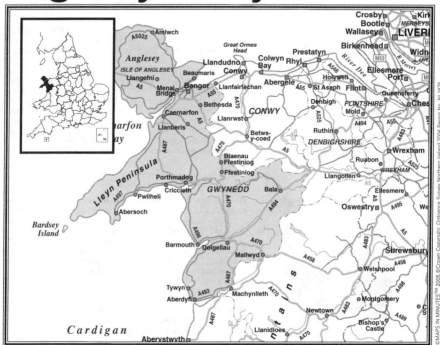

ANGLESEY
Richard and Shirley Murphy, Ingledene, Ravenspoint Road, Trearddur Bay LL65 2YU (Tel & Fax: 01407 861026).
Ingledene, a large Edwardian seaside home with magnificent views across Trearddur Bay, provides a warm and friendly welcome for your stay. Spacious twin/double rooms (two en suite), most with sea views. Relax and watch the glorious sunsets and wake up to the sound of the waves. All rooms are centrally heated with colour TV and tea/coffee making facilities. Parking is to the rear of the property with ample space for boats, etc. Holyhead ferry terminal is only 10 minutes away, with day trips to Ireland from £12. Bed and Breakfast from £22.50 per person. Open all year. Self-catering cottage (sleeps 2+2) also available.
e-mail: info@ingledene.co.uk
website: www.ingledene.co.uk

Free or reduced rate entry to Holiday Visits and Attractions – see our READERS' OFFER VOUCHERS on pages 53-90

BALA

Mrs C. A. Morris, Tai'r Felin Farm, Frongoch, Bala LL23 7NS (01678 520763). Tai'r Felin Farm is a working farm, situated three miles north of Bala (A4212 and B4501). Double and twin bedrooms available with beverage tray and clock radio. Beamed lounge with colour TV, diningroom. Central heating. Excellent base for touring Snowdonia National Park, watersports, walking, fishing, etc. National White Water Centre one mile. Hearty breakfast. Recommended for excellent cooking and friendly atmosphere. Relax and enjoy a homely welcome. Bed and Breakfast from £22 to £24. Walkers and cyclists welcome. Car essential. **WTB ★★** *FARM.*

CRICCIETH

Mrs Parker, Seaspray, 4 Marine Terrace, Criccieth LL52 0EF (01766 522373). Seaspray is a large non-smoking Victorian terrace house, situated on the sea front, west side of Criccieth Castle on the Lleyn Peninsula. Some rooms are en suite, others have private facilities, affording sea views across Cardigan Bay. Evening meals are available on request at breakfast, vegetarian meals an option. Pets are welcome. Criccieth is only a short distance away from the Snowdonia National Park, which boasts some of the most beautiful and spectacular scenery in the country. Ample facilities are available for golfers, sailors, fishermen and ramblers. B&B from £22 pppn. **WTB ★★★** *B&B.*
website: www.seasprayguesthouse.co.uk

DOLGELLAU

Mr and Mrs J. S. Bamford, Ivy House, Finsbury Square, Dolgellau LL40 1RF (01341 422535; Fax: 01341 422689). A country town guesthouse offering a welcoming atmosphere and good homemade food. Guest accommodation consists of six double rooms, four with en suite toilet facilities, all with colour TV, tea/coffee making facilities and hair dryer. The diningroom, which is licensed, has a choice of menu, including vegetarian dishes. The lounge has tourist information literature and there are maps available to borrow. Dolgellau is an ideal touring, walking and mountain biking region in the southern area of the Snowdonia National Park. Bed and Breakfast from £21, en suite from £27.
WTB ★★ *GUEST HOUSE,* **AA ♦♦♦**
e-mail: marg.bamford@btconnect.com
website: www.ukworld.net/ivyhouse

DOLGELLAU

Mrs G.D. Evans, "Y Goedlan", Brithdir, Dolgellau LL40 2RN (Tel & Fax: 01341 423131). Guests are welcome at "Y Goedlan" from February to October. This old Vicarage with adjoining farm offers peaceful accommodation in pleasant rural surroundings. Three miles from Dolgellau on the B4416 road, good position for interesting walks (Torrent, 400 yards from the house), beaches, mountains, narrow gauge railways and pony trekking. All bedrooms are large and spacious; one double, one twin and one family room, all with colour TV, tea/coffee facilities and washbasins. Bathroom, two toilets; shower; lounge with colour TV; separate tables in dining room. Reduced rates for children under 10 years. Central heating. Car essential, parking. Comfort, cleanliness and personal attention assured, with a good hearty breakfast; Bed and Breakfast from £20 per night; single occupancy from £23 per night. **WTB ★★★** *B&B.*

Readers are requested to mention this FHG publication when seeking accommodation

Anglesey & Gwynedd 319

LLANERCH-Y-MEDD

Mrs Nia Bown, Tre-Wyn, Maenaddwyn, Llanerch-y-Medd, Isle of Anglesey LL71 8AE (01248 470875). Why not spend your holiday on a traditional Welsh working farm? Tre-wyn is a lovely, spacious farmhouse and offers excellent accommodation. Bedrooms are en suite, with TV and hospitality tray. The dining room and lounge have wonderful views across the garden and rural countryside. Good base for birdwatchers, cyclists, walkers and visiting tourist attractions. Non-smoking. Open April to October. **WTB** ★★★★ *B&B*.

TALYLLYN

Gwesty Minffordd Hotel, Talyllyn LL36 9AJ (01654 761665; Fax: 01654 761517). Small 17th century Drovers' Inn at the base of Cader Idris (2697ft), ideal as a centre for touring. Enjoy a Minffordd dinner, cooked on an Aga using local Welsh produce, organic vegetables, Welsh flavouring. Residential and restaurant licence. Seven bedrooms all en suite, two on the ground floor; non-smoking. Pets welcome; no children under 12. Dolgellau six miles, Machynlleth eight. **WTB** ★★★ *HOTEL*, **AA** ★★, *FOUNDER MEMBER TASTE OF WALES, GOOD FOOD GUIDE 2000*.
e-mail: hotel@minffordd.com
website: www.minffordd.com

TYWYN

Mrs Gweniona Pugh, Eisteddfa, Abergynolwyn, Tywyn LL36 9UP (01654 782385; Fax: 01654 782228). Eisteddfa offers you the comfort of a newly-built bungalow on the Tan-y-coed Ucha Farm, situated adjacent to the farmhouse but with all the benefits of Bed and Breakfast accommodation. The bungalow, which has been designed to accommodate disabled guests, is conveniently situated between Abergynolwyn and Dolgoch Falls with Talyllyn Narrow Gauge Railway running through the farmland. Three bedrooms, two en suite and the third with a shower and washbasin suitable for a disabled person. The toilet is located in the adjacent bathroom. Tea/coffee tray and TV are provided in the bedrooms as are many other extras. We also cater for Coeliac Diets. **WTB** ★★★ *B&B*, **AA** ♦♦♦♦

Llanberis Lake Railway
Llanberis, Gwynedd
See our **READERS' OFFER VOUCHER** for details of free or reduced rate entry

---

Pili Palas - Butterfly Palace
Menai Bridge, Anglesey
See our **READERS' OFFER VOUCHER** for details of free or reduced rate entry

North Wales

BETWS-Y-COED
Jim and Lilian Boughton, Bron Celyn Guest House, Lôn Muriau, Llanrwst Road, Betws-y-Coed LL24 0HD (01690 710333; Fax: 01690 710111). A warm welcome awaits you at this delightful guest house overlooking the Gwydyr Forest and Llugwy/Conwy Valleys and village of Betws-y-Coed in Snowdonia National Park. Ideal centre for touring, walking, climbing, fishing and golf. Also excellent overnight stop en route for Holyhead ferries. Easy walk into village and close to Conwy/Swallow Falls and Fairy Glen. Most rooms en suite, all with colour TV and beverage makers. Lounge. Full central heating. Garden. Car park. Open all year. Full hearty breakfast, packed meals, evening meals - special diets catered for. Bed and Breakfast from £24 to £30, reduced rates for children under 12 years. Special out of season breaks. WTB ★★★ *GUEST HOUSE.*
e-mail: welcome@broncelyn.co.uk
website: www.broncelyn.co.uk

See also Colour Display Advertisement

BETWS-Y-COED
Brian and Enid Youe, Fairy Glen Hotel, Beaver Bridge, Betws-y-Coed LL24 0SH (01690 710269). Fairy Glen Hotel offers you a warm and friendly welcome, comfortable accommodation and excellent home-cooked food, in a relaxed and convivial atmosphere. All our rooms are well equipped with central heating, colour TV, alarm clock-radio, hairdryer and tea/ coffee making facilities. We have a TV lounge, and cosy licensed bar for our residents to relax in. Our private car park is for guests only. Evening meals available from £15 per person. Bed and Breakfast from £26 per person per night. WTB ★★ *HOTEL*, AA ★★
e-mail: fairyglen@youe.fsworld.co.uk
website: www.fairyglenhotel.co.uk

North Wales 321

BETWS-Y-COED

FRON HEULOG COUNTRY HOUSE
Betws-y-Coed, North Wales LL24 0BL
Tel: 01690 710736
e-mail: jean@fronheulog.co.uk
website: www.fronheulog.co.uk

"The Country House in the Village"

Betws-y-Coed – "Heart of Snowdonia"

You are invited to enjoy real hospitality at Fron Heulog; an elegant Victorian stone-built house with excellent non-smoking accommodation, comfortable bedrooms, all with en suite bathrooms, spacious lounges, a pleasant dining room, and full central heating. Enjoy the friendly atmosphere with hosts' local knowledge and home cooking. Sorry, no small children; no pets.

From the centre of Betws-y-Coed turn off busy A5 road over picturesque Pont-y-Pair bridge (B5106), then immediately turn left. Fron Heulog is 150 yards up ahead facing south, in quiet, peaceful, wooded, riverside scenery.

Welcome! – Croeso! Bed & Breakfast £25-£35 pppn
Holiday? Short Break? Pleased to quote.
AA ♦♦♦♦, Recommended by Which?
Jean & Peter Whittingham welcome house guests

See also Colour Advertisement

BETWS-Y-COED

Mrs Florence Jones, Maes Gwyn Farm, Pentrefoelas, Betws-y-Coed LL24 0LR (01690 770668). Maes Gwyn is a mixed farm of 90-97 hectares, situated in lovely quiet countryside, about one mile from the A5, six miles from the famous Betws-y-Coed. The sea and Snowdonia Mountains about 20 miles. Very good centre for touring North Wales, many well-known places of interest. House dates back to 1665. It has one double and one family bedrooms with washbasins and tea/coffee making facilities; bathroom with shower, toilet; lounge with colour TV and diningroom. Children and Senior Citizens are welcome at reduced rates and pets are permitted. Car essential, ample parking provided. Good home cooking. Six miles to bus/railway terminal. Open May/November for Bed and Breakfast from £22. SAE, please, for details.
e-mail: fjones@maesgwynwales.wanadoo.co.uk

BETWS-Y-COED

Mark and Joan Edwards, Bryn Bella Guest House, Lôn Muriau, Llanrwst Road, Betws-y-Coed LL24 0HD (Tel & Fax: 01690 710627). Bryn Bella is a small but select Victorian guest house enjoying an elevated position overlooking the beautiful village of Betws-y-Coed and the surrounding mountains of the Snowdonia National Park. All rooms are beautifully furnished and have en suite shower facilities. All rooms have colour TV, clock/radio/alarm, microwave, fridge, tea/coffee making facilities and hairdryer. The house enjoys glorious views of the village and surrounding mountains and has car parking for every room. Secure garaging for motorcycles and mountain bikes is also available. Free pick-up service from the local railway station. Non-smoking throughout. Bed and Breakfast from £25 per person per night. Open all year. On-line booking. WTB ★★★★ *GUEST HOUSE*, **AA** *FOUR RED DIAMONDS*.

e-mail: welcome@bryn-bella.co.uk
website: www.bryn-bella.co.uk

Visit the FHG website
www.holidayguides.com
for details of the wide choice of accommodation featured in the full range of FHG titles

BETWS-Y-COED

Mrs E.A. Jones, Pant Glas, Padoc, Pentrefoelas Road, Betws-y-Coed LL24 0PG (01690 770248). Peaceful and quiet, but with a friendly atmosphere, this sheep farm of 181 acres, with scenic views, is situated five miles from Betws-y-Coed. Ideal for touring, within easy reach of Snowdon, Bodnant Gardens, Caernarvon Castle, Llandudno, Black Rock Sands, Ffestiniog Railway, Llechwedd Slate Mines, Swallow and Conwy Falls and woollen mills. Accommodation comprises one double and one twin bedroom, both with washbasins and tea/coffee making facilities; bath and shower, two toilets. Use of colour TV lounge. Sorry no pets. Car essential, parking for three/four cars. Bed and Breakfast from £18. Open Easter to October.

CHESTER (near)

Mrs Christine Whale, Brookside House, Brookside Lane, Northop Hall, Mold CH7 6HN (01244 821146). Relax and enjoy the hospitality of our recently refurbished 18th century Welsh stone cottage. The home-from-home accommodation offers a double, twin or family room, en suite upon request. All rooms have colour TV and tea-making facilities. Within a short walk the village has an excellent restaurant and two pubs (one of which serves bar meals). Suitable for touring North Wales and Chester or just a short break away from it all. Bed and Breakfast from £35 per night single, £49 per night double. **WTB ★★★** *B&B*.
e-mail: christine@brooksidehouse.fsnet.co.uk
website: www.brooksidehouse.fsnet.co.uk/

CONWY

Glyn Uchaf, Conwy Old Road, Dwygyfylchi, Penmaenmawr, Conwy LL34 6YS (Tel & Fax: 01492 623737). Enjoy a quiet and relaxing break at this old mill house set in its own 11 acres complete with nature pond and lake, ideal centre for touring the Snowdonia National Park. Accommodation consists of three beautifully appointed bedrooms with all modern facilities, and all en suite. There is also a private lounge with widescreen TV and Sky satellite and a wide selection of videos etc. Children and pets welcome. The village is only three minutes away with good pubs and good food. Golf, fishing and the blue flag beach approximately five minutes away. Guests have ample secure off-road parking. Bed and Breakfast from £30 per person per night. **WTB ★★★**
e-mail: john@baxter6055.freeserve.co.uk

CONWY

Glan Heulog Guest House, Llanrwst Road, Conwy LL32 8LT (01492 593845). Spacious Victorian house, tastefully decorated. With off-road parking. Short walk from historic castle and town walls of Conwy. Ideally situated for touring Snowdonia and North Wales with its many attractions. We have a selection of twin, double and family rooms with en suite facilities, TV and tea/coffee making facilities. There is a large garden with seating to enjoy the far-reaching views. Children welcome. Pets by arrangement. Vegetarians catered for. Bed and Breakfast from £22–£28 per person per night. **WTB ★★★** *GUEST HOUSE*, **AA ♦♦♦♦**
e-mail: glanheulog@no1guesthouse.freeserve.co.uk
website: www.walesbandb.co.uk

The FHG Directory of Website Addresses
on pages 339-370 is a useful quick reference guide for holiday accommodation with e-mail and/or website details

North Wales 323

CONWY
Park Hill Hotel/Gwesty Bryn Parc, Llanrwst Road, Betws-y-Coed, Conwy LL24 0HD (Tel & Fax: 01690 710540). OUR HOTEL IS YOUR CASTLE. Family-run country house hotel. Ideally situated in Snowdonia National Park. Breathtaking views of Conwy/Llugwy Valleys. Renowned for excellent service, cuisine and its teddy bear collection. Indoor heated swimming pool with sauna free and exclusively for our guests. Secluded free car park. Golf course and village within six minutes' walking distance. Walkers welcome; guided walks on request. Free shuttle service to nearest railway stations. All our rooms with en suite bathroom facilities, coffee/tea tray, CTV etc. Full cooked English Breakfast. Multilingual staff. Bed and Breakfast from £28 per person per night. **WTB ★★★** *HOTEL*, **AA/RAC ★★**. *SPECIAL HOSPITALITY AWARD. ASHLEY COURTENAY AND WHICH? RECOMMENDED.*
e-mail: welcome@park-hill-hotel.co.uk   website: www.park-hill-hotel.co.uk

LLANDUDNO
Roger and Merril Pitblado, Chilterns for Non-Smokers, 19 Deganwy Avenue, Llandudno LL30 2YB (01492 875457). Catering specifically, and only, for non-smokers, Chilterns is well placed close to the Great Orme, promenade, beach and shops. Our forecourt provides invaluable parking in this beautiful seaside town. We provide Bed and Breakfast accommodation in centrally heated, en suite rooms with king-size beds, hairdryers, alarm clocks, colour TV and beverage trays. Tariff from £20 per person per night. **WTB ★★★** *GUEST HOUSE.*
e-mail: info@chilternsguesthouse.co.uk
website: www.chilternsguesthouse.co.uk

LLANDUDNO
Mrs Ruth Hodkinson, Cranleigh, Great Orme's Road, West Shore, Llandudno LL30 2AR (01492 877688). A comfortable, late Victorian private residence and family home situated on the quieter West Shore of Llandudno. Only yards from beach and magnificent Great Orme Mountain. Parking: no problem. Town centre is a short pleasant walk away. Many places of interest in surrounding area, and opportunities for sports and recreational activities. Excellent home cooked food. Two en suite rooms with bath and wc, both with views of sea and mountains. Conforms to high standards of S.I. 1991/474. Most highly recommended. Bed and Breakfast £20 per person.

RHOS-ON-SEA
Sunnydowns Hotel, Rhos-on-Sea, Colwyn Bay, Conwy LL28 4NU (01492 544256; Fax: 01492 543223). A three star hotel, situated close to the beach and shops, with car park, bar, games room, sauna, restaurant and TV lounge. All rooms en suite with remote-control TV, video and satellite channels, radio, tea/coffee facilities, hairdryer, mini-bar/refrigerator, safe and telephone. The towns of Llandudno, Colwyn Bay and Conwy are only five minutes' drive away and it is just ten minutes to the mountains and castles of Snowdonia. Dogs welcome.
e-mail: sunnydowns-hotel@tinyworld.co.uk
website: www.hotelnorthwales.co.uk

Readers are requested to mention this FHG publication when seeking accommodation

North Wales / Carmarthenshire

TREFRIW

Mrs B. Cole, Glandwr, Trefriw, Near Llanrwst LL27 0JP (01492 640431). Large country house on the outskirts of Trefriw Village overlooking the Conwy River and its Valley, with beautiful views towards the Clwydian Hills. Good touring area; Llanrwst, Betws-y-Coed and Swallow Falls five miles away. Fishing, walking, golfing and pony trekking all close by. Comfortable rooms, lounge with TV, dining room. Good home cooking using local produce whenever possible. Parking. Bed and Breakfast from £25.

Carmarthenshire

CARMARTHEN

Mrs Margaret Thomas, Plas Farm, Llangynog, Carmarthen SA33 5DB (Tel & Fax: 01267 211492). Working farm. "Welcome Host". Situated six miles west of Carmarthen town along the A40 towards St Clears. Quiet location, ideal touring base. Working farm run by the Thomas family for the past 100 years. Very spacious, comfortable farmhouse. All rooms en suite, with tea/coffee making facilities, colour TV and full central heating. TV lounge. Evening meals available at local country inn nearby. Good golf course minutes away. Plas Farm is en route to Fishguard and Pembroke Ferries. Ample safe parking. Bed and Breakfast from £22.50 per person. Children under 16 years sharing family room half price. A warm welcome awaits. **WTB ★★★ FARM.**
website: www.plasfarm.co.uk

please note

All the information in this book is given in good faith in the belief that it is correct. However, the publishers cannot guarantee the facts given in these pages, neither are they responsible for changes in policy, ownership or terms that may take place after the date of going to press. Readers should always satisfy themselves that the facilities they require are available and that the terms, if quoted, still apply.

Ceredigion

See Also Colour Display Advertisement

ABERYSTWYTH

Queensbridge Hotel, The Promenade, Aberystwyth SY23 2DH (01970 612343; Fax: 01970 617452). Aberystwyth, with its award-winning beach, is one of Wales's favourite traditional seaside towns. With many visitor attractions it is the ideal venue for touring North, Mid and South Wales. Situated at the quieter end of Aberystwyth's historic Victorian promenade, overlooking the panoramic sweep of Cardigan Bay, the Queensbridge Hotel offers guests superior comfort in 15 spacious en suite bedrooms, all with colour TV, hospitality tray and telephone. A hearty Welsh breakfast is served in the welcoming Breakfast Room where we pride ourselves on our prompt, efficient service and excellent menu choice. Established 1972 – "Our reputation for comfort and good service remains steadfast". **WTB ★★** *HOTEL,* **AA ★★★, RAC ★★**

The Golf Guide · 2006
Where to Play, Where to Stay

Available from most booksellers, **The Golf Guide, Where to Play, Where to Stay** covers details of every UK golf course – well over 2800 entries – for holiday or business golf. Hundreds of hotel entries offer convenient accommodation, with accompanying details of the courses – the 'pro', par score, length and more. Including holiday golf in Ireland, France, Portugal, Spain, the USA, South Africa and Thailand.

**Only £9.99 from booksellers or direct from the publishers:
FHG GUIDES, Abbey Mill Business Centre, Seedhill,
Paisley PA1 1TJ** *(postage charged outside UK)*
e-mail: admin@fhguides.co.uk • www.holidayguides.com

Felinwynt Rainforest Centre
Cardigan, Ceredigion
See our **READERS' OFFER VOUCHER** for
details of free or reduced rate entry

•••some fun days out in CEREDIGION

Animalarium, Borth • 01970 871224 • www.animalarium.co.uk
New Quay Honey Farm, Llandysul • 01545 560822 • www.thehoneyfarm.co.uk
Llwernog Silver-lead Mine, Ponterwyd • 01545 570823 • www.silverminetours.co.uk

Pembrokeshire

See also Colour Display Advertisement

HAVERFORDWEST
Mr and Mrs Patrick, East Hook Farm, Portfield Gate, Haverfordwest, Pembroke SA62 3LN (01437 762211). Howard and Jen welcome you to their Georgian Farmhouse surrounded by beautiful countryside, four miles from the coastline and three miles from Haverfordwest. Double, twin and family suite available, all en suite. Ground floor rooms available. Pembrokeshire produce used for dinner and breakfast. Dinner £18 per person. Bed and Breakfast from £25 to £30 per person. **WTB ★★★★ FARMHOUSE.** Cottage conversion also available from Christmas 2005, caters for two to eight people.
website: www.easthookfarmhouse.co.uk

HAVERFORDWEST
Haroldston Hall, Portfield Gate, Haverfordwest SA62 3LZ (01437 781549). Far from the madding crowd. A delightful country house set in spacious grounds amid serene rolling countryside just a mile from St Bride's Bay, Coastal Path and sandy beaches. Ideally situated to explore the beauty of Pembrokeshire's National Park. Relax and enjoy the warm, friendly atmosphere, large, comfortable, fully-equipped bedrooms and bathrooms (en suite available). Delicious legendary traditional Aga-cooked breakfast. Non-smoking. Pets must be kept in cars; not allowed in bedrooms. Parking available. Open all year. Bed and Breakfast £30 to £35 per person per night. **WTB ★★★★ COUNTRY HOUSE.**
e-mail: benjamin@stewart-thomas.fsnet.co.uk
website: www.haroldstonhall.co.uk

• • • some fun days out in PEMBROKESHIRE

Castell Henllys Iron Age Fort, Newport • 01239 891319 • www.castellhenllys.com
Heron's Brook Animal Park, Narberth • 01834 860723 • www.herons-brook.co.uk
Heatherton Country Sports Park, Tenby • 01646 651025 • www.heatherton.co.uk
Langloffan Cheese Centre, Castle Morris • 01348 891241 • www.welshcheese.co.uk

---

Free or reduced rate entry to Holiday Visits and Attractions
see our **READERS' OFFER VOUCHERS**
on pages 53-90

Powys 327

Powys

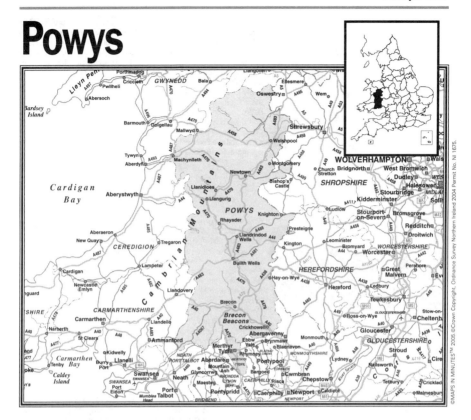

See also Colour Display Advertisement

BRECON

Gwyn and Hazel Davies, Caebetran Farm, Felinfach, Brecon LD3 0UL (Tel & Fax: 01874 754460). Working farm, join in.
A warm welcome, a cup of tea and home-made cakes await you when you arrive at Caebetran. Well off the beaten track, where there are breathtaking views of the Brecon Beacons and the Black Mountains and just across a field is a 400 acre common, ideal for walking, bird-watching or just relaxing. Ponies and sheep graze undisturbed, while buzzards soar above you. Visitors are welcome to see the cattle and sheep on the farm. The farmhouse dates back to the 17th century and has been recently modernised to give the quality and comfort visitors expect today. There are many extras in the rooms to give that special feel to your holiday. The rooms are all en suite and have colour TV and tea making facilities. The dining room has separate tables, there is also a comfortable lounge with colour TV and video. Caebetran is an ideal base for exploring this beautiful, unspoilt part of the country with pony trekking, walking, birdwatching, wildlife, hang-gliding and so much more. For a brochure and terms please write, telephone or fax. "Arrive as visitors and leave as our friends". Winners of the 'FHG Diploma' for Wales 1998 and 1999. *WELCOME HOST*.
e-mail: hazelcaebetran@aol.com   website: www.caebetranfarmhousebedandbreakfastwales.com

---

•••some fun days out in POWYS

Centre for Alternative Technology, Machynlleth • 01654 705950 • www.cat.org.uk
King Arthur's Labyrinth, Corris • 01654 761584 • www.kingarthurslabyrinth.com
Celtica, Machynlleth • 01654 702702 • www.celticawales.com

BRECON

Mrs M. J. Mayo, Maeswalter, Heol Senni, Near Brecon LD3 8SU (01874 636629). Maeswalter is a 300-year-old farmhouse in the mountainous Brecon Beacons National Park. There are tastefully decorated bedrooms, three double en suite, one family room sleeping three with private bathroom. The comfortable lounge/diningroom features exposed timbers. Visitors can roam freely through the grounds where there are seats to sit and admire the scenery and wildlife. Also private apartment (en suite double bedroom and private sittingroom). The bedrooms have colour TV and beverage tray with tea/coffee making facilities, chocolate and biscuits. Rates per room: en suite double £50 per night, family room sleeping three £60 per night; private en suite on the ground floor £60 per night. Reductions for longer stays.

BRECON

Mrs A. Harpur, Llanbrynean Farm, Llanfrynach, Brecon LD3 7BQ (01874 665222). Llanbrynean is a fine, traditional, Victorian farmhouse peacefully situated on the edge of the picturesque village of Llanfrynach, three miles south-east of Brecon. We are in an ideal spot for exploring the area - the Brecon Beacons rise behind the farm and the Brecon/Monmouth canal flows through the fields below. We are a working family sheep farm with wonderful pastoral views and a large garden. The house is spacious and comfortable with a friendly, relaxed atmosphere. We have two double en suite bedrooms and one twin with private bathroom. All have tea/coffee facilities. There is a sitting room with log fire. Bed and Breakfast from £22 per person. Excellent pub food within easy walking distance.

BUILTH WELLS (near)

Mrs Margaret Davies, The Court Farm, Aberedw, Near Builth Wells LD2 3UP (Tel & Fax: 01982 560277). Non-smokers please. We welcome guests into our home on a family-run livestock farm situated away from traffic in a peaceful, picturesque valley surrounded by hills. Lovely walking, wildlife area, central to Hay-on-Wye, Brecon Beacons, Elan Valley and very convenient for Royal Welsh Showground. We offer comfort, care and homeliness in our spacious stone-built farmhouse with traditional cooking using home produce where possible. Bedrooms have adjustable heating, hospitality trays and electric blankets. En suite or private bathroom available. Guests' lounge with TV. Bed and Breakfast from £20. Good food available at nearby village inn.

CRICKHOWELL

Les and Lucille Hill, Whitehall, Glangrwyney, Crickhowell, Powys NP8 1EW (01873 811155). A Grade II Listed Georgian manor house dating back to the 18th century. Whitehall is situated in a small village on the A40 near Abergavenny in the Brecon Beacons National Park, and within walking distance of the Black Mountains, an Area of Outstanding Natural Beauty. Consisting of three large comfortable bedrooms, two en suite and one with private shower room, all with TV/DVD and hospitality tray. Spacious dining room, guest lounge with woodburning stove and private, off-road, secure parking. Evening meals available in the Village Inn just 10 yards away. Single from £30, double/twin from £50, family from £60. Non-smoking. Open all year. **WTB ★★★**
e-mail: anna.hill@btopenworld.com
website: www.staying-in-wales.com

HAY-ON-WYE

Annie and John McKay, Hafod-y-Garreg, Erwood, Builth Wells LD2 3TQ (01982 560400). The oldest house in Wales, nestling on a wooded hillside in a Site of Special Scientific Interest, well off the beaten track, above, reputedly, the most picturesque part of the River Wye. A short drive from Hay-on-Wye 'Town of Books', and Brecon and the Beacons National Park. Alternatively, leave your car and step through our gate into a walkers' paradise, steeped in ancient Celtic history. Drink spring water from the tap, and have an enormous breakfast with our free-range eggs. Enjoy a delicious candlelit supper with log fires in the massive inglenook. Bed and Breakfast £50 per double en suite, dinner available at £16 per person.
website: www.hafodygarreg.co.uk

LLANIDLOES

Jean Bailey, Glangwy, Llangurig, Llanidloes SY18 6RS (01686 440697). Local river stone (Wye) built house offering comfortable Bed and Breakfast accommodation in beautiful countryside. Traditional English breakfast served; all home cooked evening meals; special diets catered for, vegetarians included. Accommodation comprises two doubles (can be used as family rooms as single bed also in each) and one twin bedroom with washbasin, tea/coffee facilities and storage heater (all beds have electric underblanket); bathroom, separate shower room; diningroom (separate tables per party); lounge with colour TV. Pets welcome. Parking. Central for touring and local walks. Bed and Breakfast £14 per person; reductions for children under nine years. Ideal for birdwatching – 'Kite Country'.

MACHYNLLETH

Nant yr Onog, Dinas Mawddwy, Machynlleth SY20 9JQ (01650 531470). Your friendly hosts, Pat and her daughter Georgina, will welcome you to this Bed and Breakfast accommodation in old farmhouse in the stunning Dyfi Valley, approximately two-and-a-half miles from Dinas Mawddwy. Ideal secluded and peaceful base away from main roads for walking, touring, fishing, painting or just to relax and unwind! Accommodation consists of one family apartment - double room, separate room with twin bunk beds and en suite shower room; twin room with en suite bathroom, all with excellent views of the surrounding hills. Situated on the edge of Snowdonia National Park there is a wide variety of spectacular scenery as well as places to visit; Welsh Coast, Harlech Castle and Centre for Alternative Technology within easy reach. Terms from £25 pppn, special rates for children.
e-mail: nantyronog@aol.com

FHG Guides publish a large range of well-known accommodation guides. We will be happy to send you details or you can use the order form at the back of this book.

National Cycle Collection
Llandrindod Wells, Powys
See our **READERS' OFFER VOUCHER** for details of free or reduced rate entry

MACHYNLLETH

Gwernstablau, Llanwrin, Machynlleth SY20 8QH (01650 511688). Gwernstablau is a tranquil 17th century farmhouse set in its own five acre grounds. It tastefully combines the old world charm of a wealth of beamed ceilings and open log fires with the convenience of modern central heating and en suite accommodation. Enjoy a short break or longer stay. Individual attention assured. Dinner can be enjoyed in the distinctive dining room with its galleried landing, crystal chandelier and antique furniture. Bed and Breakfast £26.
website: www.gwern-stablau.com

NEWTOWN

Mrs Vi Madeley, Greenfields, Kerry, Newtown SY16 4LH (01686 670596; mobile: 07971 075687; Fax: 01686 670354). A warm welcome awaits you at Greenfields. All rooms are tastefully decorated and are spacious in size, each having panoramic views of the rolling Kerry hills. There is a good choice of breakfast menu and evening meals can be provided by prior arrangement; packed lunches are also available. Licensed for residents. Accommodation available in twin, double, family and single rooms, all en suite (twin rooms let as singles if required). Hostess tray and TV in all rooms. The diningroom has individual tables. A good place for stopping for one night, a short break or longer holiday. Excellent off-road parking. Bed and Breakfast from £44 double or twin room, from £25 single and £70 family room. Brochure available. **WTB ★★★** *GUEST HOUSE.*

e-mail: info@greenfields-bb.co.uk
website: www.greenfields-bb.co.uk

WELSHPOOL

Mrs Joyce Cornes, Cwmllwynog, Llanfair, Caereinion, Welshpool SY21 0HF (Tel & Fax: 01938 810791). Built in the early 17th century, Cwmllwynog is a traditional long farmhouse of character on a working dairy farm. We have a spacious garden with a stream at the bottom and a lot of unusual plants. All bedrooms have colour TV and drink making facilities. Double room en suite, twin with washbasins and private bathroom. Delicious home-cooked meals cooked just for you! We can help you with routes. Open January to November. Bed and Breakfast from £22, Evening Meal £12. **WTB ★★★★** *FARMHOUSE.*
e-mail: joyce@cornes1.wanadoo.co.uk

South Wales

COWBRIDGE (near)

Mrs Sue Beer, Plas Llanmihangel, Llanmihangel, Near Cowbridge CF71 7LQ (01446 774610). Plas Llanmihangel is the finest medieval Grade 1 Listed manor house in the beautiful Vale of Glamorgan. We offer a genuine warmth of welcome, delightful accommodation, first class food and service in our wonderful home. The baronial hall, great log fires, the ancient tower and acres of beautiful historic gardens intrigue all who stay in this fascinating house. Its long history and continuous occupation have created a spectacular building in romantic surroundings unchanged since the 16th century. A great opportunity to experience the ambience and charm of a past age. Three double rooms. Bed and Breakfast from £28. High quality home cooked evening meal on request. **WTB ★★★**

GUEST HOUSE, SELECTED BY THE CONSUMER ASSOCIATION "WHICH?" AS ONE OF THE TOP TWENTY B&B'S IN GREAT BRITAIN FOR 2004.
e-mail: plasllanmihangel@ukonline.co.uk

Rhondda Heritage Park
Pontypridd, South Wales
See our **READERS' OFFER VOUCHER** for
details of free or reduced rate entry

332 South Wales

GOWER
Culver House Hotel, Port Eynon, Gower SA3 1NN (01792 390755). Nestling against the sand dunes, Culver House enjoys an idyllic location overlooking the beautiful "Blue Flag" beach at Port Eynon. The bay is extensively used for swimming and watersports and access to the beach and dunes is easy. An ideal base to explore Gower, our quiet, family-run hotel offers a licensed bar and comfortable lounge equipped with a library of interesting books to delight walkers, nature lovers and bird watchers alike. We welcome singles and do not charge a supplement. All bedrooms have en suite or private facilities, most have sea views. Ground floor rooms available. Non-Smoking. **WTB ★★** *COUNTRY HOTEL*
website: www.culverhousehotel.co.uk

MONMOUTH
Rosemary and Derek Ringer, Church Farm Guest House, Mitchel Troy, Monmouth NP25 4HZ (01600 712176) A spacious and homely 16th century (Grade II Listed) former farmhouse with oak beams and inglenook fireplaces, set in large attractive garden with stream. An excellent base for visiting the Wye Valley, Forest of Dean and Black Mountains. All nine bedrooms have washbasin, tea/coffee making facilities and central heating; most are en suite. Own car park. Terrace, barbecue. Colour TV. Non-smoking. Bed and Breakfast from £23 to £27 per person, Evening Meals by arrangement. **WTB ★★** *GUEST HOUSE*, **AA ♦♦♦**
website: www.churchfarmmitcheltroy.co.uk

MONMOUTH
Tresco Guest House, Redbrook, Near Monmouth (01600 712325). Situated in the Wye Valley. Snacks available. Packed lunches. Special rates for children. Ground floor bedrooms have views of flower gardens. Fishing, pony trekking, walking and canoeing. Parking. Bed and Breakfast £20. **WTB ★★★** *GUEST HOUSE.*

ST BRIDES WENTLOOG (near Newport)
Mrs C.A. Bushell, Chapel Guest House, Church Road, St Brides Wentloog, Near Newport NP10 8SN (01633 681018; Fax: 01633 681431) Comfortable accommodation in a converted chapel situated in a village between Newport/Cardiff, near Tredegar House. Restaurant and inn adjacent, car park available. Guest lounge with TV. Single, double and twin rooms en suite. Beverage trays, TV, shaver points in all rooms. From £26. Children under three years FREE, three to 12 year olds half price sharing parents' room. Pets by arrangement. Leave M4 at Junction 28, take A48 towards Newport, at roundabout take third exit signposted St Brides, B4239. Drive to centre of village, turn right into Church Road and left into Church House Inn car park; the guest house is on the left and a warm welcome awaits. Credit/Debit Cards accepted. **WTB ★★★** *GUEST HOUSE.*
e-mail: chapelguesthouse@hotmail.com
website: www.SmoothHound.co.uk/hotels/chapel1.hotmail/

•••some fun days out in SOUTH WALES
National Showcaves Centre for Wales, Swansea • 01639 730684 • www.showcaves.co.uk
Barry Island Pleasure Park, Near Cardiff • 01446 732844 • www.barryisland.com

IRELAND

Co. Donegal

LETTERKENNY

Nuala and Michael Duddy, Pennsylvania House B&B, Curraghleas, Mountain Top, Letterkenny (00 353 74 9126808; Fax: 00 353 74 9128905). Pennsylvania House is a luxurious smoke-free B&B overlooking the hills, valleys and mountains of Donegal, four minutes away from Letterkenny town. It is tucked away off the main road and provides a secluded retreat for those who desire the very finest in accommodation. Spacious en suite bedrooms, TV, phone, alarm clock radio, luggage racks, arm chairs, etc. Pennsylvania House is unique and truly outstanding and provides everything and more that any visitor could desire. Guests will feel right at home in this picturesque corner of the Emerald Isle, where you arrive a stranger and leave a friend. Rates from 45 euros to 55 euros per person sharing per night. No children under 12 years of age.

AA ♦♦♦♦

e-mail: info@accommodationdonegal.com   website: www.accommodationdonegal.com

---

Pets Welcome!

"THE PET WORLD'S VERSION OF THE ULTIMATE HOTEL GUIDE!" (The Times)

Now bigger than ever and with full colour throughout,
Pets Welcome! is used every year by thousands of discriminating owners who simply refuse to leave their pets "home alone".
Published twice a year in Autumn and Spring.

Only £8.99 from booksellers or direct from the publishers:
FHG Guides, Abbey Mill Business Centre, Seedhill, Paisley PA1 1TJ *(postage charged outside UK)*
e-mail: admin@fhguides.co.uk • www.holidayguides.com

Free or reduced rate entry to Holiday Visits and Attractions – see our READERS' OFFER VOUCHERS on pages 53-90

THE FHG DIPLOMA

HELP IMPROVE BRITISH TOURIST STANDARDS

You are choosing holiday accommodation from our very popular FHG Guides.
Whether it be a hotel, guest house, farmhouse or self-catering accommodation, we think you will find it hospitable, comfortable and clean, and your host and hostess friendly and helpful.

Why not write and tell us about it?

As a recognition of the generally well-run and excellent holiday accommodation reviewed in our publications, we at FHG Guides Ltd. present a diploma to proprietors who receive the highest recommendation from their guests who are also readers of our Guides. If you care to write to us praising the holiday you have booked through FHG Guides Ltd. – whether this be board, self-catering accommodation, a sporting or a caravan holiday, what you say will be evaluated and the proprietors who reach our final list will be contacted.

The winning proprietor will receive an attractive framed diploma to display on his premises as recognition of a high standard of comfort, amenity and hospitality. FHG Guides Ltd. offer this diploma as a contribution towards the improvement of standards in tourist accommodation in Britain. Help your excellent host or hostess to win it!

FHG DIPLOMA

We nominate

Because

Name ....

Address..

....

Telephone No...

SPECIAL WELCOME SUPPLEMENT

Are you looking for a guest house where smoking is banned, a farmhouse that is equipped for the disabled, or a hotel that will cater for your special diet? If so, you should find this supplement useful. Its three sections, NON-SMOKERS, DISABLED, and SPECIAL DIETS, list accommodation where these particular needs are served. Brief details of the accommodation are provided in this section; for a fuller description you should turn to the appropriate place in the main section of the book.

Non-smoking • England

LONDON, HAMMERSMITH. Anne and Sohel Armanios, 67 Rannoch Road, Hammersmith, London W6 9SS (020 7385 4904; Fax: 020 7610 3235). Comfortable, centrally located Edwardian family home. Great base for sightseeing. Excellent transport access. Bed and Continental Breakfast £24 pppn Double; £34 single. Smoking only in garden.

DEVON, BIDEFORD. Iris & Brian Chapple, Meadow Park, Buckland Brewer, Bideford EX39 5NY (01237 451511). Spacious, centrally heated and tastefully furnished accommodation providing panoramic views to the distant hills of Dartmoor and Exmoor. Non-smoking and sorry, no pets. Off-road parking. Open all year except Christmas.

DORSET, BEAMINSTER. Caroline and Vincent Pielesz, The Walnuts, 2 Prout Bridge, Beaminster DT8 3AY (01308 862211). Very well situated in this medieval town, the house has been very tastefully refurbished with en suite rooms, tea and coffee making facilities, all the comforts of home. Totally non smoking. **ETC** ◆◆◆ *SILVER AWARD.*

HAMPSHIRE, NEW FOREST. Mrs J. Pearce, "St Ursula", 30 Hobart Road, New Milton BH25 6EG (01425 613515). Ideal base for visiting New Forest; Salisbury, Bournemouth easily accessible. Sea one mile. High standards throughout. Town centre and mainline railway to London minutes away. Open all year. **ETC** ◆◆◆, *NATIONAL ACCESSIBLE SCHEME LEVEL 1.*

LANCASHIRE, BLACKPOOL. Elsie and Ron Platt, Sunnyside and Holmsdale Hotel, 25-27 High Street, North Shore, Blackpool FY1 2BN (01253 623781). Two minutes from North Station, five minutes from Promenade, all shows and amenities. Colour TV lounge. Full central heating. No smoking.

LINCOLNSHIRE, WOODHALL SPA. Barbara and Tony Hodgkinson, Kirkstead Old Mill Cottage, Tattershall Road, Woodhall Spa LN10 6UQ (01526 353637; mobile: 07970 040401). A warm welcome awaits you at this peaceful, detached, non-smoking house. Three bedrooms, two en suite, each with TV, clock radio and hot drinks tray. **ETC** ◆◆◆, *NATIONAL ACCESSIBLE SCHEME, M2, VISUAL 2, HEARING 2.*

NORTHUMBERLAND, WARKWORTH. Sue and Geoff Lillico, Aulden, 9 Watershaugh Road, Warkworth NE65 0TT (Tel & Fax: 01665 711583). Enjoy a high standard of care and hospitality. Each room has TV, hospitality tray and hairdryer. Extensive breakfast menu. Non-smoking.

OXFORDSHIRE, WITNEY. Mrs Elizabeth Simpson, Field View, Wood Green, Witney OX28 1DE (01993 705485; Mobile: 07768 614347). Set in two acres and situated on picturesque Wood Green, yet only ten minutes from the centre of town. Non-smoking. **ETC** ◆◆◆ *SILVER AWARD*

SOMERSET, BATH. Michael and Carole Bryson, Walton Villa, 3 Newbridge Hill, Bath BA1 3PW (01225 482792; Fax: 01225 313093). All bedrooms tastefully decorated and furnished with en suite facilities, hospitality tray, colour TV, hairdryer and central heating. No smoking policy throughout. **ETC** ◆◆◆

336 SPECIAL WELCOME

SOMERSET, BURNHAM-ON-SEA. Mrs F. Alexander, Priors Mead, 23 Rectory Road TA8 2BZ (Tel & Fax: 01278 782116). Enchanting Edwardian home set in half-an-acre of beautiful gardens with weeping willows, croquet and swimming pool. Peaceful location, walk to the sea, town, golf and tennis clubs. Parking. *"WHICH?" RECOMMENDED.*

SURREY, GATWICK. Carole and Adrian Grinsted, The Lawn Guest House, 30 Massetts Road, Horley RH6 7DF (01293 775751; Fax: 01293 821803). Imposing Victorian house, five minutes from Gatwick Airport. All rooms en suite with TV, hairdryer, tea/coffee/chocolate tray, direct dial phone and computer modem sockets. Central heating. Children welcome. Totally non-smoking.

SUSSEX (EAST), HASTINGS. Peter Mann, Grand Hotel, Grand Parade, St Leonards, Hastings TN38 0DD (Tel & Fax: 01424 428510 or 0870 2257025) Seafront family-run hotel; some rooms with colour TV, radio; some en suite. Unrestricted/disabled parking. Non-smoking restaurant. Licensed bar. **ETC ◆◆◆**

WILTSHIRE, MARLBOROUGH. Jackie and James MacBeth, Manor Farm, Collingbourne Kingston, Marlborough SN8 3SD (01264 850859). Attractive Grade II Listed farmhouse. Sumptuous traditional, vegetarian, gluten-free and other special diet breakfasts. Beautiful countryside with superb walking and cycling. Non-smoking. **ETC ◆◆◆◆,** *FARM STAY MEMBER*

YORKSHIRE (NORTH), SCARBOROUGH. Sue and Tony Hewitt, Harmony Country Lodge, Limestone Road, Burniston, Scarborough YO13 0DG (0800 2985840; Tel & Fax: 01723 870276). Relaxing octagonal retreat, superb 360° views of the National Park and sea. Licensed, private parking, completely non-smoking. Warm and friendly. **ETC ◆◆◆◆**

Non-smoking • Scotland

AYRSHIRE, KILMARNOCK. Mrs Nancy Cuthbertson, West Tannacrieff, Fenwick, Kilmarnock KA3 6AZ (01560 600258; mobile: 07773 226332; Fax: 01560 600914). A warm welcome awaits all our guests to our dairy farm, situated in the peaceful Ayrshire countryside. Relax in spacious well furnished en suite rooms with all modern amenities. Children welcome. **STB ★★★★** *B&B.*

AYRSHIRE, LARGS. Mrs M. Watson, South Whittlieburn Farm, Brisbane Glen, Largs KA30 8SN (01475 675881). Superb farmhouse accommodation, enormous delicious breakfasts, warm, friendly hospitality. Nominated for "AA LANDLADY OF THE YEAR 2005", and chosen by "WHICH BEST BED & BREAKFAST". All rooms en suite. Open all year except Christmas. **STB ★★★★** *B&B,* **AA ◆◆◆◆**

PERTH & KINROSS, CALLANDER. Annfield Guest House, North Church Street, Callander FK17 8EG (01877 330204; Fax: 01877 330674). Ideal as an overnight stop or as the centre for visiting the surrounding Scottish Highlands. All bedrooms have en suite facilities or private bathroom, hospitality tray and hairdryer. Private parking. No smoking. **AA ◆◆◆◆,** **STB ★★★** *B&B.*

Non-smoking • Wales

NORTH WALES, BETWS-Y-COED. Mr & Mrs M Edwards, Bryn Bella Guest House, Llanrwst Road, Lôn Muriau, Betws-y-Coed LL24 0HD (01690 710627). Small but select Victorian guest house with glorious views. All rooms en suite. Non-smoking throughout. Open all year. On-line booking. **WTB ★★★★** *GUEST HOUSE,* **AA** *FOUR RED DIAMONDS*

NORTH WALES, LLANDUDNO. Roger and Merril Pitblado, Chilterns for Non-Smokers, 19 Deganwy Avenue, Llandudno LL30 2YB (01492 875457). Centrally placed Bed & Breakfast accommodation in en suite rooms with king-size beds, hairdryers, alarm clocks, colour TVs and beverage trays. **WTB ★★★** *GUEST HOUSE.*

SOUTH WALES, ST BRIDES WENTLOOG (Near Newport). Mrs C. A. Bushell, Chapel Guest House, Church Road, St Brides Wentloog, Near Newport NP10 8SN (01633 681018; Fax: 01633 681431). Comfortable accommodation in a coverted chapel. Guest lounge with TV. Single, double and twin rooms en suite. Beverage Trays, TV, shaver points in all rooms. From £26. **WTB ★★★** *GUEST HOUSE*

Please mention this FHG Guide when enquiring about accommodation featured in these pages

Special Diets • England

LONDON, HAMMERSMITH. Anne and Sohel Armanios, 67 Rannoch Road, Hammersmith, London W6 9SS (020 7385 4904; Fax: 020 7610 3235). Comfortable, centrally located Edwardian family home. Great base for sightseeing. Excellent transport access. Bed and Continental Breakfast £24 pppn Double; £34 single. Smoking only in garden.

LINCOLNSHIRE, WOODHALL SPA. Barbara and Tony Hodgkinson, Kirkstead Old Mill Cottage, Tattershall Road, Woodhall Spa LN10 6UQ (01526 353637; mobile: 07970 040401). A warm welcome awaits you at this peaceful, sunny, detached, non-smoking house. Three bedrooms, two en suite, each with TV, clock radio and hot drinks tray. ETC ♦♦♦♦, *NATIONAL ACCESSIBLE SCHEME, M2, VISUAL 2, HEARING 2.*

SUSSEX (EAST), HASTINGS. Peter Mann, Grand Hotel, Grand Parade, St Leonards, Hastings TN38 0DD (Tel & Fax: 01424 428510 or 0870 2257425) Seafront family-run hotel; some rooms with colour TV, radio; some en suite. Unrestricted/disabled parking. Non-smoking restaurant. Licensed bar. ETC ♦♦♦

WILTSHIRE, MARLBOROUGH. Jackie and James MacBeth, Manor Farm, Collingbourne Kingston, Marlborough SN8 3SD (01264 850859). Attractive Grade II Listed farmhouse. Sumptuous traditional, vegetarian, gluten-free and other special diet breakfasts. Beautiful countryside with superb walking and cycling. Non-smoking. ETC ♦♦♦♦, *FARM STAY MEMBER*

Special Diets • Scotland

AYRSHIRE, LARGS. Mrs M. Watson, South Whittlieburn Farm, Brisbane Glen, Largs KA30 8SN (01475 675881). Superb farmhouse accommodation, enormous delicious breakfasts, warm, friendly hospitality. Nominated for "AA LANDLADY OF THE YEAR 2005", and chosen by "WHICH BEST BED & BREAKFAST". All rooms en suite. Open all year except Christmas. Packed lunches and special diets. STB ★★★★ *B&B*, AA ♦♦♦♦

DUMFRIES & GALLOWAY, WHITHORN (near). Mike and Helen Alexander, Craiglemine Cottage B&B, Glasserton, Near Whithorn DG8 8NE (01988 500594). Our rural location makes this a wonderful place to unwind. Ideal for touring. Children and pets welcome. Evening meals available on request including vegetarian or other dietary needs. STB ★★

Special Diets • Wales

SOUTH WALES, ST BRIDES WENTLOOG (Near Newport). Mrs C.A. Bushell, Chapel Guest House, Church Road, St Brides Wentloog, Near Newport NP10 8SN (01633 681018; Fax: 01633 681431) Comfortable accommodation in a converted chapel. Guest lounge with TV. Single, double and twin rooms en suite. Beverage trays, TV, shaver points in all rooms. From £26. WTB ★★★ *GUEST HOUSE.*

Visit the FHG website www.holidayguides.com for details of the wide choice of accommodation featured in the full range of FHG titles

338 SPECIAL WELCOME

Disabled • England

HAMPSHIRE, NEW FOREST. Mrs J. Pearce, "St Ursula", 30 Hobart Road, New Milton BH25 6EG (01425 613515). Ideal base for visiting New Forest; Salisbury, Bournemouth easily accessible. Sea one mile. Downstairs twin bedroom. Town centre and mainline railway to London minutes away. Open all year. ETC ◆◆◆◆, *NATIONAL ACCESSIBLE SCHEME LEVEL 1.*

LINCOLNSHIRE, WOODHALL SPA. Barbara and Tony Hodgkinson, Kirkstead Old Mill Cottage, Tattershall Road, Woodhall Spa LN10 6UQ (01526 353637; mobile: 07970 040401). A warm welcome awaits you at this peaceful, sunny, detached, non-smoking house. Three bedrooms, two en suite, each with TV, clock radio and hot drinks tray. ETC ◆◆◆◆, *NATIONAL ACCESSIBLE SCHEME, M2, VISUAL 2, HEARING 2.*

SUSSEX (EAST), HASTINGS. Peter Mann, Grand Hotel, Grand Parade, St Leonards, Hastings TN38 0DD (Tel & Fax: 01424 428510 or 0870 2257025) Seafront family-run hotel; some rooms with colour TV, radio; some en suite. Unrestricted/disabled parking. Non-smoking restaurant. Licensed bar. ETC ◆◆◆

Disabled • Wales

SOUTH WALES, ST BRIDES WENTLOOG (Near Newport). Mrs C.A. Bushell, Chapel Guest House, Church Road, St Brides Wentloog, Near Newport NP10 8SN (01633 681018; Fax: 01633 681431) Comfortable accommodation in a converted chapel. Guest lounge with TV. Single, double and twin rooms en suite. Beverage trays, TV, shaver points in all rooms. From £26. WTB ★★★ *GUEST HOUSE.*

Useful Guidance for Guests and Hosts

Every year literally thousands of holidays, short breaks and overnight stops are arranged through our guides, the vast majority without any problems at all. In a handful of cases, however, difficulties do arise about bookings, which often could have been prevented from the outset.

It is important to remember that when accommodation has been booked, both parties – guests and hosts – have entered into a form of contract. We hope that the following points will provide helpful guidance.

- When enquiring about accommodation, be as precise as possible. Give exact dates, numbers in your party and the ages of any children.
- State the number and type of rooms wanted and also what catering you require – bed and breakfast, full board etc. Make sure that the position about evening meals is clear – and about pets, reductions for children or any other special points.
- Read our reviews carefully to ensure that the proprietors you are going to contact can supply what you want. Ask for a letter confirming all arrangements, if possible.
- If you have to cancel, do so as soon as possible. Proprietors do have the right to retain deposits and under certain circumstances to charge for cancelled holidays if adequate notice is not given and they cannot re-let the accommodation.

- Give details about your facilities and about any special conditions. Explain your deposit system clearly and arrangements for cancellations, charges etc. and whether or not your terms include VAT.
- If for any reason you are unable to fulfil an agreed booking without adequate notice, you may be under an obligation to arrange suitable alternative accommodation or to make some form of compensation.

WEBSITE DIRECTORY 339

DIRECTORY OF WEBSITE AND E-MAIL ADDRESSES

A quick-reference guide to holiday accommodation with an e-mail address and/or website, conveniently arranged by country and county, with full contact details.

Golf Tours
Global Golf Tours
• **e-mail: info@ggtours.org**
• **website: www.ggtours.org**

•LONDON

Hotel
The Elysee Hotel, 25-26 Craven Terrace,
LONDON W2 3EL. Tel: 020 7402 7633
• **e-mail: information@hotelelysee.co.uk**
• **website: www.hotelelysee.co.uk**

Hotel
Queens Hotel, 33 Anson Road, Tufnell Park,
LONDON N7. Tel: 020 7607 4725
• **e-mail: queens@stavrouhotels.co.uk**
• **website: www.stavrouhotels.co.uk**

Hotel
Athena Hotel, 110-114 Sussex Gardens,
Hyde Park, LONDON W2 1UA
Tel: 020 7706 3866
• **e-mail: athena@stavrouhotels.co.uk**
• **website: www.stavrouhotels.co.uk**

Hotel
Gower Hotel, 129 Sussex Gardens,
Hyde Park, LONDON W2 2RX
Tel: 020 7262 2262
• **e-mail: gower@stavrouhotels.co.uk**
• **website: www.stavrouhotels.co.uk**

B & B
Sohel & Anne Armanios, 67 Rannoch Road,
Hammersmith, LONDON W6 9SS
Tel: 020 7385 4904
• **website: www.thewaytostay.co.uk**

Hotel / B & B
St Athans Hotel, 20 Tavistock Place,
LONDON WC1H 9RE. Tel: 0207 837 9140
• **e-mail: stathans@ukonline.co.uk**
• **website: www. stathanshotel.com**

Hotel
MacDonald Hotel, 45-46 Argyle Square,
King's Cross, LONDON WC1H 8AL
Tel: 020 7837 3552
• **e-mail: enquiries@macdonaldhotel.com**
• **website: www.macdonaldhotel.com**

Hotel
Elizabeth Hotel, 37 Eccleston Square,
LONDON SW1V 1PB. Tel: 020 7828 6812
• **e-mail: info@elizabethhotel.com**
• **website: www.elizabethhotel.com**

•BEDFORDSHIRE

Self-Catering
Bluegate Farm Holiday Cottages
Bluegate Farm, Stanbridge,
LEIGHTON BUZZARD, Bedfordshire
LU7 9JD. Tel: 01525 210621
• **e-mail: michies@bluegatecottages.co.uk**
• **website: www.bluegatecottages.co.uk**

•BERKSHIRE

Hotel
Clarence Hotel, 9 Clarence Road,
WINDSOR, Berkshire SL4 5AE
Tel: 01753 864436
• **e-mail: enquiries@clarence-hotel.co.uk**
• **website: www.clarence-hotel.co.uk**

Guest House
Bluebell House, Lovel Lane, WINKFIELD,
Windsor, Berkshire SL4 2DG
Tel: 01344 886828
• **e-mail: registrations@bluebellhousehotel.co.uk**
• **website: www.bluebellhousehotel.co.uk**

www.holidayguides.com

340 WEBSITE DIRECTORY

•BUCKINGHAMSHIRE

Caravan Park / B & B
M.J. Penfold, Highclere, New Barn Lane,
Seer Green, BEACONSFIELD,
Buckinghamshire HP9 2QZ
Tel: 01494 874505
- e-mail: highclerepark@aol.com
- website: www.highclerefarmpark.co.uk
    www.highclerefarm.co.uk

Hotel
Different Drummer Hotel, 92-94 High Street,
Stony Stratford, MILTON KEYNES,
Buckinghamshire MK11 1AH
Tel: 01908 564733
- e-mail: info@hoteldifferentdrummer.co.uk
- website: www.hoteldifferentdrummer.co.uk

•CAMBRIDGESHIRE

Golf Club
Cambridge National Golf Club,
Comberton Road, Toft, CAMBRIDGE,
Cambridgeshire CB3 7RY. Tel: 01223 264700
- e-mail: meridian@golfsocieties.com
- website: www.golfsocieties.com

•CHESHIRE

Guest House / Self-Catering
Mrs Joanne Hollins, Balterley Green Farm,
Farm Deans Lane, Balterley, Crewe
Cheshire CW2 5QJ. Tel: 01270 820 214
- e-mail: greenfarm@balterley.fsnet.co.uk
- website: www.greenfarm.freeserve.co.uk

Farmhouse B&B
Mrs Helen Sarginson, Hampton House
Farm, Stevensons Lane, HAMPTON
MALPAS, Cheshire SY14 8JS
Tel: 01948 920588
- e-mail: nick.sarginson@ukonline.co.uk
- website: www.hamptonhousefarm.co.uk

Guest House / Self-Catering
Mrs Angela Smith, Mill House and Granary,
Higher Wych, MALPAS, Cheshire SY14 7JR
Tel: 01948 780362
- e-mail: angela@videoactive.co.uk
- website: www.millhouseandgranary.co.uk

Farm House / B & B
Jean Callwood, Lea Farm, Wrinehill Road,
Wybunbury, NANTWICH, Cheshire
CW5 7NS. Tel: 01270 841429
- e-mail: jean@leafarm.freeserve.co.uk
- website: www.SmoothHound.co.uk

•CORNWALL

Self-catering
Graham Wright, Guardian House, Barras
Street, Liskeard, Cornwall PL14 6AD.
Tel: 01579 344080

Hotel
Hampton Manor, ALSTON,
Near Callington, Cornwall PL17 8LX
Tel: 01579 370494
- e-mail: hamptonmanor@supanet.com
- website: www.hamptonmanor.co.uk

Self-Catering
Cornish Traditional Cottages, Blisland,
BODMIN, Cornwall PL30 4HS
Tel: 01208 821666
- e-mail: info@corncott.com
- website: www.corncott.com

Self-Catering
Penrose Burden Holiday Cottages,
St Breward, BODMIN,
Cornwall PL30 4LZ
Tel: 01208 850277 or 01208 850915
- website: www.penroseburden.co.uk

Self-Catering
Mrs Angela Clark, Darrynane Cottages,
Darrynane, St Breward, BODMIN,
Cornwall PL30 4LZ. Tel: 01208 850885
- e-mail: enquiries@darrynane.co.uk
- website: www.darrynane.co.uk

Hotel
Wringford Down Hotel, Hat Lane,
CAWSAND, Cornwall PL10 1LE
Tel: 01752 822287
- e-mail: a.molloy@virgin.net
- website: www.cornwallholidays.co.uk

Self-Catering
Mineshop Holiday Cottages,
CRACKINGTON HAVEN, Bude,
Cornwall EX23 0NR. Tel: 01840 230338
- e-mail: info@mineshop.co.uk
- website: www.mineshop.co.uk

Self-Catering
Colin Kemp, Pantiles,
6 Stracey Road, FALMOUTH,
Cornwall TR11 4DW. Tel: 01326 211838
- e-mail: colinkemp@lineone.net
- website: www.falmouthapartments.co.uk

Self-Catering
Mrs K Terry, "Shasta", Carwinion Road,
Mawnan Smith, FALMOUTH, Cornwall
TR11 5JD. Tel: 01326 250775
- e-mail: katerry@btopenworld.com
- website: www.cornwallonline.com

WEBSITE DIRECTORY 341

Self-Catering
Mr M. Watson, Creekside Holiday Cottages,
Strangwith House, Restronguet,
FALMOUTH, Cornwall TR11 5ST
Tel: 01326 375972
* e-mail: **martin@creeksidecottages.co.uk**
* website: **www.creeksidecottages.co.uk**

Self-Catering
Mrs S. Trewhella, Mudgeon Vean Farm,
St Martin, HELSTON Cornwall TR12 6DB
Tel: 01326 231341
* e-mail: **mudgeonvean@aol.com**
* website:
www.cornwall-online.co.uk/mudgeon-vean/ctb.html

Self- Catering / Caravan & Camping
Franchis Holiday Park, Cury Cross Lanes,
Mullion, HELSTON, Cornwall TR12 7AZ
Tel: 01326 240301
* e-mail: **enquiries@franchis.co.uk**
* website: **www.franchisholidays.co.uk**

Self Catering
Trenannick Cottages Ltd, Trenannick
Farmhouse, Warbstow, LAUNCESTON,
Cornwall PL15 8RP. Tel: 01566 781443
* e-mail: **lorraine.trenannick@i12.com**
* website: **www.trenannickcottages.co.uk**

Self-Catering
Celia Hutchinson,
Caradon Country Cottages, East Taphouse,
LISKEARD, Cornwall PL14 4NH
Tel: 01579 320355
* e-mail: **celia@caradoncottages.co.uk**
* website: **www.caradoncottages.co.uk**

Self-Catering
Kaye & Bill Chapman, Coldrinnick Cottages,
Coldrinnick Farm, Duloe, Near LOOE,
Cornwall. Tel: 01503 220251
* website: **www.cornishcottage.net**

Self-Catering
Tremaine Green Country Cottages,
Tremaine Green, Pelynt, Near LOOE,
Cornwall PL13 2LT. Tel: 01503 220333
* e-mail: **stay@tremainegreen.co.uk**
* website: **www.tremainegreen.co.uk**

Self-Catering
Mrs A.Brumpton, Talehay Holiday Cottages,
Pelynt, Near LOOE, Cornwall PL13 2LT
Tel: 01503 220252
* e-mail: **paul@talehay.co.uk**
* website: **www.talehay.co.uk**

Hotel
Restormel Lodge Hotel, Castle Hill,
LOSTWITHIEL, Cornwall PL22 0DD
Tel: 01208 872223
* e-mail: **restlodge@aol.com**
* website: **www.restormelhotel.co.uk**

Self-Catering
St Anthony Holidays, St Anthony,
MANACCAN, Helston, Cornwall TR12 6JW
Tel: 01326 231357
* e-mail: **info@stanthony.co.uk**
* website: **www.stanthony.co.uk**

Hotel
The Old Coastguard Hotel, The Parade,
MOUSEHOLE, Penzance, Cornwall TR19 6PR
Tel: 01736 731222
* e-mail: **bookings@oldcoastguardhotel.co.uk**
* website: **www.oldcoastguardhotel.co.uk**

Hotel
St George's Hotel, 71 Mount Wise,
NEWQUAY, Cornwall TR7 2BP
Tel: 01637 873010
* e-mail: **enquiries@stgeorgeshotel.free-online.co.uk**
* website: **www.st-georges-newquay.co.uk**

B & B
Mr & Mrs M. Limer, Alicia, 136 Henver Road,
NEWQUAY, Cornwall TR7 3EQ
Tel: 01637 874328
* e-mail: **aliciaguesthouse@mlimer.fsnet.co.uk**
* website:
www.cornishlight.freeserve.co.uk/alicia.htm

Hotel
Boscean Country Hotel, St Just,
PENZANCE, Cornwall TR19 7QP
Tel: 01736 788748
* e-mail: **Boscean@aol.com**
* website: **www.bosceancountryhotel.co.uk**

Guest House
Greystones Guest House, 40 West End,
PORTHLEVEN, Helston, Cornwall TR13 9JL
Tel: 01326 565583
* e-mail: **mawbb@tiscali.co.uk**

Guest House
Mrs E. Neal, Tamarind, 12 Shrubberies Hill,
PORTHLEVEN, Cornwall TR13 9EA
Tel: 01326 574303
* e-mail: **lizzybenzimra@hotmail.com**
* website:
www.web-direct.co.uk/porthleven/tamarind.html

Hotel
Longcross Hotel, Trelights, PORT ISAAC,
Cornwall PL29 3TF. Tel: 01208 880243
* e-mail: **longcross@portisaac.com**
* website: **www.portisaac.com**

Hotel / Inn
Cornish Arms, Pendoggett, PORT ISAAC,
Cornwall PL30 3HH. Tel: 01208 880263
* e-mail: **info@cornisharms.com**
* website: **www.cornisharms.com**

342 WEBSITE DIRECTORY

Self-Catering
Mr Heywood, Trewince Manor,
PORTSCATHO, St Mawes, Cornwall TR2 5ET
Tel: 01872 580289
- **e-mail: bookings@trewince.co.uk**
- **website: www.trewince.co.uk**

Caravan & Camping
Wheal Rose Caravan & Camping Park,
Scorrier, REDRUTH, Cornwall TR16 5DD
Tel: 01209 891496
- **e-mail: whealrose@aol.com**
- **website: www.whealrosecaravanpark.co.uk**

B & B
Mrs Merchant, Woodpeckers, RILLA MILL,
Callington, Cornwall PL17 7NT
Tel: 01579 363717
- **e-mail: alison.merchant@virgin.net**
- **website: www.woodpeckersguesthouse.co.uk**

Caravan & Camping / Holiday Park
Chiverton Park, Blackwater, ST AGNES,
Cornwall TR4 8HS. Tel: 01872 560667
- **e-mail: info@chivertonpark.co.uk**
- **website: www.chivertonpark.co.uk**

B & B
Cleaderscroft Hotel, 16 British Road,
ST AGNES, Cornwall TR5 0TZ
Tel: 01872 552349
- **e-mail: tedellis@cchotel.fsnet.co.uk**
- **website: www.cchotel.fsnet.co.uk**

Hotel / Inn
Driftwood Spars Hotel, Trevaunance Cove,
ST AGNES, Cornwall TR5 0RT
Tel: 01872 552428/553323
- **website: www.driftwoodspars.com**

Farm B & B
Mrs D. Rundle, Lancallan Farm, Mevagissey,
ST AUSTELL, Cornwall PL26 6EW
Tel: 01726 842 284
- **website: www.lancallanfarm.co.uk**

Guest House
Sue Couch, The Elms, 14 Penwinnick Road,
ST AUSTELL, Cornwall PL25 5DW
Tel: 01726 74981
- **e-mail: sue@edenbb.co.uk**
- **website: www.edenbb.co.uk**

Farmhouse
Mrs Diana Clemes, Tregilgas Farm,
Gorran, ST AUSTELL, Cornwall PL26 6ND
Tel: 01726 842342
- **e-mail: dclemes88@aol.com**

B & B
Mrs Liz Berryman, Polgreen Farm,
London Apprentice, ST AUSTELL,
Cornwall PL26 7AP. Tel: 01726 75151
- **e-mail: polgreen.farm@btclick.com**
- **website: www.polgreenfarm.co.uk**

Caravan & Camping
St Ives Bay Holiday Park, Hayle, Near
ST IVES, Cornwall. Tel: 0800 317713
- **website: www.stivesbay.co.uk**

Hotel
Rosevine Hotel, Porthcurnick Beach,
ST MAWES, Cornwall TR2 5EW
Tel: 01872 580206
- **e-mail: info@rosevine.co.uk**
- **website: www.rosevine.co.uk**

Self-Catering
Maymear Cottage, 5 Maymear Terrace,
Bodinnick Lane, ST TUDY, Bodmin,
Cornwall PL30 3NE. Tel: 01840 213120
- **e-mail: aandr.reeves@virgin.net**
- **website: www.maymear.co.uk**

Self-Catering
Mr & Mrs C.W. Pestell, Hockadays,
Tregenna, Near Blisland, ST TUDY,
Cornwall PL30 4QJ. Tel: 01208 850146
- **e-mail: holidays@hockadaysholidaycottages.co.uk**
- **website: www.hockadaysholidaycottages.co.uk**

Self-Catering
King Harry Cottages, King Harry Ferry,
Feock, TRURO, Cornwall TR3 6QJ
Tel: 01872 861915
- **e-mail: jean@kingharry.f9.co.uk**
- **website: www.kingharry-info.co.uk**

Caravan Park
Summer Valley Touring Park, Shortlanesend,
TRURO, Cornwall TR4 9DW
Tel: 01872 277878
- **e-mail: res@summervalley.co.uk**
- **website: www.summervalley.co.uk**

B & B
The Townhouse Rooms, 20 Falmouth Road,
TRURO, Cornwall TR1 2HX
Tel: 01872 277374
- **e-mail: info@trurotownhouse.com**
- **website: www.trurotownhouse.com**

www.holidayguides.com

A useful index of towns/counties appears at the back of this book

WEBSITE DIRECTORY 343

•CUMBRIA

Self-Catering
The Eyrie, Lake Road, AMBLESIDE, Cumbria
Contact: Mrs D. Clark. Tel: 01844 208208
• e-mail: dot.clark@btopenworld.com

Caravan Park
Greenhowe Caravan Park, Great Langdale,
AMBLESIDE, Cumbria LA22 9JU
Tel: 015394 37231
• e-mail: enquiries@greenhowe.com
• website: www.greenhowe.com

Hotel / Guest House
Ian & Helen Burt, The Old Vicarage,
Vicarage Road, AMBLESIDE, Cumbria
LA22 9DH. Tel: 015394 33364
• e-mail: info@oldvicarageambleside.co.uk
• website: www.oldvicarageambleside.co.uk

Inn
The Britannia Inn, Elterwater, AMBLESIDE,
Cumbria LA22 9HP. Tel: 015394 37210
• e-mail: info@britinn.co.uk
• website: www.britinn.co.uk

B & B
Mrs C. Henderson, Highfield, Lake Road,
AMBLESIDE, Cumbria LA22 0DB
Tel: 015394 32671
• e-mail: info@highfield-ambleside.co.uk
• website: www.highfield-ambleside.co.uk

B & B
Mrs M. Lees, Rothay House, Rothay Road,
AMBLESIDE, Cumbria LA22 0EE
Tel: 015394 32434
• e-mail: enquiries@rothay-house.com
• website: www.rothay-house.com

Hotel
Crow How Hotel, Rydal Road, AMBLESIDE,
Cumbria LA22 9PN. Tel: 015394 32193
• e-mail: stay@crowhowhotel.co.uk
• website: www.crowhowhotel.co.uk

B & B
Mrs B. Houssin, Ambleside Lodge,
Rothay Road, AMBLESIDE, Cumbria
LA22 0EJ. Tel: 015394 31681
• e-mail: enquiries@ambleside-lodge.com

Self-Catering
Scalebeck Holiday Cottages, Great Asby,
APPLEBY, Cumbria CA16 6TF
Tel: 01768 351006
• e-mail: mail@scalebeckholidaycottages.com
• website: www.scalebeckholidaycottages.co.uk

Guest House
Mrs Bebbington,
Holly Cottages Guest House, Rayrigg Road,
BOWNESS-ON-WINDERMERE, Cumbria
LA23 3BZ. Tel: 015394 44250
• e-mail: info@hollycottagesguesthouse.co.uk
• website: www.hollycottagesguesthouse.co.uk

Self-Catering / Farm
Mrs J. M. Almond, Irton House Farm,
Isel, COCKERMOUTH, Cumbria CA13 9ST
Tel: 017687 76380
• e-mail: almond@farmersweekly.net
• website: www.irtonhousefarm.com

Hotel
Shepherds Hotel, Egremont Road,
COCKERMOUTH, Cumbria CA13 0QX
Tel: 01900 822673
•e-mail: reception@shepherdshotel.co.uk
•website: www.shepherdshotel.co.uk

B & B
Mrs Aspey, Grizedale Lodge, Grizedale,
HAWKSHEAD, Ambleside, Cumbria
LA22 0QL. Tel: 015394 36532
• e-mail: enquiries@grizedale-lodge.com
• website: www.grizedale-lodge.com

B & B
Mrs F. Townsend, Pepper House,
Satterthwaite, Near HAWKSHEAD,
Lake District National Park, Cumbria
LA12 8LS. Tel: 01229 860206
• e-mail: frances.townsend@virgin.net
• website: www.pepper-house.co.uk

Hotel
Ivy House Hotel, Main Street, HAWKSHEAD,
Cumbria LA22 0NS. Tel: 015394 36204
• e-mail: ivyhousehotel@btinternet.com
• website: www.ivyhousehotel.com

Hotel / Self-Catering
Woodlands Country House & Cottages,
IREBY, Cumbria CA7 1EX. Tel: 016973 71791
• e-mail: stay@woodlandsatireby.co.uk
• website: www.woodlandsatireby.co.uk

Self-Catering
Keswick Cottages, Kentmere, How Lane,
KESWICK, Cumbria CA12 5RS
Tel: 017687 73895
• e-mail: info@keswickcottages.co.uk
• website: www.keswickcottages.co.uk

Self-Catering
Lakeside Marina Apartments,
Derwent Water Marina, Portinscale,
KESWICK, Cumbria CA12 5RF
Tel: 017687 72912
• e-mail: info@derwentwatermarina.co.uk
• website: www.derwentwatermarina.co.uk

WEBSITE DIRECTORY

Guest House
Cragside Guest House, 39 Blencathra Street,
KESWICK, Cumbria CA12 4HX
Tel: 017687 73344
• e-mail:
wayne-alison@cragside39blencathra.fsnet.co.uk
• web: www.smoothhound.co.uk/hotels/cragside

Self-catering
Slee Cottage, KESWICK, Cumbria.
Contact: Orchard House, Embleton,
Cockermouth, Cumbria CA13 9XP
Tel: 017687 76257
• e-mail: info@orchardhouse.uk.net
• website: www.orchardhouse.uk.net

Self-Catering
Mrs S.J. Bottom, Crossfield Cottages,
KIRKOSWALD, Penrith, Cumbria CA10 1EU
Tel: 01768 898711
• e-mail: info@crossfieldcottages.co.uk
• website: www.crossfieldcottages.co.uk

Guest House / Self-Catering
Near Howe Hotel & Cottages,
MUNGRISDALE, Penrith, Cumbria CA11 0SH
Tel: 017687 79678
• e-mail: nearhowe@btopenworld.com
• website: www.nearhowe.co.uk

Self-Catering / Caravan
Fell View Holidays, Glenridding,
PENRITH, Cumbria CA11 0PJ
Tel: 01768 482342; Evening: 01768 867420
• e-mail: enquiries@fellviewholidays.com
• website: www.fellviewholidays.com

Self-Catering
Mr & Mrs Iredale, Carrock Cottages,
Carrock House, Hutton Roof, PENRITH,
Cumbria CA11 0XY. Tel: 01768 484111
• e-mail: info@carrockcottages.co.uk
• website: www.carrockcottages.co.uk

Self-Catering
Mark Cowell, Church Court Cottages,
Gamblesby, PENRITH, Cumbria CA10 1HR
Tel: 01768 881682
• e-mail: markcowell@tiscali.co.uk
• website: www.gogamblesby.co.uk

Guest House
Blue Swallow Guest House,
11 Victoria Road, PENRITH, Cumbria
CA11 8HR. Tel: 01768 866335
• e-mail: blueswallow@tiscali.co.uk
• website: www.blueswallow.co.uk

B & B
Mr Bell, Albany House, 5 Portland Place,
PENRITH, Cumbria CA11 7QN
Tel: 01768 863072
• e-mail: info@albany-house.org.uk
• website: www.albany-house.org.uk

B & B
Brooklands Guest House, 2 Portland Place,
PENRITH, Cumbria CA11 7QN
Tel: 01768 863395
• e-mail: enquiries@brooklandsguesthouse.com
• website: www.brooklandsguesthouse.com

Self-Catering / Caravan & Camping
Tanglewood Caravan Park, Causeway Head,
SILLOTH-ON-SOLWAY, Cumbria CA7 4PE
Tel: 016973 31253
• e-mail: tanglewoodcaravanpark@hotmail.com
• website: www.tanglewoodcaravanpark.co.uk

Guest House / Self-Catering
Mrs Jones, Primrose Cottage, Orton Road,
TEBAY, Cumbria CA10 3TL
Tel: 01539 624791
• e-mail: info@primrosecottagecumbria.co.uk
• website: www.primrosecottagecumbria.co.uk

B & B / Self-Catering
Barbara Murphy, Land Ends Country Lodge,
Watermillock, Near Penrith, ULLSWATER,
Cumbria CA11 0NB. Tel: 01768 486438
• e-mail: infolandends@btinternet.com
• website: www.landends.co.uk

Self-Catering
High Dale Park House, Satterthwaite,
ULVERSTON, Cumbria CA12 8LJ
Tel: 01229 860226
• e-mail: peter@lakesweddingmusic.com
• website: www.lakesweddingmusic.com

Self-Catering
Mr & Mrs Dodsworth, Birthwaite Edge,
Birthwaite Road, WINDERMERE, Cumbria
LA23 1BS. Tel: 015394 42861
• e-mail: fhg@lakedge.com
• website: www.lakedge.com

Guest House / B & B
Mrs D Heighton, Beckmead House,
5 Park Avenue, WINDERMERE, Cumbria
LA23 2AR. Tel: 015394 42757
• e-mail: beckmead_house@yahoo.com
• website: www.beckmead.co.uk

 FHG Guides Ltd publish a wide range of holiday accommodation guides – for details see the back of this book

WEBSITE DIRECTORY 345

•DERBYSHIRE

Inn
The Dog & Partridge Country Inn,
Swinscoe, ASHBOURNE, Derbyshire
DE6 2HS. Tel: 01335 343183
• e-mail: info@dogandpartridge.co.uk
• website: www.dogandpartridge.co.uk

Farmhouse B & B / Self-Catering
Mrs M.A. Richardson, Throwley Hall Farm,
Ilam, ASHBOURNE, Derbyshire DE6 2BB
Tel: 01538 308202
• e-mail: throwleyhall@btinternet.com
• website: www.throwleyhallfarm.co.uk

B & B
Mrs A.M. Whittle, Stone Cottage,
Green Lane, Clifton, ASHBOURNE,
Derbyshire DE6 2BL. Tel: 01335 343377
• e-mail: info@stone-cottage.fsnet.co.uk
• website: www.stone-cottage.fsnet.co.uk

B & B
Mrs M Harris, The Courtyard,
Dairy House Farm, Alkmonton, Longford,
ASHBOURNE, Derbyshire DE6 3DG
Tel: 01335 330187
• e-mail: michael@dairyhousefarm.org.uk
• website: www.dairyhousefarm.org.uk

B&B
Mrs J. Salisbury, Turlow Bank, Hognaston,
ASHBOURNE, Derbyshire DE6 1PW
Tel: 01335 370299
•e-mail: turlowbank@w3z.co.uk
•website: www.turlowbank.co.uk

Self-Catering
Burton Manor Farm Cottages,
Over Haddon, BAKEWELL, Derbyshire
Contact: Mrs R. Shirt, Holmelacy Farm,
Tideswell, Buxton SK17 8LW
Tel: 01298 871429
• e-mail: cshirt@burtonmanor.freeserve.co.uk
• website: www.burtonmanor.freeserve.co.uk

Self-Catering
P. Skemp, Cotterill Farm,
BIGGIN-BY-HARTINGTON, Buxton,
Derbyshire SK17 0DJ. Tel: 01298 84447
• e-mail: enquiries@cotterillfarm.co.uk
• website: www.cotterillfarm.co.uk

Guest House
Mr & Mrs Hyde, Braemar Guest House,
10 Compton Road, BUXTON, Derbyshire
SK17 9DN. Tel: 01298 78050
• e-mail: buxtonbraemar@supanet.com
• website: www.cressbrook.co.uk/buxton/braemar

Hotel
Charles Cotton Hotel, Hartington,
Near BUXTON, Derbyshire SK17 0AL
Tel: 01298 84229
• e-mail: info@charlescotton.co.uk
• website: www.charlescotton.co.uk

Hotel
Biggin Hall Hotel, Biggin-by-Hartington,
BUXTON, Derbyshire SK17 0DH
Tel: 01298 84451
• e-mail: enquiries@bigginhall.co.uk
• website: www.bigginhall.co.uk

Self-Catering
Mr & Mrs Hollands, Wheeldon Trees Farm,
Earl Strendale, BUXTON, Derbyshire
SK17 0AA. Tel: 01298 83219
• e-mail: hollands@easterndale.fsnet.co.uk
• website: www.wheeldontreesfarm.co.uk

Self-catering
The Flat 'Bramblegate', Tideswell Lane,
EYAM, Hope Valley, Derbyshire S32 5RD
Tel: 01433 631004
•e-mail: staffordrowland@supanet.com

Self-catering
Bridgefoot Cottage, FROGGATT, Derbyshire
Contact: Marsha North, Green Farm, Curbar,
Hope Valley, Derbyshire S32 8YH
Tel: 01433 630120
•website: www.peakdistrictholiday.co.uk

Farm / Self-Catering
J. Gibbs, Wolfscote Grange, HARTINGTON,
Near Buxton, Derbyshire SK17 0AX
Tel: 01298 84342
• e-mail: wolfscote@btinternet.com
• website: www.wolfscotegrangecottages.co.uk

Self-catering
Carloyn Wilderspin, Lower Damgate Farm
Cottages, Near ILAM, Ashbourne,
Derbyshire DE6 2AD. Tel: 01335 310367
•e-mail: damgate@hotmail.com
•website: www.damgate.com

Self-catering
Carpenter's Cottage, 1 Bentley Brook,
Bailey's Mill, MATLOCK, Derbyshire DE4 5EW
Tel: 0115 923 3455/0796 7120713
•e-mail: bobwilmot@edwalton.fslife.co.uk

www.holidayguides.com
for the wide range of accommodation featured in the full range of FHG titles

346 WEBSITE DIRECTORY

•DEVON

Self-Catering
Toad Hall Cottages, DEVON
Tel: 01548 853089 (24 Hours)
• e-mail: thc@toadhallcottages.com
• website: www.toadhallcottages.com

Self-Catering
Farm & Cottage Holidays, DEVON
Tel: 01237 479698
• e-mail: enquiries@farmcott.co.uk
• website: www.farmcott.co.uk

Self-Catering
North Devon Holiday Homes,
19 Cross Street, BARNSTAPLE,
Devon EX31 1BD. Tel: 01271 376322
• e-mail: info@northdevonholidays.co.uk
• website: www.northdevonholidays.co.uk

Self-Catering
Marsdens Cottage Holidays, 2 The Square,
BRAUNTON, Devon EX33 2JB
Tel: 01271 813777
• e-mail: holidays@marsdens.co.uk
• website: www.marsdens.co.uk

Holiday Park
Parkers Farm Holiday Park,
Higher Mead Farm, ASHBURTON,
Devon TQ13 7LJ. Tel: 01364 652598
• e-mail: parkersfarm@btconnect.com
• website: www.parkersfarm.co.uk

Self-Catering
Robin & Wren Cottages,
ASHBURTON, Devon
Contact: Mrs M. Phipps, Newcott Farm,
Poundsgate, Newton Abbot TQ13 7PD
Tel: 01364 631421
• e-mail: enquiries@newcott-farm.co.uk
• website: www.newcott-farm.co.uk

B & B
Mrs Joy Hasler, Riversmead, Newbridge,
near ASHBURTON, Devon TQ13 7NT
Tel: 01364 631224
• e-mail: eddie.hasler@virgin.net
• website: www.riversmead.net

Holiday Park
Hunters Moon Country Estate, Hawkchurch,
AXMINSTER, Near Lyme Regis, Devon
EX13 5UL. Tel: 01297 678402
• e-mail:
enquiries@huntersmooncountryestate.co.uk
• website:
www.huntersmooncountryestate.co.uk

www.holidayguides.com

B & B / Self-Catering
Mrs S.J. Avis, Lea Hill, Membury,
AXMINSTER, Devon EX13 7AQ
Tel: 01404 881881
• e-mail: reception@leahill.co.uk
• website: www.leahill.co.uk

Farmhouse B & B
Mrs H. Ayre, Kimbland Farm, Brayford,
BARNSTAPLE, Devon EX32 7PS
Tel: 01598 710352
• e-mail: info@kimblandfarmholidays.co.uk
• website: www.kimblandfarmholidays.co.uk

Self-Catering
Mr & Mrs Thorne, Bampfield Farm,
Goodleigh, BARNSTAPLE, Devon EX32 7NR
Tel: 01271 346566
• e-mail: enquiries@bampfieldfarm.co.uk
• website: www.bampfieldfarm.co.uk

Self-Catering
George & Anne Ridge,
Braddon Cottages & Forest, Ashwater,
BEAWORTHY, Devon EX21 5EP
Tel: 01409 211350
• e-mail: holidays@braddoncottages.co.uk
• website: www.braddoncottages.co.uk

Hotel
Sandy Cove Hotel, Combe Martin Bay,
BERRYNARBOR, Devon EX34 9SR
Tel: 01271 882243 / 882888
• website: www.sandycove-hotel.co.uk

B & B / Self-Catering
Mr & Mrs Lewin, Lake House Cottages
and B&B, Lake Villa, BRADWORTHY,
Devon EX22 7SQ. Tel: 01409 241962
• e-mail: lesley@lakevilla.co.uk
• website: www.lakevilla.co.uk

Self-Catering / Organic Farm
Little Comfort Farm Cottages,
Little Comfort Farm, BRAUNTON,
North Devon EX33 2NJ. Tel: 01271 812414
• e-mail: enquiries@littlecomfortfarm.co.uk
• website: www.littlecomfortfarm.co.uk

B & B
Miss Audrey Isaac, Crowborough,
Georgeham, BRAUNTON, Devon EX33 1JZ
Tel: 01271 891005
• website: www.crowboroughfarm.co.uk

Self-Catering
Devoncourt Holiday Flats, Berryhead Road,
BRIXHAM, Devon TQ5 9AB
Tel: 01803 853748
• website: www.devoncourt.info

WEBSITE DIRECTORY 347

Guest House
Woodlands Guest House, Parkham Road,
BRIXHAM, South Devon TQ5 9BU
Tel: 01803 852040
• e-mail: **woodlandsbrixham@btinternet.com**
• website: **www.dogfriendlyguesthouse.co.uk**
      www.woodlandsdevon.co.uk

Caravans & Camping
Hedley Wood Caravan Park, Bridgerule,
(Near BUDE), Holsworthy, Devon EX22 7ED
Tel: 01288 381404
• e-mail: **info@hedleywood.co.uk**
• website: **www.hedleywood.co.uk**

Touring / Camping
Holmans Wood Holiday Park, CHUDLEIGH,
Devon TQ13 0DZ. Tel: 01626 853785
• e-mail: **enquiries@holmanswood.co.uk**
• website: **www.holmanswood.co.uk**

Self-Catering / B & B / Caravans
Mr & Mrs Gould, Bonehayne Farm,
COLYTON, Devon EX24 6SG
Tel: 01404 871416/871396
• e-mail: **gould@bonehayne.co.uk**
• website: **www.bonehayne.co.uk**

Self-Catering
Watermouth Cove Cottages,
Watermouth, Near COMBE MARTIN,
Devon EX34 9SJ. Tel: 0870 2413168
• e-mail: **stay@coastalvalleyhideaways.co.uk**
• website: **www.coastalvalleyhideaways.co.uk**

Self-Catering
Watermill Cottages, Higher North Mill,
Hansel, DARTMOUTH, Devon TQ6 0LN
Tel: 01803 770219
• e-mail: **graham@hanselpg.co.uk**
• website: **www.watermillcottages.co.uk**

Self-Catering
Mrs S.R. Ridalls, The Old Bakehouse,
7 Broadstone, DARTMOUTH, Devon TQ6 9NR
Tel: 01803 834585
• e-mail: **ridallsleisure@aol.com**
• website: **www.oldbakehousedartmouth.co.uk**

Hotel
Dartmouth Golf & Country Club,
Blackawton, DARTMOUTH, Near Totnes,
Devon TQ9 7DE. Tel: 01803 712686
• e-mail: **reservations@dgcc.co.uk**
• website: **www.dgcc.co.uk**

Farm B & B
Mrs Karen Williams, Stile Farm, Starcross,
EXETER, Devon EX6 8PD. Tel: 01626 890268
• e-mail: **info@stile-farm.co.uk**
• website: **www.stile-farm.co.uk**

B & B
Welcombe-in, Welcombe Cross (A39),
HARTLAND, Devon EX39 6HD
Tel: 01288 331130 or 07714 664547
• e-mail: **WelcombeBandB@aol.com**
• website: **www.welcombe-in.co.uk**

Self-Catering / Caravan & Camping
Mrs Megan Daglish, Tamarstone Farm,
Bude Road, Pancrasweek, HOLSWORTHY,
Devon EX22 7JT. Tel: 01288 381734
• e-mail: **pets@tamarstone.co.uk**
• website: **www.tamarstone.co.uk**

Self-Catering
Jane Mason, Tinney Waters, Pyworthy,
HOLSWORTHY, Devon EX22 6LF
Tel: 01409 271362
• e-mail: **jeffmason@freenetname.co.uk**
• website: **www.tinneywaters.co.uk**

Self-Catering
Mike & Judy Tromans, Hope Barton Barns,
HOPE COVE, Near Salcombe, Devon
TQ7 3HT. Tel: 01548 561393
• e-mail: **info@hopebarton.co.uk**
• website: **www.hopebarton.co.uk**

Hotel / Guest House
St Brannocks Hotel, St Brannocks Road,
ILFRACOMBE, Devon EX34 8EQ
Tel: 01271 863873
• e-mail: **barbara@stbrannockshotel.co.uk**
• website: **www.stbrannockshotel.co.uk**

Self-Catering
Widmouth Farm Cottages, Watermouth,
Near ILFRACOMBE, Devon EX34 9RX
Tel: 01271 863743
• e-mail: **info@widmouthfarmcottages.co.uk**
• website: **www.widmouthfarmcottages.co.uk**

Self-Catering
Beachdown Holiday Bungalows,
Beachdown House, Challaborough Bay,
KINGSBRIDGE, South Devon
Tel: 01548 810089
• e-mail: **enquiries@beachdown.co.uk** or
      pets@beachdown.co.uk
• website: **www.beachdown.co.uk**

Self-Catering
Torcross Apartment Hotel, Torcross,
KINGSBRIDGE, Devon TQ7 2TQ
Tel: 01548 580206
• e-mail: **enquiries@torcross.com**
• website: **www.torcross.com**

Self-Catering
Collacott Farm, KING'S NYMPTON,
Umberleigh, North Devon EX37 9TP
Tel: 01769 572491
• e-mail: **info@collacott.co.uk**
• website: **www.collacott.co.uk**

348 WEBSITE DIRECTORY

Self-Catering
Torridge House Cottages, Torridge House
Farm, LITTLE TORRINGTON, Devon
EX38 8PS. Tel: 01805 622542
- e-mail: info@torridgehouse.co.uk
- website: www.torridgehouse.co.uk

Guest House
Dave & Anne Wilford, Gable Lodge, 35 Lee
Road, LYNTON, Devon EX35 6BS
Tel: 01598 752367
- e-mail: gablelodge@btconnect.com
- website: www.gablelodgelynton.co.uk

Farm B & B
Mrs T.M. Merchant, Great Sloncombe Farm,
MORETONHAMPSTEAD, Newton Abbot,
Devon TQ13 8QF. Tel: 01647 440595
- e-mail: hmerchant@sloncombe.freeserve.co.uk
- website: www.greatsloncombefarm.co.uk

Hotel
Riversford Hotel, Limers Lane, NORTHAM,
Bideford, Devon EX39 2RG
Tel: 01237 474239
- e-mail: riversford@aol.com
- website: www.riversford.co.uk

Farm B & B
David & Jane Pyle, Lower Nichols Nymet
Farm, NORTH TAWTON, Devon EX20 2BW
Tel: 01363 82510
- e-mail: pylefarm@btinternet.com
- website: www.pyle-farm-holidays.co.uk

Farm Guest House
Mrs Ann Forth, Fluxton Farm,
OTTERY ST MARY, Devon EX11 1RJ
Tel: 01404 812818
- website:
www.s-h-systems.co.uk/hotels/fluxtonfarm.html

Hotel / Guest House
Glenside House, Ringmore Road,
SHALDON, Teignmouth, Devon TQ14 0EP
Tel: 01626 872448
- e-mail: glensidehouse@amserve.com
- website:
www.smoothhound.co.uk/hotels/glensideho.html

Self-Catering
Mr & Mrs Dillon, Boswell Farm Cottages,
SIDFORD, Near Sidmouth, Devon EX10 0PP
Tel: 01395 514162
- e-mail: dillon@boswell-farm.co.uk
- website: www.boswell-farm.co.uk

Caravan & Camping
Harford Bridge Holiday Park, Peter Tavy,
TAVISTOCK, Devon PL19 9LS
Tel: 01822 810349
- e-mail: enquiry@harfordbridge.co.uk
- website: www.harfordbridge.co.uk

Farm B & B
Mary & Roger Steer, Rubbytown Farm,
Gulworthy, TAVISTOCK, Devon PL19 8PA
Tel: 01822 832493
- e-mail: jimmy.steer@virgin.net
- website: www.rubbytown-farm.co.uk

Hotel
The Aveland Hotel, Babbacombe,TORQUAY,
Devon TQ1 3PT. Tel: 01803 326622
- e-mail: avelandhotel@aol.com
- website: www.avelandhotel.co.uk

Self-Catering
M & T Ayre, Ratcliffe Farm, THORVERTON,
Exeter, Devon EX5 5PN. Tel: 01392 860434
- e-mail: ayre.ratcliffe@virgin.net
- website: www.devon-country-holidays.net

Self-Catering
Mrs Patricia Crawford, Baidland, Downs
Road, THURLESTONE, Devon TQ7 3NF
Tel: 01548 560688
- e-mail: jcbaidland@btinternet.com

Guest House
Mrs Arnold, The Mill, Lower Washfield,
TIVERTON, Devon EX16 9PD
Tel: 01884 255297
- e-mail: arnold5@washfield.freeserve.co.uk
- website: www.washfield.freeserve.co.uk

Self-Catering
Mrs H. Carr, Sunningdale Apartments,
11 Babbacombe Downs Road, TORQUAY,
Devon TQ1 3LF. Tel: 01803 325786
- e-mail: allancarr@yahoo.com
- website: www.sunningdaleapartments.co.uk

Self-Catering
West Pusehill Farm Cottages,
West Pusehill Farm, Pusehill,
WESTWARD HO!, Devon EX39 5AH
Tel: 01237 475638
- e-mail: info@wpfcottages.co.uk
- website: www.wpfcottages.co.uk

Golf Club
Royal North Devon Golf Club, Golf Links
Road, WESTWARD HO!, Devon EX39 1HD
Tel: 01237 473817
- e-mail: info@royalnorthdevongolfclub.co.uk
- website: www.royalnorthdevongolfclub.co.uk

Caravan & Camping
North Morte Farm Caravan & Camping Park,
Mortehoe, WOOLACOMBE, Devon
EX34 7EG. Tel: 01271 870381
- e-mail: info@northmortefarm.co.uk
- website: www.northmortefarm.co.uk

WEBSITE DIRECTORY 349

•DORSET

Self-Catering
Dorset Cottage Holidays
Tel: 01929 553443
• e-mail: enq@dhcottages.co.uk
• website: www.dhcottages.co.uk

Self-catering
Dorset Coastal Cottages, The Manor House,
Winfrith Newburgh, Dorchester, Dorset
DT2 8JR. Tel: 0800 980 4070
•e-mail: hols@dorsetcoastalcottages.com
•website: www.dorsetcoastalcottages.com

Self-Catering / B & B
Bookham Court Holiday Cottages &
Whiteways Farmhouse B&B, Bookham
Farm, ALTON PANCRAS, Dorset DT2 7RP
Tel: 01300 345511
• e-mail: andy.foot1@btinternet.com
• website: www.bookhamcourt.co.uk

B & B
Mr Edwards, Tiffany's Bed & Breakfast,
Chine Crescent, West Cliff, BOURNEMOUTH,
Dorset BH2 5LB. Tel: 01202 551424
• e-mail: tiffanyshotel@aol.com
• website: www.tiffanysbb.co.uk

Hotel
Cransley Hotel, 11 Knyveton Road, East
Cliff, BOURNEMOUTH, Dorset BH1 3QG
Tel: 01202 290067
• e-mail: info@cransley.com
• website: www.cransley.com

Self-Catering
Flat 1 - Iona, 71 Sea Road, Boscombe,
BOURNEMOUTH, Dorset BH5 1BG.
Contact: Andrew Hooper
Tel: 01202 460517 or 07967 027025
• e-mail: hoops2@ntlworld.com
• website: www.ionaholidayflat.co.uk

Farm B & B / Self-Catering
Sue Johnson, Cardsmill Farm, Whitchurch
Canonicorum, CHARMOUTH, Bridport,
Dorset DT6 6RP. Tel: 01297 489375
• e-mail: cardsmill@aol.com
• website: www.farmhousedorset.com

Hotel
The Queens Armes Hotel, The Street,
CHARMOUTH, Dorset DT6 6QF
Tel: 01297 560339
• e-mail: darkduck@btconnect.com
• website: www.queensarmeshotel.co.uk

Farm Caravan Park
Giants Head Caravan & Camping Park,
Old Sherborne Road, Cerne Abbas,
DORCHESTER, Dorset DT2 7TR
Tel: 01300 341242
• e-mail: holidays@giantshead.co.uk
• website: www.giantshead.co.uk

Hotel
Eype's Mouth Country Hotel, EYPE,
Bridport, Dorset DT6 6AL
Tel: 01308 423300
• e-mail: info@eypesmouthhotel.co.uk
• website: www.eypesmouthhotel.co.uk

Farm B & B
Mrs Gill Gosney, Kington Manor Farm,
Church Hill, Kington Magna,
Near GILLINGHAM, Dorset SP8 5EG
Tel: 01747 838371
• e-mail: gosneykm@aol.com
• website:
www.smoothhound.co.uk/hotels/kingtonmanor.html

Hotel
Cromwell House Hotel, LULWORTH COVE,
Dorset BH20 5RJ. Tel: 01929 400253
• e-mail: catriona@lulworthcove.co.uk
• website: www.lulworthcove.co.uk

Self-Catering
Westover Farm Cottages, Wootton Fitzpaine,
Near LYME REGIS, Dorset DT6 6NE
Tel: 01297 560451/561395
• e-mail: wfcottages@aol.com
• website: www.westoverfarmcottages.co.uk

Guest House / Self-Catering
The Poachers Inn, PIDDLETRENTHIDE,
Dorset DT2 7QX. Tel: 01300 348358
• e-mail:
thepoachersinn@piddletrenthide.fsbusiness.co.uk
• website: www.thepoachersinn.co.uk

Holiday Park
Cove Holiday Park, Pennsylvania Road,
ROYAL MANOR OF PORTLAND, Dorset
EX13 5UL. Tel: 01305 821286
• e-mail: enquiries@coveholidaypark.co.uk
• website: www.coveholidaypark.co.uk

B & B
Mrs C. Perrett, Folke Manor Farm, Alweston,
SHERBORNE, Dorset DT9 5HP
Tel: 01963 210731
• e-mail: folkemanorfarm@aol.com
• website: www.ruraldorset.co.uk

**Please mention this FHG Guide when enquiring about
accommodation featured in these pages**

350 WEBSITE DIRECTORY

Hotel
The Knoll House, STUDLAND BAY,
Dorset BH19 3AW. Tel: 01929 450450
• e-mail: info@knollhouse.co.uk
• website: www.knollhouse.co.uk

Farmhouse B&B / Caravan & Camping
Luckford Wood House, East Stoke,
WAREHAM, Dorset BH20 6AW
Tel: 01929 463098/07888 719002
• e-mail: info@luckfordleisure.co.uk
• website: www.luckfordleisure.co.uk

B & B
Glenthorne Castle Cove, 15 Old Castle
Road, WEYMOUTH, Dorset DT4 8QB
Tel: 01305 777281
• e-mail: info@glenthorne-holidays.co.uk
• website: www.glenthorne-holidays.co.uk

•ESSEX

B & B / Self-Catering
Mrs B. Lord, Pond House, Earls Hall Farm,
CLACTON-ON-SEA, Essex CO16 8BP
Tel: 01255 820458
• e-mail: brenda_lord@farming.co.uk
• website: www.earlshallfarm.info

B & B
Mrs W. Anderson, The Old Manse,
15 Roman Road, COLCHESTER, Essex
CO1 1UR. Tel: 01206 545154
• e-mail: wendyanderson15@hotmail.com
• website: www.doveuk.com/oldmanse

•GLOUCESTERSHIRE

Farmhouse B & B
Box Hedge Farm B & B, Box Hedge Farm
Lane, Coalpit Heath, BRISTOL BS36 2UW
Tel: 01454 250786
• e-mail: marilyn@bed-breakfast-bristol.com
• website: www.bed-breakfast-bristol.com

B&B
Jane Roper, Royland Farm Cottage, Fernhill,
Almondsbury, BRISTOL BS32 4LU
Tel: 07791 221102/07768 286924
• e-mail: jane@roylandfarmcottage.co.uk
• website: www.roylandfarmcottage.co.uk

B & B
Mrs C. Hutsby, Holly House, Ebrington,
CHIPPING CAMPDEN, Gloucestershire
GL55 6NL. Tel: 01386 593213
• e-mail: hutsbybandb@aol.com
• website: www.hollyhousebandb.co.uk

Inn
The King's Arms Inn, The Street (A433),
DIDMARTON, Near Badminton,
Gloucestershire GL9 1DT. Tel: 01454 238245
• e-mail: bookings@kingsarmdidmarton.co.uk
• website: www.kingsarmsdidmarton.co.uk

B & B
Mrs Z.I. Williamson, Kempsford Manor,
Kempsford, Near FAIRFORD, Gloucestershire
GL7 4EQ. Tel: 01285 810131
• e-mail: ipek@kempsfordmanor.co.uk
• website: www.kempsfordmanor.co.uk

Hotel
Tudor Farmhouse Hotel & Restaurant,
Clearwell, FOREST OF DEAN,
Gloucestershire GL16 8JS. Tel: 01594 833046
• e-mail: info@tudorfarmhousehotel.co.uk
• website: www.tudorfarmhousehotel.co.uk

Guest House
Gunn Mill House, Lower Spout Lane,
Mitcheldean, FOREST OF DEAN,
Gloucestershire GL17 0EA
Tel: 01594 827577
• e-mail: info@gunnmillhouse.co.uk
• website: www.gunnmillhouse.co.uk

B&B
Hunters Lodge, Dr Brown's Road,
MINCHINHAMPTON, Gloucs GL6 9BT
Tel: 01453 883588
• e-mail: hunterslodge@hotmail.com
• website: www.cotswoldsbandb.co.uk

B & B
Anthea & Bill Rhoton, Hyde Crest, Cirencester
Road, MINCHINHAMPTON, Gloucestershire
GL6 8PE. Tel: 01453 731631
• e-mail: anthea@hydecrest.demon.co.uk
• website: www.hydecrest.co.uk

Self-Catering
Orion Holidays, Cotswold Water Park,
Gateway Centre, Lake 6, Spine Road,
SOUTH CERNEY, Gloucestershire GL7 5TL
Tel: 01285 861839
• e-mail: bookings@orionholidays.com
• website: www.orionholidays.com

B & B
Mrs Wendy Swait, Inschdene,
Atcombe Road, SOUTH WOODCHESTER,
Stroud, Gloucestershire GL5 5EW
Tel: 01453 873254
• e-mail: swait@inschdene.co.uk
• website: www.inschdene.co.uk

www.holidayguides.com • for the full range of accommodation featured in FHG titles

WEBSITE DIRECTORY 351

B & B
Mrs F.J. Adams, Aston House, Broadwell,
Moreton-in-Marsh, STOW-ON-THE-WOLD
Gloucestershire GL56 0TJ. Tel: 01451 830475
• e-mail: fja@netcomuk.co.uk
• website: www.astonhouse.net

Farmhouse B & B
Robert Smith, Corsham Field Farmhouse,
Bledington Road, STOW-ON-THE-WOLD,
Gloucestershire GL54 1JH. Tel: 01541 831750
• e-mail: farmhouse@corshamfield.co.uk
• website: www.corshamfield.co.uk

Hotel
Downfield Hotel, 134 Cainscross Road,
STROUD, Gloucestershire GL5 4HN
Tel: 01453 764496
• e-mail: info@downfieldhotel.co.uk
• website: www.downfieldhotel.co.uk

Hotel / Golf Club
Tewkesbury Park Hotel, Golf & Country Club,
Lincoln Green lane, TEWKESBURY,
Gloucestershire GL20 7DN. Tel: 0870 609 6101
• e-mail: tewkesburypark@corushotels.com
• website: www.tewkesburypark.co.uk

•HAMPSHIRE

Guest House
Mrs McEvoy, Langley Village Restaurant,
Lepe Road, Langley, Near BEAULIEU,
Southampton, Hampshire SO45 1XR
Tel: 02380 891667
• e-mail: alexismcevoy@tinyworld.com
• website: www.langley-hampshire.co.uk

B & B
Mrs Arnold-Brown, Hilden B&B,
Southampton Road, Boldre, BROCKENHURST,
Hampshire SO41 8PT. Tel: 01590 623682
• website: www.newforestbandb-hilden.co.uk

Campsite
Lower Tye Campsite, Copse Lane,
HAYLING ISLAND, Hampshire
Tel: 02392 462479
• e-mail: lowertye@aol.com
• website: www.haylingcampsites.co.uk

B & B
Mr & Mrs Farrell, Honeysuckle House,
24 Clinton Road, LYMINGTON, Hampshire
SO41 9EA. Tel: 01590 676635
• e-mail: skyblue@beeb.net
• website:
www.newforest.demon.co.uk/honeysuckle.htm

Hotel
Crown Hotel, High Street, LYNDHURST,
Hampshire SO43 7NF. Tel: 023 8028 2922
• e-mail: reception@crownhotel-lyndhurst.co.uk
• website: www.crownhotel-lyndhurst.co.uk

Hotel
Penny Farthing Hotel, Romsey Road,
LYNDHURST, Hampshire SO43 7AA
Tel: 023 8028 4422
• website: www.pennyfarthinghotel.co.uk

Hotel
Bramble Hill Hotel, Bramshaw,
Near LYNDHURST, New Forest,
Hampshire SO43 7JG. Tel: 02380 813165
• website: www.bramblehill.co.uk

Caravans for Hire
Downton Holiday Park, Shorefield Road,
MILFORD-ON-SEA, Hampshire SO41 0LH
Tel: 01425 476131/01590 642515
• e-mail: info@downtonholidaypark.co.uk
• website: www.downtonholidaypark.co.uk

Hotel
Woodlands Lodge Hotel, Bartley Road,
Woodlands, NEW FOREST, Southampton
Hampshire SO40 7GN. Tel: 023 8029 2257
• e-mail: reception@woodlands-lodge.co.uk
• website: www.woodlands-lodge.co.uk

B & B
Mrs Thelma Rowe, Tiverton B & B,
9 Cruse Close, SWAY, Hampshire SO41 6AY
Tel: 01590 683092
• e-mail: ronrowe@talk21.com
• website: www.tivertonnewforest.co.uk

Guest House/B&B
Sheila Hooper, Lang House, 27 Chilbolton
Avenue, WINCHESTER, Hampshire
SO22 5HE. Tel: 01962 860620
•e-mail: stay@langhouse.co.uk
•website: www.langhouse.co.uk

•HEREFORDSHIRE

Self-Catering
Mrs Kavanagh, Whitewells Farm Cottages,
Ridgeway Cross, Near GREAT MALVERN,
Worcestershire WR13 5JR
Tel: 01886 880607
• e-mail: info@whitewellsfarm.co.uk
• website: www.whitewellsfarm.co.uk

Self-catering
Mrs Williams, Radnor's End, Huntington,
KINGTON, Herefordshire HR5 3NZ
Tel: 01544 370289
• e-mail: enquiries@the-rock-cottage.co.uk
• website: www.the-rock-cottage.co.uk

352 WEBSITE DIRECTORY

B & B
Mrs S.W. Born, The Coach House, Putley,
LEDBURY, Herefordshire HR8 2QP
Tel: 01531 670684
- e-mail: **wendyborn@putley-coachhouse.co.uk**
- website: **www.putley-coachhouse.co.uk**

Farm House B & B
Mrs Drzymalski, Thatch Close, Llangrove,
ROSS-ON-WYE, Herefordshire HR9 6EL
Tel: 01989 770300
- e-mail: **info@thatchclose.co.uk**
- website: **www.thatchclose.co.uk**

Guest House
Mrs C. A. Anderson, Lea House B & B, Lea,
ROSS-ON-WYE, Herefordshire
Tel: 01989 750652
- e-mail: **enquiries@leahouse.co.uk**
- website: **www.leahouse.co.uk**

Self-Catering
Main Oaks Farm Cottages, Goodrich, ROSS-
ON-WYE, Herefordshire.
Contact: Mrs Unwin, Hill House, Chase End,
Bromsberrow, Ledbury, Herefordshire
HR8 1SE. Tel: 01531 650448
- e-mail: **info@mainoaks.co.uk**
- website: **www.mainoaks.co.uk**

•ISLE OF WIGHT

Self-Catering
Island Cottage Holidays, ISLE OF WIGHT
Tel: 01929 480080
- e-mail: **enq@islandcottageholidays.com**
- website: **www.islandcottageholidays.com**

Hotel
Sandpipers Hotel, Coastguard Lane,
FRESHWATER BAY, Isle of Wight PO40 9QX
Tel: 01983 758500
- e-mail: **fatcats@btconnect.com**
- website: **www.fatcattrading.co.uk**

Hotel
The Country Garden Hotel, Church Hill,
TOTLAND BAY, Isle of Wight PO39 0ET
Tel: 01983 754521
- e-mail: **countrygardeniow@aol.com**
- website: **www.thecountrygarden.co.uk**

•KENT

Guest House
S. Twort, Heron Cottage, Biddenden,
ASHFORD, Kent TN27 8HH. Tel: 01580 291358
- e-mail: **susantwort@hotmail.com**
- website: **www.heroncottage.info**

Farm B&B
Bower Farm House, Stelling Minnis,
CANTERBURY, Kent CT4 6BB
Tel: 01227 709430
- e-mail: **nick@bowerbb.freeserve.co.uk**
- website: **www.bowerfarmhouse.co.uk**

B & B
Ms Frances Mount, South Wootton House,
Capel Road, Petham, CANTERBURY, Kent
CT4 5RG. Tel: 01227 700643
- website: **www.farmstay.co.uk**

Farm B & B
Alison & Jim Taylor, Boldens Wood,
Fiddling Lane, Stowting, FOLKESTONE,
Ashford, Kent TN25 6AP. Tel: 01303 812011
- e-mail: **StayoverNight@aol.com**
- website: **www.countrypicnics.com**

Hotel
Collina House Hotel, 5 East Hill, TENTERDEN,
Kent TN30 6RL. Tel: 01580 764852/764004
- e-mail: **enquiries@collinahousehotel.co.uk**
- website: **www.collinahousehotel.co.uk**

•LANCASHIRE

B & B
Mrs Val Hilton, Jepsons Farm, Moor Road,
Anglezarke, CHORLEY, Lancashire PR6 9DQ
Tel: 01257 481691
- e-mail: **enquiries@jepsonsfarm.co.uk**
- website: **www.jepsonsfarm.co.uk**

Hotel
The Chadwick Hotel, South Promenade,
LYTHAM ST ANNES, Lancashire FY8 1NS
Tel: 01253 720061
- e-mail: **sales@thechadwickhotel.com**
- website: **www.thechadwickhotel.com**

B & B
Rose Cottage Bed & Breakfast, Longsight
Road, Clayton-Le-Dale, Near MELLOR,
Ribble Valley, Lancashire BB1 9EX
Tel: 01254 813223
- e-mail: **bbrose.cott@talk21.com**
- website:
www.smoothhound.co.uk/hotels/rosecott.html

Hotel
Broadwater Hotel, 356 Marine Road,
MORECAMBE, Lancashire LA4 5AQ
Tel: 01524 411333
- e-mail: **broadwaterhotel@aol.com**
- website: **www.broadwater.co.uk**

WEBSITE DIRECTORY 353

Hotel
Rosedale Hotel, 11 Talbot Street,
SOUTHPORT, Lancashire PR8 1HP
Tel: 01704 530604
• e-mail: info@rosedale-hotel.co.uk
• website: www.rosedale-hotel.co.uk

•LEICESTERSHIRE & RUTLAND

Guest House
Richard & Vanessa Peach, The Old Rectory,
4 New Road, Belton In Rutland,OAKHAM,
Rutland LE15 9LE. Tel: 01572 717279
• e-mail: bb@iepuk.com
• website: www.theoldrectorybelton.co.uk

•LINCOLNSHIRE

B & B
Mrs D. Hickling, Woodside Farm, Long Lane,
BARKESTONE-LE-VALE, Nottinghamshire
NG13 0HQ. Tel: 01476 870336
• e-mail: hickling-woodside@supanet.com
• website: www.woodsidebandb.co.uk

Self-Catering
S. Jenkins, Grange Farm Riding School
Holiday Cottages, Waltham Road,
BARNOLDBY-LE-BECK, Grimsby,
Lincolnshire. Tel: 01472 822216
• e-mail: sueuk4000@netscape.net
• website: www.grangefarmcottages.com

Holiday Caravan Park
Orchard Holiday Park, Frampton Lane,
Hubberts Bridge, BOSTON, Lincolnshire
PE20 3QU. Tel: 01205 290328
• e-mail:
DavidMay@orchardholidaypark.fsnet.co.uk
• website: www.orchardpark.co.uk

Hotel
Branston Hall Hotel, BRANSTON,
Lincolnshire LN4 1PD. Tel: 01522 793305
• website: www.branstonhall.com

Self-Catering
Woodland Waters, Willoughby Road,
Ancaster, GRANTHAM,Lincolnshire
NG32 3RT. Tel: 01400 230888
• e-mail: info@woodlandwaters.co.uk
• website: www.woodlandwaters.co.uk

Farm B & B
Mrs C.E. Harrison, Baumber Park, Baumber,
HORNCASTLE, Lincolnshire LN9 5NE
Tel: 01507 578235
• e-mail: baumberpark@amserve.com
• website:
http://uk.geocities.com/baumberpark/thehouse

B & B
Bed & Breakfast at No19 West Street, Kings
Cliffe, Near Stamford, PETERBOROUGH,
Lincolnshire PE8 6XB. Tel: 01780 470365
• e-mail: kjhl_dixon@hotmail.com
• website: www.kingjohnhuntinglodge.co.uk

Farmhouse B & B
S Evans, Willow Farm, THORPE FENDYKES,
Skegness, Lincolnshire PE24 4QH
Tel: 01754 830316
• e-mail: willowfarmhols@aol.com
• website: www.willowfarmholidays.co.uk

B & B / Guest House
Mrs C.M. Brennan, Claremont Guest House,
9/11 Witham Road, WOODHALL SPA,
Lincolnshire LN10 6RW. Tel: 01526 352000
• website:
www.woodhall-spa-guesthouse-bedandbreakfast.co.uk

B&B
Mrs Barbara Hodgkinson, Kirkstead Old Mill
Cottage, Tattershall Road, WOODHALL SPA,
Lincolnshire LN10 6UQ. Tel: 01526 353637
•e-mail: barbara@woodhallspa.com
•website: www.woodhallspa.com

•MERSEYSIDE

Hotel
Tree Tops Country House,
Southport Old Road, FORMBY,
Near Southport, Merseyside L37 0AB
Tel: 01704 572430
• e-mail: sales@treetopsformby.fsnet.co.uk
• website: www.treetopsformby.co.uk

•NORFOLK

Bed & Breakfast
The Old Pumphouse, 2 Holman Road,
AYLSHAM, Norfolk NR11 6BY
Tel: 01263 733789
• e-mail:
tonyandlynda@oldpumphouse.fsworld.co.uk
• website:
www.smoothhound.co.uk/hotels/oldpumphouse.html

Self-Catering
Sand Dune Cottages, Tan Lane,
CAISTER-ON-SEA, Great Yarmouth,
Norfolk NR30 5DT. Tel: 01493 720352
• e-mail: sand.dune.cottages@amserve.net
• website:
www.eastcoastlive.co.uk/sites/sanddunecottages.php

354 WEBSITE DIRECTORY

Farmhouse B & B
Mrs M. Ling, The Rookery, Wortham, DISS,
Norfolk IP22 1RB. Tel: 01379 783236
* e-mail: russell.ling@ukgateway.net
* website:
  www.avocethosting.co.uk/rookery/home.htm

Self-Catering
Idyllic Cottages at Vere Lodge,
South Raynham, FAKENHAM, Norfolk
NR21 7HE. Tel: 01328 838261
* e-mail: major@verelodge.co.uk
* website: www.idylliccottages.co.uk

Self-catering
Colkirk Cottages, FAKENHAM, Norfolk
Contact: Catherine Joice, Nelson Cottage,
Fakenham, Norfolk NR21 7ND
Tel: 01328 862261
* e-mail: catherine.joice@btinternet.com
* website: www.colkirkcottages.co.uk

Hotel
Elderton Lodge Hotel, GUNTON PARK,
Norfolk NR11 8TZ. Tel: 01263 833547
* e-mail: enquiries@eldertonlodge.co.uk
* website: www.eldertonlodge.co.uk

Self-Catering
Blue Riband Holidays, HEMSBY,
Great Yarmouth, Norfolk NR29 4HA
Tel: 01493 730445
* website: www.BlueRibandHolidays.co.uk

B & B
Joanna Douglas, Greenacres Farm,
Woodgreen, LONG STRATTON, Norfolk
Tel: 01508 530261
* e-mail: greenacresfarm@tinyworld.co.uk
* website: www.abreakwithtradition.co.uk

B & B
Mrs Christine Thrower, Whincliff,
Cromer Road, MUNDESLEY-ON-SEA,
Norfolk NR11 8DU. Tel: 01263 721554
* e-mail: whincliff@freeuk.com
* website: http://whincliff.freeuk.com

Guest House
Sue Wrigley, Regency Guest House, The
Street, NEATISHEAD, Norfolk Broads,
Norfolk NR12 8AD. Tel: 01692 630233
* e-mail: regencywrigley@btopenworld.com
* website: www.norfolkbroads.com/regency

Self-Catering
Sunnybank, Blofield, NORWICH, Norfolk.
Contact: Mrs C Pritchard,
18 Danesbower Lane, Blofield, Norwich,
Norfolk NR13 4LP. Tel:01603 713986
* e-mail: gpritchard@breathe.com
* website: www.cottageguide.co.uk/sunnybank

Farmhouse B & B
Mrs Jenny Bell, Peacock House,
Peacock Lane, OLD BEETLEY, Dereham,
Norfolk NR20 4DG. Tel: 01362 860371
* e-mail: PeachH@aol.com
* website:
  www.SmoothHound.co.uk/hotels/peacockh.htm

Self-Catering
Mr & Mrs Castleton, Poppyland Holiday
Cottages, The Green, THORPE MARKET,
Norfolk NR11 8AJ. Tel: 01263 833219
* e-mail: PoppylandHoliday@aol.com
* www.poppyland.com

Guest House
Mr K. Jackman, Wroxham Park Lodge, 142
Norwich Road, WROXHAM, Norfolk
NR12 8SA. Tel: 01603 782991
* e-mail: parklodge@computer-assist.net
* website: www.norfolkbroads.com/parklodge

•NORTHUMBERLAND

Self-Catering
Mrs M. Thompson, Heritage Coast Holidays,
6G Greensfield Court, ALNWICK,
Northumberland NE66 2DE
Tel: 01670 787864
* e-mail: paul.thompson@marishalthompson.co.uk
* website: www.northumberland-holidays.com

Hotel / Self-Catering
Riverdale Hall hotel, BELLINGHAM,
Northumberland NE48 2JT
Tel: 01434 220254
* e-mail: iben@riverdalehall.demon.co.uk
* website: www.riverdalehall.demon.co.uk

Guest House
Dervaig Guest House, 1 North Road,
BERWICK-UPON-TWEED, Northumberland
TD15 1PW. Tel: 01289 307378
* e-mail: dervaig@talk21.com
* website: www.dervaig-guesthouse.co.uk

Self-catering
Doxford Farm Cottages, CHATHILL,
Northumberland NE67 5DY
Tel: 01665 579348
* e-mail: doxfordfarm@hotmail.com
* website: www.doxfordfarmcottages.com

B & B / Farm / Camping
Mrs S. Maughan, Greencarts Farm, Near
Humshaugh, HEXHAM, Northumberland
NE46 4BW. Tel: 01434 681320
* e-mail: sandra@greencarts.co.uk
* website: www.greencarts.co.uk

WEBSITE DIRECTORY

Guest House / B & B
Mrs M. Halliday, Beck'n'Call, Birling West Cottage, WARKWORTH, Northumberland NE65 0XS. Tel: 01665 711653
- e-mail: beck-n-call@lineone.net
- website: www.beck-n-call.co.uk

• NOTTINGHAMSHIRE

B & B
Mrs D. Hickling, Woodside Farm, Long Lane, BARKESTONE-LE-VALE, Nottinghamshire NG13 0HQ. Tel: 01476 870336
- e-mail: hickling-woodside@supanet.com
- website: www.woodsidebandb.co.uk

• OXFORDSHIRE

Self-Catering
Cottage in the Country Cottage Holidays Oxfordshire. Tel: 0870 027 5930
- e-mail: enquiries@cottageinthecountry.co.uk
- website: www.cottageinthecountry.co.uk

B & B
Carol Ellis, Wynford House, 79 Main Road, LONG HANBOROUGH, Oxfordshire OX29 8JX Tel: 01993 881402
- e-mail: caellis@rya-online.net
- website: www.accommodation.uk.net/wynford.htm

Guest House
K. Bradford, Hamilton House, 43 Hill Rise, OLD WOODSTOCK, Oxfordshire OX20 1AB Tel: 01993 812206
- e-mail: Kay@HamiltonHouseWoodstock.co.uk
- website: www.hamiltonhousewoodstock.co.uk

B & B
Mr & Mrs N. Hamilton, Gorselands Hall, Boddington Lane, North Leigh, between WOODSTOCK and WITNEY, Oxfordshire OX29 6PU. Tel: 01993 882292
- e-mail: hamilton@gorselandshall.com
- website: www.gorselandshall.com

Guest House
Mrs Elizabeth Simpson, Field View, Wood Green, WITNEY, Oxfordshire OX28 1DE Tel: 01993 705485
- e-mail: bandb@fieldview-witney.co.uk
- website: www.fieldview-witney.co.uk

• SHROPSHIRE

Guest House
Ron & Jenny Repath, Meadowlands, Lodge Lane, Frodesley, DORRINGTON, Shropshire SY5 7HD. Tel: 01694 731350
- e-mail: meadowlands@talk21.com
- website: www.meadowlands.co.uk

Self-Catering
Clive & Cynthia Prior, Mocktree Barns Holiday Cottages, Leintwardine, LUDLOW, Shropshire SY7 0LY. Tel: 01547 540441
- e-mail: mocktreebarns@care4free.net
- website: www.mocktreeholidays.co.uk

B & B / Self-Catering
Mrs E. Purnell, Ravenscourt Manor, Woofferton, LUDLOW, Shropshire SY8 4AZ Tel: 01584 711905
- e-mail: ravenscourtmanor@amserve.com
- website: www.internet-top.co.uk/ravenscourt

B & B
Mrs P. Morrissey, Top Farm House, Knockin, Near OSWESTRY, Shropshire SY10 2HN Tel: 01691 682582
- e-mail: p.a.m@knockin.freeserve.co.uk
- website: www.topfarmknockin.co.uk

• SOMERSET

Farm B&B / Self-Catering
Jackie & David Bishop, Toghill House Farm, Freezing Hill, Wick, Near BATH, Somerset BS30 5RT. Tel: 01225 891261
- website: www.toghillhousefarm.co.uk

B&B
Mrs C. Bryson, Walton Villa, 3 Newbridge Hill, BATH, Somerset BA1 3PW Tel: 01225 482792
- e-mail: walton.villa@virgin.net
- website: www.walton.izest.com

Inn
The Talbot 15th Century Coaching Inn, Selwood Street, Mells, Near BATH, Somerset
- e-mail: roger@talbotinn.com
- website: www.talbotinn.com

FHG Guides Ltd publish a wide range of holiday accommodation guides – for details see the back of this book

356 WEBSITE DIRECTORY

B & B
Mrs B. Keevil, Eden Vale Farm, Mill Lane,
Beckington, Near BATH, Somerset
BA11 6SN. Tel: 01373 830371
- e-mail: bandb@edenvalefarm.co.uk
- website: www.edenvalefarm.co.uk

Self-Catering
Westward Rise Holiday Park, South Road,
BREAN, Burnham-on-Sea, Somerset TA8 2RD
Tel: 01278 751310
- e-mail:
westwardrise@breansands.freeserve.co.uk
- website: www.breansands.freeserve.co.uk

Self-Catering / Caravans
Beachside Holiday Park, Coast Road,
BREAN, Somerset TA8 2QZ
Tel: 01278 751346
- e-mail: enquiries@beachsideholidaypark.co.uk
- website: www.beachsideholidaypark.co.uk

Self-Catering
Mrs Valerie Beale, Brean Sands, 53 Hillview,
South Road, BREAN, Somerset TA8 2AD
Tel: 01278 751979
- e-mail: valbeale@breansands.fsbusiness.co.uk
- website: www.somersetaccomodation.co.uk

B & B / Self-Catering
Mrs Sally Snook, Clanville Manor,
CASTLE CARY, Somerset BA7 7PJ
Tel: 01963 350124
- e-mail: info@clanvillemanor.co.uk
- website: www.clanvillemanor.co.uk

Self-Catering
Jennifer Buckland, Spring Cottage, Venns
Gate, CHEDDAR, Somerset BS27 3LW
Tel: 01934 742493
- e-mail: buckland@springcottages.co.uk
- website: www.springcottages.co.uk

Caravan & Camping Park
Broadway House Holiday Touring Caravan
& Camping Park, CHEDDAR, Somerset
BS27 3DB. Tel: 01934 742610
- e-mail: info@broadwayhouse.uk.com
- website: www.broadwayhouse.uk.com

Farm / B & B
Mrs C. Bacon, Honeydown Farm,
Seaborough Hill, CREWKERNE,
Somerset TA18 8PL. Tel: 01460 72665
- e-mail: c.bacon@honeydown.co.uk
- website: www.honeydown.co.uk

Guest House
Mrs M. Rawle, Winsbere House,
64 Battleton, DULVERTON, Somerset
TA22 9HU. Tel: 01398 323278
- e-mail: info@winsbere.co.uk
- website: www.winsbere.co.uk

Inn
Exmoor White Horse Inn, Exford,
EXMOOR, Somerset TA24 7PY
Tel: 01643 831229
- website: www.exmoor-whitehorse.co.uk

Farm Self-Catering & Camping
Westermill Farm, Exford, EXMOOR,
Somerset TA24 7NJ. Tel: 01643 831216
- e-mail: fhg@westermill.com
- website: www.westermill.com

Self-Catering
Mrs G. Hughes, West Withy Farm, Upton,
Taunton, EXMOOR, Somerset TA4 2JH
Tel: 01398 371258
- e-mail: ghughes@irisi.u-net.com
- website: www.exmoor-cottages.com

Farm Self-Catering
Jane Styles, Wintershead Farm,
Simonsbath, EXMOOR, Somerset TA24 7LF
Tel: 01643 831222
- website: www.wintershead.co.uk

B&B
Mrs C. Chauvet, Withy Road Farm,
Withy Road, East Huntspill, HIGHBRIDGE,
Somerset TA9 3NW. Tel: 01278 780226
- website: www.bbwithyroadfarm.cjb.net

Self-Catering
Mrs N. Hanson, Woodcombe Lodges,
Bratton, MINEHEAD, Somerset TA24 8SQ
Tel: 01643 702789
- e-mail: nicola@woodcombelodge.co.uk
- website: www.woodcombelodge.co.uk

Guest House / Self-Catering
Lynne Abbott & Ian Pearson,
The Old Cider House, 25 Castle Street,
NETHER STOWEY, Somerset TA5 1LN
Tel: 01278 732228
- e-mail: info@theoldciderhouse.co.uk
- website: www.ochc.co.uk

Inn / Self-Catering
The Ship Inn, High Street, PORLOCK,
Somerset TA24 8QD. Tel: 01643 862507
- e-mail: mail@shipinnporlock.co.uk
- website: www.shipinnporlock.co.uk

Self-Catering
Mrs J Greenway, Woodlands Farm,
Bathealton, TAUNTON, Somerset TA4 2AH
Tel: 01984 623271
- website: www.woodlandsfarm-holidays.co.uk

www.holidayguides.com

WEBSITE DIRECTORY 357

Guest House / B & B
Blorenge House, 57 Staplegrove Road,
TAUNTON, Somerset TA1 1DG
Tel: 01823 283005
• **e-mail: enquiries@blorengehouse.co.uk**
• **website: www.blorengehouse.co.uk**

Guest House / Farm
G. Clark, Yew Tree Farm, THEALE,
Near Wedmore, Somerset BS28 4SN
Tel: 01934 712475
• **e-mail: enquiries@yewtreefarmbandb.co.uk**
• **website: www.yewtreefarmbandb.co.uk**

Self-Catering
Croft Holiday Cottages, 2 The Croft, Anchor
Street, WATCHET, Somerset TA23 0BY
Tel: 01984 631121
• **e-mail: croftcottages@talk21.com**
• **website: www.cottagessomerset.com**

B & B / Guest House
Mrs Ann Morgan, Greenbay B&B, Greenbay,
Washford, WATCHET, Somerset TA23 0NN
Tel: 01984 640303
• **e-mail: green_bay@btinternet.com**
• **website: www.greenbaybedandbreakfast.co.uk**

Farmhouse B & B / Self-Catering
Mrs H.J. Millard, Double-Gate B&B Ltd,
Godney, WELLS, Somerset BA5 1RX
Tel: 01458 832217
• **e-mail: doublegatefarm@aol.com**
• **website: www.doublegatefarm.com**

Hotel / Self-Catering
Francesca Day, Timbertop Aparthotel,
8 Victoria Park, WESTON-SUPER-MARE,
Somerset BS23 2HZ
Tel: 01934 631178 or 01934 424348
• **e-mail: stay@aparthoteltimbertop.com**
• **website: www.aparthoteltimbertop.com**

Guest House
Mrs Margaret Ann Holt, Moorlands Guest
House, Hutton, WESTON-SUPER-MARE,
Somerset BS24 9QH. Tel: 01934 812283
• **e-mail: margaret_holt@email.com**
• **website: www.guestaccom.co.uk/35**

Farmhouse B & B
Jenny Cope, North Down Farm, Pyncombe
Lane, WIVELISCOMBE, Somerset TA4 2BL
Tel: 01984 623730
• **e-mail: jennycope@tiscali.co.uk**
• **website: www.north-down-farm.co.uk**

> **Please mention this FHG Guide
> when enquiring about
> accommodation featured
> in these pages**

•STAFFORDSHIRE

Caravan & Camping / Holiday Park
The Star Caravan & Camping Park,
Star Road, Cotton, Near ALTON TOWERS
Staffordshire ST10 3DW
Tel: 01538 702219
• **website: www.starcaravanpark.co.uk**

Farm B & B / Self-Catering
Mrs M. Hiscoe-James, Offley Grove Farm,
Adbaston, ECCLESHALL, Staffordshire
ST20 0QB. Tel: 01785 280205
• **e-mail: accom@offleygrovefarm.freeserve.co.uk**
• **website: www.offleygrovefarm.co.uk**

Guest House
Mrs Joyce Rowe, Harlaston Post Office,
Main Road, HARLASTON, Tamworth,
Staffordshire B79 9JU
Tel: 01827 383324/383746
• **e-mail: info@harlastonpostoffice.co.uk**
• **website: www.harlastonpostoffice.co.uk**

Guest House
Mrs Griffiths, Prospect House Guest House,
334 Cheadle Road, Cheddleton, LEEK,
Staffordshire ST13 7BW. Tel: 01782 550639
• **e-mail: prospect@talk21.com**
• **website: www.prospecthouseleek.co.uk**

Self-Catering / B & B
Mrs Melland, Larks Rise, New House Farm,
Bottom House, Near LEEK, Staffordshire
ST13 7PA. Tel: 01538 304350
• **e-mail:
bookings@staffordshiremoorlandsfarmholidays.co.uk**
• **website:
www.staffordshiremoorlandsfarmholidays.co.uk**

Self-catering
The Raddle Log Cabins, Quarry Bank,
Hollington, Near Tean, STOKE-ON-TRENT,
Staffordshire ST10 4HQ. Tel: 01889 507278
•**e-mail: peter@logcabin.co.uk**
•**website: www.logcabin.co.uk**

•SUFFOLK

Guest House / Hotel
Dunston Guest House/Hotel, 8 Springfield
Road, BURY ST EDMUNDS, Suffolk IP33 3AN
Tel: 01284 767981
° **website: www.dunstonguesthouse.co.uk**

Guest House
Kay Dewsbury, Manorhouse, The Green,
Beyton, BURY ST EDMUNDS, Suffolk IP30 9AF
Tel: 01359 270960
• **e-mail: manorhouse@beyton.com**
• **website: www.beyton.com**

358 WEBSITE DIRECTORY

Self-Catering
Mr P. Havers, Athelington Hall, Norham,
EYE, Suffolk IP21 5EJ. Tel: 01728 628233
- e-mail: **info@logcabinholidays.co.uk**
- website: **www.logcabinholidays.co.uk**

Guest House
The Grafton Guest House, 13 Sea Road,
FELIXSTOWE, Suffolk IP11 2BB
Tel: 01394 284881
- e-mail: **info@grafton-house.com**
- website: **www.grafton-house.com**

B & B / Self-Catering
Mrs Sarah Kindred, High House Farm,
Cransford, Woodbridge, FRAMLINGHAM,
Suffolk IP13 9PD. Tel: 01728 663461
- e-mail: **info@highhousefarm.co.uk**
- website: **www.highhousefarm.co.uk**

Self-Catering
Kessingland Cottages, Rider Haggard Lane,
KESSINGLAND, Suffolk.
Contact: S. Mahmood,
156 Bromley Road, Beckenham, Kent
BR3 6PG. Tel: 020 8650 0539
- e-mail: **jeeptrek@kjti.freeserve.co.uk**
- website: **www.k-cottage.co.uk**

Self-Catering
Southwold Self-Catering Properties.
H.A. Adnams, 98 High Street,
SOUTHWOLD, Suffolk IP18 6DP
Tel: 01502 723292
- e-mail: **haadnams_lets@ic24.net**
- website: **www.haadnams.com**

Self-Catering
Whitehouse Barns, Blythborough, Near
SOUTHWOLD.
Contact: P. Roskell-Griffiths,
66 Queen Elizabeth's Walk, London
N16 5UQ. Tel: 020 8802 6258
- e-mail: **peneloperoskell@yahoo.co.uk**
- website: **www.whitehousebarns.co.uk**

Self-Catering
Windmill Lodges Ltd, Redhouse Farm,
Saxtead, WOODBRIDGE, Suffolk IP13 9RD
- e-mail: **Julian@windmilllodges.co.uk**
- website: **www.windmilllodges.co.uk**

www.holidayguides.com
for the wide range of accommodation featured in the full range of FHG titles

•SURREY

Hotel
Chase Lodge Hotel, 10 Park Road,
Hampton Wick, KINGSTON-UPON-THAMES,
Surrey KT1 4AS. Tel: 020 8943 1862
- e-mail: **info@chaselodgehotel.com**
- website: **www.chaselodgehotel.com**
  www.surreyhotels.com

•EAST SUSSEX

Guest House
The Cherry Tree Hotel, 15 Silverdale Road,
EASTBOURNE, East Sussex BN20 7AJ
Tel: 01323 722406
- e-mail: **lynda@cherrytree-eastbourne.co.uk**
- website: **www.cherrytree-eastbourne.co.uk**

Self-Catering
Mrs Rosemary Norris, Caburn Cottages,
Ranscombe Farm, GLYNDE, Lewes,
East Sussex BN8 6AA. Tel: 01273 858062
- e-mail: **enquiries@caburncottages.co.uk**
- website: **www.caburncottages.co.uk**

Hotel
Beauport Park Hotel, Battle Road,
HASTINGS, East Sussex TN38 8EA
Tel: 01424 851222
- e-mail:
  reservations@beauportparkhotel.demon.co.uk
- website: **www.beauportparkhotel.co.uk**

Self-Catering
Mrs A. Reed, Boring House Farm,
Nettlesworth Lane, Vines Cross,
HEATHFIELD, East Sussex TN21 9AS
Tel: 01435 812285
- e-mail: **info@boringhousefarm.co.uk**
- website: **www.boringhousefarm.co.uk**

Hotel
Flackley Ash Hotel & Restaurant,
Peasmarsh, Near RYE, East Sussex
TN31 6YH. Tel: 01797 230651
- e-mail: **emma@flackleyashhotel.co.uk**
- website: **www.flackleyashhotel.co.uk**

• WEST SUSSEX

Caravan & Camping
Honeybridge Park, Honeybridge Lane,
Dial Post, Near HORSHAM, West Sussex
RH13 8NX. Tel: 01403 710923
- e-mail: **enquiries@honeybridgepark.co.uk**
- website: **www.honeybridgepark.co.uk**

WEBSITE DIRECTORY 359

Hotel

St Andrews Lodge Hotel, Chichester Road,
SELSEY, West Sussex PO20 0LX
Tel: 01243 606899
- **e-mail: info@standrewslodge.co.uk**
- **website: www.standrewslodge.co.uk**

Hotel

Cavendish Hotel, 115 Marine Road,
WORTHING, West Sussex BN11 3QG
Tel: 01903 236767
- **e-mail: reservations@cavendishworthing.co.uk**
- **website: www.cavendishworthing.co.uk**

•WARWICKSHIRE

Guest House / B & B

Julia & John Downie, Holly Tree Cottage,
Pathlow, STRATFORD-UPON-AVON,
Warwickshire CV37 0ES. Tel: 01789 204461
- **e-mail: john@hollytree-cottage.co.uk**
- **website: www.hollytree-cottage.co.uk**

Guest House

Mrs Hazel Mellor, Arrandale, 208 Evesham
Road, STRATFORD-UPON-AVON,
Warwickshire CV37 9AS. Tel: 01789 267112
- **website: www.arrandale.netfirms.com**

Guest House / Self-Catering

Mrs Elizabeth Draisey, Forth House,
44 High Street, WARWICK, Warwickshire
CV34 4AX. Tel: 01926 401512
- **e-mail: info@forthhouseuk.co.uk**
- **website: www.forthhouseuk.co.uk**

•WILTSHIRE

Farmhouse B&B

Mrs D. Robinson, Boyds Farm, Gastard,
CORSHAM, Wiltshire SN13 9PT
Tel: 01249 713146
- •**e-mail: dorothyboydsfarm@aol.com**
- •**website:**
www.smoothhound.co.uk/hotels/boydsfarm.html

Self-Catering

Mrs Susan King, Wick Farm, LACOCK,
Chippenham, Wiltshire SN15 2LU
Tel: 01249 730244
- **e-mail: kingsilverlands2@btinternet.com**
- **website: www.cheeseandcyderhouses.co.uk**

Guest House

Alan & Dawn Curnow, Hayburn Wyke
Guest House, 72 Castle Road, SALISBURY,
Wiltshire SP1 3RL. Tel:01722 412627
- **e-mail: hayburn.wyke@tinyonline.co.uk**
- **website: www.hayburnwykeguesthouse.co.uk**

Farm Guest House

Mrs L. Guild, Newton Farmhouse,
Southampton Road, Whiteparish,
SALISBURY, Wiltshire SP5 2QL
Tel: 01794 884416
- •**e-mail: reservations@newtonfarmhouse.co.uk**
- •**website: www.newtonfarmhouse.co.uk**

•WORCESTERSHIRE

Self-Catering

Mrs Kate Kavanagh,
Whitewells Farm Cottages, Ridgeway Cross,
Near MALVERN, Worcestershire WR13 5JR
Tel: 01886 880607
- **e-mail: info@whitewellsfarm.co.uk**
- **website: www.whitewellsfarm.co.uk**

•NORTH YORKSHIRE

Self-Catering

Recommended Cottages, North Yorkshire
Tel: 08700 718 718
- **website: www.recommended-cottages.co.uk**

Inn

The Buck Inn, Thornton Watlass,
Near BEDALE, North Yorkshire HG4 4AH
Tel: 01677 422461
- **e-mail: innwatlass1@btconnect.com**
- **website:**
  www.smoothhound.co.uk/hotels/buckinn.html

Hotel

New Inn Hotel, CLAPHAM, Near Ingleton,
North Yorkshire LA2 8HH. Tel: 015242 51203
- **e-mail: info@newinn-clapham.co.uk**
- **website: www.newinn-clapham.co.uk**

Farmhouse B & B

Mrs Julie Clarke, Middle Farm, Woodale,
COVERDALE, Leyburn, North Yorkshire
DL8 4TY. Tel: 01969 640271
- **e-mail: julie-clarke@amserve.com**
- **website:**
  www.yorkshirenet.co.uk/stayat/middlefarm

Hotel

The Foresters Arms, Main Street,
GRASSINGTON, Near Skipton,
North Yorkshire BD23 5AA
Tel: 01756 752349
- **e-mail: theforesters@totalise.co.uk**
- **website: www.forestersarmsgrassington.co.uk**

FHG Guides

360 WEBSITE DIRECTORY

Hotel
The Royal Oak Hotel, GREAT AYTON, North Yorkshire TS9 6BW. Tel: 01642 722361
• e-mail: info@royaloak-hotel.co.uk
• website: www.royaloak-hotel.co.uk

Caravan & Camping
Bainbridge Ings Caravan & Camping Site, HAWES, North Yorkshire DL8 3NU
Tel: 01969 667354
• e-mail: janet@bainbridge-ings.co.uk
• website: www.bainbridge-ings.co.uk

Self-Catering
Valley View Farm, HELMSLEY, York North Yorkshire. Tel: 01904 438635
• e-mail: sally@valleyviewfarm.com
• website: www.valleyviewfarm.com

Self-Catering
Abbey Holiday Cottages, MIDDLESMOOR. 12 Panorama Close, Pateley Bridge, Harrogate, North Yorkshire HG3 5NY
Tel: 01423 712062
• e-mail: abbeyholiday.cottages@virgin.net
• website: www.abbeyholidaycottages.co.uk or www.nidderdale.co.uk

Self-Catering
Dyson House Farm, Newsham, RICHMOND, North Yorkshire DL11 7QP. Tel: 01833 627365
• e-mail: dysonbarn@tinyworld.co.uk
• website: www.cottageguide.co.uk/dysonhousebarn

Guest House
Sue & Tony Hewitt, Harmony Country Lodge, 80 Limestone Road, Burniston, SCARBOROUGH, North Yorkshire YO13 0DG
Tel: 0800 2985840
• e-mail: tony@harmonylodge.net
• website: www.harmonylodge.net

Hotel
Ganton Greyhound, Main Street, Ganton, Near SCARBOROUGH, North Yorkshire YO12 4NX. Tel: 01944 710116
• e-mail: gantongreyhound@yahoo.co.uk
• website: www.gantongreyhound.com

Hotel / B & B
Mr J.M. Saville, Leeway Hotel, 71 Queens Parade, SCARBOROUGH, North Yorkshire YO12 7HT. Tel: 01723 374371
• website: www.leewayhotelscarborough.co.uk

Self-Catering
Mrs H. Sanderson, Cherry Trees Holiday Flats, 72 North Marine Road, SCARBOROUGH, North Yorkshire YO12 7PE
Tel: 01723 366142
• e-mail: info@cherrytrees.vholiday.co.uk
• website: www.cherrytrees.vholiday.co.uk

Hotel
The Golden Lion Hotel, Duke Street, SETTLE, North Yorkshire BD24 9DU
Tel: 01729 822203
• e-mail: bookings@goldenlion.yorks.net
• website: www.goldenlionhotel.net

Self-Catering
Mrs Jones, New Close Farm, Kirkby Malham, SKIPTON, North Yorkshire BD23 4DP
Tel: 01729 830240
• e-mail: brendajones@newclosefarmyorkshire.co.uk
• website: www.newclosefarmyorkshire.co.uk

B & B
Hilary & David Wells, Fern Bank B & B, Dishforth, THIRSK, North Yorkshire YO7 3JX
Tel: 01845 577460
• e-mail: hilaryanddavid@fernbankbb.freeserve.co.uk
• website: http://mysite.wanadoo-members.co.uk/fernbankbb

Self-Catering
Anne Fawcett, Mile House Farm Country Cottages, Mile House Farm, Hawes, WENSLEYDALE, North Yorkshire DL8 3PT. Tel: 01969 667481
• e-mail: milehousefarm@hotmail.com
• website: www.wensleydale.uk.com

Self-Catering
Allaker in Coverdale, WEST SCRAFTON, Near Leyburn, North Yorkshire c/o Mr A. Cave
Tel: 020 8567 4862
• e-mail: ac@adriancave.com
• website: www.adriancave.com/allaker

Guest House
Mr B.L.F. Martin, The Old Star, WEST WITTON, Leyburn, North Yorkshire DL8 4LU
Tel: 01969 622949
• e-mail: enquiries@theoldstar.com
• website: www.theoldstar.com

Self-Catering
Mr J.N. Eddleston, Greenhouses Farm Cottages, Greenhouses Farm, Lealholm, Near WHITBY, North Yorkshire YO21 2AD
Tel: 01947 897486
• e-mail: n_eddleston@yahoo.com
• website: www.greenhouses-farm-cottages.co.uk

Guest House
Ashford Guest House, 8 Royal Crescent, WHITBY, North Yorkshire YO21 3EJ
Tel: 01947 602138
• e-mail: info@ashfordguesthouse.co.uk
• website: www.ashfordguesthouse.co.uk

WEBSITE DIRECTORY

Farmhouse B&B
Mr & Mrs Richardson, Egton Banks Farmhouse, Glaisdale, WHITBY, North Yorkshire YO21 2QP. Tel: 01947 897289
• website: www.egtonbanksfarm.agriplus.net

Self-Catering
Mr N. Manasir, York Lakeside Lodges, Moor Lane, YORK, North Yorkshire YO24 2QU
Tel: 01904 702346
• e-mail: neil@yorklakesidelodges.co.uk
• website: www.yorklakesidelodges.co.uk

Guest House / Self-Catering
Mr Gary Hudson, Orillia House,
89 The Village, Stockton on Forest,
YORK, North Yorkshire YO3 9UP
Tel: 01904 400600
• e-mail: info@orrilliahouse.co.uk
• website: www.orilliahouse.co.uk

Guest House
St George's Hotel, 6 St George's Place, YORK, North Yorkshire YO24 1DR
Tel: 01904 625056
• e-mail: sixstgeorg@aol.com
• website: http://members.aol.com/sixstgeorg/

Guest House
Mrs J.M. Wood, Ascot House,
80 East Parade, YORK, North Yorkshire YO31 7YH. Tel: 01904 426826
• e-mail: admin@ascothouseyork.com
• website: www.ascothouseyork.com

Caravan Park
Alders Caravan Park, Home Farm, Alne, YORK, North Yorkshire YO61 1TB
Tel: 01347 830064
• e-mail: enquiries@homefarmalne.co.uk
• website: www.alderscaravanpark.co.uk

B & B
Mrs Caroline Barker, Cundall Lodge Farm, Cundall, YORK, North Yorkshire YO61 2RN
Tel: 01423 360203
• e-mail: caroline@lodgefarmbb.co.uk
• website: www.lodgefarmbb.co.uk

B & B
Sheila & Chris Birkinshaw, New Inn Motel, Main Street, Huby, YORK, North Yorkshire YO61 1HQ. Tel: 01347 810219
• e-mail: enquiries@newinnmotel.freeserve.co.uk
• website: www.newinnmotel.co.uk

•SCOTLAND

•ABERDEEN, BANFF & MORAY

B&B
Mrs Jane Selwyn Bailey, Drumgesk B&B, Newton of Drumgesk, Dess, ABOYNE, Aberdeenshire AB34 5BL. Tel: 01339 886203
•e-mail: info@drumgesk.co.uk
•website: www.drumgesk.co.uk

B&B
Mrs Jean Robb, Ardconnel, 6 Kinneskie Road, BANCHORY, Aberdeenshire AB31 5TA
Tel: 01330 822478
•e-mail: jsrobb@talk21.com

Self-Catering
Orton Estate Holidays, Orton,
By FOCHABERS, Moray IV32 7QE
Tel: 01343 880240
• e-mail: enquiries@ortonestate.com
• website: www.ortonestate.com

Self-catering
Newseat & Kirklea, FRASERBURGH, Aberdeenshire.
Contact: Mrs E.M. Pittendrigh, Kirktown, Tyrie, Fraserburgh AB43 7DQ. Tel: 01346 541231
•e-mail: pittendrigh@supanet.com

Guest House
Val Dickinson, An Cala Guest House, Woodlands Terrace, GRANTOWN-ON-SPEY, Highlands. Tel: 01479 873293
• e-mail: ancala@globalnet.co.uk
• website: www.ancala.info

Self-catering
J.B. and V.E. Downes, Hopeman Lodge, Lodge Road, HOPEMAN, Moray IV30 5YA
Tel: 01343 830245
•e-mail: mail@hopemanlodge.com
         viv.downes@btinternet.com
•website: www.hopemanlodge.com

Self-Catering
Val & Rob Keeble, Lighthouse Cottages, RATTRAY HEAD, Peterhead, Aberdeenshire AB42 3HB. Tel: 01346 532236
• e-mail: enquiries@rattrayhead.net
• website: www.rattrayhead.net

 FHG Guides Ltd publish a wide range of holiday accommodation guides – for details see the back of this book

362 WEBSITE DIRECTORY

Self-Catering
Mrs G. Walker, Forglen Cottages, Forglen
Estate, TURRIFF, Aberdeenshire AB53 4JP
Tel: 01888 562918/562518
• e-mail: forglen.estate@tiscali.co.uk
• website: www.forglen.co.uk

•ARGYLL & BUTE

Self-Catering / Touring Park
Resipole Caravan & Camping Park,
ACHARACLE, Argyll PH36 4HX
Tel: 01967 431235
• e-mail: info@resipole.co.uk
• website: www.resipole.co.uk

Self-Catering
Claddie Holiday Cottage, AUCHALICK BAY,
Loch Fyne.
Contact: John Rankin, 12 Hamilton Place,
Perth, PH1 1BB. Tel: 01738 632580
• e-mail: john@claddie.co.uk
• website: www.claddie.co.uk

Inn
Mr D. Fraser, Cairndow Stagecoach Inn,
CAIRNDOW, Argyll PA26 8BN
Tel: 01499 600286
• e-mail: cairndowinn@aol.com
• website: www.cairndow.com

Hotel
White Hart Hotel, Main Street,
CAMPBELTOWN, Argyll PA28 6AN
Tel: 01586 552440
• e-mail: whiteharthotel@amserve.net
* website: www.whiteh.com

Guest House
Oatfield House, Southend Road,
CAMPBELTOWN, Argyll PA28 6PH
Tel: 01586 551551
• e-mail: visit@oatfield.org
* website: www.oatfield.org

Self-Catering
Catriona O'Keeffe, Blarghour Farm Cottages,
Blarghour Farm, By DALMALLY,
Argyll PA33 1BW. Tel: 01866 833246
• e-mail: blarghour@btconnect.com
• website: www.self-catering-argyll.co.uk

Hotel
West End Hotel, West Bay, DUNOON,
Argyll PA23 7HU. Tel: 01369 702907
• e-mail: suzy@westendhotel.com
• website: www.westendhotel.com

Self-Catering
B & M Phillips, Kilbride Croft, Balvicar,
ISLE OF SEIL, Argyll PA34 4RD
Tel: 01852 300475
• e-mail: kilbridecroft@aol.com
• website: www.kilbridecroft.fsnet.co.uk

Self-Catering
Robin Malcolm, Duntrune Castle,
KILMARTIN, Argyll PA31 8QQ
Tel: 01546 510283
• website: www.duntrune.com

Self-Catering
Castle Sween Bay (Holidays) Ltd, Ellary,
LOCHGILPHEAD, Argyll PA31 8PA
Tel: 01880 770232
• e-mail: info@ellary.com
• website: www.ellary.com

Self-Catering / Guest House
June Currie, Hawthorn, Benderloch,
OBAN, Argyll. Tel: 01631 720452
• e-mail: june@hawthorncottages.com
• website: www.hawthorncottages.com

Self-Catering
Colin Mossman, Lagnakeil Lodges,
Lerags, OBAN, Argyll PA34 4SE
Tel: 01631 562746
• e-mail: info@lagnakeil.co.uk
• website: www.obanselfcatering.com

B & B
Mrs C. MacDonald, Bracker,
Polvinister Road, OBAN, Argyll PA34 5TN
Tel: 01631 564302
• e-mail: cmacdonald@connectfree.co.uk
• website: www.bracker.co.uk

Self-Catering
Linda Battison,
Cologin Country Chalets & Lodges,
Lerags Glen, OBAN, Argyll PA34 4SE
Tel: 01631 564501
• e-mail: info@cologin.co.uk
• website: www.cologin.co.uk

Self-Catering
Melfort Pier & Harbour, Kilmelford, By OBAN,
Argyll PA34 4XD. Tel: 01852 200333
• e-mail: melharbour@aol.com
• website: www.mellowmelfort.co.uk

Self-Catering
Mrs Barker, Barfad Farm, TARBERT,
Loch Fyne, Argyll PA29 6YH
Tel: 01880 820549
• e-mail: vbarker@hotmail.com
• website: www.tarbertlochfyne.com

WEBSITE DIRECTORY 363

•AYRSHIRE & ARRAN

B & B
Mrs Clark, Eglinton Guest House,
23 Eglinton Terrace, AYR, Ayrshire KA7 1JJ
Tel: 01292 264623
• e-mail: eglintonguesthouse@yahoo.co.uk
• website: www.eglinton-guesthouse-ayr.com
     www.ayrshire-guest-house.com

Self-Catering
Mrs Anne Hardie, Woodcroft,
23 Midton Road, AYR, Ayrshire KA7 2SF
Tel: 01292 264383
• e-mail: robin.hardie@virgin.net
• website:
www.selfcateringcottagesayrshire.com

Leisure Park
Laggan House Leisure Park, BALLANTRAE,
Near Girvan, Ayrshire KA26 0LL
Tel: 01465 831229
• e-mail: lagganhouse@aol.com
• website: www.lagganhouse.com

Farm Guest House
Glencloy Farm Guest House, Glencloy Road,
BRODICK, Isle Of Arran KA27 8DA
Tel: 01770 302351
•e-mail: glencloyfarm@aol.com
•website:
www.smoothhound.co.uk/hotels/glencloy

Caravans & Camping
Windsor Holiday Park, Barrhill, GIRVAN,
Ayrshire KA26 0PZ. Tel: 01465 821355
•e-mail:
windsorholidaypark@barrhillgirvan.freeserve.co.uk
•website: www.windsorholidaypark.com

B&B
Mrs M. Watson, South Whittlieburn Farm,
Brisbane Glen, LARGS, Ayrshire KA30 8SN
Tel: 01475 675881
•e-mail:
largsbandb@southwhittlieburnfarm.freeserve.co.uk
•website:
www.SmoothHound.co.uk/hotels/whittlie.html

Self-catering
Bradan Road, TROON, Ayrshire.
Contact: Mr Ward Brown Tel: 07770 220830
•e-mail: stay@bradan.info
•website: www.bradan.info

> **Please mention this FHG Guide
> when enquiring about
> accommodation featured
> in these pages**

•BORDERS

Self-Catering
Mrs Hunter, Headshaw Farm, ASHKIRK, By
Selkirk, Borders TD7 4NT. Tel: 01750 32233
• e-mail: headshaw@aol.com
• website: www.headshaw.co.uk

Self-Catering
The Old Barn, High Letham, BERWICK-
UPON-TWEED.
Contact: Richard & Susan Persse,
High Letham Farmhouse, High Letham,
Berwick-upon-Tweed, Borders TD15 1UX
Tel: 01289 306585
• e-mail: hlfs@fantasyprints.co.uk
• website: www.fishinscotland.net/letham

Self-Catering / Caravan & Camping
Neuk Farm Cottages & Chesterfield Caravan
Park, Neuk Farmhouse, COCKBURNSPATH,
Berwickshire TD13 5YH. Tel: 01368 830459
• e-mail: info@chesterfieldcaravanpark.co.uk
• website: www.chesterfieldcaravanpark.co.uk

Self-Catering
Jane Andrew, Fogo Mains, DUNS,
Berwickshire TD11 3RA. Tel: 01890 840259
• e-mail: ja@fogomains.co.uk
• website: www.fogomains.co.uk

B & B
The Bantry Bed & Breakfast, MacKays of
Eyemouth, 20-24 High Street, EYEMOUTH,
Berwickshire TD14 5EU. Tel: 01890 751900
• e-mail: info@mackaysofeyemouth.co.uk
• website: www.mackaysofeyemouth.co.uk

B & B / Self-Catering
Sheila Shell, Wiltonburn Farm, HAWICK,
Borders TD9 7LL. Tel: 01450 372414
• e-mail: sheila@wiltonburnfarm.co.uk
• website: www.wiltonburnfarm.co.uk

Guest House
Mr Brian Leask, Allerton House, Oxnam
Road, JEDBURGH, Borders TD8 6QQ
Tel: 01835 869633
• e-mail: info@allertonhouse.co.uk
• website: www.allertonhouse.co.uk

Self-Catering
Mill House, Letterbox and Stockman's
Cottages, JEDBURGH.
Contact: Mrs A. Fraser, Overwells,
Jedburgh, Borders TD8 6LT
Tel: 01835 863020
• e-mail: abfraser@btinternet.com
• website: www.overwells.co.uk

364 WEBSITE DIRECTORY

Hotel
George & Abbotsford Hotel, High Street,
MELROSE, Borders TD6 9PD
Tel: 01896 822308
- e-mail: enquiries@georgeandabbotsford.co.uk
- website: www.georgeandabbotsford.co.uk

Farm B & B/ Self Catering / Inn
Mrs J. P. Copeland, Bailey Mill, Bailey,
NEWCASTLETON, Roxburghshire TD9 0TR
Tel: 01697 748617
- e-mail: pam@baileymill.fsnet.co.uk
- website: www.holidaycottagescumbria.co.uk

Self-Catering
Arran Waddell, Lyne Farmhouse, Lyne Farm,
PEEBLES, Peeblesshire EH45 8NR
Tel: 01721 740255
- e-mail: awaddell@farming.co.uk
- website: www.lynefarm.co.uk

Self-Catering
Mrs C. M. Kilpatrick, Slipperfield House,
WEST LINTON, Peeblesshire EH46 7AA
Tel: 01968 660401
- e-mail: cottages@slipperfield.com
- website: www.slipperfield.com

•DUMFRIES & GALLOWAY

Self-catering
Laurel Cottage, BORGUE, Kirkcudbrightshire.
Tel: 01557 814130
- website: www.laurelcottage.plus.com

Hotel
Hetland Hall Hotel, CARRUTHERSTOWN,
Dumfries & Galloway DG1 4JX
Tel: 01387 840201
- e-mail: info@hetlandhallhotel.co.uk
- website: www.hetlandhallhotel.co.uk

Farm
Ceila Pickup, Craigadam,
CASTLE DOUGLAS, Kirkcudbrightshire
DG7 3HU. Tel: 01556 650233
- website: www.craigadam.com

Self-Catering
Rusko Holidays, Gatehouse of Fleet,
CASTLE DOUGLAS, Kirkcudbrightshire
DG7 2BS. Tel: 01557 814215
- e-mail: info@ruskoholidays.co.uk
- website: www.ruskoholidays.co.uk

Self-catering
Barclosh Farm Cottages, DALBEATTIE,
Kirkcudbrightshire DG5 4PL
Tel: 01556 610364
- e-mail: cook@barcloshfarm.co.uk
- website: www.barcloshfarm.co.uk

Farm / Camping & Caravans / Self-Catering
Barnsoul Farm Holidays, Barnsoul Farm,
Shawhead, DUMFRIES, Dumfriesshire
Tel: 01387 730249
- e-mail: barnsouldg@aol.com
- website: www.barnsoulfarm.co.uk

B&B
Rivendell, 105 Edinburgh Road, DUMFRIES,
Dumfriesshire DG1 1JX. Tel: 01387 252251
- e-mail: info@rivendellbnb.co.uk
- website: www.rivendellbnb.co.uk

B&B
Alan & Joan Graham, Barrasgate House,
Mill Hill, GRETNA, Dumfriesshire DG16 5HU
Tel: 01461 337577
- e-mail: info@barrasgate.co.uk
- website: www.barrasgate.co.uk

Guest House
Kirkcroft Guest House, Glasgow Road,
GRETNA GREEN, Dumfriesshire DG16 5DU
Tel: 01461 337403
- e-mail: info@kirkcroft.co.uk
- website: www.kirkcroft.co.uk

B & B
June Deakins, Annandale House,
MOFFAT, Dumfriesshire DG10 9SA
Tel: 01683 221460
- e-mail: june@annandalehouse.com
- website: www.annandalehouse.com

Hotel / B & B
Buccleuch Arms Hotel, High Street,
MOFFAT, Dumfriesshire DG10 9ET
Tel: 01683 220003
- e-mail: enquiries@buccleucharmshotel.com
- website: www.buccleucharmshotel.com

Hotel / Golf
Lagganmore Golf Hotel, PORTPATRICK,
Stranraer, Wigtownshire DG9 9AB
Tel: 01776 810499
- e-mail: lagganmoregolf@aol.com
- website: www.lagganmoregolf.co.uk

Hotel
Waterfront Hotel & Bistro, 7 North Crescent,
PORTPATRICK, Near Stranraer,
Wigtownshire DG9 8SX
Tel: 01776 810800
- e-mail: waterfronthotel@aol.com
- website: www.waterfronthotel.co.uk

Self-catering
Mr M. Andrew, Crailloch Croft Holiday
Cottages, Old Port Road, Crailloch,
PORTPATRICK, Near Stranraer,
Wigtownshire DG9 8JA. Tel: 01776 703092
- website: www.craillochcroftcottages.co.uk

WEBSITE DIRECTORY 365

Self-catering
Millbrook Cottage, ROCKCLIFFE, Dumfriesshire
Contact: Mrs Fiona Kerr, Sandhills, Annan,
Dumfriesshire DG12 6SN. Tel: 01461 203368
• e-mail: kerrfiona@aol.com

B&B / Horse-drawn Caravans
Barnhills, Kirkholm, Near STRANRAER,
Wigtownshire DG9 0QG. Tel: 01776 853236
• e-mail: info@barnhillsfarmhouse.co.uk
• website: www.barnhillsfarmhouse.co.uk

Self-catering
Old Tannery Cottage, THORNHILL,
Dumfriesshire.
Contact: Peter & Hilary Wray Tel: 01848 330116
• e-mail: prw01@globalnet.co.uk
• website: www.oldtannery.co.uk

• DUNBARTONSHIRE

Guest House
Croftburn Bed & Breakfast, Croftamie,
DRYMEN, Loch Lomond, Dunbartonshire,
G63 0HA. Tel: 01360 660796
• e-mail: johnreid@croftburn.fsnet.co.uk
• website: www.croftburn.co.uk

•EDINBURGH & LOTHIANS

B & B
Cruachan B&B, 78 East Main Street,
BLACKBURN, By Bathgate, West Lothian
EH47 7QS. Tel: 01506 655221
• e-mail: cruachan.bb@virgin.net
• website: www.cruachan.co.uk

Guest House
International Guest House, 37 Mayfield
Gardens, EDINBURGH EH9 2BX
Tel: 0131 667 2511
• e-mail: intergh1@yahoo.co.uk
• website: www.accommodation-edinburgh.com

B & B
McCrae's B&B, 44 East Claremont Street,
EDINBURGH EH7 4JR. Tel: 0131 556 2610
• e-mail: mccraes.bandb@lineone.net
• website:
http://website.lineone.net/~mccraes.bandb

Guest House
Mrs Kay, Blossom House, 8 Minto Street,
EDINBURGH EH9 1RG. Tel: 0131 667 5353
• e-mail: blossom_house@hotmail.com
• website: www.blossomguesthouse.co.uk

•FIFE

Hotel
The Lundin Links Hotel, Leven Road,
LUNDIN LINKS, Fife KY8 6AP
Tel: 01333 320207
• e-mail: info@lundin-links-hotel.co.uk
• website: www.lundin-links-hotel.co.uk

B & B
Mrs Duncan, Spinkstown Farmhouse,
ST ANDREWS, Fife KY16 8PN
Tel: 01334 473475
• e-mail: anne@spinkstown.com
• website: www.spinkstown.com

•HIGHLANDS

Self Catering / Campsite
Camusdarach Enterprises, Camusdarach,
ARISAIG, Inverness-shire PH39 4NT
Tel: 01867 450221
• e-mail: camdarach@aol.com
• website: www.camusdarach.com

Self Catering / Caravans
Speyside Leisure Park, Dalfaber Road,
AVIEMORE, Inverness-shire PH22 1PX
Tel: 01479 810236
• e-mail: fhg@speysideleisure.com
• website: www.speysideleisure.com

Self-Catering
Linda Murray, 29 Grampian View,
AVIEMORE, Inverness-shire PH22 1TF
Tel: 01479 810653
• e-mail: linda.murray@virgin.net
• website: www.cairngorm-bungalows.co.uk

Self-Catering
Glen Affric Chalet Park, Cannich, BEAULY,
Inverness-shire IV4 7LT. Tel: 01456 415369
e-mail: info@glenaffricchaletpark.com
website: www.glenaffricchaletpark.com

Self-catering
Mrs M. Ritchie, Rheindown, BEAULY,
Inverness-shire IV4 7AB. Tel: 01463 782461
• e-mail: hm.ritchie@btopenworld.com

Guest House
Mrs Lynn Benge, The Pines Country House,
Duthil, CARRBRIDGE, Inverness-shire
PH23 3ND. Tel: 01479 841220
• e-mail: lynn@thepines-duthil.co.uk
• website: www.thepines-duthil.fsnet.co.uk

A useful index of towns/counties appears at the back of this book

366 WEBSITE DIRECTORY

Guest House
Braeburn Guest House, Badabrie,
FORT WILLIAM, Inverness-shire PH33 7LX
Tel: 01397 772047
• e-mail: enquiries@braeburnfortwilliam.co.uk
• website: www.braeburnfortwilliam.co.uk

Hotel
The Freedom Of The Glen Family Of Hotels,
Onich, Near FORT WILLIAM,
Inverness-shire PH33 6RY. Tel: 0871 2223415
• e-mail: reservations@freedomglen.co.uk
• website: www.freedomglen.co.uk

Guest House
Norma E. McCallum, The Neuk, Corpach,
FORT WILLIAM, Inverness-shire PH33 7LR
Tel: 01397 772244
• e-mail:
normamccallum@theneuk.fsbusiness.co.uk
• website: www.theneuk.fsbusiness.co.uk

Self-Catering
Mr William Murray, Springwell Holiday
Homes, Onich, FORT WILLIAM,
Inverness-shire PH33 6RY. Tel: 01855 821257
• e-mail: info@springwellholidayhomes.co.uk
• website: www.springwellholidayhomes.co.uk

Inn
Glenelg Inn, GLENELG, By Kyle,
Inverness-shire IV40 8JR. Tel: 01599 522273
• e-mail: christophermain7@glenelg-inn.com
• website: www.glenelg-inn.com

Self-Catering
Invermoriston Holiday Chalets,
GLENMORISTON, Inverness,
Inverness-shire IV63 7YF. Tel: 01320 351254
• e-mail: ihc@ipw.com
• website: invermoriston-holidays.com

Hotel
Invergarry Hotel, INVERGARRY,
Inverness-shire PH35 4HJ. Tel: 01809 501206
• e-mail: hotel@invergarry.net
• website: www.invergarry.net/hotel

Caravan & Camping
Auchnahillin Caravan & Camping Park,
Daviot East, INVERNESS, Inverness-shire
IV2 5XQ. Tel: 01463 772286
• e-mail: info@auchnahillin.co.uk
• website: www.auchnahillin.co.uk

Self-Catering / Caravan
Mrs A MacIver, The Sheiling, Achgarve,
LAIDE, Ross-shire IV22 2NS
Tel: 01445 731487
• e-mail: stay@thesheilingholidays.com
• website: www.thesheilingholidays.com

Self-Catering
Wildside Highland Lodges, Whitebridge,
By LOCH NESS, Inverness-shire IV2 6UN
Tel: 01456 486373
• e-mail: info@wildsidelodges.com
• website: www.wildsidelodges.com

Self-Catering Chalets / Caravan Park
Halladale Inn Chalet & Caravan Park,
MELVICH, Sutherland KW14 7YJ
Tel: 01641 531282
• e-mail: mazfling@tinyworld.co.uk
• website: www.ukparks.co.uk/halladale

B & B / Self-Catering Chalets
D.J. Mordaunt, Mondhuie, NETHY BRIDGE,
Inverness-shire PH25 3DF. Tel: 01479 821062
• e-mail: davidm@mondhuie.com
• website: www.mondhuie.com

Self-Catering
Crubenbeg Farm Holiday Cottages,
NEWTONMORE, Inverness-shire PH20 1BE
Tel: 01540 673566
• e-mail: enquiry@crubenbeg.com
• website: www.crubenbeg.com

Self-Catering
Mr A. Urquhart, Crofters Cottages,
15 Croft, POOLEWE, Ross-shire IV22 2JY
Tel: 01445 781268
• e-mail: croftcottages@btopenworld.com
• website: www.croftcottages.btinternet.co.uk

•LANARKSHIRE

Self-Catering
Carmichael Country Cottages,
Carmichael Estate Office, Westmains,
Carmichael, BIGGAR, Lanarkshire ML12 6PG
Tel: 01899 308336
• e-mail: chiefcarm@aol.com
• website: www.carmichael.co.uk/cottages

•PERTH & KINROSS

Self-Catering
Loch Tay Lodges, Remony, Acharn,
ABERFELDY, Perthshire PH15 2HR
Tel: 01887 830209
• e-mail: remony@btinternet.com
• website: www.lochtaylodges.co.uk

Hotel
Lands of Loyal Hotel, ALYTH, Perthshire
PH11 8JQ. Tel: 01828 633151
• e-mail: info@landsofloyal.com
• website: www.landsofloyal.com

WEBSITE DIRECTORY

Self-catering
Riverside Log Cabins, Dunira, COMRIE, Perthshire PH6 2JZ. Tel: 0845 644 4830
• website: www.riversidecabins.co.uk

Self-Catering
Laighwood Holidays, Laighwood, Butterstone, BY DUNKELD, Perthshire PH8 0HB. Tel: 01350 724241
• e-mail: holidays@laighwood.co.uk
• website: www.laighwood.co.uk

Self-Catering
Gill Hunt, Wester Lix Cottage, Wester Lix, KILLIN, Perthshire FK21 8RD
Tel: 01567 820990
• e-mail: gill@westerlix.co.uk
• website: www.westerlix.co.uk

Self-catering
Killin Highland Lodges, The Sheiling, Aberfeldy Road, By KILLIN, Loch Tay, Perthshire. Tel: 0845 644 4866
• website: www.killinhighlandlodges.co.uk

Hotel
Balrobin Hotel, Higher Oakfield, PITLOCHRY, Perthshire PH16 5HT. Tel: 01796 472901
• e-mail: info@balrobin.co.uk
• website: www.balrobin.co.uk

B & B
Mrs Ann Guthrie, Newmill Farm, STANLEY, Perthshire PH1 4QD. Tel: 01738 828281
• e-mail: guthrienewmill@sol.co.uk
• website: www.newmillfarm.co.uk

Inn
The Munro Inn, Main Street, STRATHYRE, Perthshire FK18 8NA. Tel: 01877 384333
• e-mail: book@munro-inn.com
• website: www.munro-inn.com

Visit the  website

www.holidayguides.com
for details of the wide choice of accommodation featured in the full range of FHG titles

•WALES

Self-Catering
Quality Cottages, Cerbid, Solva, HAVERFORDWEST, Pembrokeshire SA62 6YE. Tel: 01348 837871
• website: www.qualitycottages.co.uk

•ANGLESEY & GWYNEDD

Self-catering
Rhyd Fudr, Llanuwchllyn, Near BALA, Gwynedd
Contact: Mrs J. H. Gervis, Nazeing Bury, Nazeing Road, Nazeing, Essex EN9 2JN
Tel: 01992 892331
• e-mail: jandmgervis@btinternet.com

Self-Catering
Mrs Jill Jones, Ogwen Valley Holidays, 1 Pengarreg, Nant Ffrancon, BETHESDA, Bangor, Gwynedd LL57 3LX
Tel: 01248 600122
• e-mail: jilljones@ogwensnowdonia.co.uk
• website: www.ogwensnowdonia.co.uk

Self-Catering within a Castle
Brynbras Castle, Llanrug, Near CAERNARFON, Gwynedd LL55 4RE
Tel: 01286 870210
• e-mail: holidays@brynbrascastle.co.uk
• website: www.brynbrascastle.co.uk

Self-Catering / Caravans
Plas-y-Bryn Chalet Park, Bontnewydd, CAERNARFON, Gwynedd LL54 7YE
Tel: 01286 672811
• website: www.plasybrynholidayscaernarfon.co.uk

Self-Catering
Mrs A. Jones, Rhos Country Cottages, Betws Bach, Ynys, CRICCIETH, Gwynedd LL52 0PB. Tel: 01758 720047
• e-mail: cottages@rhos.freeserve.co.uk
• website: www.rhos-cottages.co.uk

Caravan & Chalet Park
Parc Wernol Parc, Chwilog, Pwllheli, Near CRICCIETH, Gwynedd LL53 6SW
Tel: 01766 810605
• e-mail: catherine@wernol.com
• website: www.wernol.com

Guest House
Mrs M. Bamford, Ivy House, Finsbury Square, DOLGELLAU, Gwynedd LL40 1RF. Tel: 01341 422535
• e-mail: marg.bamford@btconnect.com
• website: www.ukworld.net/ivyhouse

368 WEBSITE DIRECTORY

Farm B & B
Judy Hutchings, Tal Y Foel, DWYRAN,
Anglesey LL61 6LQ. Tel: 01248 430977
- e-mail: judy@tal-y-foel.co.uk
- website: www.tal-y-foel.co.uk

Self-Catering
Llanberis Cottages, LLANBERIS.
Contact: Mrs A.D. Eaton, Bryn Gwyn Cottage,
9 Tai Bryn Gwyn, Tan-y-Coed, Llanrug,
Near Caernarfon, Gwynedd LL55 4RH
Tel: 01286 674481
- website: www.VisitWales.com/

Caravan & Camping
Mr John Billingham, Islawrffordd Caravan
Park, Tal-y-Bont, MERIONETH, Gwynedd
LL43 2BQ. Tel: 01341 247269
- e-mail: info@islawrffordd.co.uk
- website: www.islawrffordd.co.uk

•NORTH WALES

Hotel
Fairy Glen Hotel, Beaver Bridge,
BETWS-Y-COED, Conwy, North Wales
LL24 0SH. Tel: 01690 710269
- e-mail: fairyglen@youe.fsworld.co.uk
- website: www.fairyglenhotel.co.uk

Guest House
Glan Heulog Guest House, Llanwrst Road,
CONWY, North Wales LL32 8LT
Tel: 01492 593845
- e-mail:
glanheulog@no1guesthouse.freeserve.co.uk
- website: www.walesbandb.com

Guest House
Sychnant Pass House, Sychnant Pass Road
CONWY, North Wales LL32 8BJ
Tel: 01492 596868
- e-mail: bre@sychnant-pass-house.co.uk
- website: www.sychnant-pass-house.co.uk

Hotel
Caerlyr Hall Hotel, Conwy Old Road,
Dwygyfylchi, CONWY, North Wales
LL34 6SW. Tel: 01492 623518
- website: www.caerlyrhallhotel.co.uk

> **Please mention this FHG Guide
> when enquiring about
> accommodation featured
> in these pages**

•CEREDIGION

Self-Catering
Gilfach Holiday Village, Llwyncelyn, Near
ABERAERON, Ceredigion SA46 0HN
Tel: 01545 580288
- e-mail: info@stratfordcaravans.co.uk
- website: www.selfcateringwales.com or
        www.stratfordcaravans.co.uk

• PEMBROKESHIRE

Self-Catering / Inn / B & B
Llanteglos Estate, Llanteg, Near AMROTH,
Pembrokeshire SA67 8PU
Tel: 01834 831677/831371
- e-mail: llanteglosestate@supanet.com
- website: www.llanteglos-estate.com

Farm Self- Catering
Holiday House, BROAD HAVEN,
Pembrokeshire.
Contact: L.E. Ashton, 10 St Leonards Road,
Thames Ditton, Surrey KT7 0RJ
Tel: 020 8398 6349
- e-mail: lejash@aol.com
- website:
http://members.aol.com/lejash/thindex.htm

Farmhouse B & B
Mrs Jen Patrick, East Hook Farm,
Portfield Gate, HAVERFORDWEST,
Pembrokeshire SA62 3LN
Tel: 01437 762211
- e-mail: jen.patrick@easthookfarmhouse.co.uk
- website: www.easthookfarmhouse.co.uk

Caravan & Camping
Mrs M.A. Phillips, Upper Portclew Farm,
Freshwater East, PEMBROKE,
Pembrokeshire SA71 5LA
Tel: 01646 672112
- website:
www.caravancampingsites.co.uk/pembrokeshire
/upperportclewfarm.htm

Self-Catering
T. M. Hardman, High View, Catherine Street,
ST DAVIDS, Pembrokeshire SA62 6RJ
Tel: 01437 720616
- e-mail: enquiries@stnbc.co.uk
- website: www.stnbc.co.uk

Farm Guest House
Mrs Morfydd Jones,
Lochmeyler Farm Guest House, Llandeloy,
Pen-y-Cwm, Near SOLVA, St Davids,
Pembrokeshire SA62 6LL
Tel: 01348 837724
- e-mail: stay@lochmeyler.co.uk
- website: www.lochmeyler.co.uk

WEBSITE DIRECTORY

•POWYS

Self-Catering
Mrs E.A.A. Bally, Lane Farm, Painscastle, BUILTH WELLS, Powys LD2 3JS
Tel: 01497 851605
• e-mail: lanefarm@onetel.com
• website: www.lane-farm.co.uk

B & B
Annie McKay, Hafod-y-Garreg, Erwood, Builth Wells, Near HAY-ON-WYE, Powys LD2 3TQ
Tel: 01982 560400
• website: www.hafodygarreg.co uk

Self-Catering
Mrs Jones, Penllwyn Lodges, GARTHMYL, Powys SY15 6SB. Tel: 01686 640269
• e-mail: djones@teco4u.net
• website: www.penllwynlodges.co.uk

Motel / Caravans
The Park Motel & Campsite, Crossgates, LLANDRINDOD WELLS, Powys LD1 6RF
Tel: 01597 851201
• e-mail: info@parkmotel.co.uk

Country Hotel
Lasswade Country House Hotel & Restaurant, Station Road, LLANWRTYD WELLS, Powys LD5 4RW
Tel: 01591 610515
• e-mail: info@lasswadehotel.co.uk
• website: www.lasswadehotel.co.uk

Hotel
Brynafon Country House Hotel, South Street, RHAYADER, Powys LD6 5BL
Tel: 01597 810735
• e-mail: info@brynafon.co.uk
• website: www.brynafon.co.uk

Self-Catering
Oak Wood Lodges, Llwynbaedd, RHAYADER, Powys LD6 5NT
Tel: 01597 811422
• e-mail: info@oakwoodlodges.co.uk
• website: www.oakwoodlodges.co.uk

Self-Catering
Ann Reed, Madog's Wells, Llanfair Caereinion, WELSHPOOL, Powys SY21 0DE
Tel: 01938 810446
• e-mail: madogswells@btinternet.com

•SOUTH WALES

Guest House / Self-Catering Cottages
Mrs Norma James, Wyrloed Lodge, Manmoel, BLACKWOOD, Caerphilly, South Wales NP12 0RN. Tel: 01495 371198
• e-mail: norma.james@btinternet.com
• website: www.btinternet.com/~norma.james/

Self-Catering
Cwrt-y-Gaer, Wolvesnewton, CHEPSTOW, Monmouthshire NP16 6PR. Tel: 01291 650700
• e-mail: john.llewellywll@btinternet.com
• website: www.cwrt-y-gaer.co.uk

Hotel
Culver House Hotel, Port Eynon, GOWER, Swansea, South Wales SA3 1NN
Tel: 01792 390755
• e-mail: stay@culverhousehotel.co.uk
• website: www.culverhousehotel.co.uk

Public House / Motel
Green Acre Public House & Motel, 111 Heol Fach, NORTH CORNELLY, Near Bridgend, South Wales CF33 4LH
Tel: 01656 743041/744707
• website: www.the-greenacre.com/index.php

Guest House
Chapel Guest House, Church Road, ST BRIDES WENTLOOG, Near Newport, South Wales NP10 8SN. Tel: 01633 681018
• e-mail: chapelguesthouse@hotmail.com
• website: www.SmoothHound.co.uk/hotels/chapel1.html

Golf Club
St Mellons Golf Club, ST MELLONS, Cardiff, South Wales Tel: 01633 680408
• e-mail: stmellons@golf2003.fs.co.uk
• website: www.stmellonsgolfclub.co.uk

Hotel
Egerton Grey Country House Hotel, Porthkerry, Barry, VALE OF GLAMORGAN, South Wales CF62 3BZ. Tel: 01446 711666
• e-mail: info@egertongrey.co.uk
• website: www.egertongrey.co.uk

www.holidayguides.com

 FHG Guides Ltd publish a wide range of holiday accommodation guides – for details see the back of this book

•IRELAND

CO. CLARE

Self-Catering
Ballyvaughan Village & Country Holiday Homes, BALLYVAUGHAN.
Contact: George Quinn, Frances Street, Kilrush, Co. Clare. Tel: 00 353 65 9051977
• e-mail: george@ballyvaughan-cottages.com
• website: www.ballyvaughan-cottages.com

CO. WESTMEATH

Golf
East Coast & Midlands Tourism, Dublin Road, MULLINGAR, County Westmeath
Tel: 00 353 444 8650
• e-mail: info@eastcoastmidlands.ie
• website: www.eastcoastmidlands.ie

•CHANNEL ISLANDS

GUERNSEY

Self-Catering
Swallow Apartments, La Cloture, LANCRESSE, Guernsey GY3 5AY
• e-mail: swallowapt@aol.com
• website: www.swallowapartments.com

**www.holidayguides.com
for the wide range of accommodation featured in the full range of FHG titles**

Other specialised FHG Guides
Published annually: available in all good bookshops or direct from the publisher.

Recommended **COUNTRY INNS & PUBS** OF BRITAIN

Recommended **COUNTRY HOTELS** OF BRITAIN

Recommended **SHORT BREAK HOLIDAYS** IN BRITAIN

The bestselling **PETS WELCOME!**

FHG Guides • Abbey Mill Business Centre,
Seedhill, Paisley, Renfrewshire PA1 1TJ
Tel: 0141-887 0428 • Fax: 0141-889 7204
e-mail: admin@fhguides.co.uk
www.holidayguides.com

Family-Friendly Pubs and Inns

Family-Friendly Pubs and Inns

This is a selection of establishments which make an extra effort to cater for parents and children. The majority provide a separate children's menu or they may be willing to serve small portions of main course dishes on request; there are often separate outdoor or indoor play areas where the junior members of the family can let off steam while Mum and Dad unwind over a drink.

NB: Not all establishments featured in this section have an entry in the main section of this guide, but they appear in other FHG publications - see the FHG website www.holidayguides.com.

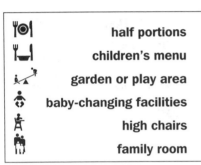

half portions
children's menu
garden or play area
baby-changing facilities
high chairs
family room

SWAN INN
Inkpen, Hungerford,
Berkshire RG17 9DX
Tel: 01488 668326
www.theswaninn-organics.co.uk

THE BULL COUNTRY INN
Stanford Dingley,
Berkshire RG7 6LS
Tel: 0118 974 4409
www.thebullatstanforddingley.co.uk

THE ANCHOR INN
Bury Lane, Sutton Gault, Near Ely,
Cambridgeshire CB6 2BD
Tel: 01353 778537
www.anchor-inn-resteaurant.co.uk

THE PHEASANT INN
Higher Burwardsley, Tattenhall
Cheshire CH3 9PF
Tel: 01829 770434
www.thepheasantinn.co.uk

CRUMPLEHORN
INN & MILL
Polperro, Cornwall PL13 2RJ
Tel: 01503 272348
www.crumplehorn-inn.co.uk

Family-Friendly Pubs and Inns

🍽	half portions
🛏	children's menu
🛝	garden or play area
👶	baby-changing facilities
🪑	high chairs
👨‍👩‍👧	family room

RASHLEIGH ARMS
Charlestown, St Austell,
Cornwall PL25 3NJ
Tel: 01726 73635
www.smallandfriendly.co.uk

THE CORNISH ARMS
Pendoggett, Port Isaac,
Cornwall PL30 3HH
Tel: 01208 880263
www.cornisharms.com

THE WHEATSHEAF
Beetham, Near Milnthorpe,
Cumbria LA7 7AL
Tel: 015395 62123
www.wheatsheafbeetham.com

THE SCREES INN
Nether Wasdale,
Cumbria CA20 1ET
Tel/Fax: 019467 26262
www.thescreesinnwasdale.com

SAWREY HOTEL
Far Sawrey,
Near Ambleside,
Cumbria LA22 0LQ
Tel & Fax: 015394 43425

THE WHITE MARE
Beckermet,
Cumbria CA21 2XS
Tel: 01946 841246
www.whitemare.co.uk

GRAHAM ARMS
Longtown,
Near Carlisle,
Cumbria CA6 5SE
Tel: 01228 791213

Family-Friendly Pubs and Inns

YORKSHIRE BRIDGE INN
Ashopton Road, Bamford in the
High Peak, Derbyshire S33 0AZ
Tel & Fax: 01433 651361
www.yorkshire-bridge.co.uk

THE GLOBE HOTEL
Fore Street, Topsham, Near Exeter,
Devon EX3 0HR
Tel: 01392 873471
www.globehotel.com

RING OF BELLS INN
North Bovey,
Devon TQ13 8RB
Tel: 01647 440375
www.ringofbellsinn.com

THE OXENHAM ARMS
South Zeal, Okehampton,
Devon EX20 2JT
Tel: 01837 840244
www.theoxenhamarms.co.uk

PORT LIGHT HOTEL
Bolberry Down, Malborough,
South Devon TQ7 3DY
Tel: 01548 561384
www.portlight.co.uk

BANKES ARMS HOTEL
East Street, Corfe Castle,
Wareham, Dorset BH20 5ED
Tel: 01929 480206
www.dorset-hotel.co.uk

THE BULL HOTEL
Market Place, Fairford,
Gloucestershire GL7 4AA
Tel: 01285 712535
www.thebullhotelfairford.co.uk

THE PLOUGH INN
Kelmscott,
Near Lechlade,
Gloucestershire GL7 3HG
Tel: 01367 253543

Family-Friendly Pubs and Inns

🍽	half portions
🛁	children's menu
🛝	garden or play area
👶	baby-changing facilities
🪑	high chairs
👨‍👩‍👧	family room

THE MALT SHOVEL
Ruardean,
Gloucestershire GL17 9TW
Tel: 01594 543028
www.maltshovel.u-net.com

THE SALUTATION INN
Market Pitch, Weobley,
Herefordshire HR4 8SJ
Tel: 01544 318443
www.thesalutationinn.co.uk

OWD NELL'S CANALSIDE TAVERN
Guy's Thatched Hamlet, Bilsborrow,
Lancashire PR3 0RS
Tel: 01995 640010
www.guysthatchedhamlet.com

THE FARMERS' ARMS
Wood Lane, Heskin, Near Chorley,
Lancashire PR7 5NP
Tel: 01257 451276
www.farmersarms.co.uk

THE HILL HOUSE
Happisburgh
Norfolk NR12 0PW
Tel & Fax: 01692 650004

THE FISHERMAN'S RETURN
The Lane, Winterton-on-Sea
Norfolk NR29 4BN
Tel: 01493 393305
www.fishermans-return.com

THE ANGLERS ARMS
Weldon Bridge, Longframlington,
Northumberland NE65 8AX
Tel: 01665 570271/570655
www.anglersarms.com

Family-Friendly Pubs and Inns

THE LUTTRELL ARMS
High Street, Dunster
Somerset TA24 6SG
Tel: 01643 821555
www.luttrellarms.co.uk

ROSE & CROWN
Woodhill, Stoke St Gregory,
Taunton, Somerset TA3 6EW
Tel: 01823 490296
www.browningpubs.com

RIVERSIDE HOTEL
Riverside Drive, Branston, Burton-upon-Trent, Staffordshire DE14 3EP
Tel: 01283 511234
www.riversidehotel-branston.com

THE BULL INN
The Street, Woolpit
Suffolk IP30 9SA
Tel: 01359 240393
www.bullinnwoolpit.co.uk

NEW INN
Clifford Chambers, Stratford-upon-Avon, Warwickshire CV37 8HR
Tel: 01789 293402
www.thenewinnhotel.co.uk

THE ROYAL OAK
Wootton Rivers, Near Marlborough,
Wiltshire SN8 4NQ
Tel: 01672 810322
www.wiltshire-pubs.co.uk

THE FAIRFAX ARMS
Gilling East, York
North Yorkshire YO62 4JH
Tel: 01439 788212
www.fairfaxarms.co.uk

THE OLD WHITE LION
6-10 West Lane, Haworth, Keighley,
West Yorkshire BD22 8DU
Tel: 01535 642313
www.oldwhitelionhotel.com

Family-Friendly Pubs and Inns

- 🍽 half portions
- 🍼 children's menu
- 🛝 garden or play area
- 👶 baby-changing facilities
- 🪑 high chairs
- 👨‍👩‍👧 family room

GRANT ARMS
The Square, Monymusk,
Inverurie,
Aberdeenshire AB51 7HJ
Tel: 01467 651226

THE VILLAGE INN
Arrochar, Loch Long,
Argyll G83 7AX
Tel: 01301 702279
www.maclay.com/VillageInn.html

THE COYLET INN
Loch Eck,
Argyll PA23 8SG
Tel & Fax: 01369 840426
www.coylet-locheck.co.uk

THE CREGGANS INN
Strachur, Loch Fyne,
Argyll PA27 8BX
Tel: 01369 860279
www.creggans-inn.co.uk

KELVIN HOUSE HOTEL
53 Main Street, Glenluce, Newton
Stewart Wigtownshire DG8 0PP
Tel/Fax: 01581 300303
www.kelvin-house.co.uk

THE CEDAR INN
20 Shore Road, Aberdour,
Fife KY3 0TR
Tel: 01383 860310
www.cedarinn.co.uk

THE INN AT ARDGOUR
Ardgour, Fort William,
Inverness-shire PH33 7AA
Tel: 01855 841225
www.ardgour.biz

Family-Friendly Pubs and Inns

THE ROWAN TREE
Loch Alvie, By Aviemore
Inverness-shire PH22 1QB
Tel & Fax: 01479 810207
www.rowantreehotel.com

BENLEVA HOTEL
Drumnadrochit, Loch Ness,
Invernes-shire IV63 6UH
Tel: 01456 450080
www.lochnesshotel.com

THE MOORINGS HOTEL
Banavie, Fort William
Inverness-shire PH33 7LY
Tel: 01397 772797
www.moorings-fortwilliam.co.uk

THE WELL COUNTRY INN
Main Street, Scotlandwell,
Kinross KY13 9JA
Tel & Fax: 01592 840444
www.thewellcountryinn.co.uk

GEORGE III HOTEL
Penmaenpool, Dolgellau,
Meirionnydd, Gwynedd LL40 1YD
Tel: 01341 422525
www.landmarkinns.co.uk

WYNNSTAY ARMS
Llangollen
Denbighshire LL20 8PF
Tel: 01978 860710
www.wynnstay-arms.co.uk

Visit the website
www.holidayguides.com
for details of the wide
choice of accommodation
featured in the full range
of FHG titles

THE WAUN WYLLT INN
Horeb, Five Roads
LLanelli, Carms. SA15 5AQ
Tel: 01269 860209
www.waunwyllt.co.uk

Family-Friendly Pubs and Inn

half portions
children's menu
garden or play area
baby-changing facilities
high chairs
family room

HUNDRED HOUSE INN
Hundred House,
Llandrindod Wells,
Powys LD1 5RY
Tel: 01982 570231

TREWERN ARMS
Nevern, Newport,
Pembrokeshire SA42 0NB
Tel: 01239 820395
www.trewern-arms-pembrokeshire.co.uk

THE CROWN INN
North Street, Rhayader,
Powys LD1 6BT
Tel: 01597 811099
www.thecrownrhayader.co.uk

GREYHOUND INN
Llantrissant, Near Usk
Monmouthshire NP15 1LE
Tel: 01291 672505/673447
www.greyhound-inn.com

THE SOMERSET ARMS
Victoria Street,
Abergavenny
South Wales NP7 5DT
Tel: 01873 852158

FHG Guides publish a large range of well-known accommodation guides. We will be happy to send you details or you can use the order form at the back of this book.

A Guide to Pet-Friendly Pubs

ENGLAND

BERKSHIRE

The Greyhound Eton Wick, Berkshire SL4 6JE
A picturesque pub with plenty of walks close by. Food served daily. Kia the Shepherd and Harvey the Retriever are the resident pets.
Sunday lunch only £5.95 between 12 noon - 3pm
Tel: 01753 863925 • www.thegreyhoundetonwick.co.uk

UNCLE TOM'S CABIN
Hills Lane, Cookham Dean, Berkshire (01628 483339).
Dogs allowed throughout.
Pet Regulars: Flossie and Ollie (Old English Sheepdog). Free dog biscuit pub.

THE GREYHOUND (known locally as 'The Dog')
The Walk, Eton Wick, Berkshire (01753 863925).
Dogs allowed throughout the pub.
Pet Regulars: Harvey (Retriever), retrieves anything, including Beer mats. KIA - German Shepherd.

THE OLD BOOT
Stanford Bingley, Berkshire (01189 744292).
Pets welcome in bar area and garden.
Pet Regulars: Resident dog "Skip" - Black Labrador.

THE SWAN
9 Mill Lane, Clewer, Windsor, Berkshire (01753 862069).
Dogs allowed throughout the pub.
Pet Regulars: Mollie and Lucy (Jack Russells).

THE TWO BREWERS
Park Street, Windsor, Berkshire (01753 855426).
Dogs allowed, public and saloon bars.
Pet Regulars: Harry (Pyrenean) and his mate Molly (Newfoundland) take up the whole bar, 'Bear' (Black Labrador), Rufus (Springer Spaniel), Mr Darcy (Poodle), Mr Darcy (Great Dane), Rosie (Chocolate Labrador), Jessie (Labrador/German Shepherd) and Lulu.

FHG
Visit the KUPERARD website
www.holidayguides.com
for details of the wide choice of accommodation featured in the full range of FHG titles

Pet-Friendly Pubs

BUCKINGHAMSHIRE

WHITE HORSE
Village Lane, Hedgerley, Buckinghamshire SL2 3UY (01753 643225).
Dogs allowed at tables on pub frontage, beer garden (on leads), public bar.

FROG AT SKIRMETT
Skirmett, Henley-on-Thames, Buckinghamshire RG9 6TG (01491 638996)
Dogs welcome, pet friendly.
Pet Regular: Resident cat "Cleo".

GEORGE AND DRAGON
High Street, West Wycombe, Buckinghamshire HP14 3AB (01494 464414)
Pet friendly.

CAMBRIDGESHIRE

YE OLD WHITE HART
Main Street, Ufford, Peterborough, Cambridgeshire (01780 740250).
Dogs allowed in non-food areas.

CHESHIRE

THE GROSVENOR ARMS
Chester Road, Aldford, Cheshire CH3 6HJ (01244 620228)
Pet friendly.
Pet Regulars: resident dog "Sadie" (Labrador).

CORNWALL

DRIFTWOOD SPARS HOTEL
Trevaunance Cove, St Agnes, Cornwall (01872 552428).
Dogs allowed everywhere except the restaurant.
Pet Regulars: Buster (Cornish Labrador cross with a Seal) - devours anything.

JUBILEE INN
Pelynt, Near Looe, Cornwall PL13 2JZ (01503 220312).
Dogs allowed in all areas except restaurant; accommodation for guests with dogs.

THE MILL HOUSE INN
Trebarwith Strand, Tintagel, Cornwall PL34 0HD (01840 770200).
Pet friendly.

THE MOLESWORTH ARMS HOTEL
Molesworth Street, Wadebridge, Cornwall PL27 7DP (01208 812055).
Dogs allowed in all public areas and in hotel rooms.
Pet Regulars: Thomson Cassidy (Black Lab), Ruby Cassidy and Lola (Black Lab).

381

Pet-Friendly Pubs

CUMBRIA

THE BRITANNIA INN
Elterwater, Ambleside, Cumbria LA22 9HP (015394 37210).
Dogs allowed in all areas except dining room and residential lounge.
Pet Friendly.

THE MORTAL MAN HOTEL
Troutbeck, Windermere, Cumbria LA23 lPL (015394 33193).
Pets allowed everywhere except restaurant.

STAG INN
Dufton, Appleby, Cumbria (017683 51608).
Dogs allowed in non-food bar, beer garden, village green plus cottage.
Pet Regulars: Sofie (Labrador) and Jeanie (Terrier).

WATERMILL INN
School Lane, Ings, Near Staveley, Kendal, Cumbria (01539 821309).
Dogs allowed in beer garden, Wrynose bottom bar.
Pet Regulars: Blot (sheepdog) and Scruffy (mongrel). Both enjoy a range of crisps and snacks. Scruffy regularly drinks Cheaston Best Bitter. Pub dog Shelley (German Shepherd). Owners cannot walk dogs past pub, without being dragged in! Biscuits and water provided.

DERBYSHIRE

THE GEORGE HOTEL
Commercial Road, Tideswell, Near Buxton, Derbyshire SK17 8NU (01298 871382).
Dogs allowed in snug and around the bar, water bowls provided.

DOG AND PARTRIDGE COUNTRY INN & MOTEL
Swinscoe, Ashbourne, Derbyshire (01335 343183).
Dogs allowed throughout, except restaurant.
Pet Regulars: Include Mitsy (57); Rusty (Cairn); Spider (Collie/GSD) and Rex (GSD).

DEVONSHIRE ARMS
Peak Forest, Near Buxton, Derbyshire SK17 8EJ (01298 23875)
Dogs allowed in bar.

---

please
note

All the information in this book is given in good faith in the belief that it is correct. However, the publishers cannot guarantee the facts given in these pages, neither are they responsible for changes in policy, ownership or terms that may take place after the date of going to press. Readers should always satisfy themselves that the facilities they require are available and that the terms, if quoted, still apply.

FHG
·K·U·P·E·R·A·R·D·

382
Pet-Friendly Pubs ■■■

DEVON

THE SHIP INN
Axmouth, Devon EX12 4AF (01297 21838).
A predominantly catering pub, so dogs on a lead please.
Pet Regulars: Kym (Boxer), Soxy (cat). Also resident Tawny Owl.

BRENDON HOUSE
Brendon, Lynton, North Devon EX35 6PS (01598 741206).
Dogs very welcome and allowed in tea gardens, guest bedrooms by arrangement.
Owner's dogs - Drummer, Piper and Angus (Labradors).

THE BULLERS ARMS
Chagford, Newton Abbot, Devon (01647 432348).
Dogs allowed throughout pub, except dining room/kitchen. "More than welcome".

CROWN AND SCEPTRE
2 Petitor Road, Torquay, Devon TQ1 4QA (01803 328290).
Dogs allowed in non-food bar, family room, lounge. All dogs welcome.
Pet Regulars: Two Jack Russells - Scrappy Doo and Minnie Mouse.

THE JOURNEY'S END INN
Ringmore, Near Kingsbridge, South Devon TQ7 4HL (01548 810205).
Dogs allowed throughout the pub except in the dining room, must be on a lead.

PALK ARMS INN
Hennock, Bovey Tracey, Devon TQ13 9QS (01626 836584).
Pets welcome.

THE ROYAL OAK INN
Dunsford, Near Exeter, Devon EX6 7DA (01647 252256).
Dogs allowed in bars, beer garden, accommodation for guests with dogs.
Pet Regulars: Cleo and Kizi.

THE POLSHAM ARMS
Lower Polsham Road, Paignton, Devon (01803 558360).
Dogs allowed throughout the pub.
Pet Regulars: Patch, owner brings his supply of dog biscuits, and Bracken (German Shepherd).

THE SEA TROUT INN
Staverton, Near Totnes, Devon TQ9 6PA (01803 762274).
Dogs welcome in lounge and public bar, beer garden, owners' rooms (but not on beds).
Pet Regulars: Buster (resident dog) partial to beer drip trays.

THE DEVONSHIRE INN
Sticklepath, Okehampton, Devon EX20 2NW (01837 840626).
Dogs allowed in non-food bar, car park, beer garden, family room and guest rooms.
Pet Regulars: Clarrie and Rosie (Terriers).

THE TROUT & TIPPLE
(A386 - Tavistock to Okehampton Road), Parkwood Road, Tavistock,
Devon PL10 0JS (01822 618886)
Dogs welcome at all times in bar, games room and patio.
Pet regulars include: Jet (black Labrador) likes biscuits and his two sons Connor and Fenrhys - sometimes misbehave. Alf (GSD) visits occasionally - but has to stay off the Guinness. Casey (Bronze Springer) - always after food. Border, Chaos and Mischief (Border Collies). Also, our own dog - Dave (Lurcher).

Pet-Friendly Pubs

DORSET

THE ANVIL HOTEL
Sailsbury Road, Pimperne, Blandford, Dorset DT11 8UQ (01258 453431).
Pets allowed in bar, lounge and bedrooms.

THE SQUARE AND COMPASS
Swanage, Dorset BH19 3LF (01929 439229).
Well-behaved dogs allowed - but beware of the chickens!

DRUSILLA'S INN
Wigbeth, Horton, Dorset (01258 840297).
Well-behaved dogs welcome.

DURHAM

MOORCOCK INN
Hill Top, Eggleston, Teesdale, County Durham DL12 9AU (01833 650395).
Pet Regulars: Thor, the in-house hound dog, and Raymond, the resident hack, welcome all equine travellers; Gem (Jack Russell); Arnie (Ginger Tom); Poppy (Jack Russell); Haflinger - the horse.

TAP AND SPILE
27 Front Street, Framwellgate Moor, Durham DH1 5EE (0191 386 5451).
Dogs allowed throughout the pub.

THE ROSE TREE
Low Road West, Shincliff, Durham DH1 2LY (0191-386 8512).
Pets allowed in bar area and garden.
Pet Regulars: "Benson" (Boxer), "Ben" (Miniature White Poodle) and "Oliver" (King Charles).

THE SEVEN STARS
High Street North, Shincliff, Durham (0191-384 8454).
Dogs welcome in bar area only.

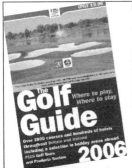

The Golf Guide · 2006
Where to Play, Where to Stay

Available from most booksellers, **The Golf Guide, Where to Play, Where to Stay** covers details of every UK golf course – well over 2800 entries – for holiday or business golf. Hundreds of hotel entries offer convenient accommodation, with accompanying details of the courses – the 'pro', par score, length and more. Including holiday golf in Ireland, France, Portugal, Spain, the USA, South Africa and Thailand.

**Only £9.99 from booksellers or direct from the publishers:
FHG GUIDES, Abbey Mill Business Centre, Seedhill,
Paisley PA1 1TJ** *(postage charged outside UK)*
e-mail: admin@fhguides.co.uk • www.holidayguides.com

ESSEX

WHITE HARTE
The Quay, Burnham-on-Crouch, Essex CM0 8AS (01621 782106).
Pets welcome.
Pet Regulars: Resident dog "Tilly" (Collie).

THE OLD SHIP
Heybridge Basin, Heybridge, Maldon, Essex (01621 854150).
Dogs allowed throughout pub.

GLOUCESTERSHIRE

THE OLD STOCKS HOTEL
The Square, Stow on the Wold, Gloucestershire GL54 1AF (01451 830666).
Dogs allowed in the beer garden, accommodation for dogs and their owners also available.
Pet Regulars: Ben (Labrador) enjoys bitter from the drip trays and Casey (Doberman) often gets carried out as he refuses to leave.

GREATER LONDON

THE PHOENIX
28 Thames Street, Sunbury on Thames, Middlesex (01932 785358).
Dogs allowed on lead in beer garden, family room. Capability 2 Grading.
Pet Regulars: Sammy (Black Labrador).

THE TIDE END COTTAGE
Ferry Road, Teddington, Middlesex (0208 977 7762).
Dogs allowed throughout the pub, except dining area.
Pet Regulars: Mimi (Labrador).

Other specialised
FHG GUIDES
Published annually: available in all good bookshops or direct from the publisher.

- **Recommended COUNTRY HOTELS OF BRITAIN** £7.99
- **Recommended SHORT BREAK HOLIDAYS IN BRITAIN** £7.99
- **Recommended COUNTRY INNS & PUBS OF BRITAIN** £7.99

FHG GUIDES LTD, Abbey Mill Business Centre, Seedhill, Paisley, Renfrewshire PAI ITJ
Tel: 0141-887 0428 • Fax: 0141-889 7204
e-mail: admin@fhguides.co.uk
www.holidayguides.com

Pet-Friendly Pubs
HAMPSHIRE

THE SUN
Sun Hill, Bentworth, Alton, Hampshire GU34 5JT (01420 562338)
Pets welcome throughout the pub.
Pet Regulars: Willow (Collie), Hazel and Purdey (Jack Russells) and "Dilweed" the cat.

HIGH CORNER INN
Linwood, Near Ringwood, Hampshire BH24 3QY (01425 473973).
Dogs, and even horses, are catered for here.

THE CHEQUERS
Ridgeway Lane, Lower Pennington, Lymington, Hants (01590 673415).
Dogs allowed in non-food bar, outdoor barbecue area (away from food).
Pet Regulars: Rusty Boyd - parties held for him. Resident pet - D'for (Labrador).

THE VICTORY
High Street, Hamble-le-Rice, Southampton, Hampshire (023 80 453105).
Dogs allowed.

HERTFORDSHIRE

THE BLACK HORSE
Chorley Wood Common, Dog Kennel Lane, Rickmansworth, Herts (01923 282252).
Dogs very welcome and allowed throughout the pub, on a lead.

THE RED LION
Chenies Village, Rickmansworth, Hertfordshire WD3 6ED (01923 282722).
Pets welcome in bar area only.
Pet Regulars: Resident dog Bobby (Terrier mixture), Luke and his sister (Boxers).

THE ROBIN HOOD AND LITTLE JOHN
Rabley Heath, near Codicote, Hertfordshire (01438 812361).
Dogs allowed in non-food bar, car park tables, beer garden.
Pet Regulars: Bonnie (Labrador), beer-mat catcher. The locals of the pub have close to 50 dogs between them, most of which visit from time to time. The team includes a two Labrador search squad dispatched by one regular's wife to indicate time's up. When they arrive he has five minutes' drinking up time before all three leave together.

FREE or REDUCED RATE entry to
Holiday Visits and Attractions — see our
READERS' OFFER VOUCHERS on pages 53-90

KENT

KENTISH HORSE
Cow Lane, Mark Beech, Edenbridge, Kent (01342 850493).
Dogs allowed in reserved area.

THE SWANN INN
Little Chart, Kent TN27 0QB (01233 840702).
Dogs allowed - everywhere except restaurant.

LANCASHIRE

ASSHETON ARMS
Downham, Clitheroe, Blackburn, Lancashire BB7 4BJ (01200 441227).
Dogs welcome.

MALT'N HOPS
50 Friday Street, Chorley, Lancashire PR6 0AH (01257 260967).
Dogs allowed throughout pub if kept under control.

LINCOLNSHIRE

THE BLUE DOG INN
Main Street, Sewstern, Grantham, Lincs NG33 5QR (01476 860097).
Dogs allowed.
Pet Regulars: Cassie (Scottie) shares biscuits with Brahms (pub cat); Nelson (Terrier), Diesel (Springer Spaniel) and Ted (Spaniel).

Pets Welcome!

"THE PET WORLD'S VERSION OF THE ULTIMATE HOTEL GUIDE!" (The Times)

Now bigger than ever and with full colour throughout,
Pets Welcome! is used every year by thousands of discriminating owners who simply refuse to leave their pets "home alone".
Published twice a year in Autumn and Spring.

Only £8.99 from booksellers or direct from the publishers:
**FHG Guides, Abbey Mill Business Centre, Seedhill,
Paisley PA1 1TJ** *(postage charged outside UK)*
e-mail: admin@fhguides.co.uk • www.holidayguides.com

Readers are requested to mention this FHG publication when seeking accommodation

Pet-Friendly Pubs
MERSEYSIDE

THE SCOTCH PIPER
Southport Road, Lydiate, Merseyside (0151 526 0503).
Dogs allowed throughout the pub.

MIDLANDS

AWENTSBURY HOTEL
21 Serpentine Road, Selly Park, Birmingham B29 7HU (0121 472 1258).
Dogs allowed.
Pet Regulars: Well-behaved dogs welcome.

NORFOLK

THE OLD RAILWAY TAVERN
Eccles Road, Quidenham, Norwich, Norfolk NR16 2JG (01953 888223).
Dogs allowed, must be on lead.
Pet Regulars: Pub dogs Flo (Scottish Terrier), Benji (Jack Russell) and Scottie (Terrier).

THE HOSTE ARMS
The Green, Burnham Market, King's Lynn, Norfolk PE31 8HD (01328 738777).
Dogs allowed throughout the pub, except restaurant.
Pet Regulars: "Augustus" and "Sweep" (Black Labradors).

THE ROSE AND CROWN
Nethergate Street, Harpley, King's Lynn, Norfolk (01485 520577).
Dogs allowed in non-food bar, car park tables. .

OXFORDSHIRE

THE BELL
Shenington, Banbury, Oxfordshire OX15 6NQ (01295 670274).
Pets allowed throughout.
Pet Regulars: Resident pub dogs "Oliver" (Great Dane) and "Daisy" (Labrador).

THE PLOUGH INN
High Street, Finstock, Chipping Norton, Oxfordshire (01993 868333).
Dogs more than welcome.
Pet Regulars: Zac (Sheepdog).

THE BELL INN
High Street, Adderbury, Oxon (01295 810338).
Dogs allowed throughout the pub.
Owner's dogs: Murphy and Dizzy (Lancashire Heelers).

FHG
Visit the K·P·E·R·A·R·D website
www.holidayguides.com
for details of the wide choice of accommodation
featured in the full range of FHG titles

SHROPSHIRE

THE INN AT GRINSHILL High Street, Grinshill, Shrewsbury SY4 3BL (01939 220410)
Set at the base of Grade II Listed Grinshill Hill, where wonderful walks can be enjoyed, nestles this newly refurbished inn. Dogs on leads are welcome in the Elephant and Castle bar, which has a separate non-smoking family room. Enjoy local fresh food from the bistro or the daily specials menu, complemented by a choice of real ales, new world wines, non-alcoholic beverages, tea, or coffee made fresh from the bean. Dog bowl and water; garden, car parking, disabled access toilet facilities available. Credit Cards welcome. Situated 7 miles north of Shrewsbury, signposted just off the A49 Whitchurch Road.
e-mail: theinnatgrinshill@hotmail.com • website: www.theinnatgrinshill.co.uk

THE TRAVELLERS REST INN
Church Stretton, Shropshire (01694 781275).
Well-mannered pets welcome - but beware of the cats!

LONGMYND HOTEL
Cunnery Road, Church Stretton, Shropshire SY6 6AG (01694 722244).
Dogs allowed in owners' hotel bedrooms but not in public areas.
Pet Regulars: Bruno and Frenzie; and owner's dogs, Sam and Sailor.

SOMERSET

CASTLE OF COMFORT HOTEL
Dodington, Nether Stowey, Bridgwater, Somerset TA5 1LE (01278 741264).
Pet friendly.

THE SPARKFORD INN
High Street, Sparkford, Somerset BA22 7JN (01963 440218).
Dogs allowed in bar areas but not in restaurant; safe garden and car park.

THE BUTCHERS ARMS
Carhampton, Somerset (01643 821333).
Dogs allowed in bar. B&B accommodation available.

HOOD ARMS
Kilve, Somerset TA5 1EA (01278 741210).
Pets welcome.

THE SHIP INN
High Street, Porlock, Somerset (01643 862507).
Dogs allowed throughout and in guests' rooms.
Pet Regulars: Include Silver (Jack Russell); Sam (Black Lab) and Max (Staffordshire). Monty (Pug), resident pet.

FHG GUIDES LTD
publish a large range of well-known accommodation guides. We will be happy to send you details or you can use the order form at the back of this book.

Pet-Friendly Pubs

SUFFOLK

THE KINGS HEAD
High Street, Southwold, Suffolk IP18 6AD (01502 724517).
Well-behaved dogs welcome.

SIX BELLS AT BARDWELL
The Green, Bardwell, Bury St Edmunds, Suffolk IP31 1AW (01359 250820).
Dogs allowed in guest bedrooms but not allowed in bar and restaurant.

SURREY

THE PLOUGH
South Road, Woking, Surrey GU21 4JL (01483 714105).
Pets welcome in restricted areas.

THE SPORTSMAN
Mogador Road, Mogador, Surrey (01737 246655).
Adopted dogs congregate at this pub.
Pet Regulars: Meesha (Border Collie) and Max (German Shepherd).

THE CRICKETERS
12 Oxenden Road, Tongham, Farnham, Surrey (01252 333262).
Dogs allowed in beer garden on lead.

SUSSEX

THE FORESTERS ARMS
High Street, Fairwarp, Near Uckfield, East Sussex TN22 3BP (01825 712808).
Dogs allowed in the beer garden and at car park tables, also inside.
Dog biscuits always available.

THE PLOUGH
Crowhurst, Near Battle, East Sussex TN33 9AY (01424 830310).
Dogs allowed in non-food bar, car park tables, beer garden. .

QUEENS HEAD
Village Green, Sedlescombe, East Sussex (01424 870228).
Dogs allowed throughout the pub.

THE SLOOP INN
Freshfield Lock, Haywards Heath, West Sussex RH17 7NP (01444 831219).
Dogs allowed in public bar and garden.

THE SPORTSMAN'S ARMS
Rackham Road, Amberley, Near Arundel, West Sussex BN18 9NR (01798 831787).
Dogs allowed in the bar area.

When making enquiries please mention FHG Guides

Pet-Friendly Pubs

WILTSHIRE

THE HORSE AND GROOM
The Street, Charlton, Near Malmesbury, Wiltshire (01666 823904).
Dogs welcome in bar.
Pet Regulars: Troy and Gio (Labradors).

THE PETERBOROUGH ARMS
Dauntsey Lock, Near Chippenham, Wiltshire SN15 4HD (01249 890409).
All pets welcome in bar.
Resident pets - Poppy, Holly and Lilly (3 generations of Jack Russell).

THE THREE HORSESHOES
High Street, Chapmanslade, Near Westbury, Wiltshire (01373 832280).
Dogs allowed in non-food bar and beer garden.
Resident Pets: Include Oscar (dog) and one cat. Three horses overlooking the beer garden.

YORKSHIRE

BARNES WALLIS INN
North Howden, Howden, East Yorkshire (01430 430639).
Guide dogs only

KINGS HEAD INN
Barmby on the Marsh, East Yorkshire DN14 7HL (01757 630705).
Dogs allowed in non-food bar.
Pet Regulars: Many and varied!

THE FORESTERS ARMS
Kilburn, North Yorkshire YO6 4AH (01347 868386).
Dogs allowed throughout, except restaurant.
Pet Regulars: Ainsley (Black Labrador).

NEW INN HOTEL
Clapham, Near Settle, North Yorkshire LA2 8HH (015242 51203).
Dogs allowed in bar, beer garden, bedrooms.

SIMONSTONE HALL
Hawes, North Yorkshire DL8 3LY (01969 667255).
Dogs allowed except dining area.
Dogs of all shapes, sizes and breeds welcome.

THE SPINNEY
Forest Rise, Balby, Doncaster, South Yorkshire DN4 9HQ (01302 852033).
Dogs allowed throughout the pub.
Pet Regulars: Wyn (Labrador) a guide dog and Buster (Staff).

THE ROCKINGHAM ARMS
8 Main Street, Wentworth, Rotherham, South Yorkshire S62 7LO (01226 742075).
Pets welcome.
Pet Regulars: Sheeba (Springer Spaniel), Charlie and Gypsy (Black Labradors), Sally (Alsatian) and Rosie (Jack Russell).

THE GOLDEN FLEECE
Lindley Road, Blackley, near Huddersfield, West Yorkshire (01422 372704).
Dogs allowed in non-food bar.
Pet Regulars: Holly and Honey (Border Collies).

CHANNEL ISLANDS/JERSEY

LA PULENTE INN
La Pulente, St Brelade, Jersey (01534 744487).
Dogs allowed in public bar.

WALES

ANGLESEY & GWYNEDD

THE GRAPES HOTEL
Maentwrog, Blaenau Ffestiniog, Gwynedd LL41 4HN (01766 590365).
Pets allowed in bar area only.

THE BUCKLEY HOTEL
Castle Street, Beaumaris, Isle of Anglesey LL58 8AW (01248 810415).
Dogs allowed throughout the pub, except in the dining room and bistro.
Pet Regulars: Cassie (Springer Spaniel) and Rex (mongrel), dedicated 'companion' dogs, also Charlie (Spaniel).

NORTH WALES

THE WEST ARMS HOTEL
Llanarmon Dyffryn Ceiriog, Llangollen, North Wales LL20 7LD (01691 600665).
Welcome pets.

PEMBROKESHIRE

THE FARMERS
14-16 Goat Street, St David's, Pembrokeshire (01437 721666).
Pets welcome in the pub area only.

POWYS

SEVERN ARMS HOTEL
Penybont, Llandrindod Wells, Powys LD1 5UA (01597 851224).
Dogs allowed in the bar, but not the restaurant, and in the rooms - but not on the beds.

Visit the FHG website
www.holidayguides.com
for details of the wide choice of accommodation
featured in the full range of FHG titles

SCOTLAND

ABERDEEN, BANFF & MORAY

THE CLIFTON BAR
Clifton Road, Lossiemouth, Moray (01343 812100).
Dogs allowed in beer garden only.

ROYAL OAK
Station Road, Urquhart, Elgin, Moray (01343 842607).
Dogs allowed throughout pub.
Pet Regulars: Jack (Collie).

ARGYLL & BUTE

CAIRNDOW STAGECOACH INN
Cairndow, Argyll PA26 8BN (01499 600286).
Pets welcome.

THE BALLACHULISH HOTEL
Ballachulish, Argyll PA39 4JY (01855 811606).
Dogs allowed in the lounge and guests' bedrooms, excluding food areas.

EDINBURGH & LOTHIANS

JOHNSBURN HOUSE
Johnsburn Road, Balerno, Lothians EH14 7BB (0131-449 3847).
Pets welcome in bar area only.
Pet Regulars: Resident dog "Topaz" (Great Dane).

LAIRD & DOG
Lasswade, Midlothian (0131-663 9219).
Dogs allowed in bar.
Pet Regulars: Many pet regulars. Drinking bowls .

PERTH & KINROSS

FOUR SEASONS HOTEL
St Fillans, Perthshire (01764 685333).
Dogs allowed in all non-food areas.

THE MUNRO INN
Main Street, Strathyre, Perthshire FK18 8NA (01877 384333).
Dogs allowed throughout pub, lounge, games room, beer garden and bedrooms (except restaurant).
Pet Regulars: Residents Jess (black mongrel with brown eyes) and Jules (white lurcher with blue eyes) have many local pals who visit including Rory, Cally, Kerry and Robbie. Bring your dog to visit! Water and dog biscuits always available.

Index of towns and counties

Please also refer to Contents pages 2 and 3

Aberdeen	ABERDEEN, BANFF & MORAY	Bishopsteignton	DEVON
Aberystwyth	CEREDIGION	Blackburn	EDINBURGH & LOTHIANS
Airdrie	LANARKSHIRE	Blackpool	LANCASHIRE
Alcester	WARWICKSHIRE	Blairgowrie	PERTH & KINROSS
Alford	LINCOLNSHIRE	Blairlogie	STIRLING & THE TROSSACHS
Allendale	NORTHUMBERLAND	Bodmin	CORNWALL
Alnwick	NORTHUMBERLAND	Boscastle	CORNWALL
Ambleside	CUMBRIA	Bournemouth	DORSET
Anglesey	ANGLESEY & GWYNEDD	Bowness-on-Windermere	CUMBRIA
Appleby	CUMBRIA	Brampton	CUMBRIA
Arisaig	HIGHLANDS (SOUTH)	Brechin	DUNDEE & ANGUS
Ashbourne	DERBYSHIRE	Brecon	POWYS
Ashbrittle	SOMERSET	Bridgwater	SOMERSET
Ashburton	DEVON	Bridlington	EAST YORKSHIRE
Ashford	KENT	Bridport	DORSET
Ashprington	DEVON	Bristol	GLOUCESTERSHIRE
Attleborough	NORFOLK	Bristol	SOMERSET
Aviemore	HIGHLANDS (SOUTH)	Brixham	DEVON
Aylsham	NORFOLK	Broadstairs	KENT
Ayr	AYRSHIRE & ARRAN	Brockenhurst	HAMPSHIRE
		Bude	CORNWALL
Bakewell	DERBYSHIRE	Builth Wells	POWYS
Bala	ANGLESEY & GWYNEDD	Burford	OXFORDSHIRE
Ballachulish	ARGYLL & BUTE	Burnham-On-Sea	SOMERSET
Balterley	CHESHIRE	Burton Joyce	NOTTINGHAMSHIRE
Banbury	OXFORDSHIRE	Burwell	CAMBRIDGESHIRE
Banchory	ABERDEEN, BANFF & MORAY	Bury St Edmunds	SUFFOLK
Barnstaple	DEVON	Buttermere	CUMBRIA
Barton-on-Sea	HAMPSHIRE	Buxton	DERBYSHIRE
Bath	GLOUCESTERSHIRE		
Bath	SOMERSET	Cadnam	HAMPSHIRE
Bathgate	EDINBURGH & LOTHIANS	Caldbeck	CUMBRIA
Beaminster	DORSET	Callander	PERTH & KINROSS
Beaulieu	HAMPSHIRE	Callander	STIRLING & THE TROSSACHS
Bebington	MERSEYSIDE	Cambridge	CAMBRIDGESHIRE
Bedale	NORTH YORKSHIRE	Campbeltown	ARGYLL & BUTE
Beetley	NORFOLK	Cannington	SOMERSET
Beith	AYRSHIRE & ARRAN	Canterbury	KENT
Belton-in-Rutland	LEICS & RUTLAND	Carlisle	CUMBRIA
Berwick-upon-Tweed	NORTHUMBERLAND	Carmarthen	CARMARTHENSHIRE
Betws-y-Coed	NORTH WALES	Carrbridge	HIGHLANDS (SOUTH)
Bideford	DEVON	Castle Cary	SOMERSET
Biggar	BORDERS	Castleton	DERBYSHIRE
Bishop's Castle	SHROPSHIRE	Chagford	DEVON

Chandler's Ford	HAMPSHIRE	Dorchester	DORSET
Chard	SOMERSET	Dornoch	HIGHLANDS (NORTH)
Charmouth	DORSET	Dorrington	SHROPSHIRE
Cheltenham	GLOUCESTERSHIRE	Dover	KENT
Chester	CHESHIRE	Driffield	EAST YORKSHIRE
Chester	NORTH WALES	Droitwich	WORCESTERSHIRE
Chipping Campden	GLOUCESTERSHIRE	Droitwich Spa	WORCESTERSHIRE
Chorley	LANCASHIRE	Drumnadrochit	HIGHLANDS (SOUTH)
Chudleigh	DEVON	Dufftown	ABERDEEN, BANFF & MORAY
Church Minshull	CHESHIRE	Dulverton	SOMERSET
Church Stretton	SHROPSHIRE	Dumfries	DUMFRIES & GALLOWAY
Churchill	SOMERSET	Dunkeld	PERTH & KINROSS
Clare	SUFFOLK	Dunsford	DEVON
Clitheroe	LANCASHIRE	Durham	DURHAM
Clun	SHROPSHIRE		
Cockermouth	CUMBRIA	Eastbourne	EAST SUSSEX
Colchester	ESSEX	Eccleshall	STAFFORDSHIRE
Colebrooke	DEVON	Edinburgh	EDINBURGH & LOTHIANS
Colyton	DEVON	Edwinstone	NOTTINGHAMSHIRE
Compton	BERKSHIRE	Ely	CAMBRIDGESHIRE
Congresbury	SOMERSET	Eskdale Green	CUMBRIA
Coningsby	LINCOLNSHIRE	Exeter	DEVON
Conwy	NORTH WALES	Exford	SOMERSET
Corbridge	NORTHUMBERLAND	Exmoor	DEVON
Cornforth	DURHAM	Exmouth	DEVON
Corsham	WILTSHIRE	Eyemouth	BORDERS
Cotswolds	GLOUCESTERSHIRE		
Coventry	WARWICKSHIRE	Fairford	GLOUCESTERSHIRE
Cowbridge	SOUTH WALES	Falkirk	STIRLING & THE TROSSACHS
Crail	FIFE	Falmouth	CORNWALL
Crediton	DEVON	Felixstowe	SUFFOLK
Crewkerne	SOMERSET	Fillongley	WARWICKSHIRE
Crianlarich	PERTH & KINROSS	Folkestone	KENT
Criccieth	ANGLESEY & GWYNEDD	Forres	ABERDEEN, BANFF & MORAY
Crickhowell	POWYS	Fort William	HIGHLANDS (SOUTH)
Crieff	PERTH & KINROSS	Framlingham	SUFFOLK
Cromer	NORFOLK	Frosterley in Weardale	DURHAM
Croyde	DEVON		
Cubert	CORNWALL	Gainsborough	LINCOLNSHIRE
Culross	FIFE	Gairloch	HIGHLANDS (MID)
		Gatehouse of Fleet	DUMFRIES & GALLOWAY
Danby	NORTH YORKSHIRE	Gatwick	SURREY
Daventry	NORTHAMPTONSHIRE	Glaisdale	NORTH YORKSHIRE
Dawlish	DEVON	Glasgow	GLASGOW & DISTRICT
Deal	KENT	Glastonbury	SOMERSET
Delabole	CORNWALL	Glencoe	HIGHLANDS (SOUTH)
Derby	DERBYSHIRE	Gloucester	GLOUCESTERSHIRE
Devizes	WILTSHIRE	Gower	SOUTH WALES
Dolgellau	ANGLESEY & GWYNEDD	Grantown-on-Spey	HIGHLANDS (SOUTH)

395

Great Yarmouth	NORFOLK	Ilfracombe	DEVON
Gretna Green	DUMFRIES & GALLOWAY	Inveraray	ARGYLL & BUTE
Gullane	EDINBURGH & LOTHIANS	Inverness	HIGHLANDS (SOUTH)
		Ipswich	SUFFOLK
Hailsham	EAST SUSSEX	Ivybridge	DEVON
Halifax	WEST YORKSHIRE		
Hamilton	LANARKSHIRE	Jedburgh	BORDERS
Harrogate	NORTH YORKSHIRE	John O'Groats	HIGHLANDS (NORTH)
Hartfield	EAST SUSSEX		
Hartland	DEVON	Kelvedon	ESSEX
Haslemere	SURREY	Kendal	CUMBRIA
Hastings	EAST SUSSEX	Kenilworth	WARWICKSHIRE
Haverfordwest	PEMBROKESHIRE	Keswick	CUMBRIA
Hawkshead	CUMBRIA	Kettering	NORTHAMPTONSHIRE
Hayle	CORNWALL	Kilmarnock	AYRSHIRE & ARRAN
Hayling Island	HAMPSHIRE	Kilsyth	GLASGOW & DISTRICT
Hay-on-Wye	POWYS	King's Cross	LONDON (CENTRAL & GREATER)
Haywards Heath	WEST SUSSEX	Kingsbridge	DEVON
Headcorn	KENT	Kingston-Upon-Thames	SURREY
Helensburgh	ARGYLL & BUTE	Kingussie	HIGHLANDS (SOUTH)
Helmsley	NORTH YORKSHIRE	Kinlochbervie	HIGHLANDS (NORTH)
Helston	CORNWALL	Kirkby Lonsdale	CUMBRIA
Henfield	WEST SUSSEX	Kirkby Stephen	CUMBRIA
Henley-on-Thames	OXFORDSHIRE	Kirkbymoorside	NORTH YORKSHIRE
Hereford	HEREFORDSHIRE	Kirkcaldy	FIFE
Hexham	NORTHUMBERLAND	Kirkmichael	PERTH & KINROSS
High Bentham	NORTH YORKSHIRE	Kirkwall	ORKNEY ISLANDS
Holsworthy	DEVON		
Honiton	DEVON	Lairg	HIGHLANDS (NORTH)
Hook	HAMPSHIRE	Lake District	CUMBRIA
Horley	SURREY	Lanark	LANARKSHIRE
Horncastle	LINCOLNSHIRE	Lancaster	LANCASHIRE
Hornsea	EAST YORKSHIRE	Langdale	CUMBRIA
Horseheath	CAMBRIDGESHIRE	Largs	AYRSHIRE & ARRAN
Hunstanton	NORFOLK	Leamington Spa	WARWICKSHIRE

please note

All the information in this book is given in good faith in the belief that it is correct. However, the publishers cannot guarantee the facts given in these pages, neither are they responsible for changes in policy, ownership or terms that may take place after the date of going to press. Readers should always satisfy themselves that the facilities they require are available and that the terms, if quoted, still apply.

FHG

·K·U·P·E·R·A·R·D·

Lechlade-on-Thames	GLOUCESTERSHIRE	Loweswater	CUMBRIA
Ledbury	HEREFORDSHIRE	Ludlow	SHROPSHIRE
Lenham	KENT	Lulworth Cove	DORSET
Leominster	HEREFORDSHIRE	Luton	BEDFORDSHIRE
Lesmahagow	LANARKSHIRE	Lydford	DEVON
Letterkenny	CO. DONEGAL	Lyme Regis	DORSET
Leven	FIFE	Lymington	HAMPSHIRE
Lewes	EAST SUSSEX	Lyndhurst	HAMPSHIRE
Leyburn	YORKSHIRE (NORTH)	Lynmouth	DEVON
Lingfield	SURREY	Lynton	DEVON
Linlithgow	EDINBURGH & LOTHIANS		
Liskeard	CORNWALL	Machynlleth	POWYS
Liverpool	MERSEYSIDE	Maidstone	KENT
Llandudno	NORTH WALES	Malmesbury	WILTSHIRE
Llanerch-y-Medd	ANGLESEY & GWYNEDD	Malpas	CHESHIRE
Llanidloes	POWYS	Malvern	WORCESTERSHIRE
Lochinver	HIGHLANDS (NORTH)	Malvern Wells	WORCESTERSHIRE
Lockerbie	DUMFRIES & GALLOWAY	Mark Village	SOMERSET
London	LONDON (CENTRAL & GREATER)	Market Drayton	SHROPSHIRE
Long Hanborough	OXFORDSHIRE	Market Rasen	LINCOLNSHIRE
Long Stratton	NORFOLK	Marlborough	WILTSHIRE
Looe	CORNWALL	Marske-By-The-Sea	NORTHUMBERLAND
Louth	LINCOLNSHIRE	Maryport	CUMBRIA

The Golf Guide 2006
Where to Play, Where to Stay

£9.99

Available from most booksellers, **The Golf Guide, Where to Play, Where to Stay** covers details of every UK golf course. Bigger and brighter than ever, with over 650 pages packed with comprehensive details of over 2800 clubs and courses in Britain and Ireland – the 'pro', par score, length and more. Including holiday golf in Ireland, France, Portugal, Spain, the USA, South Africa and Thailand. Hundreds of hotel entries offer convenient accommodation for golfers, their families, friends and colleagues.

Pets Welcome!

£8.99

"THE PET WORLD'S VERSION OF THE ULTIMATE HOTEL GUIDE!" (The Times)

Now bigger than ever and with full colour throughout, **Pets Welcome!** is used every year by thousands of discriminating owners who simply refuse to leave their pets "home alone". Published twice a year in Autumn and Spring.

Available from booksellers or direct from the publishers:

FHG GUIDES
**Abbey Mill Business Centre, Seedhill,
Paisley PA1 1TJ** *(postage charged outside UK)*
www.holidayguides.com • e-mail: admin@fhguides.co.uk

Matlock	DERBYSHIRE	Penpillick	CORNWALL
Mauchline	AYRSHIRE & ARRAN	Penrith	CUMBRIA
Melbourne	DERBYSHIRE	Penryn	CORNWALL
Melrose	BORDERS	Penzance	CORNWALL
Melton Mowbray	LEICESTERSHIRE	Perranporth	CORNWALL
Mere	WILTSHIRE	Peterborough	LINCOLNSHIRE
Mevagissey	CORNWALL	Petersfield	HAMPSHIRE
Midhurst	WEST SUSSEX	Pickering	NORTH YORKSHIRE
Milford-on-Sea	HAMPSHIRE	Plockton	HIGHLANDS (MID)
Minchinhampton	GLOUCESTERSHIRE	Plymouth	DEVON
Minehead	SOMERSET	Polzeath	CORNWALL
Moffat	DUMFRIES & GALLOWAY	Poole	DORSET
Monmouth	SOUTH WALES	Porlock	SOMERSET
Morecambe	LANCASHIRE	Port Isaac	CORNWALL
Moretonhampstead	DEVON	Porthleven	CORNWALL
Mosterton	DORSET	Portland	DORSET
Mundesley	NORFOLK	Portree	ISLE OF SKYE
Musselburgh	EDINBURGH & LOTHIANS	Portsmouth	HAMPSHIRE
Muthill	PERTH & KINROSS		
		Reading	BERKSHIRE
Nantwich	CHESHIRE	Rhos-on-Sea	NORTH WALES
Near Sawrey	CUMBRIA	Richmond	YORKSHIRE (NORTH)
New Forest	HAMPSHIRE	Rickmansworth	HERTFORDSHIRE
Newbury	BERKSHIRE	Rilla Mill	CORNWALL
Newcastle Upon Tyne	TYNE & WEAR	Ringwood	HAMPSHIRE
Newnham Bridge	WORCESTERSHIRE	Ripon	YORKSHIRE (NORTH)
Newquay	CORNWALL	Robin Hood's Bay	YORKSHIRE (NORTH)
Newton Abbot	DEVON	Romsey	HAMPSHIRE
Newtown	POWYS	Roslin	EDINBURGH & LOTHIANS
North Tawton	DEVON	Ross-on-Wye	HEREFORDSHIRE
North Walsham	NORFOLK	Rothbury	NORTHUMBERLAND
Northallerton	NORTH YORKSHIRE	Rye	EAST SUSSEX
Northbay	ISLE OF BARRA		
Norwich	NORFOLK	St Agnes	CORNWALL
Nottingham	NOTTINGHAMSHIRE	St Andrews	FIFE
		St Austell	CORNWALL
Oban	ARGYLL & BUTE	St Bees	CUMBRIA
Okehampton	DEVON	St Brides Wentloog	SOUTH WALES
Oswestry	SHROPSHIRE	St Ives	CORNWALL
Ottery St Mary	DEVON	Salisbury	WILTSHIRE
Oxford	OXFORDSHIRE	Sandown	ISLE OF WIGHT
Oxted	SURREY	Sandy	BEDFORDSHIRE
		Scarborough	NORTH YORKSHIRE
Padstow	CORNWALL	Scunthorpe	LINCOLNSHIRE
Paignton	DEVON	Sea Palling	NORFOLK
Paisley	RENFREWSHIRE	Seaton	DEVON
Pathhead	EDINBURGH & LOTHIANS	Shaldon	DEVON
Patna	AYRSHIRE & ARRAN	Shap	CUMBRIA
Peebles	BORDERS	Shrewsbury	SHROPSHIRE

Sidmouth	DEVON	Ullswater	CUMBRIA
Skipton	NORTH YORKSHIRE		
South Molton	DEVON	Wadebridge	CORNWALL
Southampton	HAMPSHIRE	Warkworth	NORTHUMBERLAND
Spalding	NORFOLK	Warminster	WILTSHIRE
Spean Bridge	HIGHLANDS (SOUTH)	Warwick	WARWICKSHIRE
Stamfordham	NORTHUMBERLAND	Washford	SOMERSET
Stanley	DURHAM	Watchet	SOMERSET
Stanley	PERTH & KINROSS	Wells	SOMERSET
Stockbridge	HAMPSHIRE	Wells-Next-The-Sea	NORFOLK
Stoke-on-Trent	STAFFORDSHIRE	Welshpool	POWYS
Stokesley	NORTH YORKSHIRE	West Linton	BORDERS
Stonehouse	GLOUCESTERSHIRE	West Lulworth	DORSET
Stowmarket	SUFFOLK	Westcliff-on-Sea	ESSEX
Stow-on-the-Wold	GLOUCESTERSHIRE	Weston-Super-Mare	SOMERSET
Stranraer	DUMFRIES & GALLOWAY	Weymouth	DORSET
Stratford-Upon-Avon	WARWICKSHIRE	Whitby	NORTH YORKSHIRE
Strathpeffer	HIGHLANDS (MID)	Whithorn	DUMFRIES & GALLOWAY
Sturminster Newton	DORSET	Wicken	CAMBRIDGESHIRE
Surbiton	SURREY	Wickham	HAMPSHIRE
Sutton-in-Ashfield	NOTTINGHAMSHIRE	Winchcombe	GLOUCESTERSHIRE
Swanage	DORSET	Winchelsea	EAST SUSSEX
Swindon	WILTSHIRE	Winchester	HAMPSHIRE
		Windermere	CUMBRIA
Talyllyn	ANGLESEY & GWYNEDD	Windsor	BERKSHIRE
Tamworth	STAFFORDSHIRE	Winkfield	BERKSHIRE
Tarbert	ARGYLL & BUTE	Winster	DERBYSHIRE
Taunton	SOMERSET	Witney	OXFORDSHIRE
Telford	SHROPSHIRE	Wiveliscombe	SOMERSET
Tenterden	KENT	Woodbridge	SUFFOLK
Tetsworth	OXFORDSHIRE	Woodchester	GLOUCESTERSHIRE
Tewkesbury	GLOUCESTERSHIRE	Woodhall Spa	LINCOLNSHIRE
Theale	SOMERSET	Woodstock	OXFORDSHIRE
Thirsk	NORTH YORKSHIRE	Woodton	NORFOLK
Tintagel	CORNWALL	Worcester	WORCESTERSHIRE
Tiverton	DEVON	Wroxham	NORFOLK
Tolpuddle	DORSET	Wymondham	NORFOLK
Tomatin	HIGHLANDS (SOUTH)		
Torquay	DEVON	Yelverton	DEVON
Totland	ISLE OF WIGHT	York	NORTH YORKSHIRE
Trefriw	NORTH WALES		
Troutbeck	CUMBRIA		
Truro	CORNWALL		
Tywyn	ANGLESEY & GWYNEDD		

Free or reduced rate entry to Holiday Visits and Attractions – see our READERS' OFFER VOUCHERS on pages 53-90

OTHER FHG TITLES FOR 2006

FHG Guides Ltd have a large range of attractive holiday accommodation guides for all kinds of holiday opportunities throughout Britain. They also make useful gifts at any time of year. Our guides are available in most bookshops and larger newsagents but we will be happy to post you a copy direct if you have any difficulty. POST FREE for addresses in the UK. We will also post abroad but have to charge separately for post or freight.

SELF-CATERING HOLIDAYS ☐
in Britain
Over 1000 addresses throughout for self-catering and caravans in Britain..

The original
Farm Holiday Guide to COAST & COUNTRY HOLIDAYS in England, Scotland, Wales and Channel Islands. Board, Self-catering, Caravans/Camping, Activity Holidays. ☐

BRITAIN'S BEST HOLIDAYS ☐
A quick-reference general guide for all kinds of holidays.

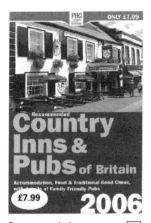

Recommended
COUNTRY INNS & PUBS ☐
of Britain
Pubs, Inns and small hotels.

Recommended
COUNTRY HOTELS ☐
of Britain
Including Country Houses, for the discriminating.

PETS WELCOME! ☐
The original and unique guide for holidays for pet owners and their pets.

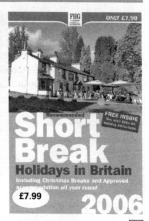

CHILDREN WELCOME! ☐
Family Holidays and Days Out guide.
Family holidays with details of amenities for children and babies.

The FHG Guide to
CARAVAN & CAMPING HOLIDAYS, ☐
Caravans for hire, sites and holiday parks and centres.

Recommended
SHORT BREAK HOLIDAYS ☐
in Britain
"Approved" accommodation for quality bargain breaks..

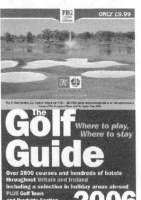

The GOLF GUIDE –
Where to play   Where to stay   £9.99
In association with GOLF MONTHLY. Over 2800 golf courses in Britain with convenient accommodation. Holiday Golf in France, Portugal, Spain, USA, South Africa and Thailand. ☐

Tick your choice above and send your order and payment to

FHG Guides Ltd. Abbey Mill Business Centre
Seedhill, Paisley, Scotland PA1 1TJ
TEL: 0141- 887 0428 • FAX: 0141- 889 7204
e-mail: admin@fhguides.co.uk

Deduct 10% for 2/3 titles or copies; 20% for 4 or more.

Send to: NAME..

ADDRESS ....
....
....
POST CODE ....

I enclose Cheque/Postal Order for £ ....

SIGNATURE..DATE ....

Please complete the following to help us improve the service we provide.
How did you find out about our guides?:

☐ Press   ☐ Magazines   ☐ TV/Radio   ☐ Family/Friend   ☐ Other